Business Environmen

Business Environment

Veena Keshav Pailwar
Professor
Institute of Management Technology
Nagpur

PHI Learning Private Limited
Delhi-110092
2017

₹ 525.00

BUSINESS ENVIRONMENT
Veena Keshav Pailwar

© 2014 by PHI Learning Private Limited, Delhi. All rights reserved. No part of this book may be reproduced in any form, by mimeograph or any other means, without permission in writing from the publisher.

ISBN-978-81-203-4890-5

The export rights of this book are vested solely with the publisher.

Second Printing ... ... **July, 2017**

Published by Asoke K. Ghosh, PHI Learning Private Limited, Rimjhim House, 111, Patparganj Industrial Estate, Delhi-110092 and Printed by Rajkamal Electric Press, Plot No. 2, Phase IV, HSIDC, Kundli-131028, Sonepat, Haryana.

To

My Father

Dr. Keshav Prathamvir

Contents

List of Figures

List of Tables

List of Boxes

List of Case Analysis Exercises

List of Cases

Preface

Business environment, which refers to the world around a business unit, is highly dynamic. Continuous changes that take place in its various constituents necessitate changes in business decisions, which include the type of product to be produced, the scale of operation, price to be charged, the amount of different types of factor inputs to be used, the level of research and development expenditure, and many other strategic decisions. For example, changes in economic structure, occurring because of globalization and liberalization process and recurrent business fluctuations, require continuous re-orientation of business practices and strategies that can help in combating competition by cutting costs and retaining profitability. Changes in laws governing business activities also force business restructuring. Along with continuous changes in economic structure and legal framework, rapid technological advancements make the environment more complex and challenging, and necessitate quick changes in the ways in which business organizations operate. They are made to relook at their hire and outsourcing policies and practices, inventory management, and the manner of communication with different stake holders. Technological changes also compel substantial spending on training of the staff so that it can deal effectively with the new technology.

Another important factor that brings changes in the business environment is demography. These changes, though gradually, bring in substantial structural changes in the environment. At present, one major demographic issue facing the world is the problem of old age population in some economies and growing young age population in other. Changes in the demographic structure alter the consumption pattern as well as affect the availability and cost of labour, and force business organizations to reorient their production structure as well as production techniques. Even the changes in natural environment, such as global warming, have a significant influence on business environment, necessitating business organizations to account for the cost of damage to natural environment, affecting their profit margins. Basic awareness about changes taking place in different constituents of business environment and understanding of their implications is crucial for recognizing current developments and taking advantages of the emerging trends for positioning of an organization and strengthening its competitive advantage in a shifting market place.

Objective

This book is primarily designed for students of management to familiarize them with the various constituents of business environment under which they would be operating once they join a business unit. However, the book is also useful for practising managers struggling to understand the rationale for various strategies adopted by their organizations. It can also be helpful as a reference material for the policy makers in early stages of their carrier assisting in designing and implementing effective policy measures. Students preparing for various competitive examinations will also find the book beneficial in understanding many concepts related to various constituents of overall environment in which a business unit and an economy operate.

Coverage

There are several layers of business environment. Broadly, these layers are – outermost layer, middle layer and innermost layer. The outermost layer of the environment is known as the macro-environment, middle layer is recognized as the meso-environment, and the innermost layer is identified as micro-environment. The focus of this book is on the outermost, i.e., macro business environment. Accordingly, the book details on various constituents of macro business environment. These various constituents that are discussed in detail in this book are economic environment, legal environment, demographic environment, technological environment, and natural environment.

Pedagogical Features

This book has adopted mix of pedagogical devices that makes it not only a valuable resource but also an interesting one. Each chapter of the book has been structured in such a way that brief theoretical underpinnings, analytical understanding and conceptual background required to understand a particular constituent of business environment precedes the applications. For serious readers, more technical details and numerical illustrations of various concepts are placed under boxes. Those readers that do not want to get into more technical details can skip these boxes without losing the basic understanding of the subject. Various illustrations focusing on the current business environment are placed under the heading Understanding Business Environment (UBE). As these illustrations follow immediately after the theoretical underpinnings and conceptual background, the readers will find these helpful in relating the concepts with a constituent of business environment to which they are referring to. These illustrations not only portray the present business scenario but also compare it with the pre-1991 scenario and show its evolvement over a period of time. However, to retain the interest of the readers, the historical data and details are kept to the minimum. Most of the numerical data is also presented in a graphical format so as to make the visualization easier and simpler.

The main points emerging from each chapter are summed up under the heading Summary. This section also emphasizes the implications of particular constituent of business environment for business decisions under the sub-section Implications for Business. To facilitate students to revise and refine their understanding of various concepts and applications, several review questions and numerical problems are placed towards the end of each chapter. To assist students in analyzing business environment using various concepts presented in this book, each chapter also consists of case analysis exercises. Each chapter ends with Further Suggested Readings. Interested reader can get more in-depth understanding of various concepts by going through these reference materials.

Companion Website

The companion website (**www.phindia.com/veenapailwar/**) to this textbook contains useful additional resources for instructors as well as students.

Instructors' resources: The instructors' resources contain more than 1000 clear, crisp, and meaningful PowerPoint Slides explaining the various concepts and business scenarios. The course outline placed under this section can be useful guide for the instructors in designing and delivering business environment course in the classroom set up. Similarly, more than 1000 multiple choice questions can be a great add for designing a question paper for Business Environment course. The instructors' resources also provide the answers to the end of chapter Numerical Problems.

Students' Resources: To further enrich the understanding of students, the students' resources on the companion website contains supporting additional resources, such as Multiple Choice Questions and hints for solving chapter-end numerical problems.

Acknowledgements

As this book is an outcome of experience of teaching the subject several years in the classroom, I owe a lot to my students and express my gratitude to all of them. Some of my past students, specifically Richa Sharma, Shafique Gajdhar, Rahul Mishra, Shreyas Shirke, Vipin Goel, Rupa Deepanju, Kratika Jain, have also assisted me in writing some cases that are now part of this book. I thank all of them for their contribution.

VEENA KESHAV PAILWAR

vpailwar@yahoo.com

vpailwar@imtnag.ac.in

CHAPTER 1

Business Environment and Its Constituents

1.1 INTRODUCTION

Established in 1945, Bajaj Auto Limited remained the market leader in the Indian two wheeler industry from 1960 to mid 1990. Largely operating in a protected environment, created by the "licensing raj", the company had a huge success with its popular scooter models like Chetak and Super, and mopeds M-50 and M-80. Chetak was so popular that it used to command a premium in the market, and after booking people used to wait for months as cars, at that time, were out of the reach of common men. Since 1990 dismantling of the licensing raj, and many other liberalization and reform measures changed the face of the auto industry. The liberalization measures made the entry of new domestic and foreign players easy, and intensified the competition. To survive in the market, new technologically superior and eye-catching models of motorcycles, scooters and mopeds were offered in the market. At the same time, as India moved away from the "Hindu growth rate", the per capita income increased. Along with the steady increase in the per capita income, demographic changes in favour of youth population brought in substantial changes in the taste and preferences of Indian consumers. Modern, technologically sophisticated fuel-efficient motor bikes caught the eyes of the Indian youth population. Once gearless two wheeler became available in the market, consumers, especially women, preferred these over the geared Bajaj scooters. Failing to see the change in the environment, Bajaj Auto remained focused and continued to invest resources and time on its geared scooters. Lethargy to tap the changing environment, and adapt according to the need of the time, led to the fall of Bajaj Auto Limited from its number one position in the two wheeler market in mid 1990s. By 2009, the sales of its scooter declined to 1,000 a month and the company decided to exit from the scooter market and concentrate on motorcycle segment, which cater to the taste of Indian youth from both rural and urban areas. Presently, the company is struggling hard to gain the number one position in the domestic market, which is witnessing fall in the growth of sales volume, by continuous product differentiating and introducing technologically superior motorcycles at the entry segment, which accounts for 65 per cent of the total motorbike market share. For deeper penetration in the new export markets, such as Indonesia and other ASEAN countries, last year the company announced a strategic alliance with Japanese Kawasaki.

Companies, like Bajaj Auto Limited, are struggling hard to survive and sustain their positions and the market shares in the continuously changing business environment by incessantly changing and evolving their strategies.

For better performance, managers need to know, what the business environment refers to. What are its constituents? What is the significance of scanning business environment? This chapter focuses on these issues. Section 1.2 defines business, outlines its objectives and specifies its functions. Section 1.3 explains the meaning of business environment and details on its components. Constituents of micro business environment are described in Section 1.4, whereas constituents of macro business environment are highlighted in Section 1.5. Section 1.6 outlines the steps involved in environmental analysis and Section 1.7 brings out the significance of macro business environment for managers.

1.2 BUSINESS: MEANING, OBJECTIVE AND FUNCTIONS

Business is an economic activity performed by business firms or organizations often with the objectives of maximizing profit. This objective is supplemented by other objectives such as sales maximization, growth maximization, maximization of market share, maximization of own benefits by the managers, building up an image, and social responsibility. The economic activities performed by business organizations include production (transformation of inputs into outputs), distribution (supply of output in a marketplace) and sales (exchange of products with buyers for money).

Profit maximization, which is one of the main objectives of business organizations, requires maximization of revenue. However, resources in the hands of business organizations are limited. Therefore, firms face the challenge of allocating existing resources among alternative uses in such a way that the maximum revenue is generated and the cost is kept to the minimum. Firms, in the process of allocation and profit maximization, have to decide on the following basic economic questions:

What to Produce?

Automobile manufacturers, for example, often face a dilemma whether to produce cars or trucks.

How Much to Produce?

Once the automobile manufacturers decide to produce both cars and trucks, they face further dilemmas—whether to produce these in equal quantities or to produce more cars or less cars.

Where to Produce?

Automobile manufacturers also have to take a decision regarding the place of setting up their manufacturing plant—whether the place should be West Bengal or Gujarat or Uttarakhand?

How to Produce?

The method of production also affects the cost, and hence, the profitability. Therefore, manufacturers also have to take a call for the method of production or the type of technology used for the production. They have to decide whether components of cars or trucks are to be assembled manually or the process is to be mechanized to save on labour cost.

When to Produce?

Time of production/supply is an important consideration in production decisions. The neglect of it may result in either the build-up in inventories or loss of customers. For example, automobiles and other products are subject to seasonal changes. In festive seasons, the demand for automobiles shoots up. Firms need to keep ready the automobiles as per the forecasted demand just prior to the arrival of festive seasons, otherwise they may lose the potential customers. On the contrary, if the production of automobiles is carried out much before the festive seasons it will simply result in a build up of inventories which definitely require maintenance cost and locking up of precious resources.

1.3 BUSINESS ENVIRONMENT AND ITS COMPONENTS

All business decisions described in the previous section are taken by firms in a given business environment.

The term **business environment** refers to all those factors that are external to a business unit, but impact business decisions. As depicted in Figure 1.1, the business environment is surrounded by the two components of environment, viz, micro business environment and macro business environment.

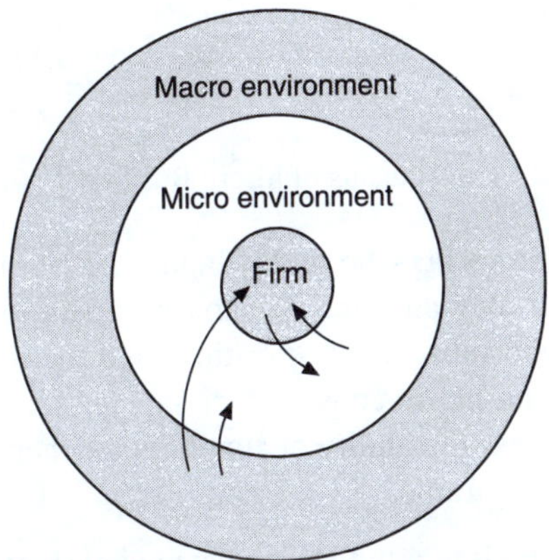

Figure 1.1 Components of Business Environment.

The **micro business environment**, also known as **task environment**, refers to the immediate surroundings of the business, whereas **macro business environment** refers to the general environment. Micro environment not only affects the operations of the firm but also get influenced by its decisions and actions. Macro environment, on the contrary, though influences business decisions, is not affected by the functioning of a business unit, making it an uncontrollable factor.

This book focuses on the macro business environment. But, to clearly differentiate the macro business environment from the micro environment, a brief overview of the constituents of the micro business environment is also presented here.

1.4 CONSTITUENTS OF MICRO BUSINESS ENVIRONMENT AND ITS SIGNIFICANCE

Micro business environment has a direct and larger influence on the working of an organization, and influences its operating performance and the efficiency with which it can serve its customers. As reflected in Figure 1.2, it includes suppliers, workers, intermediaries, competitors and public.

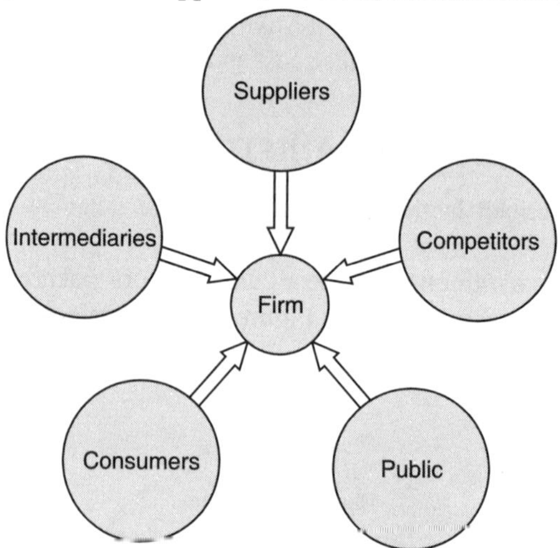

Figure 1.2 Constituents of Micro Business Environment.

1. Suppliers: **Suppliers** are the agents who supply inputs, such as raw materials and intermediate goods to an organization. They play an important role in operational efficiency. A delay in the supply of inputs can delay all the subsequent operations and the firm may fail in timely delivery of its products to customers, resulting in consumer dissatisfaction and even losing them forever. Therefore, managers need to assess the ability of suppliers for their ability to supply inputs in the required quantities in a given time frame.

2. Intermediaries: **Intermediaries** are the agents that mediate between firms and their customers. These intermediaries include physical distribution firms, resellers, and marketing intermediaries. **Distribution firms**, such as American Distribution Company, Hopkins Distribution Company and Adani Enterprises Ltd., handle movement and storage of goods from the point of origin to the point of consumption. **Resellers**, such as Walmart, Spencer, Big Bazar and Lifestyle, buy goods and services to resell to consumers for a profit. **Marketing intermediaries** consists of service agencies and financial intermediaries. **Service agencies** include marketing research and consultancy firms, advertising agencies and media firms. These agencies help consumers identify the target population and market products in most efficient and influential manner. **Financial intermediaries** include bank insurance companies and credit agencies that help companies raise finance as well as insure against various types of risks involved in production and other business operations.

3. Competitors: **Competitors** are rivals who compete with an organization in the market place. Except monopoly market structure, firms in all other market structures have one or more competitors for their products. As the number of competitors increases the competition becomes intense. Competitors not only compete for customers but also for talented staff. To prevent customers and employees from shifting to the competitors, a company needs to continuously assess consumer taste and preferences, and design the products accordingly. It also needs to design retention strategies so that the talented staff can be retained for a longer time. In a highly competitive environment, price cut and other competitive strategies fail because these strategies simply reduce profitability of each competing firm. In such situations companies end up collaborating to maximize joint profit. These collaborations take a form of joint ventures and strategic alliances such as that between Bajaj Auto Limited and Kawasaki, Microsoft and Nokia partnership for Nokia Window Phones, Chrysler and Fiat partnership to build compact and subcompact jeeps.

4. Consumers: **Consumers** comprise individuals and households that buy goods and services for personal consumption. Consumers are the most important constituents of the micro business environment as they are the demand side of the market. Without them companies cannot do their business. Identifying customer needs, retaining customers, and extending products and services to them throughout their lives are important challenges for business organizations.

5. Public: **Public** consists of all those parts of society which can directly or indirectly influence an organization's ability to achieve its objectives. Public opinion is important for a company as it can either strengthen or weaken its brand image. For example, satisfied customers are a public that spread good image about the products through word of mouth. On the contrary, activist, consumer forums, non-government agencies and even media protesting against the environmental damage done by a company is a public that can tarnish the image of a company, and weaken its brand image. Thus, managing public opinion is a crucial task for any company.

1.5 MACRO BUSINESS ENVIRONMENT AND ITS CONSTITUENTS

Macro business environment largely comprises economic environment, legal environment, demographic environment, technological environment and natural environment (Figure 1.3). These broad constituents of the business environment are described hereinafter.

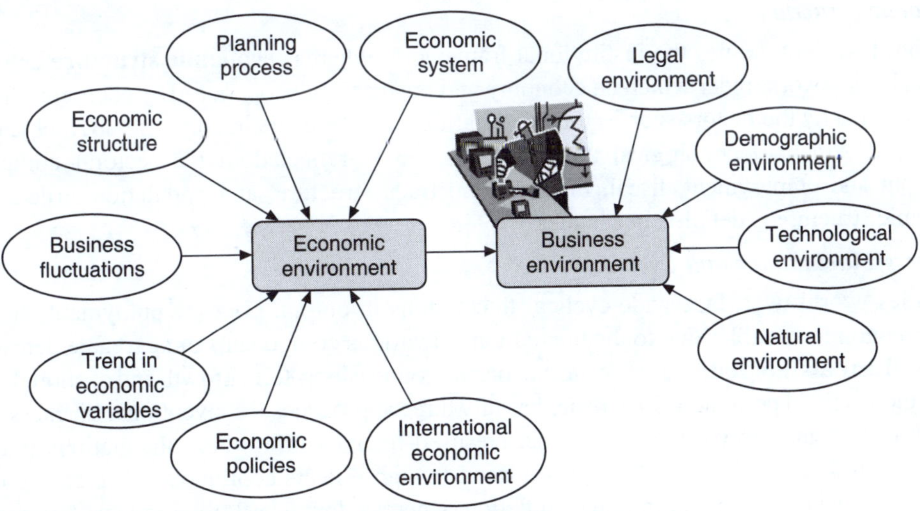

Figure 1.3 Constituents of Business Environment.

1.5.1 Economic Environment

Economic environment (as depicted in Figure 1.3) of a country is affected by the economic system, planning process, economic structure, business fluctuations, trends in macroeconomic variables, economic policies and international economic environment. These various constituents of economic environment are detailed as follows:

Economic System

An **economic system** is a set of institutions, principles and mechanisms created by a society to facilitate economic units to address their basic economic problems of allocation of scarce resources and perform their basic economic activities. Every organized society follows some or the other economic system. It is further discussed in detail in Chapter 2.

Economic systems are classified using two different approaches. One approach differentiates the systems on the basis of ownership of resources, whereas another approach classifies the systems on the basis of allocation mechanism.

On the basis of ownership of resources, economic systems are classified into capitalism, socialism, and mixed economies. Whereas on the basis of market mechanism, the systems are classified as market economies, planned economies and mixed economies.

Planning Process

Planning is needed for an efficient allocation of resources, which are limited in supply, among alternative uses. The planning process is an integral part of communist and socialist states. However, retaining their basic free market structure, even capitalist economies use planning to some extent. At present, all countries have mixed economic systems and follow planning, to a smaller or greater extent, to stimulate the level of investment, encourage technological innovations, use the resources as per national priorities and evolving economic situation, and reconcile the process of economic growth with the overall socioeconomic development of the country. The planning process is classified broadly into two categories—imperative planning and indicative planning (discussed in detail in Chapter 2).

Economic Structure

Economic system defines the institutional framework, whereas **economic structure** defines the physical framework under which an economy and business units operate. The economic structure is determined by the factors such as total population size, per capita income, demographic profile, factor endowment, technological advancement, and is reflected in the sectoral composition of output and employment, fiscal, financial and trade structure, and population structure. The economic structure is detailed in Chapter 3.

Business Fluctuations and Cycles

Countries, world over, face wide cyclical fluctuations in output, prices, employment, and other macroeconomic variables due to the fluctuations in various components of aggregate demand and supply. **Business fluctuations** are recurrent, occur around a long-term growth and of short duration, but without a fixed periodicity. There are broadly three approaches – conventional business cycles, growth cycles and growth rate cycles that are used for measuring these fluctuations (these are discussed in detail in Chapter 4). Upward trend though reflects continuously increasing output. It is also associated with a high rate of inflation, whereas downward trend reflects falling output and is associated with a high rate of unemployment, declining per capita income and misery. Fine tuning of business strategies is required as per the phase of business cycles. In a booming economy chances of success are high, but in a downturn or recession a very cautious approach is needed.

Trends in Macroeconomic Variables

General trends in various economic variables, such as national income, income distribution and poverty, inflation, employment, capacity utilization, saving, investment, fiscal deficit, money supply, balance of payment, foreign exchange reserves, exchange rate, etc., are indicative of the overall economic environment of a country. In general, the short-term trends in these variables indicate the various phases of business cycles, whereas long-term trends reflect upon the economic structure. In particular, each of these variables reflects on some specific aspect of an economy as indicated below:

An increasing trend in **national income** signifies increasing market potential/ size for business managers (national income and related concepts are discussed in detail in Chapter 5), whereas the distribution of national income affects both the market size and consumption pattern. Demand or consumption patterns widely differ across income groups, especially in those economies which are characterized by wide income disparities. In such economies, the demand from a low income strata usually concentrates on necessary and primary products, whereas an upper income group demands more of luxury items and services. On the contrary, in those economies which have less income inequality, consumption patterns are less diversified, and hence, the product mix is also narrower. As national income and its distribution play an important role in the determination of total demand and its composition, business firms can base their product mix as well as their market strategies on the basis of emerging trends in these variables.

An increasing trend in **poverty** level can derail the growth process by increasing income inequalities and subsequent unrest in the economy. Reduction in poverty levels and inclusion of various segments of the society in the growth process is essential for the sustainability of the growth process, because increasing poverty and marginalisation of a large segment of the population in the growth process can affect the quality of labour force due to malnutrition and lack of education. Through reduced level of purchasing power it also affects the demand for products (Chapter 6).

Inflation indicates the rate of change in the overall price level. A moderate rate of growth of inflation creates a conducive environment for growth. However, a very high rate of inflation, such as running inflation, galloping inflation or hyperinflation (these terms are discussed in detail in Chapter 7), creates uncertainty in the environment which jeopardizes business activities and retards economic growth.

Labour and **capital** are important factors as they influence the capacity of production. The changes in their utilization levels, reflected in employment level and capacity utilization, affect wages and interest rates. A decreasing unemployment level and increasing capacity utilization are indicative of emerging resource and capacity constraints. These also indicate that business firms may face higher wages and higher interest rates, and thus, higher cost of production. Conversely, an increasing level of unemployment and idle capital indicates underutilization of resources. Business organizations, in such a situation, can expect availability of labour and capital at cheaper rates.

Saving represents that part of the total income or resources which does not get consumed in a given period of time, and is available for additional investment. Hence, an increasing trend in saving indicates that a larger amount of funds is available easily to business units for further capital formation. While saving enhances availability of funds, investment helps in enhancing the productive capacity. Hence, an increasing trend in investment is indicative of the growing capital stock and expanding productive capacity.

Fiscal deficit, i.e., the difference between government revenue and expenditure, indicates the stance of fiscal policy. A growing fiscal deficit is indicative of expansionary fiscal policy. It adds to the existing demand and helps in employing the underutilized resources or expanding the productive capacity. However, continuous, substantial fiscal deficit, for a prolonged period of time, leads to an expansion in money supply or an increase in the debt burden of the government. Therefore, an increasing trend in fiscal deficit also hints at the inflationary pressure or increasing interest rate (cost of funds) for business firms in the coming period. (Fiscal deficit and related concepts with their implications are discussed in detail in Chapter 8.)

In modern economies, transactions take place in terms of money. Money, by making transactions possible, facilitates economic activities, such as production and consumption. Producers buy resources by making payment in terms of money. Consumers purchase goods and services by making payment in terms of money. These activities lead to demand for money. A shortage of money supply hinders and retards growth in these activities. An excess of money, conversely, leads to higher spending on goods and services, increases the overall price level, and fuels inflation. Apart from inflation, money supply also affects the availability of credit, rates of interest and, thus, the cost of credit. Thus, an increasing trend in the money supply is indicative of liquidity in the system, ease of credit, and inflationary pressure in an economy.

In the present era, each country has some trade relationship with the other countries, and hence, no economy is completely a **closed economy**. A country's transactions with the rest of the world are recorded in the **balance of payment** statement which consists of the current account and the capital account (discussed in detail in Chapter 12).

The **current account** depicts the foreign exchange earnings and outgo from a country on account of goods and services and transfer payments. The current account balance may be in deficit or surplus. In the short-run, the **current account imbalances** (deficit or surplus) may be due to cyclical fluctuations. However, a persistent current account deficit or surplus represents long-run imbalance, and indicates towards structural deficiencies. A persistent current account deficit indicates that an economy is spending more on imports of goods and services than what it is earning from exports. It implies that it is consuming more than it is earning. The converse holds true when there is persistent current account surplus.

The **capital account** depicts the foreign exchange earnings and outgo on account of capital account transactions, such as foreign direct investment, portfolio investment, external assistance, and so on of a country with the rest of the world. Though an increasing amount of foreign capital enhances the overall availability of funds for investment purpose, different types of capital flows have different implications (Chapter 14). For example, an increasing amount of Foreign Direct Investment (FDI) in the short-run enhances the overall availability of resources for domestic producers, but in the long-run, it may even lead to a higher outflow in the form of repatriation of profit and dividend. Similarly, an increasing amount of debt flows, for a prolonged period of time, may lead a country into a debt trap where it may end up borrowing from foreign sources just for making payments related to the past debt. The short-term flows, such as portfolio flows, and NRI deposits create another problem. These flows are highly volatile. Even small changes in domestic or external environment may lead to a large inflow or outflow of such capital which poses threat to the macroeconomic stability of a country.

The **foreign exchange reserves** of the central bank held in the form of foreign exchange, gold, and the Special Drawing Rights (SDRs) are an important indicator of the macroeconomic stability of a country. These reserves are used for meeting the excess of import bill over the export earnings or the current account deficit, repaying foreign debts, and stabilizing exchange rates (Chapter 15).

The **exchange rate**, which is the price of the domestic currency in terms of a foreign currency, is also an important indicator of macroeconomic stability (as elaborated in Chapter 15). Foreign trade and investment decisions are influenced by the prevailing exchange rate. Wide fluctuations in it, which is a short-term phenomena, create uncertainty in the environment, lead business units to postpone their exports, imports, and investment decisions, and thus, retard business and economic growth. Similarly, long-term trends in it reflect on the fundamental weaknesses or strengths. A continuous depreciation of the exchange rate, implying a decline in the value of the domestic currency vis-a-vis foreign currency, reflects the inherent weakness in an economy, and prevents foreigners from investing in it. On the contrary, a continuous appreciation in the exchange rate hints at the sound fundamentals and attracts foreign investors to invest in domestic currency and market.

Trends in the exchange rate, interest rate and inflation rate indicate whether the economic scenario is stable or unstable. There is an interdependency among economic variables and, therefore, instability in any of these variables leads to volatility in other variables. Macroeconomic stability is required for the growth of business organizations and the economy as a whole. The instability increases the risk of investment in domestic markets, and thus, discourages domestic business units as well as foreign companies investing into these markets. The trend in various macroeconomic indicators is depicted in UEE 1.3 using India as the case.

Apart from general trends in economic variables, the trends in socioeconomic variables also affect the business environment. People like to work in those areas or countries where basic facilities, such as health care, safe drinking water, sanitation and educational facilities are available. Business organizations, to attract talented people and to retain trained staff, like to operate from the areas where such facilities are available in plenty. Improvements in social conditions get reflected in various demographic factors such as birth rate, death rate, population growth, age, population density, age distribution, sex ratio, degree of urbanization, health factors such as fertility rate, infant mortality rate, life expectancy at birth, the incidence of major diseases like bird flu, malaria, tuberculosis, HIV/AIDS, etc., and social equality gets reflected in empowerment of women and socially disadvantaged groups. To assess overall changes in socioeconomic factors, various socioeconomic development indices (C1.1) are computed. The improvement in these indices hints at the conducive environment for business organizations.

UNDERSTANDING BUSINESS ENVIRONMENT

UBE 1.1 Trends in Macroeconomic Indicators in India

This UBE highlights the trends in macroeconomic indicators in India.

The Indian economy in 2009–10 and 2010–11 recovered, with a vigour, due to strong fiscal and financial stimuli, from the sharp deceleration in the growth rate experienced during 2008-09 (Table 1.1). However, the same stimuli also fuelled inflationary pressure with CPI based inflation rate crossing two digit figure, which necessitated tightening of the monetary policy. The marked slowdown in the growth in the last two years is partly rooted in the external environment, but is also partly attributed to the contractionary policies pursued to control inflation.

Table 1.1 Trends in Key Economic Indicators

Item	*Average* 2000–01 *to* 2009–10 *(10 years)*	*Average* 2003–04 *to* 2007–08 *(5 years)*	2008–09	2009–10	2010–11	2011–12	2012–13
Real GDP (factor cost) (% change)	7.2	8.7	6.7	8.6	9.3[2R]	6.2[1R]	5.0[AE]
Gross Domestic Saving Rate (% of GDP)	30.7	33.3	32.0	33.7	34.0	30.8	na
Gross Domestic Investment Rate (% of GDP)	31.3	33.6	34.3	36.5	36.8	35.0	na
Inflation WPI (12 month average)	5.4	5.5	8.1	3.8	9.6	8.9	7.6[d]
Inflation CPI (IW) (average)	5.9	5.0	9.1	12.4	10.4	8.4	10.0[d]
Broad Money (M3) (% change)	17.5	18.6	19.3	16.8	16.0	15.6	11.2[h]
Gross fiscal deficit (centre) (% of GDP)	4.8	3.6	6.0	6.5[i]	4.8	5.7[i]	5.1[j]
Merchandise Exports (% change) (US$)	17.7	25.3	13.6	–3.5	40.5	21.3	–4.9[d]
Merchandise Imports (% change) (US$)	19.5	32.3	20.7	–5.0	28.2	32.3	0.0[d]
Foreign exchange reserves (US$ bn.)	162	183	252.0	279.1	304.8	294.4	295.5[f]
Average exchange rate (₹/US$)	45.6	44.1	45.9	47.4	45.56	47.92	54.47[g]

Item	Average 2000–01 *to* 2009–10 *(10 years)*	Average 2003–04 *to* 2007–08 *(5 years)*	2008–09	2009–10	2010–11	2011–12	2012–13
Population (million) (year wise projected population)	na	na	1154	1170	1210[k]	na	na
Per capita Net National Income (factor cost at current prices) (₹)	na	na	40,775	46,249	54,151	61,564	68,747

Notations: na: Not Available; 1R: 1st Revised Estimates, 2R: 2nd Revised Estimates, AE: Advance Estimates, d: 2012-13 (April-January), f: At end January, 2013, g: Average exchange rate for 2012-13 (April 2012-January 2013), i: Fiscal indicators are based on the provisional actual (unadited), j: Budget estimates, k: Census 2011.

Source: Average figures are compiled from RBI (2010), Annual Report. Figures for 2008–09 to 2012–13 are compiled and estimated using data from GOI (2013), Economic Survey 2012–13.

Low levels of fiscal deficit and public debt are considered as key ingredients in the growth and stability of an economy. Operationalization of the Fiscal Responsibility Budget Management Act (FRBMA) of 2003 helped in bringing down the fiscal deficit to 2.7 per cent of GDP by 2007–08 in India. However, the rise in global commodity prices and financial meltdown necessitated fiscal stimulus to sustain domestic demand. Hence, the fiscal deficit increased to a very high level in 2008–09. With the growth reverting to the pre-crisis level, the government resumed the path of fiscal consolidation in 2010–11 with partial exit from the fiscal stimulus package and could bring back the fiscal deficit closer to the targeted levels. However, the fiscal consolidation could not be sustained further in the subsequent period as the growth faltered. The sharp deceleration in the growth rate led to a shortfall in the tax and non-tax revenue from the target levels and widened the fiscal deficit in 2011–12 and 2012–13.

Along with the deceleration in the growth momentum, there was a slowdown in the saving rate. The deceleration in the saving rate, without a commensurate decline in the investment, has resulted in a widening of the current account deficit.

Even in the periods of global turmoil, the Indian capital account surplus was more than enough to meet the current account deficit, leading to net accretion in the foreign exchange reserves. However, the year 2011–12 witnessed a mild decline in these reserves. But again in 2012–13, has registered a net accretion in the foreign exchange reserves because of improvement in net capital inflows. But, the pressure on the BOP due to the widening current account deficit and an overall weakening of the fundamentals of the Indian economy has been putting continuous pressure on the Indian rupee and resulting in a sharp depreciation in its value during the last two years.

Government Economic Policies, Activities and Legislations

Economic policies, activities and legislations pursued by the government are an important determinants of economic environment. Government policies, such as fiscal policy, monetary policy, trade policy, exchange rate policy, minimum wage legislation, safety and health norms at work, regulation, legislation for environment protection, designed to control and regulate economic activities, affect the functioning of business undertakings.

Fiscal policies try to influence the level of aggregate demand through government expenditure, taxes and subsidies. The government, through its expenditure—both consumption and investment, affects the aggregate level of income, which in turn, influences the aggregate demand. The government expenditure not only influences aggregate demand but also competes with the private sector for resources. For example, while investment on infrastructure projects by the government increases aggregate demand, enhances productive capacity, and creates an enabling and supporting environment for business houses, such activities require resources—human, raw material, machinery and finances; and hence, the government is required to compete with the private sector in the market in a free economy or have exclusive command over these resources in a command economy. Fiscal policies, especially taxes and subsidies, also indicate the priorities of the government. Such policies, apart from influencing the level of demand, are quite often used for redirecting resource allocation and income distribution in specific directions. For example, indirect taxes on commodities reduce profits of those business firms which make such commodities, and may compel them to produce the commodities which are not subject to such taxes. Thus, the government often imposes indirect taxes to discourage the production of undesirable commodities. Similarly, direct taxes, for example, higher taxes on profit income and lower taxes on wage income, along with transfer payments in the form of subsidies, scholarships, etc., lead to redistribution of income. The redistribution of income, in turn, influences consumption pattern, which business firms need to be constantly watching to remain in the business. (Fiscal policy is discussed in detail in Chapter 8.)

Monetary and **credit policies** try to influence aggregate demand, overall price level, inflation rate and interest rates by affecting the supply of money, availability of credit and working of the banking sector. These changes impact the demand for products produced by the firms, and also the cost of raw materials, cost of funds and wage rate faced by the business firms, which influence business decisions of production and investment. (Issues in monetary policy are discussed in Chapter 10).

Industrial policies (discussed in Chapter 11) specify the role of private and public sector, small, medium and large industries, and domestic and foreign enterprises in an economy. These policies aim at fostering industrial development, by creating an enabling environment for the participants, and economic growth. These also aim at correcting regional imbalances by providing incentive to business firms for setting up units in backward regions. Promoting horizontal and vertical linkages, creating competitive environment, restricting monopoly and unfair practices, promoting employment, creating, supporting and enabling infrastructure and environment are other major objectives of these policies. To achieve these objectives, the government usually pursues licensing and registration policies; reserves certain items for public enterprises and small scale industries; fixes production, quality, investment, safety and environment protection norms; regulates prices, wages and the cost of credit to various sectors; imposes taxes; provides subsidies and control; and spends on the development of infrastructure, technology, and human capital. Industrial policies determine the efficiency of production and have a direct and profound impact on the functioning of business organizations.

Trade, tariff and foreign capital policies (discussed in Chapters 12, 13, and 14) are formulated to facilitate and regulate the flow of exports, imports and capital. These policies determine the openness of an economy and the competition which domestic players face from foreign markets and foreign companies. In the countries that are trying to achieve growth through exports, these policies can take the form of various incentives in the form of subsidies, easy credit facilities, and import entitlement schemes. Exports are also facilitated through procedural simplification, trade fair in foreign countries, buyer-seller meets, and many such activities. Countries following **open door policies** usually allow liberal entry to import so as to make available quality inputs and final products at competitive prices. Business firms in such an environment have wide options of procuring raw material and other inputs required in the process of production. Such policies, allowing foreign goods, are expected to generate competition in the domestic market, and encourage domestic producers to improve the quality of their products, and reduce the cost of production. On the other hand, countries pursuing a closed door policy try to restrict the entry of imported goods to protect their industries from the foreign produced goods and allow them to develop over a period of time. Though the restrictive trade policies provide protection to domestic firms, these policies also limit the choice of inputs for them.

Similarly, policies regulating the inflow and outflow of foreign capital affect the level of competition in an economy. Easy entry and exit of foreign capital encourages foreign firms to enter and invest in domestic markets, enhances competition, and promotes efficiency and productivity. This also opens up foreign financial markets for domestic firms, and gives them a wider choice of raising resources and reducing the cost of funds.

Exchange rate policies determine the exchange rate regime (deliberated in Chapter 15). A flexible exchange rate regime promotes the market forces, encourages the flow of foreign goods, services and capital. However, such policies also subject an economy to wide fluctuations. Fixed exchange rate regime, though not so conducive for foreign trade and capital flows, provides stability to a system. In such a system, exporters, importers and investors are assured of the value of their domestic currency in the international market; and this stability assures them of protection from foreign exchange risk.

Various government policies and regulatory measures are designed, by and large, to minimize the conflicts of various agents operating in an economy. For example, firms' activities as producer and their attempt to maximize their private gains or profits, lead to considerable social costs, in terms of environmental pollution, congestion in cities, creation of slums, etc. Such social costs bring firms' interest in conflict with that of the society, and policies have to be formulated to bring in a sense of social responsibility on them.

International Economic Environment

International economic environment refers to all economic trends and conditions outside a given country. It is determined by trend in socioeconomic variables, such as GDP, inflation rate, exchange rate, economic system and policies pursued in foreign countries, the functioning of bilateral and multilateral organizations, such as the WTO, IMF, World Bank, Regional Trading Blocks, and the agreements which are arrived at these platforms.

There are no closed economies in the present era of international economic cooperation and globalization. Hence, depending on the degree of openness the constituents or determinants of international economic environment influence the working of domestic markets as described hereinafter.

Fluctuations in GDP or business activities abroad affect the demand for domestically produced goods in international markets. For example, recession in international markets reduces the income level in foreign countries, curtails the imports of foreign consumers, and thus, reduces the aggregate demand for domestically produced goods. Conversely, an expansion or a boom in foreign countries increases their income levels, demand for imported goods, and demand for domestically produced goods and services, thereby encouraging domestic business activities.

Business fluctuations in foreign countries also affect the flow of foreign capital to domestic markets. For example, recession in foreign countries pushes away capital from foreign countries to domestic markets.

Inflation rate in foreign countries also influences the cost of production in domestic markets. For example, an increase in the prices of crude oil and petroleum products affects the cost of production in the domestic market and inflation in the international markets gets imported to the domestic markets.

Similarly, agreements emerging on the platforms of multilateral, bilateral organizations and/or regional trading blocks have an immense impact on the international business environment and also on the functioning of domestic units. For example, the agreement related to patents on the WTO platform, making member countries move from the process patent to the product patent, has necessitated a change in domestic patent laws in many countries, and has also increased the cost of medicines in these countries. Similarly, the agreement to eliminate the quantitative or **quota** restrictions on textiles imposed by the developed countries has opened up wider opportunities for textile exporter countries. Likewise, tariff reduction and elimination of non-tariff barriers, mandated by the WTO, has necessitated many countries to reduce tariff and non-tariff barriers, and open up their economies for foreign goods and services.

In an open economy framework, though, the most affected units or sectors are those, that are engaged in exports and imports, the firms concentrating only on domestic markets are also not insulated from changes taking place in international scenario. This is because when foreign goods enter domestic markets they pose competition even for those firms which cater only to domestic markets. International economic integration however, not only poses problems of competition to native businesses, but also opens up technological opportunities and market abroad. Thus, the international economic environment has a significant influence on the economic environment of a country, and thereby, on the functioning of its business undertakings.

1.5.2 Legal Environment

The functioning of a company impacts its internal stakeholders such as shareholders, managers and workers as well as external stakeholders such as suppliers, consumers and the community at large. Different stakeholders have different interest in the working of an organization. At times, these interests may conflict with each other. For example, textile industry, trying to maximize its profit, may not internalize the cost of pollution of the nearby water bodies where its used chemicals are discharged. Such discharges may affect the livelihood of those who are dependent on marine life for their earnings. Hence, world over, the governments enact laws to resolve conflicting interests and minimize the harmful impacts of the functioning of companies.

Complying to these laws often necessitates changes in work practices and at times requires additional expenses on the part of the company, affecting their profitability. Lack of understanding of legal environment can lead a business organization into problems. (The issues related to the legal environment are elaborated in Chapter 16.)

1.5.3 Demographic Environment

Demographic environment is determined by population size, density, age composition, gender composition, occupation pattern, education level, family size and structure, and many such attributes of the population (described in Chapter 17).

Demographic environment affects both demand and supply sides of a market. It affects the demand side as human beings are consumers of most of the products sold in a market. The total size of the population affects the total demand for a product, whereas many other attributes of the population such as age and gender composition and economic stratification affect product mix. For example, age composition in favour of the child population creates demand for educational material, toys and baby products. Similarly, gender composition in favour of females signifies that there is a likelihood of more demand for cosmetic and other products demanded by the female population. On the supply side, population size, migration and mobility, and age structure determine the supply of labour, which is an important factor of production, whereas education profile affects the labour quality and productivity.

Importance of demography in business decisions is indisputable. Knowledge of demography can be used in various business decisions, such as site selection for production or distribution, human resource planning, market area assessment, financial planning, sales forecasting, product development and launching, target marketing and logistic planning.

1.5.4 Technological Environment

A given set of technologies available for the conduct of business determines the **technological environment** (Chapter 18) of business. Technology is the application of science, art and other fields of knowledge in various activities such as designing tools and equipments, producing goods and supplying services, communicating information and enhancing productivity.

Technological advancements are driving force behind the global developments for centuries, but they are much more rapid in the present era, making the global environment highly dynamic and challenging.

Business organizations have been an eager developer and extensive user of new technologies. They keep identifying and exploring new technologies that can reduce time and cost, improve productivity and provide them a competitive edge over their competitors. They use technological advancements for hiring and outsourcing policies, inventory management and quality control, improving security, reducing time, improving the speed of communication and widening customer reach. However, the design of an appropriate technology is a time consuming job, and requires large investment in research and development. It is also risky as high investment may not result in desirable outcomes and impose a financial burden on the investment firms. At the same time, there is a risk of inventions being copied by the competitors or development of superior technology by them which can make the existing technology outdated.

1.5.5 Natural Environment

Natural environment (Chapter 19) consists of all natural resources such as raw material, and energy sources such as water, air and climate. The business has two way relationship with the natural environment. First of all, natural environment is a source of many raw materials of almost all business organizations. A region, prosperous in the natural environment, can provide natural resources in abundance and at a cheaper rate; and, thus, becomes attractive for business units. For example, in the recent period, many multinational organizations are attracted towards the African Continent primarily because of its natural resource abundance. Second, natural environment itself is affected by business activities adversely. Often, in their drive to maximize profit, business units exploit natural resources without bothering about the environmental damage their activities may be causing. The damage is not only due to the unhindered extraction of natural resources but also due to emission of hazardous pollutants in the air and discharge of toxic waste in the water. Environmental damage is not only harmful for human beings but also for other sources of life. For example, large scale deforestation destroys fauna and fungi, which affects the livelihood of tribes living in forests, and water pollution damages marine life, which affects the livelihood of fishermen. In the long-run, by reducing the availability of natural resources environmental damage also adversely affects business activity and makes business unsustainable. Thus, for business sustainability, it is essential that business organizations are aware of environmental issues, follow environmentally sustainable practices, and internalize the cost of environmental damage.

1.6 STEPS IN ENVIRONMENTAL ANALYSIS

Environmental analysis helps managers in ascertaining threats and opportunities present in the surrounding. Given the environment, and the strengths and weaknesses of the organization, managers decide on the strategy that can help their organizations mitigate the risk from the emerging issues and benefit from the available opportunities.

Four steps are involved in environmental analysis. The steps—scanning, monitoring, forecasting and assessment—are described hereinafter.

1. Scanning: Scanning involves continuous observation and scrutiny of various socioeconomic, demographic, technological, legal and natural environmental factors from various media, such as newspaper, television, internet, and reports published by research and consultancy organizations. Exploratory in nature, scanning helps in early detection of emerging trends that are relevant for the functioning of an organization.

2. Monitoring: Scanning provides a quick idea about the direction in which some critical variables are moving. However, for decision making, we need to have a clear and accurate picture about the direction in which critical variables are tending to. Monitoring helps in this. Monitoring involves closer scrutiny and in-depth analysis of critical environmental trends unearthed during the environmental scrutiny. During monitoring data, on various critical factors, for several periods, is recorded, followed and interpreted so as to be more sure of their occurrence. The process of monitoring helps in

(i) More accurate assessment of emerging trends that could be made during scanning
(ii) Identifying the areas where further monitoring is needed
(iii) Identifying the areas where further scanning is needed

3. Forecasting: Scanning and monitoring provide the picture of the current environment. This current picture is sufficient for day to day operational decisions, which are short-term in nature. But, business organizations also need to decide for future, i.e. they have to take strategic decisions, which have long-term implication. For such decisions, it is essential for organizations to know the values of critical variables in the ensuing period. Forecasting thus is essential. Forecasting involves predicting future values on the basis of past trends using various quantitative and qualitative techniques.

4. Assessment: Current and forecasted values of critical factors, emerged from scanning, monitoring and forecasting, are used for ascertaining their likely impact on the organization. During the assessment process, not only the values but also the cause and effect relationship is analysed, i.e., an assessment of the reasons for particular emerging trend are analysed. The assessment of cause and effect relationship helps an organization in formulating strategies that can help them mitigating risk and profit from emerging opportunities.

1.7 SIGNIFICANCE OF MACRO BUSINESS ENVIRONMENT

The macro business environment, unlike the micro business environment, does not affect day-to-day operational decision of a firm, but exerts a significant influence on strategic decisions. An in depth understanding of macro environment is most essential at the higher level of management. At this level, managers have to deal with the long-term or **strategic decisions,** which provide their firms with long-run advantages. Strategic decisions, such as expansion, diversification, mergers and acquisitions, research and development, advertising, packaging, etc., have implications for sustainability, performance, and long-term growth of firms. For strategic decisions, managers need to carry out a sector-specific as well as an overall economic analysis. They need to understand economic policies of the government, and also be able to ascertain the implications of these policies for the overall structure and environment of an economy in general and for their business in particular. They need to understand demographic changes as well as technological advancements. To safeguard their interest, they should be familiar with the legal environment in which they are operating. Apart from other constituents of business environment, for sustainability of business, managers also need to give adequate attention to the impact of their activities on the natural environment. While assessing the business environment, in specific, managers need to look at the following analysis:

Specific Industry Analysis

The analysis of trends in output, prices, competition, etc., in a particular industry gives a fair idea to managers about the market structure in which they are operating, and their firm's relative position in the overall market.

Government Regulation and Policy Impact Analysis

Policies formulated by governments, like fiscal, monetary, industrial and trade policies, affect a number of key variables, such as inflation rate, tax rate, exchange rate, credit availability, interest rate, disposable income, production level, product location, and so on. These changes, in turn, have substantial impact on costs, revenues and profitability of firms.

Assessment of the Long-term Trends

The assessment of long-term trends in national income, disposable incomes, per capital income, poverty and inequality level, industrial production, capital and money markets, trade and foreign capital flows, demographic trends, and changes in natural environment, helps managers in identifying the constraints emerging from the working of an economy. Similarly, a detailed analysis of emerging trends in technology and demography, leading to changes in consumer tastes and preferences, government policies, raw material supplies, etc., facilitates them in carrying out strategic planning, and taking expansion and diversification decisions.

Business decisions taken in isolation of the macroeconomic factors and environment may lead to misguided analysis and policies, and hence, heavy losses. For example, a decision to expand a business on a large scale, in a country stagnated over a long period, and having a low per capita income and a low purchasing power, may lead to a waste of resources. Firms may not be able to cover their overheads or fixed costs and may end- up making losses in the long-run. Similarly, firms lose profitable opportunities by not diversifying their production base in the economies where the structure is continuously changing.

Given the importance of environmental analysis for business decisions, and given that it is a time and resource intense activity, many firms maintain a separate department that can continuously assess the changes taking place in the environment, and inform the authorities about the emerging threats and opportunities.

SUMMARY

The term **business environment** refers to all those factors that are external to a business unit, but impact its decisions. It comprises two components- micro business environment and macro business environment. Micro business environment refers to all those external factors that are in the immediate surroundings of a business organization. It consists of sellers, resellers, intermediaries, competitors, consumers and the public. Micro business environment affects the day-to-day operational decisions of an organization. A business organization can, to some extent, influence its micro business environment. The macro business environment consists of general external factors that are not under control of any business organization. It comprises economic environment (which is influenced by the economic system, planning process, economic structure, business fluctuations, trend in macroeconomic variables, government policies, and international economic environment), demographic environment, technological environment, legal environment and natural environment. The macro business environment, though does not affect operational decisions of a business unit, exerts significant influence on strategic decisions, such as launching of a new product, mergers and acquisitions, and research and development, which have a long-term impact.

A four step process is followed for business environmental analysis. These steps are scanning, monitoring, forecasting and assessment. The business environment exerts a significant impact on business decisions, hence, many business organizations have separate economic analysis wing that continuously analyzes the environment and updates it on possible emerging threats and opportunities.

Implications for Managers

Different components of business environment influence different types of business decisions. The micro business environment influences the day-to-day operational decisions and tactical decisions, such as selection of suppliers, resellers and intermediaries and their locations, determination of the price of a commodity and its attributes, providing services to consumers to gain their loyalty, and controlling public opinion by maintaining the quality of products, providing satisfactory services and controlling damage to external factors. The operational efficiency of an organization depends on the effectiveness with which it deals with its suppliers, resellers, distributors, advertising firms and financial intermediaries, consumers and the general public.

The macro business environment affects strategic decisions, such as expansion, diversification, advertising, and R&D. In specific, different constituents of macro environment influence different aspects of business. The economic environment influences the price, cost, quantity and profitability. The demographic environment determines the overall size of the market and the product mix. Technological environment affects the factor intensity and technique of production. Natural environment determines the availability of natural resources used by business and the environmental practices that a unit need to follow. The legal environment influences the market structure in which it has to operate, and it also imposes certain regulatory compliance on the firm, which can affect the production level, location of unit and many such aspects.

It is not only the environment that affects business decisions, but the business practices and activities also influence the overall economic environment. No single business unit, though, can influence the environment, business organizations as a whole can. For example, overall business activities determine the trend in the overall output, price, investment, employment, interest rate, exchange rate and many other economic variables. Business associations and lobbies can influence government policies through representations, deliberations, discussions and suggestions. Business practices can affect the natural environment as well as compel the government to make modifications in its legal framework to protect the environment as well as the general public interest. Research and development activities can change the technological environment.

Thus, the business environment and business decisions are interdependent and influence each other. Continuous interaction between the two infuses dynamism in the business environment and poses continuous challenges for business firms.

REVIEW QUESTIONS

1.1 What is business and its objectives?

1.2 What do you understand by the term environment?

1.3 What are the components of business environment? Differentiate between these components.

1.4 What are the main constituents of the micro business environment? What types of business decisions are affected by micro business environment?

1.5 What are the main constituents of the macro business environment? What types of business decisions are affected by macro business environment?

1.6 Which component of business environment is relevant for operational decisions?

1.7 Which component of business environment is relevant for strategic decisions?

1.8 What are the different steps involved in business environmental analysis?

1.9 What is the difference between scanning and monitoring? How far assessment is different from scanning and monitoring?

1.10 Why forecasting is required in business environmental analysis?

1.11 What is the significance of business environment for managers?

CASE ANALYSIS EXERCISE

C 1.1 Socioeconomic Development Indicators

One of the widely used indicators of socioeconomic development of a country is the **Human Development Index** (HDI).

Published by the UNDP, the HDI is a summary measure of human development. It measures the average achievements of a country in three basic dimensions of human development—health, education and knowledge, and standard of living.

While preparing the HDI, an index (*I*) is created for each of these dimensions (*x*) using the following formula:

$$I x = (x - \min(x))/(\max(x) - \min(x))$$

where,

x = Actual value of a given dimension

$\min(x)$ = Minimum value of dimension x, and

$\max(x)$ = Maximum value of dimension x

In Human Development Report of 2009, the three dimensions of HDI were measured as:

Health: Measured by Life Expectancy at birth (LE) (life).

Education and knowledge: Measured by the Adult Literacy Rate (ALR) (two-third weight) and combined primary, secondary and tertiary Gross Enrolment Ratio (GER) (one-third weight) (education).

Standard of living: Measured by the Gross Domestic Product (GDP) per capita in Purchasing Power Parity (PPP) terms in US $ (income).

The HDI was estimated as a simple average of the three dimensions (sub indices *Ix*) as:

$$\text{HDI} = (1/3)\ (\text{I}_{\text{life}}) + (1/3)\ (\text{I}_{\text{education}}) + (1/3)\ (\text{I}_{\text{income}})$$

The HDI index below 0.5 was considered to be indicative of a low level of development. A HDI of 0.8 or more was considered to be a representative of a high level of development. The HDI in the range of 0.5 to 0.8 indicated middle level of development.

Since 2010, Human Development Report (HDR) some definition and measurement related changes have been brought about in the index. The three dimensions are now measured as:

Health: Measured by Life Expectancy at birth (LE).

Education and knowledge: Measured by mean years of schooling (years that a 25-year old person or older has spent in school) and expected years of schooling (years that a 5-year old child will spend with his education in his whole life). Geometric mean of mean years of schooling index and expected years of schooling index is considered for actual value of education dimension.

Standard of living: Measured by the Gross National Income (GNI) per capita in purchasing power parity (PPP) terms in US$.

The HDI is estimated as the geometric mean of the three dimensions (sub indices *Ix*) as:

$$\text{HDI} = \text{I}_{\text{life}}^{1/3} \cdot \text{I}_{\text{education}}^{1/3} \cdot \text{I}_{\text{income}}^{1/3}$$

Unlike the old method, the new aggregation method embodies imperfect substitutability across all dimensions.

Unlike earlier Human Development Reports (HRDs), the HDR 2010 uses relative thresholds based on HDI quartiles for country classification. A country is classified into the "very high development" group if its HDI is in the top quartiles, i.e., percentiles 76–100, in the "high development" group if its HDI is in percentiles 51–75, in the "medium development" group if its HDI is in percentiles 26–50, and in the "low development" group if its HDI is in the bottom quartile.

Apart from the HDI, the UNDP also publishes **Inequality—Adjusted Human Development Index** (IHDI), **Gender Inequality Index** (GII) and **Multidimensional Poverty Index** (MPI).

The IHDI adjusts the HDI for inequality in the distribution of each dimension across the population, whereas GII adjusts the HDI for inequality between female and male achievements in these dimensions. The MPI looks at the development at the micro level and identifies multiple deprivations at the individual level in health, education and standard of living.

The HDI, IHDI, GII and MPI figures, presented in Table 1.2 , indicate that globally India ranked 136 on HDI and 132 on GII, but it is better off on IIHDI (out of 187 countries covered by the latest Human Development Report).

Table 1.2 India's Global Position on Various Socioeconomic Indicators, 2012

Country	*Country Classification/ Level of Human Development*	*Human Development Index (HDI)*		*Inequality – adjusted Human Development Index (IHDI)*		*Gender Inequality Index (GII)*		*Multidimensional Poverty Index (MPI)*
		Value	*Rank*	*Value*	*Rank*	*Value*	*Rank*	*Value*
Norway	Very High	0.955	1	0.894	1	0.065	5	Na
Australia	Very High	0.938	2	0.864	2	0.115	17	Na
Brazil	High	0.730	85	0.531	70	0.447	85	0.011
Sri Lanka	High	0.715	92	0.607	53	0.402	75	0.021
China	Medium	0.699	101	0.543	67	0.213	35	0.056
India	Medium	0.554	136	0.392	91	0.610	132	0.283
Zimbabwe	Low	0.397	172	0.284	116	0.544	116	0.172
Niger	Low	0.304	186	0.200	131	0.707	146	0.642

Note: The year of compilation for MPI value varies across countries and is as follows:
Brazil and Nigeria—2006, India 2005-06, China 2002, for Sri Lanka—2003 and Zimbabwe- 2010/2011.

Source: UNDP (2013), Human Development Report.: Tackling Inequalities in a post 2015 framework.

Questions

1. What is Human Development Index (HDI)? What are its constituents?
2. What are the drawbacks of HDI?
3. What is Inequality adjusted Human Development Index (IHDI)? Why is it estimated?
4. Why is Gender Inequality Index (GII) estimated?
5. What dimensions Multidimensional Poverty Index (MPI) captures?
6. As a manager, how would you make use of these indices in your business decisions?

C1.2 Doing Business in South Asia

South Asian countries score relatively low in terms of their position in the World Bank's *Doing Business* index with an average rank of 111 among 185 countries in the latest round, which suggests that firms in the region face a difficult business environment (Figure 1.4). The sub-indices suggest that South Asian firms encounter serious obstacles in getting reliable access to electricity, in paying taxes, and in enforcing contracts. Finding difficult to access electricity is consistent with the shortages and demand supply gaps that have characterized this sector. The obstacles in paying taxes are also reflected in the relatively narrower tax bases and lower tax revenue-to-GDP ratios in South Asian countries compared with the average for other developing countries (see South Asia Annex of the *Global Economic Prospects* June 2012 report). South Asian countries, however, score better in terms of access to credit and protecting investors than their overall rank suggests, reflecting the strength of domestic financial markets.

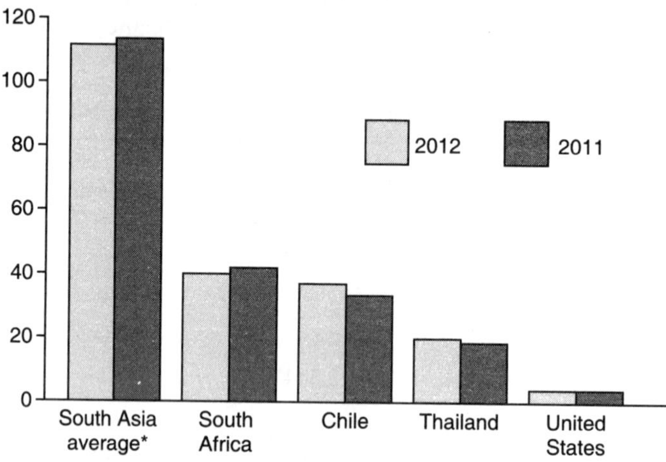

"East of doing business" rank among 185 countries
(Lower values indicate better rank)

Source: **Doing Business 2013** report, World Band
Note: South Asia average includes Bangladesh, India, Nepal, Pakistan and Sri Lanka.
See: www.doingbusiness.org for more details.

Figure 1.4 South Asia is a Difficult Place for Doing Business.

In terms of changes in ranks between the 2011 and 2012 rounds, Nepal, Pakistan, and Bangladesh fell by one, three and five notches, respectively, while India's rank held steady. Sri Lanka's rank improved from 96 to 81—making it one of the top ten countries in the world that have improved the most, in part due to improvements in the process of starting a business and getting access to credit.

Source: The World Bank (2013), Global Economic Prospects, Vol. 6, January 13, Washington D.C.: World Bank.

Questions

1. What is Doing Business Index? Who prepares this index?
2. How did South Asia fare in Doing Business Index in 2011?
3. What are the serious obstacles for business in South Asia region?
4. On what parameters South Asia region fares better?
5. In which countries of South Asia region the business environment has deteriorated over the period 2010–2011?
6. In which countries of South Asia region the business environment has improved over the period 2010–2011?
7. Find out from Doing Business 2013 Report the countries in which you prefer to set up your business?

SUGGESTED FURTHER READING

Conklin, D. (2011), The Global Environment of Business: New Paradigms for International Management, *IVEY Business Journal*, July–August.

Chakrabarty, K.C. (2013), Transit Path for Indian Economy: Six Steps for transforming the Elephant into a tiger, *RBI Bulletin*, January.

Earnest and Young (2011), Tracking Global Trends: How Six Key Developments are Shaping the Business World, (online) http://www.ey.com/GL/en/Issues/Business-environment/Six-global-trends-shaping-the-business-world.

Government of India (2013), Economic Survey 2012–13.

International Monetary Fund (2013), *World Economic Outlook*, Washington, DC, April

Khan, H.R. (2012), Turmoil in Global Economy, The Indian Perspective, *RBI Bulletin*, September.

Reserve Bank of India (2013), Macroeconomic and Monetary Developments in 2012–13, May.

Subbarao, D. (2013), India's Macroeconomic Challenges: Some Perspectives, *RBI Bulletin*, April.

United Nations Development Programme (2013), Human Development Report, The Rise of the South: Human Progress in a Diverse World, New York, USA.

CHAPTER 2

Economic System: Planning and Market

2.1 INTRODUCTION

Afghanistan is a country with plenty of minerals and other natural resources, but international investors are not willing to take a plunge and start a business there. Even the domestic business units find the system not to be very conducive for their growth and are uncertain about their fate.

What is hindering the prosperity of businesses in Afghanistan? Why investors are reluctant to invest there inspite of the immense opportunities that are available in the country? One of the major factors that has been identified behind the reluctance of the investors is the unfavourable economic system, i.e., the weak institutional mechanism or rules and regulations governing the property rights and resource allocation mechanism. The country's economic system is not business oriented. The existing economic system is not only detrimental to the growth of business units but also that of the economy as a whole.

On the contrary, business oriented economic system of Malaysia, a small economy, is a very supportive of business enterprises, domestic as well as international corporations, which has enabled the country to create strong manufacturing and export base.

Countries differ in their economic system. Business units closely look at this aspect of the economy before taking a decision to set up a unit. Hence, managers need to know what the term economic system refers to, what are the different types of economic systems, and what are their advantages and disadvantages.

Accordingly, in Section 2.2 we will look into the definition of the economic system. We will deal with classification of economic system in Section 2.3. In Section 2.4 we will discuss advantages and disadvantages of different types of economic system.

2.2 ECONOMIC SYSTEM

An economy consists of three basic economic units which perform various economic activities under given resource constraints and the rules set by their society as follows:

Consumers/Households

Households are the consumers and owners of the **factors of production** land, labour, capital, and entrepreneurship.

As consumers, households maximize utility subject to their **budget constraints**. They demand goods and services because these provide satisfaction or utility to them. Since consumption is the sole end and purpose of all production activities, the level and nature of consumer demand govern the pattern of production. The revenue of firms largely depends on the final choice made by the consumers.

As owners of factors of production, households supply factors of production in the factor market, which generate factor income for them.

Business Firms/Producers

One of the important objectives of business units is to maximize profit given the **resource constraint**. Resource constraint poses challenge before business organizations while allocating resources in alternative uses that minimizes cost, maximizes output, and hence, maximizes profit.

Governments

Governments are faced with a multiplicity of objectives, which may be in conflict with each other. For example, generally, they are motivated by the desire to maximize community welfare, but they are often influenced by the desire for power and/or sectional interests which can conflict with community welfare objective. Similarly, the short-term objectives of governments, such as full employment, price, interest rate and exchange rate stability, may conflict with its long-term objectives, such as desired composition of output, improved distribution of income and economic growth.

An **economic system** is a set of institutions, principles and mechanisms created by a society to facilitate economic units to address their basic economic problems of allocation of scarce resources and perform their basic economic activities. Every organized society follows some or the other economic system.

2.3 CLASSIFICATION OF ECONOMIC SYSTEM

Economic systems are classified using two different approaches. One approach differentiates the systems on the basis of ownership of resources, whereas another approach classifies the systems on the basis of allocation mechanism (Figure 2.1).

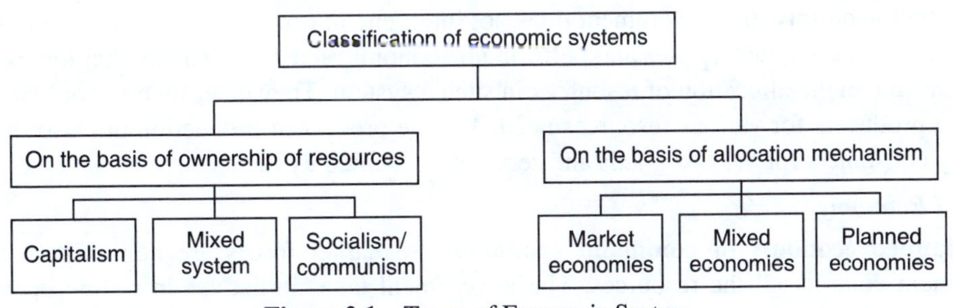

Figure 2.1 Types of Economic System.

Broadly, on the basis of ownership of resources, economic systems are classified into capitalism, socialism, and mixed economies.

Capitalism

In a capitalistic economic system, resources are owned by private individuals and organizations. Various economic decisions—production, distribution, exchange and consumption—are taken by them without any interference from the government or external body. The **market forces**, which are demand and supply forces, play a major role in economic decisions in such a system. The basic objective of capitalism is individual economic freedom and "each according to his means".

Socialism

Socialism refers to an economic system where the state owns and operates many of the nation's major industries, such as banks, airlines, railroads, telephone, electricity, and the factors of production and distribution. Planning plays an important role in such a system. The state plans for a given period of time, and decides on what to produce, how much to produce, how to produce, and at what price to supply resources and commodities to producers and consumers. The market forces are missing in such a system. The basic objective of socialism is to ensure social justice and more equitable distribution of wealth.

An extreme form of socialism is communism, where all the means of production are owned and operated by the government. However, the basic difference between communism and socialism lies in the motive behind the two systems. In socialism, the motive is "each according to his deeds", whereas communism believes in "each according to his needs".

Commonly cited examples of socialist or communist or command economies are former USSR, North Korea, Cuba, China and Iran.

Mixed Economic System

A **mixed economic system** consists of characteristics of both capitalism and socialism. In such a system, public and private ownership co-exist and decisions taken by consumers, businesses and the government determine economic activities.

Alternatively, on the basis of extent to which market mechanism is allowed in the allocation and distribution activities, the system can be characterized as market economies, planned economies and mixed economies.

Market Economy

In a **market economy**, the government does not intervene in economic activities and allows the private sector to set up enterprises and perform all economic activities. The market forces play an important role in the allocation of resources in such a system. They determine not only the prices faced by producers for various resources needed in the process of production but also the prices faced by consumers for various goods and services consumed by them.

Planned Economy

In a **planned economy** or **command economy** the market forces are non-existent and the government controls all the resources. The government takes initiatives in setting up business enterprises, and decides the prices at which resources are to be supplied to producers and commodities to be supplied to consumers.

Mixed Economy

A **mixed economy** consists of some features of a market economy and some of a planned economy. In such an economy, in priority areas the prices are fixed by the government, whereas in other areas the prices are left to be determined by the market forces.

At present, there is no country which has an economic system that is cent per cent based on either communism or socialism or capitalism. All countries today have mixed economic systems or mixed economies, with some free enterprises and some government ownership; and prices in some sectors fixed by the government and the rest determined by the market forces.

The movement of the USA, the world's largest economy, and China and India, the two leading emerging markets, towards a mixed economic system is described in UBE 2.1.

UNDERSTANDING BUSINESS ENVIRONMENT

UBE 2.1 Economic Systems in China, India and USA

Citing the examples of China, India and the USA, this UBE describes how different systems have moved more towards a mixed economic system.

During the first 30 years, after the formation of the People's Republic of China (PRC) in 1949, the world's most populous countries, China followed the system of planned economy. Planning committees of the state set targets for different spheres of economic development, allocated resources for different production units, and tightly controlled the quality and prices of various commodities. Not only factories and commercial department produced and stocked goods as per the state plans, but even farmers followed the cropping and production pattern set by the state. Though the system led to a stable planned development of the country, the economy, overall, lacked dynamism and achieved constrained growth.

From a highly communist system, China gradually started moving to more socialistic pattern in 1978, when it initiated economic reforms in rural areas. Farmers were given the right to use their land, decide the cropping pattern, and supply the products in the market independently. Prices of most of the farm products were freed. The impact of these reforms was felt on the agricultural productivity. The reform process gradually encompassed even the urban areas. With the gradual introduction of reforms in the various sectors of the economy, assigning greater freedom and importance of the non-public sectors and opening up of the economy to foreign sector, China could achieve impressive progress and could produce enough food and clothing for its people by the end of 1980s. By the end of 20th century China could quadruple the 1980's GNP. Today, Chinese population enjoys a high standard of living and modern amenities.

At present, the Chinese economic system is characterized by a socialist market economic system where the public sector plays the main role and co-exists with the private sector. The market mechanism plays much greater role in the system in the allocation of resources as compared to the pre-1978 period.

Unlike China, India has been following the mixed economic system since its independence in 1947. In the initial stages of development, planning process was emphasized and allowed limited private participation in various economic spheres. However, over a period of time, especially, after the onset of reforms in 1991, the Indian economy has become more and more liberalized and globalized. At present, in India private sector co-exists with the public sector. For example, though government control exists in the areas of procurement of foodgrains in the form of Minimum Support Prices (MSP) and the subsequent distribution of these foodgrains and pulses through the government set up known as the Public Distribution System (PDS). A parallel open market also exists for these products. Similarly, in many other areas, such as energy, telecommunication, banking, etc., private and public ownership operate and exist simultaneously. In fact there is a multiplicity of sectors—private, public, joint, cooperative, small and tiny sectors, public private partnership (PPP) (for more details of PPP refer to case analysis C1.1). A complexity in the system is present at other levels as well. For example, India has multiplicity of allocation and pricing mechanism; allocation through free market forces in some sectors co-exist with the allocation achieved through five-year plans (for more details of five-year plan refer to UEE 1.2), annual plans, rolling plans, price control and rationing, licensing, and other regulatory measures.

Inspite of major initiatives towards globalization, the Indian markets are not fully free. Various trade barriers exist which prevent dumping of cheap products by foreign countries in the domestic markets and other practices with the potential to jeopardize macroeconomic stability of the country.

Following a mixed economic system with some elements of socialism and some of capitalism, India has achieved an impressive growth in the last one decade. It is the largest emerging economy after China and is ranked fourth in terms of purchasing power parity GDP by the IMF in 2010.

Contrary to China and India, the Unites States of America (USA), the world's largest economic, military and cultural power for nearly a century and described as a capitalist economy, believes in a free market economy. Millions of independent buyers and sellers decide about what to produce, how much to produce, and what price to supply goods, services and factors of production in the market. The producers have a freedom to produce, whereas the households have a freedom to consume.

Inspite of their faith in capitalism, the principles of free market and the concept of laissez-faire, and the doctrine opposing government interference in an economy except to maintain law and order, the Americans have used the government at times to nurture new industries, protect their farmers and agricultural products, and companies from foreign competition, and also to ensure competition and free enterprise in the domestic market. The constitution (adopted in 1787) provides the government the power to regulate commerce with foreign nations and among the states, create money and regulate its value, develop road and post office network, and fix the rules regulating patents, copyrights, and bankruptcies.

At present, the US economy can be characterized as a mixed economy where privately-owned business and the government both play an important role in economic activities. Private businesses produce most goods and services. Consumers are the king in this system. Two-third of the nation's output goes to individuals for personal use and the remaining one-third is brought by the government and businesses. Though the private sector plays the lead in this system, the government is primarily responsible for the administration of justice, education, the road system, statistical reporting system, and national defence. It also plays an important role in the areas where the private system does not work or the areas which are beyond the reach of the market forces. It regulates natural monopolies, provides welfare and unemployment benefits to people who cannot support themselves, take care of aged, regulates air and water pollution, and plays a leading role in space research and technology which is too expensive for the private enterprises to handle.

Free market forces, supported by the government and the wave of technological innovations in computing, telecommunications, and biological sciences have led to the largest economic expansion during the 1990s in the US history. Inspite of its success as an economic power, the country has been subjected to business fluctuations, a characteristic of market economies. It has been through ups and downs in business activities and faced periods of prolonged recession or depression (for example, the great depression of 1929 to 1940) and downturns, and also the periods of high inflation (for example during the 1970s, and early 1980s). In the aftermath of the sub-prime lending crisis, the country faced economic challenges such as depreciation of the dollar, volatility and speculative attacks in the stock markets, burgeoning trade and fiscal deficit, and a sluggish job market.

2.4 PLANNING PROCESS

Resources, whether with a single economic unit or with an economy as a whole, are limited, and hence, **planning** is needed for an efficient allocation of these resources among alternative uses. Planning at the national level is carried out to allocate resources according to national priorities, and economic and social objectives. It requires a review of the current state as well as the level of development of the economy, an estimation of potential wealth or resources, a setting of the targets to be achieved at the end of the planning horizon in the light of long-term goals, a reconciliation of the competing demands of various productive sectors, and allocation of resources in the best possible or most efficient manner to achieve the stated goals.

The planning process is an integral part of communist and socialist states. However, even capitalist economies may adopt planning process retaining their basic free market structure. At present, all countries have mixed economic systems and follow planning, to a smaller or greater extent, to stimulate the level of investment, encourage technological innovations, use the resources as per national priorities and evolving economic situation, and reconcile the process of economic growth with the overall socioeconomic development of the country. Planning process takes up an immediate priority and plays a crucial role in underdeveloped countries facing the vicious circle of poverty.

The planning process is classified broadly into two categories—imperative planning and indicative planning.

Under **imperative planning**, there is an element of compulsion. Under such a planning process, the government or the central planning authorities dictate production, investment, distribution, consumption and pricing decisions, and hence it is incompatible with a democratic set-up where economic units enjoy freedom of ownership and decision making.

In free societies, especially the societies with mixed economic set-up, the indicative planning process is pursued and preferred over imperative planning process (as illustrated in UBE 1.2). Under **indicative planning** process, the planning body sets the broad targets in terms of sectoral investment, production, saving, exports and an overall growth rate during a specified period of time. This type of planning process tries to evolve a consensus among and cooperation from different segments (such as government, industry, trade unions, farmers, and others) for plan priorities, goals, and methods of achieving the same through wide discussions and deliberations. The government acts more as a facilitator and coordinator in the process; the success of the process depends on the level of participation at all levels.

UNDERSTANDING BUSINESS ENVIRONMENT

UBE 2.2 Planning in India

Planning has played an important part in resource allocation and achieving growth targets in the Indian Economy. This UBE sketches how India has moved from a largely imperative planning to an indicative planning process.

Capital deficiency was identified in India as one of the major obstacles in the development of the country suffering from low per capita income, high growth of population and underutilization of resources. Acceleration in the saving rate and transformation of such savings into productive investment were necessitated to boost up the level of investment in the country which was caught up in the vicious cycle of low saving leading to low investment, and hence, low income. Planning was identified as an approach to break this circle, and comprehensive development plans were advocated with specific plan targets. Planning has been used in India as an important instrument for achieving the objective of faster growth, realization of full employment, attainment of self-reliance, reduction in regional disparities and economic inequalities, modernization of various sectors of the economy, and attainment of overall economic and social development of the country.

The **Planning Commission** was set up in India in March 1950, to set a broad framework for planned development, determine plan priorities, assess the availability of resources such as, manpower, capital and others, suggest the methods of utilizing resources in the most efficient ways, identify the factors retarding growth, make periodic assessments of achievements against the targets, and devise an appropriate development strategy through five-year plans.

The Planning Commission comprises eight members: The Prime Minister as the chairman, four full time members including the Deputy Chairman, Minister of Planning, Minister of Finance, and Minister of Defence. The **National Development Council** (NDC), comprising the Prime Minister, all State Chief Ministers, and the members of the Planning Commission, is the highest national forum for planning in India. The NDC is an advisory body where all the important decisions related to planning and the draft plan prepared by the Planning Commission are discussed, debated and finally approved.

The planners initially adopted the **Harrod-Domar model** which emphasized the role of saving in promoting investment and growth. The second plan adopted the Mahalanobis framework which emphasized industrialization with stress on development of heavy industries and production of capital goods.

During the decade of 50's and 60's the planners assigned important role to the government and the public sector. The active involvement of the government was deemed necessary as private initiatives in many areas, especially, the infrastructure and heavy industries, were not coming up. Given the worldwide pessimism on the export front among the developing countries, the planners adopted a closed economy model and emphasized the strategy of import substitution rather than export promotion.

So far, India has implemented ten five-year plans. The eleventh five-year plan is currently being pursued. The objectives of these plans are briefly highlighted in Table 2.1.

Table 2.1 Five-year plans in India: Objectives, Targets and Achievements

Plan/Period	*Main objectives*	*Growth rate*	
		Target	*Actual*
First (1951–56)	To correct the disequilibrium in the economy caused by World War II and the partition. To initiate a process of all round balanced development.	2.1	3.60
Second (1956–61)	A considerable increase in the national income. Rapid industrialization with particular emphasis on the development of basic and heavy industries. A large expansion of employment opportunities. Reduction in inequalities of income and wealth.	4.5	4.21
Third (1961–66)	To achieve self sustaining growth of 5 per cent per annum. To ensure pattern of investment which could sustain this growth during the subsequent plan period. To increase agriculture production to meet the requirements of foodgrains, industry and exports. To expand basic industries like steel, chemicals, fuel, and power, and establish machine building capacity for meeting the requirements of industrialization indigenously. To utilize fully the manpower resources of the country. To establish progressively greater equality of opportunity and bring about reduction in disparities of income and wealth.	5.6	2.72

Plan/Period	*Main objectives*	*Growth rate*	
		Target	*Actual*
Fourth (1969–74)	Growth with stability. Progressive achievement of self reliance.	5.7	2.05
Fifth (1974–79)	To remove poverty To achieve economic self-reliance, eliminate special forms of external assistance, particularly, food and fertilizer imports.	4.4	4.83
Sixth (1980–85)	To control population, remove poverty, improve standard of living, reduce regional disparities and inequalities of income and wealth. To achieve economic and technological self reliance.	5.2	5.54
Seventh (1985–90)	To achieve self-reliance by increasing foodgrains production, and reducing dependence on external finance through export promotion and import substitution. To generate employment opportunities for solving the problem of unemployment. To enhance productivity and efficiency through elimination of infrastructural bottlenecks, improving capacity utilization and modernization of plants and equipments. To promote equity and social justice through alleviation of poverty and inter-class disparities. To promote speedy development of power generation and irrigation potential. To ensure growth with price stability. To decentralize planning and promote active involvement of all the sections of population in the process of development through education, communication and industrial strategies.	5.0	6.02
Eighth (1992–97)	To achieve near full employment by the turn of the century. To contain population growth. To universalize elementary education and eradication of illiteracy among people in the age group of 15 to 33 years. To provide safe drinking water and primary health care. To achieve self sufficiency in food grain and generate surplus for exports. To strengthen infrastructure.	5.6	6.02

Plan/Period	*Main objectives*	*Growth rate*	
		Target	*Actual*
Ninth (1997–02)	To accelerate growth with stable prices. To generate adequate productive employment in agriculture and rural areas. To attain food and nutritional security for all. To provide basic minimum needs of safe drinking water, primary health care facilities, universal primary education, shelter and connectivity. To contain the population growth. To ensure environmental sustainability of the development process. To empower women and all socially disadvantaged groups. To promote people's participatory institutions like panchayati raj, co-operatives and self-help groups. To strengthen efforts to build self reliance.	6.5	5.35
Tenth (2002–07)	To improve national income and per capita income for improving the public welfare. To create 100 million employment opportunities. To achieve balanced regional development. To limit population growth to 16.2 per cent.	8.0	7.2
Eleventh (2007–12)	To improve GDP and farm sector growth rate further. To create more job opportunities and to reduce unemployment among educated youth. To improve social indicators by reducing infant mortality rate and maternal death rates, improving sex ratio, providing clean drinking water, reducing air pollution, cleaning river water. To improve energy efficiency and ensuring electricity connection. To increase forest and tree cover. To expand approach road to more villages.	9.0	7.9
Twelfth (2012-17)	To achieve faster more inclusive and sustainable growth. To improve quality of infrastructure financial services. To give a boost to science and technology. To manage natural resources efficiently. To improve governance. To enhance regional equality.	8.2	–

Source: Compiled from Planning Commission, Five-year plan Documents.

The first three five-year plans emphasized **heavy industrialization** as the development strategy, and almost neglected the development of agriculture sector. As a result, the country faced severe drought conditions in 1965–66. Along with the severe drought conditions in the subsequent two years, the country faced other turmoils in the form of Indo-Pakistan conflict in 1965, devaluation of currency, a general rise in the commodity price, and erosion of resources available, and had to terminate the fourth five-year planning exercise. Instead, between 1966 and 1969, three annual plans were formulated within the framework of the draft outline of the fourth plan as interim exercise taking stock of the evolving economic scenario. The fourth plan started after three years of the third five-year plan which emphasized the development of agriculture sector through promoting the use of High Yielding Variety (HYV) seeds, fertilizers, pesticides, and irrigation facilities. The era of **Green Revolution** ushered during this plan.

In the subsequent period, the planners realized that the reduction in poverty though requires sustained growth of output, the benefits of growth do not trickle down automatically to the bottom poor. Therefore, since the mid seventies, with the onset of sixth five-year plan, a frontal attack on poverty in general and rural poverty in particular became one of the major objectives of planning in India. A number of rural development and anti-poverty programmes have been launched in the sixth and the subsequent plans. Some major poverty alleviation schemes launched over the plan period are—The Integrated Rural Development Programme (IRDP), National Rural Employment Programme (NREP), Rural Landless Employment Guarantee Programme (RLEGP), Pradhan Mantri Gram Sadak Yojana (PMGSY), Indira Awaas Yojana (IAY), Swarnjayanti Gram Swarojgar Yojana (SGSY), Sampoorna Grameen Rozgar Yojana (SGRY), Drought Prone Area Programme (DPAP), Desert Development Programme (DDP), Integrated Wasteland Development Programme (IWDP), Swarna Jayanti Shahari Rozgar Yojana (SJSRY) and Valmiki Ambedkar Awas Yojana (VAMBAY).

Like the fourth plan, due to political and economic uncertainties, the eighth five-year plan could not take-off as scheduled. The eighth plan could begin only when the situation was brought under control after two annual plans, 1990–91 and 1991–92. Fiscal consolidation, non-inflationary balanced growth for the overall well-being of the human beings, and participatory planning process are some of the important objectives of the eighth and the subsequent plans. Over the last two decades, the planning process has become more and more indicative in nature, with detailed specification of projects in the public sector and indicative sectoral targets for the rest of the economy.

The performance of planning in India can be termed as mixed. As can be seen from Table 1.2, the actual performance exceeded the growth targets in the first, fifth, sixth, seventh and eighth plans. However, achievements were far from the targets in third and fourth plans because of special circumstances such as war, famine and inflation in the third plan and high inflationary pressure in the economy during the fourth plan. The targets were missed narrowly in the second, ninth and tenth plans.

The planning process over the last 60 years has succeeded converting a largely feudal economy at the time of independence as an emerging market economy in the last decade. Over this period, the country has overcome the trap of so-called **Hindu Rate of Growth** of 3.5 per cent. During the 1980's, the country could sustain the growth rate of above 5 per cent. Reforms and restructuring process have helped India improve efficiency and productivity and accelerating the growth process. In the recent years, the country is aiming to sustain a growth of 8 to 10 per cent.

The economy has become self-sufficient in food production, has emerged strong, modern and vibrant, with diversified production base, and is steadily moving on the path of growth with a large pool of skilled manpower and talent. Over a period of time, various socioeconomic parameters have also shown remarkable improvements with increase in per capita income, consumption, reduction in poverty, increase in literacy, and improvement in life expectancy.

In spite of absolute improvement in various socioeconomic parameters, relatively, India lags behind many countries and still ranks poor on the Human Development Index (HDI). India has the highest number of illiterates in the world, and one-third of the world's absolute poor lives in India. The country is miserably lagging behind on basic amenities, such as health facilities, safe drinking water, and basic sanitation facilities. Inspite of efforts towards balanced regional development, the regional disparities still persist.

2.5 ADVANTAGES AND DISADVANTAGES OF DIFFERENT TYPES OF ECONOMIC SYSTEMS

2.5.1 Capitalism

Advantages of Capitalism

1. Wide variety to consumers: In a competitive market structure to retain customers, often producers compete with each other by differentiating their products. Consumers, thus, get a wide variety of goods.

2. Efficiency in the use of resources: To retain profitability in a competitive environment, producers try to minimize costs by adopting latest technology and management skills; this brings inefficiency in the production process.

3. Flexibility in operations and lesser delays in decision-making: There is a high degree of flexibility in the decision-making process as all the decisions are left to the individuals. Such flexibility increases the adaptability to the market changes. For example, if the demand for a commodity increases and the supply is limited, it increases the price of the commodity. Higher profit, emerging from price rise, motivates the producers to produce more; and gets supplied to the market to meet the demand.

4. Higher level of innovations: To cater to the differing preferences of consumers, producers invest heavily in research and development. Hence, in such a system large number of inventions and innovations take place, which benefit not only the producers but the society in general.

Disadvantages of Capitalism

1. Unemployment: In a capitalist or market economies profit drives the producers. Loss making activities are shut down even when they are labour intensive. Often in a slowdown or in recession, many firms, finding themselves unprofitable, close down their business units, which results in a large scale unemployment of various resources.

2. Emergence of monopolies: Profit motive, in the absence of enough regulation, results in the emergence of monopolies in capitalist economies, which can charge exorbitant prices for some essential commodities and deprive the common man of such commodities.

3. Non-availability of certain desirable goods: Certain goods such as parks, streets, though socially desirable, may not get produced if the producers find them unprofitable to produce. Community, thus, gets deprived of such goods in capitalist or market oriented economies.

4. Harmful goods may get produced: As the profit motive drives the producers in a capitalist economy, if found profitable even harmful goods, such as cigarettes and drugs, get supplied in the market.

5. Large social cost: Often private producers do not account for the social cost of their production. For example, a textile industry may pollute a nearby river by disposing various toxic chemical used in the textile manufacturing. The society ends up paying the price of polluted water either by spending on purifying the water, or incurring large medical bills on illness arising from the consumption of polluted water.

6. Large income inequalities: Resources are owned by private individuals in capitalism or market economies, which determine their income levels. Private ownership of resources, thus, increases income inequalities. In such economies abject poverty and stinking riches co-exist.

7. Uncertainty and instability: Market oriented economies are driven by market forces; optimism puts the economy on an expansionary path, whereas any adverse shock turns optimism into pessimism and derails the economy into a slowdown or recession. Thus, these economies face wide fluctuations in economic activities, which make them highly uncertain and instable.

2.5.2 Planned System

Advantages of Planned System

1. Greater economic stability: An extensive planning is carried out at the macroeconomic level regarding production, consumption, distribution, investment. The comprehensive planning makes the system highly stable and predictable. Such stability also keeps the system immune to economic fluctuations that are characteristics of market oriented or capitalist economies.

2. Basic needs met: An objective of socialist or planned economic system is to meet the basic needs of food, clothing, housing, education and health facilities. Therefore, such a system is expected to have eradicated absolute and abject poverty.

3. Egalitarian society: Socialist economies aim at egalitarian system; hence, they do not allow private ownership of resources. The state owns all the resources and allocate them as per the perceived priorities. The government provides equal opportunities for education, health care and other facilities so that all get equal opportunities to sustain themselves and no one either remain in abject poverty or enjoy too much of the wealth.

4. Low unemployment: Socialist societies strive at maximizing social welfare rather than profit maximization. As a means to achieve social welfare these societies provide employment opportunities to all even though that might come at the cost of profit. Those who remain unemployed, for whatsoever reasons, are covered under the extensive welfare program, which ensure fulfilment of basic needs of the people.

5. Better allocation of resources: In a socialist economy resources are allocated as per the priority of the society. The areas which are valued the most, get preference during the resource allocation.

Disadvantages of Planned System

1. Limited choices for consumers: Socialist economies plan to meet basic needs of their citizens rather than all types of wants. For example, an economy may plan to meet the food requirement by supplying bread. However, it may not go for different types of breads varying in size, texture, tastes, and so on. In such a system, luxuries may be thought of as unimportant or waste of resources, and the state may not produce them.

2. Lack of freedom: As almost everything is controlled by the state, individuals in planned economies have very little choice to decide on their jobs, quality and quantity of goods that they want to consume, and, at times, even the number of children that they can go for.

3. Inefficiencies in production processes: Civil servants, which look into the administration of various activities in socialist or planned economies, are paid a fixed salary. Their promotions are based on the number of years of experience rather than their performance in the field. Lack of incentive to perform and lack of competition kills the initiative to cut down on cost. Thus, these systems breed inefficiencies in the production process.

4. Delays in communication: Socialist or planned economies by their very nature are run by bureaucrats. Any decision has to pass through different layers of bureaucracy before it is finally approved. Therefore, such system faces large delays in various activities.

5. Lack of innovations from the private sector: As no one gets more than the other, there is no incentive to put in hard efforts, improve the quality of goods through inventions and innovations in socialism or planned economies.

6. Rationing and black marketing: Prices in a command economy are set by the state. To make the goods affordable to everyone, often prices are set well below the market clearing levels. The insatiated demand at the set price is met by rationing. Rationing and insatiated demand often causes black marketing and also smuggling of goods from abroad.

2.5.3 Mixed Economic Systems

Depending on the degree of extent of capitalism and socialism, in the mixed economic system the advantages and disadvantages vary from country to country.

The mixed system with a larger element of capitalism enjoys efficient allocation resources and able to provide variety to consumers at competitive prices, but at the same time such a system faces higher economic uncertainty and large income inequalities. On the contrary, the system with a larger element of socialism faces larger economic stability, lower unemployment and inequalities of income. But, such a system faces large decision and implementation delays, leading to inefficiencies in the production process. In such a system variety of products available to consumers is also limited.

SUMMARY

Economic system refers to a set of institutions, principles and mechanisms created by a society to facilitate economic units to address their basic economic problems of allocation of scarce resources and perform their basic economic activities.

It determines the pattern of ownership of resources, the role of public and private sectors, and the role of markets and the price mechanism in the allocation of resources in an economy.

Planning process, imperative or indicative, plays an important role in the allocation of resources. Though planning process is associated with the command or socialist economies, some amount of planning is done even in capitalist or market-oriented economies. However, the nature of planning differs across economic systems. In command economies, planning is imperative, whereas in more democratic or capitalist set-up planning is usually indicative.

Implications for Managers

The economic system is an important constituent of the economic environment in which business organizations operate. It affects business organizations and their decisions in many ways.

The economic system determines the ownership pattern. In a communist or socialist system and planned economies, managers have a very stable scenario. However, the profit and growth opportunities are also highly restricted. On the contrary, a capitalist system, with free markets, gives freedom of ownership of resources and opens up large avenues for profit and growth. However, in such a system, economies are subject to large market fluctuations which also pose tremendous challenges for managers. They need to continuously keep on reinventing and reorienting themselves as per the market forces to retain their competitiveness.

REVIEW QUESTIONS

2.1 What does the economic system refer to? How far a mixed economic system differs from capitalism and socialism?

2.2 *Economic system defines the institutional framework, whereas the structure of the economy defines the physical framework.* Elaborate on this statement.

2.3 What are the factors which affect the economic structure of a country?

2.4 What are the different types of planning processes?

2.5 In what direction the planning process in India has evolved over a period of time? What opportunities do you perceive in the present planning process?

2.6 In which type of economic system imperative planning process is followed?

2.7 In which type of economic system indicative planning process is followed?

2.8 What are the major advantages of capitalism?

2.9 In which type of economic system managers would expect a more stable economic environment?

2.10 What are the disadvantages of command economies or socialism?

2.11 As a manager which type of economic system will you prefer for your organization? Why?

CASE ANALYSIS EXERCISE

C2.1 Public Private Partnership

Mixed economic systems, the world over, are emphasizing **Public Private Partnership** (PPP) mode of operations to enhance their infrastructure and growth.

The PPP (or P3) is a legal agreement between government and private sector (all non-government agencies, such as the corporate sector, voluntary organizations, self-help groups, partnership firms, individuals, and community-based organizations) for the provision of assets and the delivery of services. Such contracts allocate responsibilities and business risk among various partners involved in the agreement. Under such an arrangement, the government or the public sector remains actively involved throughout the life cycle of the project and the private sector is made responsible for commercial functions, such as project design, construction, financing and operations.

The PPP differs from privatization. Under privatization, the ownership and responsibility and risk of delivering and funding a particular service rests with the private sector, whereas in the PPP the ownership of the asset may remain with the government and the responsibility and risk of delivery and funding of projects are shared by both the government and the private sector. Under privatization all the rewards accrue to the private sector, whereas the rewards are shared by the partners in the PPP.

The PPP can take various forms. Some of the forms are Service Contract, Management Contract, Lease, Concession, Build-Own-Operate (BOO), Build-Operate-Transfer (BOT), and Build-Own- Operate-Transfer (BOOT).

The PPP brings in benefit to all the parties involved. Private involvement reduces the financial burden on the government as part of the investment in the project may come from the private sector. The private sector is considered to be more efficient in managing resources—physical as well as financial. It is also expected to be equipped with the latest technology of production. Therefore, the involvement of the private sector is expected to reduce costs and bring in production efficiency. In the PPP not only do the rewards get shared but the risk also gets diversified. As responsibilities are shared, and each party is accountable to the extent of its responsibility, the projects are expected to be implemented on time. The partners from the private sector are expected to benefit from such partnerships as they get a long-term investment opportunity and get a reliable stream of revenue from the assets which they may or may not own for as long as 50 years or more. Risk sharing reduces the risk for the private sector as well. The private sector is also expected to learn from the experience of handling of the projects which otherwise were exclusively in the public sector domain. Such experiences help them in expanding their business in other jurisdictions and provide them wider market access. The society as a whole, individuals as well as business organizations, benefit from the availability of better infrastructure and uninterrupted 24-hour supply of services at cheaper rates.

It is well-recognized that the development of an economy and the creation of an enabling environment for business require well-developed infrastructure such as road, rail, air and water transport, power generation, transmission and distribution, telecommunication, water supply, irrigation and storage. Given the huge investment required for creating infrastructure, the PPP arrangements are increasingly used for construction and operation of infrastructure both in developed and developing countries.

The eleventh five-year plan in India had identified infrastructure inadequacies in both rural and urban areas as major constraining factors for achieving sustainable growth rate in the country. The plan aimed at achieving the growth rate of 8 to 10 per cent during the plan period. To achieve this target, the plan also sets an ambitious target of increasing the total investment in infrastructure from around 5 per cent in 2006–07, the base year of the plan, to 9 per cent by the terminal year 2011–12. As per its estimates, investment needed over the plan period was US $500 billion. The plan clearly realized that this amount cannot entirely come from the public sector. To support the efforts of the public sector, the plan emphasized the participation of the private sector, especially in the form of PPP, in the buildup of the physical and human capital, and technological development and diffusion. Accordingly, a number of initiatives have been taken by both the Centre and state governments to promote the PPPs in sectors like power, ports, highways, airports, tourism and urban infrastructure. Some of the illustrative projects which have been completed are indicated in Table 2.2.

Table 2.2 Some Illustrative PPP Projects in Infrastructure

S.No.	*Projects*	*S.No.*	*Projects*
1	Bangalore International Airport, Karnataka	9	Deep Draft Iron Ore Berth, Paradip Port
2	Rajiv Gandhi International Airport, Hyderabad	10	Mega Container Terminal, Chennai
3	Indira Gandhi International Airport, New Delhi	11	Multi-purpose Cargo Berths, Kandla
4	Chhatrapati Shivaji International Airport, Mumbai	12	Hyderabad Metro Rail Project, Hyderabad
5	6 Laning of Jaipur–Kishangarh National Highway	13	Colaba Bandra Metro Corridor Line-III, Mumbai
6	8/6 Laning of Delhi–Gurgaon Expressway	14	Jhajjar Power Transmission Project, Haryana
7	Hyderabad–Vijaywada National Highway	15	Mundra Port, Gujarat
8	Offshore Container Berths, Mumbai Harbour	16	Pipavav Port, Gujarat
		17	Gangavaram Port, Andhra Pradesh
		18	Krishnapuram Port, Andhra Pradesh

S.No.	Projects	S.No.	Projects
19	Vadodara–Bharuch State Highway, Gujarat	22	Jaipur–Bhilwara State Highway, Rajasthan
20	Indore–Edelabad State Highway, Madhya Pradesh	23	Delhi Western Peripheral Expressway (KMP Expressway), Haryana
21	Yedshi–Latur–Nanded State Highway, Maharashtra	24	Bridge across River Godavari between Yanam–Edurulanka, Andhra Pradesh

Source: (Planning Commission (2011), Midterm Appraisal of Eleventh Five-year plan 2007–12.

To further increase the awareness about and encourage the PPPs, a website of PPPs in India (http://www.pppinindia.com/) has been set up by the Ministry of Finance, Government of India.

Questions

1. What is the PPP? What are the different forms of PPPs?
2. Why are PPPs needed in infrastructure sector?
3. What are the benefits of PPPs for the business units participating in such agreements?
4. What are the benefits to individuals and business organizations from the PPPs approach to development? How does the PPPs help in creating a better business environment?
5. Why the eleventh five-year plan emphasized the PPPs?

SUGGESTED FURTHER READING

Chow, G.C. (2011), Economic Planning in China Princeton University , CEPS Working Paper No. 219 , June.

The Fraser Institute (online), Pencils or Candies? Planned Economies and Market Allocation, www.fraserinstitute.ca.

Planning Commission (2011), *Mid Term Appraisal of Eleventh Five-Year Plan* (2007–12).

Planning Commission (2013), Draft **Twelfth Five-Year Plan 2012–17,** Faster, More Inclusive and Sustainable Growth, Vol I.

CHAPTER 3

Economic Structure and Stages of Development

3.1 INTRODUCTION

China achieved an impressive growth rate in the last three decades. With an average 10 per cent, growth rate, it has become the second largest economy, and a major exporter and manufacturer in the world. It has become an important driving force of global growth. But three major unfavourable structural changes during this period have now started constraining its growth rate and raising doubts on its sustainability. Firstly, China's population is growing older, which will not only reduce the size of its workforce but also put pressure on social safety nets. Secondly, so far the Chinese growth is investment led, that leads to excess capacity. To achieve more balanced growth, it needs to reduce its investment to GDP ratio and improve its consumption share. Thirdly, China is growingly becoming dependent on exports for its growth, which makes it susceptible to adverse external shocks. These adverse changes are necessitating major structural changes in the Chinese economy.

Economic structure affects the performance of every economy and not restricted to China only. It is important to know the meaning of economic structure and its constituents and their implications for business organizations. Accordingly, this chapter in Section 3.2 defines the economic structure and outlines its determinants. Section 3.3 describes its constituents and points out their implications for business organizations.

3.2 ECONOMIC STRUCTURE AND ITS DETERMINANTS

Economic system (Chapter 2) defines the institutional framework, whereas **economic structure** defines the physical framework under which an economy and business units operate. Economic structure can be gauged from long-term trend in various economic variables.

The economic structure is affected by numerous factors, such as population size, income per capita, factor endowment, demographic profile and technological advancement.

The level of population affects the level of demand for goods and services. The declining size of the population reduces demand as well as growth rate, whereas the growing size is indicative of higher levels of demand, and thus, potential for higher growth.

Per capita income is a major determinant of demand for goods and services, and hence, influences the demand structure. The demand structure, in turn, influences the sectoral structure of GDP and the structure of an economy.

Factor endowment, which indicates the amount of available natural resources, human resources and capital, determines the factor intensity, production structure and the production possibility frontier. Usually, countries end up using those resources which are in plenty in their territories or producing those goods in which they have comparative advantage. For example, in the USA, capital intensity is higher because of abundance of capital, whereas in China and India, labour is used more intensively because of abundance of human resources.

Demographic profile, i.e., the age structure of the population, also has an important influence on the economic structure. Usually, the impact of 0–14 and 65 plus age group on the share of agriculture and services has been found to be positive, but the construction and heavy manufacturing industries is found to be negative.

Technology affects the method of production, i.e., the manner in which the resources are converted into output. Advancements in technology not only affect the productivity, but also influences the structure of an economy. Some of the sectors such as software and pharmaceutical industries are affected more by the changes in the technology as compared to the other sectors such as furniture and apparel.

3.3 CONSTITUENTS OF ECONOMIC STRUCTURE

3.3.1 Demand Structure

The classification of total expenditure into different expenditure components—private consumption expenditure, government consumption expenditure, investment expenditure, exports and imports—highlights the demand structure. Demand structure indicates the drivers of the growth. When the share of consumption expenditure is the highest in total expenditure then the corresponding growth is known as consumption led growth, whereas when the share of investment expenditure is the highest the growth is considered to be investment led. If the share of exports in total demand is the highest, then the growth is considered to be export led. In the long-run, it is important to achieve a balance between different items of expenditure. Otherwise constraints may appear which can hold back growth. For example, in investment led growth the productive capacity keeps increasing. If there is no corresponding increase in the output then it can result in excess capacity and deflationary pressure in the economy.

3.3.2 Production Structure

The production structure refers to the classification of output into different economic activities or sectors. It is estimated as output in an activity divided by the total national output.

Economists usually follow two three-fold classifications of production activities to analyse the **production structure** of an economy. One is the classification of activities into **primary sector**, **secondary sector**, and **tertiary sector** and the other classification is **agriculture sector**, **manufacturing/industrial sector** and **service sector**. The activities covered under these classification categories are summarized in Table 3.1.

Table 3.1 Sectoral Classification of Economic Activities

Sectors	*Activities covered*
Classification I	
Primary	Agriculture (cultivation of crops, livestock and animal husbandry); forestry, logging and fishing; mining and quarrying.
Secondary	Manufacturing; electricity, gas and water supply and construction.
Tertiary	Trade, transport and communication; financial, real estate and business services; community, social and personal services.
Classification II	
Agriculture	Agriculture and allied (forestry, logging and fishing) activities.
Industry	Manufacturing; mining and quarrying; electricity, gas and water supply; construction.
Services	Trade, transport and communication; financial, real estate and business services; community, social and personal services.

Many of the products of the primary sector are used as inputs in the secondary sector. The secondary sector converts the output of the primary sector into finished products, such as cotton into cloths, raw iron into steel rods, wood into furniture, leather into handbags, which can be used by households and business organizations as final products. Unlike the other two sectors, the tertiary sector consists of commodities which are intangible, i.e., do not have physical form. The demand for these emerges from consumers in the form of consumer services, such as tourism, health care and education, and from producers in the form of producer services, such as transport and finance.

The sectoral classification of national income or output is often used to assess the level of development of an economy. The cross-country development process has indicated that usually countries follow a typical development process. In the initial stages of development, countries largely depend on the primary sector. The value addition and, thereby, the total income generated in the economy remains low at this stage of development, which keeps saving and investment at a lower level. Thus, it restrains the productive capacity and expansion of output. The low income level also leads to a major proportion of it being spent on the agriculture and other primary products, and hence, production structure remains confined largely to agriculture and allied sectors, whereas we have already seen, value addition and income remains low. Thus, an agrarian economy gets entrapped in a vicious circle of low income and poverty until a major scientific breakthrough and technological inventions break this vicious circle by innovating new product and making it commercially useful. Usually, an **agrarian economy**, i.e., the economy where the largest share of national income or output comes from agriculture and allied activities, is considered to be in the **first stage of development**, i.e., underdeveloped.

With the advancement in the technology of production, the production structure starts moving in favour of industrial sector. Value addition being higher in the industrial sector than that in the agriculture sector, the development of the industrial sector helps in increasing the overall level of income in the country experiencing a shift in favour of industrial sector. The income elasticity of demand for manufactured products and services is relatively higher than that of the agricultural products. Hence, as the economy moves away from an agrarian structure to industrially oriented structure, the consumption basket diversifies with more of manufactured products in it. A significant transfer of resources, mainly labour and raw material, takes place from the agricultural sector to the industrial sector, which lowers the share of the agriculture sector and increases the share of the industrial sector. United Kingdom was the first country which experienced such a shift with the invention of steam power and the engine which revolutionized the textile sector and other industries and the country experienced an industrial revolution. Economies where the largest share of income comes from the industrial sector are known as industrial economies; these economies are considered to be passing through the **second stage of development**.

Once the agriculture and industry matures, further expansion in the economy, particularly the manufacturing sector, increases the demand for highly professional services, such as trade, transport, hotels, communication, banking and finance, and social services, such as education, hospitals and other infrastructure to support the industrial development. Such a shift in the demand pattern helps the country transit at the **third stage of development** where services dominate the production structure. As the value addition is the highest in the service sector, the dominance of the service sector in economic activities reflects the highest level of development.

Changes in the **production structure** of an economy also bring in changes in its **employment structure**. The changes affect not only the total level of employment but also its composition. A transition from agriculture to industry and from industry to service sector, especially when the professional services gain in importance, often displaces unskilled labour and creates more employment opportunities for skilled labour.

A **structural shift** in the production activities also affects the market structure and the level of competition in an economy, because manufacturing and other industrial activities are more open to international trade and competition. Highly industrialized countries face competition from countries which have an abundant raw material and cheap labour and are in the process of development. The countries in developing stages often take advantage of the techniques invented and knowledge developed by highly industrialized countries, and quite often reach the higher level of development faster than the countries which industrialized first, getting a second mover advantage.

Technological advancements and expansion in the knowledge sometimes help some economies to surpass the middle stage of development and transit directly from an agrarian economy to a service-oriented economy (For example, India (UBE 3.1)). Such a phenomenon is known as the **leapfrogging.** However, such an expansion is expected to constrain the sustainable growth as undeveloped physical infrastructure and industrial sector becomes a bottleneck in the expansion of service activities.

UNDERSTANDING BUSINESS ENVIRONMENT

UBE 3.1 Structural Shift in the Indian Economy

This UBE depicts the evolving sectoral composition of GDP of India and compares and contrast it with some other selected economies. It also provides the reasons for the leapfrogging process experienced by the Indian economy.

The sectoral composition of GDP is changing in India over a period of time in favour of the service sector. As can be seen from Table 3.2, the share of services in GDP has gone up from 36 per cent in 1980 to 56.4 per cent in 2011.This increase in the share of services is strikingly similar to the corresponding rise in services share in many other Asian countries between 1980 and 2011, and also in concurrence with the growth experience of many developed economies. Among some selected countries given in Table 3.2, there is an increasing trend in the share of services, to a large extent matched by a corresponding decline in the share of agriculture. However, the share of the industrial sector in the GDP appears to be particularly low in India.

Table 3.2 Movements on Sectorial Shares in GDP in Some Select Asian Countries

Country	*Agriculture*				*Industry*				*Services*			
	1980	1990	2000	2011	1980	1990	2000	2011	1980	1990	2000	2011
China	30.1	27.1	15.1	10.1	48.5	41.3	45.9	46.8	21.4	31.5	39	43.1
India	38.1	29.3	23.4	17.2	25.9	26.9	26.2	26.4	36.0	43.8	50.5	56.4
Indonesia	24.8	19.4	15.6	14.7	43.4	39.1	45.9	47.2	31.8	41.5	38.5	38.1
Korea	14.9	8.7	4.6	2.7	41.3	39.9	38.1	39.2	43.7	51.5	57.3	58.1
Malaysia	...	15	8.3	12	...	41.5	46.8	40.7	...	43.5	44.9	47.3
Pakistan	29.6	26	25.9	21.6	25	25.2	23.3	24.9	45.5	48.8	50.7	53.4
Philippines	25.1	21.9	15.8	12.8	38.8	34.5	32.3	31.5	36.1	43.6	52	55.7
Thailand	23.2	12.5	9	10.9	28.7	37.2	42	40.1	48.1	50.3	49	49

Source: Sectorial shares are computed from data available from ADB (2013), Statistical Database System (SDBS), as on 05/4/13, (online) http://www.adb.org/statistics/sdbs.asp.

Though the shift from the agriculture sector towards the service sector in India indicates that it is moving towards the advanced level of development, the almost stagnant share of the manufacturing sector is in sharp contrast with the development experience of many other countries as visualized in the theoretical literature. More or less stagnant share of the industrial sector signifies a *leapfrogging* from the agricultural phase to service phase and bypassing the industrial phase.

Advances in communication technology have allowed India to exploit its comparative advantage (Section 10.2) in services and to experience the phenomenon of leapfrogging. A large supply of trained English-speaking personnel has been one of the important factors in conferring India a comparative advantage in this field. Reforms, especially that of the financial sector, deregulation of the service sector such as communication, privatization, and opening up of the economy to Foreign Direct Investment (FDI) have provided the much needed catalyst for the growth of the service sector in India.

In spite of the decline in the share of agriculture sector, it continues to be an important sector in terms of absorbing more than half of the total workforce in India (Table 3.3). The country has also experienced a mismatch in the growth of income and employment in the service sector, i.e., income rising faster than the employment in this sector. As the service sector employs more of skilled workers than the agriculture and the manufacturing sectors, the unemployment in the country is more of unskilled than the skilled workers. The higher dependence of the labour force on the agriculture sector may be indicative of **disguised unemployment** (that is the situation when a labourer apparently looked employed in an activity, but does not contribute to the marginal productivity of it, implying that if it is removed from that activity, the total output will still remain the same.)

Table 3.3 Sectoral Share in Employment
(Level in latest available year, percentage points)

	Agriculture			*Manufacturing*			*Mining*			*Others*		
	1990	*2000*	*2011*	*1990*	*2000*	*2011*	*1990*	*2000*	*2011*	*1990*	*2000*	*2011*
China	60.1	50.0	37.0	13.3	11.2	NA	NA	NA	NA	26.6	38.8	61.9
India	62.3	60.0	56.1	15.4	16.3	18.8	NA	NA	NA	22.4	23.7	25.0
Indonesia	55.9	45.3	35.9	10.1	13.0	13.3	0.7	0.6	1.3	33.3	41.2	49.5
Korea	17.9	10.6	6.4	27.2	20.3	16.9	0.4	0.1	0.1	54.5	69.0	76.7
Malaysia	26.0	16.7	12.0	19.9	23.5	17.1	0.6	0.3	0.6	53.5	59.5	70.3
Pakistan	51.1	48.4	45.1	12.8	11.5	13.6	0.2	0.1	0.2	36.0	40.0	41.2
Phillipines	44.9	37.1	33.0	10.1	10.0	8.3	0.6	0.4	0.6	44.4	52.5	58.2
Thailand	63.3	44.2	38.7	9.7	14.9	13.8	0.2	0.1	0.1	26.7	40.8	47.4

Note: Figures for China and India in 2011 column are of 2009 as employment data for these two countries is not available for the subsequent period. Figures for mining in China and India are not available separately. In China they have been clubbed under others and that for Indian under manufacturing. Figure for 2009 for China in the other category include employment in all other sectors other than agriculture.

Source: Sectoral shares are computed from data available from ADB (2013), Statistical Database System (SDBS), (online) http://www.adb.org/statistics/sdbs.asp, as on 5/4/13.

3.3.3 Employment Structure

Classification of the employed workforce by economic activities is referred to as the **employment structure**. It can be estimated as

$$\frac{\text{Employed workforce in sector } i}{\text{Total employed workforce}} \times 100$$

As seen in the previous paragraphs, changes in the production structure along with it is also expected to bring in changes in the employment structure. Similar to production structure, the employment structure can also be used to assess the level of development. Usually, a less developed country is expected to have a greater percentage of its workforce employed in the agriculture and allied or primary activities. On the contrary, a highly developed country is expected to have a higher percentage of its workforce employed in the tertiary or service sector. However, as observed in Case UBE 3.1, due to skill mismatch this may not materialize and the service-oriented economy may find a larger proportion of its workforce employed in the agriculture and other primary activities. Due to skill mismatch, many in the workforce may remain unemployed even though in some sectors there may be high demand for the labour. Unemployment resulting from skill mismatch is known as the **structural unemployment**.

3.3.4 Fiscal Structure

Composition of the government expenditure, tax revenue, and the overall size of the government reflects the **fiscal structure**. Fiscal structure can alter the economic environment through various channels. Government expenditure in the form of production and consumption subsidies can alter the production and employment structure, and consumption pattern, whereas expenditure in physical and human capital, research and development, and public infrastructure can give a boost to overall growth. Tax structure, which reflects the composition of taxes—direct vs. indirect taxes, and tax rate structure, can affect the economy in either direction.

All taxes reduce net income; hence they are disincentive to work, save and invest, which retard economic growth. But at the same time, for a given revenue, the tax structure can be designed in such a way that it reduces income inequalities and also promote growth.

For a given tax revenue, income inequalities can be reduced by bringing in progressivity in the tax structure. From equality angle, direct taxes, which can be made progressive more easily than the indirect taxes, can be favoured.

While all taxes reduce the incentive to work, growth can be promoted by designing a tax structure that promotes investment in infrastructure, research and development, and human capital, and discourages consumption. Growth considerations suggest moving the tax structure in favour of consumption tax.

The size of the government, measured by its expenditure or income, can also affect the economic outcomes by affecting inflation rate, and quantity and cost of credit to the private sector. Though, in general, we expect the increasing government size to have a positive impact on growth (especially in case of information asymmetries (Section 9.5 and Section 11.4.2)), at times it may be growth retarding by discouraging private initiative, crowding out (i.e., discouraging private investment by higher cost of credit), reducing competition and reducing efficiency in the production process.

Fiscal structure is detailed in Chapter 8.

3.3.5 Financial Structure

As highlighted in Section 9.3.1, **financial structure** explains whether the country has a bank-based or market-based financial system.

The financial structure is categorized as **bank-based financial system** when banks and other financial intermediaries play a leading role in mobilizing savings from surplus units, like households and allocating capital to deficit units, like corporates. The bank-based system (such as that prevailing in Germany, Japan and India) gains dominance when there are large information asymmetries (Chapters 9 and 11), and deficit units or borrowers find it difficult to raise resources directly from surplus units or lenders. In the presence of large information asymmetries, banks with the help of its expert staff can generate enough information and facilitate transfer of funds from deficit units to surplus units. Due to intimidation cost (i.e., the margin of intermediaries), the cost of raising resources in the bank-based system is higher than that in the market-based system.

Box 3.1 Indicators of Financial Structure

Several indicators are available in the literature that can be used for gauging the financial structure of a country. Some of the indicators are listed hereinafter:

- *Cost Intermediation Ratio*: The cost intermediation ratio is defined as:

$$\text{Credit intermediation ratio} = \frac{\text{Loans}}{\text{External financing}}$$

The higher the value of credit intermediation ratio, the greater the importance of financial intermediaries in the financial system.

- *Market Intermediation Ratio*: The market intermediation ratio is estimated as:

$$\text{Market intermediation ratio} = \frac{\text{Securities held by financial intermediaries}}{\text{External financing}}$$

The market intermediation ratio indicates the amount of securities of different entities held by financial intermediaries rather than households and other entities. Thus, it indicates that indirectly funds are channelized through financial intermediaries. Thus, a larger value of market intermediation ratio also indicates that financial intermediaries are playing a greater role in the financial system.

- *Total Intermediation Ratio:* The total intermediation ratio is computed as:

Total intermediation ratio = Credit intermediation ratio + Market intermediation ratio

Direct and indirect contribution of the financial institutions in the financial sector is captured by this ratio.

- *Financial Intermediation Ratio*: The financial intermediation ratio is measured as:

Financial intermediation ratio = Financial assets of financial institutions (including banks) to financial assets of all domestic sectors

The financial intermediation ratio captures the significance of financial intermediation (banks as well as non-banks) in the financial system.

- *Bank Intermediation Ratio*: The bank intermediation ratio is defined as:

Bank intermediation ratio = Assets of the banking sector to assets of all financial institutions

The bank intermediation ratio only captures the significance of banks in the financial sector.

- *Claims on the Private Sector of Deposit Money Banks*: The banks claims on the private sectors are estimated as:

$$\text{Claims on the private sector of deposit money banks} = \frac{\text{Bank loans to private sector}}{\text{GDP}}$$

The importance of the banks in funding to the private sector is captured by the indicator claims on the private sector of deposit money banks.

- *Deposits to GDP Ratio:* The deposit to GDP ratio is measured as:

$$\text{Deposits to GDP Ratio} = \frac{\text{Demand, time and saving deposits of deposit money banks}}{\text{GDP}}$$

Deposits to GDP ratio indicates the resource mobilization efforts of the banking sector.

- *Stock Market Capitaization Ratio:* The stock market capitalization ratio captures the importance of financial markets in the financial system; it is defined as:

$$\text{Stock market capitalization ratio} = \frac{\text{Aggregate market value of the equity of domestic companies listed on the Stock Exchanges}}{\text{GDP}}$$

The higher the value of stock market capital to GDP ratio, the higher the importance of financial markets in the financial system of the country.

- *Share Trading Ratio:* The share trading ratio is another measure that captures the importance of financial markets and is estimated as:

$$\text{Value of share trading ratio} = \frac{\begin{array}{c}\text{Total amout of transactions}\\ \text{(Domestic and foreign including investment funds)}\end{array}}{\text{GDP}}$$

Value of share trading to GDP ratio also indicates the importance of financial markets in the financial system.

The financial structure is known as **market-based financial system** when most of the resource transfer from surplus units to deficit units takes place directly via financial markets rather than indirectly through intermediaries. Such a system gains dominance in countries with better disclosure practices, resulting in lesser informational asymmetries. Due to direct transfer of funds in the form of shares, bonds and debentures, the cost of funds is lesser in the market-based system than that in the bank-based system.

3.3.6 Trade Structure

The **trade structure** can be gauged from the sectoral export and import shares. The sectoral export share is estimated as exports from sector i to total exports. Similarly, the sectoral import share is estimated as imports of sector i to total imports. These sectoral shares and many associated measures that integrate these shares, such as the export diversification index, reflect the country's vulnerability to external trade shocks as well as its comparative advantage. Trade structure provides useful information that can be used for policy making by the country and strategic decisions by the companies involved in international trade. The trade structure is detailed in Chapter 13.

3.3.7 Population Structure or Demography

The **population structure** refers to many aspects of population ecology, such as population size, age class distribution, gender wise classification, and density. These different aspects of demography have significant impact on the business as well as the economy. For example, while the population size determines the overall market size, which affects the overall demand for products, the age class distribution, known as age structure, impacts the product mix, i.e., the type of commodities demanded. The age structure also affects the size of the labour force and spending and saving in the economy, and thus, affects its overall production capacity. The population structure is discussed in greater dctail in Chapter 17.

SUMMARY

Economic structure defines the physical framework under which an economy and business units operate. It can be ascertained from the long-term trends in various economic variables. Major determinants of economic structure are population size, income per capita, factor endowment, demographic profile and technological advancements. Some constituents of economic structure are production structure, employment structure, fiscal structure, financial structure, trade structure and population structure. Production structure refers to the share of different sectors of the economy in the total GDP. Similarly, employment structure refers to the share of different sectors in the total employment. Fiscal structure can be gauged from the contribution of direct/indirect taxes in the revenue, composition of government expenditure and the size of the government. Financial structure indicates whether a country is bank-based or market-based. Trade structure looks into the composition of exports and imports, and population structure analyzes age, gender and spatial classification of population.

Services form the largest share of India's GDP, which is indicative of the changing structure of the economy in favour of more value added activities. It also reflects that India is moving towards a more advanced stage of development.

Implications for Managers

Different constituents of economic structure have different managerial implications. Production structure highlights the stage of development. In underdeveloped countries, which are primarily agrarian economies, because of low per capita income, demand is limited to primary products and necessities; hence, managers are forced to produce more of mass consumption goods. However, in developed economies, with the largest share of the national income coming from industrial and service sectors, managers have scope for more profit by diversifying their production activities and producing luxuries and supplying services. In such economies, by concentrating only on the production of mass consumption goods, managers would be loosing lot many growth opportunities. Employment structure is indicative of the type of skill set available in the economy. In a service-oriented economy, if the largest employment is in the agriculture sector then it is indicative of skill mismatch in the economy. Companies engaged in services can face a shortage of skilled labour in such economies. Fiscal structure can give an idea about the government control in economic activities, the resources that are flowing to the public sector and how much is available to the private sector. In an economy, with a large public sector, private sector can find resource shortage. If larger share of expenditure is funded by the credit from the central bank, then managers can expect higher inflation in the economy, whereas if the government is largely borrowing from the market then private sector firms can expect the cost of credit to be high for them. Financial structure can be used for ascertaining the ways in which a firm can raise resources from the market. In a bank-based economy, managers will find it easy to raise resources in the form of loans from financial intermediaries, whereas in a market-based economy it will be convenient for them to raise resources from the market. Trade structure can be used for assessing the demand from foreign markets and accordingly products can be designed by export-oriented units. Population structure can also be used for assessing the type of goods that may be in higher demand. At the same time, it can also be used for assessing the availability of labour force.

REVIEW QUESTIONS

3.1 Economic system defines the institutional framework, whereas the structure of the economy defines the physical framework. Elaborate on this statement.

3.2 What are the factors which affect the economic structure?

3.3 What are the different constituents of economic environment?

3.4 How can we gauge the production structure of an economy?

3.5 In a service-oriented economy will you expect the share of the service sector in total employment to be higher or lower? Justify your answer.

3.6 What kind of mismatch will you expect in a service-oriented economy if the agriculture sector is the major employer?

3.7 What do you understand by the fiscal structure?

3.8 What implications you perceive for your firm if the government is meeting its resource requirement from the market?

3.9 What is the meaning of financial structure?

3.10 Who dominates in the bank-based system?

3.11 What do you understand by the market-based system?

3.12 What are the implications of bank-based financial system for managers?

3.13 In which type of financial structure resources are cheaper for firms?

3.14 What do you understand by trade structure? How would you use the information about the trade structure while taking managerial decisions?

3.15 What does the population structure refer to? Why the knowledge of population structure essential for managers?

CASE ANALYSIS EXERCISE

C3.1 Is Japan's Economic Structure Responsible for Persistent Deflation?

Japan's economic success during the post Second World War period, from 1960s to 1990s was viewed as an economic miracle. During this period the country experienced impressive economic growth with an average of 10 per cent annually in the 1960s, 5 per cent in the 1970s and 4 per cent in the 1980s. However, due to asset price bubble burst in 1990–92, the growth in the 1990s slowed down and remained low in the years ahead. Today, though Japan is one of the most highly developed economies in the world, it is marred with several structural deficiencies which are holding back its growth and keeping it under persistent deflationary pressure (Figure 3.1).

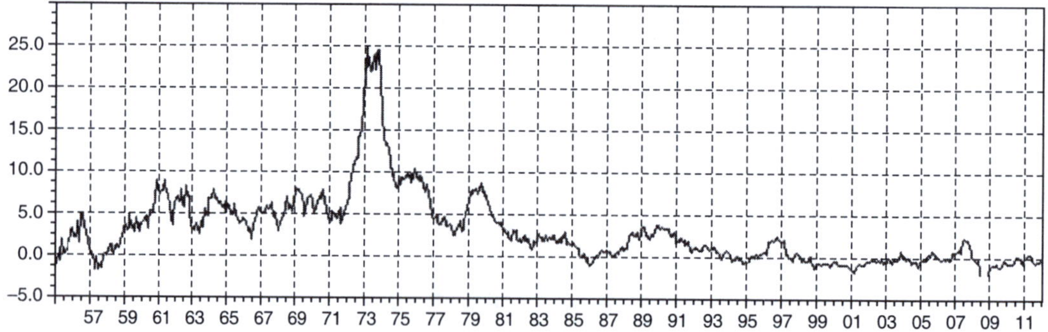

Source: inflation.eu, Worldwide Inflation Data (online), http://www.inflation.eu/inflation-rates/japan/historic-inflation/cpi-inflation-japan.aspx.

Figure 3.1 Year on Year Inflation in Japan.

Some of the structural features of Japan are outlined here:

- **Deflationary Gap:** Japan has been producing below its productive capacity now for many decades, leading to a negative output gap (Table 3.4). The negative output gap is indicative of the fact that the aggregate demand is lower than the productive capacity of the economy.

Table 3.4 Output Gap in Per cent of GDP

	1980	*2000*	*2011*	*2016*
Output gap (Per cent of GDP)	–6.485	–0.776	–4.568	–0.031

Source: Compiled from ADB (online), ADB's statistical database system.

- **Production Structure:** Japan has become a service-oriented economy with a very small proportion of GDP generated from the agricultural sector. Along with the decline in the share of the agricultural sector there has also been a decline in the manufacturing activities (Table 3.5).

Table 3.5 Structure of Output (Per cent of GDP at Current Producers' Prices)

	1995	*2001*	*2011*
Agriculture	1.8	1.5	1.2
Industry	33.0	30.0	27.5
Services	65.2	68.6	71.4

Source: Compiled from ADB (online) ADB's Statistical Database System; Ashttps://sdbs.adb.org/sdbs/index.jsp; as on 4/5/13.

- **Employment Structure:** In concurrence with the production structure, the service sector has the largest share in the total employment as well (Table 3.6). This is unlike India where though the service sector contributes largest to the GDP, its share in the employment is much lesser.

Table 3.6 Employment Structure

	1995	*2001*	*2011*
Agriculture	5.68	4.88	3.67
Manufacturing	22.55	20.02	16.68
Mining	0.09	0.08	–
Others	71.67	75.02	79.65

Source: Estimated on the basis of data available from ADB (online) ADB's Statistical Database System; Ashttps://sdbs.adb.org/sdbs/index.jsp; as on 4/5/13

- **Fiscal Structure:** The collapse of the financial system in the aftermath of the aseet price bubble burst necessitated bailout package from the government. Since then, due to the expansionary fiscal policy, the share of the government, measured by the total government expenditure as a percentage of GDP, is growing continuously, highlighting reduced opportunities for the private sector. Growing expenditure and declining revenue shares have been increasing the fiscal deficit and the public debt burden. Revenue account deficit is the major component of fiscal deficit (Table 3.7).

Table 3.7 Government Finances (Per cent of GDP at Current Market Price)

	1995	*2001*	*2010*
Total revenue	12.0	11.5	11.2
Total expenditure	16.0	17.9	18.0
Overall budgetary surplus/deficit	–4.0	–5.7	–6.7
Current surplus/deficit	–1.8	–4.0	–6.2
Capital account surplus/deficit	–2.2	–1.7	–0.6

Source: Compiled from ADB (online) ADB's Statistical Database System; Ashttps://sdbs.adb.org/sdbs/index.jsp; as on 4/5/13.

- **Financial Structure:** Japan's financial structure is bank-based rather than market-based.

After the asset prices in the early 1990s, Japanese banks suffered heavily. Unable to meet their capital adequacy requirement, many of them solved the problem by contracting credit. Contraction in the economy in the subsequent period was a logical outcome of credit contraction.

Radical liberalization and restructuring process since 1996 in Japan aimed at making the financial system market-based. But, using various indicators (Table 3.8) a study by Capelle-Blancard, G., Couppey-Soubeyran, J. and Soulat, L. (2008), claims that the system still remains bank-based.

Table 3.8 Various Indicators of the Japanese Financial System

	Data source	*1980*	*1990*	*2000*	*2004*
1a. Credit Intermediation ratio	BOJ	67%	67%	57%	49%
1b. Market intermediation ratio	BOJ	21%	20%	30%	35%
1c. Total intermediation ratio	BOJ	88%	88%	88%	85%
2. Financial assets of all domestic sectors/GDP	BOJ, IFS	6.4	10.4	11.5	11.5
3. Financial assets of FI/financial assets of all domestic sectors	BOJ	48%	52%	54%	52%
4. Financial assets of banking sector/financial assets of FI	BOJ	62%	57%	51%	50%
5. Bank loans to private sector/GDP	IFS	83%	119%	115%	100%
6. Deposits/GDP	IFS	78%	104%	113%	124%
7. Stock market capitalization/GDP	FIBV, IFS	na	89%	72%	75%
8. Value of share trading/GDP	FIBV,IFS	na	47%	61%	70%

Source: Capelle-Blancard, G., Couppey-Soubeyran, J., and Soulat, L. (2008)

- Trade Structure: Japan is the fifth largest exporter and importer in the world. It is primarily a process hub—it imports raw materials, processes them and exports the processed output. China and the USA are two major trading partners of Japan. Transport equipment, general machinery and electrical machinery are its major exports, while mineral fuels, electrical machinery and chemicals are its major imports. Over a period of time the share of exports and imports in Japan's GDP have steadily increased (Table 3.9), reflecting the growing dependence of Japan on trade for its growth. (Such a structure, at present, because of global slowdown is further adding to the negative output gap.)

Table 3.9 Japan's Exports Imports and Balance of Payment

	1995	*2001*	*2011*
Exports	8.0	9.2	13.4
Imports	5.5	7.6	13.7
Balance on goods	2.5	1.7	-0.3
Current account balance	2.1	2.1	2.0
Overall Balance	1.1	1.0	2.9

Source: Compiled from ADB (online) ADB's Statistical Database System; https://sdbs.adb.org/sdbs/index.jsp; as on 4/5/13.

- **Population Structure:** Japan is the eleventh most populated country. However, it is a shrinking economy due to falling birth rates and almost no net migration. Due to very high life expectancy, its population is also aging rapidly (Table 3.10), further threatening the productivity and growth of the economy.

Table 3.10 Population Structure of Japan (in 2012)

Population (1000)		*Age composition*			*Average annual rate of increase*	*Population density*
Female	*Male*	0–14	15–64	65+		
127,199	62,184	13.1	63.7	23.3	–0.20	343

Source: Ministry of Internal Affairs and Communications, Statistical Handbook of Japan, http://www.stat.go.jp/english/data/handbook/c02cont.htm, as on 5/5/2013.

References

ADB (online) ADB's Statistical Database System; Ashttps://sdbs.adb.org/sdbs/index.jsp; as on 4/5/13.

Capelle-Blancard, G., Couppey-Soubeyran, J., and Soulat, L. (2008), The measurement of financial intermediation in Japan, Japan and the World Economy, 20 (1).

Questions

1. What are the structural features of Japan?
2. What do you understand by deflation?
3. Which of these features according to you are responsible for persistent deflation in Japan?
4. What is output gap? What does negative output gap refers to?
5. As a manager do you think that Japanese economic structure is conducive for business? Justify your answer.

SUGGESTED FURTHER READING

Chan, H. (2012), Is India's Current Ecoonomic Slowdown due to Cyclical or Structural Factors?, VOX, http://www.voxeu.org/article/india-s-economic-slowdown-and-what-should-be-done-about-it.

Jha, R. (2011), India's Economy: Growing Rapidly and Unequally, East Asia Forum, April 28, http://www.eastasiaforum.org/2011/04/28/india-s-economy-growing-rapidly-and-unequally/

Morrison, W.M. (2013), China's Economic Rise: History, Trends, Challenges, and Implications for the United States, Congressional Research Service, http://www.fas.org/sgp/crs/row/RL33534.pdf.

Nishizaki, K, Sekine, T. And Ueno, Y. (2012), Chronic Deflation in Japan, Bank of Japan Working Paper, July, No.12-E-6, http://www.boj.or.jp/en/research/wps_rev/wps_2012/wp12e06.htm/.

CHAPTER 4

Business Cycles and Fluctuations

4.1 INTRODUCTION

The Guardian in its issue of 21 January 2013 reported that due to a slowdown in retail sales, manufacturing and many service activities, banks, investment banks and insurance brokers had registered a decline in their business volume in the end month of 2012. The paper points out that though on the basis of the contraction in the final three months of the last year, technically, the UK cannot be declared to be in a recession, a recession in the most of the euro zone, uncertainty in the USA regarding further austerity measures and disruptions in the domestic markets due to snowy weather, dampens the hope of recovery in the economy. Referring to the survey by the CBI and accountants PWC, it highlights that the overall pessimism may lead the economy into a full blown triple dip recession.

The Indian economy, which is growingly getting integrated with the world, is also not immune to developments abroad. In the last few years, it is also operating below its potential, and business units are pinning their hopes on fiscal and monetary measures that can revive the economy.

Business decisions the world over are affected by business ups and down—recovery, expansion, boom, slowdown and recession or depression—referred to as business fluctuations. Though, expansion is liked the most, and recession and depression dreaded the most, each poses different challenges for business organizations and requires different survival strategies. In spite of their significant impact, business managers lack clear understanding of the terms associated with business fluctuations and the reasons for which such fluctuations occur in an economy.

Given the significance of business fluctuations for business decisions, this chapter aims at demystifying the ambiguity surrounding the terms associated with business fluctuations and the reasons for such fluctuations. Accordingly, Section 4.2 outlines the factors causing business fluctuations. Section 4.3 highlights the measurement issues and Section 4.4 points out how various economic indicators can be used for identifying business cycles.

4.2 FACTORS LEADING TO BUSINESS FLUCTUATIONS AND CYCLES

Countries, the world over, face wide fluctuations in output, prices, employment, and other macroeconomic variables due to the fluctuations in various components of aggregate demand and supply. Empirical evidence suggests that these fluctuations are not completely random—they exhibit trend, cyclical and seasonal patterns.

The **trend** represents the long-term behaviour of an indicator, whereas **seasonal effects**, as the name suggests, influence the indicator on regular basis with fixed periodicity—annually, quarterly, monthly, etc. **Cyclical patterns** or fluctuations do not have fixed periodicity like seasonal fluctuations, and hence, cannot be easily identified. Though they cannot be easily recognized, they are recurrent and are an integral part of a market economy.

Several factors have been identified causing business cycles. Broadly, these can be classified under two categories, viz., endogenous factors and exogenous factors.

Endogenous factors are generated in the system due to frictions and unsynchronized working of an economy. Examples of such factors are inventory accumulation, money supply increase and cheap credit availability, and expectations. Endogenous factors usually affect the demand side.

Conversely, **exogenous factors**, as the name suggests, are external to the functioning of an economy. For example, war, natural calamities in the form of war, famine and epidemic, scientific breakthroughs, and technological innovations and inventions. They usually affect the supply side. Any business cycle may be caused by any of these factors or may be an outcome of more than one factor. The ways in which some of these factors cause **business cycles** and accentuate various phases of a cycle are described as follows:

Inventory Accumulation

Over production may give rise to a build up inventories above the desired level. Accumulated inventories reflect towards adverse demand conditions, and thus, compel producers to make some downward adjustments in output and employment levels. Reduced output level and retrenchment of labour, by lowering income and consumption, set in a downturn. Reduced demand for output further accentuates the adjustments. The downturn continues until the inventory level decline to the desired level and the demand resumes to be above the level of production. To maintain the desired level of inventories, and at the same time meet the demand, producers again start increasing their business, which sets in another expansionary phase.

Changes in Monetary Policy, Money Supply and Credit Availability

Expansionary monetary policy, by enhancing money supply and making credit cheaper, induces producers to expand their business and fund their activities by borrowing. Cheap credit also lures consumers to higher spending which triggers further expansion in business activities. The expansion continues until some large borrowers default on repayments of borrowed amounts, resulting in failure of many banking and non-banking financial institutions. Failure of many financial institutions reduces the availability of credit, and increases its cost. This, in turn, contracts business activities and shrinks expenditure levels, and sets in a downturn. Downturn gets accentuated, because a hike in interest rate results in more and more defaults on repayments. The expansionary phase experienced by the USA before the onset of sub-prime lending crisis (refer to UBE 9.8) and the recession in post-crisis period can be attributed to monetary factors.

Expectations

An optimism regarding a good return or expectation of higher profits motivates producers to invest more and expand their business, setting an upswing. The upswing gets strengthen when higher output results in higher profit (because wages and other cost of products increase only after a lag), higher returns on investment, and higher share prices in stock markets. The expansion and boom continues until some unexpected drop in returns and share prices occurs. Such an unexpected event easily turns optimism into pessimism, and an upturn into a downturn. Once the downturn sets in, overall pessimism takes over. Adverse expectation of profit not only discourages new investment but also results in withdrawal of already existing investment and accentuates the downturn. The process of downturn continues until some favourable event brings back the optimism.

Technological Innovations and Inventions

Scientific breakthroughs and technological innovations resulting in new products and processes make the existing ones redundant. For example, in the past, invention of steam engines changed the methods of manufacturing and transport and gave way to large investment in railways and larger ships. Similarly, invention of jet aircrafts has largely replaced passenger transports by road, rail and ships. Likewise, computers have replaced typewriters and calculators; compact disks have replaced gramophone records, fibre optic cables have replaced copper cables in telephony, and internet has replaced libraries.

To cater to the demand for new products and advanced processes, large investment in new machinery and technology is carried out. Higher investment gives a boost to production and employment, increases income and consumption levels, and sets in expansionary phase of a cycle. The initial high profits entice more and more business units to copy the innovations of the pioneer. Imitations continue until all the abnormal profits are wiped out and many firms find themselves unprofitable because of excess supply and lower price for their products. In such a situation downward adjustments in investment, output and employment take place, setting in a downturn. The downturn continues until another invention puts a break to declining demand and profits.

The expansion experienced by many countries towards the end of the last century is attributed to revolution in information technology, while the subsequent decline was the outcome of dotcom bubble burst.

4.3 APPROACHES TO BUSINESS CYCLE ANALYSIS

There are three approaches to the analysis of business fluctuations, viz., conventional business cycles, growth cycles and growth rate cycles as elaborated hereinafter:

4.3.1 Conventional Business Cycles

Attempts at understanding business cycles and making forecasts on the basis of peaks and troughs in these cycles have occupied the attention of researchers and practitioners for almost a century now. The most widely accepted definition of **business cycles** is given by Burns and Mitchel (Measuring Business Cycles, NBER, 1946).

"A cycle consists of expansions occurring at about the same time in many economic activities, followed by similarly general recessions, contractions, and revivals which merge into the expansion phase of the next cycle; this sequence of changes is recurrent but not periodic; in duration business cycles vary from more than one year to ten or twelve years".

Business cycles conventionally measure fluctuations in the absolute levels of aggregate economic activities. Broadly, there are two phases in such cycles—expansion and contraction. An expansion terminates at the **peak** (highest point in a cycle), whereas a contraction ends with the **trough** (lowest point in a cycle) in economic activities. Figure 4.1 depicts various phases in business cycles as measured conventionally. During an **expansionary phase** of a cycle (from a trough to a peak or from point A to B or C to D in the figure) business activities experience continuous expansion, whereas during a **contractionary phase** (from a peak to a trough or from point B to C or D to E) there is a continuous decline in economic activities. One complete cycle covers both the phases—expansion and contraction, and peak and trough. Thus, as shown in Figure 4.1, the movement from point B to point D depicts one complete cycle in economic activities. The expansionary phase of business cycles usually tends to be longer than the contractionary phase due to the occurrence of an upward trend in an economy.

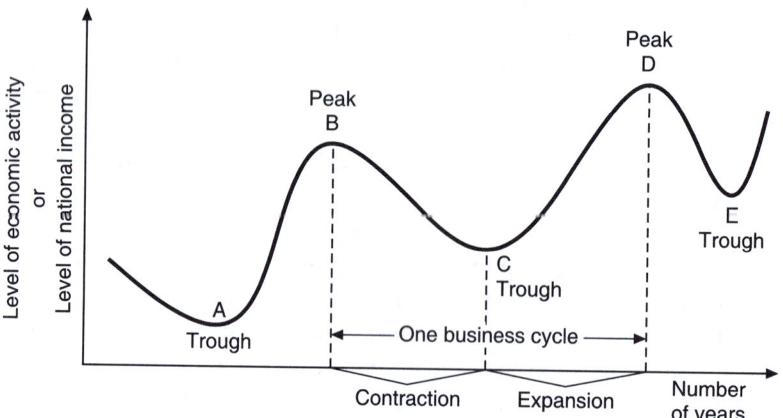

Figure 4.1 Phases in Conventional Business Cycles.

Estimation of business fluctuations requires some measurement and quantification of overall economic activities. One widely used measure is the national income. Apart from national income several other measures, such as sectoral income, employment, trade, and so on are used to represent economic activities. However, no single measure is good enough to measure wide spectrum of business and economic activities. Also, no single measure is either available for a long period or possesses all the desired attributes such as comprehensiveness, high frequency, timeliness. Hence, a composite of number of relevant indicators is used for representing economic activities.

4.3.2 Growth Cycles

An analysis of business fluctuations in terms of conventional business cycles has been found to be useful in those industrial countries which have generally experienced short expansionary and contractionary phase in levels of economic activities resulting in a low average growth rate. However, there are cases where countries, especially developing and emerging market economies, have experienced continuous expansion or contraction in levels of economic activities; leading to an appearance that these countries have not faced recessions over a very long period of time. The analysis in terms of conventional business cycles, thus, fails to identify business fluctuations or cycles in such economies.

A closer analysis, using slightly different tools, reveals that cyclicity does exist even in these cases, though they are not apparent. An increasingly accepted method of bringing out cyclical behaviour in countries experiencing very high growth, with a few or no recessions, is the **growth cycles**. A growth cycle can be ascertained from the plot of deviations of the actual growth rate of an economy from its long-run trend rate of growth or the full employment output or potential output (Box 4.1 and Box 4.2).

Box 4.1 Estimation of Trend Line or Full Employment Line

The **trend line** or **full employment output** or **potential output** is the long-run growth path of output and depicts the full employment level of output over a period of time. The full employment of output is the level of output where all the factors of production (land, labour, capital) are utilized at an optimum level (note it is the optimum level and not the maximum level).

Usually, the factors of production increase over a period of time, leading to an increase in the total output as well. Therefore, the trend line or full employment line usually is upward sloping.

The trend line or full employment output is estimated in empirical literature using parametric and/or non-parametric techniques.

Parametric techniques: Economic theory indicates that the total output (Y) of an economy at any point of time, broadly, is a function (f) of land (L), labour or population (P), capital (K) and technological improvement (T) i.e., $Y = f(L, P, K, T)$. This implies that the output varies over a period of time due to variations in L, P, K, T. Thus, the estimated and projected values of land, labour, etc., for a given timeframe, are used for estimating production function using econometric techniques. The estimated values of output provide an estimate of full employment or trend line.

Non-parametric techniques: Trend line is constructed from the basic output or GDP data by statistical techniques such as Hodrick-Prescott (HP) filter, Band-Pass (BP) filter, Phase Average Trend (PAT), etc. The smoothed GDP line is used to provide a measure of the underlying expansion or growth trend around which cyclical fluctuations occur.

Box 4.2 Estimating Potential Output and the Cyclical Position of Developing Economies

The boom-bust cycle through which developing (and developed) countries have passed in this millennium complicates the evaluation of both the level and rate of growth of potential output. Based on pre-crisis performance, developing country policy makers could easily conclude that developing-country potential GDP growth is around 7–8 per cent per year (average growth for developing countries in the 5 years through 2007 was 7.3 per cent.

Naïve measures of potential (such as moving averages of aggregate GDP growth or even statistical measures such as the Hodrik-Prescott or Kalman filters) are prone to errors (Giorno and others, 1995) – in part because they are heavily influenced by the most recent observations. If a measure is taken towards the end of a boom period it will tend to over-estimate potential, while if it is taken during a bust phase it will tend to under-estimate (Mise, Kim & Newbold, 2005).

The preferred method is to use a production function method that accounts for changes in labour supply and the capital stock as well as productivity growth (see for example OECD (2008), IMF (2005) CBO (2001)). Measures that rely on a naïve estimate of potential based pre-crisis performance give an excessively optimistic sense of sustainable growth (7.3 per cent), versus 5.9 per cent based on underlying productivity, labour force and capital growth (Figure 4.2). Importantly, the naïve measure can lead to policy errors, suggesting that substantially more slack exists in the system than do more sophisticated measures.

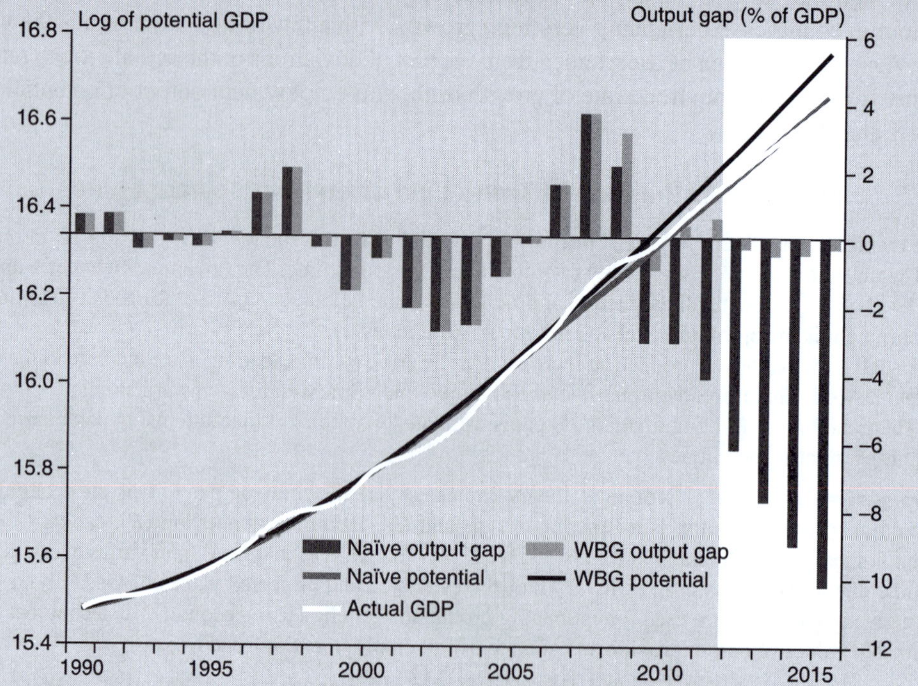

Source: The World Bank (2013), Global Economic Prospects, Volume 6, January 2013. Washington, DC: World Bank.

DOI: 10.1596/978-0-8213-9882-1 License: Creative Commons Attribution CC BY 3.0.

Figure 4.2 Using Boom Period Growth as Potential Results in a Substantial Overestimation of Slack.

Figure 4.3 depicts various phases in growth cycles. In the upper part of this figure, actual growth rate of an economy is compared with the trend growth rate, whereas in the lower part, the deviations of the actual growth from the trend growth rate are depicted. While business cycles can only be broken up into the phases of expansion and contraction with respect to peaks and troughs, growth cycles can be analyzed in terms of recovery, expansion, slowdown and recession. These phases of growth cycles are explained as follows:

Recovery: In the **recovery phase** of a cycle an economy picks up from the trough, i.e., the lowest point in the cycle, but the rate of growth remains lower than what is possible at the full employment level of output.

The recovery phase is usually associated with a mild increase in prices. The rate of increase in prices, and hence, inflation rate increases as the economy approaches the trend or full employment line. This mild increase in the inflation rate below the full employment level of output is known as **reflation**.

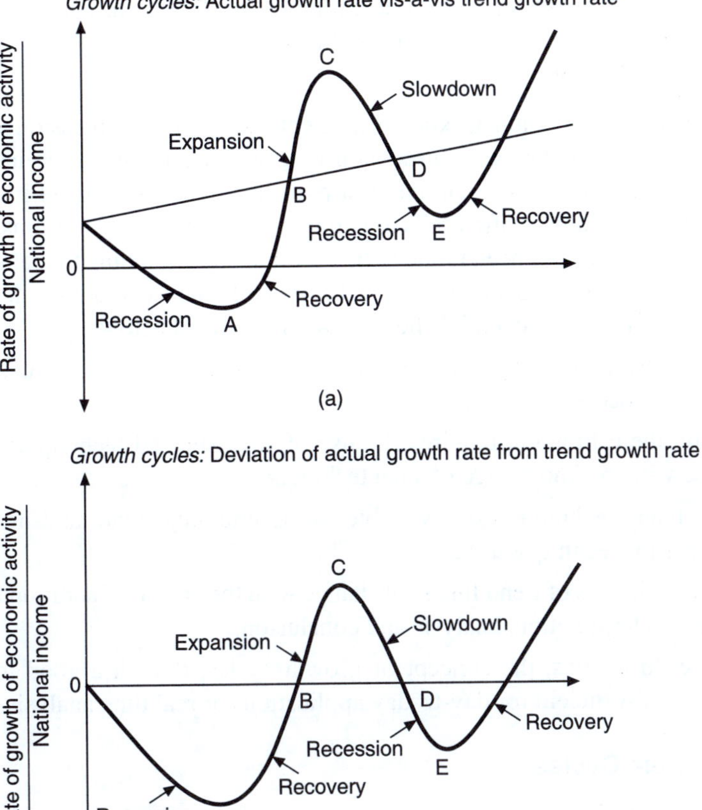

Figure 4.3 Phases in Growth Cycles.

Expansion: In the **expansionary phase** an economy expands at the rate of growth which is higher than the rate of growth at full employment level of output.

The expansionary phase is associated with rapidly increasing inflation rate. As the economy crosses the full employment level of output, wages and other prices start rising at a rapid rate and this increase gets reflected in the overall price level. The rate of increase in the price level above the full employment level is also known as **inflation**.

Slowdown: In the **slowdown phase**, an economy operates above the full employment level of output, but the rate of growth decelerates and remains less than the peak growth rate.

The slowdown is associated with a slowdown in the rate of increase in the price level, i.e., price level increases in this phase, but at a declining rate. This decline in the rate of growth of overall price level and inflation rate above the full employment level of output is known as **disinflation**.

Recession: In the **recessionary phase** there is a contraction in economic activities. The actual growth rate in this phase is lower than the growth rate at the full employment level.

In the recessionary phase prices start declining in absolute term, implying negative growth rate in prices. This situation, i.e., the absolute decline in prices below the full employment level of output, is known as **deflation.**

Depression: An acute recession is known as **depression.** The depression occurs when the recession is felt in most of the sectors of an economy (agriculture, industry, service) for a prolonged period of time with high unemployment and sharp decline in the price level in absolute term. In such a situation, the government often fails to stimulate the economy by various policy changes.

Growth cycle analysis has been found to be useful in understanding the relationship between output, inflation and unemployment. However, this type of analysis requires an estimation of the trend line which is meted with several difficulties as enumerated below:

- Firstly, an estimation of the trend line requires long time series data, which is a time consuming process.
- Secondly, the estimation requires the use of sophisticated techniques; not everyone is equipped with the knowledge of such techniques.
- Thirdly, many techniques are available for ascertaining trend, and hence, the estimate vary as per the technique used.
- Fourthly, estimates of trend line may change with the arrival of additional data, leading to changes in interpretation, analysis and conclusion.
- For these difficulties, the concept of growth cycles, though a good tool for historical analysis, is insufficient for day-to-day applications or real time analysis.

4.3.3 Growth Rate Cycles

Recognizing the problems in the estimation of trend line on a real time basis, the concept of **growth rate cycles** emerged as a solution for estimating business fluctuations in rapidly growing economies. Growth rate cycles are sustained periods of simultaneous upward (upswing) or downward (downswing) movements in the growth rate of economic activity. These cycles are estimated by plotting the growth rates at each point in time for a given time frame. The estimated growth rates are either the month to month changes or the same month year ago growth rates. The latter is preferred over the former, as the former is noisier. (i.e., it has more fluctuations).

Unlike growth cycle approach, growth rate cycle approach does not require an estimate of the trend line, because in this approach the actual growth rates are not compared with the trend or full employment growth rates. The approach distinguishes the various phases in a cycle simply on the basis of the signs of actual growth rate. Accordingly, the phases of growth rate cycle are as follows:

Expansion: **Growth rate expansion** is that phase where an economy registers sustained positive growth rate.

Recession: **Growth rate recession** occurs when a country experiences continuous negative growth rate.

Figure 4.4 depicts various phases in growth rate cycles and compares these phases with the phases in conventional business cycles. From the figure it can be ascertained that a growth rate downturn corresponds to a decline in the growth rate of economic activities (i.e., the movement from point A to C in Figure 4.3), whereas an upturn corresponds to an increase in the growth rate of economic activities (i.e., the movement from point C to E). A growth rate recession is the movement from point B to D where growth rate is negative (i.e., below zero growth rate line). It corresponds to the contraction phase of conventional business cycles (i.e. movement from point H to J). The peak (A) and trough (C) of growth rate cycles precedes the peak (H) and trough (J) of business cycles, respectively.

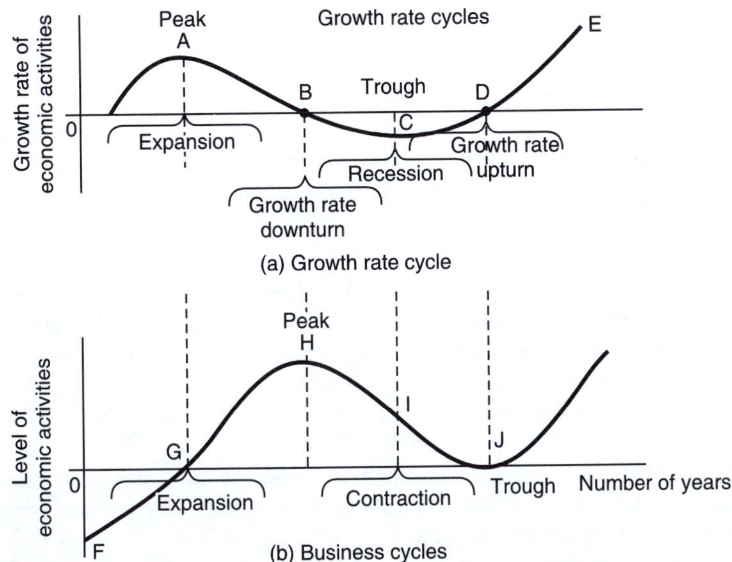

Figure 4.4 Growth Rate Cycles vis-á-vis Conventional Business Cycles.

As both conventional business cycles and growth rate cycles do not require an estimate of the trend growth rate these are jointly used for real time monitoring and forecasting of cycles.

Rule of Thumb

Even while adopting the growth rate cycle approach for an empirical estimation of recession, on a real time basis, different organizations use different rules of thumb. As per the International Monetary Fund (IMF), a country is considered to be passing through a growth rate recession when it registers a negative growth rate in two subsequent quarters in a year.

Similarly, when there is a decline in the rate of growth for two subsequent quarters, but the rate of growth is positive, the country is expected to be passing through a growth rate slowdown.

Deep and widely felt recession is also known as depression. Usually, an economy is considered to be in a depression when the real GDP declines by more than 10 per cent

4.4 IDENTIFICATION OF BUSINESS CYCLES USING ECONOMIC INDICATORS

Economic indicators or variables (Box 4.3) can be used for identifying the various phases of business cycles. Broadly, for the purpose of identification these indicators are classified as leading indicators, coincident indicators and lagging indicators (Box 4.3). Sometimes, predictions based on a single indicator are not efficient. Hence, as indicated earlier, a composite index, based on the basket of indicators, is constructed.

Box 4.3 Classification of Economic Indicators

Economic indicators such as GDP, inflation rate, employment rate, productivity, etc., help in finding various phases of and turning points in business cycles. These indicators may be classified in at least two ways. First, based on the position of their peaks and troughs—does a peak occur before the general high point in economic activity, does it follow the peak, or do they coincide? Second, based on direction of movement in indicators compared to the direction of movement of general performance of the economy— does it increase during a boom and decrease during a recession, or vice versa?

Method 1: Using position of peaks and troughs

Certain indicators may be the driving force or one of the causes behind an expansion, and so after they have witnessed a peak, the economy may start moving towards a peak in economic activity. On the other hand, the movements in some other indicators may be the result of a boom or a recession in the economy. Depending on the direction of causation, the economic indicators can be classified as follows:

Leading indicators: The indicators that hint at the likely economic scenario 12 to 15 months later are known as **leading indicators**. They provide early signals of turning points in economic activities. Some of the examples of leading indicators are—average work week, index of overtime hours, application for unemployment compensation, new companies registered, new orders, vendor performance, construction, stock prices, money supply, aggregate deposits, raw material prices, exports, consumer expectations, etc.

The information on these indicators is important for economists, business community and policy makers to make a correct analysis of economic situations and for putting in place appropriate policy measures for stabilizing output fluctuations.

Coincident indicators: The indicators the values of which change at the same time as the aggregate economic activity are known as **coincident indicators**. The economic series of these indicators have peaks and troughs that roughly coincide with the peaks and troughs in business cycles. Examples include real GDP, real non-agricultural GDP, index of industrial production, employees on non-agricultural payrolls.

Lagging indicators: The indicators values of which lag behind the turning points in aggregate economic activity are known as the **lagging indicators**. Economic series of these indicators experience peaks and troughs after that in the aggregate economic activities. Interest rate spread, ratio of manufacturing and trade inventories to sales, change in labour cost per unit output, manufacturing, commercial and industrial loans outstanding, change in CPI for services, etc., are some examples of lagging indicators.

Composite Index of Leading Indicators (CILI)

Though the values of leading indicators precede the value of overall economic activities, the exact time of change in the values of these indicators may deviate from one cycle to another cycle, which introduces an element of uncertainty in those estimates which are based on a single indicator. To minimize the element of uncertainty and for better prediction of timing of business cycles turning points a **Composite Index of Leading Indicators** (CILI) is constructed.

Method 2: Observing the direction of movement

Based on the correlation—positive or negative, between a specific indicator and the general performance of an economy, the indicators can be classified as follows:

Pro-cyclical indicators: The indicators which move in the same direction as the economy in general are known as **pro-cyclical indicators**. Their value increases during economic expansions and reduces during recessions. Examples of such indicators are: GDP, employment rate, price level, production, consumption, investment, corporate profits and capital utilization.

Counter-cyclical indicators: These indicators which are negatively correlated with the general economic performance are known as **counter-cyclical indicators**. Their value falls during expansions and rise during recessions. Unemployment rate is often cited to be an example of counter-cyclical indicators. Net exports also have been found to be in this category in certain countries.

Acyclical indicators: There are several indicators that do not exhibit any relationship with the general economic performance, and hence, are considered to be **acyclical indicators**. The correlation between the two indicators may be very close to zero. Government debt, fiscal balance, net exports, and several other indicators may or may not be cyclical, and thus, can be referred to as acyclical indicators.

The basic thread tying all the indicators is their lead-lag relationship. It can be seen from Figure 4.5 that the peak and trough in leading indicators (money supply, or aggregate deposits) precede the peak and trough in coincident indicators (IIP or GDP) and lagging indicators (interest rate). Some empirical studies indicate that the turning points in the growth of money supply lead to the turning points in the growth of an economy (coincident indicator) by about 1 to 2 years. Similarly, the peak in interest rates and inflation rate occurs within 12 months from the beginning of an economic slowdown. Furthermore, the trough in the growth of an economy leads to a rise in interest rates (lagging indicators) by about 1 to 2 years.

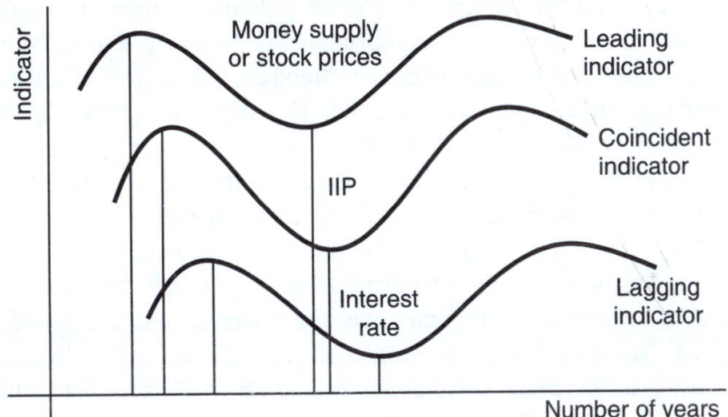

Figure 4.5 Lead and Lag Relationship among Economic Indicators.

As a leading, coincident and lagging indicators follow a well-defined and empirically established lead-lag relationship, they can be used for identifying, predicting and forecasting business cycles and future scenario. For example, leading indicators can be used for predicting turning points, whereas coincident indicators can be used for confirming the occurrence of turning points. Similarly, lagging indicators can be used for reaffirming the turning point after the occurrence of an event.

UNDERSTANDING BUSINESS ENVIRONMENT

UBE4.1 Loss of Potential Growth in India vis-à-vis Emerging Market Economies (EMEs)

This UBE depicts the growth cycles in India in the last two decades.

Potential output is generally the optimal level of output that can be achieved within natural and institutional constraints without putting pressure on inflation. Potential output has also been called the "natural gross domestic product" and, if the economy is at its potential, the unemployment rate equals the NAIRU or the natural rate of unemployment. The financial crisis often tends to affect the output of an economy through lowering financial intermediation, consumption and investments, and adversely affecting business sentiments; the extent of damage, however, depends on the severity and duration of the crisis. A recent empirical study on OECD countries over the period 1960 to 2007 by Furceri and Mourougane (2009) concludes that financial crises are estimated to lower potential output by around 1.5 to 2.4 per cent on an average. Similarly, Cerra and Saxena (2008) studied the output behaviour in 190 countries and found large and persistent actual output losses associated with financial crises, with output falling by 7.5 per cent relative to trend over a period of 10 years in the event of a banking crisis. If output loss is temporary, prompt and corrective policy initiatives are able to repair the damage and bring the output to the previous trajectory over a shorter span. On the other hand, in case output loss tends to be permanent, i.e., potential output has a structural break and has shifted to a lower trajectory, policymakers have to strive very hard and it might take longer than expected to shift back to the previous trajectory.

During the recent global crisis, the level of financial intermediation decelerated significantly in India, both in terms of bank credit and dent in equity markets. Second, the unemployment rate also went up, especially in export-oriented sectors, although official estimates are not available. Third, merchandise exports contracted at a rapid pace, possibly rendering a significant part of their capital stock and labour force idle if export-oriented enterprising units failed to shift their focus on domestic markets. Hence, in light of the above, it would be worthwhile to estimate the loss of output growth, temporary or permanent (potential), in the case of India vis-à-vis other emerging market economies.

Although, there are various methodologies to estimate potential output, obtaining a reliable measure is fraught with difficulty, and hence, the issue of appropriateness remains unsettled. Nonetheless, the Hodrick-Prescott (HP) filter has been used for deriving a long-term "trend growth" using annual as well as quarterly data to assess the loss of output growth during the current crisis. The shift in potential output growth, if any, should be construed preliminary and any inferences from the same need to be made with caveats.

The quarterly estimates of the potential growth based on the HP filter methodology shows that loss in growth, which started from the second quarter of 2008, albeit marginal, followed through the subsequent quarters with around 2.0 per cent points in Q_4 of 2008 and Q_1 of 2009 and 1.4 per cent points during Q_2 of 2009. The trends in potential growth suggest that the actual growth in industry has almost caught up with the potential level in Q_2 of 2009, indicating a temporary loss of growth. In contrast, loss of growth in the services sector continued to widen. Nevertheless, as mentioned above these results are preliminary, and therefore, should be used with great caution. Since services contribute about 60 per cent to the GDP, the potential growth in GDP seems to be following the trend in the services sector (Figure 4.6).

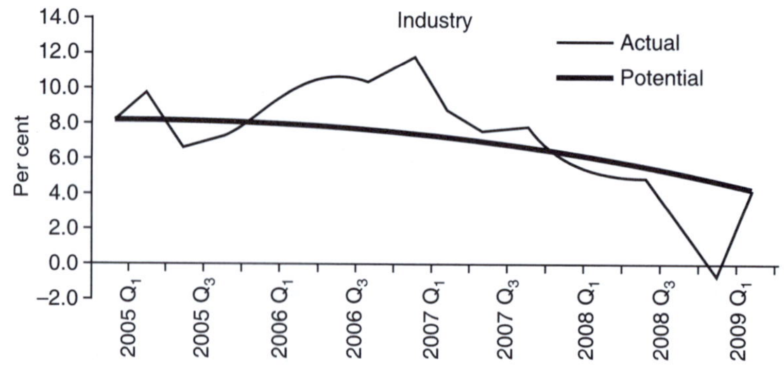

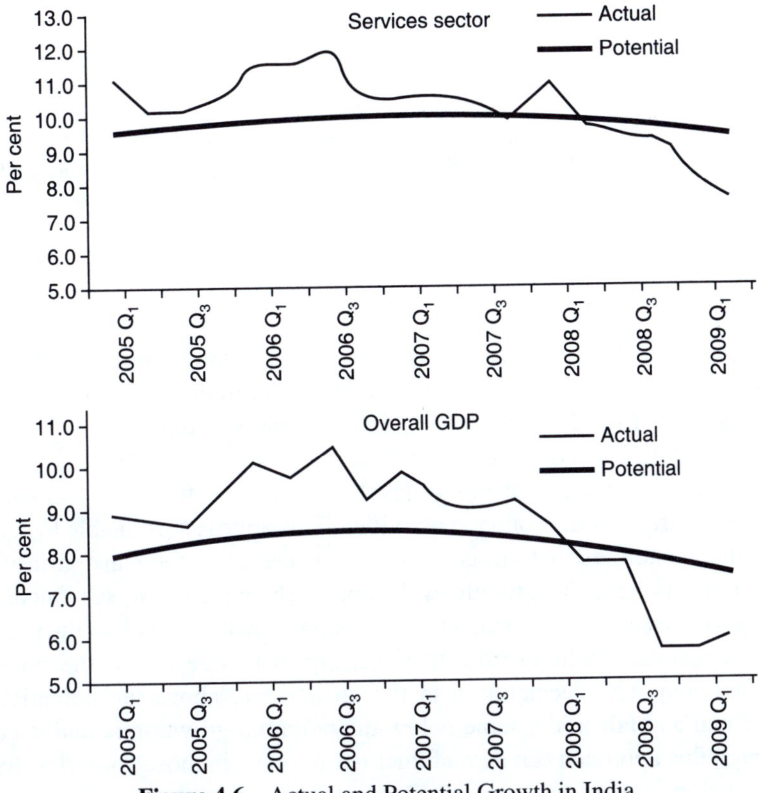

Figure 4.6 Actual and Potential Growth in India.

The potential growth in India as well as in some of the emerging market economies (EMEs) was also estimated using the HP filter with annual data from 1980 to 2008. Most of the EMEs including India have experienced loss in actual growth when compared with potential growth during 2008, whereas these countries witnessed gains in actual growth in recent years (Table 4.1). Russia had the highest growth loss followed by China, Argentina, India, Philippines and Malaysia during 2008.

Table 4.1 Growth Gap in India vis-à-vis EMEs

Country	*2001–2005*	*2006*	*2007*	*2008*
Argentina	– 1.2	2.0	1.1	– 1.6
Brazil	– 0.4	– 0.2	1.1	0.1
China	– 0.2	1.2	2.3	– 1.9
India	– 0.5	1.7	0.8	– 1.5
Indonesia	0.7	0.2	0.5	– 0.2
Malaysia	– 0.4	0.5	1.0	– 0.8
Philippines	–0.3	– 0.1	1.5	– 1.3
Russia	– 0.1	– 0.1	0.0	– 2.8

References

Cerra, V. and S.C. Saxena (2008), "Growth Dynamics: The Myth of Economic Recovery", *American Economic Review*, 98: 439–457.

Furceri, D. and Annabelle Mourougane, 2009, "The Effect of Financial Crises on Potential Output: New Empirical Evidence from OECD Countries", OECD Economic Department Working Paper 699.

Source: RBI (2010), Report on Currency and Finance 2008–09.

SUMMARY

Various endogenous and exogenous changes in business environment contribute to business fluctuations. These are, though recurrent, without fixed periodicity. Business fluctuations can be analysed using three different approaches, viz., conventional business cycles, growth cycles and growth rate cycles. The conventional business cycles analyse fluctuations in the levels of economic activities. An increase in the level of activity reflects the expansion, whereas reduction reflects contraction in economic activities. This approach is unable to deduct business fluctuations in the economies that are continuously experiencing expansion in their levels of economic activities. Hence, the growth cycle approach, which assesses fluctuations in the growth rate along the trend line growth. The increasing growth rate below the potential growth rate represents a recovery, whereas the increasing growth rate above the potential reflects an expansion or boom. The deceleration in the growth rate above the potential growth rate reflects a slowdown and fall in the same below the potential growth rate and is categorized as recession. Though this approach can deduct fluctuations even in those countries that experience continuous expansion in their activities, the necessity of making estimates of potential or full employment line devoid this approach of any practical utility. For real time analysis, therefore, the growth rate cycle approach is used. In this approach, the actual growth rate is compared with the zero growth rate. Following this approach, positive growth rate indicates expansion, whereas negative growth rate reflects recession. IMF follows this approach while declaring any country in a recession. As this approach does not require estimation of the potential growth rate, managers can easily use it for decision-making purpose. Business fluctuations can be predicted and confirmed by assessing the movements in leading, coincident and lagging indicators.

Implications for Managers

Every economy goes through business fluctuations or cycles. Understanding of leading, lagging and coincident indicators help managers to identify the phase of a business cycle a country is moving through.

Though business fluctuations impact all the sectors of the economy, the degree of the impact varies across sector and across different phases. At times the impact on different sectors may be in a different direction. For example, in a booming economy, demand for inferior goods, like coars grains may decline while that for superior goods like basmati rice may increase. The reverse may be experienced in a recession in these two sectors.

Given the differing impact of various phases of business cycles on different activities, different business strategies are necessitated to survive across business cycles. For example, the most important challenge of recovery is to retain business confidence. To benefit from the recovery, businesses need to believe that the situation is going to get better in the period ahead. Those businesses which take the risk of recruiting new staff or investing in a recovery phase find themselves better equipped to take advantage of growing demand as the recovery continues, whereas the others may simply miss the profitable opportunities.

In expansionary or booming phase, with an evergrowing demand, business confidence is high. In such a phase, firms continuing to reap profitable opportunities start experiencing skilled labour shortages and might be forced to raise wages. Pressure on the cost may be from other fronts as well. Raw material and energy prices may go up, and at the same time infrastructural constraints may start building up. Consumers with increasing purchasing power start expecting high quality products and speedy delivery. To meet such challenges businesses are required to invest in R&D that can improve the quality of their products, improve supply chain management, and devise strategies that can retain talent.

In a slowdown when demand starts decelerating, tactical adjustments, such as closing down of unprofitable activities and consolidation of not so unprofitable lines may be required to remain viable. Exploring new markets may be another way to keep up with the decelerating demand. Businesses can also continue to advertise their products to retain their brand image, the strategy that pays in the long-term, especially when the competitors are cutting on their advertisement expenditure.

A recession is the toughest time for any business. Business confidence is the lowest in the period because of continuously declining orders, late payments and mass scale business failure. Minimizing overhead costs, in the face of continuously declining demand, is the biggest challenge that the business managers face in a recession. Often this is achieved by downsizing the staff strength. In downsizing, the firms have to devise the ways in which an unproductive staff can be laid-off while the talented staff can be retained. Every recession end with a recovery. Therefore, retention of the talented staff and maintaining their morale during the tough times is crucial as that help the firms to survive a recession and prepare them for a recovery.

REVIEW QUESTIONS

4.1 What factors cause business fluctuations or cycles?

4.2 Differentiate between exogenous and endogenous factors that cause business fluctuations.

4.3 What are the different approaches to analysis of business cycles?

4.4 What are conventional business cycles? What are its various phases?

4.5 What are growth cycles? Why do we estimate them?

4.6 What is the full employment or trend line? How is it estimated?

4.7 What is the potential output? What does output gap represent? In India, how was this gap affected by the recent global financial crisis?

4.8 How far growth cycles differ from growth rate cycles?

4.9 What is the IMF rule of thumb for determining recession?

4.10 How would you differentiate depression from recession?

4.11 What are economic indicators? What are the criteria of classification of these indicators?

4.12 How are the indicators classified on the basis of position of peak and troughs?

4.13 How are the indicators categorized on the basis of the direction of the movement of indicators?

4.14 What role the leading indicators play?
4.15 Why do we prepare the composite index of leading indicators?
4.16 What role the lagging indicators play?
4.17 Why do business managers need to understand the various phases of business cycles?
4.18 How do the challenges for business differ across phases of a business cycle?
4.19 How would you vary your business strategies in different phases?

CASE ANALYSIS EXERCISE

C4.1 Will the Growth of the Service Sector Further Decelerate?

Service sector, which consists of trade, hotels and restaurants, transport, storage and communication, financing, insurance, real estate and business services, community, social and personal services, and construction, contributes the highest amount to the GDP of India. Being the backbone of the Indian economy, performance of the service sector affects the overall performance of the Indian economy.

As per RBI (2012), service sector registered its lowest growth in thirteen quarters during Q1 of 2012–13 due to the weak performance of trade, hotels, transport, storage and communication sector. The leading indicators of services sectors, such as tourist arrival, cement, cell phone connections, etc. (Table 4.2), hint towards further deceleration in the growth rate of this sector.

Table 4.2 Indicators of Service Sector Activity

Services sector indicators	*2010–11*	*2011–12*	*Apr–Sep 2011–12*	*Apr–Sep 2012–13*
1	2	3	4	5
Tourist arrivals	9.5	8.6	9.3	3.4
Cement	4.5	6.7	4.1#	5.4#
Steel	13.2	7.0	9.9#	2.7#
Cell phone connections (in million)$	227.3	107.6	46.8*	–5.7*
Automobile sales	16.8	11.2	12.0	3.6
Railway revenue-earning freight traffic	3.8	5.2	4.8	4.8
Cargo handled at major ports civil aviation	1.6	–1.7	3.1	–3.3
Domestic cargo traffic	23.8	–4.8	–5.1*	3.8*
International cargo traffic	17.7	–1.9	3.9*	–4.3*
International passenger traffic	10.3	7.6	8.8*	3.3*
Domestic passenger traffic	18.1	15.1	18.0*	–0.5*

#: Data pertains to April–August.
*: Data pertains to April–July 2012.
$: Refers to wireless subscriber additions in actual numbers.
Source: RBI (2012), Macroeconomic and Monetary Developments, October.

As different leading indicators can have different growth rate and can move in different directions, a composite of these indices is constructed and analyzed to forecast the performance of a sector or an economy during the upcoming period. The composite indicator of the service sector prepared by the RBI also confirms the deceleration in the service sector activities (Figure 4.7).

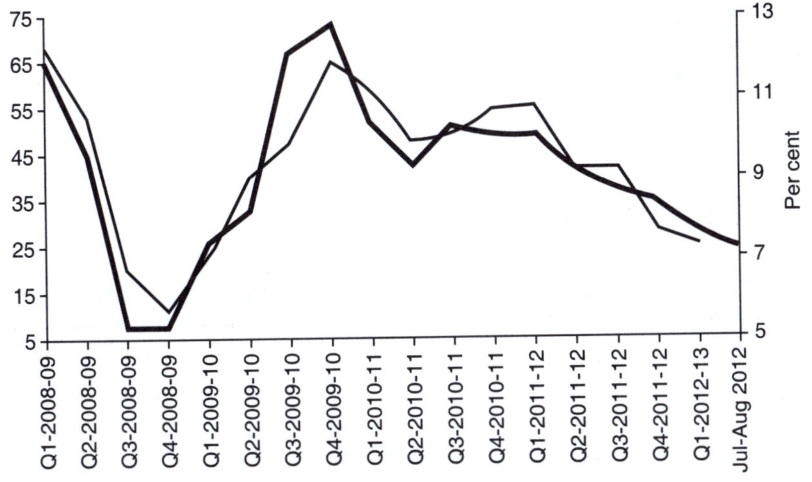

Services Sector Composite Indicator constructed by the Reserve Bank

Growth in services GDP excluding community, social and personal services (right scale)

Source: RBI (2012), Macroeconomic and Monetary Developments, October.

Source: RBI (2012), Macroeconomic and Monetary Developments, October.

Figure 4.7 Services Sector Composite Indicator.

Reference

RBI (2012), Macroeconomic and Monetary Developments, October.

Questions

1. What are the leading indicators of service sector activity?
2. In what way indicators like cement and steel are related to services?
3. What is the service sector leading indicators hinting at the performance of the service sector?
4. What are these service sector leading indicators are hinting at the overall performance of the Indian economy?

SUGGESTED FURTHER READING

Bordo, M.D. (2012), The Great Depression and the Great Recession: What Have We Learnt? *RBI Bulletin*, May.

International Monetary Fund (2012), *World Economic Outlook*, Washington, DC, October, Chapter 1.

Nagraj, R. (2013), India's Dream Run, 2003-08: Understanding the Boom and Its Aftermath, *EPW*, May 18, Vol. XLVII, No. 20.

Reserve Bank of India (2007), *Report of the Technical Advisory Group on Development of Leading Economic Indicators for Indian Economy*, January.

Reserve Bank of India (2010), *Report on Currency and Finance* 2008–09.

CHAPTER 5

National Income
Measurement and Environment Scanning

5.1 INTRODUCTION

One of the important determinants of our standard of living is our income. An increase in our income often increases our spending and improves our standard of living. Converse holds true when our income declines. A nation consists of many individuals like us. When, at the same time, many individuals experience an improvement in their income the total income or output generated in a nation enhances. This overall income or money value of total output generated in a given year, known as the **national income**, is an important determinant of aggregate consumption and investment level, and overall performance and health of a nation or an economy. An increased national income improves the aggregate consumption and overall well-being of the society, whereas converse holds true when national income declines.

National income being a determinant of aggregate consumption and investment levels, affects the overall demand for goods and services, production capacity, and hence, profitability.

As a measurement of overall economic or business activities, the movements in national income also represent business fluctuations and various phases of business cycles termed as **recovery**, **expansion**, **slowdown** and **recession** (defined in Section 5.3).

Given the importance of national income as a determinant of consumption and investment activity, and a measure of business and economic activities, business units closely watch and incorporate it in their planning, production and strategic decisions.

Data on and trends in national income and the related aggregates, such as gross domestic product, net domestic product, gross national product and net national products are placed in the **National Income Accounts**. The collection and analysis of this data is referred to as the **National Income Accounting**. While estimating, collecting and analyzing the data, economists differentiate between stock and flow variables. The flow variables are those variables that are estimated over a period of time, such as budget deficits, investment expenditure, capital formation and income (household, national, per capita). Conversely, stock variables are those variables that are estimated at a particular point of time, such as wealth (accumulation of savings), debt (accumulation of borrowings), capital stock (factories, machines and inventories), etc. National income is a flow variable, and hence, is estimated from flow variables. While estimating national income, for example, as we will see in the subsequent sections, investment (a flow variable) rather than capital stock (a stock variable) is added to other components.

At present, almost all countries have some official documents in which they record their national income and related aggregates. For example, in the US, the national income accounts are officially known as the **National Income and Product Account** (NIPA) which are constructed quarterly by the Bureau of Economic Analysis (BEA). In India, the **Central Statistical Organization** (CSO) regularly compiles and publishes the **National Account Statistics** (NAS).

This chapter details on measurement issues in national income and the related aggregates, and describes the various facets of an economy which can be ascertained from the different components of these aggregates. In particular, the process of generation of output or income or expenditure in an economy is explained in Section 5.2. The different approaches of measuring total output or income are elaborated in Section 5.3. Section 5.4 describes the various aggregates measuring the total output or income in an economy and their equivalence. Section 5.5 relates national income to personal income and outlays. Problems in the measurement of these aggregates are outlined in Section 5.6. Various uses of national income and its component are presented in Section 5.7.

5.2 ECONOMIC SYSTEM ANDGENERATION OF OUTPUT ANDINCOME

An **economy** consists of millions of consumers and firms, which interact among themselves, leading to a complex set of transactions. As an outcome of these interactions and transactions, income, expenditure and output are generated. This entire process is illustrated with the help of a circular flow in a simple economy in Section 5.2.1.

5.2.1 A Simple Closed Economy without Government, Saving and Investment

For simplicity, we have assumed that in a simple **closed economy** there is no government sector, no trade linkages with the rest of the world and no leakages and injections (defined in Section 5.2.2). There are only two economic agents, viz., households or consumers and producers or firms.

Households are assumed to own all the **factors of production**, viz., land, labour, capital and entrepreneurship. They supply these to business firms in the **factor market**. For supplying factors of production, households get remunerated in the form of **factor income**, viz., rent, wage, interest and profit, respectively. The total income of households is the sum total of these different types of factor income (also known as factor payments). Households spend their income on purchases of goods and services.

Using various factors of production, **firms** convert **intermediate products**, i.e., the goods and services that are used in the process of further production, such as coal, cement, flour, etc., into **final products**, i.e., the goods and services that are not used in further process of production, but are either consumed or invested. Final goods are sold in the **product market** by firms to households for a price. The revenue so generated is used by firms to make factor payments, i.e., rent, wage, interest and profit, and producing output in the coming period.

In the absence of saving and investment, the total income earned by households is equal to total expenditure and that, in turn, equals the value of all final goods and services produced in an economy.

This entire process of factor income moving from firms to households and then, in the form of spending, moving from households to firms appears like a circle, and hence, known as the **circular flow of income** (Figure 5.1).

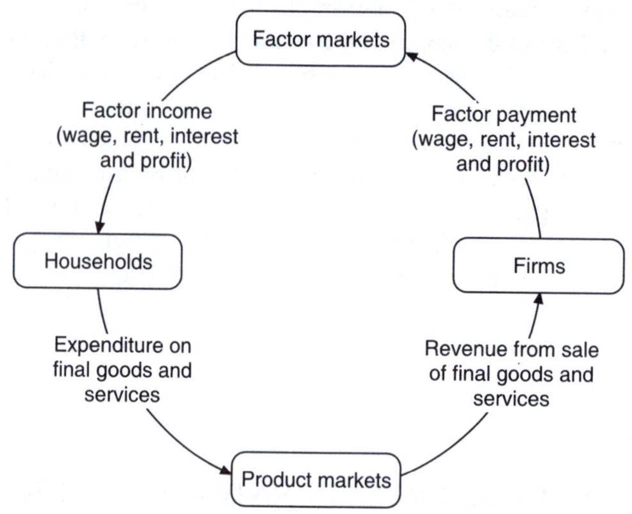

Figure 5.1 Circular Flow of Income in a Simple Closed Economy.

As long as the income that households receive from firms equals the expenditure on goods and services by households, and that equals the value of goods and services produced by firms, the following identity holds good:

$$\begin{aligned}\text{Factor payments} &= \text{Wages} + \text{Interest} + \text{Rent} + \text{Profit}\\ &= \text{Household Income}\\ &= \text{Household Expenditure}\\ &= \text{Value of Output (Final Goods and Services)}\\ &= \text{National Income}\end{aligned}$$

In this simple framework, the economy remains in a static **equilibrium** situation, i.e., there is neither a contraction nor an expansion in economic activities. Whatever households receive as factor income they spend on goods and services; whatever revenue firms receive from the sale of goods and services they spend on factor payments. There is neither excess demand nor excess supply. Hence, there are no forces which can change this equilibrium situation.

5.2.2 Savings and Investment: A More Realistic Economy

The simple economy, presented in the previous section, though clearly identifies the interactions among households and firms and explains the process of income and output creation, it is not very realistic. In reality, economic agents save part of their income and invest in plant, machinery, equipment, factory, buildings, etc. We also know that apart from households and firms, the government actively takes part in economic activities. At present, no country is completely closed, and hence, transactions with the rest of the world also play an important role in economic activities. All these features make the circular flow more complicated as depicted in Figure 5.2 and as described hereinafter.

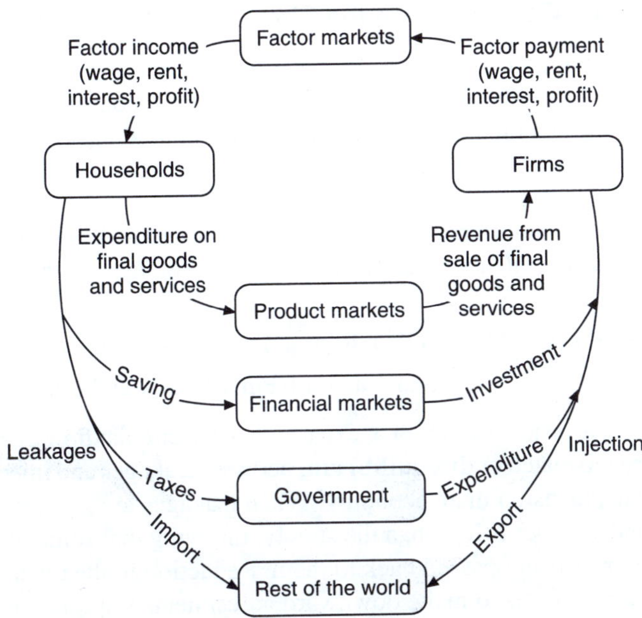

Figure 5.2 Circular Flow of Income in More Realistic Open Economy with Government.

Households save a part of their income for anticipated and unanticipated events, such as life after retirement, illness, etc. The **saving** flows from households to **financial markets** (defined in Section 9.3.2). It reduces the demand for goods and services which, in turn, reduces the revenue generated by firms and their ability to hire factors of production and generate output. Thus, we see that saving results in a contraction in economic activities, and shrinks the size of the circular flow. Hence, it is considered to be a **leakage from the circular flow**.

Financial markets supply funds to firms for investment. **Investment** generates additional demand for goods and services, expands economic activities and the size of the circular flow. Hence, it is considered to be an **injection to the circular flow**.

The government imposes **tax** (*T*) on households. Since tax reduces the income and expenditure of households it is a leakage from the circular flow. However, the government also spends on items such as administration, defence, pensions, unemployment relief, scholarship, welfare schemes, subsidies, etc. Since the **government expenditure** generates additional demand for goods and service it is an injection to the circular flow.

Transactions of an economy with the rest of the world also affect the circular flow. To take an advantage of low cost and better quality of products produced abroad, countries import (*M*) commodities. On the other hand, part of the commodities produced in the domestic markets are exported (*X*) to other countries to generate more demand for domestically produced goods. Whenever a country imports there is an outflow of income from it to a foreign country. Thus, **imports** constitute a leakage from the circular flow of income. Conversely, when a foreign country buys commodities from the domestic country there is an inflow of income into the domestic market. Thus, **exports** are considered to be an injection to the circular flow.

5.2.3 Expansion and Contraction in the Circular Flow or Economic Activities

Saving (S), taxes (T) and imports (M) cause leakages and investment (I), government consumption expenditure (G) and exports (X) constitute injections in an open economy with government. In an equilibrium, or in a static situation, total leakages are equal to total injections, i.e.,

$$S + T + M = I + G + X$$

This is considered to be an equilibrium situation, because when leakages are equal to injections total expenditure is equal to total income and also to total value of final goods and services produced in an economy, i.e.,

$$C + I + G + X - M = \text{Wage} + \text{Rent} + \text{Interest} + \text{Profit}$$
$$= \text{Total Value of Final Goods and Services}$$

In such an economy, there is no contraction or expansion in the circular flow or economic activities.

Conversely, the mismatch or **disequilibrium** between leakages and injections results either in a contraction or an expansion in an economy. When leakages are greater than injections, the demand for goods and services is less than the supply, implying that some of the income gained by households from firms is not passed back to them. Reduction in the revenue from the sale of goods and services forces firms to make downward adjustments in production in the following years. The circular flow, and hence, economic activities contract in such a situation. Contrary to this, when leakages are less than injections, there is more demand than supply, revenue generated by firms is higher than their expenditure on factor payments, which entice them to expand their production activities in the following years. The circular flow, and hence, economic activities expand in such a scenario. The contraction or expansion in an economy continues until the leakages equal injections or the economy move from a disequilibrium state to an equilibrium one.

5.3 MEASUREMENT OF AGGREGATE INCOME

While understanding the process of circular flow of income, we learnt that the aggregate income generated in an economy is always equal to the value of output produced in it, and that is equal to the total expenditure incurred in it. Therefore, the aggregate income of a country can be estimated by three different approaches as follows:

5.3.1 Expenditure Approach

The **expenditure approach** aims at measuring the total spending on final goods and services produced within a country during a given period of time, say a year. The total spending consists of not only the expenditure by domestic participants but also the foreign expenditure on domestically produced goods.

The two components of total spending are explained in more detail hereinafter.

Domestic Spending on Domestically Produced Commodities

Expenditure by the domestic participants consists of the following:

1. Consumption expenditure: **Consumption** refers to the expenditure on final commodities, i.e., goods and services, which does not result in creation of any assets. Goods are tangible items, such as wheat, mango, cycle, TV, etc., whereas services are non-tangibles, such as dry-cleaning, shoe repairing, etc. Consumption expenditure can be on durable or non-durable commodities. **Durable commodities** are those that last for long period of time and consumed over several periods. The examples of such commodities are furniture, automobiles, and household appliances. Conversely, **non-durable commodities** are those which last for a short span or consumed within a given period of time, such as soap, gasoline, food and clothing.

Consumption expenditure by private sector, consisting of households and other private entities is referred to as **private consumption expenditure** (*C*) and that by the government as **government consumption expenditure** (*G*). Therefore,

$$\text{Total consumption expenditure} = C + G$$

2. Investment expenditure or capital formation: Unlike **consumption expenditure**, investment expenditure results in a creation of an asset. It consists of expenditure on plants, machines, buildings, tools and other equipments.

Total domestic investment expenditure (*I*) can be by private sector, i.e., households and firms (*Ip*), and/or by the public sector firms owned by the government (*Ig*). The total investment expenditure can be further divided into three subcategories: business fixed investment (the expenditure on the purchase of new plants and equipments by both private and public sector firms); residential fixed investment (the expenditure on the purchase of new housing by households); and inventory investment (the expenditure by firms to increase the stock of raw materials).

Summing up the first two components, i.e., business fixed investment and residential fixed investment, we arrive at the total fixed investment. Fixed investment depreciates in value over a period of time due to wear and tear of plant, machinery, building, etc. Economists refer to the term **consumption of fixed capital** or **capital consumption allowance** to denote **depreciation.** Capital formation net of depreciation is known as the **net capital formation** whereas gross of depreciation as the **gross capital formation.**

All the above components of expenditure, i.e., *C*, *G* and *I*, do not represent the **domestic expenditure on domestically produced commodities** because each of these components have some element of domestic expenditure on foreign produced goods known as **imports** (*M*). Hence, to arrive at the estimate of domestic expenditure on domestically produced commodities, from the above components, we need to subtract the amount of expenditure on imports, i.e.,

$$\text{Domestic Expenditure on Domestically Produced Goods} = C + G + I - M$$

Foreign Spending on Domestically Produced Commodities

Domestic spending on domestically produced commodities does not give an estimate of total expenditure on domestically produced commodities, because a part of these is consumed by foreigners. To arrive at the total expenditure on domestically produced commodities we need to add the amount of expenditure by foreigners on domestically produced goods, also known as **exports (*X*).**

Thus, the total expenditure (*Y*) can be estimated by the following identity:

$$Y = C + G + I - M + X$$

By rearranging this identity, we arrive at the most commonly used expression for total expenditure in an economy as:

$$Y = C + I + G + X - M$$

where $C + I + G$ is total expenditure by domestic participants and $X - M$ is net foreign spending on domestically produced goods.

The above identity is expressed in a diagrammatic form in Figure 5.3.

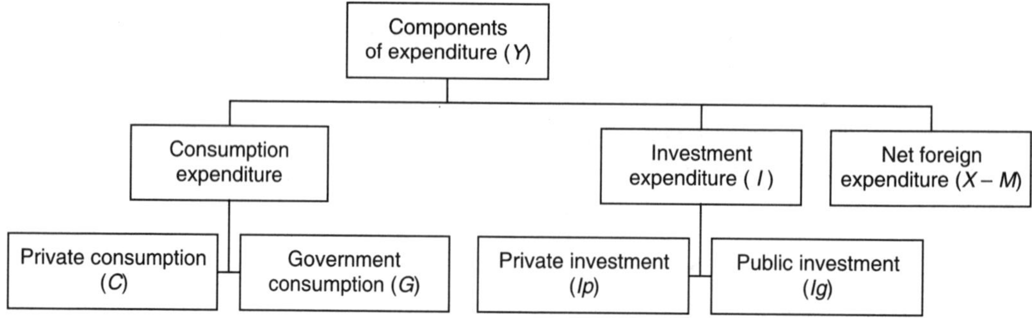

Figure 5.3 Components of Expenditure.

Changes in any of the expenditure components affect the aggregate level of demand. Some of these expenditure components depend on the level of income (such as consumption) and some are largely independent of it (such as investment, government expenditure and exports). The exogenous changes in any of the expenditure components bring in multiple changes in the aggregate income as explained in Box 5.1.

Box 5.1 Investment Multiplier

Autonomous changes in any of the expenditure components can affect the level of income. The extent of impact, however, is determined by the level of exogenous change in the given expenditure component and the value of its multiplier.

For example, an exogenous change in the level of investment brings in a change in the aggregate income which is some multiple of initial change in the level of investment.

The parameters on which the value of investment multiplier depends in a simple economy consisting of only two agents, firms and households and two expenditure components, C and I is identified as follows:

We know that in a state of equilibrium, in this simple economy, the following identity holds good:

$$Y = C + I$$

For understanding the multiplier process, investment is assumed to be an exogenous factor, whereas consumption is assumed to be related to the level of income. The relationship between consumption and income is expressed as follows:

$$C = a + bY$$

where

a = Autonomous component of consumption (mpc) expenditure unrelated to the level of income.

b = M**arginal propensity to consume** depicting the change in consumption brought by 1 percentage change in income.

Substituting for C from the consumption income relationship, the aggregate income identity can be written as:

$$Y = a + bY + I$$

By rearranging this identity we get,

$$Y - bY = a + I$$

or $$Y(1 - b) = a + I$$

or $$Y = \frac{a + 1}{1 - b} = a\left(\frac{1}{1 - b}\right) + I\left(\frac{1}{1 - b}\right)$$

Then $$\Delta Y = \Delta I\left(\frac{1}{1 - b}\right)$$

That is, a given change in investment (ΔI) brings about a multiple change in aggregate income (ΔY), and the value of the **investment multiplier** $[1/(1 - b)]$ is inversely dependent on the mpc (b).

Excluded Expenditure Categories

Before proceeding further, we should keep in mind that in the expenditure approach, while arriving at the national aggregate, only the expenditure on final goods is included. There are certain items of expenditure, which are not included while estimating total output or income through this approach. These expenditure categories are listed below:

1. Expenses in the form of transfer payments: In any economy some amount of expenditure is simply in the form of ***transfer payments***. Examples of transfer payments are expenditure on gifts, donations, scholarship to students, unemployment allowances, old age pensions, subsidies, welfare payments, personal and corporate income tax and wealth tax, sale of old paintings and used automobiles. These are one-sided transactions which do not result in the production of additional goods and services. These merely represent redistribution or transfer of income from the government to households and to business firms or from firms to households, or from households to households. Since these payments do not represent payments made for the production of final goods and services these are excluded from the estimation of aggregate income or output.

2. Expenditure on second-hand commodities: The expenditure on second-hand commodities is excluded from the estimation of aggregate output as expenditure on them was already included when the goods were bought for the first time. For example, suppose a man buys an old car then the cost of such a vehicle will not be included in the expenditure because it was already included when the car was purchased new.

3. Expenditure on intermediate products: A production process deals with both intermediate and final products. **Intermediate products** are those goods and services which are used in the further process of production. For example, apples are used to make apple juice, coal is used to make steel. On the contrary, **final products** are those, which are not used in the process of production, but are bought and used by final consumers, such as bread, books, shoes, automobiles, and hair cutting services. The value of final products is inclusive of the value of intermediate goods which are used in their production. The aggregate output, when it is estimated as the total expenditure on final goods and services, is inclusive of the value of intermediate goods. Therefore, including the expenditure on intermediate commodities, along with the final commodities, while estimating total expenditure in an economy, results in a **double counting**, i.e., counting the value of commodities more than once. Hence, while estimating the national income or output, to avoid the problem of double counting, the expenditure incurred on final products is included and that incurred on intermediate goods is excluded.

Changes in the share of different expenditure components in total expenditure affect the **demand structure** of an economy which has differing implications for the sustainability of growth as explained in UBE 5.1.

UNDERSTANDING BUSINESS ENVIRONMENT

UBE 5.1 Drivers of Growth

The share of different expenditure components in total GDP and its implications for some select countries are presented in this UBE.

The expenditure components help in understanding the ways in which the total GDP is used and the **sources of demand** or drivers of growth in a given year. The **growth drivers** in any economy are consumption expenditure (including government consumption), investment and net exports. Though the growth in any year can be increased from any of the sources, the changing share of these components reflects on the changing structure, productive capacity, government role and openness of an economy.

Though all expenditure components add to the aggregate demand and facilitate in enhancing output, different components have differing impact. A higher share of domestic consumption expenditure indicates that the output is driven by demand from the private sector, whereas a larger share of government expenditure indicates that the government is active in stimulating the economy. In the absence of enough demand coming from the domestic private sector and exports, the government expenditure can give a stimulus to the growth. A higher share of exports and imports reflects greater openness towards trade inflows and outflows. A higher share of net exports also suggests that the growth is export led. A higher share of investment, unlike the other components of demand, not only enhances the demand but also increases the potential of supply by enhancing the productive capacity.

Each type of growth process has its own pros and cons as highlighted as follows:

In an underdeveloped and developing economy, **consumption led growth** without corresponding improvement in the productive capacity may supply constraint the growth process and lead to **stagflation**– the situation in which there is simply inflation but no growth. Hence, in such economies **investment led growth** is desirable. However, in the middle income economies, with adequate level of infrastructure and productive capacity, continuously increasing share of investment only leads to a **supply glut**. In such situations, a boost to other demand components is required. In the presence of high potential supply and limited domestic demand, **export led growth** can provide avenues for sustainable growth. However, export led growth increases market sensitivity to exogenous factors and makes the country vulnerable to external shocks and business fluctuations abroad. Recession abroad can easily get transmitted in such economies. The sensitivity to such fluctuations increases if countries pursue specialization in the areas where they have comparative advantage (defined in Section 13.2.1). Specialization makes the economies potentially unstable if demand for their commodities, in which they have specialized, falls. In these situations and in the absence of enough demand coming forth from the private sector and exports, the government can provide stimulus to sustain the growth rate. However, such a growth cannot be long lasting as the pattern of financing of government expenditure can either lead to higher inflation or higher interest rate and drive out the private expenditure. Thus, though, in the short to medium term an economy can achieve a very rapid growth by enhancing the share of some components of demand, but in the long-run such growth process faces severe constraints from other components. Hence, for sustainable growth in the long-run, the balanced growth view has been gaining ground world over.

Depending on the initial conditions, evolving economic structure and changing economic scenario, different countries have been pursuing varied growth strategies. Accordingly, the share of different components of expenditure in total GDP has also varied across countries. Table 5.1 indicates the share of different components of demand in total GDP for some selected countries during the last three decades. From these figures one can get a glimpse of the evolving growth strategy adopted in these countries.

Table 5.1 Expenditure Components of GDP (Per cent share in GDP)

Year	*China*	*India*	*Pakistan*	*Singapore*	*Japan*
		Private Final Consumption			
1990	50.6	66.2	71.4	45.4	53.0
2000	46.2	63.7	75.4	41.9	56.2
2011	34.5	56.0	84.1	39.4	60.3
		Government Final Consumption			
1990	14.1	11.7	15.1	9.5	13.3
2000	15.8	12.6	8.6	10.9	16.9
2011	13.1	11.7	7.9	10.3	20.7
		Gross Domestic Capital Formation			
1990	36.1	26.0	18.9	35.1	32.7
2000	35.1	24.3	17.2	33.2	25.4
2011	48.6	35.5	13.1	22.4	19.9
		Exports			
1990	19.0	7.1	14.8	177.4	10.4
2000	23.3	13.2	13.4	192.4	11.0
2011	28.6	24.6	14.2	209.0	15.2
		Imports			
1990	15.6	8.5	20.2	167.4	9.4
2000	20.9	14.2	14.7	179.6	9.5
2011	26.0	29.8	19.2	182.3	16.1
		Discrepancy			
1990	–4.4	–2.4	…	0.0	…
2000	0.5	0.3	…	1.1	…
2011	1.2	2.0	…	1.2	…
		GDP at Current mp (billion, in national currency)			
1990	1866.8	5696.2	855.9	70390.6	442781
2000	9921.5	21023.1	3826.1	162584.1	502990
2011	47156.4	88558	18032.9	326832.4	468425

Data for GDP for Malaysia and Singapore are in million.

Sources: Computed from data from ADB (2013) Statistical Database System (online) http://www.adb.org/Economics/sdbs.asp, as on 16/5/13.

A continuously declining share of private final consumption expenditure and increasing share of investment and exports in China indicate that it has been pursuing an investment as well as export led growth.

Though Indian economy is primarily driven by domestic consumption, it is on the path similar to that followed by China. In India the share of Private Final Consumption Expenditure (C) is the largest component of expenditure, but its share has been on decline and that of Gross Domestic Capital Formation (I) is on increase. An increasing dominance of investment in the GDP indicates the growing productive capacity of the Indian economy. The government dominance in the Indian economy is also increasing over a period of time. The country is also trying to diversify its demand component by greater opening to trade flows.

Similar to India, Pakistan is highly consumption-driven economy. But, unlike India, the share of consumption expenditure is becoming more and more dominant in Pakistan. In the absence of sufficient investment coming forth, the economy is likely to face supply constraints. Inspite of domestically-driven economy, it is highly vulnerable to external shocks because of a large share of imports in the GDP.

Singapore had been primarily driven by exports. The high share of exports and imports in its total GDP also makes it susceptible to shocks in external environment.

Japan in the decade of 70's and 80's followed investment-driven path. But the increasing share of age old population made it impossible to continue such growth strategy in the coming decades. To achieve higher growth, it is gradually changing its stance from investment led growth to more diversified demand structure and more balanced growth.

5.3.2 Income Approach or Factor Income Method

Another way to measure the output of an economy is through adding the **factor payments** that firms make to the **factors of production** (land, labour, capital and entrepreneur) in the form of **rent, wages, interest** and **profits** for their contribution to the production of goods and services. Of these components, wages are often referred to as **compensation of employees**, whereas rent, interest and profit are clubbed together and termed as **operating surplus** (Figure 5.4).

Thus,

Total Factor Payments = Wages + Rent + Interest + Profit
= Compensation of Employees + Operating Profit
= Total Income

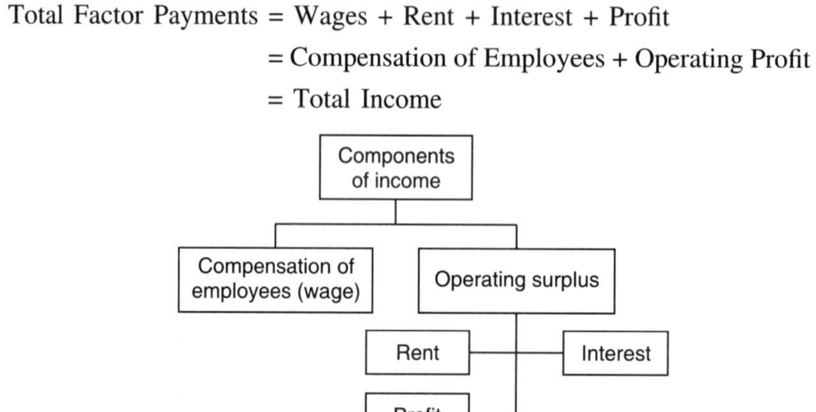

Figure 5.4 Components of Income.

While arriving at the aggregate income through this method some precautions are taken to avoid its underestimation or overestimation as detailed below:

Items Included to Avoid Underestimation

Following items are included in the estimates to avoid underestimation of national income.

First, in some countries, especially underdeveloped and developing, some producers compensate their employees partly in cash and partly in kind. For example, farmers often pay labourer in kinds, i.e., wheat, rice, pulses or any such agriculture produce. To avoid underestimation of aggregate income or output generated, payments made in kind are also included in the estimates.

Second, again in underdeveloped and developing economies, many goods and services do not appear in the market, i.e., they are not sold for a price. Contrary to this, as the economy gets developed more and more goods and services get marketed. To avoid the underestimation of the real value of goods and services generated in the economies where large amount of goods are non-marketed, along with the marketed goods, imputed value of non-marketed goods is also included in the estimate of aggregate income. For example, some people stay in their own houses, whereas others stay in rented apartments. On rented apartments the owner receives the rent which gets accounted in the aggregate income, whereas on owner occupied houses, since there is no rent paid, it remains unaccounted if care is not taken to account for it. To avoid the discrepancies and underestimation an imputed value of the rent is considered. Similarly, commodities retained for own uses, such as farm products not sold by farmers, are assigned an imputed value and that is included as income of farmers.

Items Excluded to Avoid Overestimation

The following income categories are excluded from the estimate of national income to avoid double counting or overestimation:

1. Transfer receipts: Income in the form of **transfer receipts**, such as unemployment benefits, pensions, gifts, donations, taxes, charities, fines and winnings from lotteries, are excluded from the estimate of aggregate income, because these do not result in an additional output.

2. Income from sale of second-hand goods: The income from sale and purchase of second-hand goods are also excluded because their values are already accounted when they are sold for the first time in the market.

3. Interest on loan for consumption: Aggregate income is the sum total of factor payments made to factors for their contribution during the process of production. Therefore, the interest income on loans taken for production are accounted in, whereas that on loans for consumption purpose gets excluded from the estimates of national income.

4. Income from illegal activities: Certain illegal activities, like smuggling and black marketing which provide illegal income, are excluded as it is difficult to measure and keep an account of them. In addition, these activities are outlawed by the community and are not socially useful.

5. Income from capital gains: Capital gains represent an increase in the value of capital assets resulting from an increase in the market prices of such assets. Although such gains are important for asset holders, they are not accounted in the estimates of aggregate income as they do not represent any counterpart increase in the output.

Changes in the composition of factor income have implications for income inequalities, demand pattern and government revenue as reflected in UBE 5.2.

UNDERSTANDING BUSINESS ENVIRONMENT

UBE 5.2 Trends in the Components of Factor Income

The way in which different components of factor income is accounted in the National Accounts Statistics of India and the implication of its changing composition is described in this UBE.

In India, the factor income is disaggregated into various components such as compensation of employees, operating surplus and mixed income of the self-employed.

The compensation of employees includes the total amount of wages and salaries, and supplements wages and salaries that workers receive as remuneration for their work. Wages and salaries also include the payments made in cash or kind in the form of commissions, tips and bonuses. On the other hand, supplements to wages and salaries refer to the items that the workers receive as a result of their productive work in the form of social security, private pensions, welfare funds and compensation for injuries, family allowance, insurance premium, etc.

The operating surplus includes the total income earned by firms during the production process from property and enterprises in the form of rent, interest and profit. Thus, operating surplus is the income from property plus income from entrepreneurship.

In an organized sector, proper records of different components are maintained. Therefore, the amount of compensation of employees can be segregated from the other components of income. But, in an unorganized sector, often due to lack of proper records, the distinction between employment income and operating surplus cannot be made.

In India, there are a large number of people who are self-employed (who fall under unorganized sector) in various fields, such as trade, law, proprietors, banking and insurance. As self-employed persons do not keep proper records of their income, it is not possible to classify the total income generated by such persons into wage and operating surplus. To avoid underestimation of national income due to lack of segregated data, mixed income of self-employed, which consists of wage income of own account workers, and profits and dividends of the unincorporated enterprises, is added to the estimated value of total wage and total operating surplus.

Given the difficulty in distinguishing the compensation of employees from operating surplus in the case of self employed, no clear trend in different factors of payments can be ascertained at the aggregate level as well as at the unorganized level. However, it can be ascertained that the composition of total factor income from the organized sector has moved in favour of operating surplus during the period 1990–00 to 2010–10 (Table 5.2).

Table 5.2 Percentage Share of Different Components of Factor Income in NDP at Factor Cost (at current prices)

	1999–00	*2007–08*	*2008–09*	*2009–10*	*2010–11*
	Compensation of employees				
All Sectors	37.38	32.29	34.87	35.60	35.21
Organized	24.20	20.19	22.14	23.23	22.69
Unorganized	13.19	12.11	12.74	12.37	12.52
	Operating surplus/mixed income of self employed				
All Sectors	62.62	67.71	65.13	64.40	64.79
Organized	16.35	22.21	20.20	19.99	20.13
Unorganized	46.27	45.49	44.93	44.42	44.66

	1999–00	*2007–08*	*2008–09*	*2009–10*	*2010–11*
	NDP at factor cost				
All Sectors	100.00	100.00	100.00	100.00	100.00
Organized	40.54	42.40	42.34	43.21	42.82
Unorganized	59.46	57.60	57.66	56.79	57.18
NDP at factor cost(₹ crore)	1605103	4097390	4738370	5433587	6403938

Source: CSO: National Accounts Statistics, various issues.

As low income class drives a large proportion of income in the form of wage, the changing composition of income in favour of operating surplus is indicative of increasing inequalities in the Indian economy. However, from the revenue perspective, the changing composition is indicative of better revenue collection for the government under the progressive taxation system which will be discussed in Section 8.5.1.

5.3.3 Value Added Approach or Net Product Method

Any production process deals with both intermediate and final products. As we already know that the **intermediate products** are those that are used in the further process of production. For example, wheat is an intermediate product in the process of bread making, whereas chips, keyboard, mouse all are used as intermediate products while manufacturing computers. On the contrary, final products are those that are bought and used by consumers, such as bread, stitched clothes, shoes, tables, computers, etc. The value of final products is always inclusive of the value of intermediate products. Thus, while estimating national income, if we add the value of all the products, i.e., intermediate as well as final, then it results in the problem of double counting, i.e., counting the production of a commodity more than once—first as intermediate and subsequently as final product. To overcome this problem, only the value added at each stage of production by a firm is taken into consideration. The value added by a firm at any stage of production is the difference between the revenue the firm earns by selling its products to the next stage and the amount it pays for the products of other firms it uses as intermediate goods. Thus,

Value Added by a Firm = Value of the Output Produced by the Firm
– Value of Intermediate Products Used by the Firm

Value Added in an Economy = Sum Total of Value Added by All the Firms in the Economy
= Total Income Generated in the Economy

Let us understand the concept of value added in more detail using a case of a hypothetical economy where bread, a final product, is produced using wheat flour. Production of bread goes through three stages of production—farming of wheat, milling of wheat and baking of bread. As can be seen from Table 5.3, farmers grow wheat worth ₹100 (to keep the explanation simple we can assume that they do not use any intermediate products at this stage) and sell this to the miller who converts wheat into flour worth ₹200. Thus, miller adds value of ₹100 more to the process. Thus, the value added at this stage of production is ₹100 (₹200 – ₹100). Flour is sold by the miller to the baker who converts this into the final product, i.e., bread worth ₹350. The value added by the miller is ₹150 (₹350 – ₹200). Total value added in this economy is equal to the sum total of value added at each stage of production that is equal to ₹350 (₹100 + ₹100 + ₹150).

Table 5.3 Production of Bread in a Hypothetical Economy (₹ in crores)

				Factor payment/Income				
Producers	*Output*	*Input*	*Value added*	*Wage*	*Rent*	*Interest*	*Profit*	*Total*
Farmer	100	–	100	60	10	5	25	100
Miller	200	100	100	40	5	15	40	100
Baker	350	200	150	65	15	20	50	150
Total	650	300	350	0	0	0	0	350

Thus, we can arrive at the same value of output produced in the economy by either adding the value added at each stage of production of all the products or just considering the value of all final products.

5.3.4 Equivalence of the Three Approaches

The circular flow identity presented in Section 5.2 indicates that all three approaches, i.e., the expenditure, income and value-added approaches, result in the same figure for the aggregate income or output.

Table 5.4 illustrates the equivalence of the three approaches. It can be seen that the value added, equivalent to ₹100, by the farmer results in the factor payment of ₹100 (wage ₹60, rent ₹10, interest ₹5, profit ₹25). Similarly, the value added of ₹100 by the miller results in the total factor payment of ₹100 (wage ₹40, rent ₹5, interest ₹15, profit ₹40), and value added of ₹150 by the baker results in the factor payment of ₹150 (wage ₹65, rent ₹15, interest ₹20, profit ₹50). Thus, the total value added (₹350) is equal to the total factor payment (₹350 = ₹100 + ₹100 + ₹150) in this economy, which is also equal to the value of the final product, i.e., bread worth ₹350.

Though different approaches to the measurement of aggregate income provide the same estimate, most countries [including India (UBE 5.3)] use all the three methods.

UNDERSTANDING BUSINESS ENVIRONMENT

UBE 5.3 Methods of Measuring Sectoral Output

Though all three approaches to the measurement of aggregate income provide the same estimates, not all the approaches can be used with equal ease in all the sectors, necessitating the use of different approaches in different sectors as is illustrated in this UBE using the Indian context.

It has been argued that if three different approaches of estimating national income results in the same value then why one needs to consider all the three.

The arguments in favour of use of all the three approaches are as follows, first, it provides a cross check which is required for an accurate estimate of national income. Second, the income from different sectors of an economy cannot be estimated with an equal ease using only one approach. This second aspect has been depicted here by describing the approaches that are used for estimating income from different sectors of the Indian economy.

The Indian economy is divided into three sectors, viz., primary, secondary and tertiary sectors. Depending on the nature and the extent of data available, different estimation approaches are adopted for estimating output from each of these sectors (Table 5.4).

Table 5.4 Estimation of Sectoral Income in India: Different Approaches

Method	*Sectors*
Production approach (Value-added method)	Agriculture and allied activities, forestry and logging, fishing, mining and quarrying, registered manufacturing.
Income approach	Unregistered manufacturing, gas, electricity and water supply, banking and insurance, transport, communication and storage, real estate and ownership
Expenditure approach (Commodity flow method)	Construction

For sectors like agriculture, forestry and logging, fishing, mining and quarrying, and registered manufacturing which are the commodity producing sectors, the data on output, input and prices are available on a more or less regular basis. For each of these sectors, the contribution to GDP is estimated in terms of Gross Value Added (GVA) by using the production approach. The GVA involves the estimation of total value of output at factor cost, and from there deducting the value of inputs of raw materials and services consumed in the process of production at purchasers' price. Thus, the product approach/value-added method is the most suitable for estimating the aggregate income from these sectors.

For sectors like unregistered manufacturing, gas, electricity and water supply, banking and insurance, transport, storage and communication, real estate, ownership of dwellings, trade, hotels and restaurants, public administration and defence, and other services (such as research and scientific services, medical and health services, educational services and religious and other community services, etc.), the income method is the most appropriate for estimating the national income. The data on all types of factor income for all these sectors is readily available from the published annual accounts of these undertakings, and the GVA is estimated as the sum of gross factor incomes. For example, in the case of ownership of dwellings, the GVA is obtained by estimating the gross rental of residential buildings and from there deducting the cost of maintenance and repairs, while in the case of real estate services, various components of factor income are estimated by the analysis of annual reports of the real estate companies.

The construction sector consists of contract construction by general builders, civil engineering contractors and special trade contractors. It also includes own account construction carried out by independent units of enterprises or other organizations. The estimates of GVA are derived from the estimates of value of output, which are prepared separately for *pucca* construction (urban construction) and labour intensive *kutcha* construction (rural construction).

Pucca construction is undertaken using construction materials such as cement, steel, bricks, timber, fixtures, etc., and the value of output is prepared by the commodity flow approach using the data from the Annual Survey of Industries (ASI) and the government departments. This approach estimates the supply of commodities expressed in the producer's value and also estimates disposition expressed in the purchaser's value by adding trade and transport margins and other similar expenditures.

Unlike *pucca* construction, labour intensive kutcha construction is undertaken with the help of freely available materials like mud, leaves, etc. The estimates are prepared by following the expenditure approach using data from sample surveys, budget documents of central/state government, and annual reports of public and private sector enterprises. The value of output is estimated from the survey of NSSO. Thereby, the total GVA from construction is the sum of the GVA from construction based on the commodity flow approach and the GVA from construction based on the expenditure approach.

5.4 DIFFERENT CONCEPTS OF NATIONAL INCOME AND THEIR EQUIVALENCE

The aggregate output generated in any economy can be viewed either as the output produced within its domestic territory or as the output produced by its nationals. Irrespective of the view adopted, the output can be measured either as gross of depreciation or net of depreciation. It can be valued either at **market price**, i.e., the price faced by the consumers, or at **factor cost**, i.e., the price faced by the producers. Depending on the view adopted, method used for measurement and price level used for valuation, we can get different concepts of measurements of aggregate output or income. These various concepts, the differences among them and their equivalence are discussed hereinafter.

5.4.1 Domestic Income vs National Income

The output produced within the domestic territory is known as **domestic output** (or product or income), whereas the output produced by the normal residents of a country is known as **national output** (or product or income). To grasp the two concepts, we need to understand the meaning of the terms like domestic territory and normal residents of a country more clearly.

Domestic territory refers to the territory lying within the political frontiers of a country, including territorial waters, ships and aircrafts operated by the country and embassies, government offices, consulates and military establishments of the country located abroad within the political territory of other countries. But it excludes all foreign embassies and offices of the international organizations located in the political territory of the country. Thus, the domestic output includes the output generated within the political territory including the territorial waters, income generated by the ships and aircrafts operated by the country, and also the income generated by the embassies and government offices located abroad, but excludes all the income generated by foreign embassies and offices of international organizations located in the political territory of the country.

Normal residents of a country are those individuals who normally reside in that country for a year and perform their main economic activities there and/or their main economic interest lies in that country. The normal residents of a country may or may not be its citizens. Similarly, citizens of a country may or may not be its normal residents. The normal residents of a country can generate income or output not only inside the domestic territory, but also outside it by supplying factor inputs abroad [rest of the world (ROW)].

For the supply of these factor inputs they receive factor income from abroad. For example, the salary of a professor, a resident of the domestic country, from his teaching assignment in France for three months is a factor payment received from abroad. Conversely, the normal residents of other countries also provide factor inputs to the domestic territory, and thereby, receive factor payments from it. This is referred to as the factor payments made abroad. For example, if the headquarter of an MNC sends its top most manager in its branch in India for a week, and the branch located in India makes payment for the manager for his services then this is a factor payment made abroad. Similarly, interest or dividend payments made to foreigners for their investment in India are factor payments made abroad. Thus, the **Net Factor Income from Abroad** (NFIA) for the domestic country is equal to the factor income received from abroad minus the factor payments made abroad. The net factor income from abroad, when added to the domestic income or output, gives the amount of national income or output. Thus,

National Income (or Product or Output) = Domestic Income (or Product or Output)
+ Net Factor Income from Abroad

where,

Net Factor Income from Abroad = Factor Income Received from Abroad
– Factor Payment Made Abroad

5.4.2 Gross Income vs Net Income

Domestic as well as national income can be either gross or net of depreciation. Gross figures are easier to estimate, however, net figures provide more accurate estimates of output or income for the reasons explained as follows:

We have seen in Section 3.3.1 that the **capital formation** or total investment consists of fixed capital formation and change in stock of inventories. In gross terms the identity can be written as

Gross Capital Formation (Gross Investment) = Gross Fixed Capital Formation
+ Change in Stock of Inventories

Of these two components, the **fixed capital**, i.e., machinery, plants, etc., wears out (depreciates) or becomes obsolete. Economists term this wear and tear as **consumption of fixed capital** or **capital consumption allowance**. To the extent investment in a year is used for repairing wear and tear or for replacement of the existing stock of capital, it does not add to the existing stock of capital, and hence, to total output. Therefore, to get a more accurate estimation of the output generated in an economy, we need to take account of the net value of fixed investment or net fixed capital formation. The net value can be derived from the gross value as follows:

Net Fixed Capital Formation = Gross Fixed Capital Formation – Depreciation

or Net Capital Formation = Net Fixed Capital Formation + Change in Stock of Inventories

The estimates of domestic product (or output or income) based on gross capital formation gives the estimate of **gross domestic product** as:

Gross Domestic Product (GDP) = Net Domestic Product (NDP) + Depreciation

Similarly, the estimates based on the net capital formation gives the estimate of **net domestic products** as:

Net Domestic Product (NDP) = Gross Domestic Product (GDP) – Depreciation

From the above two identities we can arrive at the **Gross National Product** (GNP) and the **Net National Product** (NNP) as follows:

GNP = GDP + Net Factor Income from Abroad

and NNP = NDP + Net Factor Income from Abroad

The natural question that can arise in our mind at this stage is whether the circular flow identity as stated in Sections 5.2.1 and 5.2.2 (i.e., Total expenditure = Total factor income = Total value of final output) holds good when there is wear and tear of capital.

The circular flow identity stated in Sections 5.2.1 and 5.2.2 holds true only if depreciation is zero. If the depreciation is greater than zero, for the circular flow identity to hold true, we need to make adjustments for it in all the approaches. However, the adjustments in the three approaches depend on whether we aim at estimating income or output at gross of depreciation or net of depreciation. If we aim at the net estimates then the adjustments required are as follows:

- First, total expenditure should be netted out for depreciation, to arrive at the net expenditure.
- Second, depreciation should be deducted from the total value added.
- Third, no adjustment is needed in the total factor payments because factor payments are in net terms.

After making adjustments for depreciation, the circular flow identity can be written as:

$$C + I - \text{Depreciation} + G + X - M = \text{Wage} + \text{Rent} + \text{Interest} + \text{Profit}$$
$$= \text{Total Value Added} - \text{Depreciation}$$
$$= \text{Net Domestic Product (NDP)}$$

Thus, when the net investment is considered one gets the net income/output of a country.

However, if we aim at the gross estimates of output/income then we need to add depreciation to the sum of factor payments. No such adjustment will be required in the case of expenditure and value-added approaches because these are gross of investment. Thus, gross domestic output or income is:

$$C + I + G + X - M = \text{Wage} + \text{Rent} + \text{Interest} + \text{Profit} + \text{Depreciation}$$
$$= \text{Total Value Added} = \text{Gross Domestic Product (GDP)}$$

5.4.3 Market Price vs Factor Cost

So far we also assumed that there is no wedge between the price faced by consumers, i.e., the **market price** (mp) and that faced by producers, i.e., the factor cost (f_c).

Before we relax this assumption and look at its implication for aggregate income or output, let us understand the concept of factor cost more clearly. Many of us get confused by hearing this term. The questions that often arise in the minds of many of us are: while producing goods and services why do we refer to the price faced by producers as factor cost when they incur cost on not only procuring factor inputs but also non-factor inputs (intermediate goods)? Do producers incur losses when they supply their products at factor cost? Do not producers make any profit when they supply products at a price which simply cover their factor costs?

We can get an answer for the first two of these questions if we understand the difference between the cost concepts at micro level and that at macro level. At the micro level, i.e., at the producer level, the cost includes both—factor inputs as well as non-factor inputs. But, at the macro or aggregate level all costs equal to factor cost; all factor and non-factor cost faced at various level of production sums upto total factor cost. The difference will be clearer if we revisit the value-added approach presented in Section 5.3.3. There we have seen that additional cost of production at each level is simply the cost of factor inputs. For example, at farming stage, the cost of production is ₹100 which is simply the cost of factor inputs. In the next stage of production, i.e., milling, the cost of production of farmers becomes the cost of intermediate products to millers. The additional cost of production for millers is again ₹100 which equals to the cost of factor inputs. At the third stage, i.e., baking stage, the miller cost becomes the cost of intermediate goods and the additional cost of production for the baker is ₹150 which is simply the cost of factor inputs.

When we sum total all the additional costs, or factor cost, of production at each stage of production, we get ₹350 as the total cost of production of bread which simply equals the total cost of production of bread at the final stage of production. If rather than adding up only the additional cost, or the cost of factor inputs at each of production, we add all the costs of production at each stage we will face the problem of double counting. Thus, at the aggregate level, the total cost of production is equal to total factor cost or total factor payments. Since products are sold in a market at factor cost, the revenue that producers get covers all the cost of production, and hence, there is no question of producer making losses.

We can get an answer to our third question if we notice that factor cost not only includes the payment to land, labour and capital but also to entrepreneurs. The remuneration to entrepreneurs is known as profit. Hence, when producers supply products in a market at factor cost they also make some profit.

Having understood the concept of factor cost, we can relax the assumption of no wedge between factor cost and market price, and assess the impact on aggregate output or income when the government imposes taxes on commodities, known as indirect taxes, and provides subsidies to producers. Imposition of indirect taxes, such as sales tax, excise duties, etc., increases the market price, whereas provision of subsidies reduces it. If the amount of indirect tax is higher than that of subsidies, the market price will overestimate national income. The converse holds true when the amount of indirect taxes is less than subsidies.

In the presence of wedge between market price and factor cost, the circular flow identity may not hold true, because in reality the different approaches use different prices while estimating national income. The expenditure approach measures the output at market price because all types of expenditure are on final goods and services which are sold in a market. On the contrary, the income approach values the output or income at factor cost because factor payments are made at the production stage, the valuation of factors is at the price faced by producers. Similarly, value-added is generated in the production process, and hence, income estimates using value-added approach are available at factor price.

For the circular flow identity to hold true, when there is a divergence between the market price and factor cost, we need to add indirect taxes to and subtract subsidies from aggregate factor payment to arrive at the estimates that are at market price. Making similar adjustments in the aggregate value added, we will get the circular flow identity as:

$$
\begin{aligned}
C + I + G + X - M &= \text{Wage} + \text{Rent} + \text{Interest} + \text{Profit} + \text{Depreciation} + \text{Net Indirect Taxes} \\
&= \text{Total Value Added} + \text{Net Indirect Taxes} \\
&= \text{GDP at Market Price}
\end{aligned}
$$

where, Net Indirect Taxes = Indirect Taxes – Subsidies

Or, alternatively, we can evaluate total expenditure at factor cost by subtracting indirect taxes and adding subsidies to the aggregate expenditure to get the following identity:

$$
\begin{aligned}
C + I + G + X - M - \text{Net Indirect Taxes} &= \text{Wage} + \text{Rent} + \text{Interest} + \text{Profit} + \text{Depreciation} \\
&= \text{Total Value Added} = \text{GDP at Factor Cost}
\end{aligned}
$$

Similarly, Net Domestic Product, Gross National Income, Net National Income can be either estimated at market price or at factor cost.

Thus, we get eight different but related concepts of total output or income produced in an economy, i.e., Gross Domestic Product at market price (GDPmp), Gross Domestic Product at factor cost (GDPfc), Net Domestic Product at market price (NDPmp), Net Domestic Product at factor cost (NDPfc), Gross National Product at market price (GNPmp), Gross National Product at factor cost (GNPfc), Net National Product at market price (NNPmp) and Net National Product at factor cost (NNPfc). The relationship of these eight measurements is presented in Figure 5.5.

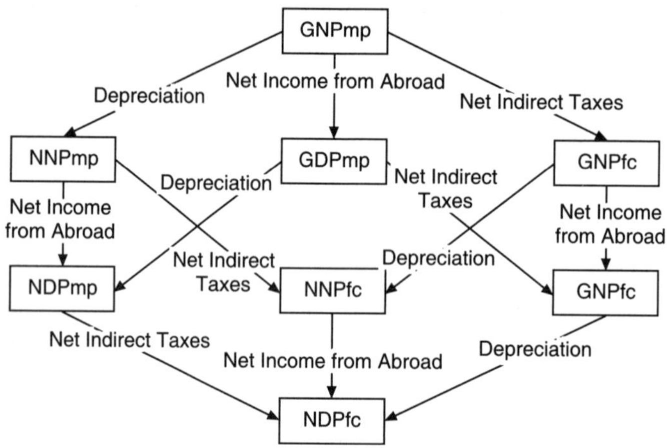

Figure 5.5 Relationship among Eight Variants of National Product Aggregates.

Of these eight measurements, economists refer to NNPfc while referring to the **national income** because it is the best available measure of aggregate output or income in an economy for the following reasons:

First, NNPfc measures the income generated by the nationals rather than simply that in the domestic territory. The income generated in the domestic territory does not include all the contribution of normal resident of a country. At the same time, it also gets biased by the contributions made by the normal resident of other countries. Improvement in the welfare of resident of a country, thus, gets better reflected in the concept of national income rather than that of domestic income.

Second, NNPfc is a net figure, i.e., it excludes the amount of depreciation, i.e., the amount used for repairing wear and tear and replacing worn out machinery. Since depreciation does not result in an additional output, the net concept of aggregate output or national income is better than the gross concept.

Third, NNPfc is estimated at factor cost, i.e., it is exclusive of net indirect taxes which are simply transfers of income from the private sector to the government. Such transfers do not result in any additional output.

5.5 NATIONAL INCOME TO PERSONAL OUTLAYS

Generally, the question that we face at this stage is, whether the national income can be estimated by summing up the personal income of all the individuals in an economy. As we have already seen in Section 3.1, the **national income** is the total income accruing to all the factors of production for their contribution to current production. However, a part of the total income that actually accrues to the factors of production is not paid out to the individuals (households) who own these factors of production. A part of it is paid to the government in the form of taxes (corporate taxes), and some of it is retained by firms in the form of **undistributed profits** or business **retained profits** to finance their investment. Thus, both corporate taxes and undistributed or retained profits, which constitute a part of factor income that accrues to the owners of productive resources, but are not actually received by the owners as a part of their personal income, are subtracted from personal income. But, not all the income that is received by individuals (households) comes from firms. A part of the income comes from the government in the form of transfer payments. These payments are unilateral transfers, like pensions, gifts, welfare payments, etc., which do not contribute to the current production of goods and services. Hence, these are excluded from the estimate of national income. The total income that is actually received by households is known as the **personal income** which represents the flow of aggregate income to households from other sectors. The relationship between personal income and national income can be expressed in terms of the following identity:

Personal Income (PI) = NNP at Factor Cost – Undistributed Profits
– Corporate Taxes + Transfer Payments (TRFP)

The personal income differs from the disposable income by the amount of direct taxes paid by individuals. After deducting personal income tax (a form of direct tax) from the personal income, we get the disposable personal income, which is actually the spendable income. One could express the relationship between disposable income and personal income in the form of a simple identity as follows:

Disposable Personal Income (DPI) = Personal Income (PI) – Personal or Direct Tax (DIR)

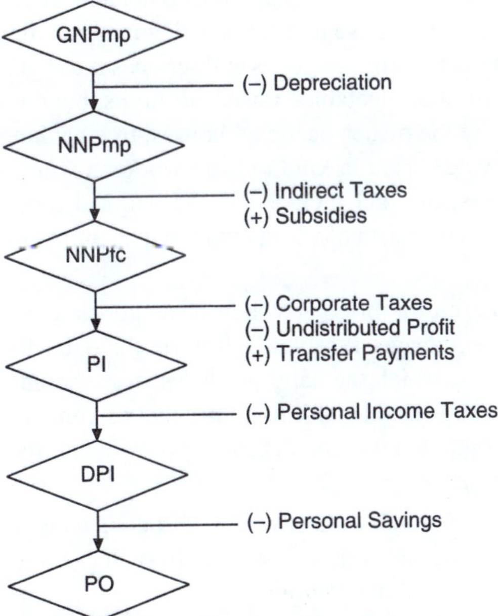

Figure 5.6 Relationship between Various Concepts of National Income and Aggregate Personal Income.

The amount of disposable income that is left after total spending in a year is referred to as **personal saving**. Thus, subtracting the personal saving from the disposable personal income one gets an estimate of the **personal outlays**.

Hence,

Personal Outlays (PO) = Disposable Personal Income (DPI) – Personal Saving (SP)

The relationship between various concepts of national income and personal income is summarized in Figure 5.6.

5.6 PROBLEMS IN THE MEASUREMENT OF NATIONAL INCOME

Exclusion of Value of Personal Services Rendered to Oneself

Most often, only the goods and services that are sold in the market get included in the measurement of national income. In the want of proper valuation method, many services rendered to one-self or to households get excluded from the estimation of national product. For example, the value of a meal cooked by a housewife inside the kitchen is excluded from the national product, while the same food cooked in a restaurant is included in the national product.

The exclusion of such activities from the national income estimates renders any comparison of national products across countries, especially between a highly developed market economy and an underdeveloped economy with substantial part of the national output remaining outside the orbit of market transactions, of doubtful validity. Development process and **marketization** of activities (i.e., the exchange of goods and services at a price) even makes the inter-temporal (over a period of time) comparison of national product difficult.

Non-market Activities and Imputation

Some goods and services, though could be marketed, do not appear in the market because they are retained for self consumption. For these non-marketed goods, an imputed value, equivalent to the market value of identical or similar goods and services is assigned while estimating national income. For example, corn and vegetables raised on farms, but consumed by farmers and their families, services yielded by the owner-occupied houses, free banking services from commercial banks to their customers, wages paid in kind to farm workers, *fringe benefits* enjoyed by highly paid top business executives, etc., get included in the national income at an imputed value.

However, there are many difficulties encountered in imputations. Some of these are as follows:

- We need to decide on the price at which these goods and services can be valued. For example, if a dairy manager receives milk from the dairy free of cost, then should it be valued at the price at which the dairy produces it or should it be valued at the price at which the dairy supplies the milk to consumers or vendors. One can get two different estimates of total output or income depending on whether the factor cost or market price is used for imputing.
- It is possible that if goods and services withheld were marketed, the market price might have fallen due to increased supply. In such cases, the valuation at market price will overestimate the national income.

- The retained output or the payments made to factor of production in kind may be either of an inferior or of a superior quality compared to the marketed output. Valuation at market price in such cases will either overestimate or underestimate the national income.
- Many government services, such as services of a judge, police and defence personnels, public parks, street lighting, etc., are provided free to the public. The imputation of these services is not possible, because there is no equivalence of many of these services in the market. Hence, most of these services are valued at their factor cost.

Changes in Inventories and Inventory Valuation Adjustment

The level of inventories changes during a given year. Government offices value inventories at an average price, i.e., the average of the price prevailing at the beginning and at the end of a year. On the contrary, business firms value these at book value. The book value of inventories changes not only due to changes in the physical volume of inventories but also due to changes in prices of goods added to the inventories. To take an account of different methods of valuation in the change in inventories, the inventory valuation adjustment becomes necessary. The inventory valuation adjustment is the difference between officially published figures and the figures obtained from business accounting data.

The purpose of this adjustment is to avoid understating or overstating of the change in inventories, which would thereby lead to a change in gross domestic investment, and hence, GNP.

Final Product—Current and Constant Rupees

The monetary value of output can change from one year to another either as a result of changes in the quantities of commodities produced or as a result of changes in the market prices or due to both of these. In such a situation, while having any meaningful inter-temporal comparison of national income or output, we face the problem of separating the part of the change that is the result of price variation from the part that is due to the variation in the **real** or physical volume.

To overcome this problem, GNP valued at current prices is deflated by a price index. The deflated GNP is referred to as **GNP at constant prices** or **real GNP.**

Any inter-temporal comparison of real product also suffers from ambiguity arising due to changes in the product mix of national output between two time periods. All the quantities increase or decrease in different percentages over time. To be able to know about the total physical quantities involved, each physical change has to be weighted by its economic value. One may use market prices as weights to remove the ambiguity in quantity comparisons. The ambiguity may, however, still exist not only with regard to the size of change, but in some cases, even as regards the direction of change if the relative prices change between different time periods.

Another problem may arise due to changes in tastes; people may shift from landline to mobile phones, postal mails to e-mails, typewriters to computers, fountain pens to ball pens, dosa to pizza, making any meaningful comparison between the two different bundles of goods at two different time periods difficult. Another serious difficulty that arises in such a comparison is from changes in the composition (the share of expenditure on each good in the total expenditure) of goods and services included in the two bundles. Even when the composition remains the same, the quality may change over time, making inter-temporal comparison difficult.

5.7 USES OF NATIONAL INCOME ESTIMATES

Having understood the measurement issues involved in national income estimation, we can grasp the implications of changes in its value and composition for an economy, in general, and for business managers, in particular. In specific, as analyzed in the following sections, national income data is useful in assessing the growth of an economy, studying the performance of its various constituents and identifying the structural changes in it, identifying business fluctuations and cycles, and also for analyzing the changes in the standard of living of its population. Such an assessment and analysis is useful for formulating economic policies, demand forecasting, and diversification and expansion of activities of business organizations.

5.7.1 Measure of Economic Growth

An increase in the level of production of goods and services reflects economic growth. The growth can be measured either in nominal terms or in real terms. The growth in nominal terms is a product of price changes and the quantity changes and may change because of either of these factors. An increase in the growth due to price changes may not add to the well-being of a society. Therefore, to get a true picture of economic improvement, the real growth, i.e., the rate of growth of national income at constant prices, reflecting the real improvement rather than simply the nominal change, is computed.

5.7.2 Indicator of Success or Failure of Planning

Many countries have adopted planning as a means of economic growth. As we have observed in Section 2.3, in a planned economy the targets of output and the rate of economic growth are set at the beginning of the planning period and resources are allocated accordingly. These targets are then compared with the actual performance of the economy in terms of sectoral and overall output. Thus, national income data helps in assessing the achievements of planning. If, by chance, the targets are not achieved the government can review the situation and take measures to overcome the constraints.

5.7.3 Indicator of Structural Changes

Sectoral classification of national income, as we have seen in Section 3.3.2, gives us an idea about the production structure. The production structure is often used for gauging the level of development of a country. Cross-country experiences have indicated that agrarian economies often are in underdeveloped state. As they develop their manufacturing or industrial sector, they attain the second stage of development. A transition from the industrially-oriented economy to service-oriented economy leads them to the third or advance stage of development. As we have seen in Section 3.3.2, many countries have surpassed the second stage of development and leapfrogged to the advanced stage of development in the recent decades. However, sustainability of such development process has been questioned because of underdeveloped state of manufacturing sector and physical infrastructure impeding further overall growth of these economies.

5.7.4 Measure of Income Inequalities

All individuals in an economy do not earn the same income due to differences in age, sex, qualification, experience, physical strength, willingness to take up risk and so on. Therefore, the aggregate income is often not shared equally by households and families. Inequalities in income distribution are not only found among different income groups and regions within a country but also among different countries. Although, there is no consensus on the manner in which income inequalities affects growth, a general view is that the relationship between the two is not linear. One group of literature suggests that though some amount of inequality is conducive for growth, the inequality above some level is likely to be growth retarding. Another group suggests that high levels of inequality are more likely to harm growth in developing than developed countries.

Support for the positive impact of income inequality on growth is based on the following arguments:

First, some degree of inequality induces individuals to work hard, innovate, undertake risky, but rewarding projects and improve their level of income, and status in their society. If there is perfect equal income distribution, such an incentive will not exist.

Second, saving rates differ among different income strata. The higher income group has higher propensity to save, and hence, some inequalities in income promote saving.

Third, infrastructure and industrial development require a large amount of investment. In the absence of well-developed financial markets, enough funds to carry out such huge investment can come only if the income distribution is highly concentrated.

However, a very high level of income inequality is considered to be growth retarding for following reasons:

First, highly unequal distribution of income, with income as well as assets concentrated in the hands of the uppermost segment of a society, brings down the per capita income of the lower and middle class to a very low level. A low level of income, along with low asset holdings, keep their saving at a lower level. In the absence of enough savings or funds, many people with potentially rewarding ideas and projects, put their ideas on a shelf, thus retarding growth process. Even when such people are able to raise funds from lenders it is usually at a very high rate, thus reducing incentive to exert efforts and enhance income and growth. In such situations, redistribution of income and wealth is growth enabling.

Second, growth requires investment not only in the sphere of physical capital but also in the sphere of human capital in the form of education and better health facilities. However, when majority of people are with very low per capita income, lack of funds, despite a high return on human capital, limits the spending on human capital, and health and hygiene. In addition to insufficient funds, the inefficient labour market also deters investment in human capital. Most of the poor people earn their income, by providing labour. However, because of their low status in the society, they command less bargaining power in the labour market, which keep their wages low. Lower wages, indicating low return on human capital, further accentuate the problem of low human capital. Poor government policies, reflecting insufficient government spending on education and health, which is often the case in developing countries, keep the return on human capital low and also accentuates the problem of lack of human capital.

Third, high income inequalities also result in social unrest and political revolts, disrupting the functioning of markets and retarding the growth process.

There are various measurements of income inequalities, some of these are elaborated in Box 5.2.

Box 5.2 Measuring Income Inequalities

Economists and statisticians have come out with a number of measures of inequality. One such measurement is the **Lorenz curve**. Plotting the cumulative percentage of population, arranged from the poorest to the highest, along the horizontal axis and cumulative percentage of income along the vertical axis, the curve shows the relationship between the percentage of income recipients and the percentage of income they receive (Figure 5.7).

The 45 degree line in Figure 5.7, also known as the **line of absolute equality**, or **egalitarian line**, shows the situation when there is an even distribution of income, i.e., bottom 10 per cent of the population receives 10 per cent of income, bottom 20 per cent of the population receives 20 per cent of income, bottom 40 per cent of population receives 40 per cent of income, and so on. This 45 degree line is a theoretical possibility; in reality it is next to impossible to get such an equitable distribution of income. However, it is a good reference point as the deviation from this line can be used for measuring extent of inequality in an economy.

The closer the Lorenz curve (the line $0abc0'$) is to the 45° line, the more equal the distribution of income is. The more the Lorenz curve bends away from the 45° line, the less equal the distribution of income. In Figure 5.7, the Lorenz curve depicts that the bottom 20 per cent of population receives less than 20 per cent of income, the bottom 80 per cent of the population receives less than 50 per cent of income and the top 20 per cent of the population receives more than 50 per cent of the income. Hence, the actual income distribution deviates from the line of absolute equality.

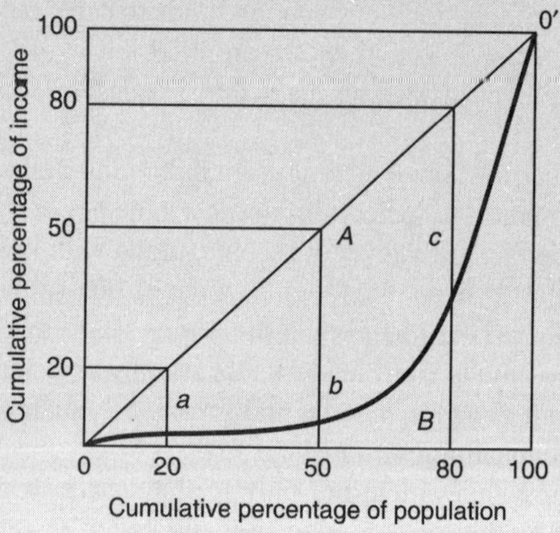

Figure 5.7 Lorenz Curve.

The Lorenz curve gives only a broad picture of inequality. To get a more precise estimate of income inequalities, statistics such as the Gini coefficient, Quantile ratio and Robin Hood index are estimated.

The **Gini coefficient** (G) is a summary statistics estimated as the ratio of the area bounded by the diagonal $00'$ and the Lorenz curve $0abc0'$ (denoted by A) and the entire area below the diagonal line (denoted by $A + B$). Thus,

$$G = \frac{A}{A+B}$$

Value of G varies between 0 and 1, with 0 depicting perfect coinciding of the Lorenz curve with the 45° line, and thus, perfect equality in income distribution, and value 1 representing complete inequality with the Lorenz curve coinciding with the straight lines at the lower and right boundaries of the box.

The **Robin Hood index** measures the level of inequality by estimating the value of maximum vertical distance between the Lorenz curve and the 45° line. The value of the index provides an estimate of the income that needs to be transferred from the population above the mean to those below the mean to achieve equality in the distribution of income.

The **Quantile ratio** is a popular descriptive index of inequality. Under the quantile measures the persons are ranked from the lowest to the highest on the basis of their income and divided into equally sized groups. Distribution of the population into five equally sized groups is termed as the **quintiles**, into 10 equally sized groups is known as the **deciles** and into 100 equally sized groups is known as the **percentiles**. Hence, the first quintile comprises the first two deciles and first 20 percentiles.

One quantile is compared with another to estimate the level of inequality, i.e., the ratio $Q(P_2)/Q(P_1)$ using P_1 and P_2 percentile. To illustrate the full spread of income distribution the percentile ratio needs to refer to the points near the extremes of the distribution. Thus, the most commonly used values for P_1 and P_2 are $P_1 = 0.25$ and $P_2 = 0.75$ (the inter quartile range or quartile ratio); $P_1 = 0.10$ and $P_2 = 0.90$ (the decile ratio) and the population median 50 for P_2.

5.7.5 Indicator of the Pattern of Consumption and Investment

We have seen in Section 5.3.1 that the national income is a sum total of different expenditure components, such as consumption and investment expenditure.

The detailed commodity-wise consumption expenditure data reveals the amount of spending on various commodity groups like food, clothing, rent, transport, medical, electricity, education and entertainment. Business organizations ascertain the consumption pattern prevailing in a country from this detailed disaggregate data and design products in concurrence with consumer preferences to avoid the mismatch between demand and supply.

Investment level affects not only the level of demand but also the productive capacity. Hence, detailed sector-wise time series data, on investment, i.e., the data on investment in agriculture, industry and service sectors, can be used for ascertaining whether productive capacity is expanding in different sectors in concurrence with the growth in demand. Investment decisions can be adjusted to avoid possible infrastructural constrain and to achieve sustained growth of an economy. Managers can take investment decisions based on such data to reap emerging profitable opportunities.

However, in the long-run, a continuous expansion in productive capacity, without matching demand coming forth, may lead to unutilized resources, large scale unemployment, excess capacity and inefficient utilization of capital, and that can constrain the growth (UBE 5.4).

UNDERSTANDING BUSINESS ENVIRONMENT

UBE 5.4 Why China's Investment Levels a Cause of Concern?

Though investment expenditure enhances productive capacity, in the long-run, demand deficiency may lead to underutilization of resources, large scale unemployment, excess capacity and inefficient utilization of capital, and also constrain the growth. Further, sustainability of growth may require reduction in the level of investment, but in an open economy framework that might impede the global growth. This UBE discusses these issues in the context of Chinese economy.

China achieved an impressive steady growth of around 10 per cent for more than 30 years. This high growth was primarily investment led. Notwithstanding year to year fluctuations, there has been an increasing trend in investment to GDP ratio in China for last many decades (Figure 5.8). In the boom period of 2005–08, the growth rate even exceeded 10 per cent. During this high growth phase, investment rate remained close to 35 per cent of GDP. The global financial crisis which reduced the export demand as well as investment expenditure, necessitated fiscal and monetary stimulus. These stimuli focused on enhancing the investment growth. As a consequence, investment rate jumped to over 45 per cent of GDP. China's investment to GDP ratio at present stands close to 50 per cent. Studies by Also Sprach Analyst (2012), Lee, Syed and Xueyan (2012) and World Bank (2013) indicate that China's present investment to GDP rate is significantly higher than the norm. Such high investment to GDP ratio are almost unprecedented, with the exception of Singapore, which achieved high levels of investment in the early 1980s . There are indications that the present investment level is unsustainable. The marginal productivity of capital in China is falling, necessitating a larger increase in investment to sustain the current growth rate. Many sectors like airports and railways are recording losses and many more like automobiles and real estate are operating much below their capacity because of collapse of external demand after the financial crisis and more recently due to the persistent euro crisis. The growth in the domestic demand is not sufficient to compensate the fall in the external demand. IMF estimates indicate that China's capacity utilization is just around 60 per cent of the capacity.

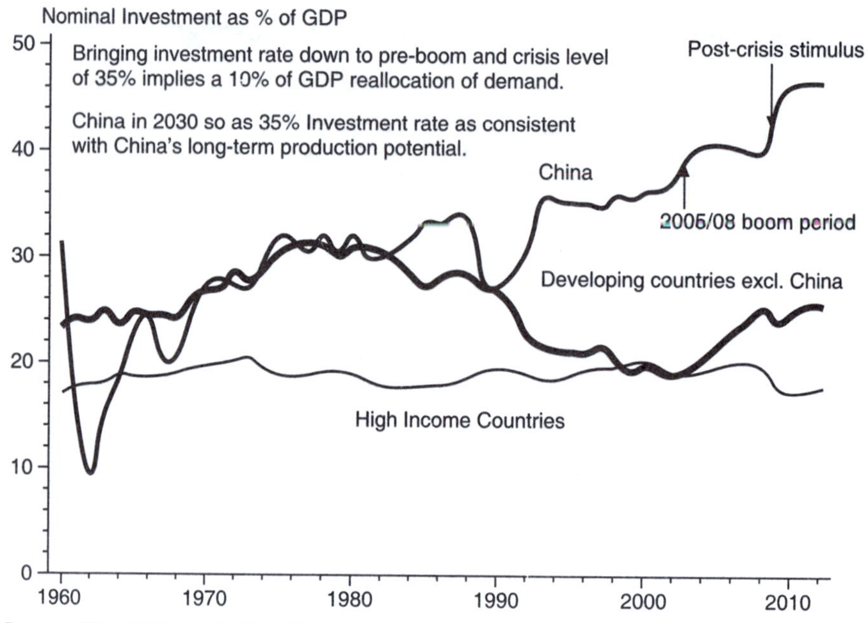

Source: World Bank (2013), Global Economic Prospects, January.

Figure 5.8 Recent Upswings in Chinese Investment Rate Pose Serious Challenges Going Forward.

To prevent under utilization of production capacity and sustainability of the growth, there is a growing realization among the Chinese authorities that the share of consumption expenditure and investment expenditure needs to be balanced. To achieve this, given the benchmark derived from the past experience of many countries, it has been pointed out that the ratio of investment to be gradually brought down by 10 percentage points over a period of time.

However, reduction in the Chinese Investment to GDP ratio will have an impact on the world economy. As a drastic reduction of 10 per cent points is unlikely in the immediate future, to assess the impact of Chinese investment to GDP ratio, World Bank (2013) carried out a simulation assuming a more reasonable reduction of 5 percentage points. The simulation results (Table 5.5) indicate the following:

Table 5.5 An Impact of Abrupt Slowing in Chinese Investment

	Real GDP	*Current account balance*	*Fiscal balance*
	(% change in level)	(% change in GDP)	
China	–1.4	1.7	–0.3
East Asia and Pacific	–1.3	1.3	–0.3
East Asia and Pacific (excl. China)	–0.6	0.0	0.0
World	–0.5	0.0	–0.2
High income countries	–0.4	–0.2	–0.2
Euro Area	–0.4	–0.1	–0.1
Developing countries	–0.7	0.4	–0.3
Developing countries (excl. China)	–0.3	–0.3	–0.2
Low income countries	–0.3	–0.2	–0.1
Middle income countries	–0.7	0.4	–0.3
Developing oil exporters	–0.4	–0.5	–0.3
Developing oil importers	–0.8	0.8	–0.2
Europe and Central Asia	–0.3	–0.5	–0.3
Latin America and Caribbean	–0.3	–0.2	–0.2
Middle East and N. Africa	–0.3	–0.4	–0.5
South Asia	–0.2	0.0	0.0
Sub-Saharar Africa	–0.3	–0.6	–0.3

Source: World Bank.

1. Chinese GDP will decline by 1.4 per cent and imports will decline by 6 per cent.
2. Reduction in Chiense imports imply reduction in global exports.
3. The world GDP will decline by 0.5 per cent and the GDP of developing countries (excluding China) will reduce by 0.3 per cent.
4. China being a major consumer of metals in the world, decline in the activities world over will reduce metal prices by 4.3 per cent and oil prices by 2.8 per cent.
5. The current account balance of the metal exporting countries, such as Chile and Peru will weaken considerably.
6. The balance of payment as a per cent of GDP in oil exporting countries, such as Nigeria, Oman and Saudi Arabia would decline by more than 0.5 percentage points.
7. Commodity exporting countries will also experience in weakening of their fiscal balance which will be a drag on growth especially of those countries which are already running large deficits.
8. Many commodity exporters are located in Sub Saharan Africa; hence the impact on this region will be strong with expected decline in current account and fiscal balance by 0.6 and 0.3 per cent of GDP.

Reference

World Bank (2013), Global Economic Prospects, Washington DC: World Bank, Vol. 6, January 2013.

5.7.6 International and Spatial Comparisons

National income data can be used for comparing the economic structure, standard of living and the overall performance across countries, i.e., **interspatial comparison**.

However, while carrying out interspatial comparison we are confronted with several difficulties as follows:

1. Population size varies across countries. In general, the total national income is higher in countries with higher population, preventing assessment of standard of living of people residing there.
2. The national income of different countries are expressed in different currencies, i.e., different units of account, rendering interspatial comparison impossible.
3. Price level varies across countries. For example, a rented two bed room apartment may cost 200 dollars in India, whereas the same may cost 800 dollars in the USA. Countries experiencing higher price level, hence, register higher nominal income without any improvement in living conditions and welfare.

Thus, for any meaningful comparison, we need to make adjustments for such variations. Some such adjustments that are often made are indicated hereinafter.

The problem of differences in population size is overcome by considering per capita GDP or per capita national income figures rather than total national income figures for comparison. The per capita figures are estimated as a ratio of total national income and total population of a country.

To account for the differences in currencies across countries, the per capita income figures are converted into a common currency, say the US dollar or Euro, at the going exchange rate. Thus, arrived figures are then used for cross-country comparison. However, such conversion results in one more problem. The variations or fluctuations in exchange rate results in variation in per capita figures expressed in a common currency, over a period of time, even when there is no change in real per capita income. This problem accentuates in the presence of large variation in exchange rates. Hence, such variations can alter the rankings of countries from one year to another. To moderate the impact of wide fluctuations in exchange rates, the three-year moving average of exchange rates (Atlas method) is used for computation.

To overcome the problem of differences in price levels across countries, the per capita income expressed in common currency is converted into common price level using purchasing power parity (Box 5.3).

Interspatial comparison of national income estimated using purchasing power parity with that estimated without purchasing power parity gives a very different picture of performance of countries involved in the comparison (UBE 5.5).

Box 5.3 Purchasing Power Parity

The **Purchasing Power Parity** (PPP) is a method of measuring the relative purchasing power of currencies of different countries.

For constructing the PPP, a common representative basket of commodities and the prices of items included in this basket across countries are selected. Using these prices, the price ratios (parities) of the same commodities in different countries are calculated. These parities are then weighted by expenditure on these commodities in a given country. The weighted parities are aggregated to arrive at the GDP or per capita income into a common currency and price level.

We can understand the basic construct of the PPP assuming that there are two countries A and B. The representative consumption basket of these two countries consists of only two commodities, food and cloth. The currency used by country A is dollar ($), whereas that used by B is rupees (₹). As shown in Table 5.6, the price of one unit of food in A is $50 and that of cloth is $100. The representative consumer in country A purchases 80 units of food, and thus, spends total $4,000 on consumption of food. He also consumes 60 units of cloth and spends $6,000 on it. Thus, total annual per capita expenditure in country A is $10,000. Similarly, the price of food in country B is ₹300. The representative consumer in country B consumes 100 units of food and spends ₹30,000 on consumption of food items. The price of cloth is ₹500. The consumer consumes 40 units and spends ₹20,000 on cloth. Thus, total per capita expenditure in country B is ₹50,000. Given the exchange rate $1 = ₹50, the per capita expenditure (or income) in country A is 10 times more than the per capita expenditure (or income) in country B.

Table 5.6 Per Capita Income using Purchasing Power Parity

	Price		*Units*		*Expenditure*		*Price ratio*	*Expenditure in $*
	A	B	A	B	A	B	$/₹	B
Food	$50	₹300	80	100	$4,000	₹30,000	50/300	₹30,000 × ($50/300) = $5,000
Cloth	$100	₹500	60	40	$6,000	₹20,000	100/500	₹20,000 × ($100/500) = $4,000
					$10,000	₹50,000		= $9,000

However, this comparison is biased as it does not take into account the differences in the price level across the countries. For more fair comparison the impact of differences in prices in two countries should be accounted for. One way to overcome this problem is to assume the same set of prices across countries and then estimate the expenditure on each commodity by multiplying the quantities of each commodity consumed in each country by the selected price level. Thus, using country A's price, the total consumption expenditure in country A remains the same as earlier, i.e., $10,000. Now using the prices of country A for country B, the per capita consumption in B can be estimated by multiplying the dollar price of each commodity with the units of each commodity consumed and summing up the total expenditure in terms of dollar on each commodity. In country B, the consumer consumes 100 units of food and 40 units of cloth. Thus, the total expenditure by this consumer in terms of prices of country A is equal to 100 × $50 ÷ 40 × $100 = $5,000 + $4,000 = $9,000. Thus, the total per capita consumption in country B is $9,000 which equals 0.9 ($9,000/$1,000 = 0.9) or 90 per cent of the per capita consumption in country A.

As the cost of comparable goods and services varies across countries, the PPP accounting for such differences in the cost of living allows a more accurate comparison of standard of living across countries.

UNDERSTANDING BUSINESS ENVIRONMENT

UBE 5.5 Richest Nations in The World

GDP per capita ($) does not take care of differences in the price level across countries. Hence, the ranking of the countries in terms of GDP per capital ($) (PPP) differs from that in terms of GDP per capita ($) as illustrated in this UBE.

Per capita income is often used for comparing the economic well-being and the standard of living across countries. As data on the per capita income based on a country's personal income are rarely available, the GDP is more commonly used for such estimates. A list of top ten countries by GDP per capita in terms of US$ and the PPP (US$) for the year 2012 is presented in Table 5.7.

Table 5.7 Richest Nations in the World

GDP per capita (US$)			*GDP per capita (PPP) (US$)*		
Country	*2012*	*Rank*	*Country*	*2012*	*Rank*
Luxembourg	1,07,206.37	1	Qatar		1
Qatar	99,731.11	2	Luxembourg	79,785.04	2
Norway	99,461.55	3	Singapore	60,409.98	3
Switzerland	79,033.03	4	Norway	55,008.77	4
Australia	67,722.59	5	Brunei Darussalam	54,388.65	5
United Arab Emirates	64,840.28	6	Hong Kong SAR	51,494.15	6
Denmark	56,202.22	7	United States	49,922.11	7
Sweden	55,157.86	8	United Arab Emirates	49,011.59	8
Canada	52,231.86	9	Switzerland	45,417.81	9
Singapore	51,161.60	10	Canada	42,734.36	10
			Memo		
India	1,491.89	142	India	3,829.70	131

Source: Based on the data from IMF (2013), World Economic Outlook Database, April, (online) http://www.imf.org/external/pubs/ft/weo/2013/01/weodata/index.aspx as on 26/5/13.

Some interesting facts to note are as follows. Luxembourg is the country with the highest standard of living in terms of US$, but it ranks 2nd in terms of the PPP (US$) values. However, some other countries that rank higher on the list in terms of nominal per capita GDP do not hold their rank in terms of the PPP per capita. For example, Denmark, which ranks seventh in terms of the GDP per capita (US$), does not appear in the list of top ten countries in terms of the GDP per capita PPP (US$).

We can also observe from the table that India ranks very low on GDP per capita terms. Out of 188 countries, considered by the IMF in its World Economic Outlook, India ranked 142 on GDP per capita (US$). It was slightly better-off in terms of GDP per capita (PPP) (US$) with a rank of 131.

5.7.7 Measurement of Business Cycles

We have seen in previous sections that the national income represents the aggregate business activities taking place in an economy in a given period of time Therefore, the movements in the levels and growth rates of national income or per capita national income are widely used to measure the various phases of business cycles across countries. For example, as noted in Section 1.3.7, the convention used by the IMF for defining the **recession** is two straight quarters of negative GDP growth [Using this criteria the world went through a recession in 2009 (UBE 5.6)].

Measurement of **business cycles**, requires high frequency data. However, quite often the data on national income or associated aggregates is not available at the desired frequency. In such cases movements in sectoral output data (which are available on higher frequency than the total national income) are taken as representative of the movements in the aggregate output. For example, the **Index of Industrial Production** (IIP), which signifies the output generated in the manufacturing and related activities, and is available at monthly frequency in most countries, is taken as a representative of business activities. However, such sectoral indicators do not give a very good picture of overall economic activities in those countries where production structure is highly diversified and any one sector cannot capture the divergent trends in other sectors. Hence, precautions should be taken while selecting indicators for representing economic activities. Sectoral indicators should not be selected in those economies where production structure is highly diversified and no sector dominate the economy as a whole. Even in those economies where the production structure is not highly diversified, the selected sectoral indicator should be related to the dominant sector, else it will not be the representative of overall economy. For example, selection of the IIP as the indicator in those economies that are primarily agrarian or service-oriented may result in faulty analysis of trends, especially when the dominant sectors are moving in different directions than the one selected for the analysis.

UNDERSTANDING BUSINESS ENVIRONMENT

UBE 5.6 Global Economic Scenario: Expansion, Slowdown, Recession and Recovery

Global economy, goes through various phases of business cycles. This UBE highlights the reasons for global recession in 2007 and the recovery in the subsequent period.

Outbreak of the US subprime crisis in August 2007 put a break on the sustained global growth of around 5 per cent during 2004–07. The global growth rate slowed down and some of the advanced economies fell into a mild recession by the middle quarters of 2008 in the face of tightening credit conditions. However, during this period the emerging and developing economies continued to grow at robust rates because of their limited exposure to the US subprime market (Figure 5.9).

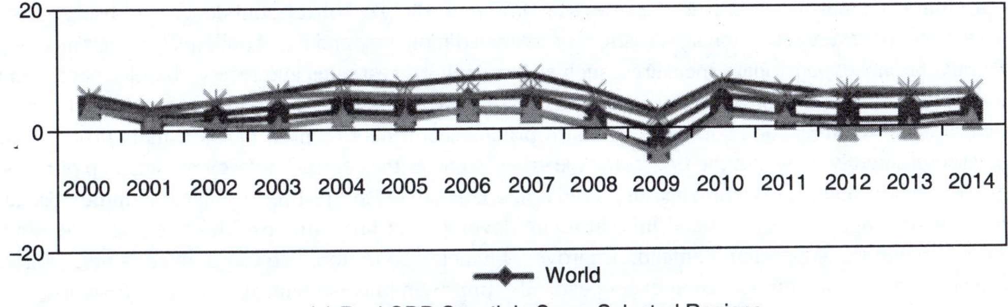

(a) Real GDP Growth in Some Selected Regions

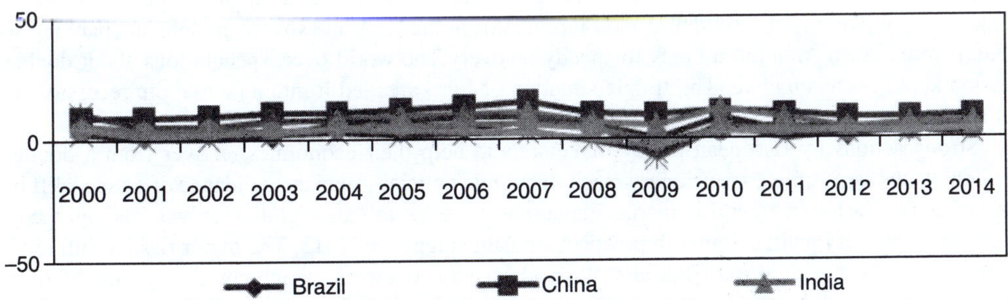

(b) Real GDP Growth in Some Selected Coutnries

Source: Prepared on the basis of Data available for IMF (2012), World Economic Outlook Database, April, http://www.imf.org/external/pubs/ft/weo/2013/01/weodata/index.aspx

Figure 5.9 Overview of Global Growth.

The situation deteriorated rapidly following the default by Lehman Brothers—a large US investment bank, and the continuous government interventions to rescue many financial institutions in the US and Europe. An increase in the amount of write-offs by the banks and their poor financial conditions raised the doubts on the solvency of many of the established financial names, resulted in a large scale withdrawal of deposits, and thus, heightened the shortage of liquid funds with them. To obtain liquid funds to meet their obligations, many of them sold off their most liquid government securities and other liquid assets which depressed yield on these assets. To improve their liquidity conditions many of the banks even slashed credit lines to hedge funds and other leveraged financial intermediaries and tightened their lending standards which resulted in a sharp decline in equity prices and disruption in the flow of trade finance and working capital. The impact of lack of credit and fund availability was the reduction in production and other economic activities.

The emerging markets that were almost untouched by these developments so far were also hit hard by a steep drop in equity prices and disruptions in trade and capital flows. The financial institutions in the US and Europe withdrew from emerging markets to meet their obligations leading to the weakening of financial institutions even in these markets.

The contraction in economic activities in crisis affected countries not only affected the flow of capital to emerging and developing countries but also reduced trade flows by reducing the demand for goods and service produced by them.

Thus, dramatic escalation of the financial crisis in 2008 led to unprecedented slowdown of economic activities and trade world over and even contraction or recession in some of the advanced economies. The impact was wide ranging and across different sectors of the crisis affected economies. But purchases of investment goods and consumer durables were hit the most by the credit disruptions and rising anxiety.

Though wide ranging policy responses succeeded, to a certain degree, to stabilize financial markets, they could not succeed in restoring consumer and investor confidence. Massive financial crisis and an acute loss of confidence put the world in a severe recession in 2009. To bolster confidence and bring back the economies out of severe recessionary situation, coordinated monetary and fiscal policies were pursued. Apart from conventional expansionary measures, such as lowering interest rates and reserve requirements, central banks pursued various unconventional measures, such as expanding eligible collateral and eligible parties for central bank facilities, and some purchases of private sector debt (central banks usually do not lend to private sector directly. However, to overcome the crisis, some of the central banks even ended up purchasing the private sector debt). Governments also intervened extensively by rolling out fiscal stimulus packages covering wide range of activities and infrastructure development programmes. Massive and wide ranging public interventions supported demand, improved financial conditions, lowered uncertainty, bolstered confidence, which helped in reducing excess capacity, improving investment. As a result, the world output registered an impressive recovery in 2010. But, the recovery could not be sustained further. Unexpected and expected adverse developments such as devastating Japanese earthquake and tsunami, unrest in oil producing Middle East and North Africa region,structural problems in the USA and sovereign debt and banking sector problems in the Euro Area put a break to speedy recovery.The world over, speculations about double dip recession kept pessimism alive. The fragile situation of Euro area led it into a double dip recession. Other advanced economies had a close escape from another recession.

Strong actions by European policy makers could help their economies recover from a double dip recession. At the same time, expansionary macroeconomic policies in Japan, avoidance of a fiscal cliff by the USA and policy easing in emerging market economies have led to recent global revival. Though the world is again on a recovery path, the growth prospects remain sluggish in 2013. The major risks to full recovery are the fiscal adjustments in the USA and other advanced economies, which could delay the recovery in emerging markets and developing countries, political problems in Italy and overall uncertainty in the Euro area.

Reference

IMF (2013), World Economic Outlook, April.

SUMMARY

The circular flow of income depicts the entire process of factor income moving from firms to households and then, in the form of spending, moving from households to firms. It shows that the total income is equal to total expenditure and also to total value of final goods and services generated in an economy in any given period.

The output generated in an economy is recorded in National Income Accounts which are known as the National Accounts Statistics in India. Total output is measured using three alternative, but equivalent approaches, known as the product approach, expenditure approach and income approach.

The product approach measures the output by adding the market values of final goods and services newly produced in an economy or alternatively sums the value added by all the producers. The expenditure approach measures output by adding the four categories of expenditure—consumption, investment, government consumption expenditure and net exports. Similarly, the income approach measures the output by adding all factor incomes in the form of wage, rent, interest and profit generated in an economy. Although each approach gives the same value for the current economic activity or output, each reflects a different dimension of an economy.

The total output generated in an economy can be viewed either as the output produced within the domestic territory or the output produced by the nationals of a country. The former is termed as the domestic product or income and the latter is known as the national product or income. The difference between the two concepts is the net factor income from abroad.

Both domestic product and national product can be measured either gross or net of depreciation. When measured gross of depreciation, these are known as GDP and GNP, respectively. Conversely, net of depreciation are known as NDP and NNP respectively.

All the above measurements of aggregate income/output can be estimated both at the factor cost and the market price. The market price differs from the factor cost by the amount of net indirect taxes. Thus, in all, we get eight different, but related measurements of total output or income. Of the eight measurements of aggregate income, economists refer to NNP at factor cost as the national income.

The national income estimates are used for measuring the growth of an economy, evaluating the performance of planning strategies, assessing income inequalities, examining production structure, understanding the composition of income and identifying the phases and turning points in business cycles.

In India, over the planning period, the composition of GDP has gradually moved from agriculture sector to service sector. Though, the share of service sector is the highest in the total output, which is indicative of high growth, the agriculture sector still supports more than 50 per cent of the employment in the country. The share of profit, interest and rent earning classes in total income is increasing over a period of time which is an indication of growing inequalities in the country.

The world as a whole witnessed continuous robust growth during 2004–07. However, the sub-prime lending crisis put a break on this high growth phase, moving the world into a recession in 2008–09. In the last two years the economy is on a recovery path, albeit slow.

Implications for Managers

National income is an important indicator that reflects on the overall health and well- being of an economy, and also the overall business activities that are taking place in it. Thus, the movements in national income help business managers in figuring out the phase through which an economy is moving and is likely to move. That is, it indicates whether an economy is going through a recovery or an expansion or a slowdown or a recession. The analysis of trend in national income helps in identifying the turning points in business cycles.

The disaggregate analysis of national income is also equally important for business managers. The analysis of national income from the expenditure side divulges the demand structure of an economy. Various components of expenditure, i.e., consumption expenditure, investment expenditure, government expenditure and net exports, reflect on the channels of growth for an economy, and the direction the economy is likely to move in the coming period. For example, in a growing economy, an increasing share of consumption expenditure indicates that the economy will continue to experience an expansion in the ensuing period, however, the expansion is likely to be constrained by the productive capacity. On the contrary, an increasing share of investment expenditure in a growing economy expected to result in a more robust and sustained expansion of output because, along with the demand, investment expenditure also increases the productive capacity. However, managers should be cautious of unrestrained expansion of investment and productive capacity. In the want of sufficient consumption and export demand such an expansion may even result in supply glut, unutilized production capacity, unplanned buildup of inventories and reduction in profitability of business organizations. Production and marketing decisions based on the comprehensive analysis of changing demand structure and balanced approach would result in better inventory management and more profits.

Expenditure components also indicate the importance of government in economic activity. The government through consumption and investment expenditure, and transfer payments affects the level of economic activities, and through taxation decisions influences the production and consumption decisions. The government spending on wages, pensions, interest and defence increases the consumption expenditure. The government transfer payments, in the form of subsidy, scholarships, etc., also increase consumption through supporting private income. It also contributes to the productive capacity by incurring substantial amount of expenditure on physical, social and economic infrastructure through spending on roads, bridges, highways, hospitals, education, entertainment, sanitation and building up markets and institutions. All these parts of government expenditure help in utilizing the idle capacity in a recessionary situation. However, in an expansionary situation, when an economy is close to or above the full employment level, the government expenditure, especially the consumption expenditure, by adding to the already existing excess demand, fuels inflation. A close scrutiny of the pattern of expenditure of the government helps managers in assessing the priorities of the government: the areas in which the government wants to expand the market, the areas of production which the government wants to discourage and the supportive structure which the government wants to come up with. All this helps managers in setting up their units in different regions of a country as well as planning their production level and production mix.

A predominant role of the government in economic activities, however, poses competition for private players as the government competes for the available resources. In many countries it has captive market for financial resources. Even in economies where the government raises resources from the market, the risk free government borrowing raises the cost of resources for private players. Thus, the government expenditure sometimes crowds out the private investment by either directly capturing the resources or raising the interest rate or prices of the resources for private players. To obviate competition, business managers need to restructure their production process and production mix, incur larger spending on R&D and upgrade technology, re-orient their strategies that can substantially cut the cost of production and the cost of raising resources from domestic and international financial markets.

The government often finances its growing expenditure by raising the level of direct and indirect taxes. These have bearing for business decisions. Direct taxes reduce the level of disposable income of households and, depending on the income elasticities, consumers generally react by reducing the demand for goods and services which contracts the size of the market for firms. Indirect taxes, on the other hand, raise the cost of inputs and the market price of final commodities which also discourage consumption and reduce the size of the market. Thus, while taking production and marketing decisions, business managers need to closely watch the taxation policies.

The understanding of implications of the level of exports and imports for business managers is equally important. The level of exports reflects on the size of the market outside the domestic market. The data on the product mix and the destination of exports divulge crucial information about potential international customers and their demand pattern. A close examination of the profile of major destination countries can help domestic firms in fine tuning their products as per the requirement of international customers. The level of imports, especially those imported commodities that are close substitutes of domestically produced ones, indicates the level of competition that the domestic producers have from foreign producers. Business managers need to look for strategies that can effectively meet this competition in terms of cost, price and quality. Foreign collaborations and higher expenditure on R&D, innovations, technological upgradation, quality improvement, advertisement, packaging, etc., can help managers in effectively dealing with such competition.

Even when imported commodities are not close substitutes of domestically produced ones, imports reduce the overall income that can be spent on domestically produced commodities. A very high level of imports may result in a large contraction in economic and business activities and lead to a slowdown or even a recession.

Net exports reflect the dependence of a country on the rest of the world for its growth. A high level of net exports indicates that the country is well integrated with the rest of the world. However, it also exposes the stability of the domestic economy to external forces. In such a situation, the domestic economy imports business cycles from the rest of the world. That is, an expansion in major trading partner countries can set in an expansion in the domestic markets and vice versa. Therefore, managers, operating in countries with greater linkages with the rest of the world, need to closely watch the changes in external economic environment.

A disaggregate sectoral or activity wise analysis reflects on the supply or production side of an economy. From the production structure managers can assess the stage of development of an economy. Primarily an agrarian economy reflects that the economy is underdeveloped or at initial level of development, whereas service-oriented economy is an indication of transition to an advance stage of development. This is important to know because the level of development affects the demand structure. In agrarian economies, the demand is more for necessities, whereas in advanced economies managers can expect higher demand for luxuries and better quality products. Various sectors of an economy are interdependent and integrated with each other through forward and backward linkages. For example, the development of agriculture sector helps creating demand for industrial products. At the same time, it eases the supply of intermediate goods used in industries. A higher level of growth of industrial sector reflects the higher demand for supporting professional services, such as transport, communication, and finance, as well as agricultural products. The development of services, in turn, helps in generating demand for agriculture and industrial products. The producers equipped with the understanding of the sectoral structure of an economy can diversify and strategically position themselves in such a way that they take advantage of the evolving structure of an economy.

REVIEW QUESTIONS

5.1 Describe the circular flow of income in a simple two sector economy framework.

5.2 Why saving, taxes and imports are considered as leakages, whereas investment, government expenditure and exports are considered as injections to the circular flow of income?

5.3 In what situations the circular flow can remain stagnant? What is needed for the circular flow to either contract or expand?

5.4 What is the difference between intermediate goods and final goods? In which of the categories do capital goods, such as factories and machines, fall? Why is the distinction between intermediate and final goods important for measuring GDP?

5.5 What is the domestic territory of a country? How is the aggregate output generated in the domestic territory represented?

5.6 Who are considered to be the normal residents of a country? Which measure indicates the total output generated by the normal residents of a country?

5.7 What are the components of total expenditure in an open economy framework with government? Define them. Why are imports subtracted from the other components of expenditure when GDP is calculated through the expenditure approach?

5.8 What is the difference between nominal GDP and real GDP? Which of these two is a better measurement of growth?

5.9 What is the difference between factor cost and market price? It is said that the GDP at market price overestimates the aggregate output in an economy. Why?

5.10 While estimating GDP at market price, indirect taxes are included, but direct taxes do not appear in the estimation. Why?

5.11 Explain the meaning of net factor income from abroad?

5.12 Define the term national income. Why is national income not equal to GDP? Why national income is considered to be the best measure of aggregate output in an economy?

5.13 Define gross domestic capital formation. Explain briefly whether the purchases and sales of second-hand assets are included in it or not?

5.14 What is the problem of double counting in the estimation of national income? Suggest measures to avoid it?

5.15 Distinguish between national income and domestic income?

5.16 Differentiate between personal income and personal disposable income. Can one get an estimate of national income by aggregating personal income of all the individuals in an economy? Why?

5.17 What items to be excluded to avoid the problem of double counting while estimating national income through income approach?

5.18 What difficulties are experienced in the estimation of national income of a country?

5.19 Define 'compensation of employees'. What are the various components of it?

5.20 What is the mixed income of the self-employed? How is it different from operating surplus? Why is the mixed income of self-employed added as a separate component while estimating national income through the income approach in India? What does the changing composition of income in India in favour of operating surplus indicate?

5.21 What are the different statistics used by economists to measure inequalities in income?

5.22 What is nominal per capita GDP? What problems are faced while using it for inter-spatial and inter-temporal comparison of standard of living? How far nominal per capita GDP differs from PPP per capita? What is the Atlas method of estimating per capita GDP? Why is it used?

5.23 Explain the basis on which production units are classified into primary, secondary and tertiary sectors in an economy. Give examples in each case. How far does this classification differ from the classification of activities into agriculture, industrial, and service sectors? What approaches have been used in the estimation of national income in these various sectors in India?

5.24 How is the composition of aggregate expenditure changing in India? What does it indicate?

5.25 What does comparatively lower export and import share in India's GDP reflect?

5.26 Is the changing structure of GDP in India in concurrence with the growth experience of other emerging markets and developed countries? What factors have attributed to the changing structure of GDP in India?

5.27 What are the implications of changing structure of GDP in favour of service sector?

5.28 What is MRPK? Why is MRPK not same across different enterprises in China? What does it indicate?

5.29 What are the reasons for lower MRPK and SOEs in China?

5.30 What were the reasons for the latest episode of the global recession? Which countries were affected the most? Why was the impact on emerging Asian economies limited?

5.31 Why do business managers need to understand the changing structure of an economy which is reflected in the changing share of different sectors in total GDP?

NUMERICAL PROBLEMS

5.1 Use the expenditure and income approaches to calculate GDP and NI from the data available in Table 5.8.

Table 5.8 Different Expenditure and Income Components

Items	*₹ crore*
Personal consumption expenditure	400
Government purchases	128
Gross private domestic investment	88
Net exports	7
Net factor income from abroad	0
Consumption of fixed capital	43
Net indirect taxes	50
Compensation of employees	370
Rent	60
Interest	48
Proprietor's income	52

5.2 Calculate GNP and GDP at factor cost, NNP and NDP at factor cost, personal income and personal disposable income and personal outlays from the data given in Table 5.8.

Table 5.9 Data on Different Aggregate Income and Expenditure Components

Variables	*₹ crore*
GNP at market prices	500
Indirect taxes	50
Subsidies	30
Net factor income from abroad	– 200
Capital consumption allowance	45
Government transfer payments to persons	15
Retained earnings of firms	30
Personal tax	25
Personal saving	75

5.3 Calculate NNP at market price from the figures provided in Table 5.10.

Table 5.10 Sectoral Data

Items	*₹ crore*
Agriculture, forestry and fishing	850
Mining and quarrying	95
Manufacturing	125
Electricity, gas and water supply	70
Construction	100
Trade, hotels, transport and communication	450
Insurance, real estate and business services	112
Community, social and personal services	115
Indirect business taxes	100
Property income received from the rest of the world	20
Property income paid to the rest of the world	60
Depreciation	74

5.4 Using the data given in Table 5.11, calculate GNP at market price by the expenditure method.

Table 5.11 Aggregate Expenditure Components

Items	*₹ crore*
Total final consumption expenditure	7,000
Gross fixed capital formation	2,000
Change in stocks	300
Errors and omissions	800
Exports	400
Imports	300
Discrepancies	– 50
Net factor income from abroad	– 200

5.5 On the basis of the data given in Table 5.12, calculate the value added by industry C and the total value added in the economy.

Table 5.12 Value Added by Different Industries

Items	*₹ crore*
Sales by industry A to industry B	40
Value added by industry B	40
Value added by industry D	30
Final sales	150

5.6 Calculate the compensation of employees from the data provided in Table 5.13.

Table 5.13 GDP and Factor Income Data

Items	*₹ crore*
Rent	40
Interest	35
Profit	15
Gross Domestic Product at factor cost	260
Consumption of Fixed Capital	60

5.7 Suppose that the autonomous component of consumption expenditure (a) is ₹1,000 crore and investment increases from ₹200 crore to ₹300 crore. Marginal propensity to consume (b) is 0.75. Estimate the value of the multiplier, change in the level of income and the new level of income.

5.8 The distribution of income in a country is presented in Table 5.14.

Table 5.14 Distribution of Income in a Country

Population	*Cumulative percentage*	
	Population	*Income*
Poorest (20%)	20	5
Next (20%)	40	20
Next (20%)	60	40
Next (20%)	80	65
Richest (20%)	100	100

What is the total percentage of income shared by the upper 40 per cent of population? What percentage of income goes to the lowest 40 per cent of population?

CASE ANALYSIS EXERCISE

C5.1 India's GDP and Associated Aggregates

The data on India's GDP and related aggregates at constant prices for the past few years is presented in Table 5.15.

It can be seen that the value of the Gross National Income (GNI) and the associated aggregates, such as the Net National Income (NNI), Gross Domestic Product (GDP), Net Domestic Product (NDP) and per capita income, is increasing over a period of time. Increasing values at constant prices are reflective of the real growth of the Indian economy.

Table 5.15 Macroeconomic Aggregates (at 2004–05 prices, ₹ crore)

Item	*2006–07*	*2007–08*	*2008–09*	*2009–10 QE*	*2010–11RE*	*2011–12 QE*	*2012–13RE*
GDP at factor cost	35,64,364	38,96,636	41,58,676	45,16,071	49,37,006	52,43,582	55,03,476
Consumption of fixed capital	3,85,700	4,27,629	4,68,904	5,21,906	5,72,054	6,24,773	6,82,350
NDP at factor cost	31,78,664	34,69,008	36,89,772	39,94,165	43,64,952	46,18,809	48,21,126
Indirect taxes less subsidies	3,07,125	3,54,311	2,57,674	2,74,776	3,59,102	3,87,797	3,14,832
GDP at market prices	38,71,489	42,50,947	44,16,350	47,90,847	52,96,108	56,31,379	58,18,308
NDP at market prices	34,85,789	38,23,319	39,47,446	42,68,941	47,24,054	50,06,606	51,35,958
Net factor income from abroad	–29,515	–17,179	–25,384	–27,757	–54,757	–46,734	–56,307
GNI at factor cost	35,34,849	38,79,457	41,33,292	44,88,314	48,82,249	51,96,848	54,47,169
NNI at factor cost	31,49,149	34,51,829	36,64,388	39,66,408	43,10,195	45,72,075	47,64,819
GNI at market prices	38,41,974	42,33,768	43,90,966	47,63,090	52,41,351	55,84,645	57,62,001
NNI at market prices	34,56,274	38,06,140	39,22,062	42,41,184	46,69,297	49,59,872	50,79,651
Private final consumption expenditure	22,59,892	24,71,397	26,49,610	28,45,303	30,88,880	33,34,900	34,72,980
Govt. final consumption expenditure	4,00,579	4,38,919	4,84,459	5,51,702	5,84,352	6,34,559	6,60,630
Exports of goods and services	8,63,459	9,14,628	10,48,140	9,99,030	11,95,764	13,79,225	14,48,883
Imports of goods and services	10,08,198	11,10,963	13,63,302	13,34,180	15,45,163	18,77,197	19,83,691
Gross domestic capital formation	14,02,369	16,56,892	15,70,333	18,41,263	21,20,377	21,31,840	32,98,551
Net domestic capital formation	10,16,670	12,29,262	11,01,430	13,19,356	15,48,322	15,07,066	23,11,523
Per capita GNI at factor cost (₹)	31,505	34,090	35,817	38,362	41,166	43,235	44,759
Per capita GDP at factor cost (₹)	31,768	34,241	36,037	38,599	41,627	43,624	45,211
Population (millions)	1,122	1,138	1,154	1,170	1,186	1,202	1,217

Source: Compiled and estimated from CSO (2012), National Accounts Statistics, (online) http://mospi.nic.in/mospi_cso_rept_pubn.htm and CSO (2013), Revised Estimates of Annual National Income, 2012-13 press note dated 7th feb http://mospi.nic.in/mospi_new/upload/nad_pr_7feb13.pdf.

Another noteworthy feature is that the values of the GDP and GNI have been higher than the NDP and NNI, respectively. The difference between the two is increasing gradually, reflecting the increasing amount of depreciation. During the period under consideration, the values of GDP and NDP are higher than the GNI and NNI respectively. This is indicative of the fact that the net factor income from abroad is negative in India. That is, the factor payment made abroad is higher than the factor income received from abroad. However, the difference is small. Hence, the growth in GNI can be used as a proxy for the growth in GDP and vice-versa.

In the period prior to global financial crisis in 2008–09, the growth in net capital formation was higher than the growth in consumption expenditure, indicating the increasing productive capacity of the economy. However, the crisis led to an absolute fall in the productive capacity of the economy. In the last two years the economy is recovering from the setback.

It can also be observed that the value of exports, during the period under consideration, had been persistently lower than the value of imports, which indicates towards persistent trade deficit on the balance of payment account of India.

Questions

1. Are the various measurements of total income reflecting real growth of the Indian economy? Substantiate your argument.
2. Why is the difference between GNI and GDP negative? What does it indicate?
3. Can we take the growth rate in GDP as a proxy for the growth rate in GNI? Why?
4. Why is the NNI lower than GNI?
5. What is the difference between gross and net capital formation? How is the net capital formation affecting the productive capacity of the Indian economy?

SUGGESTED FURTHER READING

Chakrabarty, K.C. (2011), Prospects for Economic Growth and the Policy Imperatives for India, *RBI Bulletin*, January.

Mishra, P. (2013), Has India's Growth Story Withered?, EPW, April 13, Vol. XLVIII, No. 15.

Sundaram, J.K. and Popov, V. (2013), Widening Global Income Inequality, EPW, April 17, Vol. XLVII, No. 17.

CHAPTER 6

Poverty, Growth and Inclusive Growth

6.1 INTRODUCTION

For Gokul Gaikwad, the dalit founder of Abhijeet Surface Coating, who didn't have the peer network and financial or organizational backing, it was a dream of breaking into vendor lists of large companies. Several vendor development officers from Tata Motors spent time with him at his stall at the Mumbai trade fair organized by the Dalit Indian Chamber of Commerce in December 2011, and has made his dream a reality. Not only Tata Motors but some other heavy weights industrial groups like Thermax, Forbes Marshall, and a few MNCs like Cummins India have initiated engaging and integrating dalit entrepreneurs into their supplier fold and supporting the concept of supply diversity (Economics Times, December 20, 2011).

The Future Group initiative Big Bazar's platform, Yatra, provides women from self-help groups across Maharashtra an opportunity to market their food and non-food products. The group also encourages them to branch-off from self-help groups and start their own enterprises. The Future Group has also initiated strategic partnership with Himachal Pradesh Government termed as Himachal Yatra to promote the brand Himachal by developing "source-to-market" initiatives and creating and enhancing livelihood for over 25,000 families in the state.

The ITC Ltd. e-choupal, which is the world's largest rural digital network, empowers nearly four million small and marginal farmers by giving them customized information on prices, best practices in farming, competitive channels to procure quality inputs and supply their produce at the farm gate. To help tribal and marginal farmers, the ITC has also invested extensively in research and development in Social and Farm Forestry and has developed clonal saplings, which are disease resistant, and grow much faster and in harder conditions. Besides, the company is also involved in many philanthropic programmes, such as helping in creating watershed projects covering 30,000 hectares in water-stressed areas, integrated animal husbandry services, supplementary education centres, and creating women entrepreneurship through self-help groups.

Many companies in India have set up their Business Process Outsourcing (BPO) Centres in rural areas. BPO centres in rural areas set up by the community service arm of the Tata group of companies are such initiatives. The companies' BPO centres at Mithapur in Gujarat state and Babrala in Uttar Pradesh state have already employed 200 people. Similarly, HDFC banks'

BPO centre at Tirupati in Andhra Pradesh state set up through its subsidiary Atlas Documentary Facilitators employs approximately 550 employees.

There are many activities and programmes which many companies in India and abroad are actively pursuing to integrate and involve minorities, disadvantage, deprived and disabled in productive activities and bringing them above the absolute poverty. What makes companies involve in such activities inspite of some of these being a drag on their financial bottom line? Not only developing countries but also developed countries are seriously considering inclusive growth for sustainability of their growth process. Why not only higher growth is sufficient for the development of a country? Why all the sectors and all the segments of an economy need to be integrated in the growth process? What are the dimensions of inclusive growth and how these are different than the dimensions of the growth? What are the measurements of growth, development and inclusive growth?

This chapter focuses on various questions posed in the previous paragraphs. As an attempt to answer these questions, Section 6.2 defines poverty, measures it and outlines the reasons for it. Section 6.3 brings out the difference between growth and development. This section also indicates the need for inclusive growth. Section 6.4 highlights the need for corporate involvement in the inclusive growth process.

6.2 POVERTY: DEFINITION, MEASUREMENT AND CAUSES

6.2.1 Poverty: The Meaning

Poverty reflects the pronounced deprivation of well-being of a person. It is reflected in low income and inability to fulfil basic needs of food, clothing and shelter and acquire basic services such as medical, proper sanitation and education which are necessary for the survival of a person with dignity in a society.

6.2.2 Can Poverty be Measured?

Broadly, poverty is measured in absolute as well as in relative terms.

Absolute Poverty

The **absolute poverty** measures the number of people living below a certain threshold level of income, also known as **poverty line**, which is essential for procuring certain essential goods and services. Absolute poverty is the threshold usually expressed in income terms that is sufficient for basic needs. This threshold, though, keep changing in nominal terms, remains fixed in real terms, implying that the nominal changes in the threshold level simply account for inflation. This threshold does not change with the changes in the GDP or even with the standard of living of the people.

Absolute poverty is reflected in malnutrition, short life expectancy and high level of infant mortality. Absolute poverty can be an outcome of either complete lack of resources or unequal distribution of income and wealth in the country.

The measure proposed in the World Development Report, "One dollar a day" at 1985 purchasing power parity has been extensively used as the measure of extreme or absolute poverty. In India, the measure of absolute poverty has changed over a period of time (UBE 6.1).

Relative Poverty

The **relative poverty** measures the extent to which a person's financial resources fall below the average or median income level in the economy. As the average keeps on changing with the changes in the GDP, the nominal as well as the real value of the income, under which population is considered to be poor, keep on changing with the progress of the country. As some proportion of the population of a country has been always below the average, every country faces relative poverty though it may or may not have absolute poverty.

The concepts of absolute and relative poverty are illustrated with a hypothetical illustration in Box 6.1.

Box 6.1 Absolute vs Relative Poverty: A Hypothetical Illustration

Let us understand the difference between absolute and relative poverty more clearly through a hypothetical example referring to an imaginary economy, the data related to which is presented in Table 6.1. In this imaginary economy there are seven individuals Ram, Shyam, Radha, Kavita, Babita, Madhur and Neha. They earn ₹1,000, ₹2,000, ₹3,000, ₹4,000, ₹5,000, ₹6,000 and ₹7,000, respectively in period t. Assume that the economists and statistician have estimated that the minimum income required for sustaining oneself is ₹3,000 per period. Given this threshold level of income, Ram and Shyam fall under the poverty line in period t. The average income during the same period is ₹4,000, pushing even Radha below the poverty line. Radha, though is relatively poor, is not poor in absolute terms. Let us now assume that the income level of each individual in period $t + 1$ doubles though the inflation rate remains the same. Hence, real income of all the individuals in this hypothetical economy doubles. Given the threshold level of income in real terms to be ₹3,000, Shyam is now, in period t + 1, is counted above the absolute poverty line. But with the doubling of the income level, the average income increases from ₹4,000 in period t to ₹8,000 in period $t + 1$. Since the income of Shyam remains below this average he still remains poor in relative terms. Even after doubling the income levels, Radha does not cross the relative poverty line and counted as poor. Now, further assume that the income level

Table 6.1 Absolute and Relative Poverty: A Hypothetical Example (Amount in ₹)

	Salary per period		
Person	*Period* (*t*)	*Period* (*t* + 1)	*Period* (*t* + 2)
Ram	1,000	2,000	4,000
Shyam	2,000	4,000	8,000
Radha	3,000	6,000	12,000
Kavita	4,000	8,000	16,000
Babita	5,000	10,000	20,000
Madhur	6,000	12,000	24,000
Neha	7,000	14,000	28,000
Number of the person below absolute poverty line (assuming a threshold level of income for satisfying basic necessities to be ₹3,000 per period)	2 (Ram and Shyam)	1 (Ram)	0 (None)
Number of the person below relative poverty line (given average income of ₹4,000, ₹8,000 and ₹16,000 in period t, $t + 1$ and $t + 2$, respectively)	3 (Ram, Shyam and Radha)	3 (Ram, Shyam and Radha)	3 (Ram, Shyam and Radha)

increases 4 times in period $t + 1$ compared to period t. With the quadrupling of income, everyone's income level crosses the threshold level of income depicting the poverty line, and the absolute poverty gets eradicated completely. However, the average income level increases to ₹16,000 in period $t + 2$; hence, leaving Ram, Shyam and Radha still below the relative poverty line.

From the above hypothetical example, one can ascertain that though, higher income levels can reduce or eradicate the level of absolute poverty, but are not sufficient to eradicate the relative poverty. The relative poverty can be reduced only by reducing the income inequalities. An increase in income inequalities accentuates the problem of relative poverty whereas lowering of inequalities help in reducing the number of people below the poverty line. In a system where everyone receives the same level of income, i.e., a utopian society reflecting perfectly egalitarian system, the relative poverty gets eradicated completely. As long as there are deviations from the line of absolute equality or egalitarian system, implying income inequalities (Section 5.7.4), some people will always remain below the relative poverty line.

Criticism of Measures of Poverty

Both the measures of poverty are subject to criticism. The major criticism of absolute concept of poverty is that it is time and location specific as basic needs keep on changing with the changes in time and location. For example, in urban areas, people without mobile phones, proper transport arrangements, etc., may be deprived of employment opportunities that are essential for survival. Whereas people in rural areas, employed in farming activities, without such facilities can still manage to survive. If poverty reflects the pronounced deprivation of well-being then the absolute definition of poverty is at best a partial measure. The well-being depends not only on the fulfillment of basic needs of people but also on their expectations of recognition in the society and their comparison with others. Aspiration of the general public is to reach at least this average level of income; the inability to achieve this average, at times, generates feeling of deprivation and marginalization, and loss of self esteem for some. Given this criticism of absolute poverty, perhaps, relative measurement can give a better idea of poverty. However, as the threshold average level of income keep on moving, not only in nominal terms but also in real terms, with the growth of the GDP, the relative poverty is impossible to eradicate.

Both absolute and relative poverty measures are defined in quantitative terms. However, there are various factors apart from tangible goods that determine the well-being of human beings, such as health and education. Quantification of these attributes is not easy; which makes the computation of absolute and relative poverty line difficult.

UNDERSTANDING BUSINESS ENVIRONMENT

UBE 6.1 Has Poverty Declined in India?

The methodology of estimating absolute level of poverty in India has evolved over a period of time. This UBE outlines some of the silent features of the existing methodology.

On the basis of large sample surveys of household consumption expenditure carried out by the National Sample Survey Office (NSSO), the Planning Commission in India makes absolute poverty estimates approximately every five years on the basis of methodology that is reviewed from time-to-time. Presently, the methodology adopted by the commission is based on Tendulkar Committee Report, 2009.

The Tendulkar Committee computed the poverty lines at all India level as monthly per capita consumption expenditure (MPCE) of ₹447 for rural areas and ₹579 for urban areas in 2004–05. It claimed that these estimated expenditure levels on food, education and health, are consistent with normative expenditures that can provide certain required nutritional, educational and health outcome. To make an assessment of the change in the poverty level over a period time, the committee also re-estimated the poverty level for 1993–94. The estimates which are presented in Table 6.2 indicate that there was a decline in the poverty level, as represented by the headcount ratio, by 8.1 per cent during the period 1993–94 and 2004–05.

Table 6.2 Poverty Ratio in India (per cent)

	Earlier estimates based on the Lakdawala methodology		*Estimates based on the Tendulkar methodology*		
	1993–94	2004–05	1993–94	2004–05	2009–10
Rural	37.3	28.3	50.1	41.8	33.8
Urban	32.4	25.7	31.8	25.7	20.9
Total	36.0	27.5	45.3	37.2	29.8

Source: Planning Commission (2009) and Planning Commission (2012).

Inspite of substantial changes in the methodology of computation, the estimates based on Tendulkar Committee method for 1993–94 and 2004–05 gave almost similar decline in the poverty level as that by earlier methodology, known as Lakdawala methodology. The Lakdawala methodology, which indicated that the decline was 8.5 per cent, was anchored with the per capita calorie norms of 2,400 (rural) and 2,100 (urban) per day. The reference basket that was used under this method was tied to that observed in 1973–74. As this outdated basket could not account for the rapidly changing consumption pattern of the poor, the new method was used for estimating the poverty level.

Using the Tendulkar Committee methodology and using NSS 66th round data, the commission has updated the poverty lines as MPCE of ₹673 for rural areas and ₹860 for urban areas in 2009-10. Based on these cut-offs, there has been a further decline in the poverty ratio from 37.2 per cent in 2004-05 to 29.8 per cent in 2009–10.

References

Planning Commission (2009), Report of the Export Group To Review the Methodology for Estimation of Poverty.

Planning Commission (2012), Press Note on Poverty Estimates, 2009–10, March.

Need for Poverty Estimate and Data

The definition of poverty and statistical measurement of poverty are important for the government as well policy makers in identifying the kind of poverty existing in a country, identifying the proportion of the population living in abject poverty, designing the measures and policy changes required to overcome the poverty problem especially that of absolute poverty, and selecting the target group for implementing various interventions.

International organizations also need such information for identifying the countries that are in need of international assistance and monitoring, and evaluating the impact of different types of assistance provided by them to the neediest countries.

6.2.3 Causes of Poverty

Poverty can be a result of either micro (i.e., individual) or macro (i.e., country wide) factors.

Micro-level Causes of Poverty

At the individual level, the reasons for poverty may be any of the following:

- Lack of intelligence, education, skill set and experience
- Poor health, handicap or old age
- Discrimination on the basis of sex, religion, region, etc.
- General attitude or philosophy of remaining satisfied with whatever available

Macro-level Causes of Poverty

At the country wide level, poverty can be the result of any of the following factors:

1. Overpopulation: From the perspective of poverty, rather than the absolute size it is the relative size of the population (i.e., relative to the land size or the total resources available) that matters. The relative size determines whether a country is overpopulated or underpopulated. A country is considered to be overpopulated if its population density, i.e., the ratio of population to land area, is very high, or the amount of resources per head is very low. Overpopulation has been identified as one of the major causes of poverty, because in whichever way it is defined, it reduces the per capita availability of food and other essential items. High population density often implies low resource availability per person, because a given amount of land, without improvement in productivity, reduces the availability of food and other resources per person as the population grows. However, it is not only the high population density that causes poverty. The impact of high population density can always be mitigated by adopting improved method of production. It is high population density along with the labour intensive method of production, resulting in lower productivity, that causes poverty in a country. Bangladesh, for example, has very high population density. A large proportion of its population is also engaged in labour intensive low productivity farming, which contributes to extremely high levels of poverty in the country. On the contrary, countries like the Netherlands and Belgium also have high population density, but the level of poverty is much lower in these countries because by adopting advanced modern production processes and technologies they are able to generate sufficient food and other essential items for their population.

However, low density does not ensure a larger availability of resources. Even in low density areas if people are using primitive techniques of farming and production activities, then the country can support only a few people. For example, many countries in Sub-Saharan Africa have very low population density, but still a large proportion of their population is poor. These countries though have large land, most of it is infertile. The absence of modern work practices also keeps these countries poor. Low density areas are better-off or prosperous only if they are adopting advanced techniques, and using capital intensive technique. For example, developed countries, like USA and many advanced European countries are rich not simply because of their low population density but also because of high productivity achieved through modernized techniques. These countries are able to provide large quantities of food through mechanized farming and using high yielding seeds and fertilizers. Advanced techniques of production have helped them generate resources to satisfy their basic needs.

One of the main reasons for overpopulation is the high birth rate in many underdeveloped and developing countries. In many of these countries, the largest proportion of the population is dependent on farming using labour intensive method of production. Farming communities treat their children as their assets that can be used for cultivation and producing large amounts of food grains. Preference for larger families accentuating the problem of overpopulation on the one hand and on the other hand these societal norms also make it difficult for the government to effectively bring population growth under control.

2. Lack of education: Because of lack of resources, the government of poor and developing countries find it difficult to provide quality education to each and every one, especially in rural areas, limiting the fruitful productive employment opportunities and income for the masses. Also, the children of poor people start earning at an early age by doing petty jobs to support their family members and often forgo education even when such possibilities exist in their area. Eritrea, the sixth poorest nation in the world has been facing such a situation. The country, with only around 800 schools and 2 universities, has half of its population living below the poverty line.

3. Inadequate employment opportunities: Even highly educated people remain unemployed when employment opportunities are limited. Employment opportunities in developing countries are often limited because of the low level of economic activities. In developed countries also such situations can arise due to cyclical fluctuations. In a downturn or recession, these countries also experience high levels of unemployment, which increases the number of poor people during such phases. For example, a study by Peter Saundes published by the Social Policy Research Centre in 2002 indicated that in Australia in the early 1970s, around 16.6 per cent of the unemployed were below the poverty line. The same study also indicated that those who remained unemployed during the early 1970s, could fairly quickly could overcome poverty once they returned to work, indicating that the unemployment was the major cause of their poverty.

4. Environmental degradation: Deterioration of natural environment including forests, water sources, land fertility, and atmosphere in general has been found to be one of the major reasons for poverty in some countries. Environmental degradation results in shortage of food, clean water, wood required for building shelter and many other items essential for well being of the people. People living directly on natural resources, such as those involved in forestry, fishing and mining, suffer the most by such degradations. Whereas, the countries who have already developed technology to purify air and water, and storage facility to conserve food, electricity and fuels have been able to safeguard their population, to some extent, by such degradations.

Environment degradation is often the result of overuse of natural resources. For example, excessive deforestation for meeting the ever growing requirement for wood for construction and fuel purpose, intensive farming and heavy use of inorganic fertilizers to meet the growing demand for food, which depletes soil fertility, high air pollution due to increase in polluting industrial activities, such as mining, power generation, chemical and fertilizer production and increase in the number of automobiles plying on the roads have been instrumental in environmental degradation the world over.

5. Structural and technological changes: Technological inventions and innovations often change the structure of production and employment. For example, the advent of information technology created high demand for people with a degree or diploma in computer science and technology in countries experiencing such change. However, at the same time, it also reduced demand for manual workers in manufacturing, resulting in a large decline in employment of such people. As it takes time to equip oneself with new tools and techniques, such structural changes often create large scale unemployment until the economy fully gets adjusted to absorb such changes. In the interim period, unemployment increases the income disparity and the number of poor people in the economy. In the last decade, the United States Postal Service (USPS) experienced a large decline for services provided by it because of the massive shift from postal services to email, and online and mobile communication, leading to a large scale unemployment in the postal services.

6. Demographic changes: Changes in the age structure of the population, reflecting a demographic shift, can also increase poverty. Higher ratio of children and age-old population increases the dependency ratio, because these age groups do not partake in the productive activities. Higher dependency ratio, by reducing economic activities, reduces total output as well as per capita income. Such trends also push a larger number of people under the poverty line.

7. Changes in family structure: People living in joint families share many resources, which enables them to experience economies of scale. Breakdown of joint family system and increasing trend of nuclear families require larger resources to support the same number of people, reducing the well-being of many and pushing them under the poverty line. Similarly, increasing trend in single parent families, has been causing poverty, especially in countries like the USA, UK and other western European countries. For example, a study by Levitan and Wieler (published in Economic Policy Review of Federal Reserve Bank of New York in 2008) identified shifts in family status from husband-wife families to single parent families, especially that headed by a female, causing a rapid increase in poverty during 1969-1999 in New York City.

8. Government welfare schemes: One view is that overly generous welfare programs reduce the incentive to work and discourage people to actively seek employment. Often such policies, hence, are blamed for continued high level of poverty.

9. Unfair trade: Many developed countries, including the USA, have been pursuing protective policies towards agriculture and other primary products by providing high amount of subsidies to farmers and imposing tariff barriers on imports of agriculture and other products. Due to such policies, the developing world, which enjoys a comparative advantage in these products, finds its products uncompetitative in the developed markets. Reduced demand for their exports keeps their income low. Therefore, such unfair trade practices are criticized for placing developing countries at disadvantageous footing and keeping them entrapped in high levels of poverty.

Free trade agreements among some nations are also perceived to be a form of favouritism and protectionism, which places effectively barriers on the products from the countries that are not part of such agreement.

10. Corruption: Corrupt politicians and officials often pocket a large amount of money assigned for various welfare schemes, which deters the trickling down of the impact of welfare schemes to the grass root level to the needy and poor, and makes eradication of poverty difficult.

In a corrupt system, often corporations are forced to pay bribe to procure licences to operate business, which increases the cost of production and/or deteriorates the quality of production, making cost of living higher and standard of living poor. India is often cited example of high corruption accentuating poverty in the country. Many other countries like Kenya and Pakistan are also fighting against corruption to eliminate poverty.

11. Poor governance: Inefficient management of various resources, incompetent administrative staff, poor legal and regulatory framework, along with corrupt politicians and officials, hamper the smooth functioning of activities. Such a system keeps the productivity and output low and accentuates the problem of poverty.

12. Political prejudice and inequality: Some governments differentiate among different segments of their society on the basis of race, caste, gender, ethnicity, skin colour, etc. Some groups receive favourable treatment in education, in jobs, access to public utilities, whereas others are deprived of even basic necessities; forcing these underprivileged to live under dire poverty. For example, in South African history, apartheid policies discriminated people on the basis of their skin colour. Whites were given access to public schools imparting quality education. They were also selected for high paying jobs and bestowed with liberal welfare schemes. Similarly, in Brazil, there is a social discrimination against Afro-Brazilians, keeping per capita income of this group only half that of whites and relatively higher per cent of poverty among Afro-Brazilians. Even in Indian history, Dalits, the lower caste people, were treated inhumanely and employed only for jobs like sanitation, street cleaning, leather works, plantation, etc. For ages they were suppressed and humiliated by upper castes. They were deprived the entry to schools, temples, and white collar jobs, entrapping them in deep poverty.

13. Centralization of power: The countries where political power is disproportionately centralized, i.e., one major party, politician or region dominates the decision-making process for different parts of the country, the policies are formulated without proper knowledge of the problems and requirements of the poor and underdeveloped regions. Therefore, various welfare promoting schemes fail to promote growth and eradicate poverty.

14. Colonial suppression: The governance of present day developing countries by the colonial power in the past was often highly exploitative. Colonial powers diverted natural resources from their colonies for the development of their home countries. For example, the British Empire, which was in the past one of the major colonial powers, diverted resources such as iron, coal, cotton, silk, rubber, vegetable oils, rare minerals from many Asian and African countries to build up the infrastructure of road, rail network and communication, and to support and sustain the Industrial revolution in the UK. Continuations excessive extractions of resources have been one of the main reasons for the present underdevelopment state of many such colonies.

15. External invasion and civil war: Threat of invasion due to tensions with neighbouring countries or internal strife necessitates diversion of resources that could have been used for poverty alleviation programs to military support. The actual occurrence of external invasion or civil war also causes large scale destruction of existing resources and infrastructure and retards productivity and output growth, shifting the masses to poor living conditions. For example, during the period of Desert Storm from 1990-1993, the per capita GDP in Iraq fell sharply. There was further destruction of the country's resources because of the US invasion during 2003 and 2005, increasing unemployment sharply between 25 per cent to 50 per cent and worsening the living conditions in the country.

16. Natural disaster: Natural disasters, such as earthquakes, floods, hurricanes, etc. can result in large scale devastation of natural resources and infrastructure. For example, in 2004, tsunami catastrophe resulted in huge loss of agriculture and other resources in the coastal areas of many countries in Asia and Africa. Similarly, Haiti, the poorest countries in the Americas, hit by a powerful earthquake in 12 January 2010 that killed 2,20,000 people and made one million people homeless, experienced further worsening of the poverty situation.

6.3 ECONOMIC GROWTH: A TOOL TO REDUCE POVERTY AND IMPROVING HUMAN WELL-BEING

Many countries have tried to eradicate poverty and improve the well-being of human beings by rapid growth. Some succeeded in achieving it while many failed miserably. Hence, it is essential to understand the meaning of economic growth, its measurement, its efficacy in reducing poverty and alternative approaches to reduce poverty that improve the overall well-being of human beings.

6.3.1 What is Economic Growth?

Economic growth refers to the growth of total output or income. National income, or any of its variants, such as Gross Domestic Product (GDP) or Gross National Products (GNP), can be used for measuring growth. Growth is similar to increase in size or number, i.e., it has only quantitative dimension. It makes a country wealthier in terms of man-made goods and services produced using natural resources.

6.3.2 Measuring Growth

Pro-Poor Growth

For eradicating poverty though growth is essential it is not a sufficient. For substantial reduction of poverty, growth has to be pro-poor. Broadly, **pro-poor growth** is the growth that is good for the poor. For precious measure of pro-poor growth two approaches are taken, viz., the absolute definition of pro-poor growth and the relative definition of the pro-poor growth (Figure 6.1). These two definitions of pro-poor growth are discussed further hereinafter.

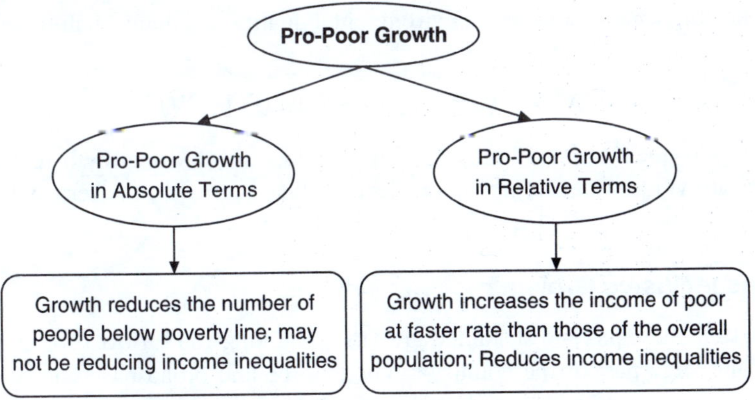

Figure 6.1 Approaches to Pro-Poor Growth.

The absolute definition of pro-poor growth targets the growth of income of only poor people, and adjudged by how fast on an average the income of the poor rise. As per this definition, overall income growth of 8 per cent with the income growth of poor households by 2 per cent can be considered pro-poor growth. On the contrary, the relative definition of pro-poor growth not only looks at the growth of income of the poor people, but even that of the not-poor people. It compares the changes in the income of the poor with that of the non-poor. By this definition, pro-poor growth is experienced when the income of the poorest people grow faster than those of the population as a whole; implying a reduction in income inequalities. As per this definition, the overall income growth of 8 per cent with the income growth of poor households by two per cent cannot be considered pro-poor. For the **relative pro-poor growth**, the income growth of poor households has to be higher than the overall growth. For example, income growth of 10 per cent for poor households is pro-poor if the overall growth is 8 per cent. Even the overall income growth of 0.5 per cent can be considered pro-poor if the income growth of poor households is more than it, say 1 per cent or 2 per cent.

Of the two definitions, the absolute definition of pro-poor growth is preferable if the objective is to bring about an absolute reduction in poverty. However, if the objective is to reduce income inequalities, then better definition is the relative definition of pro-poor growth.

6.3.3 Why Growth is not Sufficient to Improve Overall Well-Being?

Human well-being of income is dependent on not only per capita income, but many other factors, such as education and good health. Growth only reflects the quantitative aspect of well-being that is measured by the per capita income. It does not encompass qualitative aspect of well-being. Therefore, overall level of development is assessed to ascertain the improvement in human life.

Development

Development is often confused with growth. Growth is just a quantitative aspect of human well-being. Growth though enriches people it may not necessarily bring about qualitative improvement in their life. Unlike growth, development has a qualitative dimension as well and is a much wider concept. **Development** refers to an overall enrichment in the quality of life. Apart from the improvement in per capita income, it also looks into changes in the literacy level, improvement in sanitation and health, personal security, environmental quality and many such factors.

6.4 INCLUSIVE GROWTH: WHAT, WHY AND HOW?

A continued improvement in standard of living requires sustained growth and development. For sustainable growth and development we need inclusive growth, the term which is defined hereinafter.

6.4.1 What is Inclusive Growth?

Inclusive growth is the rapid and sustained growth in the long-run (at least for 30 years), which is inclusive of the large part of the country's labour force and broad based across sectors. The inclusive growth aims at achieving rapid growth rate by levelling the playing field, getting rid of constraints resulting lopsided growth, and involving every segment of the population.

The inclusive growth definition is in concurrence with the absolute definition of pro-poor growth (Section 6.3.2). However, a pro-poor growth need not result in inclusive growth. While absolute pro-poor growth can be achieved by direct income redistribution schemes, inclusive growth depends on improvement in productivity and enhancement of employment opportunities to achieve the same. Similarly, the focus of inclusive growth is not simply on poor but on utilizing more fully the labour force entrapped in low productivity activities and the population strata completely excluded from the growth process. Inclusive growth is people centred growth in which people participate in the development process, and also benefit from the policies and programmes of the government. Pro-poor growth though a necessary condition but not a sufficient one for inclusive growth. Not only the poor but also the other excluded groups, such as schedule caste and schedule tribe, other backward categories, minorities, women and physically challenged, are under the purview of inclusive growth. Inclusive growth intends to enhance the capability of excluded by providing them equal opportunities, involving them in decision making and creating productive employment opportunities for them.

6.4.2 Why Do We Need Inclusive Growth?

Though some level of growth is essential for sustained poverty reduction, an increasingly gaining view is that growth by itself is not a sufficient condition for eradicating poverty. It is possible that rather than reducing poverty, growth can marginalize the poorer sections and increase inequality in standard of living, which, in turn, can slow down and derail the growth process through political channels or conflict. Hence, for getting quality results and sustainability of growth process we need to have inclusive growth.

6.4.3 Strategies for Inclusive Growth

1. Reducing inequalities in opportunities: Extreme inequalities in opportunities affect human capabilities and go against the social justice. For example, gender bias against a girl child denies the basic human right to her to live on earth. Similarly, discrimination on the basis of gender, caste, region, ethnicity, etc. not only violates the basic principle of social justice but also goes against social cohesion and is growth retarding.

2. Higher access to basic education: To improve productivity, enrichment of human capital is essential, which can be achieved by expanding access to basic education. However, access to basic education is not sufficient; it has to be linked to skill formation to improve the employability aspect of educated youth.

3. Improving productivity in high labour intensive segment: Agriculture and allied activities and small and medium enterprises are considered to be highly labour intensive activities. Improving investment in these activities not only improve the productivity but also create fruitful employment in labour abundant countries. There are many other benefits of such an approach. For example, higher investment in agriculture not only improves the productivity and increases the income of rural poor but also that of the urban poor by lowering and stabilizing the prices of food products.

4. Incentivising remittances: Developing countries where remittance inflows have been relatively robust can further promote these flows by providing incentives. These flows can be channelled into the development of small and medium enterprises that are labour-intensive and stimulate job creation.

5. Establishing effective organizational structure: To deliver programmes for social benefit in a timely and efficient manner, we require a government that is accountable, committed to social cause and representative of different segments of the society.

6. Improving provision of basic amenities: For improved standard of living it is essential to have improvement in basic amenities like water, sanitation, electricity, roads and housing.

6.4.4 Approaches to Inclusive Growth

Inclusive growth can be pursued either as top-down approach or as bottom-up approach.

1. Top-down approach: Associated widely with the centralized economies of the Soviet era, the top-down approach is widely tested and tried. In **top-down approach**, the policies are formulated at the top, executed by the middle level machinery, and benefits the bottom of the pyramid, i.e., the poor, through trickle down phenomenon. Such an approach is effective when number of organizations involved are a few, and administrative structure are well-integrated from above rather than being dispersed. Since the beneficiaries are often not involved in policy formulation and implementation, in this approach they often feel alienated to the process which often delays the desired outcome.

2. Bottom-up approach: Contrary to top-down approach, the bottom-up approach, which is gaining ground in the recent period, views that the grass root ideas, entrepreneurial ventures and small and medium enterprises are the real engines of growth. Hence, strengthening of these is expected to lay a solid foundation for inclusive growth. Based on such an ideology, the **bottom-up approach** focuses on local implementation structures by identifying local, regional and national resources. It involves the local players/the expected beneficiaries in planning, financing and execution of strategies identified for achieving all inclusive growth.

Such an approach is effective when the number of players is large, there are administrative difficulties in identifying the public needs, capabilities, strengths, ideas, and formulating and implementing effective strategies that can benefit the society at large. As the approach to growth evolves from the grass root, the participating groups and individuals clearly understand their roles, responsibilities and the goals towards which they are striving, which enhances the inclusive growth process.

The approach aims at involving enterprises and corporations in the inclusive growth process, and follows three steps: Aggregation, systemization and fostering.

3. Aggregation: While pursuing this approach, the firms/enterprises first of all identify and collect information on the resources such as manpower, skill sets, ideas, and natural resources, available to the society.

4. Systemization: In the next step they try to document these resources and devise the processes and build up a required infrastructure through which these resources can be used.

5. Fostering: In the final step these ideas are nurtured and utilized for the benefit of all the involved parties.

6.4.5 Indicators of Inclusive Growth

As we have seen in the previous sections, inclusive growth is a very exhaustive concept. It emphasizes not only quantitative but also qualitative aspects of improvement in living standard brought about through changes in productive employment and various other processes. Inclusive growth is a process rather than simply a target to be achieved; hence, it is very difficult to measure.

Over the last few decades, several organizations are struggling to identify the parameters that can be used for assessing the level of inclusive growth achieved by a country. Some well-known attempts are that by the United Nations in the form of **Millennium Development Goals** (MDGs) developed in 2000, OECD in the form of **well-being indicators** in 2011, and ADB in the form of **framework of inclusive growth indicators** (FIGI), 2011.

At present, the MDG consists of 60 indicators that can be used for monitoring progress on 8 goals and 21 quantifiable targets (Table 6.3). The broad goals to achieve are—poverty reduction, better access to school education, gender equality and women empowerment, lower child deaths, better maternal health, control over life-threatening diseases, environment sustainability, and involvement of all stakeholders in the development process.

Table 6.3 UN's Millennium Development Goals, Targets and Indicators

Goals/ Targets	*Indicators*
	Goal 1. Eradicate extreme poverty and hunger
1a. Reduce by half the proportion of people living on less than a dollar a day	1.1 Proportion of population below $1 (PPP) per day 1.2 Poverty gap ratio 1.3 Share of poorest quintile in national consumption
1b. Achieve full and productive employment and decent work for all, including women and young people	1.4 Growth rate of GDP per person employed 1.5 Employment-to-population ratio 1.6 Proportion of employed people living below $1 (PPP) per day 1.7 Proportion of own-account and contributing family workers in total employment
1c. Reduce by half the proportion of people who suffer from hunger	1.8 Prevalence of underweight children under-five years of age 1.9 Proportion of population below minimum level of dietary energy consumption
	Goal 2. Achieve universal primary education
2a. Ensure that all boys and girls complete a full course of primary schooling	2.1 Net enrolment ratio in primary education 2.2 Proportion of pupils starting grade 1 who reach last grade of primary 2.3 Literacy rate of 15–24 year-olds, women and men
	Goal 3. Promote gender equality and empower women
3a. Eliminate gender disparity in primary and secondary education, preferably by 2005, and at all levels by 2015	3.1 Ratios of girls to boys in primary, secondary and tertiary education 3.2 Share of women in wage employment in the non-agricultural sector 3.3 Proportion of seats held by women in national parliament
	Goal 4. Reduce Child Mortality
4a. Reduce by two-third the mortality rate among children under five	4.1 Under-five mortality rate 4.2 Infant mortality rate 4.3 Proportion of 1 year-old children immunised against measles

Goals/ Targets	Indicators
	Goal 5. Improve maternal health
5a. Reduce by three quarters the maternal mortality ratio	5.1 Maternal mortality ratio 5.2 Proportion of births attended by skilled health personnel
5b. Achieve, by 2015, universal access to reproductive health	5.3 Contraceptive prevalence rate 5.4 Adolescent birth rate 5.5 Antenatal care coverage (at least one visit and at least four visits) 5.6 Unmet need for family planning
	Goal 6. Combat HIV/AIDS, malaria and other diseases
6a. Halt and begin to reverse the spread of HIV/AIDS	6.1 HIV prevalence among population aged 15–24 years 6.2 Condom use at last high-risk sex 6.3 Proportion of population aged 15–24 years with comprehensive correct knowledge of HIV/AIDS 6.4 Ratio of school attendance of orphans to school attendance of non-orphans aged 10–14 years
6b. Achieve, by 2010, universal access to treatment for HIV/AIDS for all those who need it	6.5 Proportion of population with advanced HIV infection with access to antiretroviral drugs
6c. Halt and begin to reverse the incidence of malaria and other major diseases	6.6 Incidence and death rates associated with malaria 6.7 Proportion of children under 5 sleeping under insecticide-treated bednets 6.8 Proportion of children under 5 with fever who are treated with appropriate anti-malarial drugs 6.9 Incidence, prevalence and death rates associated with tuberculosis 6.10 Proportion of tuberculosis cases detected and cured under directly observed treatment short course
	Goal 7: Ensure Environmental Sustainability
7a. Integrate the principles of sustainable development into country policies and programmes; reverse loss of environmental resources 7b. Reduce biodiversity loss, achieving, by 2010, a significant reduction in the rate of loss	7.1 Proportion of land area covered by forest 7.2 CO_2 emissions, total, per capita and per $1 GDP (PPP) 7.3 Consumption of ozone-depleting substances 7.4 Proportion of fish stocks within safe biological limits 7.5 Proportion of total water resources used 7.6 Proportion of terrestrial and marine areas protected 7.7 Proportion of species threatened with extinction
7c. Reduce by half the proportion of people without sustainable access to safe drinking water and basic sanitation	7.8 Proportion of population using an improved drinking water source 7.9 Proportion of population using an improved sanitation facility
7d. Achieve significant improvement in lives of at least 100 million slum dwellers, by 2020	7.10 Proportion of urban population living in slums

Goals/ Targets	*Indicators*
	Goal 8: A Global Partnership for Development
8a. Develop further an open, rule-based, predictable, non-discriminatory trading and financial system 8b. Address the special needs of the least developed countries 8c: Address the special needs of landlocked developing countries and small island developing States 8d. Deal comprehensively with the debt problems of developing countries through national and international measures in order to make debt sustainable in the long-term.	**Official development assistance (ODA)** 8.1 Net ODA, total and to the least developed countries, as percentage of OECD/DAC donors' gross national income 8.2 Proportion of total bilateral, sector-allocable ODA of OECD/DAC donors to basic social services (basic education, primary health care, nutrition, safe water and sanitation) 8.3 Proportion of bilateral official development assistance of OECD/DAC donors that is untied 8.4 ODA received in landlocked developing countries as a proportion of their gross national incomes 8.5 ODA received in small island developing States as a proportion of their gross national incomes **Market access** 8.6 Proportion of total developed country imports (by value and excluding arms) from developing countries and least developed countries, admitted free of duty 8.7 Average tariffs imposed by developed countries on agricultural products and textiles and clothing from developing countries 8.8 Agricultural support estimate for OECD countries as a percentage of their gross domestic product 8.9 Proportion of ODA provided to help build trade capacity **Debt sustainability** 8.10 Total number of countries that have reached their HIPC decision points and number that have reached their HIPC completion points (cumulative) 8.11 Debt relief committed under HIPC and MDRI Initiatives 8.12 Debt service as a percentage of exports of goods and services
8.e: In cooperation with pharmaceutical companies, provide access to affordable essential drugs in developing countries	8.13 Proportion of population with access to affordable essential drugs on a sustainable basis
8.f: In cooperation with the private sector, make available the benefits of new technologies, especially information and communications	8.14 Fixed telephone lines per 100 inhabitants 8.15 Mobile cellular subscriptions per 100 inhabitants 8.16 Internet users per 100 inhabitants

Source: Compiled from United Nations Website (online) http://web.undp.org/mdg/goal8.shtml

OECD, under better life initiatives, has devised well-being indicators based on the framework that distinguishes between current material living conditions and quality of life, on the one hand, and the conditions required to ensure their sustainability on the other. The framework includes eleven indicators of well-being as indicated in Table 6.4. However, the quantitative indicators for sustainability (which depends on how current human activities impact on the stocks of different types of capital (natural, economic, human and social) are excluded as suitable indicators that can account for this aspect are still missing in the literature.

Table 6.4 OECD Well-Being Indicators

Dimensions of well-being	*Indicators*
1. Material living conditions	1. Income and wealth 2. Jobs and earnings 3. Housing
2. Quality of life	1. Health status 2. Work and life balance 3. Education and skills 4. Civic engagement and governance 5. Social connections 6. Environmental quality 7. Personal security 8. Subjective well-being

Source: OECD (2011), Compendium of OECD Well-being Indicators, http://www.oecd.org/dataoecd/4/31/47917288.pdf

Focusing on the needs of developing Asian economies, the ADB has FIGI which is a set of 35 indicators. These indicators are also influenced by the MDG indicators as nearly one-third of the proposed FIGI indicators are also a part of MDG monitoring. However, the FIGI has a wider coverage. It emphasizes growth and creation of opportunities along with social inclusion, social safety nets, and good governance (Table 6.5). Some of these process indicators, such as social safety nets and good governance, which are regarded as important policy ingredients to mitigate unequal opportunities are not part of MDG monitoring.

Table 6.5 Framework of Inclusive Growth Indicators

Poverty and Inequality (Income and Non-income)	
1.1 Income poverty and inequality	1. Proportion of population living below the national poverty line 2. Proportion of population living below \$2 a day at 2005 PPP \$ 3. Ratio of income/consumption of the top 20% to bottom 20%
1.2 Non-income poverty and inequality	4. Average years of total schooling (youth and adults) 5. Prevalence of underweight children under five years of age 6. Under-five mortality rate
Pillar One: Growth and Expansion of Economic Opportunity	
Economic growth and employment	7. Growth rate of GDP per capita at PPP (constant 2005 PPP \$) 8. Growth rate of average per capita income/consumption 2005 PPP \$ (lowest quantile, highest quantile, and total) 9. Employment rate 10. Elasticity of total employment to total GDP (employment elasticities) 11. Number of own-account and contributing family workers per 100 wage and salaried workers
Key infrastructure endowments	12. Per capita consumption of electricity 13. Percentage of paved roads 14. Number of cellular phone subscriptions per 100 people 15. Depositors with other depository corporations per 1,000 adults

Pillar Two: Social Inclusion to Ensure Equal Access to Economic Opportunity	
Access and inputs to education and health	16. School life expectancy (primary to tertiary) 17. Pupil-teacher ratio (primary) 18. Diphtheria, tetanus toxoid, and pertussis (DTP3) immunization coverage among 1-year-olds 19. Physicians, nurses, and midwives per 10,000 population 20. Government expenditure on education as percentage of total government expenditure 21. Government expenditure on health as a percentage of total government expenditure
Access to basic infrastructure utilities and services	22. Percentage of population with access to electricity 23. Share of population using solid fuels for cooking 24. Percentage of population using improved drinking water sources 25. Percentage of population using improved sanitation facilities
Gender equality and opportunity	26. Gender parity in primary, secondary, and tertiary education 27. Antenatal care coverage (at least one visit) 28. Gender parity in labour force participation 29. Percentage of seats held by women in national parliament
Pillar Three: Social Safety Nets	
	30. Social protection and labour rating 31. Social security expenditure on health as a percentage of government expenditure on health 32. Government expenditure on social security and welfare as percentage of total government expenditure
Good Governance and Institutions	
	33. Voice and accountability 34. Government effectiveness 35. Corruption perceptions index

Source: ADB (2011), Framework of Inclusive Growth Indicators, Key Indicators for Asia and the Pacific 2011 Special Supplement, http://www.adb.org/key-indicators/2011/special-supplement.

6.4.6 Need for Corporate Involvement in Inclusive Growth Process

Corporates are an integral part of society and integrated with the society through various channels (Figure 6.2). They provide goods and services to the society and make their earnings and profit. However, they cannot sustain on their own; demand for their goods and services emerges from the society. The better off the societies, the higher the demand for their goods and services and higher their profits. Similarly, for input requirements, such as labour and finances, they are dependent on the society. Well-off societies, rich in physical capital and human capital, can provide highly productive inputs to the corporations. On the contrary, in a poor society, afflicted by wide income disparity, high illiteracy, poor infrastructure and pathetic living conditions, corporations can be deprived of productive inputs, which may restrain their growth in the long-run. The growing realization of these facets of growth and development is increasingly pushing the corporates to seriously devise strategies for inclusive growth process.

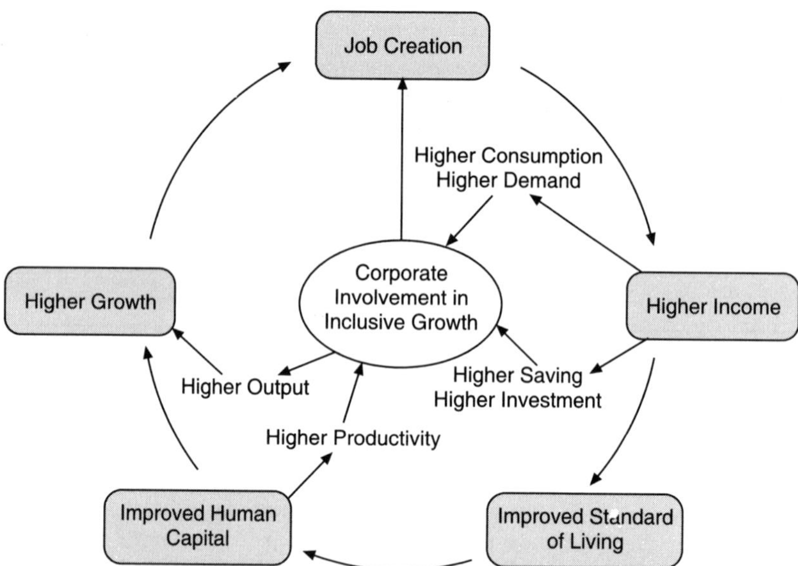

Figure 6.2 Benefits of Corporate Involvement in Inclusive Growth Process.

Some of the reasons for corporate involvement in the inclusive growth process are described hereinafter:

1. Improving corporate image and brand building: The corporate involved in social upliftment and inclusive growth are viewed with respect by different stakeholders, such as customers, employees, society, in general, and even the government. For example, Tata, Infosys, Wipro and many other corporate organizations are well-respected in India not only for their quality services but also their contribution towards the social well-being. Such an involvement helps in strengthening brand image for the companies involved. It also helps the companies in attracting and retaining talented labour force.

2. Public expectations from corporations: As corporations are an integral part of the society, public in general expects that the corporations use part of their earnings or profits for the development of the society. Since corporate activities also cause some environmental degradation, the society views that it is the responsibility of the corporations to pro-actively prevent environment degradation and use their resources for cleaning air and water, for social forestry and environmental protection in general.

3. Anti-globalization protests: Gloablization provides a wider market for corporates. However, the corporations are accused of reaping these opportunities, emerging from a greater opening of the international markets, they are indiscriminately damaging bio-diversity, rampantly using child labour and polluting air and water, which is causing adverse climate changes like global warming. Corporates involvement in inclusive growth is one way of assuring the anti-globalization protestors that corporate globalization is beneficial in those countries where such organizations are operating.

4. Domestic laws and guidelines from international forums: Some countries make the coroprates' involvement in social upliftment mandatory, whereas some are merely providing guidelines. For example, Companies Bill, 2011, in India makes it mandatory for companies to earmark 2 per cent of their average profits of preceding three years for Corporate Social Responsibility (CSR), and make a disclosure to shareholders about the policy adopted in the process. Apart from the governments, many multinational organizations have been providing guidelines regarding the corporate involvement in social upliftment and environment protection. For example, OECD guidelines announced on January 2012, endorsed by the government of 43 governments, are voluntary recommendations to multinational enterprises on responsible conduct in areas such as human rights, labour, environment, and corruption. Such pressures are compelling corporates to involve in social development and forcing them to contribute towards the inclusive growth process.

SUMMARY

Poverty, which reflects the pronounced deprivation of well-being of a person, is measured in absolute as well as in relative terms. The relative poverty measures the number of people living below a certain threshold level of living that is essential for procuring certain essential goods and services. Whereas, the relative poverty measures the extent to which a person's financial resources fall below the average or median level in the economy. Though the absolute poverty can be eradicated by achieving higher growth rate, the eradication of the relative poverty requires reduction in income inequalities.

Poverty is an outcome of various micro and macro factors. Micro factors, i.e., the factors pertaining to individuals, include lack of intelligence, poor health, discrimination and general attitude towards life. Whereas, macro factors, i.e., the factors at the country wide level, include overpopulation, lack of education, inadequate employment opportunities, environmental degradation, structural and technological changes, demographic changes, family structure, government welfare schemes, unfair trade practices, corruption and poor governance, political prejudice and inequality, centralization of power, colonial suppression, external invasions and civil wars, and natural disasters.

While economic growth is essential for poverty reduction it is not sufficient for improving the overall well-being. Growth, referring to the growth of output or income, is simply a quantitative aspect of overall well-being. Development, which reflects overall enrichment in the quality of life, is a better indicator of overall well being. Development, unlike growth, has not only quantitative dimension but also qualitative aspects. Apart from improvement in per capita income, it requires improvement in the level of education, health and sanitation, and many such parameters.

Growth or development cannot be sustained for a longer period unless it is inclusive. Inclusive growth refers to the rapid and sustained growth in the long-run, which is inclusive of the large part of the country's labour force and broad based across sectors. Growth, without inclusiveness, can marginalize the poor sections and increase inequality in standard of living and derail the growth process through political channels and conflict. Inclusive growth requires reduction in income inequalities, better access to basic education to larger section of the society, improvement in productivity in labour intensive segments, higher remittances and their channelization into the development of small and medium enterprises, effective organizational structure and improvement in the quality of basic amenities. Inclusive growth can be achieved either by top-down approach or bottom-up approach.

Inclusive growth is a process rather than simply a target, making its measurement difficult. However, some multilateral organizations have developed some indicators to assess the level of inclusiveness in the growth process. United Nations's Millennium Development Goals (MDGs), OECD's well-being indicators and ADB's framework of inclusive growth indicators are well-known attempts to measure inclusive growth.

Implications for Managers

Various resources that are required by business organizations to sustain their processes in the long-run do not grow in the same proportion as that required by these organizations. Some of these are limited in supply, such as land, and non-replenishable. Some can get polluted in the process of the production process, such as air, water and soil. Some get depleted, such as water level, forest cover, minerals, bio-diversity, etc. Unless these various resources are conserved properly, the growth process will get a severe jolt and will become unsustainable.

Business organizations are an integral part of the society. They are integrated with the society from the supply side as well as the demand side.

On the supply side, business organizations draw heavily on the societal resources in the form of human and other natural resources as well as man-made resources. The supply side can constrain the business expansion in the long-run if the supply of resources is not in commensurate with the need. However, the constraints on the productivity may emerge even in the presence of large available resources if it is not of the required quality. For example, a large pool of talented and capable people remains unemployed if it lacks the required skills and training. Business organizations can enhance their productivity and efficiency by nurturing, grooming and training the talent. The improved employment and income level is expected to enhance saving and also the availability of funds for investment purpose, further improving the productivity.Their efforts to include deprived, downtrodden minorities, outcasts, etc., will not only improve the available pool of resources but also the sense of belongingness in the population. The efforts will also help reducing stress and struggle, and building up congenial environment. When people feel a part of the growth process they try to put the best of their energy and efforts.

On the demand side, the constraints can be low population growth or low per capita income of the majority of the population or any other factor that is a major determinant of demand for business products. Business organizations can overcome these constraints, by involving masses in their production process productively, providing them gainful employment, and improving their income levels, which in turn will help them in by enhancing the demand for their products.

Given these two-way integration with the society, for their own sustainability and progress business organizations have to have a harmonious coexistence with the society and the environment in which they operate. For the sustainability of the growth process in the long-run, India Inc. has the responsibility of identifying the constrains in the sustainable growth processes, devising innovative methods to overcome the constraints, contributing to the build-up of economic, ecological and social capital through public private or community partnership though in short run such strategic alliances may not be lucrative and may hit the financial bottom line.

REVIEW QUESTIONS

6.1 How is poverty measured?

6.2 What is the difference between absolute and relative poverty?

6.3 What are the causes of poverty in India?

6.4 How is growth measured? What is the meaning of pro-poor growth?

6.5 What is the difference between growth and development?

6.6 What approach is needed for the sustainable growth or development?

6.7 What are the different strategies of inclusive growth?

6.8 What are the different approaches to inclusive growth? What are the basic differences between top-down approach and bottom-up approach?

6.9 How is inclusive growth measured?

6.10 What are the deficiencies of United Nations' indicators of inclusive growth?

6.11 What are the three pillars of inclusive growth identified by the ADB?

6.12 Why corporate involvement is essential in the inclusive growth process?

NUMERICAL PROBLEM

6.1 Table 6.6 gives the real level of income in a hypothetical society. On the basis of the given information, fill in the blanks and estimate the extent of absolute and relative poverty.

Table 6.6 Absolute and Relative Poverty: A Hypothetical Example (Amount in ₹)

Person	*Salary per period*		
	Period (t)	*Period* (t + 1)	*Period* (t + 2)
Ram	2,000	4,000	8,000
Shyam	4,000	8,000	16,000
Radha	6,000	12,000	24,000
Kavita	8,000	16,000	32,000
Babita	10,000	20,000	40,000
Number of persons below absolute poverty line (assuming threshold level of income for satisfying basic necessities to be ₹6,000 per period)			
Number of persons below relative poverty line (given average income of ₹6,000, ₹12,000 and ₹24,000 in period t, t + 1 and t + 2 respectively)			

CASE ANALYSIS EXERCISE

C6.1 How Inclusive is India's Growth?

The Indian economy is described as one of the fastest growing emerging economies in the world because of its rapid growth rate during the last two decades. However, many have doubted the sustainability of this growth process fearing that the growth is not inclusive enough to be sustained in the long-run and may become a unique chapter in India's history. Are the fears supported by the facts?

Some organizations like UN, OEDC and ADB have devised various indicators (Table 6.7) to make quantitative assessment of the inclusiveness of growth of a country. An assessment of inclusiveness of

Table 6.7 Inclusive Growth in India Vis a Vis Other South Asian Economies

Indicators	*Year*	*India* *Value (Year)*	*Bangladesh* *Value (Year)*	*Bhutan* *Value (Year)*	*Nepal* *Value (Year)*	*Sri Lanka* *Value (Year)*	*Pakistan* *Value (Year)*	*China* *Value (Year)*
				Income Poverty and Inequality				
Proportion of population living below the national poverty line	Earliest	36.0 (1994)	56.6 (1992)	31.7 (2003)	41.8 (1996)	26.1 (1991)	30.6 (1999)	6.0 (1996)
	Latest	27.5 (2005)	40.0 (2005)	23.2 (2007)	25.4 (2009)	7.6 (2009)	22.3 (2006)	…
				Non-Income Poverty and Inequality				
Prevalence of underweight children under five years of age	Earliest	50.7 (1992)	64.1 (1992)	14.1 (1999)	44.1 (1995)	21.1 (2006)	39.0 (1990)	15.3 (1992)
	Latest	43.5 (2005)	41.3 (2007)	12.0 (2008)	38.8 (2006)	21.6 (2009)	31.3 (2001)	4.5 (2005)
				Economic Growth and Employment				
Growth rate of GDP per capita at PPP (constant 2005 PPP $)	Earliest (1990–95)	3.1	2.3	5.5	2.6	4.2	2	10.9
	Latest (2005–09)	6.8	4.7	7.5	2.3	5.1	2	10.8
Employment rate (aged 15 years and over)	Earliest	55.3 (1994)	68.2 (1991)	69.8 (2003)	67.2 (1996)	42.5 (1993)	40.5 (1990)	…
	Latest	57.7 (2005)	56.0 (2005)	58.6 (2005)	91.6 (2003)	45.9 (2009)	42.8 (2007)	…
				Key Infrastructure Endowments				
Per capita consumption of electricity (kWh)	Earliest (1990)	276	44	…	35	153	277	511
	Latest (2008)	566	208	…	89	409	436	2,455

Indicators	*Year*	*India* Value (Year)	*Bangladesh* Value (Year)	*Bhutan* Value (Year)	*Nepal* Value (Year)	*Sri Lanka* Value (Year)	*Pakistan* Value (Year)	*China* Value (Year)
Paved roads (per cent of total roads)	Earliest (1990)	47.3 (1991)	7.2 (1991)	77.1	37.5	32.0 (1991)	54	72.1
	Latest (2008)	49.3	9.5 (2003)	62.0 (2003)	55.9 (2006)	81.0 (2003)	65.4 (2006)	53.5
		Access and Inputs to Education and Health						
School life expectancy (primary to tertiary)	Earliest (1999)	8.1	8.0 (2005)	7.3	8.4	12.5 (2002)	5.7 (2003)	9.9 (2001)
	Latest (2009)	10.3 (2007)	8.1 (2007)	11.0 (2008)	8.8 (2002)	12.7 (2004)	6.9	11.6
Pupil-teacher ratio (primary)	Earliest (1990)	46	63	…	39	29	43	22
	Latest (2009)	40 (2004)	47 (2005)	40 (2004)	33	23 (2008)	40	18 (2008)
Diptheria, tetanus toxoid, and pertussis (DTP3) immunization coverage among 1 year –olds	Earliest (1990)	70	69	96	43	86	54	97
	Latest (2009)	66	94	96	82	97	85	97
Physicians, nurses, and mid-wives per 10,000 population	Earliest	…	…	…	…	…	…	…
	Latest	19.0 (2005)	5.7 (2007)	3.4 (2007)	6.7 (2004)	…	13.7 (2009)	28.9 (2009)
		Access to Basic Infrastructure Utilities and Services						
Percentage of population using improved drinking water sources	Earliest (1990)	72	78	91 (2000)	76	67	86	67
	Latest (2008)	66	76	92	74	62	81	56

Indicators	*Year*	*India* Value (Year)	*Bangladesh* Value (Year)	*Bhutan* Value (Year)	*Nepal* Value (Year)	*Sri Lanka* Value (Year)	*Pakistan* Value (Year)	*China* Value (Year)
Percentage of population using improved sanitation facilities	Earliest (1990)	18	34	62	18	69	28	41
	Latest (2008)	31	53	65	31	98	45	55
			Gender Equality and Opportunity					
Gender parity in labour force participation (15 yrs and over, %)	Earliest (1990)	40.4	69.2	67.2	61.9	47.2	15.9	86
	Latest (2009)	40.4	71.1	75.7	78.8	45.6	25.6	84.5
			Social Safety Nets					
Government expenditure on social security and welfare as percentage of total government expenditure	Earliest (1995)	4.5 (1999)	0.9	...	12.1	16.3	...	1.7
	Latest (2010)	5.6 (2008)	2.9 (2008)	4.3	15.9	8.3	...	10.1
			Good Governance and /institutions					
3Corruption perceptions index	Earliest (2009)	3.4	2.4	5	3.4	2.3	2.4	3.6
	Latest (2010)	3.3	2.4	5.7	3.3	2.2	2.3	3.5

Source: Compiled from ADB (2011), Framework of Inclusive Growth Indicators, Key Indicators for Asia and the Pacific 2011 Special Supplement.

India's growth process is made here by analyzing some of the indicators proposed by ADB under the FIGI. While making such an assessment, the quality of growth in India is compared with that of other South Asian economies as well as China.

As can be seen from Table 6.7, India is not only worse than China, which has much higher growth rate than India, on most of the indicators of inclusive growth, but also many other neighbouring countries in South Asia, which have not done better than India in terms of growth rate. For example, though improvement in the growth rate of Sri Lanka is not as high as that of India, it is much better on various indicators, such as income and non-income poverty, education and health, gender parity in labour force, government expenditure on social security. Besides, Sri Lankan government is viewed as less corrupt than the Indian government. Even Bangladesh, which has much lower growth rate and high level of income poverty is doing better than India in terms of non-income poverty measures, pupil teacher ratio, and immunization coverage. It has much better drinking water and sanitation facilities. Its government is also viewed as less corrupt than that of India. In fact, in spite of very rapid growth, India's position among the South Asian countries, on many parameters of inclusive growth, such as income and non-income poverty majors, paved road, school life expectancy immunization coverage, has deteriorated.

Thus, one can infer that India has not been able to translate the increased overall revenue, emerging from higher growth, for the overall well-being of the society. The benefits of growth are not shared equally with the masses, resulting in high income inequalities in the country. It does not mean that India should not aim for high growth. Given the very low level of per capita income, rapid growth in countries like India is essential for achieving better living standard. However, rapid growth is not sufficient to achieve the better life in general. For the growth to be inclusive, it also needs to be widely shared among the different strata of the population in a way which generate productive employment. To achieve this, policy orientation needs to move towards elementary education, social securities, healthcare, agriculture and rural development, women empowerment and environment protection.

Questions

1. Has the rapid growth in India in the last two decades resulted in inclusive growth ?
2. Which are the indicators used by the ADB for assessing the inclusive growth process?
3. How is India's relative position on inclusive growth front vis-a-vis its neighbouring countries?
4. What is needed for growth sustainability in India?

SUGGESTED FURTHER READING

Bisiaux, R. (2013), Understanding the Mismatch Among the Three Definition of Poverty: New Micro-Level Evidence from Delhi Slums, EPW, Jan05, XLVIII,1.

Hirway, I. (2012), Inclusive Growth Under a Neo-Liberal Policy Framework, EPW, May 19, Vol. XLVII, 20.

Qubey, A. and Thorat, S. (2012), Has Growth Been Socially Inclusive During 1993–94 to 2009–11? EPW, March 10,Vol. XLVII, 10.

Subbarao, D. (2012), Achieving Inclusive Growth: The Challenge of a New Era, *RBI Bulletin*, October.

CHAPTER 7

Inflation and Business Environment

7.1 INTRODUCTION

In my childhood, one day my mother asked me to buy bananas which were then available for 50 paisa a dozen. Rather than spending 50 paisa on bananas I decided to save the money. A few years later I approached a banana vendor with the same 50 paisa. The vendor, however, refused to give me even a single banana because by then bananas have become more expensive, ₹12 a dozen. Also, I realized that not only prices of bananas but of almost everything have gone up. I realized that the worth of my savings has declined sharply. I became wary of rising prices, i.e., inflation.

A few years ago I noticed that one of my aunts, who was in a textile business, was very happy with the rising prices of textile products. In fact rising prices made her expand her business. I wondered why was she happy with the rising prices when the same was pinching my pockets.

In the same year of soaring pricing, one day I heard on radio our Prime Minister showing a concern on rising prices of onions, vegetables, and many other primary and manufactured products, and announcing various measures to tackle the problem at war footing. I realized that inflation matters not only to me and my aunt but also to our Prime Minister, a representative of the government.

Price movements affect all of us, consumers, households, business units and the government. These movements help consumers to adjust their demand for products, households to adjust their supply of factors of production, business units to plan their production, investment, procurement, hiring, financing and expansion decisions, and the government to formulate its taxation and expenditure policies.

Not only the government of India but also that of other countries wary sharp movements in prices, upward or downward. Inflation or deflation had always been a matter of concern world over and regarded as a major economic problem. Countries like Germany in early 1920s, Greece in early 1940s, Hungary after the end of World War II, Yugoslavia in early 1990s, Latin American countries such as Bolivia, Peru, Mexico, and Argentina in 1980s, and Brazil in early 1990s and, till very recently, African nation Zimbabwe experienced a rapid rate of increase in prices and faced a large reduction in the purchasing power of their currencies and sharp decline in the standard of living of their people in general. At the same time, deflation in the UK after the World War I, in the USA in early 1930s, in Hong Kong following the East Asian financial crisis in late 1997, and in Japan since early 1990s had accompanied by a large fall in output and employment, had posed serious socio-economic problems and strained the skills of policy makers in these countries. Though, inflation usually accompanies with an increase in employment, some countries, such as the UK in 1960s, and 1970s, and the USA in 1970s, have even experienced a very high rate of unemployment in the face of a high rate of inflation, the situation termed as stagflation.

Inflation has a tremendous impact on various macroeconomic variables, such as interest rate, exchange rate, balance of payment, and even the expectations of inflation in the forthcoming period. Not only the nominal but also the real values of these variables are affected by price changes. All these changes necessitate changes in business plans and other economic activities. Hence, this chapter makes an assessment of inflationary environment by analyzing the causes of inflation, ascertaining its impact and describing the policy tools used for controlling inflation. Though exposition, here, is in terms of inflation, a similar analysis can be carried out for deflationary situation as the impact and tools for controlling deflation are symmetrical to that of inflation. In specific, Section 7.2 defines the terms used for describing the movements in prices. Measurement issues are dealt with in Section 7.3. This section also presents the features of various price indices available in India and their uses. Description of an inflationary scenario, using various criteria, is presented in Section 7.4. Section 7.5 analyses the impact of inflation on different sections of an economy and on various macro-economic variables. Monetary and fiscal tools used for controlling inflation are described in Section 7.6.

7.2 PRICE MOVEMENTS: INFLATION, DISINFLATION, DEFLATION AND REFLATION

Prices move along with the fluctuations in business activities. These movements are termed as **inflation**, **disinflation**, **deflation** and **reflation**. **Inflation** is a persistent and substantial rise in the general level of prices after full employment level of output. We should note that inflation refers to an increase in the overall price level. The prices of different commodities may vary at different rates and in different directions. Some may increase, whereas the others may decline leading to a change in the relative prices. However, such relative price changes cannot be termed as inflation. Similarly, a one time increase in the general price level is not considered as inflation. Figure 7.1 depicts a one time increase in the price level and contrasts it with a continuous increase

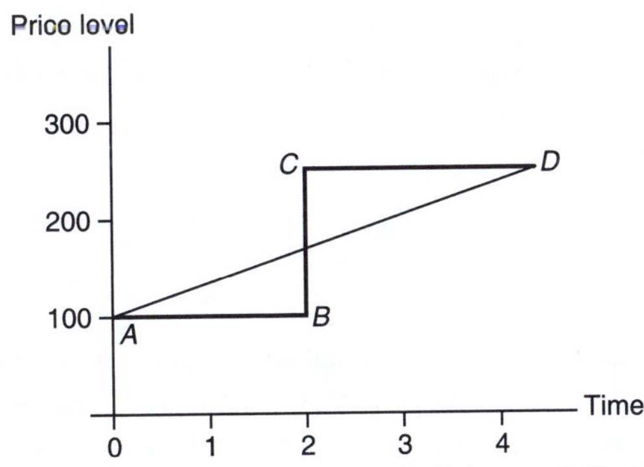

Figure 7.1 One Time Increase in Prices vs Inflation.

in the price level, termed as **inflation**. Between period 0 and period 2, the price level remains at 100 (movement from point *A* to point *B*). Then there is a sharp rise in the price level from 100 to 300 in period 2 (movement from *B* to *C*) and the overall price level again stabilizes at 300 in the subsequent period (movement from *C* to *D*). This one time increase in the price level, from *B* to *C*, cannot be termed as inflation. On the contrary, the price rise is continuous along the line *AD*, wherein the price persistently increases from 100 in period 0 to 300 in period 4. This persistent rise in the overall price level can be termed as inflation.

Inflation results in a fall in the value of money, i.e., the exchange value of money declines. Though, output, employment and income often rise in such a scenario, it reduces the purchasing power of consumers, and hence, disliked by them.

Sometimes, countries may even experience negative inflation rate. When prices of most goods and services fall over a period of time, the inflation rate turns out to be negative. This situation of persistent and substantial fall in the overall price level below the full employment level of output is referred to as **deflation**. In this state of an economy, the value of money keep on rising or the price level keep on falling. However, at the same time, there is also a fall in the output, employment, and income, and hence, such a situation is dreaded by all.

In the two extreme situations of inflation and deflation, countries also experience disinflation and reflation. **Disinflation** is a situation where an economy operates at above the full employment level of output, price level keep on increasing, but the rate of increase in price level keep on declining. On the other hand, **reflation** or **partial inflation** refers to a situation when an increase in demand at below full employment level raises not only the price level, but also the volume of output in the system. These four concepts of change in the price level are illustrated in Table 7.1

Table 7.1 Reflation, Inflation, Disinflation and Deflation: A Hypothetical Example

Period	*Inflation*		*Disinflation*		*Deflation*		*Reflation*	
	Economy above full employment output		*Economy above full employment output*		*Economy below full employment output*		*Economy below full employment output*	
	Price level	*Rate of price change*	*Price level*	*Rate of price change*	*Price level*	*Rate of price change*	*Price level*	*Rate of price change*
2001	100.0	–	100.0	–	100.0	–	95.8	–
2002	110.0	10.0	120.0	20.0	90.0	– 10.0	96.2	0.4
2003	125.0	13.6	142.0	18.3	78.0	– 13.3	96.7	0.5
2004	145.0	16.0	165.0	16.2	65.0	– 16.7	97.3	0.6
2005	170.0	17.2	190.0	15.2	54.0	– 16.9	98.1	0.8
2006	200.0	17.6	215.0	13.2	44.0	– 18.5	99.0	0.9
2007	240.0	20.0	240.0	11.6	35.0	– 20.5	100.0	1.0

Movements in the price level, along with the fluctuations in business activities, are reflected in Figure 6.2. A movement from *B* to *C* depicts the phase when an economy is operating above the full employment level of output. This phase of expansion is associated with a continuous increase in the rate of growth of price level, i.e., inflation. In phase *CD,* though the economy is above the full employment level of output, there is a continuous deceleration in the rate of growth of price level, known as **disinflation**. During the phase *DE*, the economy is below the full employment level of output and there is an absolute fall in the price level, resulting in a negative growth in the overall price level, i.e., deflation. The phase *EF* is the phase depicting recovery which is associated with **reflation**, i.e., a slow and steady increase in the price level. For simplicity, the movements in the price level and the output level are perfectly synchronized in Figure 7.2. However, in reality there may not be such exact correspondence. The diagram may not be as smooth as depicted here and there may be some overlaps, i.e., the period of inflation may start even before the end of the period of recovery and overflow partly to the period of slowdown.

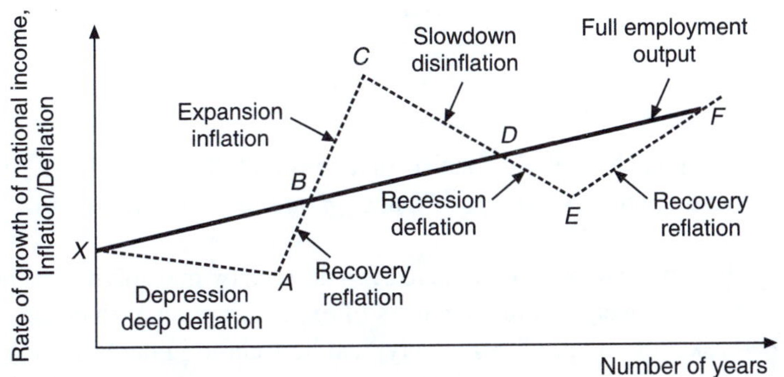

Figure 7.2 Movement in Inflation Rate over the Phases of Business Cycles.

7.3 MEASUREMENT OF INFLATION/DEFLATION

As we have seen above, the inflation is a rate of change of the overall price level in a country in a given period of time. Therefore, for estimating inflation it is essential for us to estimate the overall price level. For estimating the overall price level, the concept of price index is used.

7.3.1 Price Index

An **index** is a statistical device or measure that expresses average change in the value of something in the current period in relation to its value at a set previous time, known as the **base period**. The value of an index at the base period is always set at 100. It indicates a change without a direct reference to the actual number value of what is being measured.

If there is only one commodity and an associated price then the average price change can simply be estimated by the **price relative**, i.e., as the ratio of the price of a single commodity in a given period, known as the **current period** (P_1), to its price in some past period, known as the **base** or **reference period** (P_0).

Symbolically, the price relative can be represented as $PR = (P_1/P_0)$.

However, when in an economy consumption or production basket consists of more than one commodity, price relatives are not sufficient to estimate the overall change in the price level. In such an economy, a weighted price index is computed in which each item is given a weight according to its importance in the basket of commodities, that is chosen for computation of the price index. Two different methods, widely used for determining importance or weights, and estimating price indices are described hereinafter:

Methods of Estimating Price Indices

Two widely used methods of computing price indices are Laspeyres' method and Paasche's method. These methods compute the price indices as follows:

1. Laspeyres' method: The base year quantities are used as the weights in the Laspeyres' method. Thus, the **Laspeyres' method** computes the price index (*PIND*) in period '*t*' as

$$PINDt = \frac{\sum_{i=1}^{n} Pi_t Qi_0}{\sum_{i=1}^{n} Pi_0 Qi_0} \times 100$$

where, the basket of a typical household consists of *n* commodities, i.e., $i = 1, \ldots, n$. Pi_0 and Qi_0 are the base year prices and quantities, whereas Pi_t and Qi_t are the current year prices and quantities, respectively.

Note that the above formula we could have even derived by multiplying the price relatives by the weights (*wi*), where the weights are the shares of expenditure on each commodity in the total expenditure on the basket of commodities by a typical household in the base year.

i.e.,

$$PINDt = \left[\sum_{i=1}^{n} wi \frac{Pi_t}{Pi_0}\right] \times 100 = \left[\sum_{i=1}^{n} \left(\frac{Pi_0 Qi_0}{\sum_{i=1}^{n} Pi_0 Qi_0}\right)\left(\frac{Pi_t}{Pi_0}\right)\right] \times 100$$

$$= \left[\sum_{i=1}^{n} \left(\frac{Pi_t Qi_t}{\sum_{i=1}^{n} Pi_0 Qi_0}\right)\right] \times 100 = \left[\left(\frac{\sum_{i=1}^{n} Pi_t Qi_0}{\sum_{i=1}^{n} Pi_0 Qi_0}\right)\right] \times 100$$

2. Paasche's method: The current year quantities (Qi_t) are used as the weights in the **Paasche's method** of computation of a price index. Using this method, the price index is estimated as:

$$PIND_t = \left[\left(\frac{\sum_{i=1}^{n} Pi_t Qi_t}{\sum_{i=1}^{n} Pi_t Qi_t}\right)\right] \times 100$$

Similar to Laspeyres' formula, the above formula also we can derive by multiplying the price relatives by the weights (*wi*). Unlike the Laspeyres' method, in Paasche method the weights are the shares of expenditure on each commodity in the total expenditure on the basket of commodity by a typical household in the current period. As an exercise, readers can try it.

Estimation of Inflation Rate using Price Index

Irrespective of the method used for the computation of a price index, the inflation rate (Π) can be computed as:

$$\Pi = \{(PIND_t - PIND_{t-1})/PIND_{t-1}\} \times 100$$

The inflation rate can be calculated either on a point to point basis or on an average basis.

The **point to point estimation** (Section 2.4) involves the estimation of inflation at the same point of time in two different periods or years. For example, if a price index on 31 March 2001 is 127 ($PIND_{t-1} = 127$) and that on 31 March 2002 is 135 ($PIND_t = 135$) then inflation is 6.3 per cent = [(135 – 127)/127] × 100] in the year 2002.

On the other hand, the average estimate of inflation tantamounts to taking the average of the inflation rate at different points of time during a given period. For example, if the inflation rate is 5, 6, 7 and 8 per cent for the 4 weeks of a month. Then, the average inflation in that month is 6.5 per cent

i.e.,
$$\frac{5+6+7+8}{4} = \frac{26}{4} = 6$$

The point to point inflation helps in discounting the impact of seasonality in price fluctuations, whereas the average estimate of inflation rate moderates large positive and/or negative shocks to the price levels during a given year.

Types of Price Indices

We have seen in Section 5.4.3 that prices vary as per the stages of transactions; the prices faced by producers are different than that faced by consumers. Prices differ not only at different stages of transactions, but also for different sections of a society and different regions of an economy. Therefore, depending on the purpose, price indices are estimated at different level of aggregation, stages of transactions, groups of a society and regions of an economy by different countries. Some of the commonly computed price indices, world over, are described as follows:

1. Consumer price index: Movements in consumer prices or retail prices, i.e., the prices faced by consumers, are captured in the **Consumer Price Index (CPI)**. This measures the cost of living in a given country. The CPI is the most relevant price index for consumers as it measures the cost of the basket of only those goods and services which are directly purchased by them in a given period of time relative to the cost of the same basket of goods and services in some specified period known as the **base year**. The estimation of this index involves the following steps:

(i) *Identification of the basket of goods.* The basket covers the items of consumption in day-to-day life, such as food, clothing, housing, fuel, transport, education, medicine, electricity, telephone and entertainment.

(ii) *Determination of weights for each of the commodity covered in the consumption basket.* This involves identifying the share of expenditure on each item in the basket in the total expenditure on the basket of commodities.

(iii) *Regular monitoring of the prices.* The prices of the products covered in the consumption basket need to be collected on a regular basis through household surveys.

(iv) *Determination of the base year.* The year set as the base year has to be a normal year. Given these preliminary steps, the estimation process of the CPI is illustrated in Box 7.1.

Box 7.1 Estimation of Consumer Price Index: An Illustration

Assume that a typical household in a year spends on 4 items—food, clothing, housing. and transport. The quantities purchased by the household in the base year 2004–05, and the associated prices in years 2004–05 and 2012–13 are presented in Table 7.2.

Table 7.2 Quantities and Prices in Consumption Basket

	Quantities	*Prices (₹)*		*Expenditure (₹) (Price × Quantity)*	
	2004–05	*2004–05*	*2012–13*	*2004–05*	*2012–13*
Food	40	10	15	400	600
Clothing	20	50	40	1,000	800
Housing	10	100	125	1,000	1,250
Transport	30	20	30	600	900
Total	**100**			**3,000**	**3,550**

Over a period of time, prices of certain commodities fall, whereas those of others rise. Due to changes in the prices of commodities, the household expenditure on the basket increases from ₹3,000 in 2004–05 to ₹3,550 in 2012–13.

The quantities available for the base year, i.e., 2004-05, can be used as the weights. The Laspeyres' method, which uses the base year quantities as weights, can be used for estimating the price index. The price index in 2012–13 is

$$\frac{\sum_{i=1}^{n} Pi_t Qi_0}{\sum_{i=1}^{n} Pi_0 Qi_0} = \frac{3,550}{3,000} = 1.18 \text{, or 118 per cent}$$

As the base year price index takes the value of 100 it can be seen that the price index or inflation rate has increased by 18 per cent during 2004–05 to 2012–13.

2. Producer price index: The Producer Price Index (PPI), the index most relevant to manufacturers or producers, is designed to measure price level at an early stage of the distribution system or at the first significant commercial transaction. The prices at the early stage of distribution system are easy to collect and monitor. This makes the PPI a relatively flexible price index. In general, it frequently signals the changes in the general price level, as measured by the CPI, before they actually materialize. Thus, the PPI serves as one of the leading indicator of business cycle that is closely watched by policy makers, business managers, and even investors in share and forex markets.

Though the PPI normally can track the changes in the CPI in advance, they differ in many respect. For example, the CPI is based on retail prices, whereas the PPI is estimated on the basis of producer's prices which exclude taxes, trade margins and transportation costs. Thus, the ratio between the CPI and the PPI indicates the extent of distribution cost falling on consumers. The PPI also differs from the CPI in terms of coverage and composition as the PPI includes, for example, raw materials and semi-finished goods. The difference in the two indices, at times, lead to divergent trends in them.

3. Wholesale price index: Technically very close to the PPI, the **Wholesale Price Index (WPI)** measures the movements in the wholesale prices, i.e., the prices charged by wholesalers once these have crossed the production stage, reflecting the second commercial transactions. Besides the prices of raw materials, semi-finished and final goods, the prices of imported tangible goods are also considered in the wholesale price index if they are transacted at the wholesale level. However, it excludes the prices of exported commodities. In the countries where the government imposes taxes at ex-factory price, the wholesale prices differ from the producer prices to the extent of tax, wholesale margin and transport cost from manufacturing units to the wholesale establishments. In many countries the distinction is not made between the PPI and WPI, and the PPI is treated as the WPI. However, many countries, had been compiling the WPI, have switched over to the PPI, because it is considered to be a better measure of inflation as price changes at primary and intermediate stages can be tracked before they get built into the finished goods stage.

4. Gross domestic products deflators: The **Gross Domestic Products (GDP) Deflator** reveals the cost of purchasing the items included in the GDP during the period relative to the cost of purchasing those same items during the base year. As it is derived from the GDP data, it includes the prices of all final goods produced in the economy and excludes those of raw material and other intermediate goods. Also, since GDP measures the output produced in the domestic territory, it ignores the prices of imported goods. Similar to other indices, for this index also the base year is assigned the value 100. The deflator is estimated as follows:

$$\text{GDP deflator} = \frac{\text{Nominal GDP}}{\text{Real GDP}} = \frac{\text{GDP at current prices in the current year}}{\text{GDP at constant price in the current year}}$$

For illustration, assume that the base year is 2005–06, implying the value of GDP deflator to be 100 in this year. In 2006–07 nominal GDP is ₹50,000 crore, whereas real GDP is ₹40,000 crore. Therefore, the GDP deflator in 2006–07 is 125 ((₹50,000/₹40,000) × 100), implying that the overall price level in the year 2006–07 is 25 per cent higher than that in 2005–06.

The GDP deflator is a variable weight index as it uses Paasche's method of computation where the cost of current year's 'bundle' of production is compared at the current year's prices with that prevailing in the base period. Thus, the deflator for year 2005–06 uses output as weights of the year 2005–06, whereas deflator for the year 2006–07 uses 2006–07 output as the weights.

It is termed as a deflator because one can divide (or deflate) nominal GDP by this ratio to correct for the effect of inflation on GDP,

i.e., Real GDP = Nominal GDP/GDP deflator

Thus, the GDP deflator can be used to measure the real GDP, i.e., the GDP in rupees of constant purchasing power.

The GDP deflator is also known as the **implicit price index**, because it implies a price index which is not estimated directly, but implicitly emerges in the process of estimating real and nominal GDP.

Not all the indices described in this section are computed by all countries. The indices that are computed in India are described in UBE 7.1. Also, as these indices are broad aggregates, their behaviour is determined by their sub-components as illustrated in UBE 7.2.

UNDERSTANDING BUSINESS ENVIRONMENT

UBE 7.1 Types of Price Indices in India

Describing the various price indices available in India, this UBE points out the advantage as well as shortcomings of each of the indices.

Two sets of price indices are computed in India, viz., the price indices derived from the National Accounts Statistics and the price indices computed directly (Figure 7.3). Features of these indices are summarized in Table 7.3 and detailed hereinafter.

Directly Available Price Indices

Two sets of price indices are directly estimated in India. These are the Wholesale Price Indices (WPIs) and the Consumer Price Indices (CPIs).

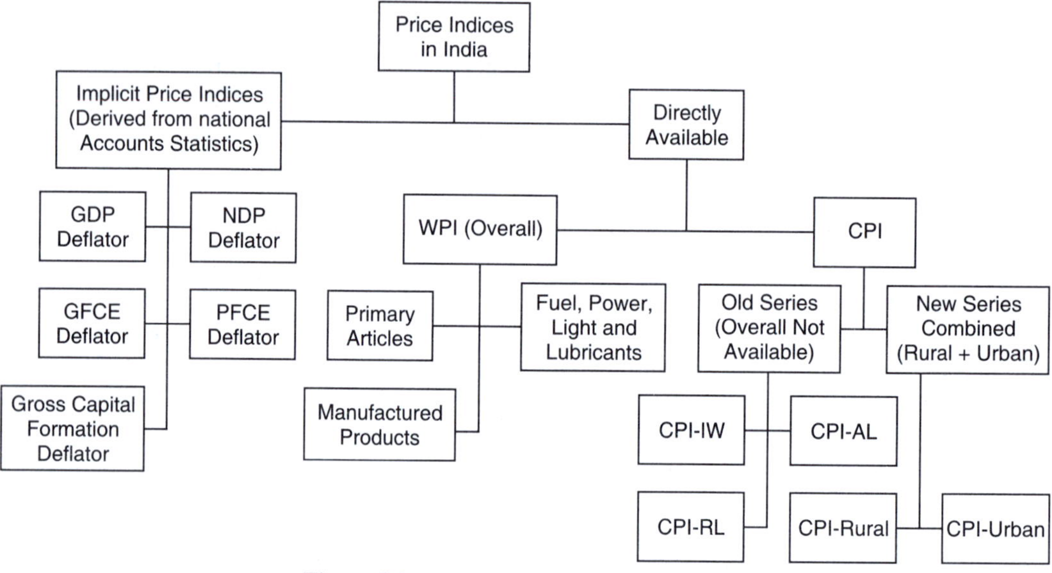

Figure 7.3 Types of Price Indices in India.

Wholesale Price Index

The WPI is the most frequently estimated measurement of price level in India. It is computed at the aggregate level as well as for major groups, subgroups and individual commodities. The WPI (overall) and the WPI for manufactured products are available only at monthly frequency, whereas the WPI for primary articles and fuel, power and lubricants are available even at weekly frequency with a lag of two weeks. Though the WPI (overall) has the widest coverage of commodities (includes even capital and intermediate goods) it does not cover services and non-tradable commodities. In the absence of any other comprehensive measure of inflation, the WPI is used for measuring headline inflation (for definition refer to Section 7.4.3) in India. It is also used by the RBI, Planning Commission and other government organizations for deflating macroeconomic aggregates, forecasting of variables for which prices are prime indicators, and working out escalation costs of projects.

Table 7.3 Price Indices: Sources of Data, Base Year, Commodity Composition and Method of Computation

	WPI	*CPI-IW*	*CPI-AL*	*CPI-RL*	*CPI-Rural*	*CPI-Urban*	*CPI-Combined (Rural +Urban)*	*GDP Deflators*
Source/ Agency	Office of the Economic Advisor/MOI	Labour Bureau/ MOL	Labour Bureau/ MOL	Labour Bureau/ MOL	CSO			NAS, CSO
Method	Laspeyres	Laspeyres						Paasche
Weights allocated on the basis of	Wholesale transactions	Consumer Expenditure Survey First 1958–59 Latest: 2001	First 1956–57 Latest: 1983	First 1983 Latest 1983	NSS 61st round			Current year quantities
Weighting diagram	Country-wide, unique	Horizontal summation of weights of centre specific indices						
Price quotations	Bulk transactions	Purchase price paid by the consumers						–
Nature of the index	Single, national	Weighted average of the centre indices						–
Current Base Year	2004–05	2001	1986–87		2010			2004–05
Number of items in basket	676	120–360	260		225	250	-	All
Major items covered	(i) Primary articles (ii) Fuel, power, light and lubricants (iii) Manufactured products	(i) Food (ii) Pan, supari, tobacco and intoxicants (iii) Fuel and light (iv) Housing (v) Clothing, bedding and footwear (vi) Miscellaneous	(i) Food beverages and tobacco (ii) Fuel and light (iii) Clothing, bedding and footwear (iv) Miscellaneous		(i) Food beverages and tobacco (ii) Fuel and light (iii) Clothing, bedding and footwear (iv) Miscellaneous	(i) Food beverages and tobacco (ii) Fuel and light (iii) Clothing, bedding and footwear (iv) Housing (v) Miscellaneous (education, medical care, transport, communication, etc.)		All items included in the GNP

	WPI	*CPI-IW*	*CPI-AL*	*CPI-RL*	*CPI-Rural*	*CPI-Urban*	*CPI-Combined (Rural + Urban)*	*GDP Deflators*
Number of centres/ quotations	5,482	78	600		1,181	310	1,491	Benchmark surveys
Time lag	2 weeks/ 1 month	1 month	3 weeks		1 month			2 years
Frequency	Weekly: Primary articles and fuel, power, light and lubricants; Monthly: Overall and all sub-heads	Monthly						Yearly

Note: CSO: Central Statistical Organization; MOL: Ministry of Labour; MOI; Ministry of Industry; NAS: National Accounts Statistics

Consumer Price Index (CPI)

At present in India, two series of Consumer Price Index (CPI) are available, viz., old series and new series. In the old series, the CPI is not estimated at the overall level. It is available only for the three categories of consumers, viz., the CPI for Industrial Workers (CPI-IW), the CPI for Rural Labourers (CPI-RL) and the CPI for Agricultural Labourers (CPI-AL) (which is considered as a subset of CPI-RL). The CPI for Urban Non-manual Employees (CPI-UNME) was also calculated in the old series, but since Feberuary 2011 its compilation has been discontinued. Of the old series, the most important one is the CPI-IW. This estimates the cost of living of industrial workers and used mainly for wage and dearness allowance of workers and employees. The coverage of this measure though not as wide as that of the WPI, it is broader than the other CPIs amongst the old series. The CPI-AL and CPI-RL are basically used for revising minimum wages for agriculture and rural labour respectively in different states. Because of the limited coverage, these measures are not considered as very robust national inflation measures. These indices reflect the fluctuations in retail prices pertaining to only specific segments rather than encompassing all the segments of population. Hence, they do not reflect a true picture of the price behaviour in the country.

To overcome the above gap, the CSO has started compiling a new series of CPIs for the entire population, viz, CPI-Rural, CPI-Urban and CPI-Combined (Rural + Urban) since January 2011 with 2010 as the base year. The new series of CPIs, thus, fills the gap of overall CPI. All the CPIs are available with a monthly frequency and a lag varying from two weeks to one month (Table 7.3). As the inflation rate computed on the basis of new series is not available even for one year, so far though the CPI based inflation is reviewed, policy decisions are still not based on this data. With the availability of long time series data, the new series, which are much wider in coverage, would be better reflecting the inflation faced by consumers, and thus, are likely to be used widely.However, it would take three to five years for the new series to stabilize and can be used for policy purposes.

WPI vs CPI-IW vs CPI (Combined)

The inflation based on these series deviates from each other not only in level terms but also in direction (Figure 7.4). Given that the three indices differ not only in terms of the base year but also in terms of methodology of data collection and computation and the coverage of basket of commodities, the deviation in level is expected. However, the large deviation in the direction of the three series, cautions towards using one series as representative of another. We can see from the figure that the deviation in the level as well as direction is much larger in case of CPI (IW) in comparison to the other two series. Hence, it cannot be very representative of the overall inflation in the country. Contrary to CPI (IW), CPI (Combined), though, seems to deviating from the WPI (overall) is moving in tandom with it. Hence, WPI (overall) can be used as a representative of the overall direction of inflation by the consumers or households.

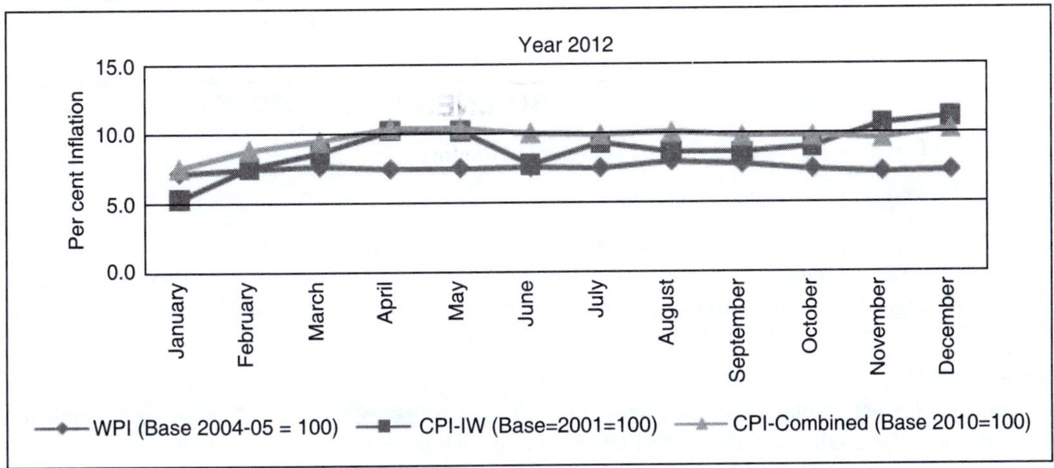

Figure 7.4 Inflation based on WPI, CPI (IW and CPI (Combined)): A Comparison.

CPI (Combined) though is a better representative of price level faced by the household, RBI for policy purpose, is still largely dependent on WPI for the following reasons.

- The WPI is computed on all India basis, whereas the CPI (combined) is just constructed for specific centres and then aggregated to obtain the all India index.
- Though services do not come under the ambit of the WPI, the coverage of non-agriculture products is better in the WPI than that in the CPI (combined). The coverage of tradable items, mainly manufactured products (weight = 64.97), is higher in the case of WPI. A wider coverage of commodities makes the WPI less volatile to relative price changes as compared to the CPI (combined).
- Though the overall WPI is now available only at the same frequency as the CPI (combined), the two sub-indices of WPI, i.e., WPI-Primary Articles and WPI Fuel, Power and Lubricants are still available with weekly frequency with a lag of fortnight. Thus, these two sub-indices can be used for ascertaining some broad estimates of overall inflation.
- Most importantly, CPI (combined) is available only for last two years, whereas WPI is estimated now for many decades. Before the CPI (combined) can be used for policy purpose it is essential to estimate its stability, which will take another four to five years.

Implicit price deflators

Implicit deflators are estimated at the aggregate (GDP deflator) as well as at sub-heads (such as for Net domestic product, Government Final Consumption Expenditure, Private Final Consumption Expenditure and Gross Capital Formation) by the Central Statistical Organization (CSO) from the National Accounts Statistics. Though the GDP deflator is the most comprehensive measure, encompassing the entire spectrum of economic activities, it is not the most widely used measure of inflation in India. A basic limitation of this measure is the low frequency and long lag of over one to two years. Even the general public is less familiar with this measurement. However, for deflating macro-economic variables, such as exchange rate and interest rate, and for research purpose the GDP deflator is widely used by various government organizations and departments.

UNDERSTANDING BUSINESS ENVIRONMENT

UBE 7.2 Inflation in India: Major Contributory Factors

This UBE highlights the major product category that caused inflation in 2009–10 and 2010–11.

In India inflation rate is estimated using various price indices. However, the Wholesale Price Index (WPI) based inflation rate continues to be the most popular measure as it is the longest available with widest coverage of commodities. It remains in the news headlines and most closely monitored by business units and policy makers. It is available for three major categories as follows:

Primary Articles

The primary products group has a weight of 20.1 per cent in the WPI series. This group incorporates major essential commodities of daily use like foodgrains, pulses, fruits, vegetables, milk, and tea. Prices of agricultural commodities are largely supply-driven and follow a seasonal pattern associated with the harvesting and marketing of these crops. Usually there is an uptrend in primary product prices during the summer months, which is the lean season, and this uptrend continues through the festival season in September–October. Thereafter, with the arrival of *kharif* crops in the market in the winter months, price rise in primary commodities gets arrested and remains subdued. Some contra-seasonal departure from this seasonal behaviour may occur on account of abnormal conditions.

Fuel, Power, Light and Lubricants

The fuel, power, light and lubricants sub-group, which has a weight of 14.9 per cent in the WPI, comprises mainly of energy products, fall within the purview of the Administered Price Mechanism (APM). However, with the dismantling of APM with effect from 2002 only prices of petrol, diesel, and kerosene and LPG are administered. Prices of other fuel products such as aviation turbine fuel, naphtha, light diesel oil, furnace oil, bitumen, etc., are market determined.

Manufactured Products

The manufactured products group, representing the core sector of the economy, has a weight of 65.0 per cent in the WPI series, and thus, is the major determinant of inflation in the country. It not only includes processed food products like sugar and edible oils but also includes other important industrial products like textiles, paper, wood products, cement, and iron and steel. The prices in this sector are considered to be demand-driven. Hence, inflation in this group is often an important consideration while formulating monetary policy which is supposed to be more effective in curtailing demand pressures than the supply shortages.

The trend in the WPI based inflation in India and major contributory factors to this trend are presented as follows:

As per GOI (2011), the headline inflation rate (Section 7.4.3) remained moderate during the last decade, with average annual inflation of 5.3 per cent. During this period the average inflation was the highest in fuel group followed by primary articles category. However, during the last five years, on an average, the primary product registered the highest rise in the price level (Figure 7.5).

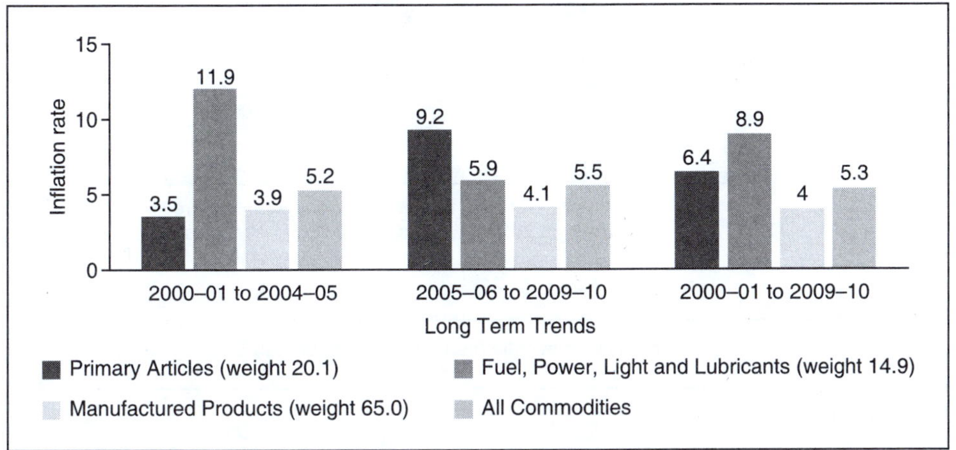

Source: Data for this figure is compiled and estimated from GOI (2011), Economic Survey 2010–11.

Figure 7.5 Average Annual and Long Term Trends in WPI-based Inflation (Base 1993–94 = 100).

Unlike the previous decadal average, the year 2010–11 and 2011–12 witnessed a sharp rise in the average inflation, with average hovering around double digit figure. Though inflation moderated in 2012–13, it still remained above the decadal average and above the comfort zone of the RBI. Both fundamental imbalances in the demand and supply factors contributed to the inflation rate.

During this period on an average all three groups of commodities, i.e., primary articles, fuel, power and lubricants, and manufactured products, recorded inflation rate higher than their decadal rates (Figure 7.6(a)). The inflation rate was the highest in the primary article category in 2010-11 (Figure 7.6(a)), but the manufacturing sector contributed the most to the inflation in this year (Figure 7.6(b)).

Shortfall in the domestic production vis-a-vis domestic demand, emanating from the high growth witnessed by the Indian economy, led to a sharp increase in inflation rate in primary products. Non-food manufactured products, mainly textiles, chemicals and metals also remained under pressure during this period due to significant increase in the cost of production led by increase in the global prices of cotton, petroleum products and metals. Though the contribution of fuel group to inflation in 2010–11 remained comparatively lower, this sector recorded substantial increase in prices due to significant increase in international crude oil and coal prices.

Inflation remained at an elevated level in 2011–12 because of an increase in food prices, a revision in the administered prices of fuel, and increased cost of manufactured products. Though slowdown in growth was expected to ease pressure on inflation during 2011–12, the extent of moderation was constrained by continuous rupee depreciation and high global commodity prices.

Though the price pressure continued to persist from food and fuel segments, inflation moderated in 2012–13, especially in the second half, reaching its lowest level in the past three years. Subdued global commodity prices and range bound fluctuations in the exchange rate helped in moderating domestic inflation, but partly it was also the outcome of slowdown in the growth and the past monetary actions taken by the RBI to contain inflationary pressures.

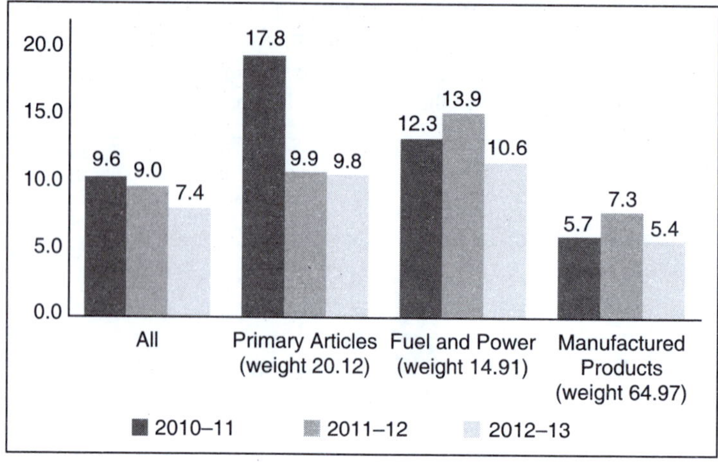

(a) Inflation in India (year to year WPI based)

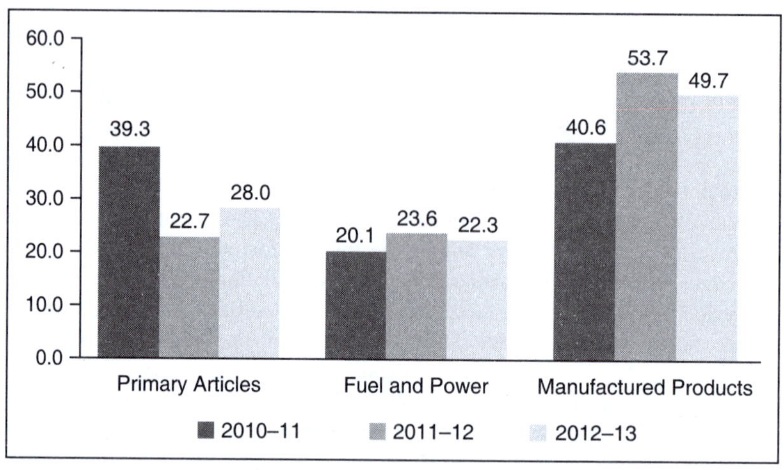

(b) Contribution to Inflation (based on WPI)

Source: Data for these figures is compiled and estimated from the WPI data available from the website of Office of the Economic Advisor, Ministry of Commerce and Industry, GOI, (online) http://eaindustry.nic.in/ as on 2/06/2013.

Figure 7.6 Average Annual Inflation: Contributory Factors (Base 2004–05 = 100).

7.4 TYPES OF INFLATION

Inflation is distinguished into different categories using various criteria. Some of these are detailed hereinafter.

7.4.1 On the Basis of Rate of Inflation

On the basis of magnitude or intensity, inflation is distinguished into four categories as outlined here. However, there is no hard and fast line of demarcation, and there may be a good deal of overlapping between these categories depending on the structure of an economy.

1. Creeping inflation: A rise in the price level at very low rate, or snail's pace, around 2–3 per cent per annum is referred to as the **creeping inflation** or **mild inflation**. In an inflationary scenario profitability of firms increases that encourages them to expand their investment and production activities. Therefore, a slow growth in prices is considered to be conducive for production activities and for an overall growth. As the slow growth in prices creates conducive environment for business and increases employment opportunities, in general, it is preferred over deflation or the zero rate of inflation.

2. Walking inflation: A sustained price increase from 3 to 7 or below 10 per cent is termed as the **walking inflation**. In this scenario, along with the prices of various commodities, wages and other cost components start rising. However, there is a lag between the increase in the prices of commodities and their cost components. This lag keeps the profitability at higher level and motivates producers to produce more even during walking inflation. The situation overall remains conducive for growth, and therefore, as such is not feared by policy makers and producers. However, it also indicates towards a possibility that if not controlled at this stage it may turn into running inflation or even hyperinflation. Thus, walking inflation, though not risky in itself, is a sign of ensuing danger and strains the skills of policy makers in designing measures to combat inflation.

3. Running inflation: A sustained price rise from 10 to 20 per cent per annum is known as the **running inflation**. Inflation above two digit level fuels speculation. Along with the prices of final commodities, their cost of production, in such a scenario, increases substantially. Firms start losing their competitiveness domestically as well as internationally. The risk in business activities and the cases of business failure increases. The overall interest rate appreciates, whereas there is a build up of pressure for depreciation of the domestic currency. It is a clear indication of a problem that requires urgent attention and formulation of strong fiscal, monetary or even direct control measures.

4. Hyperinflation: The running inflation, if not controlled, turns into the **hyperinflation**, which is also known as the **galloping** or **jumping inflation**. Prices rise at extremely rapid rate of 20–30 per cent and above. Money ceases to be useful as a medium of exchange and a store of value. People switch to barter or adopt some other country's currency as the medium of exchange or store of value. Monetary authorities lose control over inflation. People expect further rise in prices. A large uncertainty hovers around the horizons and speculative activities take over. Producers, though uncertain, in general, expect higher prices for their products in the coming period. Expecting higher prices, they withdraw the already produced goods from the market and hoard those in anticipation of higher prices in the coming period. In the process, resources, which are limited, get diverted from productive activities to speculative activities. Households become inflation conscious and spend money at a much faster rate, raising the velocity of circulation. Saving declines and the available saving is diverted in those assets which protect their purchasing power, such as real estate and gold. The Government fails to raise enough resources from borrowing, i.e., non-inflationary sources. Failing to raise resources from the market, it is compelled to opt for deficit financing, which, as discussed in Section 8.7, further fuels inflation. As there is pressure on borrowings, the rate of interest also increases.

Domestic products lose their competitiveness in the international market, which worsen the balance of payment, leading to a depreciation of the domestic currency, loss in investors' confidence in the domestic economy and flight of capital from the country. Hyperinflation, thus, can have devastating impact on real output and employment (as was the case in Zimbabwe (UBE 7.3)). It can jeopardize the macro-economic stability; and, therefore, is dreaded by all, i.e., households, producers and governments.

7.4.2 On the Basis of Degree of Control

1. Open inflation: A continuous increase in prices without any interruption and control from the government or any other authority is known as the **open inflation**.

2. Suppressed inflation: In certain economies, left to the market forces, conditions exist for a substantial rise in the price level. However, the government prevents price rise by imposing ceilings and pursuing rationing. For example, we have seen in January 2011 that the market prices of onion were ranging between ₹50 to ₹80 in different markets. The government of India intervened in the market by controlling the price of onion at ₹35 by effecting sales through its agencies NAFED and National Cooperative Consumers› Federation of India (NCCF) at that price. This situation is known as the **suppressed inflation** as there is a potential of prices flaring up on decontrol and removal of price ceilings. The symptoms of suppressed inflation are visible in the long queues of buyers waiting at the ration shops and other outlets. Suppressed inflation imposes additional administrative burden on the government. In addition to setting the prices of controlled commodities, the government needs to decide on the hierarchy of price controllers, supply officers, rationing officers, and set the rules at which rationing can be carried out. Often, rationing of goods breeds black marketing and corruption, diverts demand towards uncontrolled or un-rationed goods, and thus, shifts resources towards unproductive or undesirable channels. In the absence of enough supply, consumers are also made to postpone their present demand to a future period, which builds up an inflationary pressure in the coming period.

UNDERSTANDING BUSINESS ENVIRONMENT

UBE 7.3 Zimbabwe: A Case of Hyperinflation

Major reasons for hyperinflation in Zimbabwe have been pointed out in this UBE.

Zimbabwe, an African country, got independence in 1980. Since then it started facing rampant inflation. At the time of independence inflation stood at 7 per cent. The very next year it crossed two digit figure. By the early 21st century the situation worsened further, with the country registering three digit inflation by 2002 and four digit inflation by 2006 (Table 7.4). The latest release on year on year inflation by the Reserve Bank of Zimbabwe (RBZ), quoted the inflation rate to be 231150888.87 per cent in July 2008. Zimbabwean hyperinflation in 2008 was the second worst in the world history, next to the one in Hungary in 1946. It is difficult to assess the inflationary situation in Zimbabwe during August 2008 to November 2009, because the government stopped filing official inflation statistics. The situation came under control in December 2009 when the country experienced negative inflation rate of –7.7 per cent.

Zimbabwe was one of the strongest African nation before the beginning of this century. It maintained positive economic growth throughout the 1980s and 1990s. However, it faced continuous negative growth rate since 2000: –5 per cent in 2001, –18 per cent in 2003, –12.6 per cent in 2008. As a result of continuous negative GDP growth rate and hyperinflation, by 2005, the purchasing power of the average Zimbabwean dropped to the same levels in real terms as it was in 1953. At present Zimbabwe is one of the poorest nations in the world with unemployment of more than 90 per cent and one-fifth of the population infected with HIV/AIDS.

Table 7.4 Inflation Rate in Zimbabwe (Year on Year)

Year	*Inflation rate*	*Year*	*Inflation rate*
1990	15.5	1999	58.5
1991	24.3	2000	55.9
1992	42.1	2001	71.9
1993	27.5	2002	133.2
1994	22.3	2003	365.0
1995	22.5	2004	350.0
1996	21.7	2005	237.8
1997	18.9	2006	1016.7
1998	31.7	2007	6723.7

Source: Reserve Bank of Zimbabwe, (Online) (http://www.rbz.co.zw/about/inflation.asp), as on 20/5/2011.

Poor and unpredictable policies pursued by the government were behind the poor economic performance and hyperinflation in Zimbabwe between 2003 to 2009. These policies included the following:

Fast track land reform programme: Land reform in Zimbabwe empowered the government to buy land compulsorily for redistribution and restricted the size of the land holdings, depriving the farmers the advantage of mechanization and **economies of scale** (i.e., the advantages resulting from a large scale production) and increasing their cost of production. The programme also imposed land tax, further increasing the prices of agriculture products.

Large fiscal deficit: Government expenditure remained at unsustainable levels due to hike in salaries for soldiers, policemen and other civil servants, and payments on past borrowings. The expenditure was financed initially, by uncontrolled borrowing and, subsequently, by printing new notes, fuelling inflation year after year.

Unrealistic price controls: Government tried to control prices by setting ceilings that were nowhere closer to market reality (in February 2007, the government had declared inflation illegal), causing various distortions in resource allocation. Due to such repression the unofficial estimates put the inflation rate to be much higher than what has been quoted in official statistics.

Highly overvalued exchange rate: Zimbabwe pursued the fixed exchange rate regime, making exports uncompetitive and imports cheaper. Overvalued exchange rate, by making exports dearer and reducing demand for domestic produced goods, discouraged domestic production. At the same time, by encouraging imports it kept the domestic expenditure at higher level, thus fuelling inflation further. Hyperinflation led to a sharp decline in the value of Zimbabwean Dollar., Consequently, there was a loss in the Zimbabwean currency. Public simply refused to accept it, which made the government abandon its own currency on 1st July 2009 in favour of the major ones including Euro and the United States Dollar.

7.4.3 On the Basis of Coverage

1. Headline inflation: **Headline inflation** is the overall inflation faced by consumers. In most countries, it is estimated on the basis of overall CPI, which covers all the commodities in the consumption basket of a typical consumer.

2. Core inflation: Some of the commodities included in the basket associated with the overall CPI are subject to supply and policy shocks, flairing up the prices of these commodities and headline inflation. For example, we often notice a spurt in prices of agriculture products in the event of monsoon failure. Similarly, geopolitical tensions in Middle-East and North Africa (MENA) region often cause a big spike in oil prices. Many-a-time, the impact of such shocks is temporary, which obscures normal inflationary environment or trend in inflation.

To ascertain the trend in inflation, when it is obscured by temporary phenomenon, the core inflation is estimated. **Core inflation** is defined as the overall CPI less the prices of sensitive commodities, especially food and energy prices. It can be estimated using various methods as outlined in Box 7.2.

Box 7.2 Core Inflation: Estimation Methods

There are several methods to estimate core inflation as follows:

Exclusion method: In exclusion method, core inflation is estimated by taking out the price of a fixed, pre-specified set of items from the overall CPI basket as indicated in Figure 7.7. The excluded items are either highly price sensitive or subject to supply shocks.

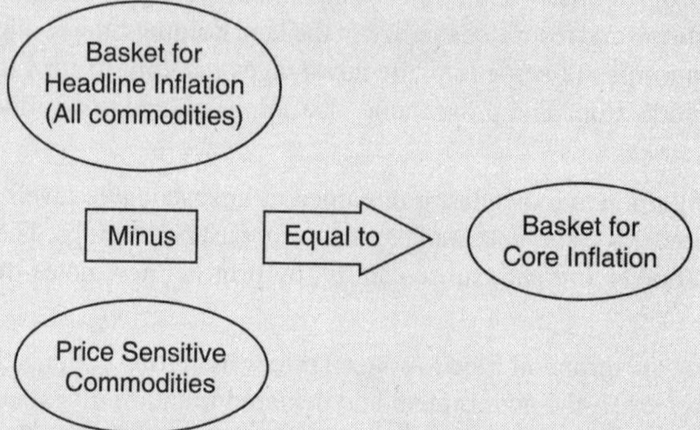

Figure 7.7 Basket for Headline and Core Inflation.

Because of its simplicity, the exclusion method is the most commonly used approach to estimate core inflation. Most countries exclude food and energy items, which are considered to be highly volatile and most susceptible to supply or external shocks, from the overall basket. For example, the US estimates excludes food and energy prices. Similarly, Japan excludes fresh food and Thailand excludes fresh food and energy from the overall CPI. However, there are other items which are also excluded by some countries. For example, Germany excludes indirect taxes from the overall CPI, whereas the UK excludes mortgage interest rates from retail price index. Peru excludes nine price sensitive commodities including chicken, potato, onion, bread, fish, eggs, citrus fruits, vegetables and urban transport.

Statistical methods: The extraction method is criticized on the ground that the basket of commodities whose prices are volatile is not time invariant, i.e., over a period of time different commodities become price sensitive. Therefore, excluding certain commodities permanently will result in loss of information about underlying inflation; it will either under or over estimate the core inflation. To overcome this problem, various statistical methods are adopted which, rather than removing certain commodities permanently, only exclude those commodities that exhibit extreme price movements during a given period. These techniques remove extreme (positive or negative) or outlier price changes from the overall inflation rate. Depending on the commodities exhibiting extreme price movements, the set of excluded commodities changes every month. Trimmed median and weighted median are two widely used statistical methods. Trimmed mean method takes the average inflation rate after excluding a specified percentage of extreme price changes, while the weighted median simply takes the median inflation rate.

Econometric methods: The methods described above, however, are devoid of theoretical interpretation, and hence, make little economic sense. Therefore, apart from exclusion and other methods, central banks internally also try to estimate core inflation by estimating relationship between inflation and the variables that have been identified to affect inflation on the basis of economic theory and reasoning. For example, the core inflation can be specified as a function of growth in money supply, output growth, change in international oil prices and the headline inflation. The estimated parameter values, along with the actual values of explanatory variables, are then used for estimating core inflation in any given period.

Monetary policy is based on the core inflation when there is a divergent trend in it and the headline inflation as illustrated in UBE 7.4.

UNDERSTANDING BUSINESS ENVIRONMENT

UBE 7.4 Does Headline Inflation Matter?

Policy makers often face a dilemma whether they should base changes in monetary policy on headline inflation or core inflation. This UBE addresses this issue by focussing on the inflationary trend in two structurally different countries.

The world had just started recovering from the recessionary conditions faced in 2009. The recovery was, however, slow and subject to downside risks. Many advanced countries were struggling hard to give a boost to their slogging economies. Similarly, many emerging market economies were striving to retain their high growth rates. The situation advocated pursuance of easy monetary policy, i.e., expansion of money supply and cheaper credit so that the demand for goods and services was enhanced. Central banks were, however, cautious in taking such a step and debated and deliberated on this issue widely, with views divided? Why?

Central banks were cautious in implementing easy monetary policy because of two reasons. First, there is a trade-off between growth and inflation. High growth is often associated with high inflation. Though a mild rate of inflation is sought after, a high inflation rate is not desirable because it jeopardizes the working of an economy by creating uncertainties and diversion of resources in unproductive areas. Second, many central banks (such as the central bank of New Zealand, the UK, Canada, Australia, South Korea, Egypt, South Africa, Iceland, and Brazil) have been pursuing **inflation targeting framework**, i.e., they pursue monetary policy in such a way that inflation does not go beyond the set targets. Easy monetary policy, endangering inflation targeting framework, places central banks at the risk of losing their credibility in controlling inflation.

In 2010 and 2011 the headline inflation rate was heading north in many advanced and emerging market economies (Table 7.5) because of increasing food and international oil prices. Containment of inflationary pressures, thus, demanded pursuance of tight monetary policy. The situation of slow recovery and contemporaneous inflation, however, made the policy choice for central bankers more difficult. Similarly, in India, in the last two years, inflation has remained at elevated level, demanding contraction in monetary policy. Slowdown in the economy, however, has constrained such a decision.

The analysis below reflects on this issue—whether governments should contain headline inflation when recovery is on its way—by analyzing the scenario of two structurally different countries—the USA and India.

Table 7.5 Global Inflation

Country/Region	*CPI inflation (y-o-y) (End March)*			
	2010	*2011*	*2012*	*2013*
Developed Economies				
Australia	2.9	2.7#	1.6#	2.5#
Canada	1.4	2.2$	1.9	1.0
Euro Area	1.6	2.7	2.7	1.7
Israel	3.2	4.2$	1.9	1.3
Japan	– 1.1	–0.5$	0.5	–0.9
Korea	2.3	4.1	2.6	1.3
UK	3.4	4.4$	3.5	2.8
US	2.3	2.7	2.7	1.5
Developing Economies				
Brazil	5.2	6.3	5.2	6.6
India	14.9	8.8$	9.4	10.4
China	2.4	5.4	3.6	2.1
Indonesia	3.4	6.7	4.0	5.9
Philippines	4.4	4.8	2.6	3.2
Russia	6.5	9.5$	3.7$	7.3$
South Africa	5.1	3.7$	6.1$	6.0
Thailand	3.4	3.1	3.5	2.7

#: Q4 (January–March)

$: February

Note: For India, data on inflation since 2012 pertain to New CPI (Combined: rural + urban). Prior to 2012 it pertains to CPI for Industrial Workers.

Source: RBI (various issues), Macroeconomic and Monetary Developments.

Inflation Scenario in the US

In the US the headline inflation remained at elevated level between October 2010 and April 2012 (Figure 7.8) because of an increase in international prices of oil as well as food, posing a question whether the monetary policy to be tightened by raising the policy rates to curtail inflationary pressures or eased to give a further boost to the economy that was underway recovery.

The policy makers and economists there were divided on this issue as detailed hereinafter.

Views Opposing Tight Monetary Policy

The group opposing tight monetary policy, including economist Paul Krugman and also policy makers like Charls Evans President of Fed Chicago, was basing its argument on the core inflation. This group was arguing that the inflation developments were obscured by price shocks in food and fuel groups that had boosted "headline" (or overall) inflation rates.

The group further argued that the working of the markets for products like food and fuel group is quite unlike the working of markets like labour market. The labour market adjusts sluggishly in response to imbalances between demand and supply, hence, wages adjust slowly and have long lasting impact on inflation. In contrast to these markets, in the markets for commodities like food and fuel the adjustments arising from demand and supply factors are faster and sharper. However, these adjustments often remain specific to those markets, without getting transmitted to other commodities. Hence, the impact of changes in prices of these commodities on overall inflation is temporary; these changes do not affect the underlying long-term trend in inflation, i.e., the core inflation. Thus, abstracting from these shocks, the group argued that, the inflationary pressures, was subdued.

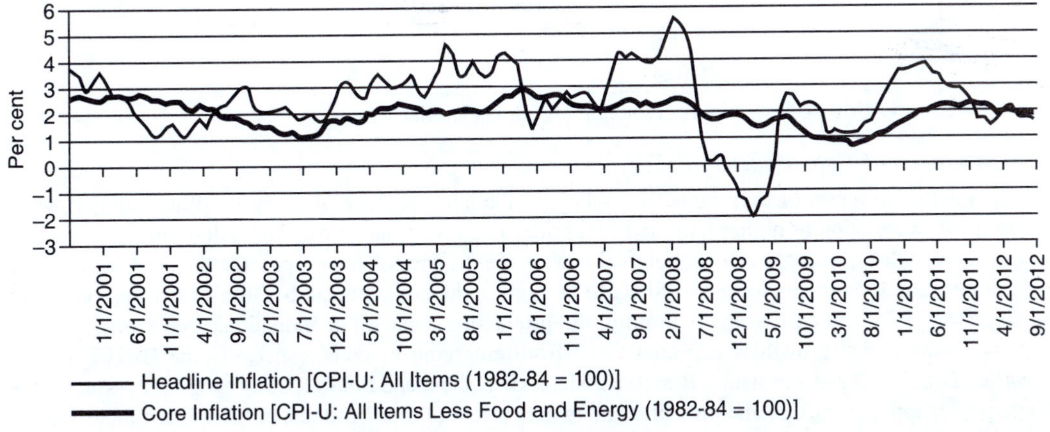

Source: The figure is plotted on the basis of data available from Federal Reserve Bank of Cleveland, (online) http://www.clevelandfed.org/research/data/us-inflation/chartsdata/index.cfm?state1=1&state2=2&state3=0&state4=0&startDate=01/01/2002&endDate=01/13/2013&datatype=2&freq=monthly, as on 2/6/2013.

Figure 7.8 Headline and Core Inflation in the USA.

Drawing on the historical observation, the group also claimed that the core inflation had been quite stable in the USA (Figure 7.8) in the last few decades. The core and headline inflation do not move in tandem. There had been no episodes of the headline inflation leading to a rise in the core inflation, implying little linkage between the two. The divergence between the two widen sharply whenever there is a sharp rise in food and fuel prices. This was the case in 2007–08 as well as in 2010 and 2011

Similar argument was made in IMF (2001) study. Though now dated, the study by relating the headline and core inflation to their lagged values, indicated that during 1965–82, the lagged value of headline inflation was one the dominant factors explaining both the headline and core inflation. However, it was no longer of a concern during 1983–2001 (Table 7.6). The results of the study implied that the price shocks that drove a wedge between the overall and core inflation were short lived and were not feeding into the core inflation. Therefore, the study supported the view that monetary policy changes can be based on the core inflation rather than the headline inflation.

Defending its views, the group further argued that the core inflation primarily reflects demand conditions, whereas increase in the prices of food and fuel items in 2010 were due to supply shocks. Since monetary policy is more effective in controlling demand pull inflation rather than the one led by supply factors, it should be based on the core inflation. Hence, monetary policy did not require tightening.

Table 7.6 Regression Results for Overall and Core CPI Inflation

Dependent Variable	*Parameter on 12-month lagged inflation*[1]	
	Overall	*Core*
	1965M1–1982M12	
US Overall	1.51 (6.7)	– 0.94 (3.6)
US Core	1.22 (7.9)	– 0.54 (3.1)
	1983M1–2001M4	
US Overall	0.14 (0.5)	0.15 (0.16)
US Core	0.14 (0.6)	0.40 (1.6)
	1997M1–2001M2	
US Overall	0.30 (1.0)	– 1.40 (2.0)
US Core	0.26 (0.4)	– 0.37 (2.3)

Source: IMF (2001), *World Economic Outlook*, October.

Views in Support of Tight Monetary Policy

The arguments in support of tight monetary policy, in the latest episode of rising headline inflation, were based on the expectation of higher food and fuel prices in the coming period. Defending its argument, the group indicated that, the continued geopolitical tensions in the MENA region posed a threat of further hike in oil prices. The food prices were also likely to be high in the period ahead because of two reasons; first, the diversion of land to cash crops is limiting the production capacity of individual food crops. Second, majority of the global growth is expected to be from emerging markets, especially the **BRICS** (group indicating Big Five States consisting Brazil, Russia, India, China and South Africa) economies which have a huge population, putting demand pressures and raising prices of food products further. These factors, apart from directly affecting the food prices, will also have second round impacts on prices in general through expectations because expected inflation often is incorporated in economic decisions. Hence, a shock that is considered to be temporary in nature will have a generalized enduring impact through second round impacts, affecting the inflationary trend, i.e., the core inflation.

Inflation Scenario in India

India has also experienced supply shocks in food and fuel prices. Statistical estimates indicate that about one-third of the total variation in the headline inflation are due to supply shocks in food and oil with impact of oil shocks having relatively greater impact. The nature of inflation, however, is different in India than that in the US. A closer look at Figure 7.9 indicates that, unlike the US, in India headline and core inflation move in tandem. Deviations between the two do occur, but gradually they merge leading to similar movement in the two inflation rates, implying that shocks to price sensitive commodities not only affect the headline inflation, but get fed into the core inflation by increasing the cost of production of non-food manufactured products. The manufacturers, in turn, are able to pass on the higher cost of production to consumers in the form of higher prices.

RBI (2010) study based on Granger causality test, which is an econometrics test, also supports this observation. Without getting into technical details, we can see that the results of the study suggest that there is a unidirectional causality with 'food and fuel inflation', reflecting the supply shocks Granger cause the changes in core inflation (Table 7.7). Thus, supply shocks in India contribute to second round effects, which often materialize with a lag and operate through inflation expectations, wage negotiations and price setting behaviour of firms, and influence the long-term inflationary trends in the country.

[1]Absolute values of t-statistics in parentheses, adjusted for MA (12) error terms. Constant terms in the regressions have been suppressed.

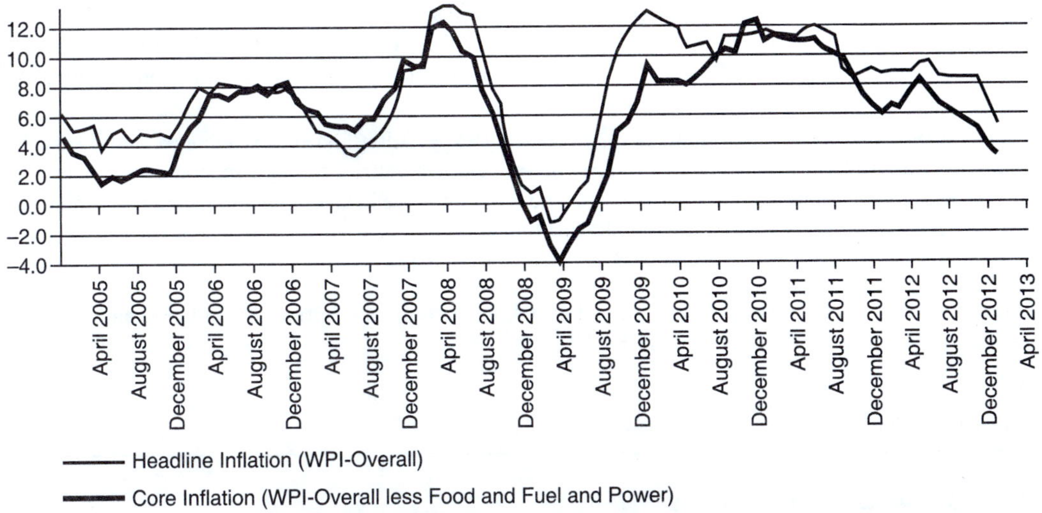

Figure 7.9 Headline and Core Inflation in India.

Note: In India, headline inflation is based on overall WPI. Estimate of the core inflation is not available from official sources on a regular basis; hence, it is estimated as WPI Overall – Weighted average of WPI of Primary and Manufactured Food Items and Fuel and Power.

Source: The WPI (overall) data for the chart is compiled and estimated from Government of India, Ministry of Commerce and Industry, Office of the Economic Advisor, (Online) http://eaindustry.nic.in/, as on 2/6/2013.

Table 7.7 Relation between Food Inflation and Core Inflation

Null Hypothesis	*F-Statistics*	*Prob.*
Core Inflation does not Granger cause food and fuel inflation	1.09	0.34
Food and fuel inflation does not Granger cause core inflation	2.73	0.07

Source: RBI (2010) Annual Report.

Thus, in India headline inflation can be used for representing long-term inflationary trend and the monetary policy can very well be based on headline inflation trend.

Lessons for Monetary Policy

So, what matters for monetary policy: headline inflation or core inflation? The answer, as we have seen from the inflationary scenario in two structurally different economies, depends on the following factors:

1. When a shock is in the market for a commodity which is subject to supply shocks leading to temporary spikes in prices (such as food and fuel), then the link between headline inflation and core inflation will be weak. In such situations, headline inflation does not matter much; the core inflation needs to be considered while formulating monetary policy.
2. Conversely, if price change is an outcome of imbalances in a market that adjusts sluggishly to demand and supply mismatch, such as labour market, then the impact of price change will be enduring, the link between headline and core inflation will be strong. In such a situation monetary policy needs to look into the headline inflation to contain inflationary pressures at the initial stages.

3. If a shock is expected to be temporary and does not have any effect on the expectations of inflation of market participants, the long-term decisions will not be influenced by it. The impact of such a shock will remain confined to headline inflation. In such a situation core inflation can guide the monetary policy changes.
4. Conversely, if a shock influences inflationary expectation and that is incorporated by market participants in their decisions then inflation gets generalized through second round effects. In such a situation, both the headline and core inflation move in tandem; hence, changes in monetary policy can be very well based on the headline inflation.

References

Evans and Fisher (2011), What are the implications of rising commodity prices for inflation and monetary policy?, Chicago Fed Letter, May 2011, No. 286.

IMF (2001), *World Economic Outlook*, October.

RBI (2010), Annual Report.

7.4.4 On the Basis of Causes

Inflation is caused by either demand pressures or supply pressures as detailed below.

Demand-pull Inflation

An autonomous or exogenous increase in any of the components of demand increases the aggregate demand in an economy. In the presence of excess capacity, an increase in the aggregate demand will not have any impact on prices. However, if the supply is limited or the economy is operating at its potential, defined by the full employment level of output, changes in the demand exert pressure on prices. Thus, an excess of aggregate demand over the full employment level of output creates an inflationary gap (Box 7.3) and drives up prices. The inflation taking place due to demand pressures is known as the **demand-pull inflation**.

The excess of demand over the supply can emerge for any of the following reasons:

1. Increase in the quantity of money: Some channels of demand pressures are the government borrowings from the central bank or borrowing of financial institutions from the central bank. The central bank often prints new notes to meet the borrowing requirements of the government or financial institutions, which increase the supply of new notes and money supply in an economy.

2. Increase in business outlays or government expenditure: An increase in business outlays or government expenditure increases money income with the public, and hence, demand, without a corresponding increase in the supply of real output.

3. Foreign expenditure on goods and services: Foreign spending on domestically produced goods and services increases exports. Given the supply of domestically produced goods, it creates an excess of demand. This is an important factor for those countries where exports form a major share of the GDP. However, if along with exports there is a matching increase in imports, the net impact on demand will be nil.

Box 7.3 Inflationary Gap vs Deflationary Gap

The **inflationary gap** refers to an excess of aggregate demand (Consumption Expenditure (C) + Investment Expenditure (I) + Government Expenditure (G)) over the available full employment level of output.

To understand this concept more clearly, refer to Figure 7.10. The 45° line in this figure represents all those points where demand is equal to supply. The intersection of this line with the aggregate demand curve ($C + I + G$) represents the full employment level of output (Yf). An autonomous increase in the government expenditure shifts the aggregate demand to $C + I + G$. Given the output at Yf, the shift in the demand curve creates an excess of demand over the available supply. This excess, represented by AB, is known as the inflationary gap as it puts pressure on prices to rise.

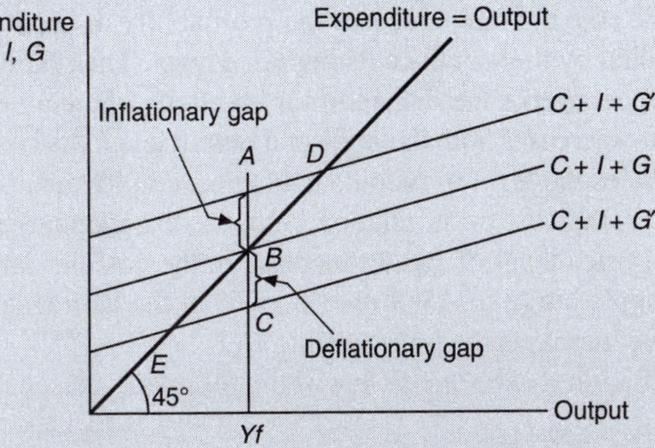

Figure 7.10 Inflationary vs. Deflationary Gap.

On the other hand, an autonomous decline in any of the demand components results in a shift in the aggregate demand curve below the full employment level of output. For example, in Figure 7.10 an autonomous decline in the government expenditure to G≤ shifts the aggregate demand curve to $C + I + G$. This creates a gap of BC between Yf and the actual aggregate demand. As an excess of supply over the demand results in lowering of prices, the gap BC is also known as the **deflationary gap**.

The demand pull inflation increases output as well as inflation. Figure 7.11 depicts this aspect of the demand pull inflation. Suppose the economy is operating at Y_0 level of output with the overall price level of P_0. An exogenous increase in any of the demand components shifts the demand curve from AD_0 to AD_1. Given the aggregate supply curve AS_0, the shift in the demand curve increases the price level to P_1.

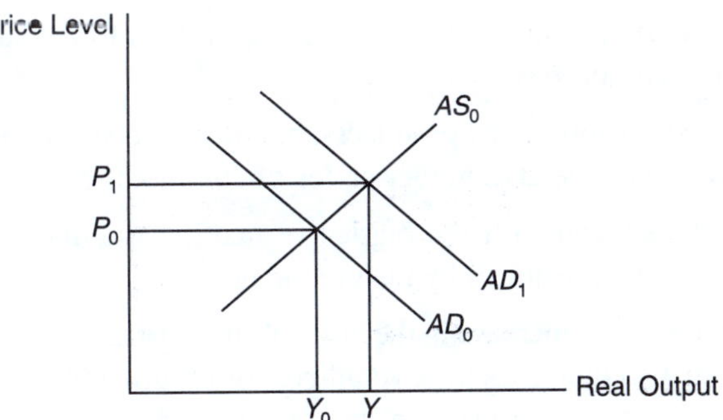

Figure 7.11 Demand Pull Inflation.

Cost-Push (or Supply Side) Inflation

An autonomous increase in any of the cost components of production, such as raw materials, intermediate goods, wages and mark-up, can increase the overall cost of production. Often, the higher cost of production gets passed on to the consumers in the form of higher prices of final commodities. An increase in the overall price level due to cost pressures is known as the **cost-push inflation**.

An increase in the cost per unit squeezes the profitability of producers. Thus, it reduces the amount of output supplied by them at the existing price level. The fall in the supply pushes up the overall price level. Hence, unlike the demand-pull inflation, where an exogenous shift in any of the demand components increases both the price and output level, the cost-push inflation increases the price level, but reduces the level of output, and hence, employment.

Figure 7.12 depicts the cost-push inflation. Suppose the economy is operating at Y_0 level of output with the overall price level of P_0. An increase in the cost per unit reduces the supply and shifts the aggregate supply curve to AS_1 from AS_0. Given the aggregate demand curve AD_0, the shift in the supply curve increases the price level to P_1.

The cost-push inflation can be due to any of the following reasons:

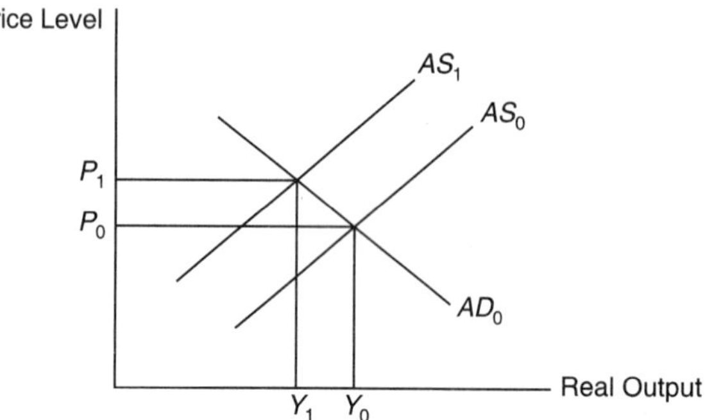

Figure 7.12 Cost-push Inflation.

1. Higher wage rates: The wage that a labourer receives reflects his productivity or contribution to the product. However, powerful trade unions, sometimes, may successfully secure higher wages for workers, even greater than their productivity. This increase in the cost of production, without corresponding increase in the productivity, often gets passed on to consumers in the form of an increase in the prices of commodities.

2. Higher profit margins: Monopolist producers, hoarders and speculators can hike their profit margins exogenously which can lead to higher prices of commodities.

3. Higher taxes: Producers can shift the burden of taxes, particularly indirect taxes, such as excise duties and sales tax, to consumers by raising the prices of goods.

4. Higher prices of inputs: An increase in the price of fuel, energy and other basic ingredients in the process of production also increases the overall cost of production that quite often gets passed on to consumers in the form of higher prices of final goods and services.

5. Other factors: A fall in agricultural production, due to insufficient or excessive or irregular rainfall or other natural calamities, like floods, droughts and famine, reduces the aggregate supply and raises the prices of agricultural goods. Similarly, a fall in industrial production, on account of strikes, lockouts, breakdown of power supply, etc., may reduce the supply of industrial output and increase the prices of intermediate goods, which may lead to the cost-push inflation.

Relationship between Demand-Pull and Cost-Push Inflation

The demand-pull and cost-push inflation are interrelated and move, quite often, in tandem. They may even co-exist (UBE 7.5).

The demand-pull inflation may increase the demand for factors of production, leading to an increase in the prices of factors of production. An increase in the prices of factors, as noted above, causes cost-push inflation.

The cost-push inflation, as a consequence of higher compensation to employees, may result in higher demand for goods and services, which may turn into the demand-pull inflation. Though the cost-push inflation can continue to grow, it cannot persist unless there is an excess demand. The cost-push inflation is difficult to control even through monetary and fiscal measures.

UNDERSTANDING BUSINESS ENVIRONMENT

UBE 7.5 Disentangling Drivers of Manufacturing Inflation: Cotton Textiles

This UBE highlights that both demand pull and cost push factors are behind manufacturing inflation in India.

Manufacturing occupies an unusually large weight (65 per cent), relative to its share in national output (and omitting services), in the WPI; hence it has exaggerated bearing on inflation measurement in India. A particular policy focus is on 'core inflation' in non-food manufacturing (Reserve Bank of India: RBI). The reason that core manufacturing inflation' occupies importance is because it is thought to be less prone to supply shocks and a more accurate gauge of demand side pressures. A standard demand-side inflation explanation: if output growth is above some sustainable potential output (supply capacity), then inflation results. This 'Phillips-curve' explanation of a short-term inverse relationship between output (employment) and prices (wages) is widely used by policymakers to gauge inflation, and take demand-side policy measures, such as tighter monetary and fiscal policy to manage inflation. This is also sometimes invoked more broadly to explain why core inflation in emerging countries such as India, China, and Brazil is recently much higher (6-9 per cent) because of their faster growth (signs of possible 'overheating'), versus low inflation (2–3 per cent) in developed countries.

While this demand-side focus may be appropriate, a complicating factor in emerging markets such as India is also the influence of unprecedented international commodity price rises in recent years as a 'cost-push' cause of manufacturing inflation. The recent rise in global commodity prices, in turn, is judged to be, at least partly, the result of very loose monetary policies in developed countries. Consider textiles, a major manufacturing sector in India. Cost-push pressures start with raw cotton prices, which spill over to yarn costs, then to woven cloth, and finally the finished products: textiles, garments, and others. A closer look at this sector would hence be useful.

Figure 7.13 shows the broad picture of what has been happening to different components of cotton textile prices (January 2008-January 2012). As is evident, raw cotton prices, which ballooned in global markets in August 2010 and reached a peak in March-April 2011 and have since been moderating, although still well above historical levels, have been a major influence on subsequent manufacturing stages' prices. What happens to prices of the output of spinning mills, cotton yarn, is heavily influenced by cotton prices. In turn, these heavily influence all subsequent stages such as cotton textiles and garments. Formal econometric tests confirm that. The point: even traditional 'core' manufacturing inflation is not without large 'supply-side' shocks from world markets in key manufacturing sectors in India (and other emerging countries); accordingly, we need to be appropriately cautious about unhesitatingly using traditional developed country theories and measures of demand-side pressures as causes of core inflation.

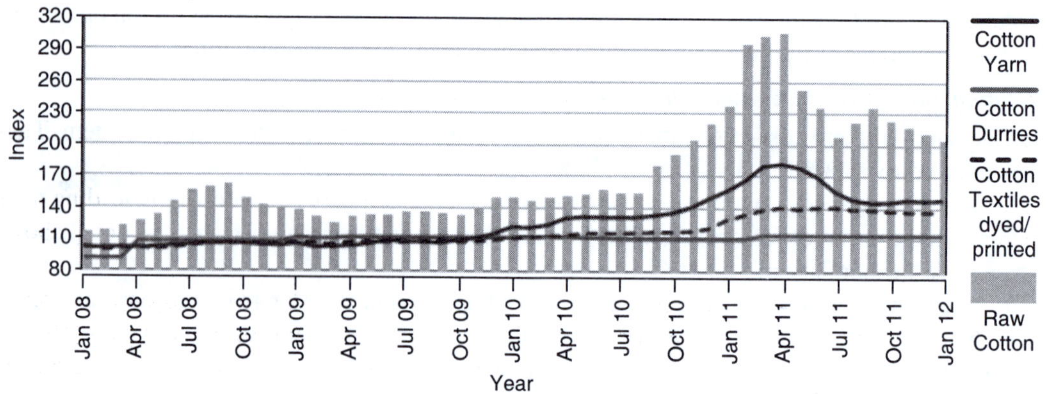

Figure 7.13 Prices of Cotton Textiles: Global Input Shocks vs Domestic Demand Pressures and Wages.

A further analytical question is: Can we disentangle raw material cost-push price pressures from, say, labour costs? Later stages of cotton textile manufacturing are especially interesting, because after raw material costs, labour costs dominate. Indeed, visually one can see that the influence of raw cotton costs drops the further down the chain one goes—say cotton textiles dyed or printed or artisanal cotton durries. Figure 7.14 shows the results of an exercise: imputed labour (and other) cost movements in textiles, using

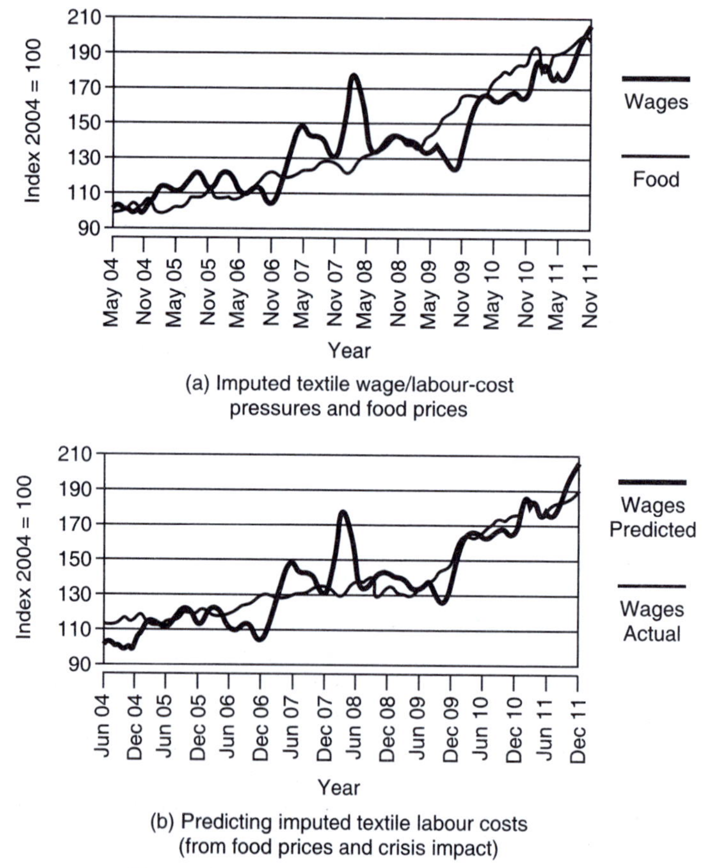

Figure 7.14 Labour Cost in Manufacturing.

the (econometric) residuals after taking out raw material costs (raw cotton, yarn, or cloth, as the case may be, at each stage). The results are also compared to food price movements. They suggest two conclusions: (1) nominal labour-cost pressures were rising prior to the global crisis in 2008, but fell sharply after the crisis (till late 2009) and have since started to rise again; and (2) real wage movements are, however, much more moderate, as labour costs appear to track food prices (with a lag). The analysis was cross-checked with other labour intensive industries (leather, wool). One further key analytical insight: traditional artisanal industries (carpet making, weaving), which employ massive numbers, are faring worst in imputed earnings with sharply rising raw material input costs and rising market costs outside.

Three broad conclusions: (a) recent very high inflation episode in India was influenced heavily by global commodity price shocks, even in 'core' manufacturing, as in textiles; (b) imputed nominal wage inflation, from labour-intensive industries, has been recovering and rising, but is influenced by rising food price inflation; and (c) whether Mahatma Gandhi National Rural Employment Guarantee Act (MGNREGA) and other pressures have independently contributed to this or were simply following food prices cannot be easily disentangled; the latter explanation is preferable. A domestic demand-side explanation of recent 'core' inflation in India may merit caution and warrants further analytical work.

Source: GOI (2012), Economic Survey, 2011–12.

7.4.5 On the Basis of Predictability of Inflation

Anticipated or Expected Inflation

Expectations play an important role in the dynamism of inflation. While taking economic decisions, economic units make predictions about the expected level of inflation in the coming period on the basis of past and present trends in price levels. While forming expectations, they also depend on the forecasts available from various reports and policy documents, and economic forecasts made by professional research organizations and business units. They closely watch the values of certain economic variables that precede inflation (known as the **leading indicators**) and provide important information regarding the movements in inflation rate. Some of these leading indicators are changes in money supply and credit availability, rates of interest, fiscal deficit and monetized deficit, changes in tax rates, movements in exchange rates, trend in wages and salaries, infrastructure and production bottlenecks, movements in the balance of payment, agricultural output and supply shocks, natural calamities, etc. The so determined rate of inflation, i.e., the **expected inflation** rate is incorporated in economic decisions by various economic agents. Labourers take into account this while negotiating for wages, consumers plan their spending taking account the expected rate of inflation, producers incorporate the expected inflation in their investment, production and financing decisions, and the government bases estimation of tax revenue, expenditure and deficit incorporating the expected rate of inflation.

The expected inflation, also known as the **inertial inflation**, is quite often self-fulfilling, i.e., the future expected inflation rate turn out to be what the economic units are expecting at present, and can persist for a long time. For example, if labourers expect 10 per cent increase in the inflation rate they will negotiate for 10 per cent higher wages, and thus, the inflation rate will increase accordingly. If consumers, in anticipation of higher expected inflation in the coming period, prepone their expenditure, the demand for goods and services will increase. This leads to a higher inflation rate. Similarly, other contracts can get formulated in such a way that the impact of inflation is neutralized.

The expected inflation, if can be incorporated in economic decisions and can be hedged sufficiently, does not affect much the relative economic outcomes, such as distribution of income or production (discussed further in Section 7.5).

Unanticipated Inflation

Economic agents can make errors in their inflation forecasts. The actual inflation may differ from the anticipated inflation; it may end up significantly above or below the expected inflation. The difference between the two is referred to as the **unanticipated inflation**. The unanticipated inflation, as it is not expected, cannot be integrated into economic and business plans, and thus, leads to unnecessary economic waste and social disruptions in economic outcomes. For example, producers expecting higher prices may respond by increasing investment and production. These decisions however, prove to be a mistake if actual inflation turns out to be lower than what had been expected. Similarly, the unanticipated inflation, as it cannot be incorporated into economic decisions, redistributes the income from creditors to debtors, fixed income earners to profit earners, from consumers to producers, and as explained in the next section, can lead to socially undesirable outcomes.

7.5 EFFECTS OF INFLATION

The expected or anticipated inflation can be incorporated in business and economic decisions or can be hedged. Therefore, it does not alter economic outcomes much. Unanticipated inflation, however, as cannot be incorporated in economic decisions, brings with it substantial changes as discussed hereinafter.

7.5.1 Effect on Production and Economic Activities

A mild inflation is not only desirable but also a necessary condition for economic growth. The widened profit margins due to mild rise in prices induce firms to invest more, leading to higher employment and resource utilization.

Inflation alters the relative prices, and thus, the profitability of different business organizations is affected differently. The firms experiencing higher profits expand their production level faster than the others. At the same time, there are also the firms where profitability remains stagnant and even fall. Finding themselves uncompetitive, they close down their production. In the process, inflation changes not only the level of production, but also its composition.

An economy benefits from such reallocation of resources if that brings it closer to its competitive advantage. However, to the extent resources get diverted to less productive areas due to changes in relative prices, it adversely affects the productive efficiency.

Though a mild inflation is conducive for economic activities, inflation beyond a certain limit creates a chaos for the following reasons:

1. A highly inflationary situation generates an expectation of higher inflation in the future. Hence, it makes the hoarding of output, with the objective of selling it in the future when prices rise, more profitable. Producers, therefore, use their limited funds for hoarding or maintaining the inventories of finished and semi-finished goods rather than using those for enhancing output. Thus, a high rate of inflation retards the growth of output.

2. A high rate of inflation erodes the purchasing power rapidly. Thus, it may even reduce the demand for commodities, necessitating certain firms to close down their operations.
3. To protect their purchasing power, even workers may resort to strikes for a wage hike which increases the cost of production and adversely affects the profitability and production levels.

7.5.2 Effect on Distribution of Income

All prices do not change at the same rate. Therefore, inflation is asymmetric in its impact. It affects different sections of a society differently as follows:

1. Producers vs consumers: In an inflationary scenario, the prices of goods rise at a much faster rate than the cost of production. Thus, profit increases in an inflationary period which benefits producers. Consumers, on the other hand, have to bear the brunt as their purchasing power declines due to increasing prices. They are required to curtail their consumption of not-so-essential or luxury items, and readjust their consumption basket in favour of essential commodities.

2. Debtors vs creditors: Debtors are those who have procured loan or are in debt. These can be households, firms, financial institutions or governments. The payment obligation of interest and principal in debt contracts are usually specified in nominal terms without taking into account the expected level of inflation that would be prevailing in the future at the time when the contract matures. In an inflationary situation, once the contract matures and the debtors pay their debts, they gain in real terms because the purchasing power of the amount borrowed declines compared to the period when the contract was made. On the other hand, creditors stand to loose on account of inflation, because they receive lesser amount in real terms from debtors. For example, a firm borrows ₹100 at the rate of interest of 10 per cent for one year. It is under obligation to repay the principal and interest payment amounting to ₹110 at the end of the year. During this period the inflation rate increases by 30 per cent. Now, though the borrower will return ₹110 at the end of the year he gains because in real terms he will return only ₹77 (₹110 – ₹33). Thus, inflation transfers ₹33 from creditors to debtors or form lenders to borrowers.

3. Holders of fixed interest security vs shareholders: Holders of fixed income securities, such as fixed income yielding bonds, debentures and deposits, receive fixed interest income on their investment. As this income is not linked to inflation, they lose in an inflationary scenario. On the contrary, in a similar scenario, equity holders benefit because the return on equity is variable. In an inflationary situation profit rises which increases the share prices, and thereby, the return to equity holders.

4. Fixed income earning class vs profiteers: Inflation reduces the purchasing power of fixed earning class (such as wage and salary earners, pensioners, fixed interest and rent earners). The workers employed in small and unorganized sectors are hit the hardest because they are unable to secure escalator clause in their wage contracts. On the other hand, the income group that depends on profit earnings benefits the most as profit increases in an inflationary scenario.

High and rising prices, although disturb all household budgets, pinch the poor the most. Though wages form the largest component of this class, they remain fixed for a fairly long period of time or do not rise in the same proportion as the inflation rate. This is also the group that uses larger proportion of its income for consumption. High growth rate accompanying high inflation rate, though brings in substantial benefit for middle and high income groups, is not good for the poor section of a society. Thus, in a country where the population below the poverty line forms a significant proportion of the total population, a moderate growth rate with a moderate inflation rate is better than a high growth rate with a high inflation rate.

5. Government vs general public: Higher growth, often accompanied by a high inflation rate, increases the nominal income. Thus, for a given tax rate it increases the tax revenue of the government. However, the increase in inflation rate escalates the cost of various projects undertaken by the government. Hence, it increases government expenditure as well. The net effect on fiscal deficit depends on how the total revenue and expenditure are affected, while the effect on the public depends on the manner in which the deficit is financed. The fiscal deficit financed through borrowing from the central bank (as we will see in Section 5.7 and Section 6.6.1) fuels inflationary pressures further and hurts the public in general. Whereas the deficit financed through taxes leads to direct increase in the burden of taxes on the public. The deficit may even be financed through market borrowing (that is the borrowing from financial institutions) which hurts the public by reducing the availability of funds for them and increasing interest rates.

7.5.3 Other Effects

Inflation also impacts an economy in various other ways as described hereinafter:

1. Uncertainty in economic activities: Businessmen defer making long-term commitments, such as investment, in a highly inflationary scenario, because it creates uncertainty regarding the prices prevailing in the future. Rather than using their limited funds for production and investment, producers and traders speculate on the prices of commodities. They divert resources from productive activities to hoarding activities in anticipation that supply of these hoarded commodities would fetch them a better price in the future. In the process, growth stagnates or retards.

2. Diversion and sub-optimal utilization of resources: Inflation influences the relative prices. Prices of luxury goods rise more than that of essential commodities. This results in a diversion of resources from the production of essential goods (the goods which are valued more by a society) to luxury goods (which are valued less by a society). Thus, by distorting relative prices, inflation results in less than optimal allocation of resources and creates shortage of essential goods.

3. Reduction in savings: Inflation also erodes the value of savings, and thus, discourages households to save more. Not only total savings but also its composition gets affected adversely. In an inflationary scenario, households tend to shift savings from financial to real assets like real estate and gold. The value of these assets rises along with inflation, which prevents erosion in the value of savings.

4. Imbalances in the balance of payment: By affecting the domestic prices vis-a-vis foreign prices inflation makes exports dearer and uncompetitive in the international market, which reduce the demand for exports. At the same time, it also makes imports cheaper for domestic participants, enhancing demand for imports. Thus, inflation adversely affects the trade account of the balance of payment (i.e., exports minus imports).

Inflation also brings in changes in the capital account of the balance of payment (i.e., inflow of foreign capital minus outflow of capital). An inflationary scenario often experiences hike in interest rates that attracts foreign portfolio flows, which are highly volatile. However, foreign firms usually keep themselves away from the countries experiencing very high rate of inflation that adversely affects the inflow of foreign direct investment which are considered to be relatively stable flows.

On balance, the countries experiencing prolonged high rate of inflation, experience highly volatile and uncertain situation.

5. Depreciation of the exchange rate: We have seen above that inflation makes domestically produced commodities dearer in the international market, shrinks exports and reduces foreign exchange earnings. On the contrary, it makes imports cheaper, enhances domestic expenditure on foreign goods and services, and increases outflow of foreign currency. A reduction in exports and an increase in imports worsen the trade account deficit, leading to a negative net inflow of foreign currency. If, at the same time, there is a capital account deficit, i.e., the outflow of foreign capital is greater than the inflow, the foreign exchange earnings will be negative even on the capital account. Thus, the total demand for foreign currency will be higher than the supply. As we will see in Section 15.3, this also implies lower demand for domestic currency than the supply in the international market. This kind of situation leads to a depreciation (i.e, reduction) in the exchange rate which is nothing but the price of domestic currency in terms of a foreign currency. Persistence in inflation rate, thus, puts continuous pressure on depreciation of exchange rate, which in the long run makes people loose confidence in their domestic currency and rush for relatively stable foreign currency to safeguard their interest.

Thus, a mild inflation is desirable as it helps oil the wheels of an economy and accelerates growth in the short-run. However, a combination of higher growth and higher inflation is not sustainable over time because of the distortions that inflation brings in its wake. The acceptable level of inflation, i.e., the level of inflation that brings in positive effect, varies from one country to another. In India, the acceptable level of inflation is estimated to be somewhere around 4–5 per cent.

7.6 CONTROL OF INFLATION

Different policy measures are used for controlling inflation depending on its source, cause and intensity. The measures aimed at controlling inflation tries to bridge the gap between aggregate demand for and aggregate supply of different goods and services. Some of the countries have even adopted inflation targeting framework to directly address the issue of inflation (Box 7.4).

Box 7.4 Inflation Targeting

Inflation increases profitability, and thus, stimulates investment and business activities. However, it distorts relative prices, leads to reallocation of resources from necessities to luxuries and brings in large inequalities of income which may not be socially acceptable. Beyond a point, it creates an uncertainty for business units and leads to a diversion of resources from productive to speculative activities. The expenditure by governments also increases in an inflationary environment. If it is not accompanied by the commensurate increase in the revenue collection, then fiscal deficit expands, further fuelling inflation or increasing an overall interest rate. Inflation also adversely affects the balance of trade, deteriorates the quality of capital account flows, puts continuous pressure on the exchange rate to depreciate, and makes the exchange rate volatile. Uncontrolled inflation, thus, has all the potential to jeopardize macroeconomic stability of a country.

Governments and central banks, thus world over, seek to control inflation by adopting conservative fiscal and monetary policies. To control inflation, which is not directly under their control, they set intermediate targets like money supply or exchange rate. However, finding it difficult to control inflation through these intermediate targets in 1990s, several countries have started focusing directly on inflation rate. This approach of controlling inflation is known as the **inflation targeting**.

Under inflation targeting, the basic objective of monetary policy is to attain and preserve a low and stable rate of inflation. The authorities set an explicit inflation target for a period ahead. Forecasting of inflation becomes essential. Therefore, a full-fledged model incorporating relevant variables and information is developed for this purpose.

One of the important channels of increase in money supply and, thereby inflation, is the government borrowing from the central bank (as we will see in Section 8.7). Therefore, the inflation targeting framework requires a considerable degree of independence of the central bank from the government and conduct of monetary policy independent of fiscal considerations, because the borrowings of the government from the central bank leads to printing of new notes and increases money supply which puts pressure on prices as we will see Section 8.7. Thus, the central bank independence mandates the restriction on fiscal deficit as well restrictions on the government borrowing from the central bank. It also necessitates the existence of well-developed markets for government securities so that the government can easily sell these and raise resources from the market rather than remaining dependent on the central bank.

Inflation targeting requires a country to forego other targets like the targeting of exchange rate or interest rate or wage rate. If any of these variables is a target variable then the monetary policy loses its control over the inflation target as will be evident from Section 15.4.

An absence of consensus on optimum inflation rate, appropriate price index as the base for inflation targeting, existence of administered prices, absence of well developed analytical framework for forecasting inflation, large fiscal deficit, lack of autonomy for the central bank, absence of well-developed financial markets often make difficult the adoption of inflation targeting framework.

7.6.1 Monetary Measures

Money supply increases the nominal income, and thus, the purchasing power of the public. Given the available supply of commodities, the higher purchasing power increases demand, and thus, results in higher inflation. The central bank of a country tries to control the demand, and hence, inflation by regulating money supply. The measures adopted by the central bank to regulate money supply, known as **monetary measures**, are described hereinafter.

Quantitative Measures

Some of the quantitative measures, as we will see in more detail in Section 8.4, are the bank rate, open market operations and variable reserve requirements.

1. Bank rate: Borrowing from the central bank is one of the ways in which financial institutions raise resources to fund their activities. However, this source of fund is not free for banks. The central bank provides financial assistance to commercial banks and other financial institutions at a rate known as the **bank rate**. Financial institution, in turn, lend to the public and the government at a rate that is influenced by their own cost of funds. By varying the bank rate, the central bank can change the cost of funds to financial institutions, and thereby, their lending rates.

To control inflation, the central bank increases the bank rate, which pushes up lending rates of financial institutions and also all other rates that are linked with or influenced by the bank rate, such as call money rate and the rate on government securities. An overall increase in interest rates makes the investment less attractive. It discourages consumption expenditure on consumer durables and thereby, chokes off the excess demand.

Effectiveness of the bank rate increases if banks do not have an easy access to other sources of fund, the other rates are sufficiently sensitive or linked to the bank rate, and investment and consumption decisions are affected to a greater extent by the changes in interest rates.

2. Open market operations (OMOs): The **Open Market Operations** (OMOs) consist of sales and purchases of government securities by the central bank from the open market (consisting of financial institution and other dealers in government securities) rather than directly to and from the government.

To control inflation the central bank performs open market sales of government securities. To pay for these securities, the public or investors surrender the domestic currency to the central bank. Thus, the sale of government securities by the central bank from its own account reduces the money supply in circulation, and thereby, the demand for goods and services.

The OMOs directly affect the money supply; therefore, they are considered to be superior to bank rate policy in their effect on money supply. However, effective implementation of these instruments requires developed secondary market for government securities. That is, there should be sufficient demand for these securities by the public as well as sufficient stock of these securities with the central bank at the time these operations are performed.

3. Variable reserve requirements: Commercial banks do not use their entire resources or funds for lending. They maintain some part of their funds, known as **cash reserves** or **cash balances**, for meeting the withdrawal requirement of their depositors as well as the statutory requirement imposed on them by the central bank. A reduction in the quantity of these cash balances enhances the funds for lending purpose, whereas an increase in the quantity has an opposite impact.

The central bank can directly impound the cash reserves of commercial banks by raising the statutory requirement known as the **Cash Reserve Ratio** (CRR). An increase in the CRR implies that the banks are expected to maintain a larger proportion of their funds (coming from demand and time liabilities) as cash in hand or deposits with the central bank. This reduces the availability of funds with the banks for the purpose of further lending, which, as we will see in Section 6.6.3, is expected to reduce availability of credit to the public. A reduction in credit is expected to reduce investment and consumption expenditure, and thereby, the aggregate demand and inflation.

Selective Control Measures

Direct credit control measures can even be adopted by the central bank by regulating consumer credit, imposing higher margin requirements and issuing directives appealing banks to restrict and direct resources only towards the desired channels as follows:

1. Regulating consumer credit: During an inflationary period, consumer credit facilities are restrained by raising the down payments and reducing the payment period of credit on selective basis.

2. Higher margin requirements: Borrowers are subjected to higher margin requirements when they approach financial institutions for credit in order to restrict the demand for credit.

3. Directives, moral suasion, publicity and direct action: The central bank may often issue directives to financial institutions to curtail the expansion of credit. Failure of such directives, at times, results in direct interventions by the central bank in the working of financial institutions.

The effectiveness of monetary measures depends on the degree of control exercised by the central bank as well as the extent of cooperation extended by commercial banks and other financial institutions.

7.6.2 Fiscal Measures

Fiscal policies, i.e., government expenditure, taxation and debt policies, are also used to curb inflationary pressures. Restrictive fiscal policies, such as a reduction in government expenditure and/or an increase in taxes, address the demand side and try to control inflation by bridging the gap between aggregate demand and supply as indicated hereinafter.

1. Public expenditure: Government expenditure is one of the important components of aggregate demand. Reduction in subsidies, wages, other administrative expenses and postponement of new projects, etc., reduces the money income of the public. Thus, it directly curtails the aggregate demand for goods and services.

While exercising this instrument, the government must keep the non-essential expenditure to the minimum rather than the development expenditure. Otherwise, not only the demand side but also the productive capacity is affected adversely.

2. Taxation: Imposition of new taxes and raising the existing tax rates, on one hand, reduces the purchasing power of the people and, on the other hand generates resources for the government. Direct taxes (defined in Section 8.5.1) like income tax, wealth tax, etc., reducing the disposable income, directly exert pressure on demand.

Raising the prices of commodities indirect taxes discourage private sector spending, and thereby, help containing inflationary pressures. However, these taxes fall heavily on the fixed income earners, who are anyway hit hard by inflation. Besides, these add on to the cost-push inflation by raising the prices of goods.

3. Public borrowing and debt: Borrowing by the government results in a transfer of funds from the private sector to the public sector. Reducing the funds available with the private sector and their demand for commodities, public borrowing helps in containing inflationary pressures.

The government needs to use such raised funds judiciously by investing these in building up the productive capacity rather than on consumption expenditure which simply fuels inflation without adding on to the production capacity. It has also been suggested that the government should avoid paying back any of its previous loans during inflation to prevent an increase in the income in the hands of the private sector and to keep a check on their expenditure levels.

7.6.3 Other Measures

1. Price control and rationing: To curb inflationary pressures, the government often directly controls the prices of sensitive commodities or of the commodities that have substantial weight in the consumption basket or production structure. This is the most popular method, but difficult to administer as it requires covering sufficient number of essential consumer goods under the rationing system. Rationing quite often encourages black marketing and rent seeking. Price controls also lead to diversion of resources from regulated to unregulated sectors, the sectors that may not be as important for the society as the regulated ones. Thus, price controls limit the freedom and welfare of consumers.

2. Wage policy: Wages, salaries as well as profit margins are controlled or frozen for a period of time during highly inflationary situations. The government defers the payment of a part of the salary to its employees to reduce the current purchasing power. Similarly, arrears on account of pay revisions are transferred to the provident funds accounts. Wage control tries to restrict the cost-push inflation by breaking the wage-price spiral.

3. Output adjustment: The Government even tries to encourage output of those goods that are the cause of inflationary pressure by inducing shift in the factors of production from the production of less inflation sensitive goods to more inflation sensitive goods. Subsidies and other incentives are provided by the government for such a shift. The government, at times, also directly regulates the allocation of resources and places a directive regarding the system of priorities. Sometimes, to enhance the domestic supply, imports are resorted to which is the most powerful and speediest way of checking cost-push inflation.

In the long-run, structural reforms in the system are implemented to boost up the level of production. For example, a greater degree of privatization and deregulation is introduced which enhances competition, efficiency, productivity and output, and helps in curbing inflationary pressures.

A combination of these measures can be adopted by a government to combat inflationary pressure in the given period of time as described in UBE 7.6.

UNDERSTANDING BUSINESS ENVIRONMENT

UBE 7.6 Measures to Contain Inflation

One of the prime objectives of monetary and fiscal policies in India is to maintain price stability in the country. The co-ordinated efforts are often made by the monetary and fiscal authorities to achieve these objectives. Various monetary and fiscal measures implemented to contain inflationary pressures in 2010–11 are outlined in this UBE

In India, inflation remained at an elevated level during 2010–11 (April–November). Though it moderated in the subsequent period, i.e., in 2012–13, it remained above the comfort level ((UBE 7.2, Figure 7.5), which is below 5 per cent for the Indian economy. During this period, weighted contribution of primary articles and fuel and power to headline inflation was relatively higher than their respective weights, while the weighted contribution of manufactured products remained lower than its weight.

The inflation persisted at above the comfort zone because of (i) higher international prices of crude, precious metals, edible oils, etc., (ii) change in dietary pattern leading to structural demand and supply mismatch for protein rich items and (iii) revision in minimum support prices for some of the essential commodities and (iv) revision in petroleum prices in September 2012.

Inflation had been due to both demand and supply factors and was a cause of concern for both the Government and the RBI. To contain inflationary pressures, as per GOI (2012), following measures were implemented, which tried to address the issue from both supply and demand sides.

I. Fiscal & Administrative Measures

- Reduced import duties to zero - for wheat, onion, pulses, crude palmolein and to 7.5 per cent for refined and hydrogenated oils and vegetable oils.
- Duty-free import of white and raw sugar was extended up to 30 June 2012; however, import duty of 10 per cent was instituted in June 2012.

- Banned export of edible oils (except coconut oil and forest based oil) and edible oils in blended consumer packs upto 5 kg with a capacity of 20,000 tons per annum and pulses (except Kabuli chana and organic pulses and lentils up to a maximum of 10,000 tons per annum).
- Imposed stock limits from time to time in the case of select essential commodities such as pulses, edible oil, and edible oilseeds and in the case of paddy and rice for specific seven states upto 30.11.2012.
- Ban on export of onion was imposed for short period of time whenever required. Exports of Onion were calibrated through the mechanism of Minimum Export Prices (MEP).
- Maintained the Central Issue Price (CIP) for rice (at ₹5.65 per kg for BPL and ₹3 per kg for AAY) and wheat (at ₹4.15 per kg for BPL and ₹2 per kg for AAY) since 2002.
- Suspended Futures trading in rice, urad, tur, guar gum and guar seed.
- To ensure adequate availability of sugar for the households covered under TPDS, the levy obligation on sugar factories was restored to 10 per cent for sugar season 2011–12.
- Government allocated rice and wheat under Open Market Sales Scheme.
- Resumed the scheme for subsidized imported pulses through PDS in a varied form with the nomenclature "Scheme for Supply of Imported Pulses at Subsidized rates to States/UTs for Distribution under PDS to BPL card holders" with a subsidy element of ₹20 per kg to be paid to the designated importing agencies upto a maximum number of BPL card holders for the residual part of the current year and extended the scheme for subsidized imported edible oils w.e.f. 1.10.2012 to 30.9.2013 with subsidy of ₹15 per kg for import of upto 10 lakh tonnes of edible oils for this period.

II. Budgetary and other measures

- A National Mission for Protein supplements in 2011–12 was launched with allocation of ₹300 crore.
- To broaden the scope of production of fish to coastal aquaculture, apart from fresh water aquaculture, the outlay in 2012–13 was stepped up to ₹500 crore.
- To help consumers and farmers by improving the selling and purchasing facilities, recently, the Government permitted Foreign Direct Investment (FDI) in multi-brand retail trading.

III. Monetary measures

The Reserve Bank of India (RBI) had also taken suitable steps to contain inflation with 13 consecutive increases by 375 bps in policy rates from March 2010 to October 2011. However, with moderation in inflation rate, repo rate was reduced by 50 basis points in April 2012 to bring it to 8 per cent.

Reference: GOI (2012), Mid Year Economic Analysis, 2012–13.

SUMMARY

Sharp movements in prices, whether upward or downward, are feared by all, the government, business enterprises and households. Price movements along the business and economic fluctuations are termed as inflation, disinflation, deflation and reflation.

Prices of different commodities move in different directions at any given point of time. Therefore, to estimate an overall price level, price indices are estimated. Some of the widely used price indices are the CPI, WPI, PPI and GDP deflators. These indices are used for estimating inflation.

Inflation is differentiated using various criteria. On the basis of intensity of price rise, it is categorized as creeping, walking, running and hyper inflation. On the basis of degree of control, it is identified as open and suppressed inflation. On the basis of coverage, it is measured as headline and core inflation. On the basis of cause, it is known as demand-pull and cost-push inflation, and on the basis of predictability, it is termed as expected and unanticipated inflation.

Inflation brings in micro-economic and macro-economic changes. It increases the profitability of producers and induces them to invest and produce more. However, it also creates uncertainty which may lead to a diversion of resources from the productive to speculative activities. It results in a redistribution of income, which benefits producers, debtors, shareholders and profiteers, but harms consumers, creditors, fixed income security holders and fixed income earners. Inflation has tremendous influence on interest rates, exchange rates, balance of payment, and even the expectations of inflation in the forthcoming period.

Monetary and fiscal policies and various other measures are implemented to contain inflationary pressures by affecting both demand and supply sides.

In India, as the PPI is not available, inflation is estimated using the WPIs and the CPIs.

During 2012–13 inflation in India remained at an elevated level. To curb the inflationary pressures, various monetary and fiscal measures, including reduction in import duties on agriculture and manufactured food products, ban on exports of edible oil, stock limits on essential items, increase in the policy rate by the RBI, were implemented.

Implications for Business Managers

Modest inflation, i.e., creeping to walking inflation, is identified to be conducive for production and business enterprises. In an inflationary scenario, the profitability of business ventures increases, which induces managers and producers to enhance their production level and expand their production capacity.

Similarly, rapid increase in inflation rate also increases the profitability of business organizations. But it also creates uncertainty regarding the price level in the coming period. In general, it generates expectation that the inflation rate is going to rise further in the coming period and the commodity sold in the next period would fetch them a better price. The uncertainty regarding the future inflation rate puts on hold the investment decisions of firms; rather producers prefer holding back the supply of already produced goods in expectation of better price for the same in the coming period.

The rapidly rising prices benefit business units only for a certain period. In the long-run, they are also affected adversely by the soaring level of prices both on demand and supply front as follows:

- A very high rate of inflation reduces the purchasing power of consumers drastically which makes them to postpone or curtail their purchasing decisions. Different firms get affected by the lowering of demand to different degrees depending on the elasticity of demand for their products.
- A high inflation rate makes domestically produced commodities dearer in the international market. Exports become uncompetitive and the demand for these declines. Inflation, thus, not only reduces the domestic demand but also contracts the demand for exports, leading to an overall decline in the demand for domestically produced commodities. An overall

decline in the demand leads to an underutilization of existing capacity, idle resources, and lay-off of certain factors of production.

- On the supply front, the cost of production goes up. To protect their purchasing power and the standard of living, workers demand for higher wages, which inflates the production cost. At the same time, prices of raw materials and other intermediate goods further strain the cost of production. This squeezes the profitability of business units.
- Cost of production also bumps upon import front in certain cases. The contraction in export demand increases the trade deficit that puts pressure on the depreciation of domestic currency. Depreciation makes imports dearer, and to the extent that these are used in the process of production, the cost of production goes up.

Inflation also increases interest rates and makes capital dearer. This further pushes up the cost of production. A high rate of inflation brings in uncertainty in economic scenario, keeps on hold the consumption and investment activity, results in excess capacity, makes the domestic business units uncompetitive in the international market, leads to trade imbalances, and results in depreciation of the domestic currency. Continuous depreciation in the domestic currency makes the holding of domestic currency unattractive. The public looses confidence in the domestic currency and rushes for other currencies to protect their interest. Thus, a high inflation rate has all the potential to jeopardize the macroeconomic stability of a country.

Business managers constantly need to monitor the inflationary build-ups in an economy while taking their production, investment and various strategic decisions. To the extent business firms are able to find a pattern in the inflationary dynamism on the basis of past trend, able to understand the factors affecting the inflation, able to project and anticipate the inflation rate in the coming period, they would be able to incorporate inflationary factors in their business decisions and protect their interest by taking defensive and protective measures.

REVIEW QUESTIONS

7.1 What is inflation? How would you differentiate inflation from deflation, and disinflation from reflation?

7.2 Does the WPI or CPI ever fall? If yes, what is the economic term used for describing such a situation?

7.3 What are the two widely used methods for calculating price indices? Which of these methods use the base year quantities as the weights?

7.4 What are the advantages of using the Paasche's method of estimating a price index? Why is the Laspeyres' method used for calculating many price indices inspite of the fact that the Paasche's method gives a better estimate of a price index in a given period?

7.5 Why is the CPI estimated? How far is it different from the PPI?

7.6 What are the differences between PPI and WPI?

7.7 What is the GDP deflator? Why is it known as the implicit price deflator?

7.8 What are the different price indices available in India? Which of these is used for estimating headline inflation? Why?

7.9 Is the overall CPI estimated in India? If yes, what does it consist of?

7.10 What is the core inflation? Why do we need to estimate it?

7.11 "Monetary policy should be based on core inflation". Comment on this statement.

7.12 What are the uses of CPI-AL and CPI-RL in India?

7.13 Which of the price index is used for working out escalation cost of projects in India?

7.14 Are services included in the CPIs and WPIs in India? If yes, which of the services are included in these indices?

7.15 Why inflation rate is estimated at both point to point basis and on the average basis. If there are large fluctuations in inflation rates at different points of time in a given year, which of the two methods will give a better picture of an inflationary scenario in a country in a given year? Why?

7.16 Why is the hyperinflation feared, though the creeping inflation is welcomed?

7.17 The cost-push inflation can exist in an economy; however, it cannot persist unless there is an excess demand. Why?

7.18 What is inflationary gap? Why does it emerge? How far is it different from the deflationary gap?

7.19 Why producers benefit from an inflationary situation?

7.20 Who gets benefitted from an inflationary situation, debtor or creditor?

7.21 "Expected inflation is not as much of a problem as unexpected inflation." Is this statement true or false? Why?

7.22 If inflation benefits certain segments of the society, then, why a government tries to control it?

7.23 What is inflation targeting? What are the essential conditions for its success?

7.24 What type of monetary instruments are used for controlling inflation?

7.25 Describe various fiscal measures used for controlling inflation?

7.26 Describe the present inflationary scenario in India? What have been the major contributory factor to inflation in India in the recent period. Is this demand driven or supply led?

7.27 "Fiscal measures only affect the demand side." Reflect on this statement.

7.28 What supply side measures had been adopted by the Government of India in 2012–13 to curb inflation?

7.29 "Only fiscal measures have been used in India in 2012–13 to curb the inflation." Comment on this statement.

7.30 Inflation increases the profitability of business firms. Therefore, as a business manager you would decide to expand your production base in an economy experiencing hyperinflationary scenario. Do you agree with this decision? Give reasons for your answer.

NUMERICAL PROBLEMS

7.1 WPI values for 2009 and 2010 are shown in Table 7.8. Find out the year on year as well as period to period inflation rates from these values.

Table 7.8 WPI Indices

Month	*2009*	*2010*	*Month*	*2009*	*2010*
January	124.4	135.2	July	128.2	141.0
February	123.3	135.2	August	129.6	141.1
March	123.5	136.3	September	130.3	142.0
April	125.0	138.6	October	131.0	142.9
May	125.9	139.1	November	132.9	143.8
June	126.8	139.8	December	133.4	146.0

7.2 As per the data available from IMF World Economic Outlook, April 2011, the GDP deflator of India rose from 130.488 in 2009 to 143.351 in 2010. Calculate the percentage rise in the price level in India (or rate of inflation) between 2009 and 2010.

7.3 Assume that the base year for estimating GDP at constant price is 2009–10. GDP of a country at current prices rise to ₹400 crore in 2010–11 from ₹350 crore in the base year. Assume that the general price level increases by 25 per cent during this period. Estimate the price index, GDP deflator and the Real GDP in 2010–11. Is there growth in the GDP in real terms?

7.4 Construct a suitable price index from the information given in Table 7.9. Which of the years you can take as the base year? Which of the two methods—Laspeyres' and Paasche's—would you apply to estimate the price index?

Table 7.9 Commodity-wise Data on Expenditure and Price

Items	*Expenditure in 2009–10 (in ₹)*	*Price per unit (in ₹)*		*Unit*
		2009–10	*2010–11*	
Wheat	30.00	1.55	3.20	kilogram
Rice	40.00	4.40	8.50	kilogram
Cloth	53.75	10.75	21.00	metre
Pulses	22.40	3.20	6.50	litre
Milk	75.00	2.50	5.50	litre
Mustard oil	51.00	6.80	16.00	kilogram
Potatoes	4.50	0.75	2.50	kilogram

CASE ANALYSIS EXERCISE

C7.1 How is the global energy landscape evolving in response to high oil prices

The landscape of the global energy map is changing rapidly. The International Energy Agency (2012) recently announced that thanks to increased production of natural gas and shale oil, the United States will become world's largest oil producer surpassing Saudi Arabia by the mid-2020s, while North America (Canada, Mexico and the USA combined) will become a net oil exporter by 2030.

These developments are to a large extent a natural market reaction to the quadrupling of international oil prices between 2000–02 and 2010–12, which saw a substantial uptick in global exploration efforts and made profitable extraction technologies.

High prices have boosted supply and moderated demand

In the United States, new techniques, such as horizontal drilling and hydraulic fracturing (—fracking), have permitted the widespread exploitation of until-now uneconomic shale oil; shale natural gas; and so-called—tight-oil deposits. As a result, US crude oil and natural gas production has increased 30 per cent during 2005–2011. Ultimately, these technologies have already added over 1 mb/d to US crude oil output so far, and they are expected to add much more. Partly as a result of these technologies, global proven reserves have risen by 33 per cent since 2000, with 70 per cent of the increase coming from increased extraction estimates (reserves growth) as opposed to new discoveries. New discoveries have also been playing an import role, accounting for about 40 per cent of production during the same period (IEA, 2012). Associated investment has contributing importantly to growth in a range of developing countries, including in Sub-Saharan Africa (see Sub-Saharan Africa regional annex).

The demand-side has also reacted, with a rapid increase in the energy efficiency of motor vehicle fleets both through the introduction of new more energy efficient technologies such as hybrid cars and reduced demand for energy inefficient vehicles. Since 2000, the average automobile mileage of new cars sold in the United States has increased by 18 per cent and that of the existing fleet by 7.7 per cent BFN 1. Similar trends are observable throughout the high-income world. As a result, OECD demand for oil has declined a total of

7.6 per cent since 2005 (IEA, 2012B). Over the long run the IEA now expects OECD total liquids demand (crude and refined hydrocarbons) demand to fall a further 11 to 21 per cent depending on policies.

Demand outside of the OECD (mainly developing countries) has been more robust, with total liquids consumption rising 3.5 per cent annually since 2005, partly reflecting rising vehicle use. More than half of global oil output is consumed by the transportation industry, which is the fastest growing component of oil demand, especially in China, India, and the Middle-East. These trends are expected to continue although at somewhat slower pace after 2020, with global oil and liquids demand rising by an annual average rate of 0.6 and 0.7 per cent between 2011 and 2035.

Yet, oil prices have remained resilient

Despite the equilibrating trends in supply and demand, world prices remain in excess of $100 per barrel, and are expected to remain above $100 over the medium-to-long term, mainly because of the elevated extraction cost of newly discovered and new-technology oil.

Yet, downside and upside risks exist. On the downside, the process of substitution away from oil and toward new extractive technologies is not yet complete. Currently US natural gas and coal trade at an 80 per cent discount to brent oil—opening up huge arbitrage opportunities, that are likely to exercise increasing downward pressure on international prices as pipeline reversals and liquefied natural gas exports begin to de-compartmentalize international markets. Over the longer-run, changes in battery technology and/or expanded use of natural gas could significantly erode the engineering advantage of crude oil products (see Commodity Annex), allowing abundant and low-cost coal to compete indirectly with liquid fuels through electrical vehicles.

A significant upside risk, stems from the environmental costs associated with new extraction techniques. For the moment, there remains a lively debate concerning the potential for geological damage pollution to aquifers from the chemicals and heavy fresh-water use of fracturing techniques.

BFN 1. Increase in new vehicle passenger car efficiency between 2011 and 2000; Increase in short-wheel base vehicles 2009–2000 Bureau of Transportation Statistics (2012).

Source: The World Bank (2013), *Global Economic Prospects*, Volume 6, January 2013. Washington, DC: World Bank.

Doi: 10.1596/ 978-0-8213-9882-1 License: Creative Commons Attribution CC BY 3.0.

Questions

1. What has caused the emergence of the United States on the global energy map?
2. What will be the global energy map scenario by 2030?
3. How high international oil prices boosted supply and moderated demand?
4. Why still international oil prices are ruling high inspite of rapid changes in energy map scenario?
5. What do you think about the movement of international oil prices in the future?

SUGGESTED FURTHER READING

Eapen, L.M. and Nair, S.R. (2012), Food Price Inflation in India (2008 to 2010), *EPW*, May 19, XLVII, 20.

Gokarn, S. (2012), Food Inflation: This Time It's Different, *RBI Bulletin*, January.

Mohanty, D. (2012), The Importance of Inflation Expectations, *RBI Bulletin*, December.

Pandey, S.J., Krishnaswamy, R, and Kanagasabapathy, K. (2013), Has Inflation Led By Food Prices Become Chronic? EPY, May 18, Vol. XLVIII, 20.

Subbarao, D. (2013), Is there a New Normal for Inflation? *RBI Bulletin*, April.

CHAPTER 8

Fiscal Policy and Environment

8.1 INTRODUCTION

An article in Economics Times, 20 May 2013 edition, indicated that the delay in the implementation of Goods and Service Tax (GST) in India is forcing many micro, small and medium enterprises to relocate their units. As per the article, three months ago Manjeet Singh, an entrepreneur, shifted his 60 lakh inverter manufacturing unit from Haryana to Delhi. For operating his unit, Singh was purchasing his inputs from Delhi and also transferring his manufactured invertors to Delhi where most of his customers are located. While moving inputs from Delhi to Haryana he had to pay 2 per cent Central State Tax (CST) and also while moving finished inverters from his unit to Delhi he was subjected to 2 per cent CST, making his cost 4 per cent higher than the competitors located just a few kms away in Delhi. This was a big enough margin, making his survival difficult. All these years he did not shift as he was expecting the implementation of CST which would have made his cost similar to that of his competitors by making all manufacturers, irrespective of the location, subject to single rate of duty.

Many business decisions, like the location decisions taken by Manjeet Singh, are affected by the level and type of taxes prevailing in the country. The government taxation decisions affect the cost and profitability of business organizations directly. Affecting profitability, the taxation also influences the dividend payment by business organizations. As it affects the disposable income of households and their total demand and the demand mix taxation has an impact on business organizations from demand side as well.

The government not only imposes taxes but also incurs expenditure on defense, subsidies, wages and scholarships. It spends on building ports, roads, rail tracks, telephone network, etc., to create physical infrastructure that can support productive activities. It also spends on hospitals to provide medical facilities, on schools to impart education to the underprivileged and weaker sections of the society, and on many other such activities that strengthen human capital. Thus, we see that the government influences economic activities not only indirectly but also directly by enhancing demand, output and creating employment opportunities.

Capitalist societies, historically, vehemently opposed the interventions by governments in economic activities because they viewed that the government interventions, by distorting relative prices, can do harm to the society. They envisaged minimum role to governments, restricting their interventions in the areas such as national defence, and domestic law and order. However, the Great Depression, following the Second World War, made it clear that the governments can play an important role in boosting the level of employment, controlling inflation, and stabilizing business activities by affecting the aggregate level of demand.

Modern societies acknowledge the positive and supportive role played by the government. These societies are characterized by mixed economic system where, though the central role is played by the private sector, the government involvement facilitates its activities and supports the market mechanism. Government participation, in these economies, is not confined to just traditional activities of maintaining law and order, but has expanded its reach to include the provision of social infrastructure, such as education, health, entertainment, social security and physical infrastructure, such as airports, roads, parks, water and sewage system.

The governments raise revenue by levying taxes to finance their expenditure. The expenditure that governments undertake and the ways in which they finance their expenditure are covered in fiscal policy. **Fiscal policy** is defined as a set of principles and decisions of a government in setting the level of public expenditure and the ways of financing it.

Fiscal policy affects an economy both at micro and macro levels. At the micro-economic level, it is used for making the distribution of wealth and income more equitable, providing equitable access to social services, meeting the basic needs of poor, influencing relative prices and cost conditions in order to discourage some activities and encourage others, and enhancing the efficiency of production and competitiveness of domestically produced output. At the macro-economic level, the balance of tax revenue and expenditure influences the aggregate demand, which, in turn, influences output, employment, overall price level, inflation, rate of interest, and many other variables.

Fiscal policy, thus, has a profound impact on business conditions and competitiveness. Managers need to continuously and closely watch fiscal policy developments to take not only strategic decisions but also micro decisions of procurement, production and distribution. Hence, various aspects of fiscal policy are detailed in this chapter. The objectives of fiscal policy are elaborated in Section 8.2. Section 8.3 describes the types of fiscal policy, whereas Section 8.4 emphasizes the role of fiscal policy as a counter cyclical device. Section 8.5 analyzes the instruments of fiscal policy. It also details on the trends in and composition of tax revenue and public expenditure in India and the various tax and expenditure reform measures initiated in the post-1991 era in India. Section 8.6 outlines the various concepts of deficits and their implications for an economy. This section also briefs us on the impact of efforts taken for fiscal consolidation in India. Section 8.7 deals with the various methods of financing government deficit and their implications for an economy.

8.2 OBJECTIVES OF FISCAL POLICY

Fiscal policy has both macro and microeconomic objectives. In developed countries, the focus of fiscal policy is on maintaining full employment and stabilizing growth, whereas in developing countries it is used to create an environment for rapid economic growth. The various objectives of fiscal policy are as follows:

1. Mobilization and efficient allocation of resources: Developing countries are characterized by a low level of income and investment; thereby entrapped in a vicious circle of poverty. Fiscal policy aims at breaking this circle by mobilizing and generating resources through taxes and borrowing, and investing these resources in efficient ways.

2. Minimization of inequalities of income and wealth: Fiscal tools are used with the objective of bringing about redistribution of income in favour of the poor by taxing the rich and spending the so raised revenue on various social welfare activities including education, health, water and sanitation.

3. Increasing employment opportunities: The level of employment influences the aggregate output and income, and thus, general standard of living of the populace. Fiscal policy in developing countries, thus, strives at increasing the level of employment, while in developed countries it aims at sustaining the full employment.

4. Increasing output and accelerating economic growth: Fiscal policy aims at directing the resources to socially desired channels with high yield so as to boost output and accelerate economic growth.

5. Economic stability: Fiscal policy is often employed, especially in developed countries, to moderate business fluctuations or cycles. During an upswing, taxes are hiked to curb the rising demand for goods and services, whereas these are lowered in a recessionary phase to boost up the level of demand.

6. Price stability: Economic stability is largely dependent on overall price stability. A stable price level creates conducive environment for production, output and employment. Fiscal policy aims at reducing price fluctuations and maintaining stable price level by containing inflationary and deflationary tendencies. In an inflationary situation, government expenditure is curtailed and taxes are increased to reduce disposable income and expenditure of the private sector. Conversely, in a deflationary situation, the government enhances its own expenditure and induces the expenditure of the private sector by reducing taxes and enhancing the disposable income.

8.3 TYPES OF FISCAL POLICY: CONTRACTIONARY OR EXPANSIONARY

Depending on the impact of fiscal policy on economic activities, fiscal policy is described as contractionary or expansionary. If the policy aims at reducing the aggregate economic activities it is known as the **contractionary fiscal policy**. Conversely, if it aims at enhancing aggregate economic activities it is described as the **expansionary fiscal policy**.

The stance of the policy can be gauged from **fiscal balance**, which is the difference between government expenditure and government revenue. Therefore, if the fiscal balance is in surplus (i.e., the revenue is higher than the spending) and it is increasing, or the extent of deficit is decreasing compared to previous periods then the fiscal policy is contractionary. It takes the form of lowering government spending and/or raising taxes. A reduction in government expenditure reduces the aggregate demand, and hence, the output directly. On the contrary higher taxes force households and consumers to pay larger proportion of their income towards taxes, which reduces their disposable income and expenditure. From the GDP identity $Y = C(Y - T) + I + G + X - M$, it can be seen that an increase in tax (T) and/or reduction in government expenditure (G), given all other variables (such as consumption (C), Investment (I), Exports (X), Imports (M)) as fixed, reduces the aggregate demand, puts downward pressure on prices, and reduces output (Y) and employment. Thus, a contractionary fiscal policy reduces the output, employment and inflation rate in an economy by increasing taxes and reducing government expenditure. Such policies are pursued to stabilize a booming economy, experiencing a high growth rate of output but also a high rate of inflation.

On the contrary, if the fiscal balance is in deficit (i.e., the government spending is higher than the government revenue) and the extent of deficit is increasing, or the extent of surplus is decreasing compared to previous period then the fiscal policy is considered to be expansionary. It is implemented by lowering taxes and expanding government spending. Such policies increase the aggregate demand. Consequently, they raise the overall price level and inflation rate, and boost up the output, income and employment level. Such policies are pursued by the government in an economy experiencing recession—represented by a negative growth rate of output, deflation and high level of unemployment.

Expansionary as well as contractionary fiscal policies affect the national income. But the extent to which a given change in tax and expenditure brings about in the overall national income is determined by the values of tax and expenditure multipliers (Box 8.1) and the length of policy lags (Box 8.2).

Box 8.1 Fiscal Policy Multipliers

In the context of fiscal policy there are two multipliers, viz., expenditure multiplier and tax multiplier The **expenditure multiplier** assesses the impact of a given change in government expenditure on aggregate output. That is, it quantifies by how much the total output increases when there is a given amount of change in the government expenditure.

From the GDP identity ($Y = C + I + G + X - M$), which we have seen in Section 3.3.1, we can arrive at the expenditure multiplier as follows:

To arrive at the expenditure multiplier, for simplicity, we assume that all the components of expenditure, except private consumption expenditure, are exogenous to the system. Further assuming that the consumption expenditure (C) depends on **disposable income**, i.e., the income (Y) net of direct taxes (T), or $Y - T$, we can relate the consumption to income as follows:

$$C = b(Y - T)$$

where, b is the marginal propensity to consume (mpc), determined by the consumption behaviour of the public.

For simplicity we also assume that the government does not impose taxes, i.e., T is zero. Hence,

$$C = bY$$

By substituting for C in the GDP identity we arrive at

$$Y = bY + I + G + X - M$$

or

$$Y(1 - b) = I + G + X - M$$

Hence,

$$\Delta Y = \frac{1}{1 - b}\Delta G$$

or

$$\Delta Y = m\Delta G$$

where

$$m = \frac{-b}{1 - b}\Delta T$$

Thus, a given change in the government expenditure results in some multiple change in the aggregate output or income. The value of the multiplier depends on the mpc. For example, if the marginal propensity to consume (b) is 0.8, then the value of income multiplier is 5. Thus, in this case, a one rupee increase in the expenditure increases the income in the economy by ₹5.

Similar to the expenditure multiplier, the **tax multiplier** can be derived from the GDP identity. The tax multiplier assesses the impact of a given change in the tax on output,. To derive this multiplier, we assume that consumers pay income tax, which creates a wedge between their income and disposable income. Since consumption is related to disposable income, we can specify consumption relation as $C = b(Y - T)$. For simplicity, we also assume that all other expenditure components, i.e., I, G, X and M are constant.

Substituting for consumption in the GDP identity we arrive at

$$Y = b(Y - T) + I + G + X - M$$

or

$$Y(1 - b) = - bT + I + G + X - M$$

Hence,

$$\Delta Y = \frac{-b}{1 - b} \Delta T$$

or

$$\Delta Y = m \, \Delta T$$

where

$$m = \frac{-b}{1 - b}$$

Thus, the tax multiplier is $- b/(1 - b)$. It indicates that the effect of an increase in the tax is in the opposite direction to that of an increase in the government spending. A one rupee change in the tax changes disposable income ($Y - T$) by one rupee, but changes the consumption by only a fraction of rupee determined by the propensity to consume. Thus, for b of 0.8 the tax multiplier is equal to 4, implying that a one rupee reduction in the tax rate increases the income by ₹4.

The tax multiplier is one less in absolute value than the government expenditure multiplier because a tax has a smaller per rupee impact on equilibrium income than a change in a spending. Thus, the balanced budget multiplier, i.e., a one rupee increase in the government spending financed by a one rupee increase in a tax, increases equilibrium income by one rupee. The balanced budget multiplier is the sum total of expenditure and tax multipliers, i.e.,

$$\frac{\Delta Y}{\Delta G} + \frac{\Delta Y}{\Delta T} = \frac{1}{1 - b} + \frac{-b}{1 - b} = \frac{1 - b}{1 - b} = 1$$

As equilibrium income can be affected by the changes in government spending and taxes, fiscal instruments can be varied to offset the undesirable changes and to stabilize an economy.

Box 8.2 Policy Lags

Government policies can be used for addressing a number of issues and achieving various objectives. However, there can be a fairly long and variable time, known as the **time lag**, between the time at which policies are implemented and the time their impact is felt on the targeted variables. These lags in policies can be inside or outside as depicted in Figure 8.1 and as described hereinafter.

Inside lags take place because the changes in policy actions, to resolve an issue, do not take place instantaneously with an occurrence of a shock. The **inside lag**, thus, is the time between an occurrence of a shock or disturbance and the corrective/remedial action implemented by the government or the central authority. It occurs because of the data lag, recognition lag, decision/legislative lag, and action/implementation lag. The data or information, documenting the state of an economy, reaches policy makers with a lag. The acquisition of information is a time and resource consuming process. Surveys are required to be conducted on fairly regular intervals to collect the data. The time required collecting or gathering information results in the **data lag**. The processing and analysis of data and documentation of the existence of a problem takes time, and thus, delays the recognition of an economic problem. This, along with the recognition that the problem warrants policy action response, leads to the **recognition lag**. Identification of corrective policy legislation and decision making process leads to the **decision lag**. Finally, it takes time to implement an appropriate policy response, leading to the **implementation lag** or **action lag**. To understand the concept of the inside lag, we can consider a situation when there is a sudden hike in the international oil prices, leading to an increase in the cost of production of manufactured goods and a slowdown in the growth of output in this sector. The IIP data, which captures the movements in the manufacturing output, arrive in the office of data compilers after a month's time and compilers often take a fortnight to assimilate this data, leading to the data lag of six weeks or one and half month. The central bank and the government, on the receipt of this data, analyzes it along with the data on other related variables, resulting in the recognition lag of say a fortnight. If a slowdown is identified on the basis of the data analysis, the government and other policy makers debate on the nature of the problem and try to assess whether the problem is temporary in nature or long lasting and warrants any policy action, leading to the decision lag. Once the policy action is identified in the form of higher subsidies to the manufacturers by the government, it takes time to receive an approval from the parliament, causing the implementation lag.

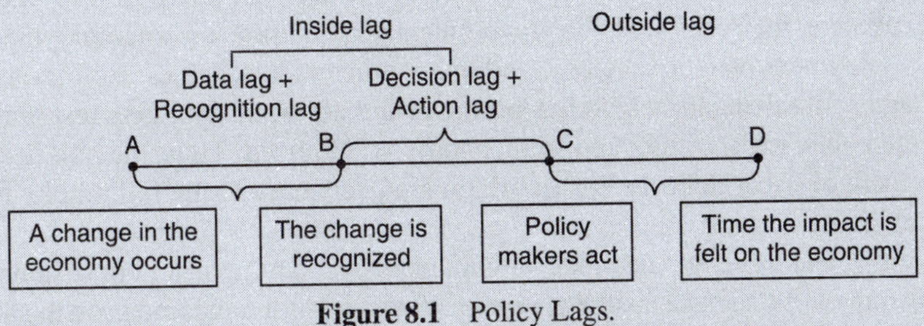

Figure 8.1 Policy Lags.

Unlike the inside lag, the **outside lag** occurs after the policy is implemented. It is the time that elapses between the approved policy measure is implemented and the impact of it is felt on the targeted variables. In the context of our previous example, once manufacturers receive subsidies from the government, manufacturers take time to adjust their output level, leading to the outside lag.

For a policy measure to be effective both the inside and outside lags should be minimized. Otherwise, the very purpose of policy action is often defeated.

For fiscal policy the inside lags have been identified to be relatively longer than the outside lags. It takes relatively longer time to get an approval and implement a fiscal policy measure, which increases the inside lag. However, once the policy measure has been implemented its impact on the economy is felt relatively swiftly. On the contrary, for monetary policy the inside lag is comparatively shorter than the outside lag.

8.4 FISCAL POLICY AS A COUNTER CYCLICAL DEVICE

Fiscal policy has two elements: one is non-discretionary or automatic and the other is discretionary.

The **non-discretionary component of fiscal policy** is an endogenous component, which changes along with business fluctuations. It automatically changes the amount of public expenditure and revenue, and thus, the size of fiscal balance. In a downturn such elements automatically increase the public spending and reduce the tax revenue collection. On the contrary, in an upturn the public expenditure declines and tax revenue increases automatically. The reasons for the automatic changes in the expenditure and revenue are explained hereinafter.

The public expenditure increases automatically in a downturn. For example, many governments have employment guarantee programmes, which provide employment or unemployment benefits to the unemployed. In periods of slowdown and recession the number of people registering with employment exchanges for unemployment benefits increases sharply. Thus, as the level of unemployment increases the government expenses on such schemes automatically increases without there being any change in the fiscal policy. The higher expenditure by the government on unemployment benefits gets infused in the form of higher income that increases the aggregate demand. Similarly, many governments operate state run hospitals and provide medical benefits to poor and underprivileged at subsidzed rates. The number of people visiting such hospitals increases in a downturn, thus, increasing the public expenditure on subsidies provided to such hospitals. Likewise, many governments also supply subsidized foodgrains and other essential items through ration shops. The number of households purchasing items from such shops increases in a downturn. In a downturn, where the deficiency of demand is a problem, such non-discretionary elements of fiscal policy, by raising public expenditure, create additional demand and help in moderating the slowdown or recession. Conversely, in an upward phase of a business cycle, the level of employment increases and the government expenditure on unemployment guarantee schemes, unemployment benefit schemes, and many other such schemes declines automatically. The level of aggregate demand, which has been causing an expansion, gets restrained through a reduction in the public expenditure, and the economy is stabilized. Thus, the non-discretionary or automatic element of fiscal policy helps in bringing an economy to the full employment level of output and stabilizing it.

The government revenue declines automatically in an upturn. For example, under a progressive income tax structure, as the economy slows down the income growth slows down as well. Income tax being progressive, the taxpayers pay less tax and spend larger proportion of their income on goods and services. The aggregate demand, thus, increases and this helps in moderating the downturn. On the contrary, in a booming economy the income level increases. The income tax being a progressive tax, the number of tax payers falling in a high tax bracket also increases and they end up paying more taxes. This constraints the amount of expenditure by the private sector, and thus, helps in moderating the boom.

The non-discretionary or automatic component of fiscal policy, thus, helps in moderating the ups and downs in business activities and stabilizing the economy automatically; hence, it is also known as the **automatic stabilizer**.

A fallout of automatic stabilizers is that they automatically change the size of fiscal deficit over various phases of business cycles. The deficit increases in downturns as the government expenditure increases and tax revenue falls. On the other hand, in upturns, government spending declines and the revenue increases, which reduces the size of fiscal deficit.

Unlike the non-discretionary component, the **discretionary component of fiscal policy** is exogenous to the system and emerges from the deliberate policy actions of a government. The government pursues discretionary changes in the policy to achieve certain stated objectives, especially when self correcting mechanism in the form of automatic stabilizer is not sufficient enough to bring in desirable changes. For example, in a downturn, if sufficient expansion does not take place automatically, the government can give a boost to an economy by introducing fiscal stimulus packages. As a part of these packages, a new employment generation programme can be introduced or the coverage of the existing employment guarantee programme can be enhanced. Or, alternatively, the government can reduce tax rates or eliminate existing taxes on various commodities or activities to enhance the disposable income of household and net profit of corporations to give a boost to aggregate consumption and investment demand. This we have seen in the recent episode of global recession when many governments ended up introducing fiscal stimulus packages in their countries. Conversely, in an upturn, if sufficient contraction in government expenditure does not take place, then the government can exit from the existing lines of programmes. For example, it can eliminate the existing employment guarantee schemes or reduce their coverage. Alternatively, the government can even enhance the tax rates to contract private consumption or investment expenditure. This also we have seen in 2010–11, when the governments of many countries, with the recovery of their economies, started withdrawing from the fiscal stimulus package which they had introduced during the recessionary period. Since these policies are not in-built and do not become operative automatically these are known as **discretionary fiscal policies**.

8.5 INSTRUMENTS OF FISCAL POLICY

Fiscal policy uses two main instruments, viz., public revenue and public expenditure (Figure 8.2), to achieve its various objectives. These instruments are laid down in the **Annual Financial Statement** of a government (UBE 8.1) and are discussed in this section.

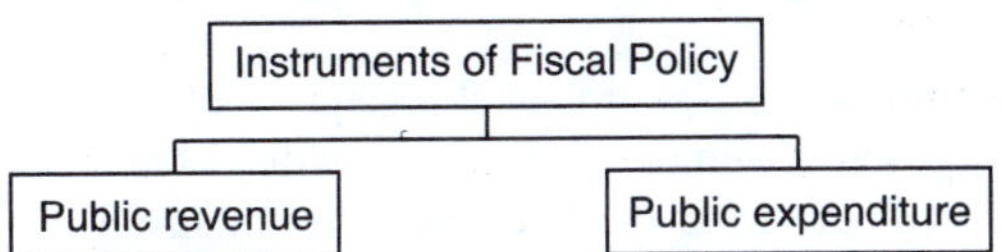

Figure 8.2 Instruments of Fiscal Policy.

UNDERSTANDING BUSINESS ENVIRONMENT

UBE 8.1 Union Budget

The stance of fiscal policy can be gauged from the Annual Financial Statement of a government. To understand this document, it is essential to know its subheads and the items accounted under them. This UBE explains the subheads of the Annual Financial Statement of the Government of India.

The statement of estimated receipts and expenditure of the Government of India, reflecting its policies, is titled as the **Annual Financial Statement** which is also known as budget.

The Union Budget for the ensuing financial year is presented each year normally on February 28 in the Lok Sabha for approval. The most of the budget proposals become operative at the start of the financial year, i.e., 1st April. The budget summarizes the receipts and expenditures of the government for the previous year and presents the estimates for the ensuing year. It enunciates the government's long-term economic policy, and immediate taxation proposals. The budget document is drafted by the budget division of the Finance Ministry taking into consideration the proposals from various ministries and departments and the available funds.

The Annual Financial Statement is sub-divided into three sub-heads as follows:

Consolidated fund of India: The **consolidated Fund of India** is one big reservoir where the government pools in all its funds together. The inflow to this account is from all tax and non-tax sources. Fresh borrowings as well as recoveries of outstanding loans also form a part of this account. All payments from this fund require prior authorization from the parliament.

Contingency fund of India: The utilization of amount from the **contingency fund of India** is placed at the disposal of the President of India. The amount is utilized for meeting urgent and unforeseen expenditure. This fund helps the government tide over difficult situations. Though prior authorization is not required, the ex-post approval for withdrawal of an equivalent amount from the consolidated fund is obtained, and the amount that is withdrawn from the contingency fund is recouped to the fund. At present, the authorized corpus of the fund is ₹500 crore.

Public account fund of India: The amount in the **public account fund of India** does not belong to the government. The government just acts as a banker of the public funds such as transactions relating to provident funds, small savings collections, other deposits, etc. Since the amount does not belong to the government, the authorization for repayment, to the persons and authorities who deposited them, from this account is not required.

The Annual Financial Statement distinguishes the expenditure on revenue account from other expenditure categories, and thus, comprises:

Revenue budget: The **revenue budget** comprises the revenue receipts and the expenditures incurred from these revenue receipts. The revenue receipts consist of both tax and non-tax receipts, such as interest and dividend on investments made by the government, fees and other receipts for services rendered by the government. The expenditure on revenue account is for the normal running of government departments and various services, interest charges on debt incurred by the government, subsidies and grants given to state governments and other parties, etc.

Capital budget: The **capital budget** consists of capital receipts and payments. The main items of capital receipts are the loans raised by the government from the public, which are also known as the **market loans**, borrowings by the government from the RBI and other financial institutions, loans from foreign governments and bodies, and recoveries of loans granted by the Central Government to state governments, union territories and other parties. On the contrary, the capital payments consist of capital expenditure on assets such as land, buildings, machinery, equipment, and investment in shares, loans and advances granted by the Central Government to state governments, union territories, government companies and other parties. The transactions in the public account are also a part of the capital budget.

8.5.1 Public Revenue

The own revenue of a government comprises revenue receipts (both tax and non-tax receipts) and own capital receipts (Figure 8.3).

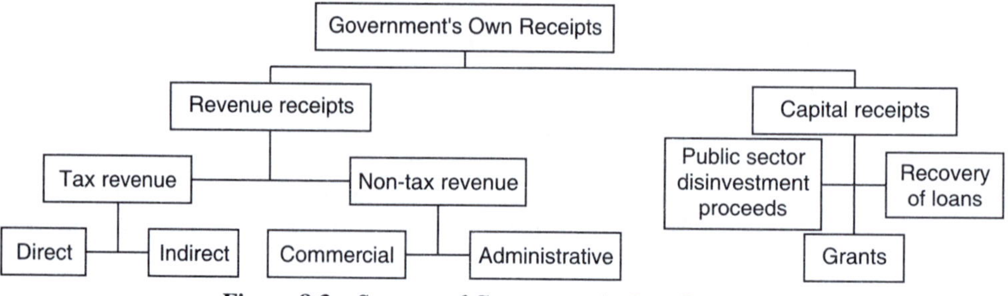

Figure 8.3 Sources of Government's Own Revenue.

Revenue Receipts

The **revenue receipts** can be either in the form of tax revenue or non-tax revenue.

Tax revenue: A government generates **tax revenue** by imposing taxes. A **tax** is a levy imposed by a government on economic agents/legal entities. It is a duty of taxpayers to pay it. A tax is the amount withdrawn from the private sector without leaving the government with a liability to the payee. Also the contribution, received from taxpayers, may even be used for non-tax payers.

Total tax revenue collection is an outcome of the tax rate and the tax base. The **tax rate** is the tax expressed in percentage terms. It can be marginal or average, or *ad valorem* or specific (Box 8.3). The **tax base**, on the other hand, is the amount on which the tax is levied. For example, for income tax the base is the income of an individual while for corporate tax the base is profit of a firm. Similarly, for an excise duty the base is the total output produced by a firm, for a value added tax the base is the value added by a firm, and for a sales tax the base is the total value of an item sold.

Box 8.3 Tax Rate

The **tax rate** is a tax expressed in percentage terms. It can be marginal or average. The **marginal tax rate** refers to the change in the tax payer's liability as the taxable income changes.

$$\text{Marginal tax rate} = \frac{\Delta(\text{Total tax liability})}{\Delta(\text{Total taxable income})}$$

The **average tax rate** or **effective tax rate**, on the other hand, refers to the total tax liability as a percentage of total taxable income.

$$\text{Average tax rate} = \frac{\text{Total tax liability}}{\text{Total taxable income}}$$

For example, if the tax rates are: 10 per cent for income level up to ₹1,00,000, 20 per cent for income slab of ₹1,00,000 to ₹2,00,000, and 30 per cent for income slab of ₹2,00,000 to ₹3,00,000, then for the taxpayer with income of ₹2,50,000 the total tax liability, marginal tax rate, and average tax rate are as follows:

Total tax liability = (0.10 × 1,00,000) + (0.20 × 1,00,000) + (0.30 × 50,000) = 45,000

The marginal tax rate is 30 per cent.

The average or effective tax rate is (45,000/2,50,000) = 0.18 or 18 per cent

Marginal or average tax rates are generally referred to in the context of income tax. In most countries, marginal tax rates increase along with the increase in income, leading to progressivity in the taxation system. Marginal tax rates play an important role in determining the incentive to earn. Higher marginal tax rates discourage individuals to earn more. At 100 per cent marginal tax, individuals will not have any incentive to earn more income, and this may even reduce the total tax revenue collected by the government as we will see while discussing the **Laffer curve**.

Apart from income, commodities are also subject to taxes. Taxes on commodities can be specific or *ad valorem*.

The **specific tax** is a flat or fixed rate tax. Under the specific tax the tax base is the quantity of certain commodity. The base is not affected by the value of the commodity under this tax . For example, the licence fees is a specific tax. The owner of, say, a scooter is required to pay the fixed amount to obtain the driving license which is irrespective of the value of the scooter. Similarly, the tax on cigarettes is a specific tax, it is levied as certain fixed amount per 1,000 sticks and does not vary with the value of cigarettes. Likewise, fuel and liquor are often subject to specific taxes whereby tax is per litre of petrol and per pint of beer respectively. Specific taxes are clear and simple to administer. They involve greater degree of certainty and involve less administrative cost. There are less chances of evasion or avoidance as there are fewer loopholes in flat taxes. However, flat taxes are inherently regressive; they impose higher burden on the poor than on the rich. These taxes are also less flexible and are not effective as automatic stabilizers.

On the contrary, under the ***ad valorem* tax (for definition refer to Box 8.5)**, the base is the value of a commodity. Under this type of tax, rather than the amount of tax, the rate of tax is fixed. For example, a tax at the rate of 10 per cent of the value of a television set is an *ad valorem* tax. It increases the amount of tax revenue collected if the value or the price of the commodity on which it is levied increases. The property tax is an *ad valorem* tax where an owner of real estate or other property pays tax as per the value of the property. Similarly, custom duty, sales tax and value added tax are examples of an *ad valorem* tax.

Ad valorem taxes, though difficult to administer, provide greater revenue to the government whenever the value of a product increases. They are progressive in their impact because the higher income group usually buys expensive gadgets, such as luxury cars, travels in luxury—such as first class compartment; hence, under this type of tax system, it pays more tax than the poor income group. Conversely, the poor income group buys less expensive gadgets, travels in economy mode and ends up paying lesser tax if the tax is an *ad valorem* tax.

Principles of Good Tax Policy

Traditionally, the basic objective behind imposing taxes is to raise revenue. However, in modern economies these have become an important instrument of fiscal policy to achieve other objectives, such as equity and growth. The objective of equity is achieved by redistribution of income among individuals or different population groups. For example, taxes are imposed on working population to support the poor, the disabled and the retired. Similarly, to attain higher growth, macroeconomic performance is influenced by diverting resources, such as capital and labour, in certain desired channels, such as investment in infrastructure and production and consumption of essential goods, by imposing lower rates of taxes or by providing various tax concessions. Sometimes, taxes are also used for influencing the behaviour of taxpayers. For example, alcohol and cigarettes pose a risk to public health; taxes can be used to discourage the consumption and production of such products. If designed prudentially, the above objectives can be achieved efficiently by taxation policy. However, hasty and carelessly designed taxation policies can have an adverse impact on an economy and can even jeopardize the social system and bring in political instability. To evolve an efficient and fair tax system, the noted economist Adam Smith suggested four principles of taxation as equity, certainty, convenience and economy. Modern economists advocate some more principles as elaborated hereinafter:

1. Equity and fairness: The **principle of equity** and fairness implies that the similarly situated taxpayers should be taxed similarly and taxes imposed should be in proportion to the ability to pay. Tax system should be able to maintain horizontal and vertical equity.

2. Horizontal equity: It implies that the two taxpayers with equal abilities to pay should pay the same amount of tax. They should not be discriminated on the basis of the source of income or any other criteria. For example if Ram is earning ₹1 lakh from agricultural activities and Shyam is earning the same amount from manufacturing activities, then both Ram and Shyam should be subjected to the same amount of tax. On the contrary, **vertical equity** implies that the person with greater ability to pay should pay more tax. For example, if Neeraj is earning ₹2 lakh then he should pay higher amount of tax than Ram and Shyam. Such a system is fair as people do not mind paying as per their capacity.

3. Certainty: The **principle of certainty** implies that the tax rules should be clear enough to enable tax payers to identify the items/transactions that are subject to a tax liability. Tax rates should be stable, i.e., should not be changing every now and then. Procedures and mode of payment of a tax should leave no room for ambiguity and dependence on tax consultance. They help taxpayers to determine their tax liability with certainty.

4. Convenience of payment: Tax payments should be due at a time that is most convenient for taxpayers to pay taxes. For example, sales tax can be assessed at the time of purchase when consumers have the choice to buy or not to buy goods and pay the tax. Similarly, income tax can be deducted at source, i.e., from employees' salary cheques. Likewise the tax on interest rates on deposits can be deducted by banks before making interest payments to their depositors. The **principle of convenience of payment** ensures a better compliance with a tax system.

5. Economy of collection: Tax collection imposes certain costs on both the government and the taxpayers. These costs are administrative costs and compliance costs. **Administrative costs** are the expenses incurred by a government on the revenue officers. On the contrary, **compliance costs** are incurred by taxpayers in visiting tax offices and consulting tax consultants. The complexity in a tax system increases administrative costs as well as compliance costs. The **principle of economy of collection** suggests that such costs should be minimized.

6. Simplicity: The **principle of simplicity** indicates that the tax laws should be simple to understand and easy to comply with. Complex tax laws (for example too many tax slabs, or a large variety of taxes or too many types of tax payers) lead to errors in the assessment of liability, induce evasion, reduce compliance, and increase the cost of collection.

7. Neutrality: Taxation of some commodities and activities while leaving the others out of the tax net results in diversion of resources from the taxed areas to non-taxed areas, and thus, causes distortions in consumption and production choices. The **principle of neutrality** suggests that the tax system should aim at minimizing such distortions. The primary purpose of a tax should be restricted to raising the revenue for a government rather than affecting business and personal decisions and activities.

8. Economic growth and efficiency: A tax system should be in concurrence with and support the national goals of economic growth and efficiency. A taxation system favouring a particular industry or commodity, for example, may divert the flow of capital, labour and other resources in particular industries at the cost of other industries as well as that of the economy as a whole. The **principle of economic growth** suggests that the taxes should lead to allocation efficiency and should promote economic growth.

9. Transparency: The **principle of transparency** suggests that thc taxpayers should know clearly about the tax rates applicable on any transaction or activity, and their total tax liability. They should also be able to analyze the impact of these on them. Ambiguities in a taxation system affect the tax revenue collection and divert it to unintended parties.

10. Flexibility: The **principle of flexibility** argues that the tax system should be able to adopt to changing circumstances. It should act as an automatic stabilizer without external interferences and any new legislation.

11. Minimum tax gap: A **tax gap** is the difference between taxes that are owed and taxes that are voluntarily paid. A tax gap can be due to intentional or unintentional errors. Intentional errors are an outcome of under reporting of income, overstating of permissible deductions, omission of certain taxable transactions, non-filing of returns. Whereas, unintentional errors are an outcome of complex, ambiguous and multiplex tax laws resulting in a lack of understanding of rules and estimation mistakes. The **principle of minimum tax gap** argues that the tax system should be simple and should incorporate penalties for non-compliance so as to minimize the tax gap.

12. Stability and predictability: The principle of stability and predictability indicates that the tax system should be stable, predictable and reliable. It should enable the government to estimate the expected amount of tax revenue in the coming period with a greater degree of confidence. The predictability of tax revenue is important for the government to determine its expenditure level. The tax revenue from different types of taxes get affected differently when the structure of an economy and economic environment is continuously evolving and changing. Some of the taxes are more sensitive to economic fluctuations than the others. Thus, the fluctuations in total tax revenue collection can be minimized by imposing a mix of taxes.

Some of these principles may be in conflict with each other. Countries decide to emphasize one or the other principles depending on the structure of their economies, economic environment, and social and political priorities. Usually a multiple tax system is preferred over a single tax system so as to avoid large fluctuations in tax revenue collection occurring due to income/output fluctuations. However, large multiplicity is avoided to keep the tax system simple. While judging a tax system, a holistic view needs to be taken that fits into the economic organization of a society.

Nature of Taxes

Different taxes affect different sections of the population differently. Some taxes impose higher burden on the lower income strata while the others on the higher income strata. A tax system can be either progressive or regressive or proportional as described hereinafter.

1. Progressive tax system: Under the **progressive tax system** the tax rate increases as the amount to which the rate is applied increases. The progressive tax is based on the concept of ability to pay. It takes a larger proportion of income from a high income group than a low income group. For example, under a progressive tax system the low income group may be subject to a 10 per cent tax rate, the middle income group to a 20 per cent tax rate and the high income group to a 30 per cent tax rate. The progressive tax reduces the tax incidence (Box 8.6) on people with lower income.

2. Regressive tax system: Under the **regressive tax system** each taxpayer, regardless of his or her income, pays the same amount of tax, say ₹100 for any income level. This implies that the tax rate decreases as the amount to which the rate applied increases. The lower income group, under this type of system, pays a larger proportion of its income as tax than the higher income group. For example, a tax of ₹100 on an income of ₹1,000, ₹10,000 and ₹1,00,000 implies a tax rate of 10 per cent, 1 per cent and 0.1 per cent, respectively. Specific taxes (Box 8.3), such as taxes on tobacco, alcohol, petrol, travel, etc., impose a larger burden on the lower income group than on the higher income group. Similarly, various user fees, such as fees for licences, tolls for roads and bridges, parking charges, which are charged per item or quantity, make the lower income group to pay a higher proportion of their income. The regressive tax system reduces the tax incidence on people with higher incomes.

3. Proportional tax system: Under the **proportional tax system**, taxpayers are subject to fixed or flat rates of tax, i.e., individuals or households pay taxes proportional to their income. For example, all the categories of households, low income group, middle income group and high income group, under this tax system, may be subject to say, a 10 per cent tax rate. The sales tax is a good example of a proportional tax because all consumers, regardless of their income, pay the same fixed rate.

Flat or proportional taxes are considered to be regressive in nature as they take away a larger proportion of income of lower income group. For example, a 10 per cent sales tax on a TV worth ₹10,000 implies a larger incidence of tax on the person with income of ₹1 lakh per annum than the person with income of ₹10 lakh per annum.

Figure 8.4 depicts the above three forms of taxes.

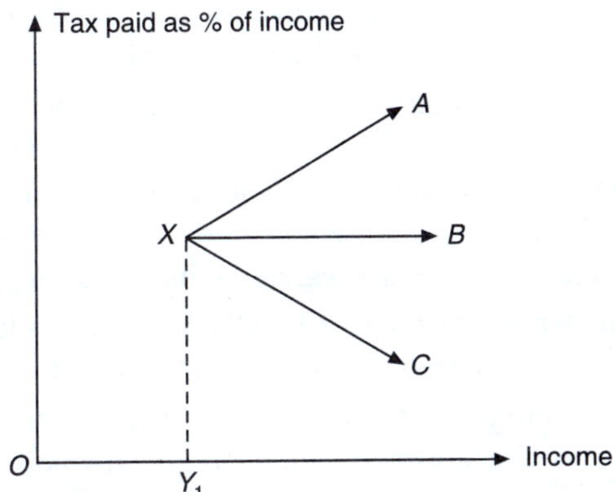

Figure 8.4 Progressive, Proportional and Regressive Income Tax System.

In Figure 8.4, the income below OY_1 is exempted from income tax. The tax rate increases as the income increases along the ray *XA* reflecting the progressive tax system. Along the ray *XB* per cent of income paid in taxes remains the same, indicative of the proportional income tax. The ray *XC* represents a regressive tax system, where the income tax rate falls as the income increases.

Types of Taxes

Broadly taxes are classified into two categories, viz., direct taxes and indirect taxes (Figure 8.3).

1. Direct tax: **Direct taxes** are the one that are paid by the people or organizations on whom they are imposed. The examples of such taxes are as follows:

(i) *Capital gains tax:* The **capital gains tax** is a tax which is levied on the profit arising from the sale of a capital asset like a bond or a share.

(ii) *Corporate tax:* The **corporate tax** is levied on the profits or net income of a company or an association.

(iii) *Inheritance tax:* The **inheritance tax** is a tax on the amount of inheritance received by a person. It is also known as the **estate tax** or **death tax**.

(iv) *Personal income tax:* The **personal income tax** is levied on the income of a person. These taxes are often levied on the total income of an individual with some permissible deductions.

(v) *Poll tax:* The **poll tax** is also known as the **per capita tax** or **capitation tax**. It is a specific tax and is levied as a set of fixed amount per individual. The poll tax is easy to compute and involves less administrative cost. This tax even discourages couples to have more children reducing the population over a period of time. However, it is strongly regressive as the poorer section of a society ends up paying a higher proportion of its income than the richer under this tax.

(vi) *Property tax:* The **property tax** is a tax imposed on the value of property, generally real estate, such as land and buildings, owned by a person.

(vii) *Retirement tax:* In many countries, the **retirement tax** is used for funding social security system meant for providing income to retired workers. This differs from a comprehensive income tax as it is levied only on the specific sources of income generally wages and salaries. It is sometimes also known as the **payroll tax**. Retirement benefits to workers are quite often linked to their contribution to this type of tax.

In certain countries, workers, irrespective of their income, pay this tax at the same rate up to a specified cap. Income above the cap is not taxed making the tax regressive in its impact. Moreover, this tax often excludes investment earnings and other forms of income that usually form a major component of income of the higher income group. Therefore, such a tax escalates the regressive impact of the tax.

(viii) *Wealth tax:* The **wealth tax** is levied on the wealth of individuals and companies that has a potential to yield return or income year after year to the wealth holder.

The incidence of direct taxes cannot be shifted to another party (Box 8.4), implying that the incidence of direct taxes lies on the party on whom it is levied. For example, if the government levies a tax on the income of Ram then he cannot shift it to Shyam. It is easier to bring in an element of progressivity in such taxes by increasing the marginal tax rates.

Box 8.4 Tax Burden and Tax Incidence

Tax burden is defined as the total tax payment as a proportion of the total income in a given period. Thus, an imposition of a tax by a government imposes some tax burden on taxpayers or persons on whom it is legally levied.

The burden of a tax can be shifted by the person who is legally responsible for paying the tax to another party who is not legally subject to the tax. **Tax incidence** indicates the person who actually bears the burden of a tax. The person who ultimately pays for a tax, or put alternately, the person who bears the incidence of a tax, is determined by the market place, specifically by the elasticities of demand and supply. Depending on the values of the elasticities of supply and demand, tax burden can be absorbed by sellers (in the form of lower post-tax prices), or by buyers (in the form of higher post-tax prices). If the elasticity of supply is high (low), less (more) of the tax burden is borne by sellers or suppliers. Conversely, if the elasticity of demand is high (low), less (more) of the tax burden is borne by consumers.

To understand the above process, suppose that there is no tax on commodities and assume that the equilibrium price of a commodity, i.e., the price determined by the intersection of demand and supply curves, is ₹100 as indicated in Figure 8.5. When there is no tax on the commodity, both sellers and consumers face the same price of ₹100, i.e., consumers pay ₹100 and producers also receive ₹100. Suppose the government levies a specific tax of ₹50 on sellers. The tax on sellers increases their cost of production and forces them to supply lesser units for each given price. This results in a shift in the supply curve from S_0 to S_1. The vertical distance between S_0 and S_1, at any given quantity, indicates the amount of tax. The shift in the supply curve, given the demand curve at D_0, increases the equilibrium price to ₹110. This is the price consumer will pay once the government charges tax on sellers. Sellers will pay ₹50 from this amount and will be left with only ₹60 per unit as the price. Post tax, consumer face price of ₹110, ₹10 higher than the pre-tax price, whereas producers face ₹60 because they pay ₹50 from ₹110 to the government as tax. Since neither of the curves is perfectly elastic (parallel to horizontal axis) or inelastic (parallel to vertical axis) the incidence of this tax falls partly on consumers and partly on sellers.

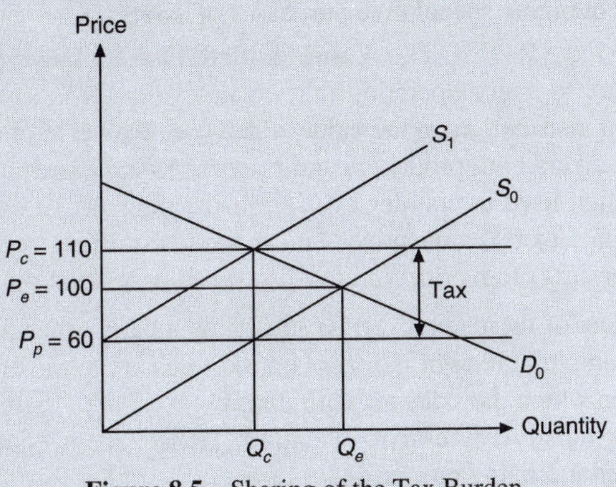

Figure 8.5 Sharing of the Tax Burden.

2. Indirect tax: **Indirect taxes** are often collected from someone other than the person presumably responsible for paying the taxes. Some examples of indirect taxes are as follows:

(i) *Countervailing duties:* The **countervailing duty** is imposed on imports to raise the prices of imported commodities in domestic markets. It is imposed with the intention of discouraging unfair trading practices, such as dumping by other countries and protecting domestic manufacturers.

(ii) *Custom duties or tariffs:* The **custom duty** or tariff is a tax on import or export of commodities. Though the import duty is used mainly as source of revenue, it is often used by governments to protect domestic industries or goods produced within the domestic boundaries.

(iii) *Excise duty:* The **excise duty** is a tax imposed on the production of goods within the country at the manufacturing stage. The excise is based on the quantity and not the value of the product produced. Though, most often, it is levied by the government to raise the revenue, sometimes it is levied to discourage the production of those goods which are believed to have an adverse impact on public health or environment. For example, excise duty on cigarettes, alcoholic drinks, tobacco, etc., are quite often imposed to discourage the consumption of these commodities.

(iv) *Sales tax:* The **sales tax** is imposed at the stage when a commodity is sold to its final consumer. A flat rate or specific rate of sales tax tends to be regressive as people with lower income end up spending a larger proportion of their income on goods and services. To minimize the regressive impact, quite often, essential commodities are exempted from sales tax and luxury items are taxed heavily.

(v) *Stamp duty:* The **stamp duty** is levied on the purchase or sales of shares and securities, and transfer of land, currency transactions (stamp duty on currency transactions is known as **tobin tax**) or some such transactions. This duty increases the cost of purchase or sales transactions.Thus, preventing such transactions, the duty reduces the liquidity of the instruments on which it is levied. Given such an impact of a stamp duty, most often it is levied for discouraging speculative purchases of assets.

(vi) *Value Added Tax (VAT):* The **Value Added Tax** applies the equivalent of excise and/or sales tax to every operation that creates value. It is assessed at each stage of production and distribution on the value added (i.e., the value of output minus the value of input) and covers both producers and traders. As indicated in Box 8.5 and Box 8.6, the VAT is often used to counter evasion in the sales tax or excise. It minimizes the cascading impact of taxes on prices and market distortions resulting from the excise duty. However, it is often criticized for discouraging production.

The incidence of any of these taxes can be shifted on a party other than the party on which these are levied. For example, a retailer can pass on the sales tax to his customers by hiking the prices of commodities on which the sales tax is imposed.

Indirect taxes are mostly regressive in nature. Hence, from equity and growth view, economists favour higher and rising proportion of direct taxes rather than that of indirect taxes in the total tax revenue collection. This implies that as the GDP increases the ratio of direct to indirect taxes should keep on increasing to retain the equity element in the system as well increasing the total tax revenue collection for the government.

Box 8.5 VAT Liability: Method of Estimation

The **Value Added Tax** (VAT) is a percentage tax on the value added in each stage of production or distribution of a good or service. Three different methods have been used to compute liability under the VAT. These are the cost subtraction method, tax credit or invoice method and cash flow method.

Cost subtraction method: Under the **cost subtraction method**, the VAT liability is calculated by multiplying the value of output (sales) net of the value of intermediate goods purchased at each stage of the production (distribution) process with the given VAT rate. For example, for a firm producing the output worth ₹100 using the inputs worth ₹50, the value added is ₹50. This firm would be liable to pay a tax of ₹5 if the VAT is 10 per cent.

Tax credit method: The **tax credit method** or **invoice method** is the most common method of computing the VAT liability. Under this method, the VAT liability is calculated by multiplying the total production (sales) at each stage of production (distribution) process by the given tax rate. Thus, the total tax liability turns out to be the same as in the case of excise (excise taxes the value of total production). However, under this method, a taxpayer receives a credit (i.e., a rebate) for any tax paid on intermediate goods in the process of production (distribution). To this extent the VAT liability turns out to be lesser than the excise liability. To obtain the credit on tax paid on inputs, taxpayers need to submit the proof in the form of invoice of purchases of inputs and tax paid thereon. Following this method, for a firm producing output worth ₹100, the tax liability will be ₹10 if the tax rate is 10 per cent. If the firm is paying a tax of ₹5 on inputs it will get credit of ₹5 and its tax liability will be simply ₹5 under the VAT. Had the firm not paid any tax on inputs it would have been subject to a tax of ₹10 under the tax credit method of VAT.

Cash flow method: The VAT is calculated on the cash flow for a firm under the **cash flow method**. Following equation is used to determine the cash flow of a firm

$$S + K^{+} = L + M + K^{-}$$

where

S = Value of output or sales

L = Payments for labour

M = Value of intermediate goods

K^{+} = Capital inflows including equity and borrowing

K^{-} = Capital outflows including dividend, interest and debt repayments

Rearranging the above equation one gets

$$V = S - M = L + K^{-} - K^{+}$$

$S - M$ gives the VAT liability under the cost subtraction method. This may also be calculated as payments to labour plus net capital outflows. Under this system interest, dividend, and any other capital outflows are taxed.

Box 8.6 VAT, MODVAT and Excise: A Comparison

The **excise** is a tax on the value of output produced by a firm. The **Value Added Tax** (VAT) is a tax on the value added at each stage of production and distribution where the value added is estimated through the cost subtraction method.

Under the excise tax system, since the tax is on the value of output that is inclusive of the value of input, the amount of inputs used in the production process also gets taxed. And if the producers of intermediate goods have paid any tax on the value of these goods then excise implies not only the tax on the value of intermediate goods but also on the tax paid on these goods. This type of taxation results in a number of distortions which are indicated as follows:

1. It discourages outsourcing and ancillarization. Since under excise producers are made to pay taxes on taxes paid on inputs, often to minimize their cost of production produces rather than outsourcing the production of inputs to **ancillaries** (i.e., the units which focus on the production of parts and components which are used by larger industries) prefer producing these in-house, leading to vertical integration of firms. The economy as a whole, however, gets deprived of the economies of scale which exist in ancillaries. Ancillaries produce not only for one company, but supply the same items to many companies and clients. Thus, these units produce the same item in bulk, and, reap the benefits arising from a large scale production known as **economies of scale**.

2. Since excise results in tax on tax paid on inputs, it increases the tax liability. Higher tax liability results in tax evasion and avoidance (Box 8.8) and affects the tax compliance which in turn affect the total tax revenue collection negatively.
3. Under the excise regime, as can be noticed from Table 8.1, the tax on tax results in cascading impact on market prices because the higher tax liability often gets passed on to consumer in the form of higher price.

Table 8.1 Impact of Excise, VAT and MODVAT on Prices: An Illustration

(₹ in crore)

Case 1: No Tax on Inputs						
	Input	*Tax on Input*	*VA*	*Output*	*Tax*	*Market price*
Excise (10%)	45	0	50	95	9.5	104.5
VAT (10%)	45	0	50	95	5	100
MODVAT (10%)	45	0	50	95	9.5	104.5
Case 2: Tax on Inputs of ₹ 5 (for simplicity tax on inputs is kept as specific, i.e., fixed amount)						
Excise (10%)	45	5	50	100	10	110
VAT (10%)	45	5	50	100	5	105
MODVAT (10%)	45	5	50	100	5	105

Price of Commodity	*Excise*	*VAT*	*MOD-VAT*	*Difference Exc-VAT*	*Difference Exc-MVAT*	*Difference MVAT-VAT*
Case 1: No Tax on Input	104.5	100.0	104.5	4.5	0.0	4.5
Case 2: Tax on Input	110.0	105.0	105.0	5.0	5.0	0.0

Notations

VA: Value Added: Value of Output – Value of (Non-factor) Input; Inp: Input

VAT: Value Added Tax: Tax on Value Added

MVAT: MODVAT: Modified Value Added Tax

Inferences

1. The market price of commodities is higher in the case of Excise.
2. Increase in the price in the case of Excise is higher when there is a tax on inputs. Therefore: There is a cascading impact on prices in the case of Excise
3. When there is no tax on inputs the MODVAT is similar to the Excise.
4. When there is a tax on inputs the MODVAT is similar to the VAT.

Given the drawbacks of excise tax system, the VAT is preferred for the following reasons:

1. By taxing only the value added, VAT treats inputs produced in-house and that produced by ancillaries equally. Thus, it does not distort production and is neutral in its effect on businessman's decision as to the way he carries out his business.
2. By taxing only the value added it reduces the cascading impact of taxes on prices. Hence, consumers face lower price under the VAT regime than that prevailing under the excise regime (Table 8.1).
3. Since the VAT is only on the value added (which is lower than the total value of output), the liability under the VAT turns out to be smaller than that under the excise. As tax payers prefer

paying lower amount of tax than the higher, it improves tax compliance and also reduces the extent of tax avoidance.

4. Compliance with the VAT requires proper documentation of the value of output and inputs. Thus, it prevents underreporting of the value of output and tax evasion which improves the revenue collection.

However, the requirement of maintaining proper records under the VAT had often resulted in protests against implementation of it from businessmen. They have argued that to maintain proper records of their transactions they are required to employ an accountant which increases their cost of production.

The **Modified Value Added Tax** (MODVAT) is a simplified form of the VAT where the tax liability is estimated through the tax credit method. The VAT enables the deduction of entire value of inputs, whereas under the MODVAT, credit is given in respect of only on the duty paid on inputs. As illustrated in Table 8.2, when there is no tax on inputs the MODVAT is similar to the excise. However, with a tax on inputs, the MODVAT gives a similar amount of tax liability as the VAT. An ease of computation and compliance has led to adoption of the MODVAT by many countries.

Tax Impact

1. Revenue impact of tax rate changes: Changes in a tax rate have two effects on tax revenue, viz., arithmetic effect and economic effect. The **arithmetic effect** implies that if a tax rate is lowered (increased), tax revenue (per dollar of tax base) will also be lowered (increased). The **economic effect**, on the contrary, recognizes the positive (negative) impact that a lower (higher) tax rate has on work, output, employment, and thereby, on the tax base by providing incentive to increase (decrease) these activities. The arithmetic effect always works in an opposite direction of the economic effect. Hence, the combined impact of economic and arithmetic effects on total tax revenue can be positive or negative depending on the strength of each of these effects at any given tax rate.

The impact of these effects on tax revenue is captured in a bell-shaped **Laffer curve** (Figure 8.6). The Laffer curve indicates that initially the arithmetic impact dominates the economic effect. Hence, an increase in the tax rate, say from t_1 level, increases the revenue; i.e., percentage increase in the tax revenue is larger than the percentage increase in the tax rate, implying positive tax elasticity. But, after a given level of tax rate, say t^*, known as the **optimum tax rate**, the

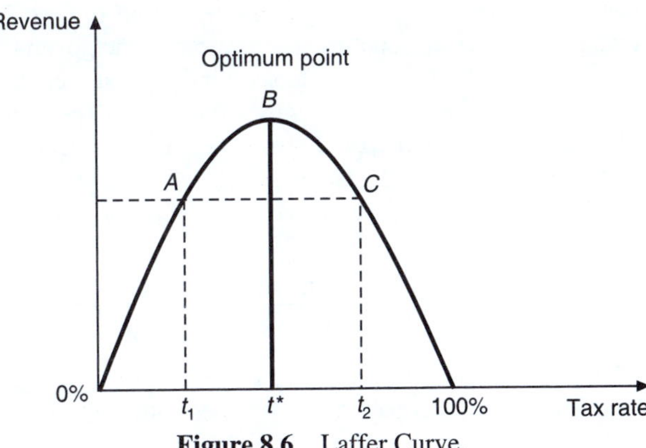

Figure 8.6 Laffer Curve.

economic effect dominates the arithmetic impact. Hence, any further increase in the tax rate, say to t_2, decreases the revenue, implying negative tax elasticity. At a tax rate of zero per cent, the government collects no tax revenues, no matter how large the tax base is. Similarly, at a tax rate of 100 per cent, the government collects no revenue, because no one is willing to work for an after tax wage of zero eroding the entire tax base. There are also two rates, for example t_1 and t_2, that return the same amount of revenue, a huge tax rate on a small tax base (t_2) and a low tax rate on a large tax base (t_1).

Revenue response to a tax rate change, known as the **tax elasticity** (Box 8.7), at a point of time varies from one economy to another and depends on a host of factors such as the type of tax system in place, prevalence of legal and accounting loopholes, penalty for non-compliance, avoidance and evasion (Box 8.8).

Box 8.7 Tax Elasticity and Buoyancy

The tax elasticity and tax buoyancy are important tools in evaluating the responsiveness of tax revenue to a tax rate and effectiveness of a country's tax strategy.

The **tax elasticity** measures the responsiveness of tax revenue to changes in a tax rate, and is defined as the percentage change in tax revenue resulting from a 1 per cent change in tax rate. Thus, the tax elasticity (e_t) is:

$$e_t = \frac{\text{\% Change in tax revenue}}{\text{\% Change in tax rate}}$$

or

$$e_t = \frac{(\Delta TR/TR) \times 100}{(\Delta t/t) \times 100}$$

or

$$e_t = \frac{\Delta TR}{\Delta t} \cdot \frac{t}{TR}$$

where, ΔTR = Change in tax revenue; TR = Total revenue before the change in tax rate; Δt = Change in tax rate; t = Original tax rate.

The value of e_t varies from positive infinity to negative infinity. The value of elasticity of greater than unity indicates that a one percentage change in tax rate results in more than one percentage change in tax revenue, implying that the system is capable of meeting the rising expenses of a government by increasing the tax rate. Conversely, the value of elasticity of less than one signifies an inelastic system incapable of automatically meeting growth in fiscal expenses.

To understand the concept further, assume that a government wants to raise its revenue to meet its growing expenditure requirement. Various options are available to the government; taxing petrol is one of those. To explore this option, the government looks at the previous year data when it has raised the tax on petrol by 20 per cent. In the last year, it recorded a growth of 40 per cent in tax revenue from petrol. It realized that the elasticity of petrol tax is 2 (i.e., 40 per cent/20 per cent). Realizing that the tax is elastic it decides on further enhancing the tax on petrol.

The **tax buoyancy** is defined as the percentage change in tax collection caused by a given percentage change in the tax base, i.e.,

$$e_b = \frac{\text{\% Change in tax revenue}}{\text{\% Change in tax base}}$$

Thus, it is a measure of increase in the actual tax revenue from a given change in the tax base. The **tax base** is an amount on which a taxpayer pays taxes. It varies with the type of tax. For example, in the case of personal income tax the base is income of individuals or households; for the corporate tax it is corporate profits, for the custom duty the tax base is the amount of imports; for the excise it is manufacturing output and for an overall tax buoyancy the tax base is the GDP.

The tax buoyancy is adversely affected by various exemptions available in the tax base. Exemptions narrow the tax base, and therefore, the tax revenue may not increase proportionately with an increase in the GDP. The value of less than one for the tax buoyancy implies that the GDP is growing at a faster rate than the growth in the tax revenue. This suggests that the tax structure needs a reform. On the other hand, the value of greater than 1 implies that tax structure or discretationary tax policies of the government affecting the tax structure is supportive of the growing expenditure requirement of the government.

To understand the applicability of the concept of tax buoyancy, consider a situation where the government is expecting a GDP growth of 10 per cent in the coming period. The estimate also indicates that given the tax structure, i.e., if the government does not change the tax structure, it will result in 8 per cent growth in the tax revenue. From these two estimates the government ascertains that the tax buoyancy is less than one (i.e., 8 per cent/10 per cent = 0.8). Hence, the GDP growth rate will not automatically meet its growing expenditure requirement. To improve tax collection, hence, it needs to change the tax structure. The structure can be changed either by widening the tax coverage, i.e., the coverage of commodities or activities on which the tax can be levied, or by enhancing the tax rates.

Box 8.8 Tax Avoidance and Tax Evasion

Tax avoidance takes place when a taxpayer uses tax laws to reduce the tax liability applicable on him. Tax avoidance is legal because business and individuals are entitled to take all lawful steps to minimize their tax liabilities. For example, to reduce the tax liability an individual can make use of various standard deductions permissible under a tax system; he can claim a rebate on the donations made by him, or he can seek a tax rebate on interest income or interest paid on loan taken from financial institutions. Corporate entities can reduce their tax liability by using a part of the profit for Research and Development (R&D) activity, using provisions for depreciation allowances, setting up units in backward areas, forming charitable trusts, etc.

Tax evasion, on the other hand, occurs when a taxpayer uses illegal means to reduce his tax liability, improperly claiming deductions that are not authorized. A taxpayer can deliberately misinterpret tax laws, underreport his income or profit from various sources. For example, corporate units can falsely claim that the company has invested ₹1 crore in R&D or show ₹10 lakh towards personal expenses. Similarly, individuals may falsely report a larger part of their income coming from agriculture sector, or as gifts from elderly to evade the tax. Tax evasion is treated as a crime and involves fines or even imprisonment.

2. Economic effects of taxation: Taxes affect an economy by influencing production, distribution of income and wealth, and inflation as detailed hereinafter:

(i) *Effect on production:* The effect of taxation on production depends on its impact on the ability to work, save and invest, willingness to work, save and invest and diversion of economic resources between different uses and localities as described as follows:

- *Impact on production through ability to work, save and invest.* A tax reduces consumption expenditure by reducing the disposable income. The malnourishment, resulting from reduction in consumption expenditure, reduces the ability and efficiency of a person to work, and hence, affects the production. The impact is severe when a tax is imposed on the poorer section of a society. The reduction in the income of this group generally lowers both the present efficiency of adults and the future efficiency of children. This argument applies to direct taxes on small incomes and indirect taxes on necessities.

A tax, by reducing the disposable income of a person, also reduces saving, and hence, the availability of funds for investment. Consequently, it adversely affects production through contraction in productive capacity.

- *Impact on production through willingness to work, save and invest.* The impact of a tax on willingness to work, save and invest and through these on production is not very clear, because the impact of a tax on these can be in any direction. One line of argument suggests that a tax, is a disincentive to work because it reduces the disposable income. Another line of argument, on the contrary, suggests that a tax by reducing the disposable income, makes people work more to maintain their standard of living. However, both the lines of arguments indicate that a tax is always a disincentive to save and investment.

  Not only the direction of tax change but also the extent of it determines whether a tax would be an incentive or a disincentive. The impact may go either way depending on whether the change is small or large. This also impacts a person's elasticity of demand for income. Highly elastic demand for income makes taxes a disincentive to the desire for work and save. Tax on a particular commodity will be slightly (highly) disincentive, if a small (large) proportion of the tax payer's marginal income is spent on it.

  Also, different types of taxes have different degree of impact on incentives to work, save and invest. There are some taxes which are neutral, in the sense that they have hardly any effect on the desire to work and save. A general tax on income, including saving, acts as more disincentive, especially to saving, than taxes on commodities (i.e. indirect taxes) which fall on expenditure only and not on saving. Hence, in the interest of enhancing saving, investment, and production, it has been suggested that the saving should be exempted from income tax and dissaving to be taxed.

  The tax structure is equally important while assessing the impact. In general, the progressive tax system is more disincentive than the proportional income tax which, in turn, is more disincentive than the regressive tax system. The poll tax, which is a regressive tax, from the point of incentives is one of the best forms of taxes, because it is neutral in its effect on production. Even the inherent tax does less damage to work and saving than an income tax.

- *Impact on production through diversion of economic resources between different uses and localities.* Taxes also affect production through diversion of resources as the producer, subject to taxes, seeks to escape these by diverting resources to some other uses which either are untaxed or taxed less. Often the taxes which fall with equal weight upon all uses of economic resources are neutral in their impact as they give no inducement to diversion. For example, taxes on windfall gains, taxes on value of land, taxes on profit of monopoly, etc., are neutral in their impact. Windfall gains are unexpected, and thus, do not affect desire to work and save. The land tax falls on the landowner irrespective of the use to which it is put. Since the supply of land is fixed by nature, the land tax also does not have any impact on the supply of land. Similarly, a tax on a monopoly profit does not alter monopoly output or selling price and is neutral in its impact. It is not essential that taxes, by diverting resources, always reduce production. On the contrary, these may stimulate production. For example, taxes on harmful drugs, diminishing their consumption and improving health and efficiency, give stimulus to production activities. Similarly, a tax on a monopoly, inducing him to increase his output and lowering his selling price, may be more productive than forcing him to operate in a competitive environment.

(ii) *Effect on distribution:* The impact of a tax on income also depends on a variety of factors varying from the tax structure to the type of taxes to the manner in which such taxes are computed.

The regressive tax and the proportional tax structure tend to increase the inequality of incomes, whereas the progressive tax structure tends to reduce it. The sharper the progression in the tax system the stronger is the reduction in inequalities. Thus, the consideration of income distribution supports a steeply progressive tax system. This also implies that the taxation should be according to the ability to pay. However, the considerations of production may make a sharply progressive tax system undesirable, because it also acts as a disincentive to work.

Income, inheritance and property taxes can be easily made progressive by introducing increasing marginal rates. On the contrary, indirect taxes, specifically which are specific, are mostly regressive, though some amount of progressivity prevails in them when taxes are *ad valorem* rather than specific. Some amount of progressivity is also introduced by taxing those commodities heavily that are primarily consumed by the richer income group, such as luxuries, and taxing those commodities lightly the expenditure on which form a larger proportion of the income of the lower income group, such as necessities.

(iii) *Effect on inflation:* Direct and indirect taxes affect prices, and hence, inflation differently. Direct taxes are supposed to be non-inflationary as an increase in direct taxes reduces the demand for goods and services, and thus, leads to a reduction in prices.

On the contrary, indirect taxes affect the cost of production which may get passed on to consumers in the form of higher market prices. The extent of pass through of a tax on a market price depends on the elasticity of demand for and supply of goods and services as discussed in Box 8.4. A large part of the incidence of a tax falls on producers if the taxed goods have a high elasticity of demand and low elasticity of supply. This reduces the profit of producers, and thus, checks inflation. However, for those taxed goods which have a low elasticity of demand and a high elasticity of supply, the incidence of tax gets shifted on to the buyers, leading to higher prices and higher inflation. Such taxed goods increase the cost of living and may force consumers to demand higher wages. To the extent wages rise, the cost of production of goods which are not taxed also increases. This leads to an increase in the overall price level induced by the increase in the cost of production.

Indirect taxes generate cost push inflation, and, quite often, have a cascading impact on prices. A multi point tax, such as the excise, has a higher cascading impact than a single point tax such as the VAT. Similarly, *ad valorem* duties are more inflationary than specific duties.

To minimize the impact of indirect taxes on inflation, a judicious choice has to be made regarding the commodities which are to be taxed as well as the rate at which these to be taxed.

To minimize the distortionary impact of taxes often reforms are introduced in the tax system as described in UBE 8.2 using India as the context.

UNDERSTANDING BUSINESS ENVIRONMENT

UBE 8.2 Tax Distortions, Reforms and Rationalization

Tax system tries to achieve multiple but often conflicting objectives. Emphasis on one objective, at the cost of others, leads to distortions and hampers growth in the long run. Reforms are introduced to minimize distortions and balance the objectives. This UBE highlights the Indian experiments with tax reforms.

India has a tax structure with a three-tier federal structure consisting of the Union Government, State Governments, and local bodies. The Union Government is empowered to levy taxes on non-agriculture income and wealth, corporate profits, custom duties, excise duties except those on alcohol, and service tax. State Governments can levy taxes on agriculture land, income and wealth, sales tax, excise on alcohol and taxes on motor vehicles, goods, and passengers, duty on entertainment, stamp duties and registration fees. Local bodies are empowered to tax properties, impose octroi, and charge for utilities.

Tax Distortions: Pre-1991 Period

In the pre-reform period, the tax policy addressed multiple objectives conflicting with each other. On the one hand, it aimed at raising resources for meeting public sector consumption and investment requirements, and on the other hand, motivated to achieve the socialistic pattern of society by bringing steep progressivity in the tax system.

The multiplicity of objectives complicated the tax system, narrowed the tax base, made the system inefficient, enlarged the horizontal inequity and led to a large scale evasion and avoidance of taxes. Some of these deficiencies and characteristics of the tax system have been detailed hereinafter.

High and multiple tax rates, narrow base and complex tax system: Before the full-fledged comprehensive tax reforms in the country began, different layers of the government developed tax system independently with no coordination with each other leading to multiple taxation of certain commodities, cascading impact on prices, various anomalies and loopholes in the tax system.

In the direct tax arena, the income tax rates, both personal and corporate income, kept on increasing. In 1973–74, for instance, the number of personal income tax slabs were as high as eleven, with marginal rates monotonically increasing from 10 per cent to 85 per cent. Including the surcharge of 15 per cent, the highest effective rate stood at 97.5 per cent. Even after rationalization and reduction in these rates, the highest marginal income tax rate was 50 per cent with effective rate standing at 56 per cent in 1991–92.

Similarly, corporate profit tax rates varied for widely-held companies and closely-held companies. Though the process of rationalization of these tax rates had started in 1983–84, in the year 1991–92 widely- and closely-held companies were still subject to tax rate of 45 and 50 per cent, respectively. They were also subject to a surcharge of 15 per cent. Foreign companies were subject to tax rate of 65 per cent on their profits.

High marginal rates of personal income tax, wealth tax, and corporate profit tax were disincentive for work, save and invest. These rates also provided a large incentive for tax evasion and avoidance. Various exemptions and incentives narrowed the tax base and went against the principle of horizontal equity. For example, inspite of high rates of corporate taxes, liberal depreciation and investment allowances made it possible for some companies to bring down their tax liabilities to zero.

The indirect tax system was also afflicted by the multiplicity of types and rates of taxes. For example, by the mid 70s, the excise tax structure was a mix of specific and *ad valorem rates*. There were 24 different *ad valorem* rates varying from 2 per cent to 100 per cent. Taxes were levied at different levels, input, capital goods, as well as final goods; with varying rates leading to cascading impact on the prices of final goods. Special treatment to the small scale sector, under the excise taxation, had been a source of substantial tax evasion. Also, the applicability of excise only up to the manufacturing stage was tempting for producers to underestimate the values of their products, and become a way to avoid tax.

The trade of goods was also subject to the sales tax which comprised General Sales Tax (GST) and Central Sales Tax (CST). The former is levied on intra-state sales by the states. The latter is legislated by the Centre, and applies to inter-state sales. It is collected and retained by the exporting states. During the pre-reform period, the rate structure of sales tax varied widely across the states. There was no tax coordination among the states or between the centre and the states. The tax rate varied not only from commodity to commodity but also with the end use of commodities. Each state allowed a large number of concessions and exemptions which kept the tax base narrow. In 1989–90, the rate of sales tax varied across the states form 4 to 12 per cent. The sales tax is imposed on the price which is inclusive of excise, and thus, proliferates the cascading impact of excise.

The indirect taxes on international trade also reflected the same complexity. International trade was subject to a large number of quantitative restrictions in the 1950s, 1960s and 1970s. However, in pursuit of raising revenue, custom duties were considerably raised in the late 1980s. Gradual tarrification, i.e., the replacement of quantitative restrictions with tariffs, made the custom structure a complex set by the mid 80s, with differentiated rates and rates varying with the stage of production, lower rates on inputs and higher rates on finished goods. Weighted average rate stood at 87 per cent in 1989–90. By 1990–91, the duty rates ranged from 0 per cent to as high as 300 per cent *ad valorem,* the bulk of imports fall in the range of 50 to 150 per cent with average effective rate working out to be 85 per cent.

Wide ranging exemptions, granted by issuing notifications, in various spheres also further complicated the indirect tax system.

Large share of indirect taxes: Indirect taxes dominated the tax revenue (Figure 8.7). Indirect taxes have a large cascading impact on prices. As the larger share of income of poor people goes in paying indirect taxes, the tax system had turned out to be highly regressive in nature.

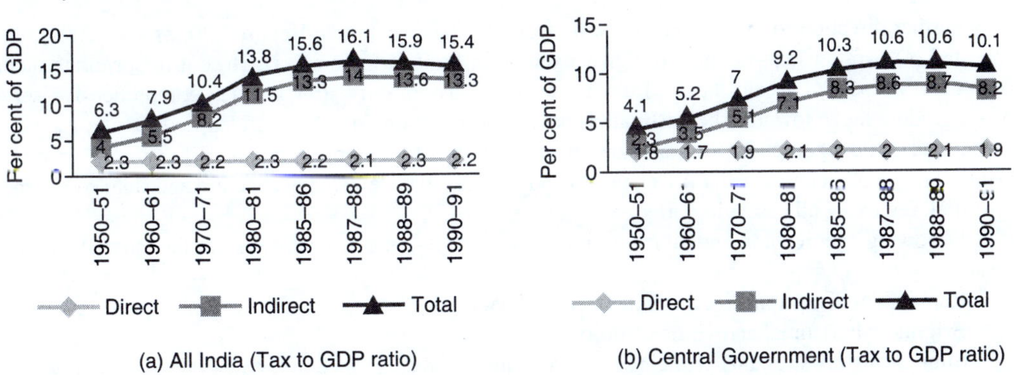

(a) All India (Tax to GDP ratio) (b) Central Government (Tax to GDP ratio)

Figure 8.7 Tax to GDP Ratio: Pre Reform Period.

Allocative inefficiency: The indirect taxes basically taxed the manufacturing commodities and left the services out of the tax purview. A low tax base resulted in higher and higher tax rates on manufactured products in order to maintain the tax to GDP ratio. By discriminating against the manufacturing sector, the tax system affected consumers and producers choices in favour of services, and thus, adversely affected the allocative efficiency. The system also perpetuated the regressive nature of the Indian taxation system, as a higher proportion of income by the poorer section of the society is spent on goods than on services. It is the higher income group that spends a larger fraction of their income on services and benefits from the lower tax rates on these.

Inequity: Though the rates of income tax were quite progressive and many necessities were exempted from indirect taxes and luxuries were taxed at a higher rate, the vertical and horizontal equity was grossly violated by a large scale evasion. Various concessions and exemptions narrowed the base which was against the principle of horizontal equity. The horizontal equity was also compromised as income from certain sectors of the economy, such as agriculture sector, remained out of the tax net. The indirect taxes were also limited to manufactured products leaving services untaxed. A lower income group spends a larger proportion of its income on manufactured goods than services. Thus, leaving the services out of the tax net had inflicted a larger burden on the lower income group than the higher income group. The various anomalies in the tax system, thus, propagated horizontal inequity and compromised on vertical equity.

Inadequacy: Though the tax system as a whole exhibited a good deal of buoyancy and elasticity (Box 8.7) it had not been able to meet the expenditure needs of the government. It resulted in a continuously growing deficit which was met through deficit financing and ever increasing amount of public debt.

Inefficient: The cost of tax collection as well as compliance was very high because of the existence of a large number of slabs, concessions and exemptions which led to classification problems, disputes and litigations.

The tax system was one of the major contributory factors to the inefficient functioning of the Indian economy in the pre-1991 period and was a stumbling block to accelerating the growth of the economy.

Tax Reforms: Post-1991 Period

Attempts were made to simplify the tax system and bring in efficiency in it in the pre-reform period However, consistent and full-fledged comprehensive reforms in the country began only in 1991–92 and tax reforms had been an integral part of these. Initially, the tax reform strategy was largely based on the recommendations of Raja Chelliah committee report (1992) which has recommended: (a) reduction in the tax rates; (b) enlargement of the tax base by reducing exemptions and concession; (c) transformation of the taxes on domestic production into a value added tax; (d) simplification of laws and procedures to make the administration and enforcement of the tax system more effective.

Further direction to the tax reform came from Kelkar Committee Reports (2002) and (2004) which suggested (a) two-tier tax system and higher exemption limit for income tax; (b) cut in corporate income tax rates; (c) repeal of wealth tax; (d) three rate basic custom duty structure; (e) comprehensive service tax; (f) gradual move towards the destination based consumption type value added taxes at the state level; (g) removal of tax exemptions, rationalization of incentives for savings, and simplification of procedures (h) introduction of an integrated VAT on goods and services to be levied by the centre and state governments in parallel, removing all cascading effect of taxes.

Following the recommendations of these committees, the tax reforms in the post-1991 period aim at:

Removal of distortions in economic decision-making.

Briging in horizontal and vertical equity.

Simplifying tax structure, reducing marginal rates to preserve incentive to work, save and invest, and encourage compliance.

Broadening the tax base with limited concessions.

Bringing in considerable improvement in tax administration and enforcement.

Some of the tax reforms implemented in the post-1991 era as follows:

Reforms in the Direct Tax System

There has been a drastic reduction in personal income tax rates and tax slabs, and continuous increase in the tax threshold. The number of tax brackets has been reduced to three of 10, 20, and 30 per cent. Corporate income tax rates have also been reduced from 40 to 35 per cent for domestic companies, and from 50 to 48 per cent for foreign companies. However, corporate income tax is still not broad based mainly due to tax holidays and large depreciation available on various investment activities. Wealth tax rates have also been reduced and exemption limit for gift tax has been enhanced.

Reforms in the Indirect Tax System

Indirect tax structure has also been greatly simplified and rationalized.

Union excise duty structure has been simplified and rationalized by reducing the number of rates and progressively switching from a specific to an *ad valorem* levy. The tax base has been broadened by removing many of the exemptions. Reforms in this era had started in 1986–87 itself when the Modified Value Added Tax (MODVAT) was introduced in the country, whereby excise paid on many inputs became eligible for credit against tax payable on output. In the post-1991 era, a major reform had been to make capital goods eligible for the MODVAT credit. In addition to it, with the reduction in import duties, almost all imports had been made subject to countervailing duty which, in turn, been made eligible for the MODVAT credit like the excise duty. The MODVAT was replaced by the Central Value Added Tax (CENVAT) in 2000–01 budget with the objective of eliminating the complexity by having a single basic rate of 16 per cent levied by the Central Government and making all inputs eligible for a set off/reduction. The CENVAT in India was primarily a VAT up to the manufacturing stage. However, subsequently, not only the manufacturers of final products but also the providers of taxable services are allowed to take credit of duty of excise as well as of service tax paid on any input received in the factories or any input service received by manufacturers of final products. The tax paid on capital goods is also eligible for set off, with the set off being spread over a two-year period. At present, the general CENVAT rate is 10 per cent. In addition, there are special excise rates which cannot be set off. However, area based excise duty exemptions, Small Scale Industries' (SSI) excise duty exemption scheme, and the low rate on selected products continue to have a major bearing on excise duty collection.

The import duty structure has been simplified and rationalized by an amalgamation of basic and auxiliary duties. To align the custom duties with the ASEAN level (4 per cent to 5 per cent) by 2010, the peak tariff rate has been drastically reduced from 300 per cent in 1991–92 to 10 per cent on non-agricultural goods in the budget of 2007–08. It remained at the same level in the subsequent budgets from 2008–9 to 2011–12. With the reduction of the peak rate, there has also been a general reduction in the average level of rates. However, the number of tax slabs is still numerous.

To widen the tax net and make the system of taxation more progressive, a tax on specific services (telephones, non-life insurance and stock brokerage) was introduced in 1994–95. Subsequently, a large number of services were brought under the tax net and tax rate was gradually increased to 12 per cent in 2008–09 budget. However, to give a boost to economic activities, in the face of severe slowdown, the rate was brought down to 10 per cent. But, with the subsequent recovery again the rate has been brought back to 12 per cent in 2012-13. To make the service tax comparable with the CENVAT applicable on manufactured goods, the input tax credit for goods entering into services and vice versa has been extended. However, a more comprehensive service tax still yet to come in place.

Tax reforms in India were initially mainly implemented at the Centre. The state tax reforms could not coincide with those at the Centre. Major landmark so far at the state level came in the form of the state VAT from 1 April 2005. By January 2008, all the 33 States/UTs introduced the VAT. There are two basic rates of 4 per cent and 12.5 per cent besides an exempt category and a special rate of 1 per cent for a few selected items. The items of basic necessities and goods of local importance (up to 10 items) have been put in the zero per cent or the exempted schedule. Uniformity in the rates reflects a better coordination among the Centre and the states.

Impact and Assessment

The tax reforms have improved the progressivity of the Indian tax system as visible from the higher share of direct taxes in the total revenue collection in the post 1990–91 period (Figure 8.8(a)). In post reform period, before the onset of global financial crisis, there was continuous improvement in the direct tax to GDP ratio (Figure 8.8(b)). Both personal income and corporate taxes contributed to this increase. However, a severe slowdown in the economy in the post global crisis period has somewhat reduced its share in the total tax revenue.

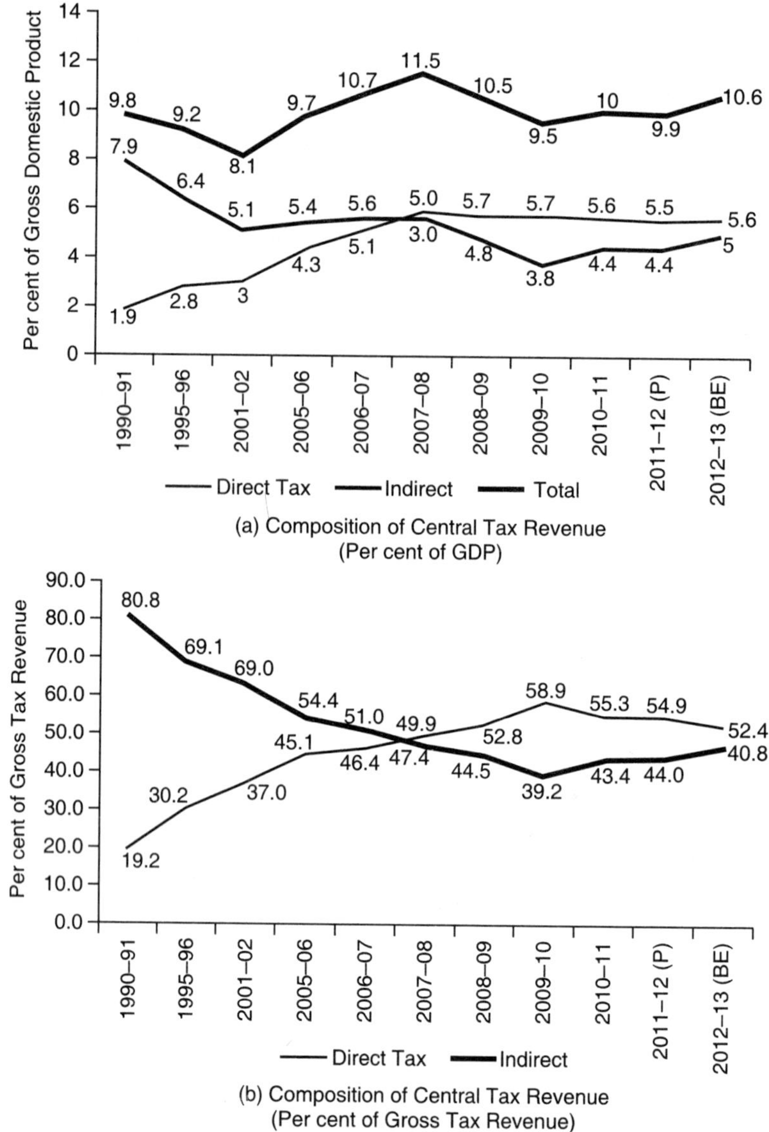

Figure 8.8 Composition of Central Tax Revenue in the Post Reform Period.

During the first two decades of reforms, there was also a decline in the indirect tax to GDP ratio. Both excise and custom revenue were responsible for this fall. The decline in the excise to GDP ratio was attributed to lowering of the rates and shift to MODVAT/CENVAT with credit extended for taxes on inputs. Whereas the fall in the customs revenue to GDP could be explained by a sharp reduction in the peak custom duties above 300 per cent prior to reforms to 10 per cent by 2007–08 as a part of the removal of protectionist policies and a move towards the ASEAN levels of tariffs.

The continuation of various exemptions to small scale units and area wise concessions, inspite of reductions in the rates, were also responsible for the fall in indirect tax to GDP ratio.

Structural changes in the composition of GDP were also partly responsible for the declining trend in the indirect tax to GDP ratio. In the post-1997–98 period the share of service sector in India's GDP continued to expand whereas that of the manufacturing sector remained almost stagnant. During this period of structural shift, the manufacturing sector remained the focus of indirect taxes and services largely remained out of the tax net or subjected to a lower tax rate. Inspite of more than 50 per cent contribution towards the GDP, the service tax accounted only 0.5 per cent of the GDP in 2004–05, and therefore, the decline in the indirect tax to GDP ratio could not be contained by the increase in service revenue. Apart from its adverse impact on the tax revenue to GDP ratio, at the micro level, the untaxed service meant that the traders using these services were unable to claim the VAT credit on service inputs, leading to cascading impact on prices. Such a tax treatment also encouraged businesses to develop in-house services rather than outsourcing these, causing to inefficient allocation of resources. Selective taxation of a few services also led to definitional ambiguities, administrative hurdles and rent seeking.

Keeping in view the dominance of services in the GDP, to improve the buoyancy of the tax system, the government has been expanding the scope of the service tax. With the increase in the coverage of services under the tax net and the increase in the tax rates there has been a marked improvement in the service tax to GDP ratio since 2005–06 which prevented the deceleration in indirect tax to GDP ratio and also the total tax revenue to GDP ratio. Inspite of reduction and rationalization during the last two decades, the total tax revenue collection is not commensurate with the government expenditure requirements. The various exemptions, incentives, anomalies and the narrow base of taxes are some of the reasons behind the low collection.

There has been a general consensus that further broad basing and simplification of the tax system is needed. This warrants withdrawal of tax exemptions and concessions given for specific activities, abolition of surcharge from income tax, pulling out of area-based concessions for infrastructure for backward area development, reduction in depreciation allowances from corporate taxes, and elimination of exemptions for export trading zones, free trade zones and technology parks, and strengthening of the taxation provisions for international transactions.

Equally important are the reforms in the tax administration. High compliance cost, along with the poor state of tax administration and information system, has led to a low compliance, continuous interface of taxpayers with the officials, corruption and rent seeking. Thus, it is essential that the system is evolved to put together the information received from various sources to improve tax enforcement. This involves improving the information networking by getting the data from various sources such as banks and other financial institutions on various assesses, exchange of information between the direct and indirect tax administrators, and between the centre and the state governments.

Reform Measures in Process

Two major reform processes—the Direct Taxes Code (DTC) and the Goods and Service Tax (GST)— are under the process of implementation in India which aim at addressing and removing the existing deficiencies in the tax system.

On direct tax front, the Direct Taxes Code Bill, 2010, aims at establishing economically efficient, effective and equitable direct tax system Some salient features of the DTC are:

- It consolidates and amends the laws relating to all direct taxes.
- It expects to improve compliance by reducing the corporate tax rate from the current effective rate of 33.2 per cent to 30 per cent and raising the exemption limits and broading the personal income tax rates.
- It is expected to provide stability to direct tax rates by obviating the need for an annual finance bill.

- It is expected to strengthen the taxation provisions for international transactions by:
  - Introducing advance pricing agreements with the tax administration in case of **transfer pricing** (i.e., the amount used in accounting for transfer of goods or services from one responsibility centre to another or from one company to another which belongs to the same group),
  - Bringing tax neutrality between a branch and a subsidy of a foreign company in India by charging the same tax rate of 30 per cent on the profit of foreign and domestic companies and levying a branch profit tax (in lieu of dividend distribution tax which is applicable on domestic companies) at the rate of 15 per cent.
  - Taxation of assets of the residents held abroad such as deposits in the bank account.
  - Alignment of the concept of residence with India's tax treaties by introducing the concept of "place of effective management" instead of "wholly-controlled in India".
  - Phase out profit-linked tax incentives and replacing them by investment linked incentives for specified sectors to minimize the incidents of tax avoidance and enhancing productive capacity.
  - Rationalizing tax incentives for saving by limiting the tax deduction to ₹1 lakh and only in investment in approved provident funds, superannuation funds and pension funds.
  - Introducing General Anti Avoidance Rule to curb aggressive tax planning
  - Taxation Non-Profit Organization set-up for charitable purpose on their surplus at the rate of 15 per cent.

On the indirect tax front, the Goods and Service Tax (GST) is expected to replace the CENVAT and the service tax levied by the Centre and the VAT levied by the states. The GST is a single rate of tax on goods and services levied at the point of destination. The introduction of GST is likely to be the biggest reform in the country, is expected to would revolutionize the indirect tax system in the country. Advantages of the GST are:

1. It is equitable because it taxes both goods and services equally,
2. It is efficient because a single rate of duty reduces the discretionary power of tax authorities, reduces corruption, and improves compliance,
3. It removes cascading impact of taxes on prices as it is levied only at the destination point and not at various points from manufacturing to retail outlets,
4. It discourages tax evasion as it is simple to comprehend,
5. It unifies markets across the country as there is only a single rate of duty.

The introduction of GST in India is, however, getting delayed because of the state government reluctance to cede taxation powers to the Central Government. They want that the "dual" GST to be levied concurrently by both the levels of the government which can preserve the fiscal autonomy of the Centre and states, and at the same time, harmonize the tax system in the country.

Non-tax Revenue

The revenue generated by a government by providing commercial and administrative activities is known as **non-tax revenue**, the details of which are as follows:

1. Commercial revenue: In many countries the government, rather than confining itself to traditional role of maintaining law and order, is also involved in commercial ventures and activities. Prices paid for government produced commodities and services form a part of **commercial revenue** for a government. Examples of this type of revenue are payments for postage, tolls, electricity charges, railway fare, telephone tariff, etc.

2. Administrative revenue: The revenue earned from various administrative services by a government is classified as **administrative revenue**. It includes:

(i) *Fines and penalties:* Infringement of a law results in fees and penalties imposed by a government. For example, often people driving two wheelers are fined for not complying with the requirement of wearing helmet. Similarly, people smoking in public places are fined.

(ii) *Licence fee:* For simply conferring a permission of a privilege, a government charges licence fees. For example, while issuing a driving licence the state governments in India charge a licence fees.

(iii) *Forfeitures:* Penalties imposed by courts for the failure of individuals to appear in the courts, to complete contracts as stipulated, etc., are known as forfeitures.

(iv) *Escheat:* A government may acquire the property of persons who die without having any legal heirs or without leaving a will. This also adds to the resources of a government.

(v) *Special assessment:* Special assessment is levied on property owners for bringing in improvements in their property by providing various civic amenities, such as installing drinking water lines, electricity or telephone cables, constructing concrete roads, or parking structure, and so on.

(vi) *Gifts and grants:* Contributions from private individuals or non-governmental or governmental donors to government funds for specific purpose, such as relief fund, defence during a war or an emergency, etc., also add to the revenue of a government.

Own Capital Receipts

1. Disinvestment of Public Sector Units: Disinvestment involves a reduction in the government's stake in the PSU through the sale of equity capital invested by it in the Public Sector Units (PSUs) to the general public. It is similar to the case where households generate revenue by selling their past accumulated assets, such as buildings, vehicles and gold. Since governments are the owners of Public Sector Units (PSUs) the proceedings emerging from their sales form a part of the own receipts of governments.

2. Recoveries of loans: The Central Government often gives loans to state and local governments and even to foreign governments. Once, after the maturity period, the government receives the loans back these become a part of its own capital receipts.

3. Grants: Capital account grants received by a government in the form of concessional loans or donations for investment purpose also form a part of the capital account receipts. These grants are different from the grants received on the revenue account in the form of food grains, medicines and other items used for providing relief to famine or flood affected areas.

8.5.2 Public Expenditure

Public expenditure refers to the expenses incurred by governments either for their own maintenance or for the welfare of their countries.

Effects of Public Expenditure

Effects of public expenditure are as follows:

1. Effect on production and growth: Public expenditure affects an economy from demand as well supply sides. Thus, it can be used for enhancing the production as well as productive capacity of an economy.

Developing economies usually are constrained by the unavailability of skilled labour and physical and social infrastructure. Public expenditure can be used for stimulating investment, creating physical, social and economic infrastructure, and developing basic and key industries. Expenditure on these adds on to the productive capacity. Besides, the availability of social overheads and physical infrastructure brings in an all round reduction in various bottlenecks and cost of production. Thus, it creates an enabling environment for private producers. An improvement in infrastructure, both social and physical, integrates different regions and sectors, and thus, stimulates the process of economic growth.

Public expenditure brings about higher production and enhances growth not only through higher expenditure level but also through the reallocation of investable resources from less to more desirable lines of production. Public expenditure can be in the form of subsidies (such as agriculture input subsidies, subsidies for investment in backward areas) for those investments which are commercially non-viable, but which are very stimulating for economic growth. Indirect effect of public expenditure can also be equally strong. The public expenditure in education and various social activities can bring about an awakening which increases the willingness to work, invent and explore. Thus, public expenditure can stimulate economic activities and lead an economy on the path of higher economic growth.

In developed countries, the availability of productive capacity is not a constraint, but fluctuations in economic activities often result in either excess or shortage of demand over the production capacity constraining the stability of growth. In such countries, the expansion and contraction in public expenditure help in stabilizing the growth rate at the full employment level of output as well as in maintaining stable inflationary scenario.

2. Effect on distribution: Public expenditure can even be used for achieving an equitable distribution of income and wealth. Such a distribution is sought by incurring public expenditure on the schemes that are expected to benefit the poorer section. The expenditure in the form of free education, health, water, and sanitation immensely helps the poor. Similarly, the expenditure on various social security schemes, such as unemployment benefits, old age pensions, medical benefits, and subsidized food, helps in bringing about a more equitable distribution. The government can intervene in the market for those goods which are in a short supply but essential, by either producing or importing them. Production subsidies can even be granted to augment the supply of these merit goods. The expenditure on various employment generating schemes helps in improving the employment level as well the income distribution.

3. Economic stability: If left to the market forces, economies often experience wide fluctuations in income, employment and prices. In a booming phase, there is an excess of aggregate demand over the available production, whereas in a recession there is deficiency of aggregate demand resulting in an idle capacity. Governments can follow anti-cyclical measures to stabilize their economies. Public expenditure, in a downturn, adds to the effective demand and, through income multiplier, the initial public expenditure results in an all round increase in demand and income, which helps overcome a downturn. In a booming phase, on the contrary, the need is to curb excess demand to contain inflationary pressures. Curtailment of the public expenditure, during an upturn, helps in restraining the inflationary pressures.

Public expenditure acts as an effective stabilizing device only in a well-integrated economy where the effect of initial change in the expenditure trickles down to other sectors and markets in a desired manner and to a desired extent. In the economy suffering from technical and other rigidities, the changes in public expenditure may not be able to bring in desired effects. For example, various types of institutional and legal restrictions, shortage of particular materials, absence of industries and inadequate productive capacity may prevent a quick market response. In such cases, the impact of higher public expenditure, even in downturns, may be inflationary.

Classification of Public Expenditure

Traditionally, governments have been following the accounting classification of their expenditure, whereby the expenditure is reflected against government departments. This classification reflects the organizational structure of governments and enables them to maintain an effective control and check over the diversion and misappropriation of public expenditure in unidentified activities. The accounting classification though helps in keeping a check on possible leakages and wastage of resources, it cannot be of much use for analyzing the effects of government expenditure on an economy.

For a more meaningful assessment of government activities and functions and impact of these on an economy, the government expenditure is classified into various categories (Figure 8.9). Some of the commonly used classification categories are elaborated hereinafter.

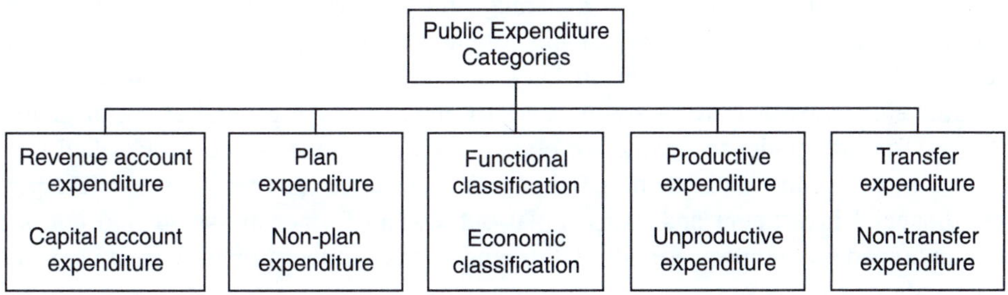

Figure 8.9 Categories of Public Expenditure.

1. Expenditure on revenue and capital account: The expenditure that does not result in a creation of any asset, but simply affects the money balances of a government is treated as the **revenue account expenditure**. It includes government spending on goods (such as stationery, medicines), services (such as defence, civil administration, social and development services), and transfer payments (such as food and fertilizer subsidies, unemployment benefits, pensions and interest payment). The revenue account expenditure has only a short-term impact. On the contrary, the expenditure that leads to variations in physical and financial assets of a government is accounted as the capital account expenditure. It includes government spending on new roads, buildings and structures, machines and equipment, discharge of debt, capital outlay on non-development items such as defence, and development items such as railways, civil aviation, irrigation and multipurpose river schemes, civil works and industrial development. The **capital account expenditure**, unlike the revenue account expenditure, adds to the growth and has long-term implications.

2. Plan and non-plan expenditure: Budget provisions for various schemes or programmes that have been included in five-year plans are shown under the **plan expenditure**. In a five-year plan, the financial allocation among different heads or categories of expenditure is made on a five-year basis. Within these broad parameters, an annual allocation is made in the government budget. The **non-plan expenditure**, on the contrary, includes both development and non-development expenditure which is not included in a plan. It comprises expenditure that is obligatory in nature (such as interest payments and pensions) and expenditure that is an essential obligation of the state (such as defence, internal security, and transfer to states). It also consists of expenditure on assets created in previous plans. Once a plan scheme becomes fully operative or a plan project is completed, its maintenance or operational expenses are shifted to the non-plan budget. Even the expenditure on continuing services and activities at levels already reached in a given plan period is shifted to the non-plan expenditure (for example, expenditure on maintaining health facilities and continuing research projects, and operating expenses of power stations). Normally, all populist programmes of a government are launched under the head of non-plan expenditure.

3. Functional and economic classification of public expenditure: The **functional classification** allocates expenditure from the point of view of its destination, regardless of the agent responsible or the economic implication of the same. Under this classification, the government expenditure is organized according to various activities and policy objectives. The UN Department of Economic Affairs has suggested the functional classification of expenditure under five heads, viz., general services (such as general public services, defence, public order and safety), community services (such as education, health, social security and welfare), social services (housing and community amenities, recreational, cultural and religious services), economic services (such as fuel and energy, agriculture, forestry, fishing and hunting, mining and mineral resources, manufacturing and construction, transport and communication, and other economic services) and unallocable. The **economic classification,** on the contrary, shows the government expenditure by economic categories that are of significance for analyzing the general effect of government transactions. Broadly, under the economic classification, the expenditure is classified into three broad categories of final outlays, transfer payments (interest payments, subsidies, pensions, etc.) and financial investment and loans. Final outlays are further classified into consumption expenditure (expenditure on wages and salaries, and goods and services for current use) and gross capital formation (Table 8.2).

Table 8.2 Components of Functional and Economic Classification

Functional classification	*Economic classification*
General services	Final outlays
Community services	Consumption expenditure
Social services	Gross capital formation
Economic services	Transfer payments
Unallocable	Financial investment and loans

The functional and economic classifications are complementary to each other and cut across various government departments and agencies. They help in highlighting the involvement of a government in various spheres, such as capital accumulation, health, education, and so on.

4. Productive and unproductive expenditure: The classification of public expenditure into productive and non-productive categories is based on whether it is in the nature of consumption or investment. It is the investment expenditure that improves the productive capacity of an economy, and hence, considered to be productive expenditure. Apart from the expenditure on the addition to capital stock, the expenditure on creation and maintenance of assets which increases the productive efficiency, such as parks, water works, and the expenditure on building up human capital, such as education, training, health, hygiene, are considered to be productive investment.

Consumption expenditure, such as expenditure on administration, defence, justice, law and order maintenance, is considered to be unproductive expenditure. The productive as well as the non-productive expenditure can be either on the revenue account or the capital account.

5. Transfer and non-transfer expenditure: The **transfer expenditure** or **transfer payments** are unilateral payments, i.e., the payments without corresponding receipts of goods and services. Interest payments, subsidies, old age pensions, unemployment benefits, scholarships by a government are some examples of transfer payments. Through these payments a government simply transfers the right or claim to certain goods and services to certain sections of the society. On the contrary, the **non-transfer expenditure** is a payment for the purchase of goods and services. The expenditure by a government on administration, defence, education, roads, ports are examples of the non-transfer expenditure. In the case of transfer payments, the beneficiary decides the use of resources made available to him, whereas in the case of non-transfer payments, the government making such payments decides the use of resources with it.

Canons of Expenditure

Governments use public resources, and hence, are responsible for the overall betterment of their countries. To assure that the scarce resources are not wasted or diversified and used most efficiently and judiciously to achieve the stated objectives, a number of canons have been suggested. These canons are as follows:

1. Canon of economy: The resources available in an economy are scarce. For the progress of an economy and society these resources need to be used efficiently and judiciously. The **cannon of economy** suggests that the wastage of resources should not occur in the case of public expenditure which is simply a counterpart of the resources available with the other sections of a society. For an efficient utilization of the resources, governments should use techniques like Programme and Performance Budgeting (PPB) (Box 8.9) and Zero Base Budgeting (ZBB) (Box 8.10).

Inefficiencies in the allocation of the expenditure can occur for various reasons, such as faulty planning and execution, and delays in sanctioning the amount for planned and approved activities. The delays, quite often, increase the cost of commodities, and hence, the cost of execution. For continuous check on the efficiency of usages, various costing methods and cost benefit analysis be used by governments. However, governments are constrained in the use of these techniques as they cannot be applied for all kinds of government expenditures. For example, certain expenditure categories are contractual in nature and some are obligatory for governments, such as pension payments and interest payments. Governments are under obligation to incur expenditure on these; hence, the question of an economy in their use does not arise.

2. Canon of sanction: The **canon of sanction** suggests that the public funds should not be used without proper authorization. They should be used only for the purpose for which these have been sanctioned. Such a norm is expected to avoid a wasteful expenditure and misappropriation and diversion of funds.

Box 8.9 Performance and Programme Budgeting

The principle of economy suggests that governments should be using resources most economically and efficiently. The choice of projects, hence, should be based upon cost-benefit analysis, and the actual performance of the selected projects should be reviewed against their expected standards. This implies that the decision to select and spend on a particular project should first comprise programming or a stagewise sequence of steps for executing it known as **Programme Budgeting**, and then, it should go through the test of factual performance known as the **Performance Budgeting**. When the programme goes through both these stages, it is known as the **Performance and Programme Budgeting** (PPB).

The Programme Budgeting and the Performance Budgeting, though technically similar and interlinked, are not identical with each other. Programme budgeting consist of the following steps:

(a) Defining the objective of various fiscal measures and identifying the programmes from which the selection has to be made.

(b) Making an assessment of selected programmes using a cost-benefit analysis, ranking them and selecting the best, given the available resources.

(c) Adopting a forward looking approach by preparing a time schedule for financial flows and other activities together with the expected achievement of targets.

The performance budget, on the other hand, makes an assessment of achievements and failures of the programme budget.

The PPB helps in achieving a more effective and efficient allocation of scarce resources in the public sector. It provides a system of feedback which can be improved over a period of time. However, it also poses a number of conceptual and other problems.

One of the problems faced in implementing the PPB is that the quantification of results of many programmes in fields such as health, hygiene and education is not possible. The PPB cannot be implemented at the national or aggregate level, such as for the agriculture and industrial sector as a whole.

An efficient functional classification of a budget, well-integrated with the accounting system extended to the level of departments and other organizations that can provide timely and current data for the appraisal of performance of various activities and programmes, is needed for the implementation of the PPB.

Box 8.10 Incremental Budgeting vs Zero Base Budgeting

Under the incremental budgeting, each Ministry assumes that all its activities and organizations are there to stay. They add on each year some additional expenditure over and above the existing amount of expenditure and submit a budget expenditure. Under this system, although budget documents contain targets, both physical and financial, they lack in analysis of progress or performance in detail. The progress of schemes/projects in terms of their physical achievements against the background of clearly indicated objective is monitored, however, the evaluations of the programmes and projects does not take place. A lot of emphasis is placed on new projects; old items of expenditure are normally taken for granted without justifying their existence and continued in the coming period.

The Zero Base Budgeting (ZBB) is an innovative technique of budgeting that aims at reducing the wastage in public expenditure. It reviews and evaluates every item of expenditure assuming that the expenditure at the time of review is zero. The need for every item of expenditure has to be justified and the level of expenditure evaluated in order to achieve set objectives. Following steps are involved in the ZBB in an organization:

(a) Goals and objects of the organization are evaluated.

(b) Functions and various activities of the organization are analyzed.

(c) Units for facilitating the ZBB are identified.

(d) Decision packages are evolved assessing the financial requirements to support a particular level of operation.

(e) Decision packages are examined.

(f) They are ranked by the decision unit head and sent to the higher management.

(g) Ranking is completed at the department level and budget proposals are finalized.

The ZBB has the following advantages over the incremental budgeting:

- Entire budgeting exercise is expected to be more realistic as it is based on a comprehensive analysis of priorities, goals and implementation of the ZBB.
- Cost effective.
- Ensures better participation of the executives and lead to better communication.
- Helps in improving the operational efficiency of the entire organization.
- Results in a perceptible cut in a budget as obsolete schemes are dropped out.

Though the ZBB has several advantages, one of the important pre-conditions for its implementation is that the organization should be in a position to provide all the information including the necessary cost data. Also, the development and successful implementation of the ZBB requires more than a year. Therefore, the analysis and evaluation of programmes often result in substantial time losses.

3. Canon of benefit: The **canon of benefit** argues that the public expenditure should be incurred only if it collectively maximizes social benefits. Thus, each category of expenditure should be viewed against the benefits expected from it. Also, the reallocation of resources needs to take place that enhances social benefits by various effects on income and wealth distribution.

4. Canon of surplus: As per the canon of surplus the government is expected to be prudent in its use of resources and meet its current expenses from the current revenue, and avoid incurring deficit, i.e., borrowing.

However, as the public expenditure plays an important role in economic stabilization, the choice of deficit or surplus budget is to be decided on the merit of each case. Thus, during recession, to give a boost to economic activities, governments can do well by running budget deficits. On the contrary, during expansions surplus budgets can be aimed at for stabilization. Also, in underdeveloped economies, the resource mobilization efforts may necessitate governments to depend on deficit financing.

Developing countries in order to achieve various socio-economic objectives often end up compromising on various canons of expenditure listed above. This is illustrated in UBE 8.3 using Indian context.

UNDERSTANDING BUSINESS ENVIRONMENT

UBE 8.3 Trends in Public Expenditure

This UBE highlights the extent of deviation of the public expenditure in India from the canons of public expenditure and the government's attempt to improve the composition of its expenditures.

The government consumption and investment expenditure is an important constituent of aggregate demand in the Indian economy. It affects not only the demand side but also the supply side of the economy and also plays an important role in an equitable distribution of income in the economy. The Investment component of public expenditure is self-sustaining as it increases the productive capacity leading to higher income and higher tax and non-tax revenue for the government in the forthcoming period. However, the investment expenditure has a long gestation period, and thus, a higher expenditure leads to short-term fiscal imbalances building up either inflationary pressures in the economy or increasing the burden of public debt. Thus, important consideration for any government is to keep the expenditure within the limits that is supportive of growth with equity, but at the same time it should not destabilize the economy by building up inflation or debt payment pressures. Whether the government of India has been able to maintain proper composition of its expenditure has been highlighted below:

The development and growth requirements of the Indian economy led to a continuous increase in the public expenditure in the pre-1991 era, resulting in the combined expenditure of Central and state governments at 34.3 per cent of GDP in 1990–91 (Figure 8.11(c)). Various steps taken to compress the expenditure lowered this ratio in the initial years of reform with the ratio declining marginally to 33.5 per cent by 1996–97. However, the expenditure correction during this period had been brought mainly through the compression in capital expenditure. During 1990–91 to 1996–97, though, the revenue expenditure increased by 1.8 per cent, capital expenditure registered a steeper decline of 2.6 per cent. Also, the success in reducing the total expenditure could not be sustained in the ensuing period, the trend reversed and the expenditure to GDP ratio started rising again.

Concerned with the high rate of growth of non-development expenditure, the government viewed that lasting solution to this problem required substantial downsizing in the government expenditure. To carry out the process of downsizing in a systematic way, an Expenditure Reform Commission was constituted in 2000. The commission suggested a number of steps for expenditure correction. These included the minimization of cost of buffer stock operations, rationalization of fertilizer subsidies, optimizing the government staff strength, introduction of the VRS, retraining and redeployment of surplus staff in various government departments and autonomous institutions. In the light of these recommendations and proposals, a number of steps have been taken over a period of time to rationalize the level of expenditure. Some of these are as follows:

- Optimizing the government staff strength by restrictions on fresh recruitments to 1 per cent of the total civilian staff strength over the four years beginning fiscal 2002–03.
- Introduction of a new pension scheme of defined contribution for new recruits in the budget for 2003–04.
- Rationalization of various subsidies through various measures as follows:
- *Oil Subsidy*
  - Dismantling of the Administered Price Mechanism (APM) in the petroleum sector and the oil pool account effective from April 2002.
  - Decontrolled the pricing of petrol in June 2010
  - Putting a cap on LPG cylinders in 2012
  - Proposed deregulation of diesel and other fuel prices
- *Food Subsidy*
  - Allowing the Food Corporation of India (FCI) to access market loan carrying lower interest rate.
  - Encouraging private trade in food grains.
  - Liquidating excess food grain stocks.
  - Adopting a targeted approach to food subsidies, i.e., making these subsidies available only to the population below poverty line (BPL).
  - The government is aiming to move towards direct transfer of cash subsidy to people living below poverty line in a phased manner.
- *Fertilizer subsidy*
  - Withdrawing unit based pricing scheme
  - Gradual move towards nutrient based subsidy: subsidy is fixed per tonne on key non-nitrogenous fertilizers

Along with these steps, the bindings on expenditure followed by the Central and state governments under the Fiscal Responsibility Budget Management (FRBM) Act led to some moderation in the total expenditure. With the harmonized fiscal policies pursued by both the Central and state governments in the FRBM era, there was some reduction in the revenue expenditure to GDP ratio and change in the composition of expenditure in favour of the capital expenditure during 2003–04 to 2006–07. During this period, the public expenditure had been reoriented towards creation of productive assets through expansion of physical infrastructure, such as roads, highways, ports, power, railways, water supply, sewage treatment and sanitation, and through health and education. However, this shift had come mainly on account of expenditure by the state governments (Figure 8.10(b)). Capital expenditure at the Centre declined to pathetical low level at 1.7 per cent in 2006–07 (Figure 8.10(a)).

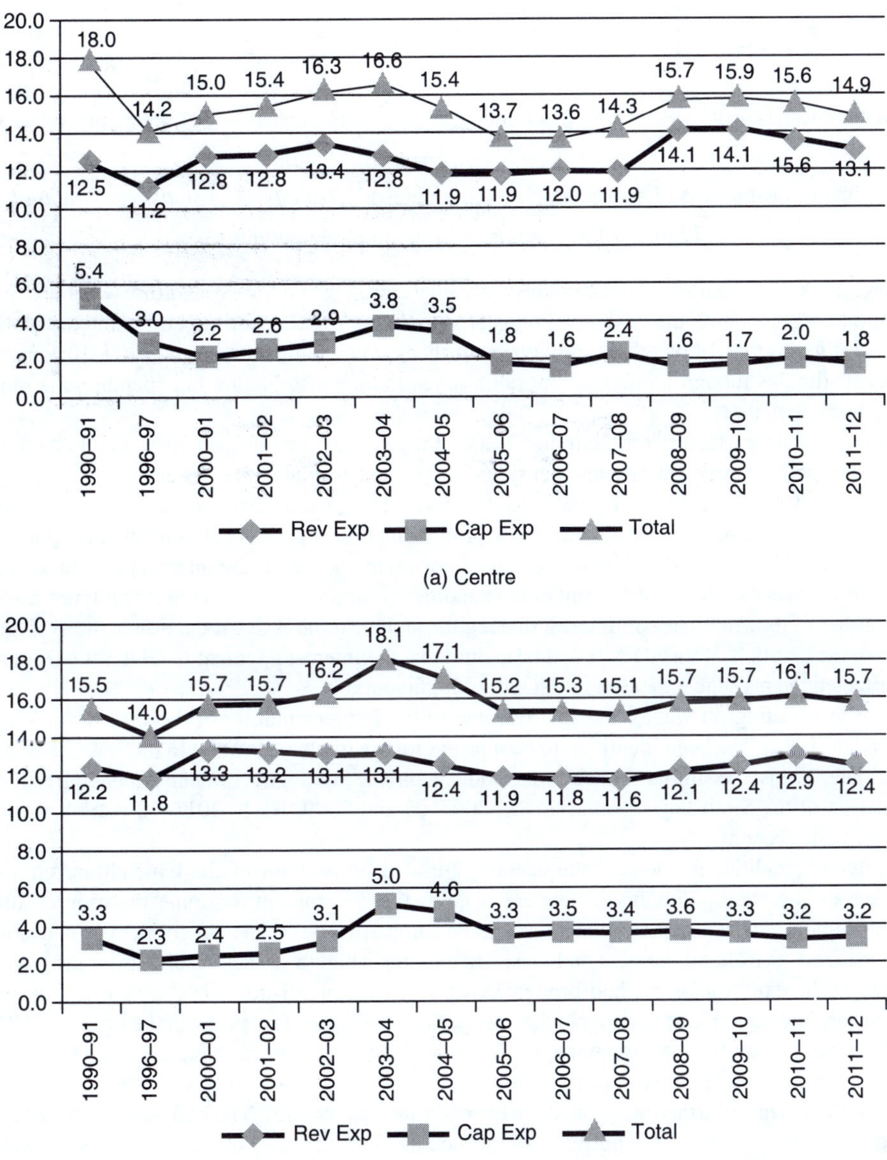

(a) Centre

(b) State

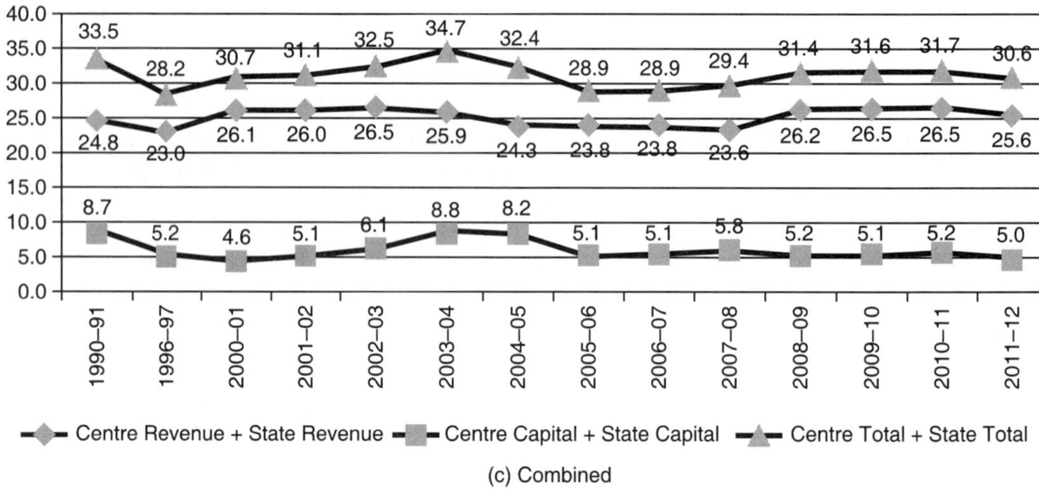

(c) Combined

Source: Estimated on the basis of data available from RBI (2012), *Handbook of Statistics of Indian Economy*.

Figure 8.10 Trends in Government Expenditure.

The year 2007–08 again experienced substantial increase in the public expenditure with the expenditure to GDP ratio almost touching the peak level registered in the pre-FRBM period. Following the global crisis and the fiscal stimulus that followed, this proportion further increased in 2008–09 and 2009–10. Partial rolling back of fiscal stimulus though moderated the ratio, much more consolidation in expenditure is required to contain the fiscal deficit.

Major contributory factors for the higher share of revenue expenditure are identified to be the interest payment, spending on wages, salaries and pensions, and expenses related to subsidies.

In the early 1990s, a substantial fiscal consolidation led to a decline in the debt to GDP ratio. However, the weighted average interest rate in this period rose, following the progressive alignment of coupon rates with the market rates. In the late 1990s, though the cost of borrowing declined, the interest payment continued to rise due to the existence of sizeable amount of outstanding liabilities contacted at higher interest rates during the initial phases of reforms. The soft interest rate regime and the progressive reduction in the average cost of borrowing in the first half of this decade had brought down the interest payment to GDP ratio (Figure 8.11). This has affected the revenue expenditure to GDP ratio, favourably.

A rise in spending on wages and salaries, due to the implementation of the Fifth Pay Commission towards the late 1990s, has been identified to be a prime source of abnormal rise in the revenue expenditure during the late 1990s. A similar impact was noticed on the total government expenditure due to the implementation of the Sixth Pay Commission in 2008–09 and 2009–10. In 2011–12 there has been some moderation in this account.

Downward rigidities in the revenue account are also on account of the expenditure on subsidies. Subsidies are an important policy instrument and used by the government for domestic resource allocation, income distribution, export efficiency and international competitiveness. The government provides subsidies for food, fertilizers, petroleum, interest on loans, and exports. Though conscious efforts by the government, by phasing out the export subsidy, had brought down the level of subsidies in the first half of 1990s the expenses on subsidies again started rising in the later period. In the past few years, in the light of FRBM rules, along with a reduction in the interest payments, fiscal corrections have been brought about by a reduction in the expenses on subsidies. However, the twin shocks of 2008–09 (global commodity price shock and global financial turbulence) have further burgeoned the expenditure on subsidies. The high level of international oil prices, and high carrying cost of the buffer stock of food has kept the level of subsidies at elevated levels in the last year.

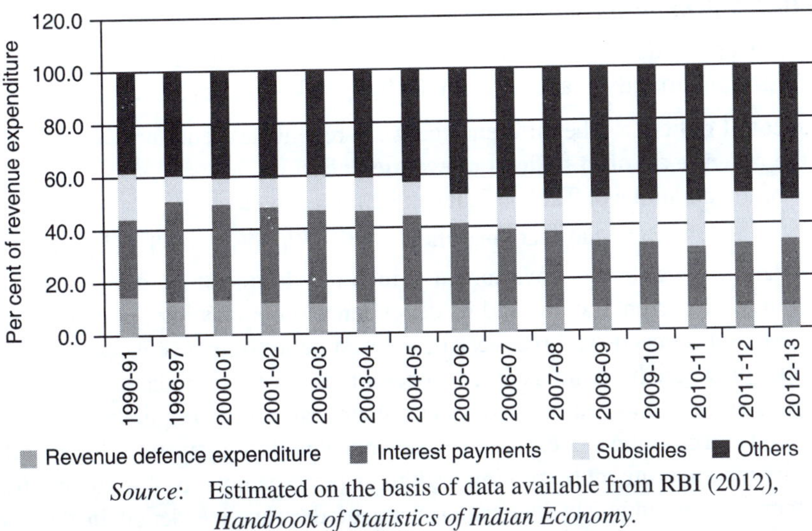

Source: Estimated on the basis of data available from RBI (2012), *Handbook of Statistics of Indian Economy.*

Figure 8.11 Components of Revenue Expenditure of Central Government.

8.6 MEASUREMENT OF GOVERNMENT DEFICIT: VARIOUS CONCEPTS

The term government deficit refers to the difference between government expenditure and government's own revenue. However, this difference can be estimated for different types of expenditure and revenue categories (Table 8.3) given the objective behind estimating it. The different concepts of deficits have different implications for an economy in terms of their impact on output, money supply, prices, productive capacity and economic structure.

Table 8.3 Revenue and Capital Receipts of the Government

Receipts	*Notation*	*Disbursement*	*Notation*
A. Revenue receipts	RR	**A. Revenue expenditure**	RE
1. Tax Receipts	R_1	1. Interest Expenditure	E_1
2. Non Tax Receipts (2a + 2b)	$R_2\ (R_{21} + R_{22})$	2. Other Expenditure	E_2
2a. Interest Receipts	R_{21}		
2b. Non Interest Earning	R_{22}		
B. Capital receipts	CR	**B. Capital expenditure**	CE
1. Grants	R_3	1. Domestic Lending	E_3
2. Recovery of Loans	R_4	2. Other Expenses	E_4
3. Disinvestment Receipts	R_5		
4. Borrowing (4a + 4b)	$R_6\ (R_{61} + R_{62})$		
4a. Domestic	R_{61}		
4b. Foreign	R_{62}		
Aggregate receipts	$RR + CR$	**Aggregate expenditure**	$RE + CE$

Concepts of Deficit Estimated from Budget Documents

Though many concepts of deficit are estimated, only some are available from the budget documents. The concepts that are normally available from the budget documents are as follows:

1. Revenue account deficit: The difference between revenue expenditures and revenue receipts is known as the **revenue account deficit** or **revenue deficit**.

In terms of the notations of Table 8.3, it can be represented as:

$$\text{Revenue account deficit} = RE - RR = (E_1 + E_2) - (R_1 + R_2)$$

The revenue deficit reflects the government's inability to meet its day-to-day expenditure requirements out of its current income and its dependence on borrowing or other capital receipts, such as disinvestment proceeds and recovery of the past debt, to finance its consumption. This is similar to a situation where households borrow or sell their past accumulated assets, such as gold, land, buildings, shares and debentures, to meet their consumption requirement or expenses on items such as food and clothing. An existence of revenue deficit is against the golden rule of public finance, whereby the government borrowing or other capital receipts to be used only for financing public investment. A continuously increasing share of the revenue deficit in the **fiscal deficit** (i.e. total borrowing) adversely affects public investment. Hence, it has an adverse impact on the productive capacity in the long-run. Conversely, a falling revenue deficit, for a given level of fiscal deficit, implies that the borrowed funds or other capital receipts are used for capital formation or build up of assets. It is a healthy trend as it enhances the productive capacity.

2. Capital account deficit: The difference between capital expenditure and own capital receipts is known as the **capital account deficit**. It can be represented as:

$$\text{Capital account deficit} = (E_3 + E_4) - (R_3 + R_4 + R_5)$$

The capital account deficit reflects that the receipts on the capital account are not sufficient to meet the investment requirements of the government. It also implies that the government is borrowing or using its surplus on the revenue account (if any) for funding its investment in physical assets and social and economic infrastructure. This type of deficit, since used for funding assets that add on to the productive capacity and production efficiency, is not considered to be of a great worry as far as it is self-sustaining.

3. Fiscal deficit: The **fiscal deficit** captures an excess of total expenditure over total revenue and can be estimated as:

$$\begin{aligned}\text{Fiscal deficit} &= (\text{Revenue expenditure} + \text{Capital expenditure}) \\ &\quad - (\text{Revenue receipts} + \text{Own capital receipts}) \\ &= \text{Borrowings} \\ &= (E_1 + E_2 + E_3 + E_4) - (R_1 + R_2 + R_3 + R_4 + R_5) = R_6\end{aligned}$$

This can be rearranged further as follows:

$$\begin{aligned}\text{Fiscal deficit} &= (\text{Revenue expenditure} - \text{Revenue receipts}) \\ &\quad + (\text{Capital expenditure} - \text{Own capital receipts}) \\ &= \text{Revenue account deficit} + \text{Capital account deficit} \\ &= [(E_1 + E_2) - (R_1 + R_2)] + [(E_3 + E_4) - (R_3 + R_4 + R_5)] \\ &= R_6\end{aligned}$$

The fiscal deficit, thus, is a sum total of revenue account and capital account deficits. The fiscal deficit captures the entire shortfall in government's own receipts over its expenditure that is expected to be met by domestic and or foreign borrowing.

The fiscal deficit can be curtailed by reducing the revenue deficit and/or capital account deficit. Corrections in the fiscal deficit, brought about by a reduction in the revenue deficit often leads to compression in the capital expenditure; thus, adversely affecting the productive capacity.

4. Primary deficit: One of the major components of government expenditure is interest payments. Though interest payments in the current period are obligatory, they are on the outstanding public debt that is an outcome of past policies. In any given period, though the government may be following the policy of fiscal contraction and consolidation, the amount of interest payment may be large due to a substantial amount of outstanding public debt. Fiscal deficit, which is the difference between total receipt and total expenditure including the expenditure on interest payments, hence, does not reflect on the current fiscal stance. It is unable to reflect on the extent to which the current discrepancy in fiscal operations improves or worsens the government's net indebtedness. Hence, the concept of **primary deficit**, which is the fiscal deficit net of interest payment is estimated. The primary deficit can be estimated as:

Primary deficit = Gross fiscal deficit – Interest payment
= (Revenue expenditure + Capital expenditure)
– (Revenue receipts + Capital grants + Recovery of loans
+ Disinvestment proceeds) – (Interest payments)

$$= (E_1 + E_2 + E_3 + E_4) - (R_1 + R_2 + R_3 + R_4 + R_5) - E_1$$
$$= (E_2 + E_3 + E_4) - (R_1 + R_2 + R_3 + R_4 + R_5) = R_6 - E_1$$

The primary deficit occurs when the government's own revenue is not sufficient to meet the government non-interest expenditure. For a given level of fiscal deficit, the rising interest payments lowers the primary deficit and vice-versa. A falling primary deficit implies that new borrowings are being used to meet old debt liabilities. A persistent increase in the primary deficit over a period of time indicates the further accumulation of public debt and worsening of the interest payment burden. On the other hand, a zero primary deficit indicates that the government is able to meet its non-interest expenditure out of its own revenue, i.e., non-borrowed receipts, without any further debt build-up. A primary surplus, on the other hand, implies that the government is not only able to meet its non-interest expenditure out of its revenue but is also able to bring in a reduction in the level of its outstanding debt. A large primary surplus, thus, helps in bringing down the level of outstanding debt.

5. Gross vs net deficit: In the context of developing countries, a sizeable part of Central Government borrowings is lent to other sectors—state and local governments, public sector enterprises and the like. When net domestic lending (loans and advances minus repayments/recoveries) are deducted from the gross fiscal deficit and gross primary deficit the residual is referred to as the **net fiscal deficit** and **net primary deficit**, respectively. Thus,

Net fiscal deficit = Gross fiscal deficit – Net domestic lending
= Gross fiscal deficit – Domestic lending + Recoveries

$$= R_4 + R_6 - E_3$$

and

$$\text{Net primary deficit} = \text{Gross primary deficit} - \text{Net loans and advances}$$
$$= \text{Gross primary deficit} - \text{Loans and advances} + \text{Recoveries}$$
$$= R_4 + R_6 - E_1 - E_3$$

When the Central Government is the focal point of analysis, the concept of net fiscal deficit/net primary deficit is more meaningful than the gross fiscal deficit/gross primary deficit. It can be noted that in the terminology of IMF, the fiscal deficit refers to the gross fiscal deficit.

Concepts of Deficit Estimated Independently

The concepts of deficit that are normally not available from the budget documents are as follows:

1. Monetized deficit: The various measures of deficit explained above do not reveal the extent of a government's dependence on the borrowing from the central bank. Borrowing of a government from the central bank is often met by printing new notes. Hence, such borrowing increases the money supply and inflation. Borrowing from other sectors does not have such an impact. Therefore, the concept of **monetized deficit** is estimated which measures the level of support the central bank provides to the government's borrowing programme. However, the monetary concept of government deficit is suitable only for analyzing the monetary impact of fiscal operations. It falls short of the coverage needed to capture the full impact of current fiscal stance on the overall indebtedness of a government, which is reflected in the fiscal deficit.

2. Cyclical and structural deficit: The actual fiscal deficit in any country is a result of both temporary and permanent factors. Transitory effects are due to cyclical movements. In an upward phase of a business cycle, the actual output growth is above the trend or full employment output or potential growth. During this phase, the expenditure on unemployment benefits and other welfare programmes falls, whereas tax revenue rises through higher corporate profits, wages, and consumer expenditure on goods and services without any change in either the government expenditure policies or tax rates. The reverse applies in a downturn when the actual output growth is below the trend or potential growth.

The component of deficit occurring because of cyclical reasons (i.e., deviations in the actual output from the potential) is known as the **cyclical deficit** (Figure 8.12). The magnitude of the cyclical component gets determined by the size of the deviation of an economy from its potential (which is reflected in the trend) and the responsiveness of expenditure and revenues to the deviation. The cyclical deficit is a temporary phenomenon and does not necessitate a change in the fiscal stance.

The cyclical component, however, obscures the fiscal stance or the medium term orientation (i.e. whether the government is aiming at an expansionary or a contractionary policy). Hence, to understand the medium-term orientation of fiscal policy one needs to make adjustments in the actual fiscal deficit. The fiscal deficit adjusted for cyclical component is known as the **structural deficit**. It reflects the deficit that exists even when an economy is operating at its potential or full employment level of output. Structural deficiencies in a system cause such a deficit. For example, if existing tax rates are very low, then even when the economy experiences rapid growth the government may not be able to raise large revenue, resulting in a deficit. Similarly, other structural problems, such as a large share of children or ageing population in the total population, non-coverage of rapidly growing sectors of an economy under the tax net, etc., can result in the structural deficit.

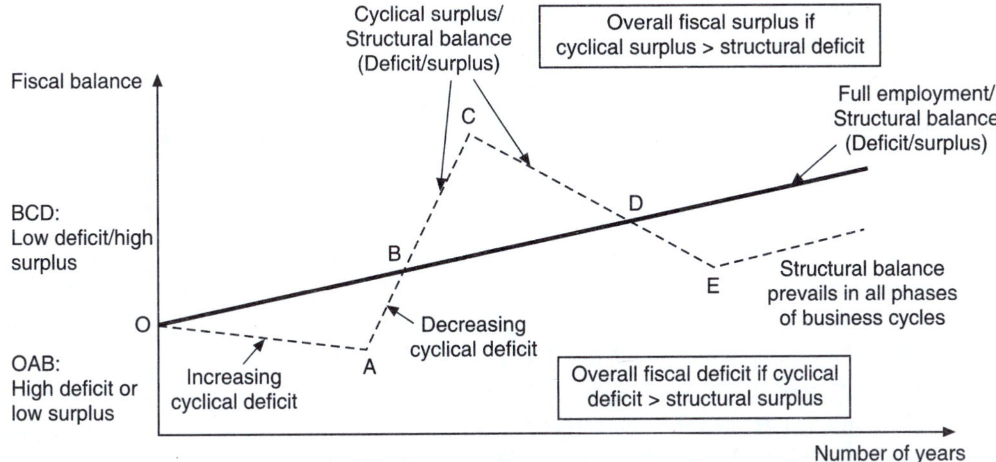

Figure 8.12 Cyclical and Structural Deficit.

Structural deficit is an outcome of structural deficiencies. Hence, it causes persistent fiscal deficit which can result in continuous inflationary pressures and other associated problems. It requires urgent policy attention and correction. Knowing that such a deficit can hamper the long-term growth and destabilize an economy, many multilateral organizations emphasize a correction in structural deficit to get a membership of that group. For example, IMF (Maastricht Treaty) stipulates that the member countries need to maintain either fiscal balance or surplus over the medium term (referring to underlying or structural fiscal position) and the actual fiscal imbalance (deficit) below 3 per cent of GDP in a given year except in the case of unusually large shocks. This stipulation implies that the member countries need to strive for structural balance or surplus. However, they can incur cyclical deficit of up to 3 per cent in a given year to automatically stabilize the economy from cyclical fluctuations. The estimation of cyclical and structural balance involves the following steps:

1. Estimation of potential output: For the estimation of potential output, the following two methods are used world over:
   - *Statistical methods to estimate trend output:* Statistical methods usually depend on the Hodrick-Prescott (HP) time series filtering method to estimate the trend line.
   - *Econometric methods to estimate production function:* Parameters estimated using econometric techniques are combined with actual (or projected) values of the determinants of output (capital, labour and total factor productivity) in the production function to obtain underlying potential output.
2. Quantification of the cyclical component of expenditure and revenue:
   - *Revenue:* The cyclical component is obtained by adjusting the observed revenue using the elasticities of major tax items and taking into account the gap between actual and potential output.
   - *Expenditure:* It is assumed that only a fraction of the government expenditure is sensitive to output fluctuations. Only the outlays on unemployment benefits are taken into consideration while estimating the effects of cyclical variations in unemployment. These are adjusted in proportion to the gap between the actual and natural rates of unemployment.

3. The subtraction of cyclical expenditures and revenues from their observed levels so as to obtain the normal level of expenditure and revenue.

The structural balance, if in a deficit, highlights the extent of fiscal correction needed. However, while interpreting the structural budget balance following points need to be kept in mind:

1. In the estimation of structural balance, the effect of inflation is ignored.
2. The structural balance captures the direct budgetary effects of changes in interest rates which normally are not under the immediate control of fiscal authorities. To that extent, structural imbalance is overstated in an environment of a generalized increase in interest rates. In such circumstances the primary (i.e., net of interest payments) structural budget balance is a better indicator.
3. The budgetary elasticities (i.e., tax and expenditure elastcities) are assumed constant over a medium-term. However, substantial structural changes can result in significant changes in these elasticities. If not adjusted as per the changing environment, these elasticities may not reveal the correct structural budget balance of a country.
4. The structural balance is not an indicator of the effects of fiscal policy on an economy as it excludes the budgetary effects of automatic stabilizers.

Given these deficiencies, many countries are not publishing the extent of structural deficit on a regular basis. However, concepts of cyclical and structural deficits are very useful analytical tools. Hence, occasionally governments make an assessment of these. The concept of cyclical deficit helps them to assess the extent of discretionary policy changes which are required if there is a deviation of actual output from the potential output (UBE 8.4). The concept of structural deficit, on the contrary, helps governments in identifying the extent of structural deficiencies in the system and the correction required thereof.

UNDERSTANDING BUSINESS ENVIRONMENT

UBE 8.4 Discretionary Component of Fiscal Policy in India

Given the small size of cyclical component in India, this UBE suggests that the government needs to often resort to discretionary fiscal actions, resulting in substantial structural deficit to stabilize the economy.

Fiscal policy consists of two components, discretionary and non-discretionary. The discretionary component reflects the **stance of fiscal policy**. That is, it indicates whether the policy is expansionary or contractionary. Changes in fiscal balance, as a result of discretionary policy, affect the output. The non-discretionary component, on the contrary, does not result in the change in the fiscal stance, i.e., the government does not bring in any change in the fiscal policies. However, due to fluctuations in economic activities, the fiscal policies in vogue automatically change the level of government expenditure and revenue, and hence, the overall fiscal balance.

The pertinent question is whether non-discretionary changes or automatic components of fiscal policy are sufficient enough to moderate business cycles and bring back an economy on its trend growth path or some discretionary changes are needed to achieve the same. This aspect of fiscal policy is usually employed by decomposing the actual fiscal deficit into a structural component which is unresponsive to business cycles, and a cyclical component, which is responsive to cycles.

Cyclical component of fiscal deficit is often **counter-cyclical**. That is, it moves in the opposite direction of business fluctuations. For instance, during a slowdown of an economy, the revenue of the government, at unchanged tax rates, declines while expenditure on schemes such as unemployment guarantee schemes and anti-poverty schemes increases. Thus, in a downturn, the cyclical component of fiscal deficit turns negative. Given no change in the structural component, the actual fiscal deficit widens in the event of a slowdown. The cyclical component of fiscal deficit boosts up the level of aggregate demand and the economy gets stabilized automatically. Hence, it is also known as **automatic stabilizer** or **built in stabilizer**. Predominance of cyclical component in fiscal deficit averts the need for changing the fiscal stance or pursuing non-discretionary policies. On the other hand, in the absence of sufficient automatic stabilizers, the government has to intervene by discretionary policy changes, such as changing the tax rates and/or level of public spending or combination of both for moderating business fluctuations.

In the context of Indian economy, RBI (2002) indicated that the structural deficit is a predominant component of fiscal deficit. More recent studies, RBI (2009) and GOI (2011), indicate that the structural component continues to dominate the fiscal deficit even in the post-FRBMA period. Cyclical component, though present, is not large in magnitude. As per GOI (2011), during the period 1990–1991 to 2009–2010, the cyclical component ranged between a deficit of 0.4 per cent of GDP and a surplus of 0.4 per cent of GDP as against actual gross fiscal deficit which ranged between 2.5 to 7.8 per cent of GDP (Figure 8.13).

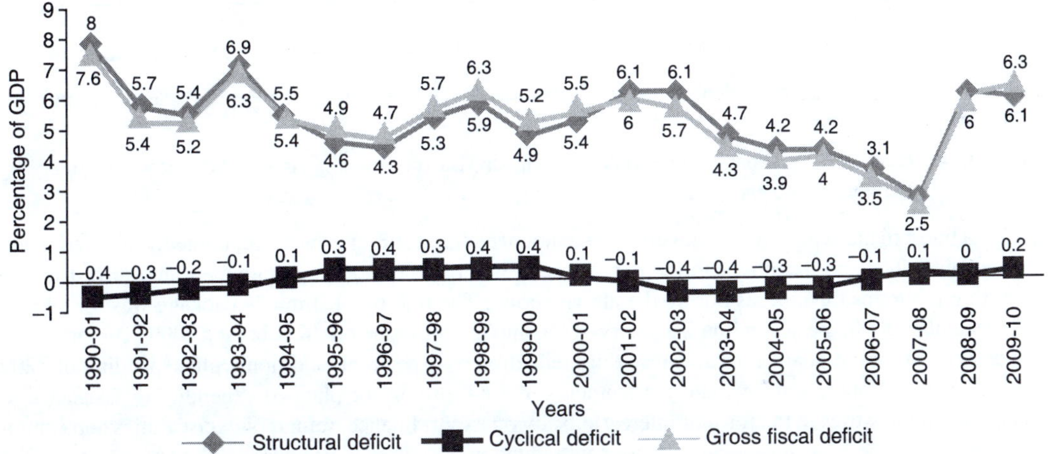

Note: '–' value indicates surplus.

Source: Based on the data available from GOI (2011), Economic Survey 2010–11.

Figure 8.13 Cyclical, Structural and Fiscal Deficit in India.

The data available from IMF, as presented in Figure 8.14, indicates that in comparison to other countries also India's overall fiscal deficit and **structural deficit** (also known as **cyclically adjusted balance** or deficit) is much higher. It is also higher than that prevailing in advanced economies.

Given the small size of cyclical component in India, the findings suggest that the government needs to resort to discretionary fiscal actions to stabilize the economy. The government, hence, has been using the discretionary fiscal policy to give a boost to the economy whenever required as is evident from the write up below.

During the high growth phase that the Indian economy experienced during 2002–03 to 2007–08, the discretionary fiscal actions remained relatively weak up to 2007–08. However, unprecedented global crisis in 2008–09, triggered by sub-prime lending crisis in the USA, and the subsequent slowdown experienced in India in 2008–09 and 2009–10 necessitated significant increase in the discretionary component.

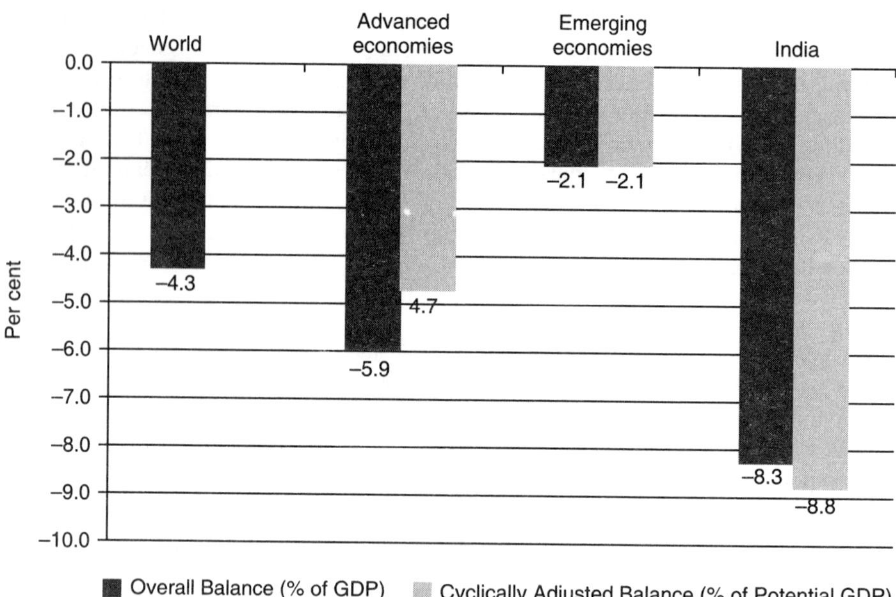

Source: IMF (2013), Fiscal Monitor April Data Base, (Online), http://www.imf.org/external/pubs/ft/fm/2013/01/fmindex.htm.

Figure 8.14 Overall Fiscal Balance and Cyclically Adjusted Balance in India vis a vis Advanced and Emerging Economies—Year 2012.

To give a boost to the economy, the government announced fiscal stimulus package, in the form of reduction in taxes and duties and incentives to the export sector and expenditure on employment and infrastructure generating programs three times during the above period. The first fiscal stimulus package was introduced on 7 December 2008, the second on 2 January 2009, and the third one on 24 February 2009. The measures included an across-the-board central excise duty reduction by 4 per cent, additional plan spending of ₹200 billion, additional borrowing by state governments of ₹300 billion for planned expenditure, assistance to certain export industries in the form of interest subsidy on export finance, refund of excise duties and central sales tax, other export incentives, and a 2 per cent reduction in central excise duties and service tax, i.e., the combined reduction of 6 per cent in central excise duties. As per RBI (2010), the fiscal stimulus measures amounted to 2.4 per cent in 2008–09, which moderated to 1.8 per cent in 2009 ((RBI 2010)).

References:

GOI (2011), Economic Survey 2010–11.

RBI (2002), Report on Currency and Finance 2000–2001.

RBI (2009), Annual Report.

RBI (2010), Annual Report.

8.7 FINANCING OF PUBLIC DEFICIT

The excess of expenditure over revenue, known as the **deficit**, can be financed by a government from domestic (central bank and domestic market participants) as well as foreign borrowing as indicated in Figure 8.15. The impact of each form of borrowing on an economy is described here.

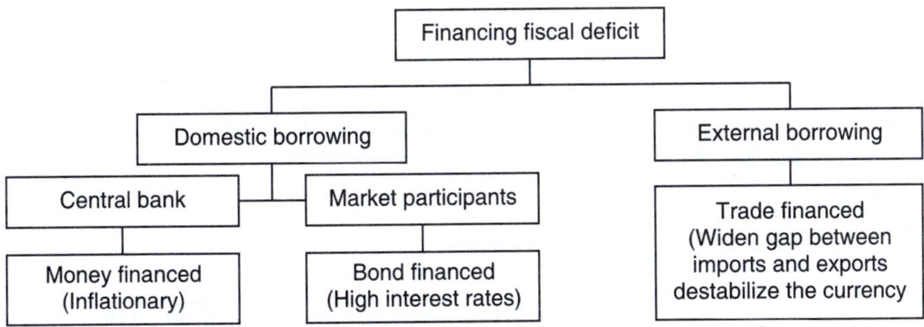

Figure 8.15 Financing of Fiscal Deficit and Its Impact.

Borrowing from the Central Bank

A government can sell its securities to the central bank to finance its expenditure. This amounts to a purchase of government securities by the central bank from the primary market. The central bank has the power to print domestic currency; hence, whenever it purchases government securities and pays for it by printing new notes the money supply increases. Thus, the financing of the government deficit by borrowing from the central bank, also known as the **monetized deficit**, increases the money supply.

Depending on the existing structure of an economy, an increase in the money supply affects output as well as price level. In the presence of excess capacity it increases output by making more resources available to domestic agents and enhancing their demand for goods and services. However, if there is no excess capacity in an economy and the supply of goods and services is limited, the increase in the demand, because of an increase in money supply, simply pushes up the price level. This can be noted from the equation of exchange, i.e., $MV = PY$, which implies that

$$p = m - g + v$$

where,

p = Percentage change in prices (P) (inflation)

m = Percentage change in money supply (M)

g = Percentage change in output (Y)

v = Percentage change in velocity (V) (average frequency with which a unit of money spent in a given period)

Given that the velocity remains stable in the short-run and the output is fixed (i.e., $g = 0$) due to the capacity constraint, the prices change in the same proportion as the change in money supply.

Thus, in a recessionary situation, in the presence of excess capacity, the deficit financing, i.e., the borrowing of a government from the central bank, can stimulate and enhance total output. However, if the supply is limited, and the economy is facing severe capacity constraint, the impact will be largely on the price level. The economy under such circumstances will be under severe inflationary pressures if the government opts for money financing of its deficit. Though a mild inflation rate is conducive for business expansion and economic activity, a high rate of inflation is not. As has been noted in Section 4.5.2, the high rate of inflation changes relative prices, distorts allocation of resources and income, increases income inequalities, leads to a diversion of resources to unproductive channels, makes the domestic goods uncompetitive in the international market, fuels further inflationary expectations, further deteriorates fiscal deficit, and leads to a loss of public faith in government policies. Thus, a high level of monetized deficit needs to be restrained if the capacity of production is under a strain. In a recession though a government can resort to a higher borrowing from the central bank, it, however, should be highly cautious towards such financing in an already booming economy.

Do empirical estimates validate the relationship between fiscal deficit and inflation? UBE 8.5 explores the issue in the Indian context.

UNDERSTANDING BUSINESS ENVIRONMENT

UBE 8.5 Fiscal Deficit and Inflation

In the long run, governments often resort to central banks to finance their deficit which fuels inflation; this UBE substantiates this observation.

The relationship between fiscal deficit and inflation is a complex one. Often the distinction is made between short and long-run to analyze the dynamism of inflation. In a short-run, higher deficit may not lead to inflation as it can be financed by additional borrowing. However, in a long-run, borrowing puts pressure on interest rates and becomes politically difficult. Therefore, in a long-run, most often the fiscal deficit gets financed by borrowing from the central bank. The monetized deficit adds to the purchasing power without creating additional supply sparks and sustains inflation, and often causes high and hyper inflation.

IMF (2007), drawing on the study of IMF staff, substantiate this phenomenon and indicates that there is statistically significant positive relationship between the size of the fiscal deficit scaled by narrow money and inflation for a sample of 23 emerging market economies (Argentina, Brazil, Chile, China, Colombia, Egypt, Hungary, India, Indonesia, Israel, Korea, Malaysia, Mexico, Morocco, Pakistan, Peru, Philippines, South Africa, Thailand, Turkey, Uruguay, Venezuela, and Zimbabwe) during 1970–99 (Table 8.4). This implies that the higher the inflation the higher the fiscal imbalances (ratio of government deficit over GDP), and/ or lower the size of the inflation tax base (proxied by the ratio of narrow money to GDP). This relationship is identified to be quite stable to the inclusion of other variables (such as indicators of openness, political instability, exchange rate regime, changes in oil prices, changes in non-oil commodity prices, and world inflation) as well as the exclusion of countries that experienced hyper inflation episodes in the late 80s/early 90s (such as Argentina, Brazil, and Peru). In addition to the government deficit, changes in world oil prices and world inflation were found to be significant. On the other hand, the impact of pegged exchange rate regime and inflation had been identified to be statistically insignificant. The report indicates that a reduction in the government deficit by 1 percentage point of GDP is associated with a drop in inflation by 2 per cent to 6 per cent points depending on the level of private sector's holding of narrow money. A 10 per cent reduction in oil prices brings about four-fifths of a percentage point reduction in the inflation rate, whereas a 10 per cent change in the world inflation translates into a reduction in domestic inflation of almost 3 per cent.

Table 8.4 Long-run Relationship between Inflation, Fiscal Deficit, and Changes in World Prices

	Coefficient	*t-ratio*
Government deficit/Narrow money	0.32	18.1
Changes in world oil prices	0.08	9.4
World inflation	0.29	7.3

Source: IMF (2007), *World Economic Outlook*, April.

In the Indian context, RBI (2010) indicates that though there is a positive relationship between inflation and **seigniorage** (i.e. the change in the monetary base or printing new notes) in the short run, it is not significant. The same study, however, estimating the co-integrating long-run relationships through bound testing (ARDL) approach (which is an econometrics approach) during 1952 to 2009 indicates the following:

(i) Government resorts to seigniorage to finance its deficit in the long-run:

One per cent change in gross fiscal deficit (GFD) is estimated to cause half a per cent change in seigniorage 'S', defined as change in real reserve money:

$$\text{Log S} = -3.19 + 0.51 \text{ Log GFD} - \text{Dummy 1975–76}$$
$$-(10.7) \quad (16.6) \qquad\qquad (-2.8)$$

(ii) Resorting to the seigniorage for financing the deficit influences the price level:

A one per cent change in seigniorage is estimated to cause about one-third of a per cent change in the price level (WPI):

$$\text{Log WPI} = 4.53 + 0.32 \text{ Log S} + 0.05 \text{ Trend}$$
$$(17.6) \quad (1.7) \qquad\qquad (4.0)$$

(iii) Government deficit increases aggregate demand which has direct causal impact on the price level:

One per cent change in fiscal deficit is estimated to cause about one-quarter of a per cent change in the price level:

$$\text{Log WPI} = 3.0 + 0.25 \text{ Log GFD} + 0.044 \text{ Trend} + \text{Dummy 1974-75}$$
$$(5.1) \quad (2.1) \qquad\qquad (2.9) \qquad\qquad (2.6)$$

Thus, in India, in the long-run, inflation is influenced either directly by deficit itself or through the creation of money via deficit financing, or a combination of both.

References

IMF (2007), *World Economic Outlook*, April.

RBI (2010), Annual Report.

Borrowing from the Domestic Open Market

The government can even raise funds from the open market, i.e., by issuing government securities to other domestic participants, such as commercial banks and other financial institutions. Like central bank these other domestic participants do not have the power to create money. Hence, the government borrowing from these sources does not result in higher money supply. The government borrowing from the market, however, increases the demand for funds, and thus, puts pressure on the overall interest rates. Higher interest rates affect business activities and general economic environment on various fronts as analyzed as follows:

1. Interest rate is one of the important factors affecting investment in an economy. Interest rate and investment are inversely related. Higher government borrowing from the market leads to an overall higher interest rate which may crowd out private investment if it is sensitive to interest rate. It has been observed that the private investment is more efficient than the public investment. Thus, a higher interest rate, as an outcome of higher borrowing by a government, also implies a replacement of more productive investment by less productive one (if the government is using borrowed amount for investment). In the long-run, such a shift adversely affects the growth rate.

2. The interest rate differentials, i.e., the difference between interest rates in the domestic market vis-a-vis that in the rest of the world, affect the inflow of foreign capital (detailed in Section 14.2.3). Given the level of interest rate abroad, interest rate differentials attract foreign capital in the domestic market. A higher inflow of foreign capital increases the supply of foreign currency. As this currency gets converted into the domestic currency by domestic players the demand for domestic currency increases. Thus, given the supply of domestic currency, an increase in the demand for it increases its price in terms of a foreign currency. This is known as the **appreciation** of domestic currency (Section 15.2). The appreciation adversely affects the export competitiveness. Again this is not a very conducive scenario for business organizations as the demand for their products in the international market suffers.
3. The higher level of interest rate increases the expenditure of a government on interest payment in the ensuing period which further deteriorates the fiscal deficit and leads to further build-up of public debt. Sometimes, the debt burden itself may become unsustainable in the sense that the government may be required to borrow simply to repay its past debt. Macroeconomic stability gets jeopardized by the unsustainable level of debt.

However, as elaborated hereinafter, the government borrowing from the market may even be very conducive for the overall business and economic growth under certain scenarios, especially when the economy is in an underdeveloped state, the investment is not very sensitive to interest rate, and there are large under-utilized capacities.

In underdeveloped economies, the infrastructure which supports business activities is usually missing. The government borrowing that is used for financing investment in infrastructure reduces the cost of business. Thus, rather than crowding out, the public investment may crowd in the private investment.

Interest rate though an important determinant of investment, in certain economic scenarios investment may not be very sensitive to it. Prospects of future growth and general enabling environment may positively affect the level of investment even in the presence of overall high interest rate. Thus, if the public borrowings are supporting the overall growth, it may not adversely affect the private investment even though it may be increasing the overall interest rate.

The government borrowings increase the demand for goods and services, Thus, it increases the overall level of demand. In business downturns, due to lack of demand from the private sector the resources remain unutilized. In such a scenario, market borrowing by the government though increases the demand for goods and services, may not drive up the overall interest rate.

The government borrowings may not adversely affect export competitiveness, rather it may be export enhancing if the funds mobilized by the government are used for increasing the overall efficiency of production.

Thus, it can be ascertained that the government borrowing, if used judiciously for increasing investment and infrastructure, creates an enabling environment for business and may be self-sustaining. However, the extended level of government borrowing, used for financing mainly the consumption expenditure, may not be self-sustaining. In a booming economy, when the demand for the funds from the private sector is very high, the government borrowing puts further upward pressure, implying that the government should restrain itself from incurring deficit in such a scenario.

Borrowing from External Markets

Government borrowing from abroad can be from bilateral sources (government of another country), multilateral sources (World Bank, IMF, ADB, etc.), and/or foreign private organizations. Foreign borrowing adds to the available domestic resources. If used for enhancing productive capacity, such borrowing does not create much of a problem for an economy. However, servicing the build-up of foreign debt may drain out the resources from the country in the long run.

The government borrowing, whether domestic or foreign, if used for unproductive expenditure, may lead an economy under a debt trap, a situation where the government borrows for repaying its past debt, and jeopardize the macro-economic stability. In such a situation, the public loses faith in fiscal policies and may not be willing to lend to the government. The government also loses credibility in external markets, which makes it difficult to borrow from external sources. Constrains on the borrowings may force the government to monetize its deficit. However, that puts inflationary pressures on the economy.

External borrowings also have impact on trade flows. External borrowings increase inflow of foreign currency. Once foreign currency is converted into domestic currency, the demand for the domestic currency increases, which appreciates the value of the domestic currency. Consequently, imports become cheaper and exports dearer, leading to widening of the trade deficit. Hence, external borrowings are considered to be trade financed

Government deficit, hence, we can see that may fuel inflationary pressure, raise interest rates, crowd out more efficient private investment, widen trade deficit and may drain out the domestic resources. It may pose a threat to macroeconomic stability and growth of an economy. Therefore, the governments experiencing persistent of fiscal deficit try to reform their fiscal structure. Fiscal corrections can be brought about by tax reform (UBE 8.2), expenditure corrections (UBE 8.3) and even by institutional reforms (UBE 8.6).

UNDERSTANDING BUSINESS ENVIRONMENT

UBE 8.6 Institutional Reforms for Fiscal Consolidation

Persistent fiscal deficit either fuels inflation or crowds out private investment. Hence, Fiscal discipline is essential to achieve sustainable growth. As described in this UBE the FRBM Act 2003, is an institutional mechanism that aims at strengthening fiscal discipline in India.

The fiscal deficit plays an important role in creating demand in a demand deficient economy, and thus, leading the economy towards a high growth trajectory. However, a continuous high level of deficit becomes a cause of concern for several reasons as follows:

1. The persistent high level of fiscal deficit preempts a larger share of public resources for debt servicing, thereby, leaving that much less for capital expenditure, thus, reducing the funds for physical infrastructure (such as roads and power) and social infrastructure (such as education and health).
2. The composition of fiscal deficit is equally important. A higher proportion of revenue deficit in the fiscal deficit indicates that the borrowed resources are used for current consumption, implying the diversion of funds for unproductive activities. Though large consumption expenditure adds on to the aggregate demand and raises growth in the short-run, it reduces funds available for investment purposes, thus, adversely affecting the long-term growth. For sustainability of growth, it is essential to balance the revenue account and use the borrowed funds for investment purpose.

3. The government borrowing programme also reduces the availability of funds to the private sector, and crowds out the private sector investment. Given the differences in the efficiency of production in the two sectors, the diversion of resources to the public sector has an adverse implications for growth. A balance needs to be struck between the availability of funds to the government and the private sector.
4. Depending on the ways in which fiscal deficit is financed, an increasing fiscal deficit can have implications for the level of interest rate or inflation in a country. If the deficit is financed by government borrowing in the domestic market it puts pressure on the domestic interest rate. On the other hand, if the government finances the deficit by borrowing from the central bank (thus, resulting in printing of new notes) it fuels inflation.
5. The revenue deficit also leads to inter-temporal equity concerns as it gives pleasure of spending to the current generation the cost of which is born by the later generations.

The government has been playing an important role in India since independence by supporting economic activities. Though the active involvement of the government has helped the country enhance its productive capacity, a large amount of expenditure has been on unproductive activities. At the same time, inspite of sufficient tax buoyancy, the anomalies in the tax system, has restrained the government efforts to mobilize revenue sufficient enough to meet its expenditure requirements.

The unproductive expenditure and tax distortions resulted in continuously high level of fiscal deficit in India in the pre- FRBM act period (Figure 8.17). The high fiscal deficit, a large part of which had been on the revenue account, was financed either by the borrowing from the RBI and/or by market borrowing from commercial banks and other financial institutions which was almost captive. These borrowings put inflationary pressure and build up of high level of outstanding public debt, threatening the stability of the economy. The persistent high fiscal deficit, thus, constrained the economy from realizing its full growth potential in the past and necessitated fiscal corrections and consolidation.

Attempts were made in the 1990's to reduce the fiscal deficit by reducing, rationalizing and consolidating taxes. However, the efforts at fiscal consolidation, after an initial spurt of success of bringing down the fiscal deficit of the Central Government as a proportion of GDP from 6.6 per cent in 1990–91 to 4.1 per cent in 1996–97 (Figure 8.16(a)), waned in the face of strong sectoral demand for resources. The fiscal deficit again rose to 6.2 per cent in 2001–02. During this period the quality of fiscal deficit further deteriorated as indicated by the substantial increase in the proportion of revenue deficit to fiscal deficit from 49.4 per cent in 1990–91 to 74.4 per cent in 2002–03 [Figure 8.16(b)].

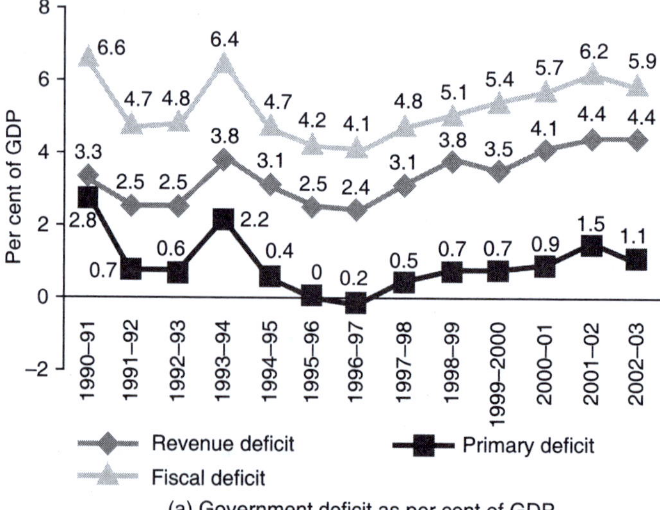

(a) Government deficit as per cent of GDP

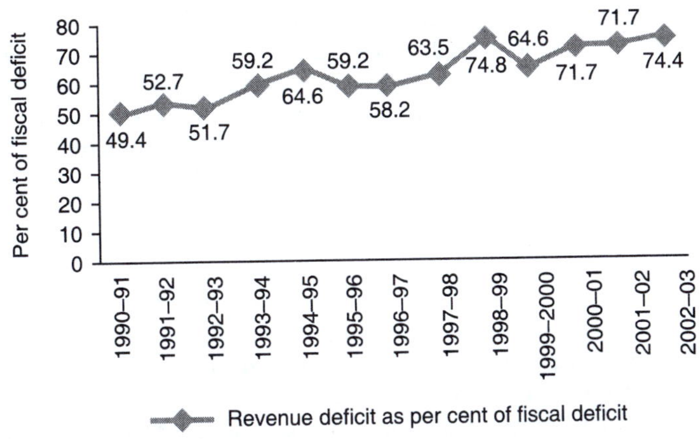

(b) Revenue deficit as per cent of fiscal deficit

Source: Based on the data from GOI (Various Issues), Economic Survey and Union Budget.

Figure 8.16 Trends in Deficit of the Central Government in the Pre-FRBM Period.

Given the problems associated with the continued high level of fiscal deficit, the Government of India enacted the Fiscal Responsibility and Budget Management (FRBM) Bill 2000, to place in institutional mechanism that strengthens fiscal discipline and binds the government to pursue a prudent fiscal policy and enhance the credibility of fiscal stance and transparency of fiscal operations. The bill was revised in 2003. The FRBM rules, instigated in 2004, commit the government to a deficit or debt reduction path into the future (Table 8.4).

Table 8.4 Requirements of the FRBM Act 2003 and FRBM Rules 2004 (as amended through the Finance Act 2004)

Requirement	*Enactment date*
Revenue deficit	
Date for elimination	31/3/2009
Minimum annual gain (reduction)	0.5% of GDP
Fiscal deficit to GDP	
Ceiling	3% by 31/3/2009
Minimum annual gain (reduction)	0.3% of GDP
Contingent liabilities (maximum annual issuance)	0.5% of GDP in any financial year
Total additional liabilities (including external debt at current exchange rate)	9% of GDP in 2004-05
Annual reduction	1% of GDP
RBI primary market purchases of GOI bonds	Cease on 1/4/2006

One of the major objectives of the FRBM Act was to affect a shift in the composition of total expenditure in favour of capital expenditure. Therefore, the FRBM rules stipulated the elimination of revenue deficit by 31 March 2009 through a reduction of minimum of 0.5 per cent of GDP per annum, and thereafter, build up of an adequate revenue surplus. The FRBM rules also set to achieve a reduction in gross fiscal deficit by 0.3 per cent or more of GDP every year so that it did not exceed 3 per cent of GDP by the end of March 2009. To reduce the monetization of deficit, the FRBM prohibited the government from borrowing directly from the RBI from the year 2006–07 onwards except in the form of the ways and means advances to meet temporary mismatches in receipts and payments or unexpected circumstances. This was also expected to remove fiscal constraints on the conduct of monetary policy and debt management. The RBI, however, allowed buying and selling of government securities in the secondary market. The FRBM Act limited the contingent liabilities (contingent liabilities are possible obligations that may emerge for an organization in the future if certain uncertain events occur. Governments too have certain contingent liabilities. For example, many public sector banks are owned by the government. Often, in the event of failure of such financial institutions, the Central Government come to their rescue. Some governments provide free earth quake insurance resulting in contingent liability for them. Even when state guaranteed infrastructure project runs into difficulty it results in contingent liability for the government) of the Central Government by restricting these to 0.5 per cent of GDP in any financial year. It also stipulated that the additional liabilities shall not exceed 9 per cent of GDP for the year 2004–05. In each subsequent year, the limit of 9 per cent of GDP to be progressively reduced by at least one per cent point of GDP.

The FRBM Act, however, had some built-in-flexibility in achieving revenue and fiscal reduction targets. It had a provision that the specified limits may be exceeded on the grounds of national security or national calamity or such exceptional grounds as the Central Government may specify. The Act also contained the provisions to enhance transparency in the Central Government's fiscal operations by requiring the government to place before the parliament the quarterly progress in receipts and expenditures in relation to the budget estimates.

The enactment of FRBM rules succeeded in fiscal consolidation. The revenue and fiscal deficit as a proportion of GDP declined in the post FRBMA period and reached to 1.1 per cent and 2.7 per cent respectively in 2007–08. Contingent liabilities were 0.64 per cent, 0.07 per cent and –0.02 per cent in 2004–05, 2005–06 and 2006–07, respectively. Barring on the revenue deficit front, the progress with regard to the realization of the targets was satisfactory. Given the overall improvement in the quality of the fiscal deficit during the period 2003–04 to 2004–05, there was a temporary deterioration in ratio of fiscal deficit and revenue deficit to GDP ratio in 2005–06 arising from the devolution of resources to state governments as laid down by the Twelfth Finance Commission and implementation of the state level Value Added Tax (VAT).

The fiscal consolidation path had to be suspended in 2008–09 because of an unprecedented global financial crisis and unfavourable developments in the global arena, such as substantial increase in prices in the world commodity market (which required higher provision for food, fertilizer and petroleum subsidies). Thereafter, in 2009–10, the global recession resulted in a significant slowdown in economic activities in India which required large expenses on fiscal stimulus package causing substantial increase in the fiscal deficit as well as the share of revenue deficit in fiscal deficit (Figure 8.17).

With the global recovery and the improvements in the domestic activities, the government since 2010–11 has started the process of gradual withdrawal from the fiscal expansion carried out in the period of crisis. It is trying to follow the revised roadmap for fiscal consolidation suggested by the Thirteenth Finance Commission (Table 8.5). As per the recommendation of the commission it is also enclosing statement, detailing the three year rolling targets, to the annual budget. In the budget 2011–12, the government aimed at achieving the target set for 2011–12 under the thirteenth Finance Commission. However, there were slippage over the projection due to adverse developments after the budget presentation. Elevated global crude prices and fertilizer prices and sticky high inflation scenario in the domestic economy kept the government expenditure high, and sharp growth deceleration led to decline in direct tax revenue collection. Besides, sluggish financial market conditions hampered the government's attempts to raise funds from divestment program and worsened fiscal position.

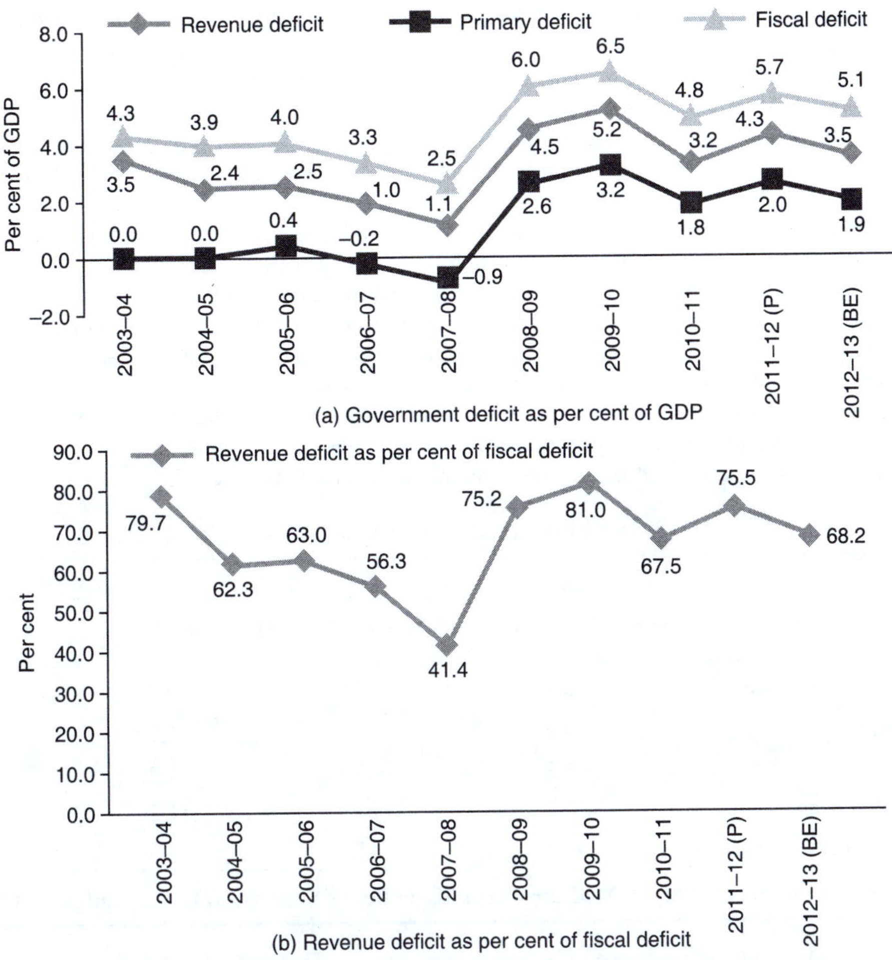

Figure 8.17 Deficit of the Central Government in the Post-FRBM Period.

Table 8.5 Fiscal Consolidation Path for 2009–10 to 2014–15

	2011–12	2012–13	2013–14	2014–15
Revenue deficit				
MTFP	4.4	3.4	2.8	2.0
13th FC	2.3	1.2	0.0	– 0.5
Fiscal deficit				
MTFP	5.9	5.1	4.5	3.9
13th FC	4.8	4.2	3.0	3.0
Outstanding debt				
MTFP	45.7	45.5	44.0	41.9
13th FC	52.5	50.5	47.5	44.8

Notations: MTFP: Medium Term Fiscal Policy; FC: Finance Commission

Source: Compiled from GOI (2012), Medium Term Fiscal Policy statement, **Union Budget 2012–2013**.

The fiscal stress continued in 2012–13, leading to appointment of Kelkar Committee in August 2012 to suggest Roadmap for Fiscal Consolidation. Based on the committee's report, aiming to reduce fiscal deficit to 3 of GDP, the government announced a roadmap for fiscal consolidation during the period of 12th plan, i.e., 2012–13 to 2015–16 (Table 8.6) and initiated slew of measures to improve fiscal position,which include consolidation of both plan and non-plan expenditure, better efforts to raise both tax and non-tax revenue, and improving revenue collection by disinvestment in Hindustan Copper Ltd., NALCO, SAIL, RINL, BHEL, OIL, MMTC and NMDC.

Government since the budget of 2011–12 is targeting to eliminate effective revenue deficit rather than the total revenue deficit. The **effective revenue deficit** is the revenue deficit net of grants given by the union government for creation of capital assets. The reason for considering the effective revenue deficit rather than revenue deficit are as follows. As per the present accounting system, all grants form the union government to state governments, union territories, and other bodies are treated as revenue expenditure even though some of these are used for capital creation. Such revenue expenditure, since results in a creation of asset and contribute to the growth of the economy, should not be treated as unproductive. Therefore, rather than eliminating entire revenue deficit, the government has targeted the elimination of effective revenue deficit. The new roadmap for fiscal consolidation also target this as indicated in Table 8.6.

Table 8.6 Fiscal Consolidation Plan

	2012–13	*2013–14*	*Targets for*	
	(Revised Estimates)	*(Budget Estimates)*	*2014–15*	*2015–16*
Effective Revenue Deficit	2.7	1.8	0.9	0.0
Revenue Deficit	3.9	3.3	2.7	2.0
Fiscal Deficit	5.2	4.8	4.2	3.6
Gross Tax Revenue	10.4	10.9	11.2	11.5
Total Outstanding Liabilities	45.9	45.7	44.3	42.3

Source: Compiled from GOI (2013), **Medium Term Fiscal Policy Statement, Union Budget 2013-14.**

SUMMARY

Fiscal policy consists of revenue and expenditure policies of a government. These policies can be used for achieving micro as well as macro objectives, such as mobilization and allocation of resources, equitable distribution of income, increasing growth, and promoting macroeconomic stability.

Fiscal policy has discretionary and non-discretionary components. The discretionary component reflects whether the policy is contractionary or expansionary and, thus, highlights the stance of fiscal policy. The non-discretionary component, though, does not reflect on the medium to long-term stance of the policy, is used for automatic stabilization of an economy. Hence, it is also known as the automatic stabilizer. The extent to which these policies affect any economy is determined by the tax and expenditure multipliers. The efficacy of these policies is also affected by the inside and outside lags.

Fiscal policy affects government receipts as well as expenditure.

Government receipts are on revenue as well as on capital accounts. One of the important sources of revenue account receipts is the tax, both direct as well as indirect. The tax is a compulsory levy imposed for raising resources and achieving the objectives of fiscal policy. Taxes can be progressive, regressive or proportional. The impact of a given percentage change in the tax rate on the total revenue of the government depends on the value of the tax elasticity or buoyancy. A government also receives revenue from non-tax sources such as commercial and administrative revenue.

The capital account receipts are partly owned by the government such as grants, recoveries of loans and disinvestment proceeds, and partly borrowed funds from domestic as well as foreign sources.

On the expenditure side, the public expenditure is classified into various heads, such as revenue and capital account, plan and non-plan, productive and unproductive, transfer and non-transfer expenditure, and functional and economic categories. Public expenditure can have a profound impact on growth, distribution of income and economic stability. To assure that the public resources are used efficiently and judiciously the canon of economy, canon of sanction, canon of benefit and canon of surplus have been suggested by economists.

By affecting the receipts as well as expenditure of a government, fiscal policy also affects its deficit. Various concepts of government deficit are estimated depending on the purpose of analysis. Some of the widely used concepts are revenue deficit, fiscal deficit, primary deficit, monetized deficit, cyclical deficit and structural deficit. The government deficit can be financed through borrowing from the central bank, other domestic participants and external sources. The borrowing from the central bank is often inflationary in its impact, whereas the borrowing from the domestic market participants puts pressures on the average interest rate and foreign borrowing leads to drains of domestic resources in the long-run.

In India, the pre-1991 period, i.e., pre-reform period, is characterized by deficiencies in the tax system in the form of multiplicity of taxes and tax rates, very high marginal tax rate, large vertical and horizontal inequities resulting from inadequate coverage of income from agriculture and services, various concessions and exemptions resulting in large scale avoidance and evasions and narrow tax base, and a large share of indirect taxes in total tax revenue making the tax system highly regressive.

On the expenditure front, the revenue account expenditure, consisting of interest payments, wages and salaries, and subsidies, was a substantial proportion of total expenditure. It was also highly inelastic in nature bringing in downward rigidities in the revenue account expenditure.

The revenue deficiencies and downward rigidities in expenditure had led to persistent and substantial fiscal deficit in the pre-reform era which had exposed the country to high inflationary and interest rate pressures, led to a build-up of large outstanding debt, and threatened the macroeconomic stability of the country.

To overcome the problem of large persistence fiscal deficit, comprehensive fiscal reforms, including tax reforms, expenditure reforms and institutional reforms have been initiated in the country since 1991–92. Tax reforms have been introduced in the form of reduction in tax rates and slabs, introduction of VAT and inclusion of number of services in the tax net; whereas expenditure reforms have addressed the issues of optimizing government staff strength through restrictions on fresh recruitments, dismantling of the administrative price mechanism, introduction of new pension scheme of defined contribution, rationalization and reduction of budgetary subsidies.

Institutional reforms, in the form of enactment of the FRBM Act (2003) and FRBM Rules (2004), have been introduced to bring in more discipline in government functioning.

These reforms succeeded in improving the share of direct taxes in the tax revenue collection and also improving the tax to GDP ratio. There was also substantial rationalization of the government expenditure in the post 1990–91 period. The reforms also succeeded in fiscal consolidation exercise in the post-FRBMA, 2003 era. However, the slowdown experienced by the country in 2009, in the aftermath of sub-prime lending crisis in the USA, put a hold on such an exercise and the country recorded substantial increase in the fiscal deficit. The consolidation efforts again seem to be on its long-term trajectory.

To achieve further consolidation of fiscal deficit, further simplification, rationalization and broad-basing of the tax system is required. Government aims at improving the tax system by enacting the Direct Tax Code and implementing the Goods and Services Tax in the coming years. On expenditure front, the efforts are required to curtail the revenue account expenditure.

Implications for Business Managers

Fiscal policy is one of the important drivers of business environment and overall macroeconomic stability of a country. The levels of government expenditure, taxes and deficit affect both the demand and the supply side of an economy and have profound impact on economic and business decisions as summarized as follows:

The government expenditure is one of the important components of aggregate demand. In a recessionary situation, when the deficiency of demand is the problem, the government consumption and investment expenditure boost up the level of aggregate demand and encourage business firms to produce or supply more. This helps in utilizing the idle capacity of business units and maintaining their profit levels. The government expenditure also affects the supply side as investment expenditure leads to an improvement in physical and social infrastructure which supports business activities and creates an enabling environment for business in general.

Taxes also affect the demand and supply side of an economy. Taxes affect the disposable income and purchasing power of individuals and business units. Thus, they affect private consumption and investment expenditure which is important for business organizations to plan their production activities. Taxes affect the supply side as they largely direct the procurement, production, employment, investment and diversification decisions of business organizations. Taxes, by affecting the relative prices, and thus, the relative profitability of producing different commodities, also affect the allocation of resources by business units in favour of those commodities that are taxed less. Taxes also guide business enterprises in deciding the location for setting up their units.

The level of fiscal deficit also affects the overall macroeconomic and business environment. Fiscal deficit affects inflation in the country, especially when there is no excess capacity and the deficit is financed through printing domestic currency. Fiscal deficit, if financed from borrowing from the domestic market participants, affects the average level of interest rates. Both inflation and interest rates are important variables in business decisions. These variables affect the production, investment and financing decisions of business organizations and private producers.

For these reasons, business firms and private producers closely watch budget announcements and fiscal developments. They continuously monitor the trends in the ratio of fiscal deficit to GDP, proportion of revenue deficit in total deficit, share of interest payments in total expenditure of the government, and the share of capital expenditure in total expenditure, debt to GDP ratio to ascertain whether the fiscal operations are sustainable, or there are inherent threats to macroeconomic stability on fiscal front. Many strategic decisions, including expansion and launching of new products, and diversification of product lines, are based on the close assessment of fiscal environment of different regions and countries.

REVIEW QUESTIONS

8.1 What is fiscal policy? What are its objectives?

8.2 Differentiate between the discretionary and non-discretionary components of fiscal policy giving illustrations? Which of these components help in ascertaining the medium to long-term stance of fiscal policy? What are the automatic stabilizers?

8.3 How would you differentiate an expansionary policy from a contractionary fiscal policy? Can you assess whether the policy is expansionary or contractionary on the basis of non-discretionary component of fiscal policy? Give reasons for your answer.

8.4 What are fiscal policy multipliers? Why do we need to know their values? Why does the large value of marginal propensity to consume imply the large value of expenditure multiplier?

8.5 What are policy lags? Why is it important to know the duration of these lags? Which of the lag is of longer duration for fiscal policy?

8.6 Is fiscal policy helpful in stabilizing an economy? If yes, how?

8.7 What are the sources of public revenue? What is the basis of differentiating revenue receipts from capital receipts?

8.8 What is tax? What are the principles of good tax system?

8.9 Differentiate between the marginal tax rate and the average or effective tax rate.

8.10 What are the differences between an *ad valorem* duty and a specific duty?

8.11 Distinguish between the progressive and regressive tax systems? Is the proportional tax system progressive or regressive in nature? Which of these tax systems is needed for equity purpose? Which of the system is more efficient for production? What would you suggest to make the tax system progressive?

8.12 What are the differences between direct and indirect taxes?

8.13 What is the VAT? What are the different methods of calculating the VAT liability?

8.14 Is the MODVAT similar to the VAT or excise? In what type of a tax system the cascading impact on prices is higher? Which of these tax systems promote vertical integration of firms?

8.15 How would you measure the tax burden? What do you understand by the incidence of a tax? Is there any relationship between the elasticity of demand and supply and the incidence of a tax falling on a party? If yes, please elaborate.

8.16 What is the Laffer curve?

8.17 How would you estimate tax elasticity and tax buoyancy? How far the two differ? Why are these two statistics needed?

8.18 How does taxation impact economic variables, such as production, distribution and inflation?

8.19 Distinguish between the tax evasion and tax avoidance. Which of these is illegal?

8.20 What are the sources of non-tax revenue for a government?

8.21 What constitutes the own capital receipts of a government?

8.22 How does public expenditure affect an economy?

8.23 What are the main categories in which public expenditure is classified? What do these classifications reflect?

8.24 Differentiate between the plan and non-plan expenditure.

8.25 What are the canons of public expenditure?

8.26 Why performance and programme budgeting are carried out? What are the steps involved in the two?

8.27 Differentiate between incremental budgeting and zero base budgeting.

8.28 Would you prefer the revenue account deficit or capital account deficit? Why?

8.29 Why fiscal deficit is known as the broader concept of deficit? What does it reflect?

8.30 What is the economic rational of estimating the primary deficit?

8.31 Why is the monetized deficit estimated?

8.32 To ascertain the current fiscal stance, which concept of government deficit will you be looking at?

8.33 Why do we estimate the net fiscal and primary deficits?

8.34 Differentiate between the cyclical and structural deficits? Why are these estimated? Which of these acts as an automatic stabilizer?

8.35 What are the different ways of financing public deficit? What are the implications of these different methods of financing for an economy?

8.36 Why does the borrowing of a government from the central bank results in inflationary pressures in an economy?

8.37 Why does the government borrowing from domestic market participants result in higher average interest rate in an economy?

8.38 In what form the VAT has been implemented in India? Answer clearly distinguishing between the MOVDAT and CENVAT.

8.39 Please describe the emerging trends in the tax revenue collection in India. Is the composition of taxes changing in India? Is this changing composition favourable for the economy? Why?

8.40 What reforms have been initiated in India on tax front and why?

8.41 What had been the impact of rationalization of tax rates in India? What further steps need to be taken to improve the tax performance in the country?

8.42 What steps have been implemented to bring in expenditure correction in the Indian Economy?

8.43 How have the FRBM act and rules strengthened the institutional mechanism that aims at fiscal consolidation in the Indian economy?

8.44 Is substantial expenditure correction been achieved in the post-reform period in India?

8.45 What are the issues which need to be addressed for further correction on expenditure front?

8.46 How far reforms have been able to bring compositional changes in the fiscal deficit in India?

8.47 "Automatic stabilizers are missing in India". Comment and analyze this statement.

8.48 How far fiscal consolidation attempts have succeeded in India?

8.49 "Fiscal deficit fuels inflation in the long-run". Substantiate this finding using cross-country empirical studies.

8.50 Why is the understanding of fiscal policy important for business managers?

NUMERICAL PROBLEMS

8.1 Receipts and expenditures of the Central Government of a country are presented in Table 8.7.

Using the above information answer the following questions:

(i) Estimate the revenue deficit, gross fiscal deficit and gross primary deficit. Also, write the formula for each of these concepts.

(ii) Is the information given in the table sufficient for estimating monetized deficit? Specify the reasons for your answer. If the information is sufficient then calculate the extent of monetized deficit.

(iii) If the loans and advances by the Central Government to the State Governments is equal to1 ₹5,000 crore then what will be the net primary deficit?

Table 8.7 Receipts and Expenditure of the Central Government

(₹ in crore)

Item	*Amount* (₹)
I. Revenue receipts (a + b)	4,03,465
(a) Tax revenue	3,27,205
(b) Non-tax revenue	76,260
II. Capital receipts (a + b + c)	1,60,526
(a) Recovery of loans	8,000
(b) PSU disinvestment	3,840
(c) Borrowings and other liabilities	1,48,686
III. Total receipts	5,63,991
IV. Revenue expenditure (a + b)	4,88,192
(a) Interest payments	1,39,823
(b) Non-interest expenditure	3,48,369
V. Capital expenditure	75,799
VI. Total expenditure	5,63,991

8.2 What change in total output will you expect if the government increases spending on various anti-poverty programme by ₹20 crore. The marginal propensity to consume for the economy is estimated to be 0.8.

8.3 Suppose that the marginal propensity to consume is 0.8. Government announces a tax cut of ₹20 crore. Estimate the impact of this tax cut on output.

8.4 When a person's income increases from ₹90,000 to ₹1,00,000 per annum, his tax liability increases from ₹27,000 to ₹31,000. For this tax liability, estimate the marginal tax rate applicable to him.

8.5 Suppose the tax slabs and marginal tax rates are as given in Table 8.8.

Table 8.8 Income Tax Structure

(₹ per annum)

Tax status	*Marginal tax rate* (%)
0–10,000	10
10,001–20,000	20
21,000–30,000	30
31,000 and above	40

Estimate the total tax liability for an individual having an income of ₹35,000. What is the marginal tax rate he is facing? What is the average (effective) tax rate on his income?

8.6 The government raises its expenditure by ₹4 crore, and at the same time, levies a lump sum tax of ₹4 crore. What impact of these changes in fiscal policy you expect on the total output?

CASE ANALYSIS EXERCISE

C8.1 Output Gaps and Fiscal Space

In the boom years prior to the financial crisis, with GDP growth exceeding potential, large positive output gaps developed, reaching 3.8 per cent of GDP by 2008 in developing countries. This strong (cyclical) boost to activity raised tax revenues (in US dollar terms) in developing countries by nearly 26 per cent in 2007 alone.

Fortunately, most developing countries were pursuing a cautious fiscal policy, and used the cyclical tax proceeds to reduce fiscal deficits, which actually turned to surpluses of 0.1 and 0.8 per cent of GDP in 2007 and 2008, respectively. With this conservative, counter cyclical fiscal policy, developing-countries created the fiscal space that in turn allowed deficits to rise counter-cyclically during the crisis—helping to mitigate the downturn.

The speed with which developing countries recovered from the crisis nicely illustrates the advantages of having ample buffers. Indeed, looking across regions there is a strong negative correlation between the size of fiscal surplus in 2007 and the size of the GDP hit countries took, with regions that were in surplus having generally experienced a larger fluctuation in their fiscal deterioration and a smaller decline in GDP (relative to potential) (Table 8.9). The notable exception to this pattern was the Europe and Central Asia region, which unlike other regions had been caught up in the financial excess of the boom period and therefore suffered both an external and a domestic shock.

Table 8.9 Output Gaps and Fiscal Balance Responses Following the Financial Crisis

	Developing countries	*EAP*	*ECA*	*LAC*	*MNA*	*SAS*	*SST*
Fiscal Balance in 2007	0.0	0.4	3.0	–1.3	–0.1	–4.1	0.4
Change in output gaps (A)	–4.0	–1.4	–10.7	–5.4	–0.1	–2.0	–3.1
Change in fiscal balances (B)	–3.8	–2.7	–7.2	–3.0	–3.8	–1.6	–6.8
Elasticity (B to A)	0.9	1.9	0.7	0.5	29.4	0.8	2.2

Notations: EAP: East Asia and Pacific; ECA: Europe and Central Asia, LAC: Latin America and Caribbean, MNA: Middle East and North Africa, SAS: South Asia; SST: Sub Saharan Africa.

Source: World Bank (2013), *Global Economic Prospects*, Volume 6, January 2013. Washington, DC: World Bank. Doi: 10.1596/978-0-8213-9882-1 License: Creative Commons Attribution CC BY 3.0

Questions

1. What do you understand by positive output gap?
2. Was the revenue increase in 2007 cyclical or structural in nature?
3. How does fiscal surplus in 2007 and 2008 helped developing countries in the downturn followed by the global financial crisis?
4. What is the relationship between fiscal surplus during a boom and the capacity to withstand shocks in a downturn?
5. Why Europe and Central Asia region suffered the most during the crisis period?
6. What would you expect for a country in a downturn if it is having large fiscal deficit in a booming phase?

SUGGESTED FURTHER READING

Kanagasabapathy, K., Vaidya, D.S. and Tilak, V.G. (2013), Budgeting for Fiscal Consolidation, *EPW*, 27 April, Vol. XLVII, 17.

Khan, H.R. (2013), Promoting Retail Investor Participation in Government Bonds, *RBI Bulletin*, February.

Padmanabham, G. (2012), Governance Deficit and Financial Crisis, *RBI Bulletin*, March.

Papadimitriou, D.B. and Antonopopulos, R. (2012), Economic Turbulence in Greece, *EPW*, 4 February, Vol. XLVII, 5.

Rao, M.G. (2005), Tax System Reform in India: Achievements and Challenges Ahead, Presented in the International Symposium on Tax Policy and Reform in Asian Countries, Hitotsubhashi University, Tokyo, Japan, July 1–2.

Sharma, J.V.M. and Bhaskar, V. (2012), A Road Map for Implementing the Goods and Services Tax, *EPW*, 4 August, XLVII, 31.

Subbarao, D. (2012), Price Stability, Financial Stability and Soverign Debt Sustainability: Policy Challanges from the new Trilemma, *RBI Bulletin*, February.

CHAPTER 9

Financial System, Crisis and Reforms

9.1 INTRODUCTION

In primitive economies, without proper access to financial institutions, such as banks, savings were maintained by individuals mainly in the form of cash, gold, cattle and many such other assets. The fear of theft and inconvenience of storage of such items kept the amount of saving at a very low level. The lack of enough information and the inability to assess the project viability of borrowers also constrained the amount of lending. The low saving mobilization and low investment restrained capital formation and income generation. Such economies also used barter or commodity money or cash for transaction purpose. The clumsy and time consuming process of transactions limited the volume of transaction and economic activities at a lower level, and thus, constrained the growth process.

In contrast to this, in modern era we find that the public have an access to a variety of financial institutions, varying from commercial banks to mutual funds to insurance companies, providing an array of saving instruments to individuals, such as deposits of varying maturity period, mutual funds of different types, such as equity fund, gilt fund, debt fund and balanced fund, life insurance, pension funds, etc. Catering to varied preferences through these instruments, financial institutions are able to mobilize a large amount of funds. These institutions, with the help of their trained and professionally qualified staff, are also able to assess the viability of projects put up with them for seeking credit. With the help of large amount of resources and qualified and trained staff, they can also efficiently lend resources. In such economies, we find that corporates need not depend entirely on their internal saving and resources to carry out production and investment activities. They can easily access funds from financial institutions and even directly from the public by issuing deposits, bonds, debentures and shares in financial markets. They can also access a variety of financial services from different institutions. Also, in such economies, the availability of sophisticated payment mechanism, such as cheques, mobile and internet fund transfer facilities, make a large number of transactions possible within no time. Such a payment mechanism, hence, increases consumption and production activities tremendously.

Thus, we see that a well-developed financial system, consisting of financial institutions, financial instruments, financial markets and financial services, can help in the growth of an economy by mobilizing saving and making available funds as per business requirements. It also supports the process of growth by providing alternative and efficient means of payment such as cheques and electronic fund transfer facilities.

However, at the same time we see the banks running, and financial crises taking place in several economies. The most recent episode of such a crisis was the sub-prime lending crisis which triggered the worldwide failure of financial institutions and led the world economy into a recessionary situation. The crisis highlighted that a poorly managed and supervised financial system can result in severe contraction in economic activities and can bring in misery to masses for several years.

As the costs associated with financial crises are very high it is very important for us to know. What the constituents of a financial system are? How do they operate? What causes weaknesses in them? What did the risk of a fragile financial system are? Accordingly, this chapter provides an overview of a financial system and outlines the need for an efficient and well-functioning financial system. This chapter also details on the reforms that can be carried out to strengthen the financial system. In specific, Section 9.2 briefs on the functions of a financial system. The various constituents of a financial system are described in Section 9.3. The reasons for financial sector weaknesses are highlighted in Section 9.4. The risk of a fragile financial system and the need for implementing reforms are indicated in Section 9.5. The measures initiated in India to strengthen the financial system and the impact of these measures on the functioning of the financial intermediaries and financial markets are also indicated in this section.

9.2 FUNCTIONS OF A FINANCIAL SYSTEM

Encouragement of Saving

An economy consists of surplus units which spend less than their income and, thus, save. It also consists of deficit units which spend more than their income and, thus, borrow. Households are usually surplus units, whereas the government and producers are usually deficit units.

Saving implies future consumption. The preferences for saving or future consumption vis-à-vis present consumption depend on a number of factors such as liquidity, maturity, safety and expected returns as explained hereinafter. The saving retained in the form of cash, ornaments and some such assets is subject to theft. Therefore, when safe avenues for saving are not available then surplus units get discouraged to save. People like to save more when they are sure of the safety of their saving. Similarly, people like their saving to be available whenever they want it in the future. If they are assured of the liquidity or availability of their saved amount whenever they want, they are encouraged to save more. Different people have different future consumption horizon. Some of us want to use our saving for consumption after one month, while others might like to use it after 1 year, 5 years or 10 years. If the saving is made available to savers as per their time preference or maturity preference, they are encouraged to save more. Saving kept in the form of cash, gold or some such items do not result in any return. Thus, over a period of time their value remains stagnant. On the contrary, if the saved amount provides some return than that increases the value of the saved amount. People prefer to save more when they expect to receive some good returns on their saved amount and compensated for postponing their consumption for future.

In the absence of instruments with desirable features, economic agents are either not motivated to save enough or their saving get diverted to unproductive instruments such as gold.

For example, suppose only available financial assets are government securities maturing after ten years. This instrument, though safe and provide reasonable return, does not meet the requirements of those surplus units which need money before ten years and have preference for liquid assets.

A financial system, by designing and offering a wide range of financial instruments with different combinations of risk, return, maturity and liquidity, encourages economic agents to save more.

Mobilization of Saving and Resources

In an underdeveloped financial system, the choice of instruments in which surplus units can keep their saving is limited to instruments like cash, gold, land, etc. The limited number of buyers for and sellers of these instruments restricts the trading of instruments in the markets, and hence, reduces the liquidity of these instruments. The resources mobilized in such a system are limited, which constrain the sufficient availability of funds to the productive sectors. The funds remain with the surplus units unutilized, and hoarded in the form of unproductive assets. Producers and investors, constrained by the availability of their own funds, quite often resort to high cost informal sources such as relatives and moneylenders.

A well-developed financial system, consisting of efficient financial intermediaries which employ skilled staff with an ability to assess the credit worthiness of their clients, can generate trust among surplus units that their funds are in safe hands and are utilized judiciously. Such a system is able to mobilize large amount of saving or resources from surplus units. It smoothens the process of flow of funds from savers to investors and promotes saving by providing an array of financial instruments meeting the preferences of different surplus units.

Resources are mobilized in a financial system directly through financial markets in the form of **primary securities**, i.e., those securities that are issued by the borrowers to the lenders, such as shares, bonds, and debentures. These are also mobilized indirectly through financial intermediaries in the form of **secondary securities**, i.e., those issued by the intermediaries to the surplus units, such as deposits, mutual fund units, etc., with the help of a well-trained marketing personnels who can convince the savers with the features of their financial instruments on offer and safety of their amount.

Efficient Reallocation of Financial Resources

In traditional financial systems, mostly moneylenders and endogenous bankers provide funds to deficit units. They often lack skills to evaluate the credit worthiness of their clients and the productivity of their projects. They operate in unorganized and unregulated set-up and charge varied and very high interest rates. Though this can be partly attributed to higher risk involved in their operations, but ignorance and lack of access of small borrowers to the alternative sources of finance is often the main factor behind the high rates. Another deficiency of such systems is the lack of integration among different constituents of this market, consisting of money lenders, endogenous bankers and more organized lenders like banks. The lack of integration obstructs the flow of information from one region to another, from one market to another and from one organization to another organization. It results in an inefficient allocation of resources. For example, suppose in Maharashtra many entrepreneurs are interested in operationalizing their ideas, that seem very revolutionalizing and productive than the activities pursued in other regions, say Bengal. However, in the absence of proper integration, such information is not available to all lenders across the country. On the one hand, in such a situation the deficit units in Maharashtra are not able to collect enough funds because resources in any of the areas are limited. On the other hand, the lenders in Bengal and other areas are forced to lend only to the deficit units in their own localities that are not very efficient, productive and using funds simply for marriages, naming ceremonies, shraadh, etc. Thus, we can see that in the absence of proper integration, there is an inefficient allocation of resources compromising the social and growth priorities.

Contrary to the underdeveloped financial systems, financial intermediaries and financial markets under well-developed financial systems operate in an organized format and are well-integrated with the other segments of the system. Because of enough integration among markets and intermediaries, all the relevant information required for allocating resource is available to all the participants in such a system. In a well-integrated system funds move to most productive areas, say Maharashtra, from not that much productive regions, say Bengal.

Also, in a transparent and well-functioning system, deficit units like corporates are made to disclose enough information to the public through their quarterly or annual reports. Such a disclosure makes it possible for the surplus units to assess their credit worthiness and supply their surplus funds directly to the corporates rather than through financial intermediaries. As no intermediary is involved in such a direct recourse to funds, there is no intermediation charges and the cost of funds is lower for the corporates.

Diversification and Risk Reduction

Saving of an individual investor is usually too small. Investment in most of the financial instruments requires some transaction cost, such as broker fees in case of purchases of shares. Transaction cost, usually, is a fixed amount; it does not vary with the amount of investment. Therefore, small savers, to avoid incurring large transaction costs, end up placing their saving in limited number of assets like cash, deposits, and/or shares of one or two companies. However, narrow portfolio, either exposes them to higher **market risk** (arising from the fluctuations in the price of financial instruments) or compromises on return. For example, suppose Ravi is able to save only ₹1,000 every month. He has the option of keeping his saving in deposits and shares of various companies. Value of investment in deposits is not subject to market fluctuations. Hence, these assets are comparatively safer, but the return on these is also low. On the contrary, investment in shares provides high return, but share prices keep fluctuating widely and, hence, are subject to large market risk. However, not all share prices fluctuate in the same direction at the same time. A sharp reduction in the prices of some shares gets moderated by a reduction in the prices of other shares. Hence, the impact of wide fluctuations in share prices on earnings can be mitigated to a large extent by diversifying the portfolio of assets. The portfolio can be diversified by investing in different types of financial instruments rather than investing in only a single share or a single financial asset. Ravi has this knowledge, and in the market shares of different types of companies are also available. However, because of small amount of saving and high transaction cost of investing in shares of many companies, to save on the transaction cost, he decides to invest only in the shares of an automobile company say "Truth". Since he didn't had an expertise to assess the worthiness of companies issuing shares, he selects shares of this company without looking at the company's fundamentals. He decides on his choice by looking at what his friends Dharma and Karma, were investing in. One day he realized that his entire saving is wiped out because of a sudden crash in the share prices of "Truth" due to a financial fraud deducted in the company. He could have averted such a situation by placing his saving in deposits, but that would have returned a very low saving and his dream of becoming a millionaire would have shattered.

Financial intermediaries pool in small savings and in the process mobilise large amount of resources. Since they deal in large volumes, they are able to employ legal and technical experts who have expertise in assessing the performance of companies offering shares. Given their dealings in large volumes and expert staff, financial intermediaries can reduce per unit transaction cost of their investment, and diversify their portfolio by judiciously selecting shares and other financial instruments. Thus, they can reduce the risk of investment and, at the same time, improve the return on their investment which is not possible for individuals, especially small savers.

Enhancement of Investment and Capital Stock

To carry out production processes, firms need to build up capital stock through investment in plant and machinery. Investment requires a corresponding amount of saving. Production and investment processes require skills that every economic unit does not possess. As the amount saved by a single entity is small, and if the investment has to be financed from the own saving of an investor or the internal saving of a firm, then the amount of investment taking place in an economy remains low. For example, assume that Dheeraj is an entrepreneur equipped with technical skills to carry out production and manage resources. He wants to set up a glass factory, but does not have enough savings. To supplement his resources he borrows from Ankit, but his savings are too small to meet the resource requirement of Dheeraj. So, on the recommendation of Ankit, Dheeraj approaches Sanchit, a large saver. But he does not have trust in Dheeraj's ability to manage his proposed project and to repay the borrowed amount. Therefore, unable to borrow from Sanchit and raise enough resources, Dheeraj keeps his plans of investing in a glass factory aside. In an underdeveloped financial system there are many budding entrepreneurs like Dheeraj, who find themselves unable to raise enough resources, thus restricting the amount of investment or capital formation in the economy.

A financial system breaks this vicious circle of limited saving and limited investment on the one hand, it achieves this by mobilizing the saving of surplus units like Ankit and Sanchit, not interested and not capable of investment activities, and on the other hand by placing these resources at the disposal of entrepreneurs like Dheeraj, engaged in production and investment activities.

A financial system encourages the aggregate amount of investment by offering borrowers a wide range of financial liabilities and services to suit their needs and preferences. In a well-developed financial system, borrowers can borrow for short-term or long-term, raise funds in the form of debt or equity, or from financial intermediaries or financial markets. The availability of a large number of instruments and a large channels of interactions among borrowers and lenders increases the amount of funds mobilized and lent in the system.

A financial system helps in segregating investment decisions from saving decisions implying that Dheeraj, the investor, need not save, and Ankit and Sanchit, the savers, need not get involved in production and investment. Thus, a financial system helps in the specialization of functions of saving and investment. Those who are not willing to save or those do not have capability to invest, may entrust their savings to others directly through financial markets or indirectly through financial intermediaries. The resources, thus, get transferred to those who are willing to take risk and have capabilities of carrying out investment, production and technological innovations.

In the absence of a well-developed financial system, resources get either unutilized, or investment and production get limited to the extent of the internal saving of firms or producers. The segregation of saving and investment decisions, as we see in a developed system, on the one hand, eases the resource constraints and, on the other hand, prevents the wastage of resources and promotes large-scale investment, which enhances the capital stock and productivity in an economy.

Promotion of Technological Innovations

Technological innovations require large resources. Often these do not take place because of small amount of resources available with innovators. By easing the finance constraints, and making credit available in time, and in adequate quantity a financial system also encourages technological innovations.

Supporting Payment Mechanism

Financial institutions like banks provide cheque facilities on their demand deposits. They also provide credit cards, debit cards and electronic fund transfer facility. All these instruments are widely used as means of payment in modern economies. Such payment mechanism makes transactions easier and helps in saving a lot of time which could be used for enhancing output and growth further.

Facilitating Growth and Development

The level of production is determined by the level of land, labour, capital, entrepreneurship and technological advancement. A financial sector, by promoting the level of capital stock and technological innovations, helps in shifting the production possibility frontier (which reflect the potential output; defined in Section 13.2.1), and thus, creates the possibility of enhancing output and growth further.

The impact of financial sector development on economic growth is illustrated in UBE 9.1 referring to the Indian context.

UNDERSTANDING BUSINESS ENVIRONMENT

UBE 9.1 Does Stock Market Promote Economic Growth in India?

It has been argued that the development of financial sector helps in the economic growth of a country. This UBE assesses the validity of this hypothesis by referring to econometric studies in the Indian context.

In order to establish relationship of various components of the financial sector, viz. banking sector and stock market, with economic growth in India, regression technique has been used. As the monthly GDP series is not available, seasonally adjusted monthly Index of Industrial Production (IIP) was used as a proxy for economic activity. Before carrying out the regression analysis using Ordinary Least Square (OLS), the monthly data were adjusted for seasonality and then the variables were log transformed. As an indicator of the capital market development, market capitalization (MCAP) as a percentage of GDP, which measures the size of the market, and Value Traded Ratio (VTR), which reflects the liquidity of the market, have been used. For the banking sector, Bank Credit (BCR) as a percentage of GDP has been taken as a measure of banking sector development. The period of the analysis was from April 1995 to June 2006.

It is found that both the stock market and the banking sector abet the level of economic activity in the country (Eq. 9.1). However, the relationship between stock market and economic activity is not strong as the coefficient of stock market activitiy, viz. MCAP and VTR, though significant, are very small. On the other hand, bank credit plays a very significant role. This confirms the bank dominated financial system in India.

$$\underset{(16.9)}{\text{LIIP} = 1.27} + \underset{(2.2)}{0.02\ \text{LMCAP}} + \underset{(5.0)}{0.02\ \text{LVTR}} + \underset{(34.4)}{0.43\ \text{LBCR}} + \underset{(6.0)}{0.47\ \text{AR}(1)} \tag{9.1}$$

Adjusted $R_2 = 0.99$; F-statistics = 3240.7; DW-statistics = 2.24
(Figures in parentheses represent t-statistics.)

It is also found that both the banking sector and the economic growth promote stock market activity in India (Eq. 9.2).

$$\underset{}{\text{LMCAP}} = \underset{(-3.2)}{-9.01} + \underset{(2.7)}{1.25\ \text{LIIP}} + \underset{(4.7)}{1.32\ \text{LBCR}} + \underset{(25.9)}{0.89\ \text{AR (1)}} \tag{9.2}$$

Adjusted $R_2 = 0.97$; F-statistics = 904.6; DW-statistics = 2.28
(Figures in parentheses represent t-statistics.)

References

Nagaishi, M. (1999), Stock Market Development and Economic Growth: Dubious Relationship, *Economic and Political Weekly*, July 17.

Shah, A. and Susan Thomas (1997), Securities Markets: Towards Greater Efficiency, *India Development Report*, Oxford University Press.

Source: RBI (2007), Report on Currency and Finance 2005–06, Chapter 7.

9.3 CONSTITUENTS OF A FINANCIAL SYSTEM

A financial system consists of financial institutions, financial markets, financial instruments and services, and the rules governing their functioning and interactions with each other (Figure 9.1). These various constituents are described hereinafter.

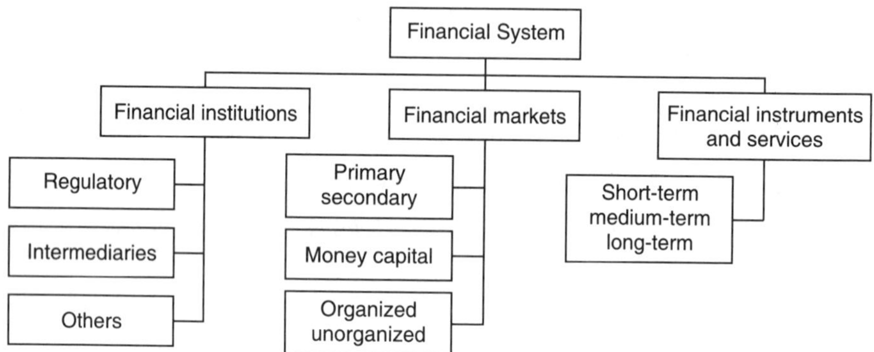

Figure 9.1 Constituents of Financial System.

9.3.1 Financial Institutions

Financial institutions, as depicted in Figure 9.1, can be regulatory institutions, financial intermediaries and others.

Regulatory institutions try to ensure smooth functioning of financial intermediaries, financial markets and other constitutes of the financial system by imposing prudential norms on them. Though usually monetary authority is assigned the task of regulation, a variety of such institutions and acts can exist in an economy regulating different segments of the financial institutions as illustrated in UBE 9.2. and UBE 9.3.

Financial intermediaries are the business organizations that act as mobilizers and depositors of savings and as purveyors of credit and financial services.

Financial intermediaries can be differentiated from non-financial organizations on the basis of their primary activities. **Non-financial organizations**, such as manufacturing units, are engaged in productive activities. They deal in real assets, such as machinery, equipment, stocks of goods, real estate and so on. Therefore, fixed assets dominate their balance sheets. Unlike non-financial organizations, financial intermediaries or institutions in general are involved in providing financial services. They deal in financial assets, such as deposits, loans, securities, etc. Therefore, financial assets dominate the balance sheet of these institutions.

Financial intermediaries are distinguished using various criteria (Figure 9.2). One of the important ways of distinguishing financial intermediaries is the primary functions performed by them. On the basis of primary functions performed by financial institutions, they are classified into banking and non-banking institutions. These two types of institutions can be distinguished from liabilities as well as assets sides.

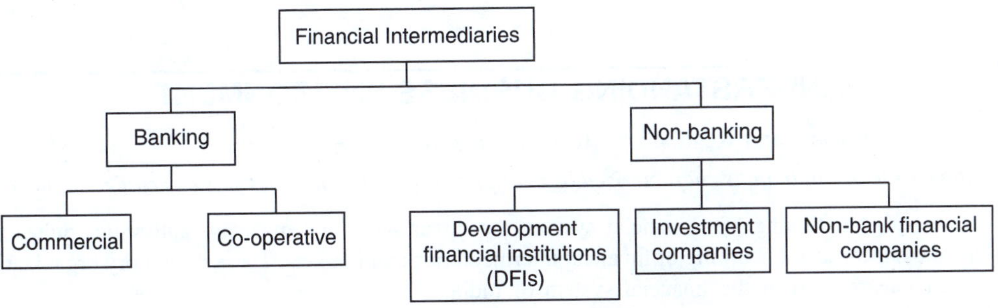

Figure 9.2 Types of Financial Intermediaries.

On the liabilities side, demand deposits are one of the major liabilities of **banking institutions**. Banks provide cheque facility against their deposits which can be used for making payments. Thus, banking institutions participate in an economy's payment mechanism, i.e., they provide transaction services. Banking institutions by supporting payment mechanism, facilitate consumption and production activities. Banks, operating under fractional reserve requirements, can create credit, deposits; hence,they can even influence money supply.

Traditionally, banking institutions are supposed to provide credit mainly for short-term, i.e., for meeting the working capital requirements of corporates. The assets side of the balance sheet of banks is, therefore, dominated by short-term credit.

Unlike banks, **non-bank financial institutions** do not provide cheque facilities on their deposits; hence, they do not partake in payment mechanism, and their liabilities are not money. On the assets side, their balance sheet is dominated by development loans or long-term loans which are primarily used for investment in machinery, plant, building, etc. or purchasing durables, such as automobile, television, refrigerator, etc.

These two broad categories of financial institutions can be further distinguished into various categories. For example, banking intermediaries can be classified as commercial banks or co-operative banks. **Commercial banks** operate on profit motive, whereas **co-operative banks** operate for the benefit of a group of people who have formed these. Similarly, non-bank financial intermediaries can be differentiated as Development Financial Institutions, Investment Companies and Non-Bank Financial Companies. **Development Financial Institutions** (DFIs) provide primarily long-term loans for development purpose. **Investment Companies**, like insurance companies and mutual funds invest in marketable securities. **Non-Bank Financial Companies** (NBFCs) consist of heterogeneous group of companies including nidhis, housing companies and lease hire purchase companies.

Apart from financial intermediaries, a financial system may consist of various other financial institutions providing a variety of financial services. Examples of such intermediaries are **venture capital, which** provide startup capital for new firms, and **merchant banks, which help** in international trade finance and provide business advisory services.

Countries differ in terms of dominance of financial intermediaries or financial markets in their financial system. Dominance of financial intermediaries is referred to as the **bank-based system**, whereas the system dominated by financial markets is referred to as the **market-based system**. Even in a bank-based system, it can be the banks or non-bank financial intermediaries that can dominate the system. For example, in India it is the banking intermediaries that dominate the system (UBE 9.4).

UNDERSTANDING BUSINESS ENVIRONMENT

UBE 9.2 Supervisory and Regulatory Structure in India

Regulatory structure in India is characterized by multiplicity of authorities and acts as detailed in this UBE.

For the smooth functioning of a financial system, the government and monetary authorities quite often regulate and supervise the working of financial intermediaries and markets. These regulatory organizations are also an integral part of the financial system of India.

In India, though there is a multiplicity of regulatory and supervisory authorities (Figure 9.3). With some amount of overlapping in the coverage, the financial system is regulated and supervised mainly by two government agencies under the Ministry of Finance, viz., the **Reserve Bank of India** (RBI) and the **Securities and Exchange Board of India** (SEBI) with the help of various acts and policies.

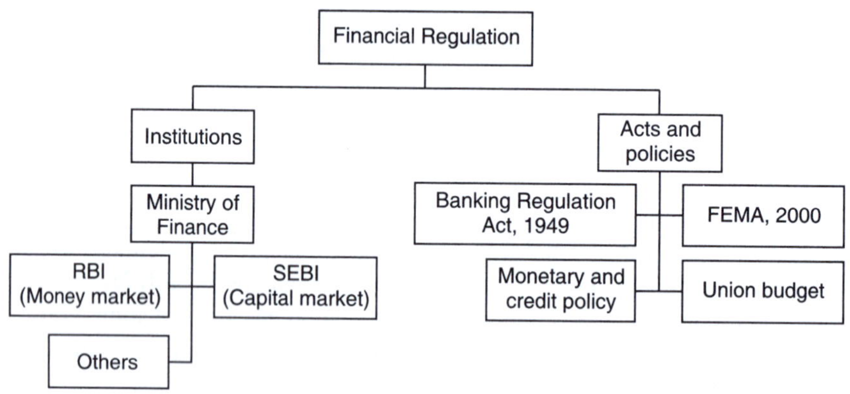

Figure 9.3 Supervisory and Regulatory Structure in India.

The RBI mainly regulates the functioning of money market and financial intermediaries. It deals with the government bond issuance and supervises the Over the Counter (OTC) trading (Section 9.3.2) for government bonds and currencies. It regulates the operations of the payment system and the operations of the depository for government bonds. On the other hand, the regulation of capital markets is under the purview of SEBI. The supervision of exchange trading for securities, excluding derivative based on commodities, are also under its purview. The supervision of finance companies, such as mutual funds and brokerage firms, also falls under its ambit.

Apart from the RBI and the SEBI, there are other institutions which supervise and regulate particular segments of the financial sector. For example, the **Insurance Regulation and Development Authority** (IRDA) regulates and supervises the working of insurance companies. The supervision of exchange trading futures with underlying assets as commodities are under the purview of the **Forward Markets Commission**. The **Department of Company Affairs** (DCA) regulates the working of limited liability firms.

Some of the important acts and policies are the **Banking Regulation Act** of 1949, guiding the regulation of bank intermediaries; the **Monetary and Credit Policy** regulating the supply of money, and cost and availability of credit in the country; the **FEMA** 2000, facilitating the foreign exchange transactions; the **Union budget** levying taxes and tariffs.

UNDERSTANDING BUSINESS ENVIRONMENT

UBE 9.3 Reserve Bank of India

Central Banks world over perform multiple functions. Performing these functions, they support various sectors of their economies. This UBE details on the functions performed by the RBI, the central bank of India.

The Reserve Bank of India is the central bank of India. It was established on 1 April 1935, in accordance with the provision of the RBI Act of 1934. Though originally privately owned, since nationalization in 1949 it is fully owned by the Government of India (GOI).

Functioning of the RBI is governed by a central board of directors appointed by the GOI for a period of four years. The board comprises four full time official directors, the Governor and four Deputy Governors and non-official directors–10 directors from various fields and one government official nominated by the GOI and four directors one each from the four local boards located in four regions of the country in Mumbai, Calcutta, Chennai and New Delhi. The RBI has 22 regional offices—most of them in State capitals. It also has six training establishments.

The RBI functions as a monetary authority, regulator and supervisor of the financial system, manager of foreign exchange, issuer of currency, and also assumes the development role as follows:

1. As the monetary authority, the RBI formulates, implements and monitors the monetary policy with the objective of maintaining price stability and ensuring adequate flow of credit to productive sectors.
2. As the regulator of the financial system, with the objectives of maintaining public confidence in the system, protecting depositors' interest and provision of cost-effective banking services to the public, it prescribes the broad parameters of banking operations within which the country's banking and financial system functions.

To facilitate external trade and payment, and to promote orderly development and maintenance of foreign exchange market in the country, the RBI manages the Foreign Exchange Management Act (FEMA) 1999.

The RBI is an issuer of the currency. To give the public adequate quantity of currency notes and coins in good quality, it issues and exchanges or destroys currency and coins not fit for circulation.

The RBI has also been instrumental in setting up, designing and developing many institutions in the country.

Apart from the above core functions, it has some other subsidiary functions to perform.

The RBI acts as a banker to the Central and state governments and provides them merchant banking services. It is also a banker to the banks. It maintains accounts of all the scheduled commercial banks.

UNDERSTANDING BUSINESS ENVIRONMENT

UBE 9.4 Dominance of Banks in the Indian Financial System

In India, there are variety of financial intermediaries, but this UBE shows that commercial banks still dominate.

Historically, the financial system in India has been dominated by financial intermediaries—banks and non-banks.

The banking system consists of commercial and co-operative banks. However, it is the commercial banks that dominate the system in terms of assets, deposits, advances and investment (Table 9.1). Commercial banks can be further distinguished on the basis of their origin as Indian or foreign. Indian commercial banks can also be differentiated on the basis of their ownership. Either they are owned by the public sector or private sector. When the majority shareholding of **public sector banks** is in the hands of government then these are known as **nationalized banks**. The public sector banks located in rural areas with ownership in the hands of the Central Government, state government and the sponsoring nationalized banks in the ratio of 50:15:35 are known as **regional rural banks** (Figure 9.4).

Table 9.1 Financial Assets of Banks and Financial Institutions*
(End March 2010)

Type of institution	*Number of institutions*	*Share in total assets*
A. Commercial Banks	**173**	**92.49**
(a) Scheduled Commercial Banks (excluding RRBs)	87	45.58
(i) Public Sector Banks	26	33.16
(ii) Private Sector Banks	20	9.21
(iii) Foreign Banks	41	3.20
(b) Regional Rural Banks	82	1.33
(c) Local Area Banks	4	0.01
B. Co-operative Banks	**96,149**	**4.86**
C. Non-Banking Financial Institutions	**12,410**	**2.64**
(a) Financial Institutions**	4	1.85
(b) Non-Banking Financial Companies#	12,385	0.68
(c) Primary Dealers	21	0.11

*Excludes insurance companies regulated by Insurance Regulatory and Development Authority (IRDA) and mutual funds regulated by Securities and Exchange Board of India (SEBI)

**Data pertain to four FIs, viz. NABARD, NHB, SIDBI, and EXIM Bank. IIBI Ltd. was under voluntary winding up as on 31 March 2010

#Data pertain to Residuary Non-Banking Companies, Deposit taking NBFCs (NBFC-D), and non-deposit taking systemically important NBFCs (NBFC-ND-SI)

Source: Compiled from RBI (2012), Report on Trend and Progress of Banking in India. Data on no. of commercial banks is compiled from RBI (2012), Basic Statistical Returns of scheduled Commercial Banks in India, Vol. 40.

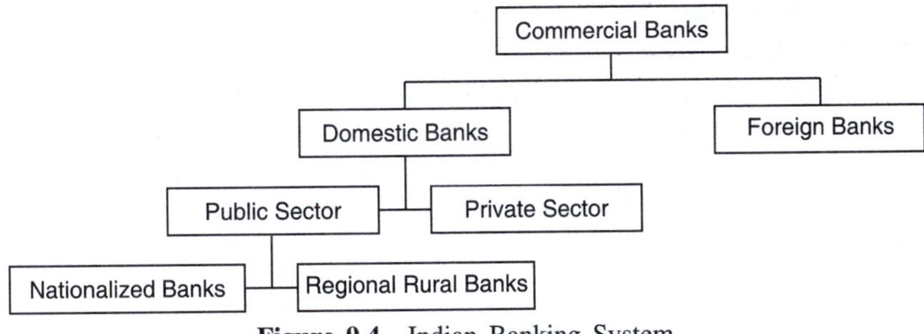

Figure 9.4 Indian Banking System.

The banking institutions in India have confined their operations to their traditional function of short-term and medium-term lending. The main argument against the participation of commercial banks in long-term or even medium-term lending is that since their deposits are largely of short-term nature, it would be risky if a bank locks up its resources in term lending. However, deregulation of the banking industry, in the post reform era, has opened up new opportunities for banks to increase revenue by diversifying into investment banking, securitization, factoring, depository services, credit cards, etc. The opening up of the banking sector to private players and foreign participants has infused a large degree of competition in the system and created more competitive environment for the banking sector.

In India, non-banking financial intermediaries consist of Development Financial Institutions (DFIs), also known as Term Lending Institutions (at national level NABARD, SIDBI, EXIM Bank, IIBI, NHB, and state level SFCs and SIDCs), Investment Companies (LIC, GIC), Primary Dealers (PDs), capital market intermediaries (such as mutual funds) and Non-Banking Financial Companies (NBFCs) such as nidhis and hire purchase companies. A brief description of these financial institutions is given hereinafter.

The DFIs were established in India, mostly by the government, to resolve the problem of shortage of long-term resources arising from the risk aversion of savers and creditors to part funds for long gestation periods. These institutions provide financial assistance in the form of term loans, underwriting, direct subscription to shares/debentures and guarantees. The short-term lending by these institutions is limited only to the extent that they are permitted to lend for the purpose of working capital requirement. The conditions of these institutions have been deteriorating over a period of time and their importance in the Indian financial system has declined to a very low level as can be seen from Table 9.1.

Investment institutes pool in small savings of the households. They invest in a well diversified portfolio of fixed income (debt) and variable income securities (equity), and invest in shares and debt market. These, thus, provide households an option for portfolio diversification with relatively less risk.

The NBFCs, proliferated between the late 1980s and the mid-1990s, are a heterogeneous group of finance companies engaged in a variety of fund and non-fund (fee) based activities. They are broadly classified as **deposit taking NBFC** (NFCs-D) and **non-deposit taking NBFCs** (NBFCs-ND). These are asset finance companies (AFCs), investment companies and loan companies. Some prominent NBFCs are SBI Capital Markets, Kotak Mahindra Finance, Enam Financial Consultants Private Limited, ICICI Securities Limited. Though these are large in number and are a significant source of institutional finance to the unorganized sector and small borrowers at the local level, their importance in the total institutional finance in the country is almost insignificant.

9.3.2 Financial Markets

Financial markets are the centres or arrangements that provide facilities for buying and selling of financial instruments, such as shares, debentures, credit, and financial services. The corporations, financial institutions, individuals and governments trade in financial products in these markets either directly or through brokers and dealers on organized exchanges or off-exchanges. The participants in these markets are financial institutions, agents, brokers, dealers, borrowers, lenders, savers and others. All these participants are interlinked by the laws, contracts and communication networks.

Financial markets can be classified into different categories (Figure 9.1) using various criteria as follows:

Money Markets and Capital Markets

The distinction of financial markets into money markets and capital markets is based on the differences in the period of maturity of financial assets issued in these markets.

1. Money market: The **money market** is a centre for dealings in financial instruments or assets of short-term nature which have an initial maturity period of less than one year. Because of short maturity period they are highly liquid. Therefore, they compete closely with monetary assets (i.e., cash and deposits) which are the most liquid assets in the portfolio of households and other economic units. The money market provides a platform for meeting of these surplus units that want to depart funds only for short duration with those deficit units that want funds only for working capital or any other short-term requirements. Thus, this market provides an avenue for equilibrating the supply of and demand for short-term funds.

Apart from mobilizing short-term savings, the money market plays an important role in the **monetary transmission mechanism,** the mechanism through which changes in monetary policy affects the various economic variables (Box 9.1).

Box 9.1 Role of the Money Market in the Monetary Transmission Mechanism

The money market forms the first and the foremost link in the transmission of monetary policy impulses to the real economy. Policy interventions by the central bank along with its market operations influence the decisions of households and firms through the **monetary transmission mechanism**. The key to this mechanism is the total claim of the economy on the central bank, commonly known as the **monetary base** or **high powered money** in the economy. Among the constituents of the monetary base, the most important constituent is bank reserves, i.e., the claims that bank hold in the form of deposits with the Central Bank. The banks' need for these reserves depends on the overall level of economic activity. This is governed by several factors—(i) banks hold such reserves in proportion to the volume of deposits in many countries, known as **reserve requirements**, which influence their ability to extend credit and create deposits, thereby limiting the volume of transactions to be handled by the bank, (ii) bank's ability to make loans (asset of the bank) depend on its ability to mobilize deposits (liability of the bank) as total assets and liabilities of the bank need to match and expand/contract together, and (iii) banks' need to hold balances at the central bank for settlement of claims within the banking system as these transactions are settled through the accounts of banks maintained with the central bank. Therefore, the daily functioning of a modern economy and its financial system creates a demand for central bank reserves which increases along with an expansion in overall economic activity (Friedman, 2000b).

The central bank's power to conduct monetary policy stems from its role as a monopolist, as the sole supplier of bank reserves. The most common procedure by which central banks influence the outstanding supply of bank reserves is through "open market operations" that is, by buying or selling government securities in the market. When a central bank buys (sells) securities, it credits (debits) the reserve account of the seller (buyer) bank. This increases (decreases) the total volume of reserves that the banking system collectively holds. Expansion (contraction) of the total volume of reserves in this way matters because banks can exchange reserves for other remunerative assets. Since reserves earn low interest, and in many countries remain unremunerated, banks typically would exchange them for some interest bearing assets such as treasury bills or other short-term debt instruments. If the banking system has excess (inadequate) reserves, banks would seek to buy (sell) such instruments. If there is a general increase (decrease) in demand for securities, it would result in increase (decline) in security prices and decline (increase) in interest rates. The resulting lower (higher) interest rates on short-term debt instruments mean a reduced (enhanced) opportunity cost of holding low interest reserves. Only when market interest rates fall (rise) to the level at which banks collectively are willing to hold all of the reserves that the central bank has supplied with the financial system reach equilibrium. Hence, an "expansionary" (contractionary) open market operation creates downward (upward) pressure on short-term interest rates not only because the central bank itself is a buyer (seller), but also because it leads banks to buy (sell) securities. In this way, the central bank can easily influence interest rates on short-term debt instruments. In the presence of a regular term structure of interest rates and without market segmentation, such policy impulses get transmitted to the longer end of the maturity spectrum, thereby influencing long-term interest rates, which have a bearing on household's consumption and savings decisions, and hence on aggregate demand.

There are alternative mechanisms of achieving the same objective through the imposition of reserve requirements and central bank lending to banks in the form of refinance facilities. Lowering (increasing) the reserve requirement, and therefore, reducing (increasing) the demand for reserves has roughly the same impact as an expansionary (contractionary) open market operation, which increases (decreases) the supply of reserves creating downward (upward) pressure on interest rates. Similarly, another way in which central banks can influence the supply of reserves is through direct lending of reserves to banks. Central bank lends funds to banks at a policy rate, which usually acts as the ceiling in the short-term market. Similarly, central banks absorb liquidity at a rate which acts as the floor for short-term market interest rates. This is important, since injecting liquidity at the ceiling rate would ensure that banks do not have access to these funds for arbitrage opportunities, whereby they borrow from the central bank and deploy these funds in the market to earn higher interest rates. Similarly, liquidity absorption by the central bank has to be at the floor rate since deployment of funds with the central bank is free of credit and other risks. Typically, the objective of the central bank is to modulate liquidity conditions by pegging short-term interest rates within this corridor.

While the above mechanism outlines how central bank can influence short-term interest rates by adjusting the quantity of bank reserves, the same objective can be achieved by picking on a particular short-term interest rate and then adjusting the supply of reserves commensurate with that rate. In many countries, this is achieved by targeting the overnight inter-bank lending rate and adjusting the level of reserves which would keep the inter-bank lending rate at the desired level. Thus, by influencing short-term interest rates, central bank can influence output and inflation in the economy, the ultimate objectives of monetary policy.

Source: RBI (2007), Report on Currency and Finance 2005–06.

Some of the constituents of the money market are repo market, treasury bill market, call money market and commercial bills market. These instruments are described in Section 9.3.3.

2. Capital market: The **capital market** deals in long-term instruments or assets. These are the assets that have initial maturity period of more than a year. Governments and corporates raise funds from capital market for their investment expenditure or expansion. As described in Section 9.3.3, some of the constituents of capital market are equity market and government securities market.

Primary Markets and Secondary Markets

1. Primary markets: The primary market deals in new financial claims or new securities issued by the corporate sector. Therefore, it is also known as the **new issues market**. The new issues may take the form of equity shares, preference shares or debentures. The firms raising funds by issuing new securities may be new companies or existing companies planning expansion. The public sector, consisting of Central and state governments, various Public Sector Units (PSUs), statutory and other authorities such as state electricity boards and port trusts, also issue bonds and shares in this market especially as a part of **disinvestment** of government holdings, implying the reduction in the government stake in these organizations.

The primary markets mobilize savings and supply fresh or additional capital to business units. Floatation of new issues involves three distinct services:

(i) *Origination*: **Origination** requires a technical evaluation of the proposal.

(ii) *Underwriting:* The business unit has to identify a financial institution which can underwrite its issue of shares. The business unit has to identify a financial institution which can underwrite its issue of shares. **Underwriting** guarantees the purchase of a stipulated amount of a new issue at a fixed price if the expected sale to public does not materialize. Such an approval of a new issue proposal, by a well-established financial institution, improves the acceptability of the new issue by the investing public.

(iii) *Distribution of new issues*: Distribution consists of the sale of new issue to the public. It can be in any of the following forms:

- *Issue of prospectus to the public.* **Issue of prospects to the public** is an open invitation to the public by the company issuing shares to subscribe to its issue. The process consists of offer of ordinary shares by the company to the general public for subscription by issuing a prospectus consisting the necessary information about the company, opening and closing dates of subscription, minimum subscription amount required, names of the brokers, underwriters and agents, and their obligations. Under this method a fixed number of shares are allotted among the applicants in a non-discriminatory manner.
- *Sale offer.* Under the **sale offer**, the shares are offered to the public indirectly through some intermediary such as a merchant bank. A fixed amount of shares are first sold by the issuing company to selected intermediaries at a fixed price, which, in turn, offer these to the public at a higher price. The process saves time of the issuing company and also the hassles of mobilizing funds from the public.
- *Private placement.* Under **private placement**, the issue is not offered to the public for subscription, but is placed privately with a few big financers consisting of financial institutions or individual investors. As the sale of securities is almost assured, under this process the underwriting of the issue is usually not required. Though this leads to concentration of shareholding in few hands, it saves a lot of expenses involved in the public issue. This method is usually preferred by the small companies that cannot afford the cost of public issue or by the companies that are not sure of raising

enough funds through the public issue. (The private placement market is illustrated in UBE 9.5).

- *Rights issue.* The process of **rights issue** involves invitation to the existing shareholders of an old corporation to subscribe to a part or whole of a new issue in a fixed proportion to their shareholding. Often the shares are offered at a discount to the current market price by reputed and well-established companies, the shares of which are widely held and listed on the stock exchanges. This method also leads to concentration of shares in the hands of existing shareholders.
- *Book building.* Under the **book building method**, the demand for a new issue and the price at which it could be offered in the market are assessed by a lead manager, appointed by the issuing company, through a survey. The lead manager is usually an investment bank providing underwriting and other advisory services. Sometimes, the prospective investors are given incentives to participate in a shadow auction of the shares. Such auctions help in assessing the demand for the issue from the behaviour of the investing public. They also help in setting the price at which a new public offer can be made. This process is usually followed by a company which is not sure of the demand for its shares and the price at which the shares can be offered to the public.

2. Secondary markets: The secondary market deals in securities already issued or existing or outstanding. Thus, it is similar to second hand or resale market for goods.

Unlike primary market, secondary market does not help in mobilizing additional saving, Therefore, it does not directly lead to higher investment or capital formation. However, it provides a continuous market for existing securities where these can be bought and sold in volume with little variation in the current market price. Thus, it provides liquidity to the initial buyers in the primary market to re-offer the securities to any interested buyer at any price, if mutually accepted. By assuring the existing security holders of the liquidity of their investment, an active secondary market promotes the growth of the primary market and capital formation.

The secondary markets consists of organized stock exchanges and Over the Counter (OTC) markets.

The **stock market** or **stock exchange** is an organization where buying and selling of listed or approved existing securities takes place. The organization is an association of persons or firms that provides the stock brokers an exchange floor, and regulates and supervises the transactions that take place on its platform. Prices of traded stocks are settled by open bids and offers on the floor of the exchange.

The **Over The Counter** (OTC) is an informal arrangement between stock brokers and dealers and middle man who deal in the securities that are not listed on an organized stock exchange through telephone, facsimile or electronic network. These are usually the securities of small companies which have only limited market. Unlike the securities traded on organized stock markets, the prices of the securities traded on the OTC are determined through direct negotiations between stock brokers.

The major players in the secondary market are the stock brokers, who are the members of the stock exchanges, mutual funds, financial institutions, foreign institutional investors, and individual investors.

Organized and Unorganized Markets

1. Organized markets: The financial transactions which take place within well-defined arrangements constitute the **organized markets**. These markets function within a legal framework where participants are expected to be well-informed of the procedures and rules of participation. Transactions in these markets are systematic, and well-recorded and documented. Stock markets are examples of such markets.

2. Unorganized markets: The financial transactions that take place outside the well-established exchanges or without systematic or orderly structure or arrangements constitute the **unorganized markets**. The markets in rural areas are usually of this nature. However, some of the markets in urban areas are also unorganized in nature. Inter-bank money markets and most foreign exchange markets do not have organized exchanges, but they are not unorganized markets in the same way the rural markets are. Similarly, the OTCs are unorganized markets.

Parts of the unorganized markets are informal markets involving families and small groups of individuals lending and borrowing from each other.

9.3.3 Financial Instruments/Assets/Securities

Financial instruments or assets or securities represent a claim to the payment of a sum of money sometime in the future (repayment of principal) and/or a periodic (regular or not so regular) payment in the form of interest or dividend.

Financial instruments or assets can also be classified using various criteria as depicted in Figure 9.5 and as described hereinafter.

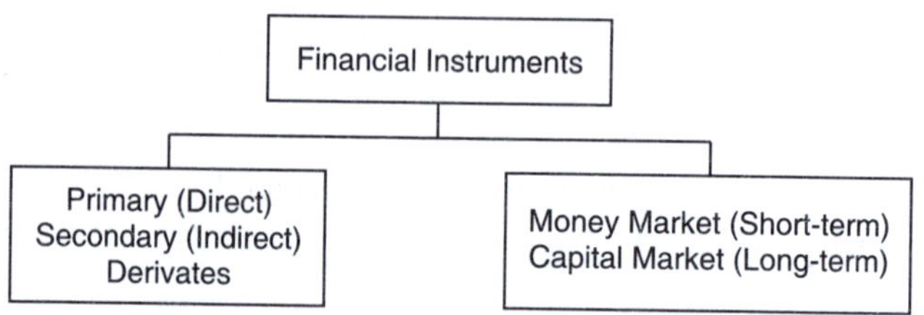

Figure 9.5 Types of Financial Instruments.

Primary (Direct) Securities, Secondary (Indirect) Securities and Derivatives

The financial instruments are categorized and explained as follows:

1. Primary securities: **Primary securities** or **direct securities** are issued directly by ultimate investors to the ultimate savers. Examples of such securities are ordinary shares and debentures.

2. Secondary securities: **Secondary securities** or **indirect securities** are issued by financial intermediaries to ultimate savers. The examples of such securities are bank deposits, mutual funds units, insurance policies, and so on. These are better suited to the requirements of the small investors who do not have expertise or risk taking capacity required for investing in primary securities.

3. Derivatives: Liberalized financial markets, by their very nature, are characterized by high volatility arising out of large fluctuations in the prices of securities traded in these markets. **Derivative** instruments help in partially or fully transferring risk by locking in asset prices for the future period. These are the instruments whose value is derived from the value of one or more underlying assets, which can be primary or secondary security, or index or reference rate. The most commonly used derivatives are forwards, futures and options.

A **forward contract** is an agreement to exchange an asset or instrument for cash at a predetermined future date at a price contracted today. These are private bilateral contracts. Hence, each contract is customized and is unique in terms of contract size, expiration date, asset type and quality.

A **futures contract**, on the contrary, is standardized tradeable contract between a seller (writers/shorts) and a buyer (longs). Like forward contracts, these contracts obligate the seller to deliver to the buyer and the buyer to receive the given asset in the specified quantities of specified grades, at a fixed time in the future, at the contracted price. As these contracts are standardized, secondary market for these is more liquid.

An **option** is the contract that gives the holder the right (not the obligation) to buy (call option) or sell (put option) securities at a pre-determined price (strike/exercise price) within/at the end of a specified period (expiration period). For the holder of call/put options, the exercise of the right becomes profitable only if the price of the underlying securities rise/fall above/below the exercise price.

Money Market Instruments and Capital Market Instruments

Apart from financial instruments, there are money market instruments and capital market instruments as follows:

1. Money market instruments: **Money market instruments** have maturity period of one day to one year. These instruments can be easily sold in the market without much loss in their value; hence, they are highly liquid. Some important money market instruments are described here (features of these instruments are described in more detail in Section 10.4).

2. Capital market instruments call and notice money: In the **call money market** or **notice money market** funds are lent for a very short period. Funds borrowed or lent for a day are known as **call money or overnight money**, whereas funds borrowed or lent for more than a day and up to 14 days are known as **notice money**. Intervening holidays and/or sundays are excluded for the purpose of calculating maturity. No collateral security is required for trading in these instruments. Risk involved for investors, hence is supposed to be more. Interest rates on these instruments are market-determined.

These instruments have been designed basically to enable banks and other institutions to even out their day-to-day deficits and surpluses of funds. The call rates are subject to large volatility because banks depend on this unsecured (because no collaterals required) market heavily for meeting their temporary mismatches in demand for and supply of funds arising out of cash reserve requirements, arbitrage opportunities in other markets, sudden supply of funds from other participants, and other occasional disturbances in the financial system. The central bank keeps a close watch on call rates, and intervenes in the market to avoid large volatility.

Apart from banks, primary dealers are also allowed to participate in this market both as borrowers and lenders in India.

3. Inter-bank term money: The **inter-bank term money** is exclusively available for banks. Banks borrow and lend funds for a period of 14 days and generally upto 90 days, without any collateral security, at market determined rates.

4. Treasury bills: At the short-end, the lowest risk category instruments are the **Treasury Bills (TBs)**. These are promissory notes issued by a government, at a prefixed day and for a fixed amount, at a discount, for a period of 14 days, 91 days, 182 days and 360 days, to raise funds to meet temporary mismatches in its cash flows. However, these also help the monetary authority to regulate liquidity in the system as well as signal the interest rate movement to the market through the auctions of treasury bills. Based on the bids received at the auctions, the central bank decides the cut-off yield, and accepts all the bids below this yield. Because of their short maturity, treasury bills closely compete with call money funds. The yield on TBs, hence, is mainly dependent on the rates prevalent in call/notice money market.

In India, a considerable amount of borrowing of the Central Government takes place through this instrument. Banks are the major investors in these instruments as these are highly liquid assets, and provide a safe avenue for their short-term funds. At the same time, the amount invested in TBs is counted towards various statutory requirements (such as SLR requirement in India). Beside banks, the other investors in TBs are mutual funds, insurance companies, primary dealers, other financial institutions and foreign institutional investors. As the amount involved is very large, the participation of small investors, such as households, is ruled out in this market.

5. Collateralized borrowing and lending obligations: The **Collateralized Borrowing and Lending Obligations** (CBLO) is an instrument which provides an alternative avenue for managing short-term liquidity to those participants who are restricted from participating in call money market. Borrowing in the CBLO segment is fully collateralized. The rates in this segment, hence, are expected to be comparable with the repo rates described below.

6. Commercial bills: Bills of exchange are drawn by a seller on a buyer for the value of goods delivered to him. Such bills are called **trade bills**. When trade bills are accepted by commercial banks they are called **commercial bills**. If the seller is in a need of funds he may approach his bank for discounting the bills. The bank receives the maturity proceeds of the discounted bills from the drawee.

Scheduled commercial banks, all India financial institutions, mutual funds, select scheduled state co-operative banks and scheduled urban co-operative banks are approved participants in this market in India.

7. Certificate of deposits: Issued at discount to the face value, in large denomination, by banks and other financial institutions, **Certificate of Deposits** (CDs) are negotiable term deposit certificates which carry very low risk. These provide large resources to banks, especially in tight liquidity situations, at attractive market determined rates to large corporates and high net worth individuals. Highly liquid and risk-free instrument, CDs compete with one year bank deposits and the funds traded in call money market, interest rate on one year deposit acting as a floor and the call rates as a ceiling.

In India, the RBI allows CDs upto one year maturity; however, the maturity that is most traded in the market is for 90 days.

8. Commercial papers: Issued by well rated corporate entities to raise funds for short-term working capital requirements directly from the market instead of borrowing from financial institutions, **Commercial Papers** (CPs) are unsecured promissory notes with fixed maturity. Freely transferable, these are sold at a discount to the face value. As the borrowers can directly borrow from the market at a market determined rate, rather than through financial intermediaries, CPs issue involves disintermediation.

Through CPs, well-rated companies can raise funds at a cheaper rate than that prevailing on the loans from financial intermediaries. Compulsory rating imparts safety to this instruments.

9. Inter corporate deposits: **Inter Corporate Deposits** (ICDs) are unsecured loans, extended by one corporate to another, mainly as a refuge for low rated companies. Better rated companies can borrow from banks and lend in this market. The interest rate in this market, hence, is higher than those in the other markets. In India this market is not well-organized.

10. Repo: **Repo**, which is a short form of, **repurchase agreement** or **buyback** or **ready forward**, is a contract in which a seller of securities, such as treasury bills, agrees to buy them back at a specified time and price, making available the funds temporarily for the party agreeing for the sale contract (for details refer to Section 8.4). The difference between sale and purchase price, the latter being slightly higher, is the interest earned by the investor or lender. The term **reverse repo** is also used for repo transaction when the deal is viewed from the perspective of the supplier of funds. It implies that the securities are bought with an agreement to resell them at a fixed price on a future date.

Repo is a short-term collateralized instrument; hence it has been widely used by banks to meet their short-term liquidity requirements, specifically when they have to meet the statutory requirements, like cash reserve ratio, imposed by the central bank.

The central banks also use it widely for adjusting short-term liquidity and stabilizing interest rates. Internationally, the term repo/reverse repo are viewed from the market side. Therefore, repo implies that the central bank purchases securities with an agreement to resell it after a stipulated period of time. Through this process, it infuses liquidity for a short period of time and also indicates the short-run orientation of the monetary policy.

Presently, repo transactions are permitted in India against all GOI securities, treasury bills, public sector units bonds and the units of Unit Trust of India.

The RBI is an active participant in the repo market and performs repo/reverse repos to achieve stable liquidity in the system by evening out the mismatches between the demand for and the supply of short-term funds.

Banks are also major players in this market as the instrument is very convenient to those banks which have surplus Statutory Liquidity Ratio (SLR; Section 8.4.1) securities but CRR deficit. Non-bank entities having Subsidiary General Ledger (SGL) account with the RBI, Discount and Finance House of India (DFHI) and primary dealers in this market are permitted to participate in reverse repos with banks.

11. Capital market securities: Broadly two types of securities are traded in capital markets, government securities and corporate securities. These are described hereinafter.

(i) *Government securities.* **Government securities** are issued by the Central Government, state governments and local bodies and even Public Sector Units (PSUs). Also known as **bonds** or **fixed income securities**, these securities are debt securities. Government securities are almost default free as payment from the government is assured. These securities are also highly liquid as these can be easily sold in the market at the going market price.

The government securities market is dominated by financial institutions as the amount involved is very large, which small investors cannot afford to invest.

(ii) *Corporate securities.* Corporates issue both **debt instruments**, known as **debentures**, and **ownership securities**, known as **equity shares** (ordinary, perpetual or other). On bonds or debentures, the holder receives both the regular periodic payments and the repayment of the principal at a fixed date. Whereas on equity shares—ordinary shares or perpetual bonds—only periodic payments are received (which are regular in the case of perpetual bond but may be irregular in the case of ordinary shares).

Contrary to general perception, equity constitutes a small proportion of total volume traded in capital markets.

9.4 WEAKNESSES IN THE FINANCIAL SYSTEM

Cyclical downturn and/or structural deficiencies often prevent the efficient functioning of a financial system. The channels through which these factors weaken a financial system are described as follows:

9.4.1 Cyclical Downturn

A cyclical downturn (Figure 9.6), especially a recession, often leads to the weakening of the balance sheets of corporate organizations by reducing the demand for their products and, in turn,

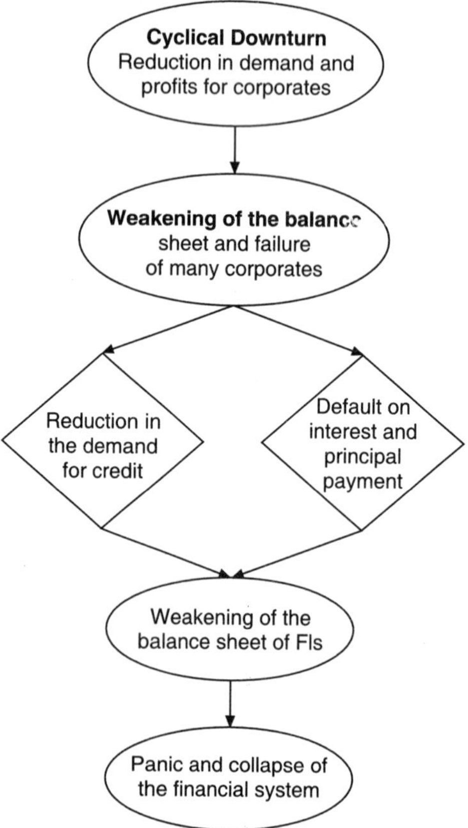

Figure 9.6 Cyclical Downturn and Financial System Crisis.

their profitability. A severe recession also leads to a failure of many of them. A recession, thus, on the one hand, reduces the demand for credit from Financial Institutions (FIs) and, on the other hand, reduces the quality of their assets as many corporate organizations fail to pay either the interest or the principal. Therefore, large Non Performing Assets (NPAs) accumulate on the balance sheets of financial institutions, leading to deterioration in their health, and eventually, collapse of many of them.

9.4.2 Structural Weaknesses

Structural weaknesses in a financial system may arise because of the following reasons:

Financial Repression

Government regulations and discretionary policies, quite often, suppress the functioning of market forces, and distort financial prices and interest rates (illustrated in UBE 9.5). **Financial repression** can exist in the form of administered interest rates and directed lending programmes. Under **administered interest rate** regime, the government fixes interest rates rather than leaving the determination of these to the market forces. Under **directed lending programmes**, the government directs the allocation of credit rather than leaving that to the market forces.

In an administered system, quite often, to promote investment, real interest rates are fixed at a lower level than that would prevail in a system where the rates are market determined. However, this discourages saving and mobilization of resources. The lower amount of saving keeps the amount of investment low inspite of lower real interest rates. As can be seen from Figure 9.7, fixing of the interest rate at r_{la} (i.e., below the market determined or clearing rate of r_{le}) increases the demand for funds from Q_2 to Q_3. However, the fixed rate of interest is able to mobilize resources only to the extent of Q_1. In such a system, supply of funds limits the credit and the investment to Q_1, rather than increasing it to Q_3.

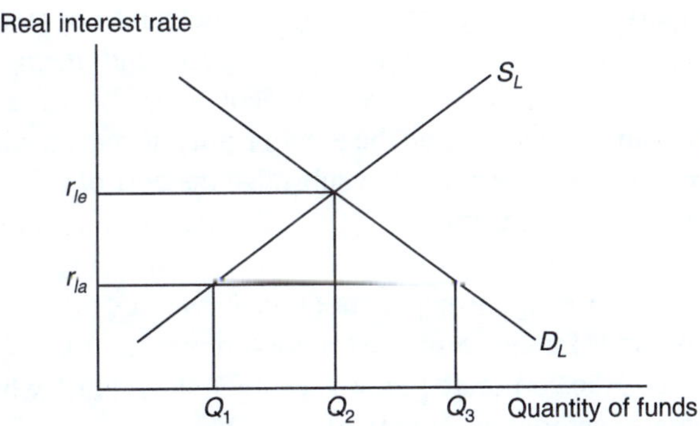

Figure 9.7 Administered Interest Rate in Loanable Funds Market and Supply Constraint on Investment.

To overcome the problem of adverse impact of low administered interest rates on the supply of resources, the government also, often, ends up regulating interest rates on deposits. Interest rates on deposits are fixed above the equilibrium level to mobilize higher amount of saving. However, the fixation of deposit rate at r_{da} (above the equilibrium rate of r_{de}), as depicted in Figure 9.8(a), and that of lending rate r_{la} (below the equilibrium rate of r_{le}) [Figure 9.8(b)] compresses the spread, i.e., the difference between interest income and interest expenditure, from $(r_{le} - r_{de})$ to $(r_{la} - r_{da})$, reducing the profitability of financial institutions.

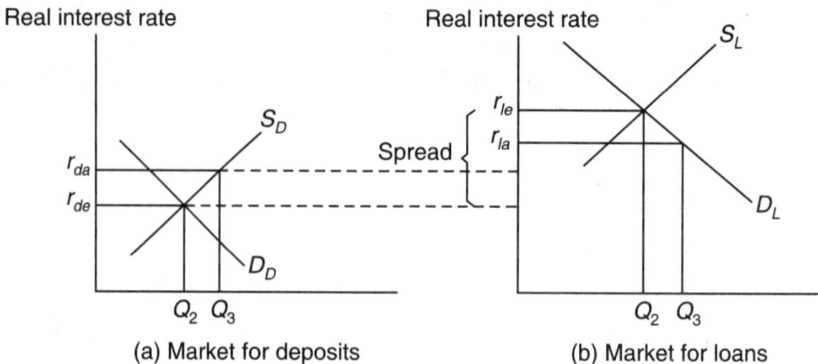

Figure 9.8 Administered Rate Structure in Deposit and Loanable Funds Markets.

Adoption of the system of directed lending programmes further distorts the allocation of resources. Under such a system, credit is allocated to various units not on the basis of productivity and viability of their projects, but on considerations other than economic efficiency. Such a system, thus, hinders the process of resource allocation in an efficient manner.

Quite often, directed credit programmes also involve **cross-subsidization** of credit which implies that the cost of subsidy given to one sector is born by another sector rather than that by the government or any other external agency. The credit to the government and priority sectors, such as small scale industry, farmers and exporters is often subsidized. To maintain the viability of lending organizations, the cost of this subsidy is passed on to the "free" portion of the credit, which is often the credit to corporate sector, in the form of higher rate of interest.

Figure 9.9 highlights the extent of cross-subsidization in a financially repressed economy. Left to the market forces, given the market demand curve D_M and supply curve S_M, the market clearing rate is r_{le} and quantity supplied and demanded of funds is Q_e (Figure 9.9(a)). The government, in a repressed economy, makes an assessment of the demand and supply curves and conjectures on the equilibrium rate and quantity. Growth and social equity considerations compel the government to subsidize the cost of credit to the priority sector (the sectors that are considered to be important from the socio-economic point of view but are weak) by charging a lower rate of interest of r_{lp} (Figure 9.9(b)). However, the huge demand for funds, at this rate, is met by rationing the supply at Q_p level. Supply of funds to the priority sector reduces the availability of funds for the corporate (or non-priority) sector to $Q_e - Q_p$ (Figure 9.9(c)). Given the demand curve D_C, the corporate sector is charged the rate r_{lc}, which clears the demand for funds from the corporate sector at the supply of $Q_e - Q_p$.

The higher cost of funds weakens the position of corporate organizations, and results in defaults on payments, which, in turn, weakens the balance sheet of financial intermediaries.

Deposit Insurance

To protect the interest of depositors, in many countries, it is mandatory for banks to get insured their deposits. Deposit insurance enhances the public confidence in banking organizations and reduces their fragility by eliminating the possibility of self-fulfilling panics.

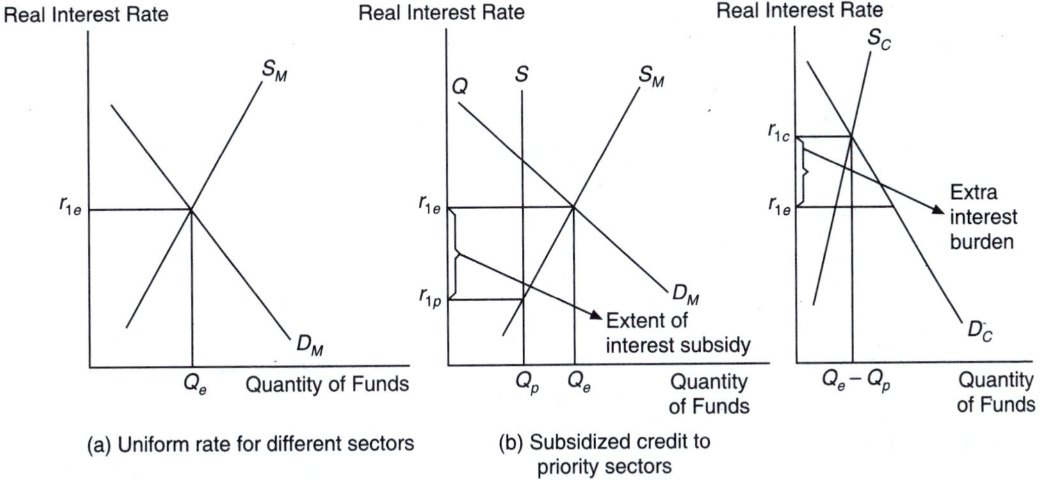

Figure 9.9 Directed Lending Programmes, Cross-subsidization, and Interest Burden on Corporate Sector.

However, such a regulation makes depositors neutral to the quality of assets in which financial institutions invest. Depositors, assured of the safety of their deposited amount, do not differentiate between a financial institution which has invested in quality assets than the one which has invested in risky assets. Rather, they invest their money on the basis of the return offered to them, In the absence of enough monitoring from the depositors, to show an improved performance and to attract a large amount of deposits, financial institutions tend to increase the risk (risk and return are inversely related) of their portfolios. However, deteriorating quality of assets increases the chances of bank failures.

Lack of Prudential Norms

Absence of **prudential norms**, such as capital adequacy ratio (Box 9.2), provision for non-performing assets (NPAs) (Box 9.3), etc., leads to a low level of capitalization, inefficient operations and functioning, encourages excessive risk taking, unsound lending practices, asset-liability maturity mismatch, currency mismatch, and poor governance. The process through which the absence of sufficient prudential norms weakens a financial system is explained as follows:

1. Capital is a non-borrowed ownership liability for any organization; hence, it is a more stable source of funds. At the time of crisis, when heavy withdrawal of borrowed liabilities (especially deposits) takes place, the ownership capital provides the cushion and protection for an organization from a collapse and bankruptcy. However, a high level of capitalization reduces the **return on equity** (i.e., the ratio of profit to equity capital), one of the ratios which is widely used for assessing the performance of a company. Hence, to show higher and better performance, organizations try to minimize the amount of ownership capital on their balance sheets. A low level of capitalization, however, reduces the risk absorption capacity of financial organizations, especially that of banks, as they operate on very thin margins and have high debt to equity ratio.
2. In the absence of prudential norms, banks often end up investing in assets that are high on return, but at the same time are risky. The credit allocation by financial institutions,

without considering the viability and profitability of projects, increases the amount of NPAs on their balance sheets. At times, in search of higher returns, they also end up locking their funds in long-term instruments, but in the process compromise on the liquidity of their asset portfolio. Also, in an open economy, investment may be in foreign assets leading to currency mismatch in the asset portfolio. The problem becomes severe when financial institutions are likely to face bankruptcy as managers and owners end up taking more risk in the expectation of higher return.

Financial Liberalization

Financial liberalization is expected to promote competition and efficiency in the working of a financial system and, hence, economic growth. However, financial liberalization, without prudential regulation and supervision in force, encourages excessive risk taking by managers and may result in crises. The problem is more severe when deposits are insured.

Financial Opening

Financial sector opening is expected to be welfare improving as external financing is expected to alleviate the scarcity of saving, promote higher investment, and thus, higher growth. However, such an opening of the economy subjects the country to a large amount of volatility. Even small changes in the external or internal environment, in such an economy, lead to a large amount of capital inflows and outflows and destabilizes the economy as discussed in Section 15.4.2.

Financial institutions also become subject to fluctuations in exchange rate, especially, when they borrow in foreign currency and lend in domestic currency. An unexpected depreciation of the domestic currency threatens the profitability of financial institutions and even leads to a collapse of some of them.

UNDERSTANDING BUSINESS ENVIRONMENT

UBE 9.5 Financial Repression in India: Genesis of Reform

India was a classic case of financial repression which resulted in serious inefficiencies in the system as indicated in this UBE.

With the objectives of achieving social justice, equity and growth, the Government of India kept on increasing expenditure on various social and developmental activities, resulting in continuously growing fiscal deficit in the pre-1991 period. As the resources available in the domestic market were limited to meet the ever-growing demand for funds, the fiscal deficit was primarily financed by the government through borrowing from the RBI. Often, for funding the short-term (temporary) mismatches between the expenditure and revenue, the government resorted to the issue of ad-hoc 91 days treasury bills, which, in the absence of a well-developed market for government securities, were absorbed by the RBI, causing in continuous and automatic monetization of deficit and continuous inflationary pressures in the economy. As a result, the WPI-based inflation rate accelerated gradually from an annual average of 1.7 per cent during the 1950s to 9.0 per cent in the 1970s, before moderating to 8 per cent in the 1980s. It reached to above 13 per cent in the year of crisis of 1991–92.

To contain the inflationary pressures, and at the same time meet the resource requirement of the government, the RBI followed the route of statutory pre-emption in the form of Cash Reserve Ratio (CRR) and Statutory Liquidity Ratio (SLR). The CRR, which was initially pegged to 4 per cent, was gradually increased to 15 per cent by the end of 1980s (the then statutory maximum) to control the excess liquidity emerging from government expenditure. On the other hand, the SLR was continuously raised from initial

20 per cent to 38.5 per cent (reaching almost the then statutory maximum of 40 per cent) during the same period, to make the resources available to the government without inflationary pressures. The CRR and SLR taken together pre-empted 63.5 per cent of resources.

An administered interest rate structure was also pursued to achieve the above stated objectives. Growth priority required greater mobilization of resources and higher capital formation and investment. Hence, to enhance the level of saving and to improve the mobilization of resources, deposit rates were fixed above the equilibrium rates. To give a boost to the investment, credit (especially to the priority sector) was subsidized by fixing the lending rates below the equilibrium rate. To keep the cost of borrowing for the government low, the interest rate on government securities was also kept at a lower level.

The system of directed lending programme was also used for the benefit of poorer and weaker segments of the society, the segments which otherwise find it difficult to raise resources from the open market. Under the directed credit programme, it was made mandatory for banks to lend 40 per cent of the total credit to the priority sector, such as agriculture, small scale industries, small transport operators, and export sectors. The quantitative priority sector lending targets were often combined with the administered interest rate structure so that the credit is available to these sectors at affordable rates.

To provide an access to the banking and financial facilities to wider population, the government nationalized many private banks.

To develop a variety of institutions, matching with the maturity spectrum of liability portfolio of financial institutions, the market for short-term funds was reserved for banks and that for long-term funds was kept under the exclusive domain of Development Financial Institutions (DFIs).

These socially-oriented policies had several positive facets. The country experienced a large expansion in the bank branch network and development of various types of financial institutions catering to the demand of different types of customers. The wider bank branch network improved the level of monetization in the country and enhanced the resource mobilization by increasing the level of deposits. The development of DFIs enhanced the investment rate in the economy, which supported the industrialization process. There was also an improved flow of credit to the earlier deprived sectors, such as agriculture and small scale industries.

Notwithstanding these positive facets, the repressive policies had serious impact on the financial health and viability of financial institutions as elaborated below:

The ever-growing statutory pre-emption, in the form of CRR and SLR, created a situation of under supply of credit to the private sector; the CRR by reducing the overall availability of funds for lending purpose and the SLR by diverting the resources from the private sector to the government which is considered to be less efficient in the utilization of resources.

The system of priority sector lending led to market segmentation, created excess capacity in certain sectors and deprived the rest, and added to the problem of misallocation of resources. Besides, the directed credit often did not reach the desired areas, because of leakages in the system. Priority sector lending not only compromised the growth aspect by diverting resources from the more efficient and productive sectors to the less efficient ones, but also weekend the balance sheets of financial institutions by increasing the non-performing assets on their balance sheets.

The administered interest rate system, which was meant to reduce the cost of funds for the priority sector and the government, turned out to be highly complex because of the multiplicity of rates. On the deposit front, the rates varied by the type and tenure of deposits. On the lending front, the lending rate structure consisted of six categories based on the size of loans. Under each category, a minimum lending rate was prescribed. Multiplicity of interest rates made the system very difficult to comprehend, leaving interpretational ambiguities.

The administered interest rate system also resulted in low productivity and efficiency in the financial system. The fixation of deposit rates above the market clearing level and that of lending rates below the equilibrium level put pressure on the margins or spread (difference between interest earning and interest expenditure) of financial institutions, weakening their balance sheets. To maintain their profitability, financial institutions, often, on the 'free' portion of their loans charged the rate higher than that of equilibrium rate, leading to cross-subsidization of credit and high cost of credit to the corporate sector. This not only weakened the balance sheets of corporate organizations, but also increased the chances of adverse selection of borrowers by financial institutions, because high risk borrowers are often the one willing to pay higher rates; thus, deteriorating the quality of assets on their balance sheets.

The administered interest rate structure, especially the subsidized rates, obstructed the development of various markets (for example low interest rates on government securities prevented the development of market for these securities) and hampered their integration.

The pre-emption of credit in the form of statutory pre-emptions and priority sector lending, tight control over interest rates, subsidized credit to weaker sections, demarcation of markets by type of customers and by category of loans, thus, reduced the level of competition, resulted in misallocation of resources and widespread market segmentation, preventing integration and development of financial markets in the country.

Against this background, the reforms in the financial sector were initiated in the early 1990s in India (UBE 9.8).

Box 9.2 Capital Adequacy Norms

Most banks operate on thin **spread**, which is the difference between interest income and interest expenses. They fund their operations mostly from deposit liabilities which are highly liquid and can be easily withdrawn by depositors. Therefore, banks are vulnerable to collapse if not managed prudentially. Bank capital, which is owned by banks, provides a cushion against downturn emerging from sudden withdrawal of funds or large losses from their lending operations. Capital, being an ownership fund, ensures that the shareholders of banks have sufficient funds at risk so that they take more care in supervising the functioning of banks and the use of depositors' funds. Central banks in many countries, thus, impose minimum capital adequacy requirements on financial institutions.

Capital Adequacy Ratio (CAR), also known as **Capital to Risk Weighted Assets Ratio** (CRAR), is a measure of the amount of a bank's capital expressed as a percentage of its Risk Weighted Assets (RWAs). The amount of capital that needs to be maintained when CRAR is 8 per cent is illustrated here.

Suppose that ABC bank has assets totaling ₹100 crore which consists of cash ₹20 crore; Government Bonds ₹40 crore; Mortgage Loans ₹10 crore, and Other Loans ₹30 crore. Also suppose that the central bank of the country where this bank is located has indicated 0 per cent risk weights to cash and government bonds (government bonds are guaranteed by the government and, hence, are default risk free), 50 per cent of the risk weight to mortgage loans, and 100 per cent risk weight to other types of loans.

Given the risk weights and the amount of each type of assets of ABC bank, the Risk Weighted Assets (RWA) of this bank will be:

$$RWA = 20\left(\frac{0}{100}\right) + 40\left(\frac{0}{100}\right) + 10\left(\frac{50}{100}\right) + 30\left(\frac{100}{100}\right)$$

$$= 0 + 0 + 5 + 30 = ₹35$$

The 8 per cent of RWA = (8/100) 35 = ₹2.8 crore.

The bank, thus, needs to maintain ₹2.8 crore on its balance sheet to meet the minimum CRAR imposed by the central bank.

Minimum capital adequacy requirement set by the Basel Committee on Banking Supervision I, II and III at the Bank for International Settlement (BIS) has provided a level playing field with standardized definition of capital and the standard weights to the assets categories. Basel I set 8 per cent as minimum capital for meeting the capital adequacy requirement. It divides capital into Tier 1 capital (consisting of the shareholders equity and retained profits) and Tier 2 (comprising subordinate debt, undisclosed reserves and general loss reserves). Basel I did not discriminate between different levels of risks while assigning weights to different assets.

Basel II tried to rectify the defects of Basel I by getting rid of old risk categories that treated all the corporate borrowers the same. Instead, it adopted a three pillar approach. Pillar 1 sets out the minimum capital requirement for banks, to cover **credit risk** arising arising from the default on payment of principle and or interest, **market risk** arising from changes in the prices of assets, such as prices of shares in stock markets, and **operational risk** emerging from the people, systems and process through which a company operates. Pillar 2 created a new supervisory review process, which required financial institutions to have their own internal processes to assess their capital needs and appoint supervisor to evaluate an institution's overall risk profile. Pillar 3 aimed at improving market discipline by requiring firms to publish certain details of their risks, capital and risk management. The objective of Basel II, thus, was on macro-prudential regulation of banks.

Basel III, developed in response to the global financial crises, not only focuses on macro-prudential regulations of banks (i.e., regulation of individual banks) but also on macro-prudential stability (i.e., the financial stability of the system as a whole). Basel III aims at achieving this by improving the quality and increasing the quantity of capital, and hence,

1. It has raised the share of Tier 1 capital to 6 per cent from the existing 4 per cent of RWA.
2. It makes it mandatory for banks to maintain **capital conservation buffer** of 2.5 per cent of RWA(thus raising the total minimum capital requirement of 10.5 per cent from the existing 8 per cent) to absorb losses during periods of prolonged financial and economic stress (such as one month of liquidity shortage).
3. It also makes it mandatory for banks to maintain a **counter-cyclical buffer** within a range of 0 per cent to 2.5 per cent of common equity. This buffer can be buildup in good times and can be used during periods of stress in downturn or recession. It is expected to prevent excess credit growth in periods of boom.

In the event of default on points 2 and 3 banks will be restricted paying out bonuses, dividends, etc., to their shareholders.

Box 9.3 Non Performing Assets and Provisioning

The level of Non Performing Assets (NPAs) indicates the quality of bank assets, the level of credit risk banks are exposed to and the efficiency in allocation of resources to productive sectors of the economy by banks.

There is no uniform system of classification of assets. Many countries have adopted delinquency period as the main benchmark for classifying assets into various categories and define a NPA as an asset where principal and/or interest are more than 90 days overdue.

To improve the quality of bank assets, a differential treatment is followed while accounting the income on NPAs and provisioning is made for the potential loss that the bank may incur on these assets. For the purpose of income recognition and provisioning, the NPAs are further classified on the basis of delinquency (i.e., default) period as substandard assets, doubtful assets and loss assets.

Sub-standard assets: The **sub-standard assets** are the NPAs for a period of not exceeding 180 days, i.e., 6 months (in India, less than 1 year).

Doubtful assets: The **doubtful assets** are the NPAs where principal and/or interest are at least 180 days past due (in India, more than 1 year).

Loss assets: The **loss assets** are the assets where principal and/or interest are at least 1 year past due (more than 2 to 3 years) and the losses have been identified by the bank or internal or external auditors or by the supervisory authorities of the central bank on these assets.

In some countries, banks are advised not to show interest received on NPAs on accrual basis (i.e., when they are due for receipt), but reflect it only once the cash payment is actually received by them. Interest received on NPAs is restored on an accrual basis only after the full settlement of all delinquent principal and interest.

To strengthen the quality of assets, most of the countries have adopted the standard requirements of provisioning which require provisioning of 20 per cent (10 per cent in India) for outstanding balance of sub-standard assets, 50 per cent (In India, 10 to 100 per cent depending on the period for which the asset has remained doubtful) with respect of doubtful assets, and 100 per cent of loss assets. Some countries also have 0.25 per cent provisioning requirement for **standard assets**, i.e., the assets which do not disclose any problem and which do not carry more than normal risk attached to the business.

9.5 FRAGILE FINANCIAL SYSTEM, CRISIS AND REFORMS

Financial sector weaknesses cause failure of, initially, some banks and financial institutions. Panic, set by the failure of some of the financial institutions, generates the belief that some more financial institutions will collapse soon, subsequently resulting in a large scale withdrawal of funds and collapse of many of them even though otherwise they may be financially sound and operating efficiently. The contraction in available funds reduces the credit creating capacity of financial institutions, especially that of the banks, which rely primarily on deposit funds to carry out their lending business. As a result, the supply of credit reduces in the market which adversely affects the investment by corporates.

Failure of banking financial institutions also distresses the payment mechanism. Banks play an important role in the payment mechanism as the cheques supported by demand deposits are widely used as a means of payment in modern economies. Loss of faith in the functioning of banking organizations and financial system, leading to a large scale withdrawal of deposits and multiple contractions in money supply, disrupts the payment mechanism, which hampers transactions and production activities.

Financial institutions, given their expertise, have better information about their customers and the viability of their projects. The collapse of many banks and financial institutions, at the same time, also leads to a loss of information generation capacity which they in general possess. In the absence of enough information, the market is dominated by **asymmetry of information**, i.e., the situation where one party has better information than the other. For example, managers have better information about the performance of their organizations than shareholders or public in general; borrowers have better information about the viability of their projects than lenders. An asymmetry of information increases the **moral hazard problem** of borrowers, implying that the funds may be used by the borrowers in the areas other then the one for which those were lent. It also accentuates the chances of **adverse selection** by lenders implying that the lenders may end up selecting the borrowers who are not only willing to pay higher interest rate, but are also highly risky. Thus, realizing that these problems dominate in a scenario of insufficient information, in general, lenders are not willing to depart with their funds, and overall supply of funds contracts in the market. The mobilization of saving reduces, which shrinks the investment.

Thus, a financial crisis, causing a large scale failure of banks and other financial institutions, reduces overall mobilization of saving, increases moral hazard and adverse selection problems, reduces lending and investment activities, disrupts the payment mechanism and trading and production processes. The overall impact of a financial crisis is a reduction in output, employment, and growth of an economy (Figure 9.10).

As financial sector crises leads to the collapse of an entire economy and imposes heavy cost in terms of economic and social suffering (UBE 9.6), the government, the central bank and other regulators, and policy makers, world over, try to prevent such crises from occurring by bringing in structural changes and strengthening the financial sector by implementing various reform measures (as illustrated in UBE 9.7 and UBE 9.8 using India as an example).

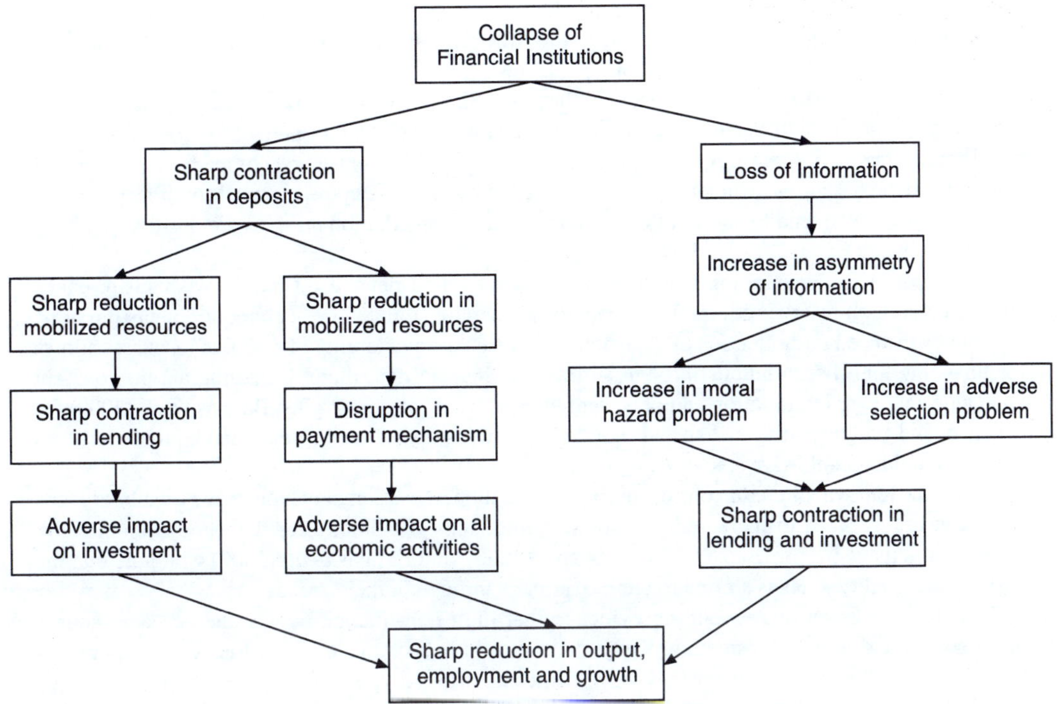

Figure 9.10 Ramifications of Collapse of Financial Institutions.

Financial sector reforms aim at deepening and widening the system by liberalizing the economy and allowing the market forces to play a greater role in the allocation of financial resources. They try to improve the efficiency in the system by opening up the economy to private and foreign sectors and infusing competition. At the same time, they attempt to strengthen the market by addressing the moral hazard and adverse selection problems by imposing prudential norms, such as minimum capital requirement directly related to the risk of the loan portfolio, and by bringing in force a proper supervisory system to enforce regulation and publicize the information (Box 9.4).

Box 9.4 Spreads in the Banking Sector

A central objective of financial deregulation is to encourage competition among financial institutions in order to improve the efficiency and the stability of the financial system. In this context, the difference between the interest rate charged to borrower and the interest rate paid to depositors, which reflects the cost of intermediation, is an important indicator of efficiency. A high differential may adversely affect domestic savings and jeopardize economic growth. Financial deregulation, by enhancing competition, is expected to narrow this gap.

Financial systems in developing countries typically exhibit significantly high and persistent spreads (Barajas *et al.*, 2000). These high margins have persisted even though most countries have undertaken financial liberalization. It has been observed that in many sub-Saharan African countries, the range of financial products remain extremely limited, interest rate spreads are wide, capital adequacy ratios insufficient, and the share of non-performing loans quite high. Similarly, Brock and Rojas-Suarez (2000) remark that most policymakers in Latin America have been disappointed by the fact that spreads have failed to converge to international levels.

Several arguments have been advanced for the same. First, high interest rates may persist if financial sector reforms do not significantly alter the structure within which banks operate. Several studies have noted that competitive pressures that arise from conditions of free entry and competitive pricing will tend to raise the functional efficiency of intermediation by decreasing the spread. More recent studies on bank spreads also tend to support the hypothesis that intermediation margins are positively related to market power (Barajas *et al.*, 1999).

Second, in many developing countries without an explicit deposit insurance mechanism, banks are subject to high reserve requirements, even post-liberalization. While such requirements might be dictated by the need for protection of depositors' interests, the availability of a pool of resources allows for financing high fiscal deficits through an implicit financial tax, thereby creating an environment that can promote rising inflation and persistent high intermediation margins. Barajas *et al.* (2000) for instance, find evidence of a positive and significant relationship between spreads and liquidity reserves in the Columbian banking system.

Third, the removal of credit controls during financial liberalisation may worsen the quality of loans that may, in turn, lead to increased risks of systemic crisis. Testimony for the same is empirically evidenced in the work of Brock and Rojas-Suarez (2000), and Barajas *et al.* (2000) who note that the cost of poor quality loans is shifted to bank customers through higher spreads.

Fourth, there is an overwhelming evidence that high non-financial costs also act as a source of persistent and wide intermediation spreads in developing countries. Non-financial costs reflect variations in physical capital costs, employment and wage levels. Demirgic-Kunt and Huizinga (1999), find evidence of a positive relation between net interest margin and overhead costs. Similarly, Brock and Rojas-Suarez (2000), also find significant evidence of a positive relation between spreads and wages or non-financial costs.

Fifth, Saunders and Schumacher (2000), note that the capital which banks hold to cushion themselves against expected and unexpected risks may lead to higher spreads. The cost of high regulatory and/or endogenously determined capital ratios may be covered through widening the spread between lending and deposit rates.

Sixth, macroeconomic instability and the policy environment may also affect the pricing behaviour of commercial banks. In order to capture the effects of the macroeconomic and policy environment, spread equations include, among others, inflation and growth of industrial output as control variables. For instance, there is an evidence to suggest that inflation is positively associated with intermediation spreads, particularly in developing countries with high and variable inflation rates (Demirgic-Kunt and Huizinga, 1999; Mlachila and Chirwa, 2002).

In summary, while financial liberalization should generally lead to a lowering of spreads, whether they actually decline or not ultimately depend on a number of factors. Generally, lending rates relative to deposit rates can increase or remain high, depending on the level of reserve requirements, the competitiveness of the banking system, the cost structure of the market, and the macroeconomic environment. On the other hand, if the banking system is characterized by excess liquidity, deposit rates are unlikely to increase much following financial liberalization because the marginal cost of mobilizing resources is high, while the marginal profit is negligible. Thus, the spread may actually rise, rather than fall, after financial liberalization

References

Barajas, A., Steiner R. and Salazar, N. (1999), Interest Spreads in Banking in Columbia, 1974–96, *IMF Staff Papers*, 46, pp. 196–224.

Barajas, A., Steiner R. and Salazar, N. (2000), The Impact of Liberalisation and Foreign Investment in Columbia's Financial Sector, *Journal of Development Economics*, 36, pp. 157–196.

Brock, P.L. and Rojas-Suarez, L. (2000), Understanding the Behavior of Bank Spreads in Latin America, *Journal of Development Economics*, 63, pp. 113–134.

Demirgic-Kunt, A. and Huizinga H. (1999), Determinants of Commercial Bank Interest Margins and Profitability: Some International Evidence, *World Bank Economic Review*, 13, pp. 379–408.

Mlachila, M. and Chirwa E. (2002), Financial Reforms and Interest Rate Spreads in the Commercial Banking System in Malawi, *IMF Working Paper* No. 6, IMF: Washington.

Ramaiah, M. and Ghosh S. (2002), Understanding the Behaviour of Bank Spreads in India: An Empirical

Analysis, *Prajnan*, 31, pp. 7–19.

Saunders, A. and Schumacher L. (2000), The Determinants of Bank Interest Rate Margins: An International

Study, *Journal of International Money and Finance*, 19, pp. 813–832.

Source: RBI (2002), Report on Trend and Progress of Banking in India.

UNDERSTANDING BUSINESS ENVIRONMENT

UBE 9.6 Sub-prime Mortgage Crisis and Global Recession

Financial sector weakness trigged the sub-prime mortgage crisis and caused worldwide recession as illustrated in this UBE.

Recording the recovery from the previous slowdown in 2001 triggered down by the burst of IT bubble, the USA economy stumbled into another period of slowdown since 2006 which turned into a period of global recession in 2009.

The global recession of 2009 is attributed to the sub-prime mortgage crisis in the USA and the consequent financial instability world over. Below, the US **sub-prime mortgage crisis** and its impact on the global economy are analyzed.

The US Sub-Prime Mortgage Crisis

Traditionally, in the USA, banks financed their mortgage lendings through the funds raised from customers' deposits. This restricted bank lending to the amount available from deposit liabilities.

The decade of 1990s saw a sea change in the method of financing mortgage loans. Banks rather than entirely depending on deposit liabilities, discovered new ways of financing loans. They started raising funds through securitizing loans and selling these in the mortgage bond market. This new method of raising funds enhanced the supply of funds in the loanable funds market and made credit easily available for housing purpose even to the borrowers who could not avail credit from the 'prime' lenders such as the government sponsored agencies like Freddie Mac. The mortgage lending to the borrowers with low income, poor credit history and high risk (low probability of full repayment) is referred to as **sub-prime lending**.

House hunters were lured to borrow funds by offering relatively low interest rates than what would have been applicable to the borrowers with higher risk of default. These rates were kept fixed for the initial two years of the period of loans and variable thereafter. The borrowers were not clearly explained that flexible interest rate, after the completion of two years, could imply much higher interest rates on the same loan.

The easy availability of credit (made possible by accommodative monetary policy pursued by the US Federal Reserve), with misleadingly low rates of interest, led to a sharp increase in demand for housing in the USA during 1996–2006. Many borrowers invested in housing the amount of which was much more than their income and the expected savings. Some estimates place the increase in the demand to be 9 per cent in 1996 to 20 per cent in 2006. The consequent increase in housing prices (Figure 9.11) further boosted the growth of housing market. Increased demand for housing credit got reflected in the interest rates applicable to such loans. On some of the loans, the variable interest rates after the initial period of two years even got doubled.

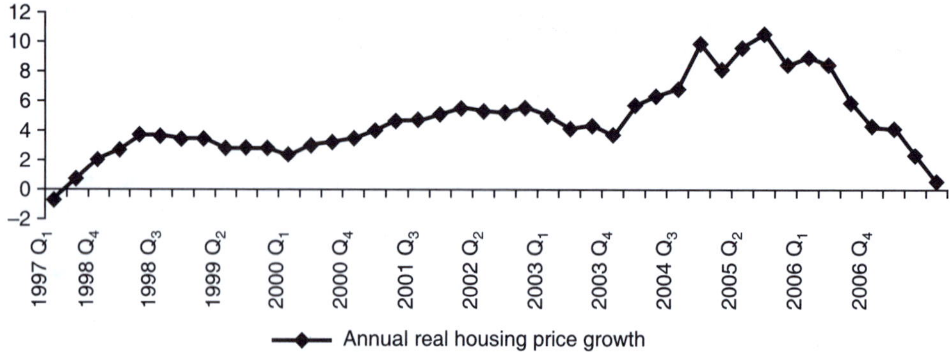

Source: Based on the data from IMF (2007), *World Economic Outlook*, October.

Figure 9.11 Annual Real Housing Price Growth in USA.

Inflationary pressures started surfacing in the USA in 2004, which led to a gradual withdrawal of liquidity by the central bank by pursuing tight monetary policy in the subsequent period. The tightening of monetary policy in 2006 resulted in a substantial increase in the interest rates. The considerable escalation in the interest rates on sub-prime loans not only flattened the demand for housing and the housing prices, which were sky-rocketing, but also increased the defaults and delinquencies (Figure 9.12). The burst of the bubble of housing prices and large defaults on sub-prime mortgage loans, on the one hand, deteriorated the balance sheet of the financial institutions who had retained the credit risk with them and, on the other hand, led to a sharp depreciation in the value of the bonds floating in the market which wiped out the net worth of the individuals and the institutions (especially the pension funds, hedge funds and the banks) who had heavily invested in sub-prime mortgage bonds.

Several structural weaknesses in the financial system, such as a prolonged period of low interest rates, lack of prudential norms on financial institutions, lack of transparency and underestimation of risk contributed to the boom of the sub-prime market. However, these weaknesses were also behind the burst of the bubble, leading to a weakening of several major financial institutions in the USA such as government sponsored enterprises Fannie Mae and Free Mac, insurance company American International Group (AIG), investment bank Merrill Lynch, Morgan Stanley, Goldman Sachs, thrift institution Washington Mutual, Commercial bank Wachovia, and also the failure of some of the biggest financial institutions such as Lehmann Brothers.

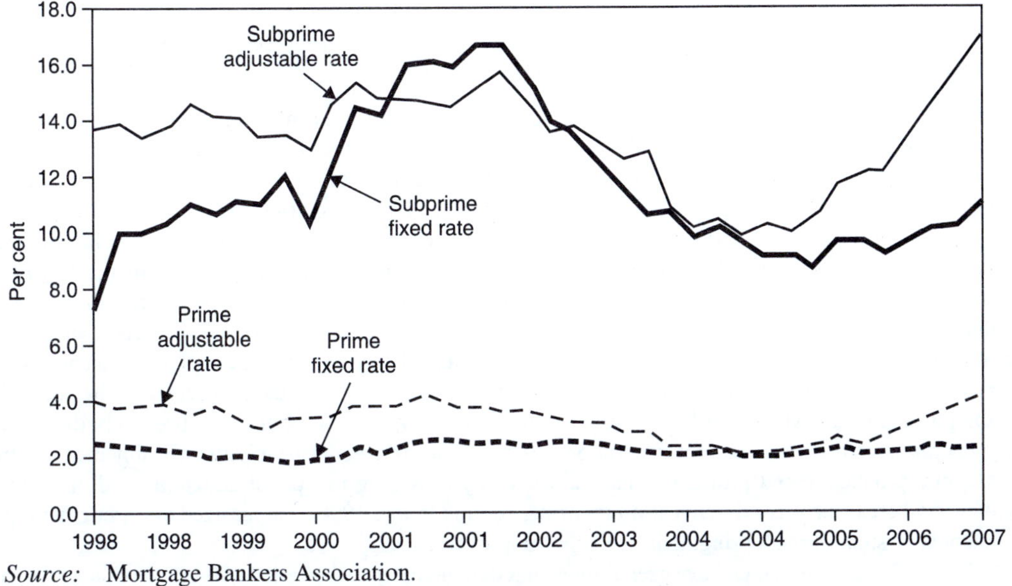

Source: Mortgage Bankers Association.

Figure 9.12 Prime Versus Sub-prime Delinquency Rates.

Spread of the Crisis

The investors, who had borrowed funds against the value of their assets and invested in the sub-prime assets, were made to sell off their other assets such as equities to repay the loans when the value of their sub-prime assets fell drastically. Not only the domestic equities but even the emerging market equities and other foreign currency denominated assets were used to pay-off the loans. Direct exposure of some European and Asian banks and other financial institutions, such as BNP Paribas, Barclays Bank, Hong Kong and Shanghai Bank, to the US sub-prime market also contributed to the spread of the crisis to other developed and emerging markets. The impact of this financial crash was felt in the equities market worldwide.

Global Recession

The financial crisis, reflected in the lack of confidence in the financial system, heightened risk aversion and increased volatility, reduced the availability of funds with the banks. The difficult terms and conditions of the credit, and overall credit crunch and liquidity shortage jeopardized the working of the real segment of the US economy. Overall lack of demand led the USA economy to another slowdown in 2006 which hit not only business equipments but also consumer goods segment. The slowdown finally turned into a recession in the USA by the end of 2007.

The US financial crisis had a spillover effect over other economies through trade and capital flows. The US economy, being largely an open economy, is highly integrated with the rest of the world. The US slowdown which surfaced in 2006–07 and turned into a recession in 2007, affected the growth of most economies of the world through compression in their exports, heavy outflow of capital flows and contraction in the economic activities. Though emerging market economies could avoid recession, the advanced economies and the global economy as a whole could not avert it (refer to Figure 5.9).

Reference

IMF (2009), *World Economic Outlook*, April.

UNDERSTANDING BUSINESS ENVIRONMENT

UBE 9.7 Financial Sector Reforms in India

This UBE details on financial sector reforms in India which attempt to overcome the weaknesses in the financial system which had crept-in it in the pre-1991 period.

Financial sector reforms in India were neither driven by any banking crisis nor were they an outcome of any external support package. They were an integral part of economic restructuring initiated in the early 1990s. The reforms in the financial sector have encompassed all the segments of the financial system. The objectives of the reforms had been to strengthen the functioning of financial intermediaries, to promote the development of new financial instruments and services so as to meet the varied needs of investors, to develop financial markets so as to bring about a transformation in the structure, stability and efficiency of financial markets, to facilitate a greater integration of markets with the objective of enabling the process of price discovery by the market determined interest rates that enhances the efficiency in the allocation of resources, and to lead the economy on higher growth path. The reforms in the financial sector have been implemented carefully in a gradual, sequential and consistent manner in tandem with the reforms in the real sector of the economy. For the purpose of analytical clarity, the reforms since the early 1990s in India have been classified as the first generation reforms and second generation reforms. The **first generation reforms** aimed at creating an efficient, productive and profitable financial sector by providing functional autonomy and operational flexibility, whereas the **second generation reforms**, starting in mid 1990s, emphasized the strengthening of the financial system through bringing in structural improvements.

The major reforms which have been implemented in India, since the early 1990s, in the financial sector have been enumerated as follows:

Reforms in the Banking Sector

Reforms in the banking sector aimed at improving the operational efficiency, financial viability and competitiveness with the objective of achieving allocative efficiency of resources through removing financial repression, providing more operational flexibility by reductions in statutory pre-emptions and strengthening of the banking organizations through prudential regulations and better supervision.

Competition, in a predominantly government-owned sector, has been infused in the post-1990 period, by allowing public sector banks to raise capital from equity market upto 49 per cent, allowing entry of new banks in the private sector, setting up a roadmap for entry of new foreign and joint venture banks with more transparent norms, allowing foreign direct investment upto 74 per cent and portfolio investment in the financial sector and issuing transparent guidelines for mergers and amalgamation of private sector banks and NBFCs.

Operational flexibility in the portfolio management of banks has been brought about by the removal of financial repression through a deregulation of interest rates and a reduction in pre-emption of resources through a substantial reduction in reserve requirements in the form of SLR and CRR. The SLR has been gradually reduced from a peak of 38.5 per cent to 24 per cent at present. The CRR was reduced from its peak of 15 per cent in 1989, to 4.5 per cent of net demand and time liabilities in 2003. Though in the light of emerging economic conditions, the CRR had been revised upwards to 6 per cent in the subsequent period, the objective of reducing it further in the long-term remains intact. Along with these, a market determined pricing for government securities and other interest rates, development of pure inter-bank call money market, auction-based repo/reverse repos for short-term liquidity, and improved payment and settlement system have enabled banks in efficient allocation of resources.

International best practices and norms in the form of risk weighted adequacy requirement, accounting, income recognition, provisioning for Non-Performing Assets (NPAs) and market exposure have been introduced to improve the transparency of the bank balance sheet. The minimum CRAR has been set at one per cent above the international norm at 9 per cent. Apart from default risk or credit risk, a separate capital charge for market risk has also been introduced in 2004. (Place the timeline of capital adequacy Basel III norms)To expand and augment their capital base, banks have been permitted to access the capital market in the form of innovative perpetual debt instruments, perpetual non-cumulative preference shares, redeemable cumulative preference shares, and hybrid debt instruments. Classification of NPAs into sub-standard assets, doubtful assets and loss assets, and provisioning not only for the non-performing assets, but also for standard assets, better risk management practices, enactment of Securitization and Reconstruction of Financial Assets and Enforcement of Security Interest (SARFAESI) Act, 2002, and setting up of Debt Recovery Tribunals, Lok Adalats, Asset Reconstruction Companies, corporate debt restructuring mechanism have been carried out to reduce the level of non-performing assets on bank balance sheets. The setting up of **Credit Information Bureau of India Limited** (CIBIL) for information sharing on defaulters and other borrowers is helping banks to reduce their exposure to bad credit risk.

To further improve the balance sheet of banks by fine tuning the risk management system, the guidelines on asset-liability management and risk management have been issued to them from time-to-time.

The supervisory and regulatory system has been revamped by establishing the **Board of Financial Supervision** as the apex supervisory authority which can give undivided attention to supervision and ensure an integrated approach to supervision of commercial banks, financial institutions and non-banking financial companies. The supervision has been further strengthened by introducing **Capital Adequacy**, **Asset Quality**, **Management**, **Earnings**, **Liquidity and Systems** (CAMELS) supervisory rating system, risk based supervision and Off-site Monitoring and Surveillance (OSMOS) as a part of crisis management framework for Early Warning System (EWS) and as a trigger for on-site inspection of vulnerable institutions. In more recent period, the focus has also been on ensuring good governance through diversified ownership and "fit and proper" owners, directors and senior managers.

For a smooth functioning of payment and settlement system and for reducing the risks in payment, the **Real Time Gross Settlement** (RTGS) has been operationalized in 2004. This has facilitated a final settlement of individual inter-bank fund transfers on a gross real time basis during the processing day which enables minimizing the systemic risk in the financial system.

However, some challenges have emerged in the liberalized and globalized scenario that need further reforms and strengthening of the financial system. Globalization of financial markets, especially an opening up of the capital account to capital outflows, exposes banks to greater market volatility and liquidity risk, interest rate risk, currency risk, counter party risk and country risk. There is a need for the strengthening of risk management practices in the country and a better cross-border supervision of financial intermediaries. Implementation of Basel III would lead to a refinement of risk management system and an improvement in capital efficiency.

There is also a need for further strengthening the corporate governance for effective risk management in banks.

Derivatives activities are increasing at a rapid rate in the country. These put banks at a higher risk, and thus, there is a necessity for clear accounting guidelines in this area.

There is an increasing trend towards entry of some of the bigger banks into other financial segments like merchant banking, insurance, etc. Though the Reserve Bank of India has introduced consolidated accounting and other quantitative methods to facilitate consolidated supervision, there is a need to evolve a framework to cover banks in mixed conglomerates where the parent organizations may be non-financial entities or financial entities coming under the jurisdiction of other regulators.

All round development of the country necessities that all the segments of the society get access to banking and financial services on equitable basis. Thus, it is essential to encourage a greater degree of financial inclusion in the country. At the same time, there is a need to strengthen the mechanism for ensuring fair treatment of consumers and effective redressal of customer grievances.

Reforms in the Financial Markets

Financial markets, especially the money market, government securities market and forex market, play a critical role in the transmission mechanism of monetary policy (Section 8.6) and have significant public policy implications for an emerging market economy. Development and strengthening of various financial markets facilitate greater integration of markets and efficient price discovery of interest rate and exchange rate. The reforms in financial sector are graduated and calibrated and addressed from all directions with emphasis on improvement in the market micro-structure and institutional and infrastructure strengthening.

Given the critical role of the short end of the financial market in the transmission mechanism, a number of initiatives have been taken to develop the call money market as pure inter-bank money market by restricting the participation in this market to banks and primary dealers only. At the same time, efforts have been to strengthen and develop the collateralized segment of the money market. Restrictions on the participation in the call money market have helped in reducing the volatility in this market, and have helped in diverting the funds from call money segment, which is un-collateralized segment, to repo and CBLO markets which are collateralized segments.

The money market has been widened and deepened by introducing various money market instruments and activating and developing the market for a number of such instruments by liberalizing the norms of participation in these instruments.

For meeting the demand for long-term funds, especially that for infrastructure requirements, a developed capital market is needed. Along with the reforms in the money market, the reforms in this market have been initiated with the objective of boosting competitive conditions, improving price discovery process, reducing transaction costs, reducing information asymmetries and strengthening institutional infrastructure.

To strengthen the institutional framework, the Security and Exchange Board of India (SEBI) was given statutory powers with the mandate of protecting investors' interests and ensuring the orderly development in the capital market in 1992. Apart from stock exchanges, various intermediaries such as mutual funds, stock brokers, merchant bankers, registrars to issue, share transfer agents and venture capital funds have been brought under the purview of the SEBI.

The market mechanism has been strengthened by repealing the Capital Issues (Control) Act, 1947, in 1992, and allowing the issuers of securities to raise capital from the market without any consent from any authority. However, to protect the interest of investors, the norms for public issue have been strengthened by improving the disclosure standards. Also, to improve the availability of information to investors, all listed companies are required to publish unaudited financial results on a quarterly basis.

The trading platform has been modernized by replacing open outcry system with screen based, automatic, anonymous, order-driven system. The setting up of the **National Stock Exchange** (NSE) of India Ltd. as a electronic trading platform, establishment of the **National Securities Depository Ltd.** (NSDL) and **Central Depository Services (India) Ltd.** (CSDL) for dematerialization of scripts and introduction of the **Electronic Fund Transfer** (EFT) Facility, have facilitated the move towards modern practices. The trading system has been further strengthened initially by shortening trading and settlement cycles from 14 days to 7 days, and subsequently, shifting to the system of **rolling settlement** with shortening the trading cycle in a gradual but in a rapid pace from T + 5 to T + 3 to T + 2 within the span of two years with the objective of reducing risks associated with unsettled trades due to market fluctuations.

Inconvenience and problems related to physical custody and transfer of scrips such as late delivery, risk of forgery and frauds have been resolved by dematerialization of the scrips. Ninety nine per cent of the scrips in the market are now dematerialized and almost 100 per cent of the trading is in a dematerialized form.

Mark to market and Value-At-Risk (VAR) daily margining and exposure limits, online trading, monitoring of margins and provisioning, clearing corporation and settlement guarantee fund mechanism for settlement have increased transparency and strengthened the risk management system and functioning of the stock exchanges. Trading in derivatives, both index and scrip based such as stock index futures, stock index options, and futures and options in individual stocks, has been permitted to hedge and manage the risk in the capital market.

To mitigate the impact of vested interest and to reduce the concentration of power in the stock exchanges, the move has been towards corporatization and demutualization of stock exchanges. The NSE has been set up as a demutualized corporate body with ownership, management and trading rights in the hands of three different sets of groups. Similarly, the stock exchange, Mumbai has been corporatized and demutualized and renamed as the Bombay Stock Exchange Ltd. (BSE).

The level of competition in the capital market has been enhanced by opening up the mutual fund industry to private sector in 1992, which was the monopoly of the Unit Trust of India (UTI) and the mutual funds set by the public sector financial institutions.

Simultaneously, the efforts have been to develop the other segments of financial markets, especially the government securities and foreign exchange markets, so as to enable the process of efficient price discovery in respect of interest rate and exchange rate.

The market for government securities plays an important role in the functioning of the economy for various reasons. First, the government's dependence on the RBI for funding fiscal deficit often results in an increase in money supply and higher inflation in the economy. The development of the government securities market helps the government in raising funds from the market and mitigating the impact of fiscal deficit on money supply and inflation. Second, the government securities are by default, risk free. Therefore, yield on these sets the benchmark for other rates. Third, in a deregulated environment, the government securities market also plays an important role in the transmission of monetary policy impulses.

Thus, for creating and developing the market for government securities, the **Primary Dealers** (PDs), which are the agents who are willing to sell and purchase the securities all the time, were introduced as market makers. With the objective of better price discovery, the administered interest rate system on government securities has been replaced by an auction-based system. The phasing out of ad hoc 91 days TBs by 1997, and complete withdrawal of the RBI from the primary market auction with effect from 1 April 2006 have further strengthened the market mechanism in this segment.

Government security market has been widened by increasing the instruments such as 91 days Treasury Bills, Zero Coupon Bonds, Floating Rate Bonds, Capital Indexed Bonds, exchange traded interest rate futures and OTC interest rate derivatives like IRS/FRA. To deepen the market, Foreign Institutional Investors (FIIs) have been allowed to invest in government securities. Introduction of automated screen based trading in government securities through the Negotiated Dealing System (NDS), setting up of risk free payments and settlement system in government securities through the Clearing Corporation of India Limited (CCIL), introduction of the Real Time Gross Settlement (RTGS) system, introduction of trading in government securities on stock exchanges, permitting non-bank participants in repo market, introduction of NDS-OM and T + 1 settlement norms have helped in further developing this market.

Globalization of the economy necessitated a greater integration with global financial markets. A move towards market-based exchange rate regime in 1993, adoption of current account convertibility in 1994, and since then the gradual move towards capital account convertibility (Section 12.4) are the major initiatives in restructuring the Indian foreign exchange market. The replacement of Restrictive Foreign Exchange Regulation Act (FERA), 1973, with the market-friendly Foreign Exchange Management Act (FEMA), 1999 (UBE 15.6), and delegation of considerable powers to the Authorized Dealers (ADs) to release foreign exchange for a variety of purposes have helped in strengthening the institutional framework of this market.

The development of rupee foreign currency swap market and introduction of additional hedging instruments such as cross currency options, Interest Rate Swaps (IRS) and currency swaps, caps/collars and Forward Rate Agreements (FRAs) in the international foreign exchange market have widened the market. The liberalization measures, such as permission to various participants in the foreign exchange market, Indian's investing abroad, FIIs to avail forward cover and enter into swap transactions, permitting FIIs and NRIs to trade in exchange traded derivatives contracts have been implemented with the objective of better integration with the financial markets abroad.

A number of initiatives have been taken to develop even the corporate bond market which is still not as developed as the government securities market. The initivtatives, such as rationalization of listing norms, implementation of delivery vs payment settlemet of corporate bonds, reduction in the shut period, setting up of reporting platform by FIMMDA to promote transparency, introduction of repo in corporate bonds, introduction of credit default swaps (CDS) to facilitate hedging credit risk, permitting banks to invest in unrated bonds of companies engaged in infrastructure activities, etc. Has considerably increased the primary as well secondary market trading of corporate bonds.However, participation in this market is primarily confined to institutional participants, such as banks, primary dealers, mutual funds, insurance companies, pension funds, corporates, etc., Though retail investors are gradually entering the market their participation is almost negligible.

UNDERSTANDING BUSINESS ENVIRONMENT

UBE 9.8 Impact of Financial Sector Reforms

This UBE describes how the financial sector reform have widened, deepened and strengthened the financial sector in India.

Financial sector reforms in India have lead to an emergence and trading of a large number of financial instruments. Availability of variety of financial instruments, easing of restrictions on transactions, development in trading technology, and reduction in transaction costs have widened and deepened the size of the market in terms of number of participants and the amount traded in various markets.

Impact on the Banking Sector

Scheduled commercial banks continue to be on an expansion path in the post-reform period, with some decline in the number of commercial banks since 2005 as a result of consolidation of some of the weak banks with the strong banks. The expansion is clearly evident from the number of bank offices, per capita deposits mobilized and per capita credit distributed by commercial banks in India (Table 9.2). The continuous expansion and spread of banking is an indication of financial deepening in the country.

Table 9.2 Spread of Commercial Banks in India

	1969	*2003*	*2004*	*2005*	*2006*	*2007*	*2008*	*2009*	*2010*	*2011*
Number of Commercial Banks	89	294	291	288	222	183	175	170	169	169
Number of Offices of Scheduled Commercial Banks in India	8,262	66,535	67,188	68,355	69,471	71,839	76,050	80,547	85,393	90,263
Population per office (in thousands)	64	16	16	16	16	15	15	14.5	13.8	13.4
Per Capita Deposits of Scheduled Commercial Banks	88	12,554	14,550	16,091	19,276	23,468	28,327	33,471	38,062	43,034
Per Capita Credit of Scheduled Commercial Banks	68	7,143	8,166	10,440	13,774	17,355	20,928	24,230	27,489	32,574

Source: RBI (2012), Basic Statistical Returns of Scheduled Commercial Banks in India, Vol. 40.

The reforms in the banking sector along with the favourable economic conditions before the onset of the global financial crisis helped banks to improve their efficiency, productivity and profitability. The efficiency gains are reflected in intermediation cost and spread. The **intermediation cost**, defined as the ratio of operating expenses to total assets, has registered a continuous reduction, brought about by a reduction in labour expenses and expenses on physical capital. This improvement is inspite of large expenditure incurred by Indian banks on installation and upgradation of information technology and implementation of voluntary retirement scheme. As a result of greater competition and enhanced efficiency, the **spread**, defined as net interest income (interest income – interest expenditure) to asset ratio, has reduced significantly over the reform period (Table 9.3).

Table 9.3 Select Performance Indicators of Commercial Banks in India

(Per cent)

	1996-97	*2000-01*	*2009-10*	*2010-11*	*2011-12*
Net Interest Margin (spread) (as a percentage of average assets)	3.22	2.84	2.17	2.91	2.9
Return on assets	0.66	0.5	1.05	1.1	1.08
Return on equity	10.25	9.61	14.31	14.96	14.6
Net NPAs to advances	8.05	6.17	1.11	1.1	1.4
CRAR					
(I) BASEL-I	8.7	13.07	13.6	13.02	12.94
(II) BASEL-II	na	na	14.5	14.19	14.24

Source: Compiled from RBI(various),Report on Trend and Progress of Banking in India.

Reforms have also brought about a significant improvement in asset quality and capital positioning of Indian scheduled commercial banks. As an outcome of several institutional measures initiated by the RBI and also a strong macroeconomic performance, both gross NPAs and net NPAs (net of provisioning) have declined in absolute terms as well as percentage of advances, reflecting better allocation of funds and better recoveries by banks.

The risk absorption capacity has also improved in the banks as reflected in their capital positioning. During the last one and half decade, the banking sector has been consistently maintaining CRAR well above the stipulated norm of minimum 9 per cent, which is an outcome of better profitability as well as the better access of the banks to capital markets.

One can also notice that the global financial crisis did not have a very significant impact on the profitability, efficiency, and soundness indicators, reflecting the capability of the financial sector to withstand shocks.

Impact on the Financial Markets

In the pre-reform period, many of the financial markets were either non-existent (such as forex market and derivates market) or the volume traded was negligible. The reform measures have been able to create markets that were non-existent. The reforms have also been able to bring insignificant transparency and improvement in the functioning of various markets. As a result there is a substantial improvement in the depth (measured by average daily volumes) of these markets (Table 9.4).

The liberalization and deepening of the markets have enabled a greater integration of various segments of money market. There is a greater integration not only among the different segments of the money market but also between the money market and capital market. There is a higher degree of correlation between yield on long-term government bond and short-term treasury bills, which is an indication of emergence of term structure of interest rates in the financial markets. Also, now there is a better integration of the foreign exchange market with the money market and the government securities market, resulting in a better management of the external sector through money market. However, the integration between the equity market and the money market is still low in India.

The reforms in financial markets in India have resulted in a relatively deep, liquid and vibrant money market. However, in the context of fuller capital account convertibility there is a need to develop the money market further by infusing better ALM practices by banks and other market participants, encouraging banks to limit their exposure to the call money market on the basis of internal control system, expanding the eligible set of underlying collateral securities for repo transactions.

Table 9.4 Depth of Financial Markets in India—Average Daily Volumes

(₹ in billion)

Month	*Money Market*						*Bond Market*		*Forex Market inter-bank (US$bn)*	*Stock Market ##*
	LAF	*Call Money*	*Market Repo*	*CBLO*	*Commercial paper**	*Certificate of Deposits**	*G-sec***	*Corporate Bond#*		
Mar 12	–1,574	175	112	380	912	4,195	99	26	21	152
Jun 12	–913	152	180	376	1,258	4,252	258	30	19	117
Sep 12	–517	143	185	502	1,706	3,572	260	36	21	143
Dec 12	–1,231	142	147	398	1,818	3,328	197	39	19	139
Jan 13	–930	170	192	456	1,998	3,251	466	25	20	128
Feb 13	–1,136	158	246	431	1,923	3,011	355	29	19	134
Mar 13	–1,093	194	216	480	1,093	3,896	307	43	23	133

* Outstanding position

** Average daily outright volume traded in Central Government dated securities

Average daily trading in corporate bonds

Average daily turnover in BSE and NSE

Note: In Column 2, (-) ve sign indicates injection of liquidity into the system

Source: Compiled from RBI (2012), Macroeconomic and Monetary Developments, May, Ch. V

The reforms in the capital market have brought about a visible improvement in trading and settlement infrastructure, increased transparency and brought in a better risk management system in place, which has brought about a considerable reduction in the transaction costs and improved the liquidity in the capital markets. However, the size of the public issue has remained small as corporates prefer the international market and the private placement rather than the public issue segment. The corporate bond market has remained even more underdeveloped. Possible reasons for the lack of participation in this market are the narrow investor base, insufficient liquidity, lack of standardization, lack of sufficient tools to manage credit, market and liquidity risk, absence of robust bankruptcy framework, absence of suitable institutional mechanism for enabling small and medium enterprises and other corporate with lower credit rating to access the corporate bond market. The corporate debt market needs strengthening by increasing the number of investors and increasing the size of the issue, strengthening the institutional framework, refinement of the trading framework and innovations to develop it further. Similarly, the government securities market though has widened and deepened, a lot has to be achieved in creating liquidity in this market which has remained concentrated on a few securities. Though the yield curve has emerged, it is not liquid at the longer end of the market. Even at the shorter end, liquidity remains low and banks remain the major investors. The development of this market is utmost important as the interest rate on government securities serves as the benchmark for pricing other debt market instruments and helps in monetary transmission process across the yield curve.

SUMMARY

A financial system, consisting of financial intermediaries, financial instruments and financial markets, helps in mobilizing higher savings, allocating resources in an efficient way, facilitating payments mechanism, enhancing the level of investment and capital stocks, encouraging technical innovations. It, hence, promotes economic growth and development.

However, banking weakness, emerging from cyclical downturn and/or structural weakness arising from financial repression, lack of prudential norms, deposit insurance and financial sector opening to private and foreign participants, may lead to financial sector crises. Such a crises, often, have long lasting and enduring adverse impact.

Indian financial system, characterized by financial repression in the pre-1991 era, has been reformed with the objective of improving the operational efficiency, viability and profitability of financial intermediaries by removing financial repression, infusing competition, strengthening the balance sheets by imposing minimum capital requirement and provisioning requirement for assets, enforcing better on-site and off-site supervision, and widening and deepening the financial markets by introducing new instruments, increasing the number of participants and strengthening the trading and settlement mechanism.

The financial sector reforms in India have improved the operational efficiency, the quality of the financial assets, and the profitability of financial intermediaries. The reforms in the financial sector have deepened and widened and improved the liquidity in the financial markets.

However, the globalization of the economy, with a move towards greater capital account convertibility, larger participation in the derivative markets and diversification of the banks into non-traditional activities such as merchant banking, insurance, etc., has exposed the banks and financial markets to a greater volatility and risk. There is, therefore, a need for further strengthening of risk management practices in financial institutions, corporate governance, and consolidated supervision and accounting framework. Equally important is greater financial inclusion as overall development of the country requires the availability of financial services to all the segments of the society.

Implications for Managers

The availability of funds, the forms in which resources can be raised, and the cost of funds all gets determined by the structure of financial system and the level of development of the financial system of a country.

In an underdeveloped financial system, the funds mobilized in the economy are small, which limits the availability of funds for investment purpose for business organizations. At the same time, small amount of resources and high demand for investible funds keep the real interest rates high, which increase the cost of production. Domestically produced goods become uncompetitive in the international markets because of the high cost of production.

On the contrary, a developed financial system is not only able to mobilize a large amount of savings and increase the supply of funds for business organizations, but also makes available these funds at a lower cost which reduces the cost of production for organizations. In a developed system, business organizations have a wide range of financial instruments available for raising resources. Given the wide choice, firms can raise funds in a most efficient way. In such a system, large well-established firms need not depend for funds on financial intermediaries. They can raise funds directly from financial markets either in the form of debt instruments or shares because of their credibility and reputation. Direct access to the markets reduces the cost of funds as financial intermediation increases the cost due to intermediation charges. Small firms and new firms usually find it difficult to raise funds directly from the market because of information asymmetry, i.e., the business managers having more information than the investors. The presence of information asymmetry and limited exposure make it difficult for entrepreneurs and managers to fund their projects by issuing shares to investors directly in the markets. Thus, even viable projects get deprived of funds in such situations. Financial intermediaries make credit available to small firms or even to new enterprises as they can access more information regarding the firms and the projects with the help of expert staff at their disposal. They can arrange funds for such firms at a cheaper rate than that would be available to them in the market if they try to access it directly.

Various financial and advisory services help business organizations in allocating their funds in most efficient ways. Financial institutions have a pool of skilled staff which can evaluate the viability of a proposed project, can guide firms regarding the profitability of a particular venture, and even help in pricing, offloading and selling their securities in the market.

With the help of a developed financial system, business organizations can even carry out international transactions. Financial intermediaries facilitate international trade by providing advance credit, guaranteeing their payments, and insuring their products.

REVIEW QUESTIONS

9.1 How does developed financial system promote growth of an economy?

9.2 Differentiate bank and non-bank financial intermediaries from both asset and liability sides. Which type of financial intermediaries help in payment mechanism?

9.3 What is the difference between primary market and secondary market? It is argued that efficient primary market results in higher saving mobilization in an economy. Secondary markets do not add on to the existing level of saving in an economy. Why do then we need to promote the secondary markets in an economy?

9.4 What is the money market? How does it help in the monetary transmission mechanism?

9.5 "Primary securities are traded only in the primary market." Analyze this statement.

9.6 Differentiate between short-term and long-term financial instruments.

9.7 Define financial repression? Why financial repression is considered to be against economic efficiency?

9.8 What do you understand by the system of administered interest rate structure? How far is this different from the cross subsidization of credit?

9.9 How does deposit insurance lead to a weakening of the financial system?

9.10 Weak regulatory and supervisory system can weaken a financial system. Why?

9.11 What is the capital adequacy ratio? How does it strengthen the balance sheet of the financial intermediaries?

9.12 What are the Non Performing Assets (NPAs)? How do these assets weaken the balance sheet of financial intermediaries? What prudential norms have been suggested by the BIS to reduce the NPA on bank balance sheets?

9.13 What does the term 'spread' refer to in the context of banking sector? Why is it used as a measure of banking sector efficiency? Inspite of financial liberalization in many developing countries, spread is significantly high. Why?

9.14 Has the development of the financial sector contributed to the growth of the Indian economy? Which segment of the financial sector has significant influence on the Indian economy?

9.15 What are the main financial sector regulatory authorities in India? How far the areas of coverage of the RBI differ from that of the SEBI? Which segment of the financial sector is supervised by the IRDA?

9.16 Describe the main functions of the RBI?

9.17 What is the private placement of securities? Why corporates in India prefer this process of issuing securities over other methods?

9.18 What necessitated reforms of the financial sector in India?

9.19 What reforms have been implemented in India in the post-1991 era?

9.20 How have the financial sector reforms affected the working of the banking industry and financial markets in India?

9.21 What are the reasons for the Sub Prime Mortgage Crisis in the USA? How has the crisis affected the global economy?

9.22 Why understanding of the working of a financial system and the level of financial development is important for business managers?

NUMERICAL PROBLEM

9.1 Suppose bank XYZ has Tier I capital equal to ₹3 crore and Tier II capital equal to 10 crore. The bank has assets worth ₹200 crore which includes cash ₹30 crore, government securities ₹50 crore, housing loans ₹40 crore, other loans ₹80 crore. The risk attached to cash and government securities is 0. Housing loans carry 50 per cent risk, whereas other loans have 100 per cent risk. The bank is required to maintain minimum Tier I equity to risk weighted assets of 4 per cent and minimum Tier II equity to risk weighted assets of 8 per cent. On the basis of given information answer the following questions:

(a) Estimate the Risk Weighted Assets (RWA) of the bank.

(b) Estimate the minimum amount of Tier I and Tier II capital the bank should be maintaining on its balance sheet?

(c) Does the bank have sufficient capital on its balance sheet?

CASE ANALYSIS EXERCISE

C9.1 Financial Conditions Index

There is a large body of literature on extracting signals about the real economy from financial variables. Economists and analysts have often used different financial prices as lead indicators of the future course of the economy. Interest rates and interest rate spreads are considered to be useful in predicting the course of the economy (Bernanke, 1990). The shape of the yield curve, i.e. the term structure of interest rates, contains information about the expectations of market participants about the state of the economy in the future. The yield curve contains considerable information on the future path of inflation for horizons of more than one year.

Similarly, the spread between three-month commercial paper (CP) and three-month Treasury bill (T-bill) depicts the credit default risk associated with corporates (if liquidity spread can be ignored). Stock and Watson (1989) have found that the spread between CP and T-bill rates, 10-year and 1-year government bond, housing starts, manufacturer's unfulfilled orders in durable goods industries and growth of part-time work are good predictors of business cycles.

Studying the movements in different financial assets in isolation, however, may be of limited use as each price contains information only about a certain aspect of the economy and does not necessarily reveal much about other aspects. This problem can be overcome by constructing an index using the relevant financial variables. This kind of index is usually called a Financial Conditions Index (FCI) and it summarises information about the future state of the economy contained in current financial variables (Hatzius et al., 2010). In essence, the FCI analyses the synthesis of various, sometimes contradictory, signals from financial markets.

Indices, such as the Bank of Canada's Monetary Conditions Index, Macroeconomic Advisers Monetary and Financial Conditions Index (MFCI), Bloomberg Financial Conditions Index (BBFCI), Goldman Sachs Financial Conditions Index (GSFCI), Federal Reserve of Kansas City Financial Stress Index (KCFSI), OECD FCI, and Monetary Conditions Index for India (Kannan et al., 2006) have been constructed at various times. Drawing from the literature, a FCI for India has been constructed in a principal components analysis framework using monthly data between January 2004 and March 2012. While indices have been computed for money market, bond market, forex market and stock market, an aggregate financial conditions index that covers all segments is also computed (Table 9.5).

Table 9.5 Components of the Financial Conditions Index

<table>
<tr><td>Call Spread (Call Rate - Effective Policy Rate)
CBLO Spread (Effective Policy Rate - CBLO Rate)
Market Repo Spread (Effective Policy Rate - Market Repo Rate)
Short Spread (3m CP - 3m T-Bill)</td><td>Money Market FCI</td><td rowspan="4">Aggregate FCI</td></tr>
<tr><td>10 yr G-Sec Yield
Long Spread (10 yr AAA Corp Bond - 10 yr G-Sec)
Medium Spread (5 yr AAA Corp Bond - 5 yr G-Sec)</td><td>Bond Market FCI</td></tr>
<tr><td>Exchange Rate
3-month Implied
Volatility Forex CMAX</td><td>Forex Market FCI</td></tr>
<tr><td>S&P CNXNifty Annual Returns
PE Ratio of S&P CNX Nifty
S&P CNX Nifty Market capitalisation to GDP Ratio</td><td>Stock Market FCI</td></tr>
</table>

The index has been constructed so that high values depict accommodative financial conditions, whereas low values depict tight financial conditions. It may be seen from Figure 9.13 that the financial conditions index captures the stressed financial conditions in the wake of the global financial crisis.

Evidently, the index shows highly stressed financial conditions in October 2008, just after the collapse of Lehman Brothers. The usefulness of the FCI should be appreciated in the context of its ability to forecast or explain economic variables like GDP, IIP and inflation. The correlation of FCI with growth rates of GDP and IIP are 0.43 and 0.60, respectively, which are statistically significant. The recovery in financial conditions has broadly been in line with recovery in the IIP and GDP growth rates (Figure 9.14). However, more research is called for to establish the link between the aggregate financial conditions index and economic variables.

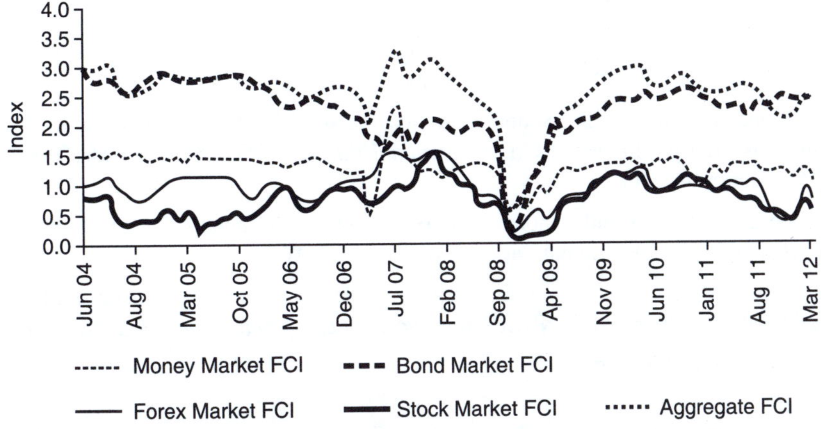

Figure 9.13 Movement in Financial Conditions Index for India.

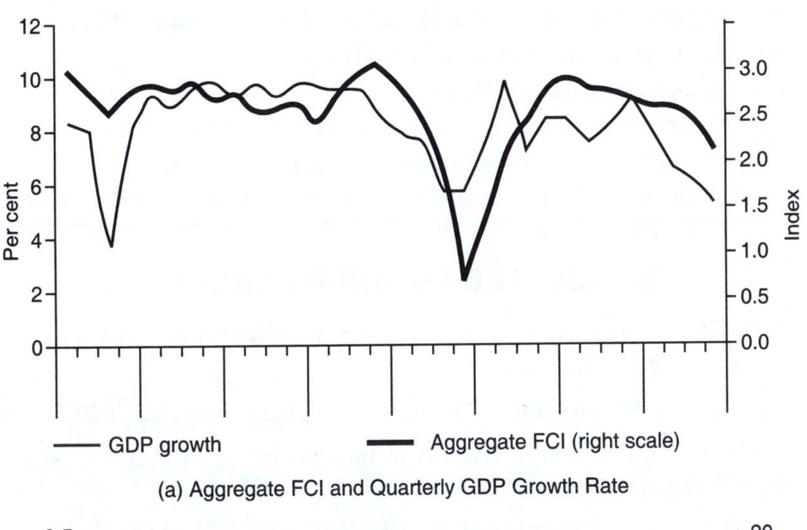

(a) Aggregate FCI and Quarterly GDP Growth Rate

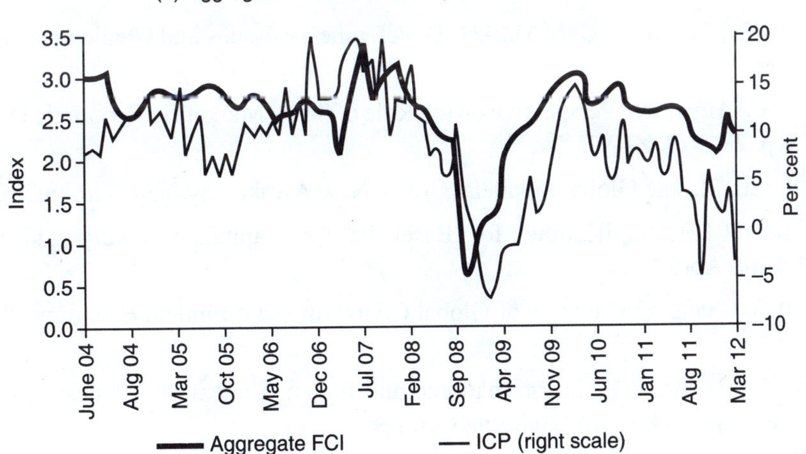

(b) Aggregate FCI and IIP Annual Growth Rate

Figure 9.14 Trends in FCI, GDP and IIP.

References

Bernanke, Ben S. (1990), "On the Predictive Power of Interest Rates and Interest Rate Spreads." *New England Economic Review*, November/December, pp. 51–68.

Hatzius, J.P., Hooper F., Mishkin K., Schoenholtz and Watson M. (2010), "Financial Conditions Index: A Fresh Look after the Financial Crisis", *National Bureau of Economic Research*, Working Paper, No.16150, Cambridge, July.

Kannan, R., Siddhartha Sanyal and Binod Bihari Bhoi (2006), "Monetary Conditions Index for India", *Reserve Bank of India*, Occasional Papers, Vol. 27, No. 3, Winter

Stock, J. and Watson M. (1989), "New Indexes of Coincident and Leading Economic Indicators," in O. Blanchard and S. Fischer (Eds.), NBER *Macroeconomics Annual* (*Cambridge*, MA: MIT), 352–94.

Source: RBI (2012), Annual Report.

Questions

1. Which financial indicators can be used for predicting the course of an economy?
2. Which indicator depicts the credit default risk associated with corporates? Why?
3. Which indicators are good predictors of business cycles?
4. Why is a financial condition index prepared?
5. What are the different financial condition indices available in the literature?
6. What are the sub-components of financial condition index (FCI) in India?
7. What does the high value of FCI indicate? How would you interpret the low value of the FCI?

SUGGESTED FURTHER READING

Chakrabarty, K.C. (2013), Contemporary Issues in Banking: Reflections on Viewpoints of a Bank Economist, *RBI Bulletin*, January.

Chakrabarty, K.C. (2013), Indian Banking Sector:Pushing the Boundaries, *RBI Bulletin*, March.

Chakrabarty, K.C. (2012), Crisis Preparedness in Interconnected Markets: Prevention is Better than Cure, *RBI Bulletin*, February.

Khan, H.R. (2012), Corporate Debt Market: Developments, Issues and Challenges, *RBI Bulletin*, November.

Kohi, V. (2012), A Historical Perspective on the Role of Stock Markets in Economic Development, *EPW*, Sep. 28, Vol. XLVII, No. 36.

Mahapatra, B. (2012), The Global Financial Crisis: New Awakening, *RBI Bulletin*, February.

Mahapatra, B. (2012), Implications for Basel III for Capital, Liquidity and Profitability *RBI Bulletin*, April.

Sinha, A. (2012), Changing Counters of Global Crisis: Impact on Indian Economy, *RBI Bulletin*, April.

Subbarao, D. (2012), Basel III in International and Indian Context: The Questions We Should Know the Answers For, *RBI Bulletin*, October.

CHAPTER **10**

Monetary Policy and Economic Environment

10.1 INTRODUCTION

Recently, the Reserve Bank of India in its Annual Monetary Policy for 2011–12, raised the **repo rate** (i.e., is the rate at which it lends to banks and other financial institutions) and **reverse repo rate** (i.e., the rate at which it borrows from financial institutions) by 50 basis points to 7.25 per cent and 6.25 per cent, respectively. It also announced a hike in the saving deposit rate from 3 per cent to 4 per cent.

Bankers, corporates and industry groups all reacted strongly to such announcements. The bankers, heading major commercial banks like the SBI and the ICICI, indicated that the increase in the rates would be passed on to their customers. Corporates and industry groups, reflecting negative sentiments, hinted that the hike will affect the most the interest sensitive sectors such as housing, automobiles and consumer durables, and constrain capacity expansion. The overall strong negative sentiments on the rate hike led to a sharp correction in the BSE Sensex by a whopping 463 points.

After some days of announcement, one of my colleagues, looking stressed, pointed out that he has not been able to sleep properly for last several days and having a headache. The reason for his headache was simply the increase in the lending rates by commercial banks as a reaction to the hike in the repo and reverse rates by the RBI. Three months ago, when he had started searching for a flat, the interest rate was around 8 to 9 per cent. Recently his search for the flat was over and he approached the bank with all the relevant documents. To his disappointment, he realized that meanwhile the rate has increased and the flat will cost him much more than what it was when he had started his search. Finally, in the wake of hike in the lending rates, he decided to postpone his plans of purchasing a flat.

The monetary policy announcements resulting in the hike in the saving deposit rate made me also readjust my saving pattern. I have started keeping more of my saving in my savings account (which gives now slightly better return) than cash in hand (which does not provide any return).

Thus, we see that monetary policy changes do affect our economic decisions. Monetary policy is an important instrument of influencing economic activities and economic management. It affects economic activities by managing the supply of money as well as influencing the demand for money by altering the cost and availability of credit. Households and business units make spending and investment decisions based upon current and expected income, wealth, price and interest rates, all of which are influenced by past, current and expected future monetary policy actions. By affecting the demand side of an economy, monetary policy tries to moderate business fluctuations—economy-wide recessions and booms arising from changes in aggregate demand. Though considered to be an effective instrument in managing demand, it is not viewed to be very effective in managing the supply side issues, such as enhancing productive capacity, improving the production of agriculture or other goods.

Given its significant influence on economic environment, in this chapter we will try to understand in greater detail what monetary policy means, what are its objectives, how it is implemented and operationalized and through what mechanism it influences the different sectors of an economy. Accordingly, Section 10.2 outlines the objectives of monetary policy. Section 10.3 briefs on the types of monetary policy which can be pursued in different economic scenarios and set-ups. Instruments of monetary policy and their mechanism of operations are described in Section 10.4. This section also describes the operating mechanism of various policy instruments used by the RBI, the central bank of India. Section 10.5 details on the monetary policy framework and elaborates on the operating procedure of monetary policy in India. Channels through which monetary policy affects the various constituents of financial sector and the economy as a whole are described in Section 10.6.

10.2 OBJECTIVES OF MONETARY POLICY

Monetary policy is conducted with varied objectives (Figure 10.1, UBE 10.1). These objectives are outlined as follows:

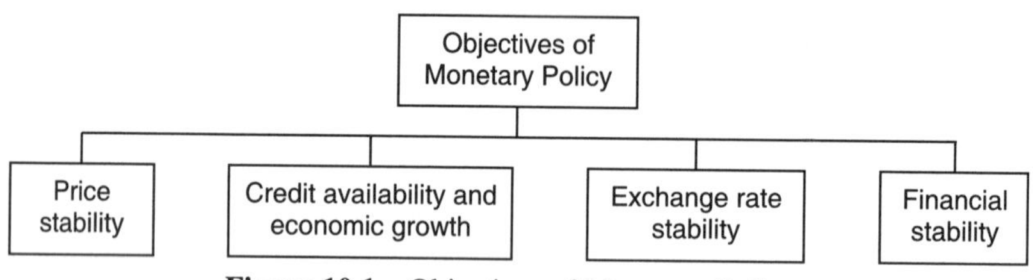

Figure 10.1 Objectives of Monetary Policy.

Price Stability

Sustained economic growth requires capital formation, which in turn depends on the level of saving. The stable price level, defined as low and stable inflation, creates conducive environment for saving, investment and growth. Thus, price stability is considered as a key objective of monetary policy.

Credit Availability and Sustained Economic Growth

Broadly speaking, sustained growth implies a sustained increase in per capita income. Two conditions are essential for sustained economic growth. First, there should be an expansion in productive capacity. Second, there should be corresponding increase in the demand for goods and services produced through this enhanced capacity. A mismatch between the two leads either to an underutilization of capacity, idle resources, unemployment and overall recession or an excess of demand fueling inflation. Either of these situations acts as a barrier to sustained high rate of economic growth. Thus, a sustained high rate of economic growth requires the demand for goods and services increasing at the same rate as the productive capacity. Monetary policy promotes sustained economic growth by minimizing fluctuations in business activity and fine tuning credit availability and money supply in concurrence with growth requirements. That is restricting credit and money supply when total demand for goods and services raises prices to unsustainable levels and expanding these when deficiency of money threatens the underutilization of resources.

Exchange Rate Stability

In an open economy framework, monetary policy is also entrusted with stabilizing the value of domestic currency vis-á-vis foreign currency as changes in exchange rates, as we will see in Section 12.4, can have a large destabilizing impact on an inflow of trade and capital flows as well as on inflation, employment and output. At the micro-level, the changes in the exchange rate also affect the balance sheet of the residents by affecting their transactions in foreign currency.

Financial Stability

Financial stability implies uninterrupted financial transactions, confidence in the financial system amongst all the participants, and absence of excess volatility in financial markets. A weak and unstable financial system leads to financial crises, and adversely affects the functioning of an economy. For an uninterrupted growth it is utmost important to have an efficient and stable financial system.

UNDERSTANDING BUSINESS ENVIRONMENT

UBE 10.1 Objectives of Monetary Policy in Developed and Emerging Market Economies

Multiple objectives can be achieved through monetary policy. However, objectives of monetary policy differ widely in developed countries vis-a-vis emerging market economies as described in this UBE.

Price stability though remains the core objective of monetary policy in most countries; many countries operate monetary policy to achieve multiple economic and social objectives (Table 10.1).

Table 10.1 Objectives of Monetary Policy

Central bank	*Objective*
	Developed Economies
Australia	Stability of the currency, maintenance of full employment, and economic prosperity and welfare.
Canada	Low and stable inflation.
ECB	Price stability primary objective. Without prejudice to the objective of price stability, also support the general economic policies with a view to contributing to a high level of employment and sustainable and non-inflationary growth.
Japan	Price stability and stability of the financial system.
New Zealand	Maintaining a stable general level of prices.
UK	Monetary stability—meaning stable prices and confidence in the currency and financial stability.
USA	Maximum employment, stable prices and moderate long-term interest rates.

Central bank	Objective
	Emerging Market Economies
China	Stability of the currency and thereby promote economic growth.
India	**Price stability and credit availability.**
Indonesia	Achieve and maintain currency stability by maintaining monetary stability and by promoting financial system stability.
Malaysia	Safeguard the value of the currency, promote monetary stability and a sound financial structure and influence the credit situation to the advantage of the country.
Mexico	Price stability.
Russia	Stability of currency, development of banking system and efficient settlement system.
South Africa	Financial stability.
Thailand	Maintain monetary stability.

Source: RBI (2005), Report on Currency and Finance 2003–04.

Amongst advanced economies, the US Federal Reserve, for example, has assigned multiple objectives to monetary policy. Monetary policy is carried out with the objective of price stability, maximum employment, and moderate long-term interest rates.

Some countries follow hierarchical objectives. For example, for the European Central Bank (ECB) the primary objective of monetary policy is price stability. However, it also pursues certain other objectives such as high level of employment and sustainable growth given the stable price level.

On the other hand, countries like Canada and New Zealand operate their monetary policies with the sole focus on price stability.

Price stability also remains a key objective of monetary policy in emerging market economies. However, given their key role in promoting economic growth, central banks of many of these countries pursue multiple objectives. Growing liberalization and opening up of these economies have also necessitated the pursuance of exchange rate and financial stability as the goal of monetary policy. For example, in Indonesia and Malaysia the monetary policy is pursued with the objective of achieving exchange rate and financial stability.

However, many of the emerging market economies have adopted inflation targeting (Box 7.3) framework during the 1990s, and thus, price stability remains the sole objective of monetary policy in these countries.

The emphasis of monetary policy in India is on price stability, provision of adequate credit for growth and curbing the use of credit for unproductive and speculative purposes, and financial stability. Besides these core objectives, the monetary and credit policy in India, also aims at strengthening the financial system of the country and achieving the objective of social justice.

10.3 TYPES OF MONETARY POLICY

Monetary policy design changes as per the goals set for it and the emerging economic scenario. Monetary policy is characterized as expansionary policy, contractionary policy, counter cyclical policy, rule based policy and discretionary policy as described hereinafter.

Expansionary Monetary Policy

An **expansionary monetary policy**, also known as easy monetary policy, aims at expanding economic activities. An expansion is achieved by encouraging spending on goods and services by making credit available in larger quantities and cheaper rates.

Contractionary Monetary Policy

Conversely, contractionary or **tight monetary policy** aims at contracting economic activities with the objective of containing inflation. A contraction is achieved by reducing the amount of credit and increasing the cost of obtaining it.

Countercyclical Monetary Policy

A **countercyclical monetary policy** tries to contract economic activities during an expansionary phase and expand economic activities in a contractionary phase of a business cycle. The objective behind such a policy is to moderate cyclical fluctuations and stabilize an economy around its trend path.

Rule-based Monetary Policy

Under a **rule-based monetary policy**, money supply and related variables are controlled by pre-determined rules, norms and standards. For example, the rules can be that the country should pursue monetary policy in such a way that inflation rate does not cross 5 per cent per annum. Or the rule can be that the money supply growth should be adjusted periodically in concurrence with the GDP growth. Under such a regime, the central bank cannot use its discretion to change the values of these variables even when the existing economic scenario demands so. Hence, under a rule-based set-up, monetary policy plays a passive role.

Discretionary Monetary Policy

When the central bank, after assessing the emerging economic scenario and using its own judgment, changes the values of money supply and related variables rather than getting constrained by the pre-set rule, then the monetary policy is considered to be discretionary. It allows the central bank greater autonomy and an active role in the conduct of monetary policy.

10.4 INSTRUMENTS OF MONETARY POLICY

Monetary policy tries to regulate money supply. In broad terms, the **money supply** (M) consists of currency with the public and deposits of the public with the banks. Since the extent of currency or deposits that the public wants to keep with itself depends on the behaviour of the public, the central bank cannot directly control the money supply. However, money supply is related with the **high powered money** (H) (also known as the **base money**), which consists of currency with the public and reserves of commercial banks, can be more directly influenced by the central bank. The central bank influences H by influencing reserves, which can be manoeuvred by changing the policy instruments cash reserve ratio (CRR) (described in Section 10.4.1). M is related with the H by a multiplier, known as the money multiplier (m) (M = m.H). Given that the public maintains currency and deposits in some fixed proportion and banks hold reserve as some fixed proportion of deposits, money multiplier can be estimated by the following equation:

$$m = \frac{1 + Cr}{Cr + Rr}$$

where

Cr = Currency to Deposit Ratio = CRR

Rr = Reserves to Deposit Ratio

Apart from the CRR, other instruments of monetary policy are also used for influencing the behaviour of the public and commercial banks. However, the impact of various policy instruments is dependent on the structure of the economy, level of development of the financial sector, extent of integration of the financial markets and many such factors including the varying time lags (Box 8.2). The ways in which various monetary policy instruments are used for bringing in desirable changes are described hereinafter.

Broadly, monetary policy instruments can be classified into two broad categories, general or quantitative measures and selective or qualitative measures (Figure 10.2).

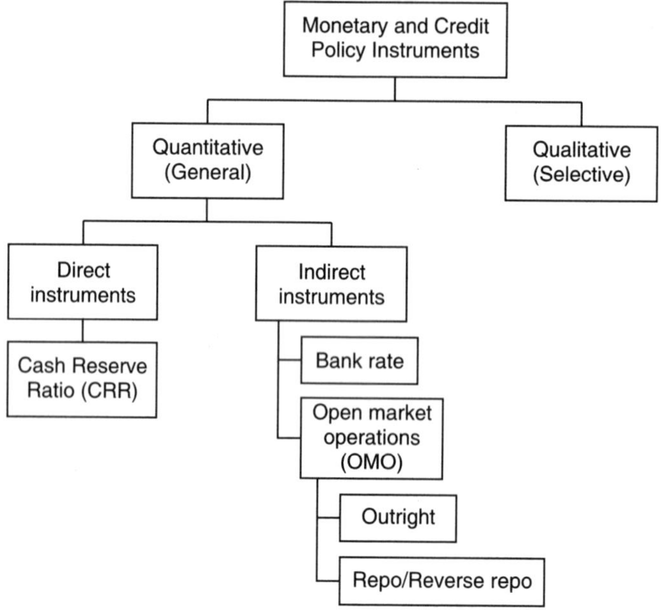

Figure 10.2 Monetary and Credit Policy Instruments.

Quantitative instruments, such as Cash Reserve Ratio (CRR), Bank Rate, Open Market Operations (OMOs) affect the total volume of credit by influencing the credit creating capacity of commercial banks; directly impounding or releasing resources with the banks or indirectly through their excess reserves.

Unlike the quantitative or general instruments of monetary policy, which affect the total volume of credit, the qualitative or selective credit control instruments affect the types of credit extended by banks. Rather than affecting the size of the portfolio of banks, these instruments affect the composition of it. The objective of imposing selective credit controls is to channelise the resources to priority areas by restricting their allocation to unproductive directions, by regulating both the amount and the terms of credit extended.

The broad characteristics of monetary policy instruments and their mechanism of operations are described hereinafter.

10.4.1 Direct Instruments

Direct instruments function according to regulations authorized to the central bank. These directly affect the volume, and via changes in the volume, the cost (interest rate) of bank reserves, credit and money supply. Thus, quantity of credit plays an important role in affecting the economy when direct instrument of credit control are employed by the central bank.

Cash Reserve Ratio

The proportion of total bank liabilities required to be kept as cash in hand or as balances with the central bank is known as the **Cash Reserve Ratio** (CRR). World over, banks are enforced, either by law or custom, to keep certain percentage of their total deposits with the central bank in the form of minimum cash reserves. Though by imposing the CRR the central bank assures itself that the bank is safe and has the liquidity for servicing its depositors, the variations in it also helps the central bank to regulate liquidity and, hence, money supply.

Mechanism of Operation

Alterations in the CRR affect the cash in the hands of banks and can have the effect on their credit creating capacity and thereby total money supply and overall liquidity in the system. For example, in a situation of excess liquidity, the central bank can raise the minimum CRR requirement. An increase in the cash reserve requirement increases the Required Reserves (RR) and reduces the Excess Reserves (ER), i.e., the funds available with the banks for the purpose of lending (Figure 10.3). Depleted cash reserves adversely affect the credit creation capacity of banks; banks would not renew the existing loans, call back part of the existing loans and not issue fresh loans leading to an overall decline in the credit (CR). We have seen that there is an inverse relationship between the reserves to deposit ratio and money multiplier. Thus, a hike in the CRR requirement, by reducing money multiplier, leads to a contraction in credit, and hence, money supply (Ms) in the system.

$$\uparrow CRR \longrightarrow \uparrow RR \longrightarrow \downarrow ER \longrightarrow \downarrow CR \longrightarrow \downarrow Ms$$

Figure 10.3 Impact of Increase in CRR on Money Supply.

Conversely, a reduction in the CRR increases the money multiplier and leads to an expansion of bank credit and total money supply and improves liquidity in the system.

The CRR is a quick way of controlling money supply. However, it is not without its drawback and may not be successful in achieving the desired objectives. The limitations of CRR are as follows:

1. The CRR may be ineffective in regulating money supply in an increasing interest rate scenario, especially when banks have excess reserves in their vault, i.e., they are already retaining the CRR much above the stipulated requirement. The opportunity cost of holding excess reserves rises in the increasing interest rate scenario. In such a scenario, the banks may circumvent the impact of a higher CRR requirement by utilizing their excess reserves for extending credit. Conversely, a reduction in the CRR may also fail to induce the banks to lend funds in a recessionary scenario where the demand for funds is not forthcoming inspite of low cost of credit.

2. The use of CRR as a tool of monetary policy may often bring inefficiency in the system. It impounds the resources available with the banks and reduces their maneuverability in portfolio allocation.
3. The CRR imposes an implicit tax on the banking system because the statutory reserves often do not carry any interest. Sometimes, this implicit tax is passed on to borrowers by banks in terms of higher interest rate on loans.
4. In many countries there are legal restrictions, in the form of minimum and maximum CRR, that limits the use of this instrument for policy purpose. For example, if the minimum statutory limit on CRR is 3 (implying that the central bank cannot reduce the CRR below this limit), then even in a very tight liquidity situation, where the requirement is to infuse credit and money supply in the economy, the central bank cannot reduce the CRR below 3 per cent, thus restricting the use of this instrument.

10.4.2 Indirect Instruments

Indirect instruments, rather than affecting the cost or volume of credit directly, influence these indirectly through the market mechanism. When market mechanism is allowed to play a role, it is the changes in the price rather than the quantity which bring in equilibrium in the market. Similarly, the price channel plays an important role in affecting an economy when indirect instrument of credit control are used by the central bank.

Bank Rate

The central bank provides credit to various financial institutions, but in many countries it is not direct credit, it is only through discounting process. That is, financial institutions can sell their already existing loans or other assets, such as securities of the government at a discounted price to the central bank to raise resources when they are in tight liquidity situations. The discount rate at which the financial institutions get their assets discounted and raise resources from the central bank is known as the **bank rate**. Thus, in simple terms, the bank rate is the minimum rate at which the central bank extend credit to financial institutions against the securities of the government and other approved first class securities. The changes in the bank rate, thus, affect the cost of borrowing for financial institutions. Given that the financial institutions set their lending rates (Box 10.1) taking into account the cost of borrowing, the changes in the bank rate are expected to affect the entire gamut of interest rates in an economy varying from lending rates to deposit rates.

Box 10.1 Lending Rates: Prime Lending Rate, Prime Term Lending Rates, Benchmark Prime Lending Rate and Base Rate

In most countries, financial institutions determine some base or benchmark rate which becomes the basis for determining the rates on their lending for different purposes and tenures. Some countries decide this rate for their most credit worthy customer while others decide the minimum which they can charge and still remain viable. Accordingly, the term used for this basic rate varies. Some of these terms are explained below:

Prime Lending Rate: The **Prime Lending Rate** (PLR) is a rate at which banks are expected to lend to their most creditworthy customers/borrowers. The PLR apart from covering the cost of funds, covers the risk premium perceived by banks on their most creditworthy customers. This way of determining rates lacks transparency as the extent of risk premium charged to each customer is not clearly revealed.

Prime Term Lending Rates: The **Prime Term Lending Rates** (PTLRs) are tenure-based PLRs. That is, for different slabs of maturity period there can be different PLRs.

Benchmark Prime Lending Rate: The **Benchmark Prime Lending Rate** (BPLR) is a rate around which banks lend money. The BPLR reflects the actual cost and is calculated on the basis of four fundamental and transparent parameters as follows:

- Actual cost of funds
- Operational cost
- A minimum margin to cover regulatory requirement of provisioning/capital charge (dividend outgo and coupon rate in the case of tier II capital)
- Profit margin

This rate, though similar to the PLR, is more transparent, because it does not include the risk attached to the most creditworthy customer.

It is referred to as the **benchmark rate** because it acts as a benchmark. All other rates set by financial institutions can be below or above this rate depending on the tenure of the loans and the risk involved in it.

Base Rate: The **base rate (BR)** includes all those elements of the lending rates that are common across all categories of borrowers. The formula for calculating the base rate takes into account the cost of deposits, cost of complying with CRR and SLR requirements (the money notionally lost by the bank in statutory obligations that throw off no interest), general overhead costs and the profit margin. The actual rate charges on a loan can be a sum of two costs: a base rate plus borrower specific charges, i.e., the tenure of the loan (implying higher cost for longer duration loans) and credit risk attached to a particular borrower (implying that an unsecured loan will face a higher cost than that secured by a collateral).

This rate appears to be very similar to the BPRL. However, there is a fundamental difference between the two. The BPLR is the benchmark rate. The actual rate can be lower or higher than this rate, while the base rate is the minimum rate. Theoretically, the actual rate cannot be below this. Thus, this is the minimum rate which financial institutions can charge and still remain viable.

India has experimented with all these rates. With a view to provide banks more freedom to determine their interest rates, the banks were allowed in October 1997, to prescribe separate Prime Term Lending Rates (PTLRs) with the approval of their boards for term loans of three years and above, apart from the freedom to fix separate PLRs for cash credit and loan components. However, with the introduction of BPLR in 2003, as all the lending rates could be determined with reference to this rate, the system of tenor linked PLR was discontinued. The BPLR was the ceiling rate for credit upto ₹2 lakh. Banks could determine the lending rates on loans and advances with limits in excess of ₹2 lakh with respect to the BPLR. Home loans and other personal loans were fixed independent of the BPLR. Banks offered the loans below the BPLR to exporters and other creditworthy borrowers (including the public enterprises). While experimenting with this rate it was realized that 70 per cent of the bank customers received loans below the BPLR. The BPLR system lacked transparency because customers could not know very clearly why they were charged below or above the benchmark rate. To bring in more transparency, the BPLR has been replaced by the BR effectively from 1 July 2010.

Different banks call their BPLR and base rate by different names. For example, ICICI BPLR is known as I-BAR whereas its base rate is known as the I-BASE.

Thus, changes in the Bank Rate (BR) affect credit creation by banks through altering the cost of credit.

To the general public, the bank rate acts as a barometer of economic activities and indicates the stance of monetary policy. A rise in the bank rate indicates that there is too much liquidity in the economy which the central bank wants to control (tighten) by pursuing tight or restrictive monetary policy. Conversely, a reduction in the bank rate is reflective of an easy monetary policy which the central bank pursues when there is a liquidity shortage in the economy.

Mechanism of Operation

Changes in the bank rate affect the cost of funds for banks and other financial institutions. The changes in the cost of funds of financial institutions then get reflected in their lending rates which are important determinants of demand for credit. Thus, by making appropriate changes in the bank rate, the central bank can indirectly influence the lending rates, and thereby, regulate indirectly the demand and volume of total credit. The channels through which the bank rate affects money supply is explained as follows:

In times of excess liquidity, for example, by raising the bank rate, the central bank makes the funds/reserves available from it costlier for financial institutions. This can affect money supply in two ways.

1. An increase in the Bank Rate (BR) may discourage financial institutions to get rediscounted their bills and to borrow funds (FBR) from the central bank. Limited resources constrain the ability of financial institutions to expand credit (CR) and contract the supply of money (Figure 10.4).

↑BR → ↓FBR → ↓CR → ↓Ms

Figure 10.4 Impact of Increase in Bank Rate: Quantity Channel.

2. Financial institutions may not reduce the demand for funds, but to remain viable and profitable they may pass on the higher cost of funds to their customers in the form of higher Lending Rates (LR), discouraging customers to seek credit from them and in the process reducing the supply of money (Figure 10.5).

↑BR → ↑LR → ↓CR → ↓Ms

Figure 10.5 Impact of Increase in Bank Rate: Price Channel.

In either case, if the alternative sources of funds (i.e., the funds in the form of deposits) are equally difficult to access, the money supply will contract.

On the contrary, in a situation of liquidity shortage, the bank rate is reduced by the central bank to encourage financial institutions to approach it more frequently for rediscounting of their bills and access resources. The money supply increases as more bills discounting results in excess reserves or funds for lending purpose with financial institutions.

Alternatively, reduction in the bank rate, reduces the cost of funds for financial institutions, which is passed on to their customers in the form of lower lending rates. A reduction in lending rates increases demand for credit from financial institutions and, thereby, enhances money supply. Thus, the bank rate affects money supply indirectly rather than directly.

Limitation of Bank Rate as an Instrument of Monetary and Credit Policy

The bank rate is an indirect instrument of credit control and its impact depends on the behaviour of various economic agents. In a highly expansionary situation, when businessmen are expecting booming economy and high profitability, there is an overall optimism. As businessmen do not mind paying higher interest rate on their credit in a booming economy. Therefore, the central bank may not be able to limit the borrowings by increasing the bank rate in an expansionary situation. The central bank, hence, sometimes control credit by refusing to rediscount bills or by imposing tight prudential norms on the banks resorting to this route too often. On the contrary, in a slowdown or recession, when there is an overall pessimism, nobody looks for funds even at cheaper rates. Hence, such a situation the reduction in the bank rate may not be able to induce the public to borrow more from financial institutions.

Open Market Operations (OMO)

Open Market Operations (OMO) refer to the sales or purchases by the central bank of a variety of assets, such as foreign exchange, gold, and government securities. These operations or transactions are either outright or repurchase agreements as depicted in Figure 10.6 and described as follows:

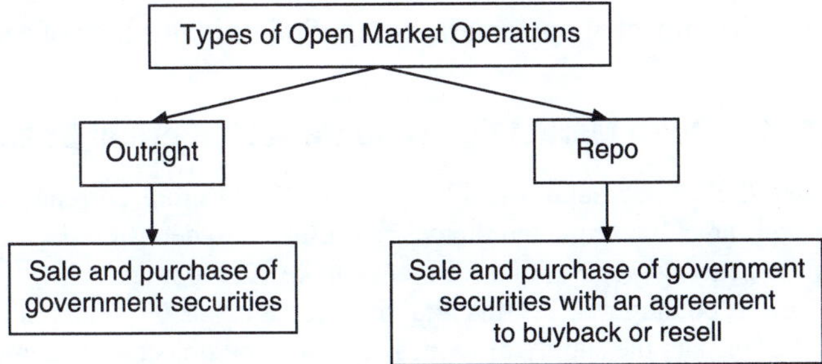

Figure 10.6 Types of Open Market Operations.

1. Outright OMO: The outright sale of any of the assets by the central bank, from its own account, leads to an absorption of liquidity and reduction in money supply from the market forever by impounding the resources of financial institutions in these securities. Conversely, the outright purchase of any of these assets leads to an injection of liquidity or expansion of money supply in the system for a prolonged period of time. OMOs are the most convenient and flexible tools that the central bank has for affecting money supply. However, as these are carried out most often using the government securities, these can be employed on a regular basis only by the central banks of those countries that have developed markets for these securities, implying that there are enough buyers and sellers for these securities at any point of time.

2. Mechanism of operations: During an expansionary and booming economy, to mop up the excess liquidity from the system, the central bank sells government and other approved securities (GS) from its own portfolio (we should remember that the central bank also acts as the banker to the government, and hence, it also trades in government securities on behalf of the government. Such operations are not OMOs because here the trade is not from its own account). The buyers of these securities pay to the central bank by writing a cheque on their deposits held with their commercial banks for payment. After clearance, the amount of deposits with the bank declines by the amount of the value of the government securities purchased by the public from the central bank, which in turn reduces the bank reserves (RE). The reduction in the bank reserves implying, a reduction in cash in hand, adversely affects their credit (CR) creating capacity. Money supply in circulation gets reduced and the expansionary process gets choked in the due course (Figure 10.7).

↑GS ⟶ ↓RE ⟶ ↓CR ⟶ ↓Ms

Figure 10.7 Impact of OMOs: A Link.

Conversely, to fight a slump, the central bank buys the government and other approved securities from domestic agents. It pays for these securities by issuing cheques drawn on itself. The agents, purchasing these securities, deposit the cheques with their respective banks. The central bank honours these cheques, on presentation, often by printing new notes. On the one hand, this increases the financial assets as well as monetary liabilities on the balance sheet of the central bank leading to an expansion in the high powered money. On the other hand, it expands the excess reserves of the banking organizations and their credit creating capacity. The expansion in the credit enhances money supply and boosts up the investment and employment opportunities and helps recovering from the slump.

Box 10.2 explains the impact of open market operations with the help of a numerical example.

Box 10.2 Open Market Operations: A Numerical Example

Suppose in a country the money supply is ₹1,500 crore (₹500 crore currency and ₹1,000 crore deposits). Bank reserves are ₹100 crore and the desired reserves to deposit ratio is 0.1. Consumption and production requirement puts the demand for money to be ₹2,000 crore.

The central bank of the country realizes this liquidity shortage, i.e., the situation where the demand for money is much higher than the supply of money. To meet the objective of economic growth, the central bank plans to bridge this gap by infusing liquidity. It makes an assessment of money multiplier which, given that the reserves to deposit ratio is 0.1, turns out to be 10, implying that an increase of ₹1 in the base money would lead to an expansion of money by ₹10. Given the money multiplier of 10, the central bank decides to bridge this gap of ₹500 crore between the demand for money and the supply of money. It decides to infuse this liquidity by purchasing government securities worth ₹50 crore through open market operations.

Open market purchases by the central bank put additional ₹50 crore with the public. Assuming that the public wants to keep only ₹500 crore as currency, it deposits the entire ₹50 crore with the banks raising the reserves of the banking system from ₹100 crore to ₹150 crore. Finding themselves with excess reserves the banks extend credit to their clients. The multiple rounds of lending and deposits ultimately raise the bank reserves and deposits to ₹1,500 crore (₹150 crore/0.1) and money supply to ₹2,000 crore (₹500 crore (currency) + ₹1,500 crore (deposits)).

3. Limitation of the OMO as a tool of monetary and credit policy: The success of OMO depends on the expansion of credit by banks in the event of additional cash in hand with them and the contraction of credit by them in a situation of reduction in their cash balances. However, this may not materialize as the expectations play an important role in economic decisions. In a booming economy, the public expects higher profit and, hence, does not mind paying higher interest. Therefore, in such a situation even if the central bank hikes the policy rates it will not discourage the public approaching their banks for credit. Since customers are willing to pay higher rates the banks will oblige them by extending credit and will not lock up their funds in securities offered under the OMO. On the contrary, in a slump, business failures are frequent occurrence and lending becomes risky. In such a situation, banks rather than lending prefer either holding more cash in hand or park their excess funds in government securities. Therefore, the central bank may not be successful in purchasing government securities from banks and other financial institutions through the OMO.

Thus, the success in infusing liquidity through this route may be constrained. As the limited stock of government securities may constrain the effectiveness of this instruments, countries like India have devised some special shemes (such as Market Stabilization Scheme (UBE 10.4) for manoeuvering sudden surge in liquidity especially emerging from large inflow of foreign capital.

Repo/Reverse Repo

The repo stands for the **repurchase agreement** and is also known as the **buyback**. It is a contract in which a participant acquires funds by selling securities, such as treasury bills. Simultaneously, he agrees to buy back or repurchase the same at a specified time and price known as the repo rate. Thus, in a repo transaction the party which sells securities with an agreement to repurchase it after a given time period in effect is borrowing funds for a short period by pledging the securities. Therefore, as we can see from Figure 10.8 a repo transaction simultaneously combines the sale/purchase of securities and also a short-term/money market borrowing/lending operations. As the lending and borrowing activity is backed up by underlying transaction in securities, the repo is also known as the **collateralized borrowing/lending**. A key distinguishing feature of the repo is that it can be used either to obtain funds or to obtain securities. As repos are short-term collateralized instruments, repo markets have strong links with interbank market, other money markets, securities markets and derivative markets.

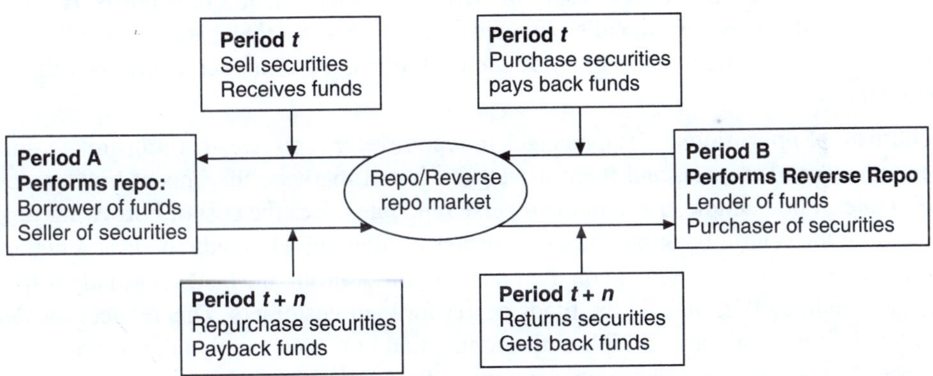

Monetary flows underlying the transactions are shown by arrows

Figure 10.8 Schematic Diagram of Repo Transaction.

The reverse repo is a mirror image of repo transaction. The reverse repo implies the purchase of securities with an agreement to sell them at a stipulated period of time and at a stipulated price. Looked from the angle of participant A (in Figure 10.8) the transaction is the repo transaction whereas, the same transaction, from the angle of participant B is the reverse repo.

The repo/reverse repo is attractive as a monetary policy instrument for two reasons. First, it carries a low credit risk or default risk, because it is backed up by the underlying government securities or other approved well-rated securities. Second, it is a very flexible tool because, unlike outright repo, this instrument absorbs or injects liquidity only temporarily. Hence, it can be used for manoeuvering liquidity on a day-to-day basis. Therefore, central banks often regularly use it for injecting and withdrawing liquidity from the market when they expect the liquidity problem to be only for a short-term, i.e., a day or so.

Internationally, the practice is to define repo/reverse repo from the side of the market participants. Thus, the repo by a central bank implies the purchase of securities from the market leading to an injection of liquidity, and the reverse repo implies the sale of securities leading to an absorption of liquidity from the market. In a situation of tight liquidity, where the need of the hour is to improve liquidity situation, the central bank purchases government securities from market participants. To make the payment for the purchases of these securities the central banks often print new notes. Therefore, repo transaction by the central bank often results in a higher money supply and higher liquidity. Conversely, in a situation of excess liquidity, the central bank mop ups the liquidity by performing reverse repo, i.e., by selling government securities with an agreement to buy back these after a stipulated period of time. The purchasers of these securities pay the central bank. Thus, money supply is withdrawn from the market for stipulated period of time. Injection/absorption of liquidity get reversed when repos/reverse repos mature. Thus, central banks can absorb/inject liquidity simply by not renewing some fraction of repos/reverse repo falling due.

In some cases, the repo and reverse repo are used for signaling the stance of monetary policy to the market participants. Central banks perform a fixed rate auction when they want to indicate the desired level of rates or signal a change in the policy. Sometimes repo and reverse repo rates are used to define an upper and a lower limit for short-term market interest rates such as that prevailing in call money market or treasury bill market or on certificates of deposits. A shift in the monetary policy stance is then signalled by adjusting the limits of the band explained as follows: Some repo rates, rather than being fixed by the central bank, are market determined through an auction system.

1. Mechanism of operations: The changes in repo/reverse repo rates get transmitted, initially, to other money market rates, and then in well-integrated markets, the impact trickles down to long-term rates. For example, a rise in the reverse repo rate raises the cost of borrowing funds for banks because the central bank purchases securities or alternatively lends funds at a higher rate. To nullify the impact of this increase on their net margins or profit, the banks normally respond by raising their lending rates, making the funds dearer for their customers. This reduces the demand for credit and, through money multiplier, the contraction in money supply takes place.

Since changes in repo/reverse repo get transmitted to other rates, these are used for absorbing and influencing liquidity as follows:

In the presence of excess liquidity, reflecting the excess of supply of funds over the demand, the call rates and other money market rates keep on declining continuously. A sharp reduction or increase in any price or rate is never desirable. Hence, to prevent further deceleration in money market rates, the central bank may intervene in the market by performing reverse repo, i.e., selling securities and creating artificial demand for funds in the market and absorbing the excess liquidity from the system. Thus, reverse repo rate sets a floor to money market rates. On the contrary, in the presence of severe shortage of funds in the money market, the central bank performs repo, creates artificial supply of funds and prevents money market rates reaching a very high level. Thus, repo/reverse repo rates provide an interest rate corridor within which the money market rates are allowed to move.

For example, a situation of easy liquidity leads to a downward/leftward shift in the demand curve from D_0 to D_2 for loanable funds (i.e. loans) and the interest rates fall from r_0 to r_2 in Figure 10.9(a). As a sharp fall is not desirable, to prevent further fall in the rates, the central bank intervenes in the market by creating an artificial demand for funds by performing the reverse repo, i.e., it sells securities and borrows funds from the market. Such an intervention by the central bank shifts the demand curve for loanable funds from D_2 to D_1, increases the interest rate from the considerably low level of r_2 to the perceived reasonable floor rate of r_1. Conversely, in a situation of tight liquidity, when because of exogenous changes in the system the demand for short-term funds increases to a very high level resulting in a sharp increase in money market rates, the central bank performs repo (Figure 10.9(b)). This artificially increases the supply of domestic currency or funds in the system and shifts the supply curve of loanable funds downward/rightward and lowers the money market interest rates from a very high level, say r_4, to the reasonable rate of r_3 , i.e., a desired cap rate.

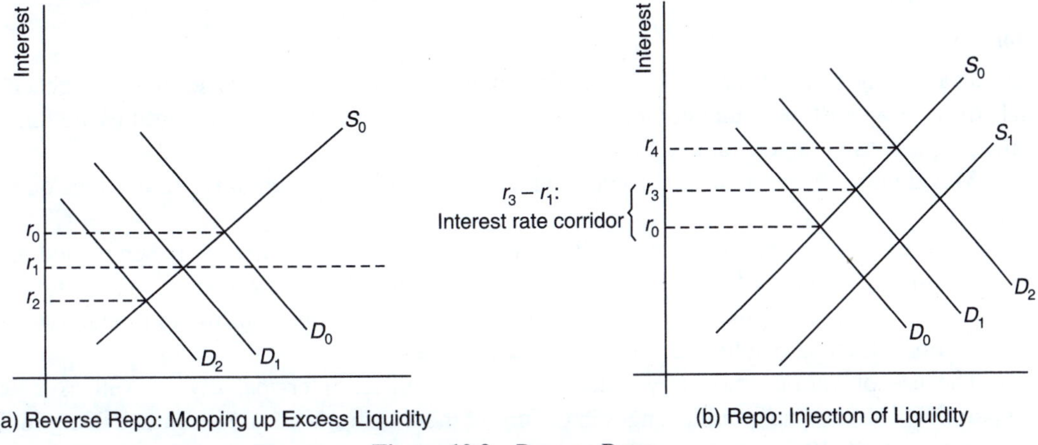

(a) Reverse Repo: Mopping up Excess Liquidity

(b) Repo: Injection of Liquidity

Figure 10.9 Reverse Repo.

2. Limitation of the repo as a tool of monetary and credit policy: The success of repo/reverse repo technique to control liquidity and money supply depends on the availability of sufficient stocks of government securities/other quality securities and the reverse repos maturing on appropriate days.

10.4.3 Qualitative or Selective Measures

Qualitative control measures are in the form of selective credit control measures or in the form of moral suasion.

Selective Credit Control Measures

Selective credit control measures adopted by the central bank try to fix the quantum as well as the cost of credit flowing to different areas of an economy. These can take various forms as follows:

1. Priority sector lending: The central bank sometimes imposes restrictions on financial institutions and makes them provide certain part of their total credit to the areas that are the priority to a country such as farmers, small scale industry, public sector units and exports. Such lendings are known as the priority sector lendings.

2. Differential interest rates: Depending on the priorities, the rates of lending to different sectors, at times, are specified by the central bank. For example, the lending to farmers, exporters or public sector units is often cross subsidized by charging lower rates to these sectors and higher rates to the other sectors.

3. Margin requirements: Higher **margin requirements** (i.e., the amount of funds as a proportion of total loans which the borrowers should have in hand) are sometimes fixed by the central bank to limit the supply of credit to unproductive (such as investment in stock market) or non-priority areas. These requirements often also vary with underlying securities.

4. Restrictions on bill rediscounting: The central bank may impose an upper limit on the bills that can be rediscounted by financial institutions with it. Sometimes, a higher rate of interest is charged to those financial institutions that frequently resort to the bill rediscounting process for accessing funds.

Moral Suasion

Periodically, letters are issued to banks urging them to exercise control over credit in general, and advances against particular commodities or unsecured loans. Sometimes priorities are hinted through speeches or in general discussions.

Moral suasion can be used for both qualitative control and quantitative restrictions on the credit.

Many of these measures can have a direct impact on the extent or direction of credit and may be very effective in times of emergency. The direct allocation of credit, however, may distort the market mechanism, may give wrong signals, and thus, may bring in distortion in production and consumption structure, resulting in sub-optimum outcomes.

The use of various monetary policy instruments differ inter-spatially as well as inter-temporarily. The inter-temporal changes in the use of these instruments are illustrated using India as the case in UBE 10.2.

UNDERSTANDING BUSINESS ENVIRONMENT

UBE 10.2 Monetary and Credit Policy Instruments in the Hands of RBI

The RBI, the central bank of India, has moved gradually from the direct instrument of credit control, such as the CRR, to the indirect instruments of credit control, such as the bank rate and repo rate, as described in this UBE.

In the pre-reform period, given a largely underdeveloped state of the financial system, regulated nature of financial markets and plan priorities, the RBI often resorted to the direct instruments of monetary policy, such as the CRR and SLR for allocating credit and regulating money supply in the economy. During this period, a very large part of the total credit available was diverted to the public sector through statutory requirements and other means. The cost of the credit was regulated through administered interest rate structure; the interest rate burden on the government and other priority sectors was kept low by subsidizing the credit to these sectors while charging higher rates to corporate entities, i.e., by **cross-subsidization**. Statutory pre-emptions in the form of CRR, SLR and priority sector lending impounded the resources of commercial banks, reduced the allocative efficiency of resources and adversely affected the viability of banks. These statutory pre-emptions imposed an indirect tax on the banking system because the CRR balances carry either no interest or very nominal interest, and the SLR investment provided a lower return because of artificially suppressed government and other securities qualified for this purpose.

Gradual liberalization and globalization of the Indian economy, strengthening and development of the financial system, restrictions on the automatic monetization of fiscal deficit, and various other changes in the economy made it possible for the RBI to operate with the indirect instruments of monetary policy, such as the bank rate, repo rate and OMOs. Accordingly, there has been a distinct shift in the monetary policy framework and operating procedures from direct instruments of monetary control to market based indirect instruments in the recent years. The thrust has been to provide the market mechanism a greater role in credit allocation, to provide banks more operational flexibility and to bring in an allocative efficiency in the economy. Below, the specific characteristics of various monetary policy tools available with the RBI are described. The changes taking place in these instruments have also been enumerated.

Cash Reserve Ratio: Banks in India are statutorily required to maintain certain proportion of their net demand and time liabilities (NDTL) (net of inter-bank liabilities) as cash in hand or balances with the RBI. In the pre 2006 period, the minimum **cash reserve requirement** (CRR) imposed by the statute was 3 per cent and the maximum was 15 per cent. These limits constrained the use of CRR as an instruments of monetary policy. With the amendment to the RBI Act, 1934, effective from 22 June 2006, the RBI permitted to fix the CRR for Scheduled Commercial Banks (SCBs) without any floor rate or ceiling rate for monetary stability considerations. It is also no longer obligatory for the RBI to pay interest on the CRR balances maintained by the scheduled commercial banks (SCBs).

The CRR remained a powerful instrument of monetary policy in the pre-reform period as financial markets were not developed for indirect instruments such as open market operations. The RBI used this instrument more frequently than the other instruments in this period for the reasons discussed hereinafter. The continuously increasing fiscal deficit and its monetization had put large pressure on inflation rate. To combat inflationary pressures, the RBI resorted to the CRR frequently which impounded the resources of commercial banks and helped the RBI to control money supply. However, the continuous increase in the CRR resulted in it reaching the statutory maximum of 15 per cent of NDTL on 1 July 1989 (Table 10.2). It remained at that level till 8 October 1992. The CRR being a non-earning asset, an increase in its value, in effect increased the implicit tax on banks which was passed by them on to the private corporate sector in the form of higher and higher PLR.

In the post-liberalized period, with a number of financial sector reforms in place, the RBI is attempting to reduce the emphasis on the use of CRR as an instrument of monetary control. Pursuing the medium-term objective of reducing the CRR, the RBI had reduced the CRR progressively from the peak of 15 per cent of NDTL in 1992, to 4.5 by 2003. However, the CRR has remained as one of the important tools of monetary policy even in the post-reform period, and has been used for liquidity management and stabilization, taking into account the liquidity conditions, inflation trends and other macroeconomic developments. For example, the reserve requirements were increased temporarily in 1997 to combat pressures arising from the contagion from the East Asian financial crisis. Again, the period from September 2004 till August 2008 witnessed a gradual increase in the CRR. During this period, the CRR was raised by 450 basis points to combat inflationary expectations. However, in response to the knock on effect of the global financial crisis on the Indian economy, the RBI reduced the CRR by a cumulative 400 basis points, to 5 per cent in four stages between 11 October 2008 and 17 January 2009. With the recovery of the economy and the build-up of inflationary pressures in the subsequent period, the CRR was gradually increased to 6 per cent by 24 April 2010. However, after a quick recovery in the post-crisis period the Indian economy faced a severe slowdown in 2011–12 and 2012–13, necessitating continuous infusion of liquidity by easing CRR. As on 22 May 2013 the CRR stood at 4 per cent.

Table 10.2 Cash Reserve Ratio on Some Selected Dates

Effective date	*Rate*	*Effective date*	*Rate*
16-09-1962	3.00	26-04-2008	7.75
22-09-1973	7.00	10-05-2008	8.00
21-08-1981	7.00	24-05-2008	8.25
01-07-1989	15.00	05-07-2008	8.50
17-04-1993	14.50	19-07-2008	8.75
25-10-1997	9.75	30-08-2008	9.00
6-12-1997	10.00	11-10-2008	6.50
24-02-2001	8.25	25-10-2008	6.00
25-08-2003	4.50	08-11-2008	5.50
18-09-2004	4.75	17-01-2009	5.00
02-10-2004	5.00	13-02-2010	5.50
23-12-2006	5.25	27-02-2010	5.75
06-01-2007	5.50	24-04-2010	6.00
17-02-2007	5.75	28-01-2012	5.50
03-03-2007	6.00	10-03-2012	4.75
14-04-2007	6.25	22-09-2012	4.50
28-04-2007	6.50	3-11-2012	4.25
04-08-2007	7.00	9-2-2013	4.00
10-11-2007	7.50		

Source: Compiled from RBI (2012), *Handbook of Statistics on Indian Economy and RBI* (2013), *Macroeconomic and Monetray Developments in 2012–13.*

Statutory Liquidity Ratio: Apart from the average daily balances that are required to be maintained in the form of CRR, the SCBs in India are also required to maintain the **Statutory Liquidity Ratio** (SLR). This can be maintained in the form of cash or gold, valued at a price not exceeding the current market price, or in unencumbered approved securities (i.e. those securities that are not already pledged somewhere else) valued at a price as specified by the RBI from time-to-time. For SLR requirement, which needs to be met on a daily basis, the demand and time liabilities as on the last Friday of the second preceding fortnight is considered. Before the amendment to the Banking Regulation Act, 1949 in 2007, the minimum and maximum SLR investment requirements were 25 per cent and 40 per cent, respectively at the end of any business day. However, the amendment removed the statutory minimum requirement of SLR with effect from January 2007.

The objectives of imposing SLR are two-fold.

1. It augments the investment of banks in government securities and makes available funds easily for the government.
2. Since government securities are default risk-free, by making bank investment in safe and more liquid assets it ensures solvency of banks.

The SLR was actively used in the pre-reform period. In this period continuously increasing government expenditure kept on increasing the government's borrowing requirement. Not only there was a large supply of government securities but, also the interest rate on these securities were maintained at artificially lower level by the **administered interest rate** regime. Underdeveloped structure of the market for government securities and the regulation of interest rate at artificially low level dampened the demand for these securities. Thus, to meet the continuously increasing government borrowing requirement, a very large part of the total funds available with banks were diverted to the government and the public sector through hikes in the SLR. The SLR became an instrument of mobilizing resources for the government from the captive financial system. The SLR reached to a peak of 38.50 per cent with effect from 22 September 1990 (Table 10.3).

Table 10.3 Statutory Liquidity Ratio on Some Selected Dates

Effective date	*Rate*	*Effective date*	*Rate*
16-03-1949	20.00	25-10-1997	25.00
16-09-1964	25.00	08-11-2008	24.00
05-02-1970	26.00	07-11-2009	25.00
25-09-1981	34.50	18-12-2010	24.00
06-02-1993	38.00	11-08-2012	23.00

Source: RBI (2012), *Handbook of Statistics on Indian Economy and RBI* (2013), *Macroeconomic and Monetary Developments in 2012–13.*

However, with the deepening and widening of the market for government securities in the post 1991 period, the SLR was gradually brought down to 25 per cent in 1997, the then statutory minimum. The SLR remained at that level almost for a decade. The unprecedented developments in 2008 consequent to the global financial crisis, however, mandated a further reduction in the SLR, and the ratio was reduced by 100 basis points to 24 per cent of banks NDTL effective from 8 November 2008. With the recovery in the sight, to contain inflationary pressures, the RBI kick started its accommodating monetary policy by increasing the SLR to 25 per cent in November 2009. However, in the face of acute liquidity crunch it was further revised downward to 24 per cent in December 2010. A persistent severe slowdown in economic activities in 2011–12 and 2012–13 further necessitated a downward revision in it. Accordingly, the SLR was eased to 23 per cent on 11 August 2012.

Bank Rate: In India, the **bank rate** is an administered rate, set by the monetary authority, and is not market determined. The bank rate acts as a signaling device and changes in it are aimed at reflecting changes in the medium-term stance of the policy. Changes in the bank rate are contemplated by the RBI taking into account the macroeconomic developments and the developments in the financial markets (expected growth rate in real GDP, rate of inflation and demand for money). However, in the pre-1997, the bank rate was not actively used as a monetary policy instrument. It got activated in 1997 and used frequently till 2003.

In the subsequent period, with discretionary liquidity being provided at the repo rate (as deliberated below) as and when required, the importance of the bank rate as a signalling rate reduced. The changes in the bank rate took place less frequently (after 2003 it was changed only in 2012), reflecting only the medium-term stance of the policy (Table 10.4). It emerged that, whereas, earlier changes in the repo rate were preceded by the changes in the bank rate, in the subsequent period the bank rate was changed after the changes in the repo rate. In a move to graduate towards single policy rate, since May 2011, a new monetary policy operating procedure has been adopted by the RBI. The new operating procedure has aligned bank rate as well as the reverse repo rate with the repo rate, which is the only independtly varying policy rate now. The bank rate, as of now, is aligned at 100 basis point above the repo rate and is not set independently.

Table 10.4 Bank Rate on Some Selected Dates

Date	*Bank rate*	*Date*	*Bank rate*
05-07-1935	3.50	02-03-2001	7.00
09-01-1971	6.00	23-10-2001	6.50
12-07-1981	10.00	30-10-2002	6.25
09-10-1991	12.00	30-04-2003	6.00
16-04-1997	11.00	14-02-2012	9.50
17-02-2001	7.50	11-08-2012	9.00

Source: RBI (2012), Compiled from *Handbook of Statistics on Indian Economy.*

In India, till recently the bank rate used to be the basic refinance rate at which the RBI used to refinance financial intermediaries, banks as well as non-banks, and provide liquidity support. With the activation of the bank rate in the late 1990s, the rates on various sector specific refinance facilities—food credit refinance, export credit refinance, government securities refinance, discretionary refinance, standby refinance, etc., were linked to the bank rate. However, over a period of time, with the objective of shifting monetary policy intervention from direct to indirect methods, many of these sector specific and discretionary refinance facilities have been consolidated and phased out. The move is towards a general refinance/liquidity adjustment facility. Export credit refinance and liquidity support to PDs are the only standing facilities available today, and they are now linked to the repo rate. Ways and means advances to the Centre and state governments have also been delinked from the bank rate and have been aligned with the repo rate. The bank rate is now mainly linked to certain specific operations of the RBI such as the CRR/SLR defaults, the Rural Infrastructure Development Fund (RIDF) and the general line of credit (GLC) scheme to the NABARD.

Open Market Operations

In India, Open Market Operations (OMOs) are conducted in government securities. However, a limited stock of government securities basically constrains the ability of the RBI to carry out the OMOs. In the pre-1991 period, the scope was further limited because of the underdeveloped government securities market and repressed interest rates.

In the pre-1991 period, OMOs were applied essentially to serve as an instrument of credit control and were primarily used to assist the GOI in its borrowing operations. Also, for the effective operations of the monetary policy the well-developed secondary market is essential. The greater degree of control of the RBI over the operations of commercial banks prohibited the functioning of the market for government securities. However, with the development of the government securities market, OMOs have been used effectively by the RBI to manage the medium-term liquidity. To maintain ample liquidity in the system, distressed from the spillover of the global crisis during 2008–09, along with other measures, the OMO (especially the purchases) were also carried out (Table 10.5). In the subsequent period in 2009–10 and 2010–11, to contain inflationary pressure, again OMO were used by reducing the purchases and increasing the sales. In the recent past in 2011–12 to overcome a severe slowdown, the RBI tried to infuge liquidity in the market by increasing OMP (purchase) and reducing OMO (sales).

Table 10.5 Open Market Operations by the Reserve Bank of India

(Amount in ₹ Crore)

Year	*OMO purchases*	*OMO sales*
1996–97	623	11,206
1997–98	467	8,081
1998–99	—	26,348
1999–00	1,244	36,614
2000–01	4,471	23,795
2001–02	5,084	35,419
2002–03	—	53,780
2003–04	—	41,849
2004–05	—	2,899
2005–06	740	4,653
2006–07	720	5,845
2007–08	13,510	7,587
2008–09	1,04,480	9,932
2009–10	85,399	9,931
2010-11	78,799	11,575
2011-12	1,42,272	8,187

Source: Compiled and estimated from RBI (2012), *Handbook of Statistics on Indian Economy.*

Repo/Reverse Repo

In India, two types of repo are in operation: inter-bank repo and RBI repo. The inter-bank repos are permitted under regulated conditions and used for raising funds to meet short-term mismatches between the demand for and the supply of funds. Besides banks, primary dealers are allowed to undertake both repo/reverse repo transactions. Non-bank participants are allowed in the repo market only as lenders. They can lend funds to other eligible participants. All government securities are eligible for repo. Repos have also been permitted in PSU bonds and private corporate securities provided they are held in the dematerialized form in a depository and the transactions are done in the recognized stock exchanges.

All Scheduled Commercial Banks (excluding the Regional Rural Banks (RRBs)) and Primary Dealers (PDs) having current account and SGL account with the RBI, Mumbai, are eligible to participate in the repo and reverse repo auctions.

As the tenure of repo/reverse repo in India is 1 to 14 days, this instrument has been used by the RBI for managing day-to-day or short-term liquidity. Over a period of time, the repo/reverse repo rates, set by the RBI, have become a sort of signalling rates along with the bank rate. These rates provide a corridor for the call money market (as seen in Figure 10.9). The quantity and the rate (Table 10.6) reflect the liquidity conditions prevailing in the market. Repo and reverse repo rates are also used as a part of the Liquidity Adjustment Facility (LAF) operations, which reflect the day-to-day pressure of marginal liquidity in the system. These rates constitute the interest rate corridor under the LAF. Any variation in these rates, hence, is perceived by the market as short-term interest rate signal arising from a change in the stance of the RBI. Since the implementation of the new operating system, the RBI sets only repo rate independently. The reverse repo rate is aligned to it, and maintained 100 basis point below the repo rate.

Table 10.6 Movements in Repo/Reverse Repo Rates

Effective since	*Repo rate*	*Reverse repo rate*
27-07-2010	5.75	4.50
16-09-2010	6.00	5.00
02-11-2010	6.25	5.25
25-01-2011	6.50	5.50
17-03-2011	6.75	5.75
03-05-2011	7.25	6.25
16-06-2011	7.50	6.50
26-07-2011	8.00	7.00
16-09-2011	8.25	7.25
25-10-2011	8.50	7.50
17-04-2012	8.00	7.00
29-01-2014	7.75	6.75
19-03-2013	7.50	6.50

Source: Compiled from RBI (2012), *Handbook of Statistics on Indian Economy and RBI* (2013), Macroeconomic and Monetary Developments, May.

10.5 MONETARY POLICY FRAMEWORK

Monetary authorities are responsible for achieving various objectives of monetary policy varying across countries and over a period of time from price stability to exchange rate stability to output growth. However, the implementation of monetary policy is encountered with several difficulties. The foremost difficulty is that the values of various variables that monetary policy aims at stabilizing are determined by the working of and interactions among various economic agents, which are in crores, and hence, cannot be monitored instantaneously and controlled directly. Another important problem is that it can take several years to impact these goals, during which the economic scenario may change and may require a different type of policy action than that was initiated in the previous scenario. For example, suppose an economy is facing a recession and the central bank implements an expansionary policy to overcome the problem. Suppose it takes 6 months of time for the expansionary monetary policy to impact the economy. Now, assume that after the implementation of the policy, because of good monsoon, the economy faces an expansion in economic activities and also some build-up of inflationary pressure. The expansionary policy initiated six months before, due to a lag of six months, will start showing its effect now and add on to the ongoing expansion. Such a policy will aggravate the problem of inflationary pressures.

Since ultimate or the final objectives or **goals of monetary policy** are not in direct control of monetary policy, the central bank often targets certain variables, known as **policy variables**. These variables have a close bearing on the **ultimate goals** and can be addressed directly by the central authorities. These **policy targets**, an example of which is interest rate, are **proximate goals**. Though these are not objectives in themselves, but if attended, help in achieving the ultimate goals. The policy targets are classified as intermediate targets and operating targets.

The **intermediate targets** are also not in direct control of monetary authorities. They cannot be hit very accurately and involve a substantial time lag. But, these have close bearing with the final objectives. The examples of intermediate targets are various monetary aggregates, such as M_1, M_2, M_3, and long-term interest rates, such as prime lending rate and treasury bond yields.

The **operating targets**, on the contrary, are tactical goals, can be influenced more directly and can be affected in much short duration by the central bank. The operating goals, such as bank reserves, base money and short-term benchmark rates, have a close bearing on the intermediate targets, such as various monetary aggregates and long-term interest rates. Therefore, though the intermediate targets cannot be affected directly, they can be influenced by affecting the operating targets using various monetary instruments.

Monetary policy instruments are the tools used by central banks to influence money market and credit conditions and pursue various monetary policy objectives by affecting the operating targets.

Thus, central banks, while conducting monetary policy, have to make decisions at both strategic and tactics (i.e., implementation) level (Figure 10.10). At the strategic level, the emphasis is on the minimization of the gap between goals and performance, whereas at the tactical or day-to-day basis central banks have to deal with the use of various policy tools for achieving the desired values of operating targets.

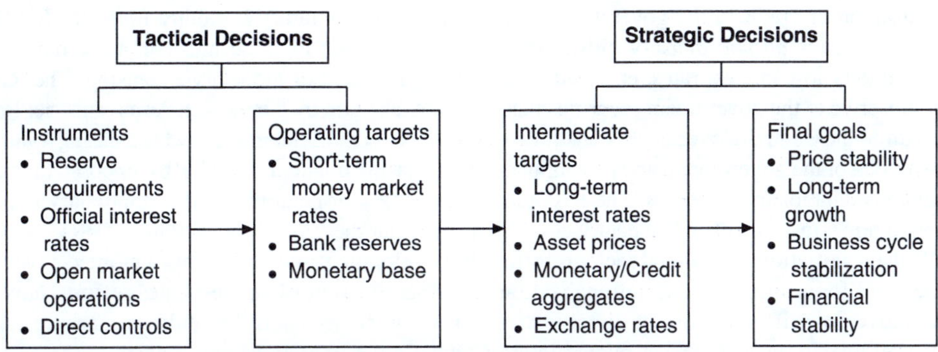

Figure 10.10 Monetary Policy Framework.

The operating procedure refers to the tactical or daily implementation of monetary policy by central banks. These cover the choice of monetary policy instruments (direct vis-a-vis indirect), width of a corridor for market interest rates (i.e., the range between minimum and maximum under which interest rates can be allowed to vary), monetary policy operating targets (money markets rates vis-a-vis bank reserves or price channel or quantity channel), the nature, extent and frequency (daily or weekly or fortnightly) of different money market operations and the manner of signalling policy intentions (bank rate or repo rate or OMO or CRR). The major challenge in day-to-day management is the selection of an appropriate level of operating target, and policy instrument that has stable and known relationship with the operating target. However, the success in this direction is not always guaranteed as the level of operating target can get affected by the market movements that may bring in instability and unpredictability in the relationship between the operating target and the instruments.

The success is also dependent on the stability of relationship between operating target and intermediate target. In the **monetary target framework**, this boils down to the stability and predictability of money multiplier, whereas the **interest targeting framework** requires a greater degree of relationship between short-term and long-term interest rates. For a successful conduct of monetary policy, equally important is the stable relationship between intermediate targets and final goals.

The **monetary policy framework** is illustrated in UBE 10.3 and UBE 10.4 using Indian context.

UNDERSTANDING BUSINESS ENVIRONMENT

UBE 10.3 Operating Procedure in India: Liquidity Adjustment Facility

Efficient operating procedure is required for desirable and timely impact of monetary policy on various economic problems. This UBE details on how the operating procedure has evolved over a period of time in India.

In the pre-reform period in India, the financial markets were highly segmented and regulated. Interest rate regulation, selective credit control and the CRR remained the main monetary policy instruments during this period. The administered interest rate regime kept the yield rate on government securities very low and the dispensation of credit to the government took place via the Statutory Liquidity Ratio (SLR). During this period, 91 days *ad hoc* treasury bills, and subsequent funding of these into non-marketable special securities at very low interest rates, emerged as the principal source of monetary expansion. The RBI had even to subscribe to the government securities that were not taken up by the market. As a result, net Reserve Bank credit to the Central Government constituted over 92 per cent of the monetary base during 1980s. The growing deficit of the government, and its continuously increasing financing by the RBI, exposed the country to continuous inflationary pressures. The RBI addressed the task of neutralizing the inflationary impact by resorting to direct instruments of monetary control, in particular the Cash Reserve Ratio (CRR).

With the initiation of financial sector reforms, the development and deepening of money, government securities and forex markets, and rationalization and liberalization of interest rates, efforts have been made to move away from the use of direct instruments of monetary control to indirect measures such as open market operations and market-related interest rates. In the liberalized era, especially the post-1997 period, the operational target of monetary policy continues to be bank reserves, which are controlled by changes in reserve requirements effected mainly through the use of CRR. However, the CRR has been progressively brought down, the bank rate has been reactivated and the liquidity management in the system is carried out through open market operations, both outright and repo/reverse repo. During this period, initially the liquidity was made available to banks in the form of various sector specific schemes or discretionary refinance at the bank rate or at the fixed rates which were linked to the bank rate. Often the fixed rate of refinance largely deviated from the cost of equivalent short-term funds in the market. This led to non-egalitarian distribution of interest rates at the short end of the market. Further, the amount of refinance available under various refinance schemes was preset. Liquidity support was also made available to Primary Dealers (PDs) at the bank rate. Apart from the bank rate, the RBI also used reverse repo to manage liquidity in the market (here we should know that in the pre-2004 period the RBI defined repo and reverse repo from its own side and used the word repo to show withdrawal of liquidity where reverse repo to indicate the injection of liquidity. However, since 2004, it has adopted international parlance for these words and has been defining them from the side of market participants—using the term repo to indicate injection of liquidity and the term reverse repo to show the withdrawal of liquidity from the market. Throughout this book we have used these words as per their internationally accepted uses).

In such a system, reverse repo rate effectively set a floor and the refinance rate/bank rate a cap making an interest rate corridor in the inter-bank call money market rate. Effectiveness of the RBI in maintaining this corridor was, however, restricted by the fact that, at times, call money rates breached the reverse repo rate because the reverse repo rate was a 3–4 day rate, whereas the call rate operates on overnight basis. Market uncertainties and different perceptions in the overnight rates also led to such a breaching of the limits.

Though refinance system was easier to operate, to do away with the deficiencies of refinance system, the multiplicity of rates at which liquidity was available and to better manage the short-term liquidity mismatches in the system, the committee on banking sector reforms (Narasimham Committee II) in 1998, recommended the introduction of the **Liquidity Adjustment Facility** (LAF). Under this scheme, the RBI was expected to conduct auctions periodically, if required daily, and reset its repo/reverse repo rate to provide a reasonable corridor for the money market rates.

The full fledged LAF, as suggested by the committee, could not be implemented immediately because (i) the repo/reverse repo operations required enough securities with the banking organizations over and above the SLR requirement and (ii) it also required efficient settlement system in the repo market. Instead, the **Interim Liquidity Adjustment Facility** (ILAF) was introduced in April 1999. With the introduction of ILAF, repos and reverse repos were formalized; the general refinance facility was withdrawn and replaced by the Collateralized Lending Facility (CLF) up to 0.25 per cent of the fortnightly average outstanding of aggregate deposits in 1997–98, for two weeks at the bank rate. The **Additional Collateralized Lending Facility** (ACLF) for an equivalent amount of CLF was also made available to banks at 2 per cent above the bank rate. These facilities could be extended for another two weeks at a penal rate of 2 per cent. Even under this new system, export credit refinance for scheduled commercial banks was retained at the bank rate. The system also provided liquidity support to PDs against the collateral of government securities at the bank rate.

The full fledged LAF was introduced in three phases. The first phase began on 5 June 2000. In this phase, the ACLF and level II support to PDs was replaced by variable rate repo auctions with the same day settlement. The CLF and level I liquidity support for banks and PDs was replaced by variable rate repo auctions. With effect from 29 March 2004, a revised LAF scheme was operationalized under which the reverse repo rate was reduced to 6 per cent and aligned with the bank rate. With the full computerization of the Public Debt Office (PDO) and the introduction of the **Real Time Gross Settlement** (RTGS), the third phase of full fledged LAF begun.

The LAF, since 2004, operated through overnight fixed rate repo (liquidity injection rate) and reverse repo (liquidity absorption), and provided a corridor for the informally targeted call money rate. The system provided necessary guidance to the market determined rate but lacked on two counts.

1. Absence of single policy rate: The operating policy rate alternated between repo and reverse repo rate depending on the prevailing liquidity situation. It created confusion among the market participants about the stance of monetary policy.
2. Absence of a firm corridor: In the absence of a firm corridor, in the extreme liquidity conditions, informally targeted effective call rate crossed the boundaries of the corridor.

To overcome these deficiencies, a revised LAF was put in place in May 2011. Under the revised LAF, repo is the only independently declared policy. The other short policy rates—bank rate, marginal standing facility (MSF) rate (under MSF scheduled commercial banks can borrow overnight at 100 basis points above the repo rate upto 1 per cent of their respective net demand and time liabilities) and reverse repo rate are linked to the repo rate. The new LAF provides a fixed corridor to formally targeted weighted average call rates. This fixed corridor has a fixed width of 200 basis points. The repo rate is placed in the middle of the corridor, the reverse repo rate at 100 basis points below and the MSF and bank rate at 100 basis points above it (Figure 10.11).

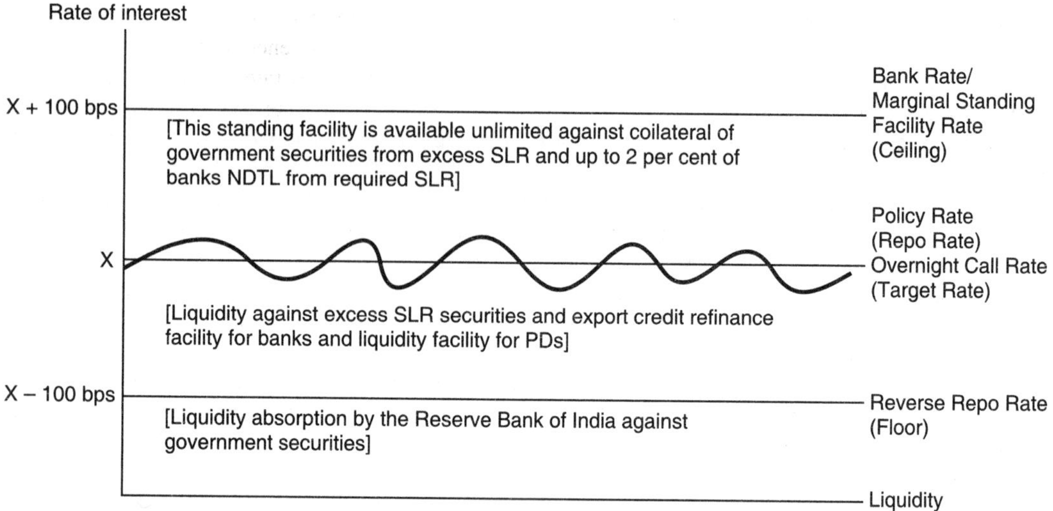

Source: Mohanty, D. (2011), Changing Counters of Monetary Policy in India, *RBI Bulletin*, December.

Figure 10.11 Revised LAF Framework.

As repo/reverse repo injects/absorbs liquidity for a short period of time, the full fledged LAF is essentially a tool of adjusting marginal liquidity. This cannot be used for absorbing the liquidity of enduring nature from the system.

Modus operandi of LAF

The Financial Markets Committee (FMC) under the aegis of the RBI, meets every day in the morning, assesses the liquidity conditions in the light of net inflows and outflows on account of forex operations, current account balances of the banks against the CRR requirements, open market operations, redemption of loans and coupon payments, announcement of new issues by the government, undrawn liquidity support on account of refinance, collateralized lending facilities to banks, and level I refinance to PDs, and the overall situation of the call money market. The LAF operations are conducted on a daily basis (except Saturdays) in the forenoon between 9.30 a.m. and 10.30 a.m. On Fridays, the auctions are held for three days to cover the following Saturdays and Sundays. In addition to the overnight repos, the RBI has the discretion to introduce longer term repos upto 14-day period as and when required. The rate of interest is determined on the basis of the bids received from the market. The minimum bid size for the LAF is ₹5 crore and multiples of ₹5 crore. While setting cut-off rates and the quantum in the repo market, the RBI keeps in mind the overall liquidity conditions in the market and not bank-wise liquidity positions. The RBI monitors the bids submitted by the borrowers, and also ensures that the funds are used only for meeting short-term mismatches and not diverted to finance more permanent assets. The RBI has also been using time-to-time the **Second LAF** (SLAF) to fine tune the liquidity during the second half of the day. The SLAF was first introduced on 28 November 2005. It was discontinued from 6 August 2007 but was reintroduced from August 1, 2008 on Reporting Fridays and from 17 September 2008 on daily basis. The SLAF, on daily basis, has again been discontinued from 6 May 2009. It is now being conducted on Reporting Fridays with effect from 8 May 2009 between 4.00 p.m. and 4.30 p.m. The mechanism of SLAF is similar to that of LAF. Both the LAF and SLAF are conducted separately and on gross basis.

The securities used under repo/reverse repo transactions are counted for the SLR purpose.

UNDERSTANDING BUSINESS ENVIRONMENT

UBE 10.4 Market Stabilization Scheme

Insufficient stock of government and other approved securities in the own account of the central bank often limits the effectiveness of the OMOs to manage liquidity in the event of large inflow of foreign capital. The Market stabilization scheme (MSS) has been introduced in India to overcome this constraint of the OMOs as described in this UBE.

With the opening up of the Indian economy to foreign capital flows, the economy has been experiencing a large inflow of foreign capital and foreign exchange. Interventions in the market by the RBI, in an effort to stabilize the exchange rate or the value of the rupee, results in purchase of foreign currency from the market and pumping of domestic currency in the economy. Thus, an inflow of foreign capital often results in an excess of liquidity in the system and makes the economy subject to a high inflationary scenario. To stabilize the economy and to sterilize the system of the impact of these capital flows, the RBI often resorts to the OMO. However, the ability of the RBI to conduct the OMO is limited by the availability of government securities in its own stock.

Considering the limited effectiveness of OMO to absorb the liquidity from the system in the event of large capital flows, a Working Group on Instruments of Sterilization (Chairperson Smt. Usha Thorat) recommended an introduction of **Market Stabilization Scheme** (MSS).

The MSS is operational in India since April 2004. The scheme operates on the same principles as the OMO. In both the cases, T-bills and dated government securities are used for absorbing liquidity from the system. However, unlike the OMO operations under the MSS the government securities are not owned by the RBI. The Government of India issues treasury bills and or dated securities under the MSS in addition to its normal borrowing requirements for absorbing liquidity from the system. These securities, though not owned by the RBI, are issued by it to the public by way of auctions. These securities have all the attributes of existing treasury bills and dated securities and are eligible for the Statutory Liquidity Ratio (SLR), repo/ reverse repo and Liquidity Adjustment Facility (LAF).

Proceeds from the sale of these securities under the MSS are held by the government in a separate identifiable cash account (MSS Account) maintained and operated by the RBI. This amount can be appropriated only for the purpose of redemption and/or buyback of the treasury bills and/or dated securities issued under the MSS as per the Memorandum of Understanding (MOU) on the MSS between the RBI and the GOI signed on March 2004. However, the MOU was amended on 26 February 2009 to enable the transfer of a part of the amount in the MSS cash account to the normal cash account as part of the Government's market borrowing programme for meeting the government's approved expenditure.

The payment of interest on the MSS securities as well as the receipts, due to premium and or accrued interest, are not shown into or credited to the MSS account, but get reflected in the budget under separate subheads.

The MSS has given a greater freedom and flexibility to the RBI in liquidity management by short-term instruments such as 91-day, 182-day and 364-day T-bills, and also the medium-term dated government securities. Short-term instruments are preferred as they provide more flexibility. The MSS has empowered the RBI to absorb liquidity on a more enduring, but still on temporary basis. This enables the use of the LAF for daily liquidity management and the OMO for managing liquidity of enduring nature.

The differences between the MSS, LAF, and OMOs have been highlighted in Table 10.7.

Table 10.7 Schemes to Manage Liquidity in the Economy

Scheme	*Liquidity addressed*	*Underlying instrument*	*Impact on the economy*
LAF	Day-to-day/ short-term liquidity: Liquidity of temporary nature/ Not designed for sterilization of large capital flows.	Repo/reverse repo	Tenure of repo/reverse repo is from 1 to 15 days. The government securities purchased/sold under repo have to be resold/repurchased by the RBI after the stipulated period of time. Thus, the impact of the LAF operations is for a short period. Therefore, the LAF can be used for fine tuning the liquidity on day-to-day basis and stabilizing the short-term interest rates.
OMO	Liquidity of enduring nature.	Outright purchase/ sale of government securities: T-bills as well as dated securities from RBI's own account.	The securities underlying the OMOs are issued by the government to meet its expenditure requirement, and hence, are a result of its borrowing programme. To the extent these are purchased by the RBI, these can be used for the OMOs as a policy instrument for absorbing/injecting liquidity in the system. As there is no repurchase agreement in the OMOs, the effect of these operations last for a longer duration than the repo operations. These operations can be used for managing the liquidity of enduring nature. However, the ability of the RBI to manage liquidity through this method gets constrained because of limited stock of government securities with the RBI on its own account. The cost of the OMO (interest payment/transaction cost) falls on the RBI.
MSS	Medium-term/ enduring liquidity: ssentially a tool to sterilize the impact of large foreign capital flows.	Outright purchase/sale of government securities: T-bills as well as dated securities from MSS account managed by the RBI.	Heavy inflows and outflows of foreign capital flows destabilize the economy. A limited stock of the government securities on the RBI's own account is found to be insufficient to sterilize the impact of these flows. The MSS allows the use of government securities, which are created not to meet the borrowing requirements of the government but specially created for stabilization purpose, for managing the liquidity of enduring nature but still on temporary basis. The cost of these programmes is borne by the government.

10.5.1 Communication Policy

Expectations play an important role in the efficacy of monetary policy in bringing about desirable changes. Therefore, incorporating expectations in the monetary policy as well as managing them is one of the challenges that central banks face. To incorporate expectations, central banks involve wider range of stake holders—from internal staff to corporate to external experts. To manage expectations central banks disseminate the stance of monetary policy and changes in it through various medium as illustrated in UBE 10.5 using Indian context.

UNDERSTANDING BUSINESS ENVIRONMENT

UBE 10.5 Monetary Policy Making Process and Dissemination in India

This UBE describes the way in which the RBI maintains transparency and disseminates the monetary policy changes to the public to manage expectations.

Traditionally, the monetary policy making process in India has confined to internal discussions and deliberation with only the end product being disseminated to the public. However, over a period of time, in the post-reform period, the internal process has become more market-oriented and technical savvy. There is a greater coordination, horizontal management and rapid responses, with overall process becoming more analytical, introspective, elaborative, consultative and participative with external orientation. There is now a greater degree of transparency. Of late, the process of monetary policy formulation is based on the information content of a large host of domestic or international macroeconomic developments.

At the apex of policy making process is the Governor, assisted closely by the Deputy Governors and guided by the Board of Directors. Monetary, economic and financial conditions are reviewed every week by a Committee of the Board and decisions are made in the light of emerging economic scenario. Several other standing committees or groups of the board and the **Board for Financial Supervision** are in place that guide in institutional development and policy formulation process. The **Financial Markets Committee** (FMC), constituted in 1997, focuses on tactical aspects. It monitors market developments, makes an assessment of market liquidity on the basis of inflows and outflows from the Reserve Bank balance sheet as a result of its operations with the banking sector, financial institutions and the government and recommends day-to-day market operations. On the other hand, the **Monetary Policy Strategy Group** is responsible for analyzing the strategies on ongoing basis. Periodic consultations with the Government, mainly with the Ministry of Finance, ensure the co-ordination between monetary and fiscal policies. There is a greater degree of external orientation with various Technical Advisory Committees and Standing Committees, comprising academicians, market participants and financial intermediaries, meeting and advising periodically. The **Technical Advisory Committee on Monetary Policy** (TACMP), set up in July 2005 (reconstituted in April 2007 and then again in July 2009) with external experts, meets at least once in a quarter to review the macroeconomic and monetary developments and advises the RBI on the 'stance' of monetary policy. The views of the TACMP are discussed in the following meeting of the Committee of the Central Board. *Ad hoc* working groups, again with external experts, are appointed by the RBI to look into the specific issues. There are also regular resource management discussions with the banks.

There is a greater and faster dissemination of the policy making process in a variety of ways. Information and data is released at regular periodicity—daily, weekly, monthly, quarterly, six monthly, and annually, and also through occasional publications of draft reports and studies (Table 10.8).

One of the important ways in which the stance and rational of monetary policy is communicated to the public is through the annual monetary policy statement made public in April and the mid-term review in October. Since July 2005, the RBI has begun a system of quarterly reviews in addition to bi-annual statements. The statements and the reviews have become more analytical and include not only the stance or measures but also elaborate on institutional and structural aspects. The policy statements are announced by the Governor in the meetings with the leading bankers where each banker present interacts with the Governor to express his or her views on the policy announcements. The rational for various monetary policy measures undertaken is also communicated to the public through the Press Releases and through the Statements made by the Governor and the Deputy Governors. After the policy announcement, the Governor addresses the press conference in the afternoon and gives interviews to print and electronic media over the next few days. On the day of the policy announcements, the Deputy Governor, in charge of the Monetary Policy Department, gives live interviews to all the major TV channels. However, as of now, unlike budget announcements, there is no practice of live telecast of Governor's monetary policy announcements.

Table 10.8 Dissemination of Policies: Some Important Modes

Mode	*Release period*	*Content*
Policy Statements of the RBI Governor		
Annual Policy Statement	April	Details on the monetary policy and development and regulatory policies in the coming one year
Mid-term Review	October	Reviews the Annual Policy statement in the light of emerging economic scenario
First Quarter Review Third Quarter Review	July January	Reviews the monetary policy and provides structured overlook of evolving market scenario, greater flexibility to take specific measures in the light of evolving circumstances.
Statutory Publications		
Annual Report	August	Details on the state of the economy and makes an assessment of the evolving economic scenario. Details on the working of the Reserve Bank and its impact on the balance-sheet of the Reserve Bank in the financial year of the RBI July to June.
Report on Trend and Progress of Banking in India	November/ December	Reviews the policies for and performance of the financial sector for the preceding year from April to March.
Non Statutory Publications		
Report on Currency and Finance	December	Since 1998–99 the report deals with a particular theme and presents a detailed economic analysis of the issues related to the theme against the recent theoretical developments and cross country empirical evidence.
Handbook of Statistics on Indian Economy	Annual	Provides time series data (annual/quarterly/monthly/ fortnightly/daily) pertaining to various economic variables.
Macroeconomic and Monetary Developments	A day before the Annual Policy Statement/ Mid-term/ Quarterly Reviews	Provides an analytical review of macroeconomic and monetary developments during the period under review providing the necessary information and technical analysis.
RBI Bulletin	First Week of Every Month	Publishes data relating to the economy, analytical articles based on the data collected by the RBI, speeches of the Governor, Deputy Governors and Executive Directors, press releases and circulars issued by the different departments.
Weekly Statistical Supplement	Every Friday at 5 p.m.	Presents weekly balance sheet of the RBI and the other data relating to the financial, commodity and bullion markets.

Mode	*Release period*	*Content*
Press Releases	Daily	Contain information on money market operations and reference rate for four major currencies, namely the US dollar, Euro, Pound Sterling and the Japanese Yen. Certain press releases are related to general public interest such as new currency notes, important banking regulations, etc.
Occasional Papers (Published thrice in a year)	Every Quarter	Carries the papers prepared by the professional staff of the RBI.
Committee Reports	Occasional	Published for feedback and wider dissemination of information.
Database on Indian Economy ((http://dbie.rbi.org.in)	Online	Provides access to the RBI data warehouse in an interactive mode and Excel/ CSV/PDF format
RBI website (http://www.rbi.org.in)	Updated several times in a day	All the information released by the RBI is made available on the website in pdf and word formats and the data is placed in excel format.

Source: Compiled from http://www.rbi.org.in/scripts/righttoinfoact.aspx

The policy changes are communicated to the regulated entities through departmental circulars which are also placed on the RBI website without any delay.

Apart from these policy statements, speeches of the Governor and Deputy Governors, on various national and international platforms, brief on the policy measures and their rationales. Several statutory, non-statutory publications, and committee reports also deliberate on the stance and rational of monetary policy appraising the financial structure and emerging economic scenario. Over a period of time, these have become more analytical, transparent and forward looking.

The RBI website, consisting of all the publications of the RBI, rated as one of the best among central bank websites. It is a rich source of information on not only the financial segment but also the overall developments in the economy. Policy changes are disseminated through the website almost on a real time basis. For example, the results of the Liquidity Adjustment Facility (LAF) of the day are posted on the website by 12.30 p.m. of the same day, the reference exchange rates are posted by 12.45 p.m. on every working day, and the press release on money market operations are made public by the next day morning by 9 a.m. All the regulatory and administrative circulars of different departments are placed on the website within half an hour of its finalization. Weekly Statistical Supplement, consisting of latest monetary and financial sector data, is placed by 5 p.m. every Friday, and the RBI Bulletin is out by the first week of every month on the website.

10.6 MONETARY POLICY TRANSMISSION MECHANISM

Monetary policy is implemented with the objectives of achieving growth with price stability. The basic presumption behind the use of monetary policy for achieving various objectives is that there exists some stable relationship between monetary policy instruments and monetary aggregates and various other economic variables Presumption is also that by bringing out changes in monetary policy instruments the central banks can influence the other segments of their economies. Since central banks can print new notes, they can affect the quantity as well as the rate (or cost) of credit to their governments, commercial banks and other financial institutions, and hence, can influence money supply and liquidity in their economies. These changes in turn, can affect the entire spectrum of short-term and long-term interest rates, exchange rates and various asset prices leading to changes in consumption and investment decisions, exports and import decisions, and thus, affecting the aggregate demand, output gap and inflation. Though overall changes in the monetary policy measures have an impact first on the financial system and then on the real sector, the extent of reactions to changes in the central bank policy rate varies across countries and across time period depending on the structure of the economy (which in turn depends on demographic profile, institutional structure, technology and many such factors) and interactions among its various constituents.

The process or channel through which changes in monetary policy instruments affect inflation, output and other economic variables is known as the **transmission mechanism** (Figure 10.12). There are numerous channels and the influence of each of these individual channels varies across countries and time (as illustrated in UBE 10.6). Also, several channels may operate simultaneously. Thus, an understanding of the transmission process is essential not only for the appropriate design and implementation of monetary policy but also for undertaking business decisions and strategic formulation. Here the mechanism of these different channels is summarized.

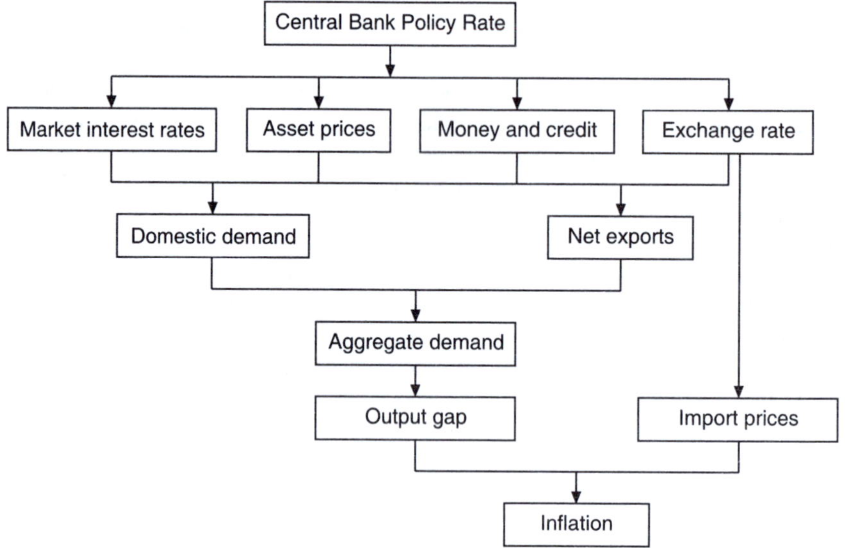

Figure 10.12 Transmission Mechanism of Monetary Policy.

10.6.1 Interest Rate

Financial institutions have alternative avenues available for raising short-term funds, varying from access to funds from the central bank to funds from inter-bank market or from deposit from the public. Interest rate channel indicates that the impact of a change in the interest rate in any of the money markets gets spilled over to the other money market and capital market segments. Thus, a change in the central bank policy rate (say repo rate) can have an immediate impact on other interest rates. For example, a rise in the policy rate (say bank rate or repo rate) often reduces the demand for funds from the central bank and shifts the excess demand from it to other markets like call money, treasury bills, bonds and share markets, which in turn increases the interest rates even in these other markets. However, the extent of hike depends on the maturity profile of assets and the level of risk involved in them as well as the level of integration across markets. The interest rate on short-term assets of commercial banks generally rise faster as these are, to a large extent, traded in the money market. A hike in the policy rate also results in a hike in the deposit rates. Therefore, often the spread between the return on bank assets and the deposits remain unchanged in the event of policy changes. A change in the policy rate also alters long-term rates.

Given nominal wage and price rigidities, a hike in the policy rate, resulting in a general rise in the spectrum of interest rate, raises the real interest rate, which in turn discourages expenditure on durable goods by households and investment expenditure by firms, leading to a decline in the aggregate demand. Given the supply of output, the output gap decreases and, given all other factors as same, the inflation rate gets suppressed.

10.6.2 Other Asset Price Channel

We have seen in Box 6.1 that there is an inverse relationship between the price of an asset and interest rate on it. Therefore, a change in the policy rate also affects the prices of various financial and physical assets, including bond prices and prices of real estate. **Other asset price channel** indicates that the variations in the prices of various assets, in turn, affect aggregate demand through various routes as follows:

1. Changes in asset prices affect aggregate demand via q-theory of investment pioneered by James Tobin. As per the *q*-theory, investment decisions are dependent on the market price (measured by equity or share prices) of a firm relative to the replacement cost of its capital. Monetary policy, by affecting equity prices, affects the market prices of firms relative to the replacement cost of their capital. Thus, it can alter the level of investment in an economy.
2. Changes in asset prices can affect the level of demand by affecting the net worth (i.e., the value of assets minus the value of borrowed liabilities or in simple terms the wealth) of households and enterprises. These entities like to keep certain proportion of their wealth in the form of liquid assets (like cash) in hand to meet the situation of distress or urgent/unexpected/unforeseen expenses. Changes in asset prices, altering the net worth of households and enterprises, affect the proportion of liquid assets to total assets, making them to adjust their consumption and investment level. For example, a fall in equity and bond prices may reduce the value of liquid assets available with households and firms making them more vulnerable to a financial distress and unforeseen events arising from illiquid assets. To restore the amount of liquid assets on their balance sheets, households and firms often cut down on their consumption and investment expenditure, leading to a fall in the aggregate demand and a lowering of inflationary pressures.

10.6.3 Exchange Rate Channel

Changes in interest rates in the domestic markets, brought about by monetary policy changes, affect the relative return on domestic assets vis-a-vis foreign assets. Consequently, these changes affect the amount of inflow of foreign currency and the value of exchange rate. For example, an increase in the policy rate, and the consequent increase in the spectrum of interest rate on domestic assets, makes domestic financial assets more attractive than comparable foreign assets. This increases the investment in domestic assets not only by the domestic participants but also by foreigners. Investment in domestic assets by foreigners increases the inflow of foreign currency which gets converted by the domestic participants in the domestic currency. Thus, as we will analyze in greater detail in Chapter 12, an inflow of foreign currency increases the demand for domestic currency, and given the supply of it, the exchange rate (i.e., the price of domestic currency in terms of foreign currency) appreciates.

The changes in the value of exchange rate or **exchange rate channel** can affect an economy in two distinct ways—the relative price effect and the balance sheet effect.

1. Relative price effect: The changes in the exchange rate alter the relative prices of domestically produced goods vis-a-vis imported goods. An appreciation in the exchange rate implies that the domestic agents can get more of a foreign currency for per unit of the domestic currency. Alternatively stated, they have to pay lower units of the domestic currency to procure one unit of a foreign currency. Thus, an appreciation lowers domestic prices of imported goods and makes those cheaper. At the same time, it increases the prices of exported commodities for foreigners and adversely affects the external competitiveness of an economy. The subsequent decline in net exports (i.e., exports—imports) reduces the aggregate demand and the output gap (i.e., the gap between demand for and supply of output), moderates the inflationary pressures.

2. Balance sheet effect: The changes in the exchange rate can even alter the balance sheet or the net worth of domestic agents, especially when households and firms hold significant amount of foreign currency debt on their balance sheets. As we have seen above, the changes in the balance sheet can lead to adjustments in borrowing as well as spending, and real side effects. For example, when domestic residents are net debtors (i.e., they have borrowed more than what they have lent) to the rest of the world, an appreciation of the exchange rate leads to a reduction in their liabilities in terms of domestic currency and improves their balance sheet position, which in turn, expands domestic demand and price level.

Thus, the balance sheet effects tends to offset the relative price effects.

10.6.4 Credit Channel

Credit channel views that the monetary policy affect aggregate demand by altering the quantity of credit rather than its price or cost.

This channel is especially significant for countries where financial markets are either underdeveloped or suffering from a large asymmetry of information or are subject to tight government regulations on cost and quantity of credit, preventing mobilization of sufficient saving and lending activities. Economies get affected through two distinct routes as per this view as described hereinafter.

Bank Lending Channel

We have seen that banks and other financial intermediaries, play an important role in those economies where there are **asymmetries of information**, i.e., one party has more information than the others. It has been observed that usually those who undertake risky projects are the ones willing to pay high interest rate on their borrowings. The chances of defaults from these borrowers, known as high credit risk, are also high. Thus, high interest rate scenario signals the lenders that more credit risks are trading in the market. In the absence of proper information, in high interest rate scenario, many of the lender withdraw from loanable funds markets. Therefore, even the projects that are viable remain unfunded due to absence of sufficient information. Small firms often find it difficult to raise funds directly from the market, because they cannot afford to hire technical staff that can assess the viability of their projects and communicate the same to lenders. Therefore, they need to depend on banks and other financial intermediaries, for external funds. Banks, with their expertise in project appraisal and lending, can overcome the problem of adverse selection arising out of asymmetric information to a large extent and become the main source of finance for small firms. By reducing the bank reserves and the funds available for lending, a tight monetary policy, in economies with large asymmetry of information, hits the small firms and borrowers the most, because they cannot borrow directly from the market. During tight monetary conditions, banks do not completely depend on the increase in the interest rates to ration credit because that increases the chances of **adverse selection**, i.e., selecting the borrower who though willing to pay high rate is high credit risk. Rather, they partly resolve the issue by tightening creditworthiness standards, such as high margin requirement. Thus, it is the aggregate credit or **bank credit channel**, rather than the interest rate, that influences the level of aggregate demand in an economy.

Balance Sheet Channel

Monetary policy can even affect the availability of credit more directly through its effects on the value of assets of both borrowers and lenders through balance sheet channel. We have seen that by altering the prices of assets, monetary policy alters the value of net worth of borrowers or collateral. Banks while providing loans often look for collateral. Hence, by changing the value of collateral, monetary policy also alters the access of borrowers to credit. Tight monetary policy, thus, increasing the interest rates (and reducing the price of assets) erodes the value of collaterals. Banks also charge higher interest rates to those borrowers who do not have sufficient collateral with them. Thus, a reduction in the value of collateral further increases the cost of external funds for firms. At the same time, a tight monetary policy also reduces the net worth of banks by reducing the value of their assets and imposes a hard budget constraint on them. Banks often go for credit rationing in such a situation. All these factors together adversely affect investment and aggregate demand. The decline in demand further reduces the cash flows of firms, value of their collateral, availability of funds and further accentuates the deceleration in demand and overall prices level.

Monetary policy transmission mechanism varies across countries and across time period. The evolvement of such a mechanism in the Indian context is depicted in UBE 10.6.

UNDERSTANDING BUSINESS ENVIRONMENT

UBE 10.6 Changing Structure and Evolving Monetary Transmission Mechanism in India

Credit channel was the most dominant channel of monetary transmission in India. However, as highlighted in this UBE, with the reforms in place, interest rate channel and exchange rate channel are also emerging to be crucial channels.

Monetary policy is expected to affect output, employment and inflation through a number of channels. Though these channels are not mutually exclusive, the relative importance of each of these channels varies from one economy to another and one time period to another. The structure of an economy, level of financial development, degree of financial market integration, instruments available with the central bank for the conduct of monetary policy, fiscal stance and pattern of financing of fiscal deficit, autonomy to the central bank in the conduct of monetary policy, mechanism of determination of interest rate, exchange rate and various other prices, and the degree of openness are some of the important factors that determine the path through which monetary policy impulses get transmitted to the different parts of an economy. Broadly, the monetary transmission channels can be classified into financial price channels (interest rates, exchange rates, and other asset prices) and financial quantity channels (money supply and credit aggregates).

Of all the channels, the interest rate channel has been identified to be the dominant transmission mechanism of monetary policy, especially in those markets where prices are determined by market forces. Changes in interest rate, by affecting the cost of credit, not only directly affect consumption and investment decisions but also induce changes in asset prices, and thus, affect the net worth or the value of collaterals of individuals and firms. These also have implications for consumption and investment decisions.

The credit channel, most often is, found to be a dominant channel in those economies where the system is characterized by repressed or underdeveloped financial markets and large asymmetry of information resulting in an adverse selection problem. In such markets, monetary policy operates on aggregate demand through changes in the availability of loanable funds from financial institutions, especially those from the banks.

With the changing structure of the Indian economy, the transmission mechanism is also evolving over a period of time in India.

The credit channel was believed to be the most dominant channel in India right from the 1950s. It was realized that higher growth can be achieved through heavy industrialization that required a large scale investment in heavy plant and machinery. Lack of private initiatives in these spheres accorded primary role to the fiscal policy in stepping up investment rate and growth and development of the country. The monetary policy played an accommodative role by meeting all the credit requirement of the government. Inflationary pressures, emerging from the continuous financing of the government expenditures by the monetization of deficit, were tackled by curbing credit to commercial sector and impounding the resources of banks in the form of higher and higher CRR and SLR requirement.

Fiscal dominance during the decade of 1970s and 1980s made the credit rationing an integral part of development planning in India. Food credit was given the first foremost priority followed by the priority sector lending. Sectoral limits were imposed on credit deployment. At the same time, selective credit control methods were adopted for preventing credit over flowing to non-priority areas. Directed credit programme, impounding of resources in the form of higher CRR and SLR requirements, administered interest rate regime, underdeveloped state of financial system, lack of financial market integration, control over prices and exchange rate, and lack of openness of the economy made the credit channel as the dominant channel of monetary policy transmission in India. It prevented financial price channels, such as interest rate and exchange rate channels, from operating or playing an important role. The directed credit control methods reduced the portfolio flexibility of financial institutions and brought inefficiency in the allocation of scarce resources. With the objective of infusing efficiency in the system, a number of reform measures were introduced during the decade of 1990s. The attempt has been to shift from a planned and administered interest rate system to a market-oriented financial system by introducing various reform measures. Some of these reform measures are as follows:

(i) Phased deregulation of interest rates
(ii) Reactivation of the bank rate since 1997
(iii) Phasing out the ad hoc treasury bills, replacing those by ways and means advances and introducing Fiscal Responsibility Management Bill (FRMB) to limit the monetization of fiscal deficit
(iv) Activating and developing the market for government securities; putting the market borrowing programme of the government through auctions

(v) Activation and development of markets for various money market instruments, such as CDs, CPs and short-term TBs

(vi) Reduction in the CRR and SLR requirements

(vii) Development of repo market and introduction of the Liquidity Adjustment Facility (LAF)

With the liberalization of the economy and the integration of financial sector reforms, monetary policy is increasingly relying on the use of indirect instruments, such as repo rate and open market operations, for regulating the liquidity in the system and stabilizing the economy. In contrast to the earlier reliance on reserve requirements and credit ceilings/sectoral credit allocation, during the post reform period, the modulation in policy rates, i.e., bank rate, repo rate and reverse repo rate, have emerged as a principal instrument of signalling monetary policy stance. The RBI is now able to influence the interest rates at the short end of the markets by modulating the liquidity in the system through the LAF operations.

With the reforms in place and the changes taking place in the structure of the economy, monetary transmission channels in India have undergone a significant transformation. Financial price channels are getting identified in the Indian context. RBI (2005), and Mohan (2007), indicate that, in addition to monetary and credit aggregates, financial prices—interest rate and exchange rate–are emerging to be crucial monetary transmission channels in India. RBI (2005) study indicates that the lags in transmission have got reduced, with the peak effect of an interest rate shock on output as well as price occurring around six months after the shock. The short transmission period, however, could be attributed to a number of factors such as wage price indexation and supply side measures, especially the role of public distribution system, to contain inflation. Similarly, exchange rate pass through transmission channel is also quite quick with 60 per cent of exchange rate pass through taking place within one year of the monetary policy impulse and 80 per cent of the pass through is completed within two years of a shock to the exchange rate. A recent study, Mohanty (2012), using a quarterly structural vector autoregression model indicated that in recent years in India an increase in policy rate resulted in decline in output growth after a lag of two quarters and moderated inflation after a lag of three quarters. The overall impact lasted for 8 to 10 quarters.

References

Mohan, R. (2007), Monetary Policy Transmission in India, *RBI Bulletin*, April. Mohan, R. (2007), Monetary Policy Transmission in India, *RBI Bulletin*, April.

Mohanty, D. (2012), Evidence on Interest Rate Channel of Monetary Policy Transmission in India, paper presented in Second International Research Conference, on Monetary Policy, Sovereign Debt and Financial Stability: A New Trilemma, held during 1-2 February 2012, Mumbai.

RBI (2005), Report on Currency and Finance.

SUMMARY

Monetary policy influences economic activity and prices by regulating the quantity as well as the cost of credit to producers and consumers.

The core objective of monetary policy is price stability. However, quite often it is pursued to achieve multiple objectives of price stability, exchange rate stability, financial stability, output stability, economic growth and social justice.

Central banks cannot directly control the final goals of monetary policy. Hence, they often set intermediate targets which have a close bearing on the final goals. As intermediate goals also cannot be achieved with great accuracy, central banks set operating targets which have close bearing on the intermediate targets. Central banks try to achieve these targets with the help of quantitative instruments, such as cash reserve ratio, bank rate and open market operations, and qualitative instruments such as selective credit control methods and moral suasion.

The process or the channel through which changes in monetary policy instruments affect inflation, output and other economic variables is known as the monetary policy transmission mechanism. Monetary policy, in general, affects an economy through changes in interest rate, other asset prices, exchange rate and credit availability.

In India, in the post-1991 era, though price stability and growth remain the core objective of monetary policy, attaining financial stability and exchange rate stability are also becoming crucial. Along with the direct instruments, the RBI is also increasingly using the indirect instruments of credit control. The repo/reverse repo rates have emerged basic signalling device of the monetary policy stance in the country. The RBI is using different schemes and processes to manage the liquidity in the system. The LAF is used for fine tuning the day-to-day liquidity, whereas the MSS has been used for managing the liquidity of enduring nature on temporary basis and the OMOs are used for managing the liquidity with enduring nature. In the emerging scenario, in addition to monetary and credit aggregates, financial prices—interest rate and exchange rate—are emerging to be the crucial monetary transmission channels in the country.

Implications for Business Managers

Business units usually need to depend on external sources, such as financial intermediaries and financial markets for financing their investment expenditure and working capital requirements. The availability and cost of credit are some of the important determinants of investment by them.

Monetary policy aims at regulating the cost and availability of credit. Changes in monetary policy in the form of changes in the bank rate or repo rate affect the cost of funds for financial institutions, which in turn, get passed on by them to their customers by bringing in changes in their lending rates. As the changes in interest rate affect the borrowing costs and, hence, the profit of corporations, monetary policy is very important for them. Similarly, changes in monetary policy in the form of CRR and SLR signal to business organizations whether there will be an overall reduction in the quantity of credit to private sector or not. An increase in these ratios indicates that the central bank wants to restrict the credit supply. In such cases, business organizations can expect some rationing of credit either by hike in the lending rate and/or by hike in margin requirements or some such changes.

The priority sectors, such as exporters, small scale industry, etc. of the economy closely watch the monetary policy announcements, because they are governed by special financing schemes. For example, exporters look forward to monetary policy because the central bank always makes an announcement on export refinance or the rate at which the central bank will lend to commercial banks that have advanced pre-shipment credit to exporters. A reduction in these rates leads to a fall in the lending rates of commercial banks on export credit, and thus, lowers borrowing costs for exporters.

Changes in monetary policy also have profound impact on stock markets. An easy monetary policy boosts up the market sentiments, increases the trading volumes in stock exchanges and helps corporates in raising finances directly from the markets. Conversely, a restrictive monetary policy brings in pessimism in financial markets, reduces trading volumes and makes it difficult for corporates to raise funds directly from the market.

In a flexible exchange rate regime and in an open economy framework, monetary policy also affects exchange rates. For example, an increase in domestic interest rates, due to monetary policy tightening, makes the domestic assets more attractive for foreigners and increases their investment in these assets as well as the inflow of foreign currency in the domestic markets. This leads to an appreciation of exchange rates. Business organizations dealing with international transactions get affected the most by such changes in exchange rates.

The knowledge of monetary policy framework (i.e., instruments, operating procedure and goals) and of monetary policy transmission process helps managers to assess and predict the impact of monetary policy not only on an economy but also on their balance sheets and financial positions, and helps them in adjusting their production and planning processes.

REVIEW QUESTIONS

10.1 Define monetary policy.

10.2 What are the basic objectives of monetary policy?

10.3 What are the different instruments of monetary policy? What are the basic differences between quantitative and qualitative instruments of credit control?

10.4 Differentiate between the CRR and SLR. Which of these regulates the money supply in a country?

10.5 Explain the mechanism of open market operations?

10.6 What is the difference between the outright OMO and repo/reverse repo?

10.7 What is the bank rate? How far is this different from the repo rate? Which one of these two signals the stance of monetary policy to the public?

10.8 What do you understand by the operating procedure?

10.9 What are tactical decisions and strategic decisions in the context of monetary policy?

10.10 What is the need for setting targets by the central bank? Differentiate between the intermediate and operating targets?

10.11 What do you understand by the transmission mechanism of monetary policy?

10.12 What are the different channels of monetary policy transmission mechanism?

10.13 Which of the monetary transmission mechanisms dominate the financially repressed system afflicted with asymmetry of information?

10.14 How far is the operating target in India different from the post-liberalized period when compared with the pre-liberalized period?

10.15 How does the RBI manage short-term liquidity mismatches and long-term liquidity mismatches?

10.16 What is the LAF? Why had the LAF been introduced in India? What changes in the economy have facilitated the introduction of the LAF in India?

10.17 What is the MSS? Why had this been introduced in India?

10.18 Of the LAF, OMO and MSS, which is the best way of managing liquidity surplus emerging from a large inflow of foreign capital?

10.19 What changes have taken place in the monetary transmission channels in India?

10.20 Briefly describe the monetary policy making process in India?

10.21 What are the different modes of dissemination of the monetary policy stance in India?

NUMERICAL PROBLEM

10.1 Suppose in a country the money supply is ₹1,500 crore. Public wants to hold only ₹500 crore in the form of currency and the rest in the form of deposits. Bank reserves are ₹100 crore and the desired reserves to deposit ratio is 0.1. The demand for money to meet consumption and production requirement is ₹1,000 crore. The excess supply of money is putting inflationary pressures on the economy. To curb inflationary pressures and stabilize the price level in the economy, the central bank sells the government security worth ₹50 crore from its own account in the market.

On the basis of the given information answer the following questions:

(a) Estimate the value of money multiplier for this economy.

(b) Estimate the amount of deposits and money supply in this economy when the central bank performs open market operations by selling government securities worth ₹50 crore.

(c) Show that by selling the government securities worth ₹50 crore the central bank will be able to fill the gap between money supply and money demand.

CASE ANALYSIS EXERCISE

C10.1 Monetary Policy in India: Objectives, Targets and Framework

Monetary policy is an important tool of macroeconomic policy in India. It is designed and formulated by the Reserve Bank of India in order to achieve its various objectives. It consists of all measures, direct and indirect, that can have an impact on the cost, availability and allocation of credit, supply of money, overall liquidity in the system, and development and overall efficiency of the financial system.

Substantial changes have taken place in the monetary policy framework in the post-1991 period compared to the pre-1991 period (Table 10.9).

In the pre-1991 period the monetary policy focussed on the objective of provision of credit for growth along with price stability. In the post-1991 period also the prime objectives of monetary policy remains the same.

The emphasis between the objectives of price stability and growth has, however, varied over time depending on the evolving price-output situation. In the initial years of development, after independence, there was a widespread consensus that public investment is required for rapid growth. Therefore, credit allocation to the government became an overriding concern, and a more direct involvement of the central monetary authority in the allocation of credit to the non-government sector became an important element of national economic policy. However, continuous deficit financing associated with public investment began to spill over into inflation during the 1960s, and took a threatening shape in the 1970s and 1980s. With the deregulation of prices and interest rates, and the liberalization of trade and capital flows, the economy became subject to more price fluctuations. Hence, in the early years of liberalization, price stability was perceived to be a critical factor for the sustainability of reform process. However, during the slowdown period of second half of the 1990s, inflation and inflationary expectations moderated substantially. To stabilize the level of output, monetary authorities pursued an accommodative (i.e., expansionary) monetary policy during this period.

With the recovery of the economy and substantial increase in international food and oil prices, in the recent years, maintaining confidence in price stability, has been emphasized to be a continuing policy objective.

Price stability and growth though have remained the prime objectives, the liberalization and opening up of the economy has necessitated that the monetary policy also addresses some new issues, such as maintaining financial stability, exchange rate stability and impact of market rate on the cost of public debt. With the growing globalization and financial integration with the rest of the world, the Indian economy has become subject to large and sudden movements in capital flows which have implications for financial and exchange rate stability in the country. Therefore, beyond the traditional trade off between inflation and growth there is now growing challenges to financial stability for the country. Similarly, in the pre-reform period the credit to the government was available at much lower real interest than that prevailed in the open market. The deregulation of interest rate and withdrawal of the RBI from the primary market for government securities have resulted in substantial increase in the cost of credit to the government. Therefore, the issue of cost of public debt has become an important consideration for the monetary policy.

Table 10.9 Monetary Policy Matrix in India

	Pre-1991 era	*Post-1991 era*
Objective	Price stability, Provision of appropriate level of credit for growth.	Price stability, Provision of appropriate level of credit for growth and financial stability.
Framework	Monetary targeting framework	Multiple indicator approach (MIA)/ Augmented multiple indicator approach
Intermediate Targets	Till the mid 1980's: Credit targeting: Bank credit: Aggregate as well as sectoral 1985–1990's: Monetary Targeting: Broad Money (M_3)	Since April 1998: Multiple Indicators: Interest rates in different markets, currency, credit extended by banks and financial institutions, broad money, fiscal position, trade, capital flows, inflation rate, exchange rate, refinancing and transactions in foreign exchange, output.
Operating Targets	Base money/ Bank reserves	Reserve Money, Short-term policy interest rates, informal targeting of effective call money rate. Since May 2011, formal targeting of effective call money rate.
Operating Instruments	Interest rate regulation, selective credit control and reserve requirements	Reserve requirements, standing facilities, Open market operations (outright and repo) affecting the quantum of marginal liquidity. Policy rates: Bank rate and reverse repo/repo rates affecting the price of liquidity. Since May 2011: Single policy rate: repo rate.

With the deepening, widening and strengthening of the financial sector, the RBI has also been actively using the indirect instruments of monetary policy, such as the bank rate and OMOs which have become more or less inactive in the pre-1991 period. In the pre-reform period, the RBI resorted more to selective credit control methods, reserve requirement and interest rate regulations.

In the pre-1991 period, India followed a **monetary targeting framework**, under which broad money acted as an intermediate target. However, in the post-1991 period, the processes of financial liberalization and innovations have activated the market forces and the interest rate channel. It has been realized that the demand for money in the coming period would be dependent not only on real income but interest rates will also exercise some influence on the decisions to hold money. It has also been realized that the relationship between money and other economic variables such as aggregate output and price level may not remain as precise as it used to be in the pre-1991 era. Therefore, in April 1998, the RBI formally adopted a **Multiple Indicator Approach** (MIA). Under this approach, besides broad money, which remains an information variable regarding liquidity in the economy, a host of other factors available at high frequency, such as interest rates in different markets, credit extended by banks and financial institutions, fiscal and balance of payment condition, inflation rate, exchange rate, currency in circulation, refinancing and transactions in foreign exchange, are examined and juxtaposed with the output data to assess the mismatch between demand for money and supply of money and draw policy inferences and initiatives.

In the subsequent period, further refinements were continuously introduced in the approach and the approach was augmented by forward looking indicators and a panel of parsimonious time series models.

In the current framework of monetary policy, known as **Augmented Multiple Indicator Approach (Figure 10.13)**, the forward looking indicators are drawn from the Reserve Bank's Industrial Outlook survey, capacity utilization survey and inflation expectation survey. The assessment from quantity variables, rate variables, forward looking indicators and models feeds into the projections of growth and inflation.

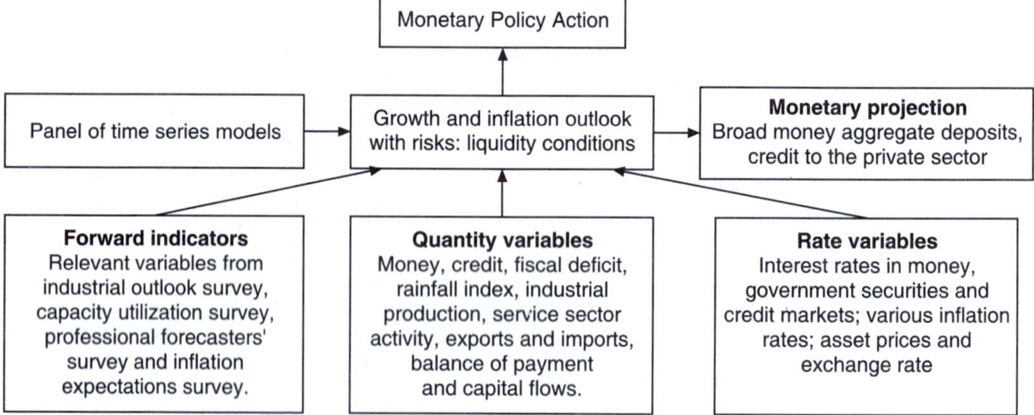

Source: Mohanty, D. (2010), Monetary Policy Framework in India: Experience with Multiple Indicators Approach, *RBI Bulletin*, March.

Figure 10.13 Augmented Multiple Indicator Approach.

With the shift away from the monetary targeting framework towards the augmented multiple indicator approach, there has also been a significant shift in the operating procedure of monetary policy. In the current environment, short-term interest rates have emerged as operating instruments to signal the stance of monetary policy. The RBI addresses the market liquidity with a mix of policy instruments consisting of changes in reserve requirements, standing market facilities, and open market operations, which affect the quantum of liquidity and changes in policy rates, such as bank rate and repo/reverse repo rates, which impact the price of liquidity.

Under the augmented multiple indicator approach, in May 2011 a new operating procedure was adopted, which has two key features. First, it explicitly recognizes the weighted average (effective) call money rate as the operating target. Second, repo rate is the only policy rate declared independently. All other policy rates, such as bank rate, MSF rate and reverse repo rate, are linked to the repo rate.

Questions

1. "Growth and price stability remains the sole objective of monetary policy in India in the post-reform period". Comment on this statement.

2. What is the monetary policy framework in India in the post-1991 period?
3. What variables are considered while determining the policy inferences and actions under the multiple indicator approach in India? How far "Augmented Multiple Indicator Approach" different from "Multiple Indicator Approach"?
4. What does the monetary targeting refers to?
5. Why is India not pursuing the monetary targeting framework in the post-reform period?
6. What is the monetary operating target at present?
7. What is the monetary policy rate at present?

C10.2 Recent Monetary Policy Developments

Central banks around the world intensified their efforts to stimulate growth through policy rate cuts and liquidity injections beginning in the second half of 2011 after an earlier period of monetary tightening. Brazil and Turkey were among the first large developing economies to reduce their policy rates by 50 basis points each in August 2011. The majority of other monetary authorities have implemented a series of policy rate cuts since then, including the European Central Bank (ECB) and the central banks of Australia, Brazil, China, Indonesia, Kazakhstan, South Africa and many others (Figure 10.14). By the third quarter of 2012, nominal policy rates worldwide were actually lower than in 2009 during the worst of the financial crisis. Key policy rates settled at 7.25 per cent in Brazil, at 6 per cent in China, at 5.75 per cent in Indonesia and at 5 per cent in South Africa.

*BFN*1: In Turkey key policy rate used under the inflation-targeting framework is one week repo auction rate. In addition, interest rate corridor and required reserve ratios are also used as policy instruments.

Policy rate cuts were complemented by liquidity injections by major economies, where already low level of interest rates prevented further policy-rate cuts. Currently, policy rates remain below one per cent in Japan (since September 1995), in the US (since December 2008) and in the UK (since April 2009). Euro Area policy rates dropped below one per cent only more recently — in July 2012. Among the most recent monetary easing actions, a third round of quantitative easing involving central bank purchases of mortgage backed securities) in the United States, and the European Central Bank's commitment to conduct Outright Monetary Transactions if necessary were particularly notable.

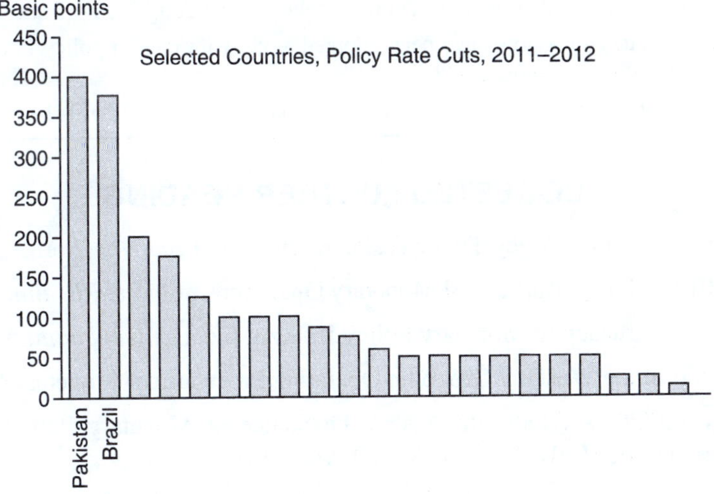

Figure 10.14 *Contd....*

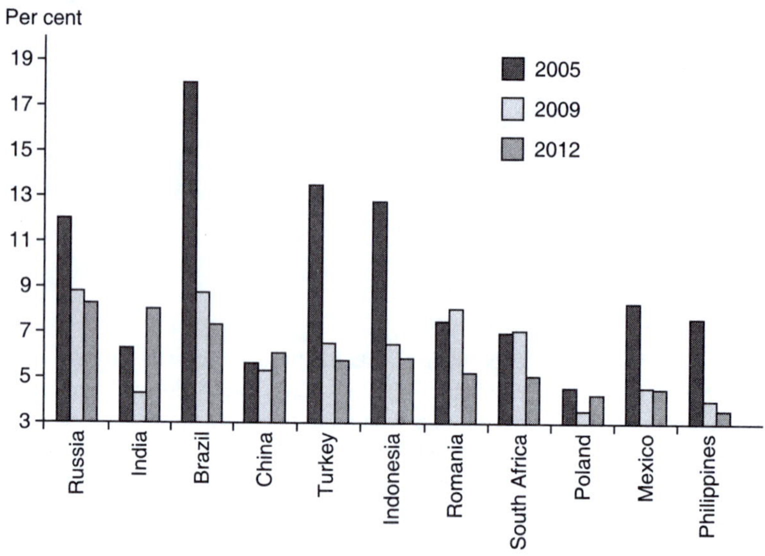

Source: World Bank, Bloomberg, Central Bank News, Central Bank Rates.

Figure 10.14 Policy Rate Cuts (peak-less trough), Jan. 2011– Sep. 2012. Key policy rates, selected years

Given the weak economic outlook, G3 and other high income countries' policy rates are expected to be left loose, and central banks are expected to continue with unconventional monetary policy throughout 2013–2014, and possibly till mid-2015.

Source: The World Bank (2013), Global Economic Prospects, Volume 6,January 2013. Washington, DC: World Bank.

Questions

1. Why the central banks world over have cut their policy rates during 2011–12 and 2012–13?
2. What complementary measures have been adopted along with cuts in policy rates? Why are these complimentary policy measures used?
3. What type of monetary policy the central banks are likely to pursue in 2013–14?

SUGGESTED FURTHER READING

Mohan, R. (2007), Monetary Policy Transmission in India, *RBI Bulletin*, April.

Mohanty, D. (2013), Money Market and Monetary Operations in India, *RBI Bulletin*, January.

Mohanty, D. (2013), Efficacy of Monetary Policy Rules in India, *RBI Bulletin*, April.

RBI (2011), Report of the Working Group on Operating Procedure of Monetary Policy.

Samantaraya, A. (2009), An Index to Assess the Stance of Monetary Policy in India in the Post-Reform Period, *EPW*, Vol. 44, No. 20, May 16.

Stiglitz, J.S. (2013), A Revolution in Monetary Policy: Lessons in the Wake of Global Financial Crisis, *RBI Bulletin*, February.

CHAPTER 11

Industrial Structure, Policy and Business Environment

11.1 INTRODUCTION

Automobiles, pharmaceuticals, medical equipment, IT and software, mobile handsets and many such products manufactured in India have hit the market abroad and have been well-received by the foreign consumers. Tata motors, a company of Indian origin, sells its passenger car Indica in the UK. Mahindra and Mahindra, an Indian multinational, is one of the most successful companies in farm equipment sector and is a well known brand in the world. Kirloskar brand of pumps sells very well in Egypt, Kenya, in some countries in Middle-East and Laos. Indian pharmaceutical company, Cipla, is able to sell its drugs to treat arthritis, cardiovascular, depression and many more diseases to almost every country in the world. Similarly, Himalaya's drugs are known world over, with 40 per cent of the total revenue of the company coming from its global business. Moser Baer, again an Indian company, is a well-known brand abroad for optical storage devices like CDs and DVDs. Raymond group, India's largest branded fabric and fashion retailer, exports to over 55 countries including Canada, Europe, Japan, Middle-East and the USA.

Being a country rich in resources and cheap labour, India has attracted many Multinational Companies (MNCs) to set up their manufacturing units in the country. Many of these units are not only manufacturing to cater to the Indian market but also supplying goods from their manufacturing units located in India to markets located abroad. General Motors, a multinational originated in the USA, wants to supply abroad its car engines manufactured in its unit located in Talegaon near Pune in Maharashtra state. *Maruti Suzuki* India Limited, a *subsidiary of* Suzuki Motor Corporation, Japan, is catering not only the Indian market but also selling some of its models in Europe. Hindustan Unilever (HUL), owned by British-Dutch company Unilever, is marketing its water purifier Pureit to markets like Indonesia, Bagladesh, Sri-Lanka, Brazil, Mexico, and Nigeria. It is also supplying its brand Annapurna to Ghana and Wheel detergent powder in Bangladesh and skin whitening cream Fair & Lovely to 30 countries across the world. And there are many such success stories.

But, what is disappointing is to know that in spite of impressive performance by automobile industry, pharmaceutical giants, software industries, India is lagging behind many of its close competitors, which started their growth path with similar initial conditions: huge population, low manufacturing base, low income and more or less closed economic system.

India adopted heavy industrialization as the development strategy after independence. In spite of considerable emphasis on developing its industrial base, in general, and manufacturing sector, in particular, and many reforms in the industrial sector since mid 1980's, the industrial sector in India still accounts for just around 26 per cent of GDP and 15 per cent of employment. The underdeveloped manufacturing sector has already started imposing constraints on the further growth of the service sector and the overall growth of the country. What has gone wrong with the industrial/manufacturing sector in spite of all the resources available in the country for its growth? What is hampering its growth? What can improve its share in the total GDP? What can be done to improve its competitiveness in the international market? These are some questions that the country is facing, now, for more than half a century.

To get an answer for some of these questions, this chapter first provides some conceptual background. Accordingly, Section 11.2 defines the terms industry and industrial structure, and helps in understanding the different ways in which industries are classified. Industrial clusters emerge only in some specific locations. Section 11.3 details on the factors that determine industrial location. Industrial policies are used for affecting the industrial structure and location. Section 11.4 defines industrial policy and outlines the reasons for which we need such policies. This section subsequently briefs on the objectives and instruments of industrial policy and the various parameters that can be used for assessing the industrial performance. Simultaneously, through cases it briefs on the policies pursued by India in the pre- and post-reform period, the consequences of such policies and the further reforms needed to develop the Indian industrial sector.

11.2 INDUSTRY: DEFINITION AND CLASSIFICATION

The term **industry** refers to the people or manufacturers or companies or firms engaged in any type of economic activity producing goods or services that are close substitutes of each other. The activities can range from the production of goods to the extraction of minerals to provision of services. For example, the cement industry is engaged in production of goods, coal mining industry extracts minerals and information technology industry provides services.

11.2.1 Classification of Industries

Industries are classified using various criteria as follows:

Size

On the basis of size, industries are classified as the small scale industry, medium scale industry and large scale industry. The definition of small, medium and large scale industry varies across countries. Various parameters, such as the number of employees, annual turnover, and investment are used for differentiating industries on the basis of size. At times, size classification of industries varies across sectors and even regions within a country (Box 11.1).

Box 11.1 Small and Medium Scale Industry

There is no standard way of classifying industry on the basis of size. The definition varies across the countries.

For example, in the USA, in wholesale trade, a small scale industry is the one that employs up to 100 workers, whereas in manufacturing and mining the number is between 500 to 1,500. In the

European Union, as indicated in Table 11.1, a general distinction is made between micro, small and medium sized businesses using the number of employees and either turnover or balances total as the criteria.

Table 11.1 Classification of Industries in the European Union

Type of industry	*Number of employees*	*Turnover*	*Balance sheet total*
Micro Business	< 10	≤ € 50 m	≤ € 43 m
Small Business	< 50	≤ € 10m	≤ € 10 m
Medium Size Business	< 250	≤ € 2 m	≤ € 2 m

Source: European Commission Enterprise and Industry, (online) http://ec.europa.eu/cgi-bin/etal.pl; as on 25/2/13.

In India, in contrast, the classification is based on the amount of investment as indicated in Table 11.2.

Table 11.2 Classification of Industry in India

Classification	*Manufacturing enterprises**	*Service enterprises***
Micro	₹2.5 million/₹25 lakh	₹1 million/₹10 lakh
Small	₹50 million/₹5 crore	₹20 million/₹2 crore
Medium	₹100 million/₹10 crore	₹50 million/₹5 crore

*Investment limit in plant and machinery; **Investment limit in equipments
Source: Compiled from Ministry of Micro, Small and Medium Enterprises (online) http://msme.gov.in/MSME_Development_Gazette.htm

Though the definition of small, medium and large scale industries is available explicitly, the same is not the case with the definition of large scale industry. The firms that do not fall in the category of small and medium scale are considered to be in the large scale industry. These firms invest heavily in capital goods and employ a large workforce. Firms manufacturing fertilizers, iron and steel, cement, ships, automobiles, textiles, natural gas, consumer durables like television, washing machines, require heavy investment and, hence, fall under this category. Tata Iron and Steel Company (TISCO), Ambuja Cement Ltd., and Reliance Petroleum Limited are some examples of large scale industries in India.

Small and medium industries are considered to be labour intensive, whereas large scale industries are more capital intensive. Hence, when the objective of the policies is to generate higher employment in the country, the size distribution of industries is analyzed.

Ownership

On the basis of ownership, industries are classified as follows:

1. Private sector industries: **Private sector industries** are owned and operated by individuals and households. Most often the profit motive governs the operations of the units operating in the private sector. Prices of commodities offered by this sector is usually determined by the market forces. In the USA, McDonalds and Microsoft Corporations are private sector industries, while in India Reliance petrochemicals, Tata Consultancy and Infosys fall under private sector.

2. Public sector industries: Government is also involved in many productive activities in many countries with the prime objective of achieving higher social welfare. The industries that are owned and operated by the government are known as **public sector industries**. The government not only owns and operates but also sets the prices of the commodities supplied by the public sector. In India, Air India, Bharat Heavy Electricals Ltd. and HMT Ltd. are some companies that fall under the public sector.

3. Joint sector industries: **Joint sector Industries** comprise undertakings wherein the ownership control and management are shared jointly by the government, the private entrepreneurships and the public at large. Though the firms in these industries operate on profit objective, socio-economic considerations also play an important role in their workings. The objective behind setting up such industries is to enhance efficiency and productivity in the production process without compromising on the social objectives. Maruti Udyog, Bharat Sanchar Nigam Limited (BSNL), Cochin Refineries, Gujarat State Fertilizers, Automobile Products of India Ltd., etc., fall in the joint sector in India.

4. Co-operative sector industries: Enterprises in co-operative sector are autonomous democratic associations of persons united voluntarily to meet their common economic, social and cultural goals. **Co-operative sector industries** follow more open, transparent, democratic and inclusive process in their operations than the ones operating on profit motives. Amul **Gujarat Co-operative Milk Marketing Federation Ltd.** (GCMMF), popularly known as Amul, Shri Mahila Griha Udyog, popularly known as Lijjat, and Indian Farmers Fertiliser Co-operative Limited (IFFCO), are some such organizations in India that follow co-operative principles.

Source of Raw Material

1. Agro-based industries: The industries using raw material from agriculture are referred to as **agro-based industries**. Cotton textile, jute and sugar industries are some industries that fall under this category.

2. Mineral-based industries: The industries using minerals like iron and steel, and cement are classified as **mineral-based industries**.

3. Forest-based industries: Paper, plywood, furniture, sports industries are classified as **forest-based industries** as their raw material comes from forests.

4. Pastoral resource-based industry: The **pastoral-based industries** such as shoes, bags and dairy, depend on animal products such as skins, hides, etc.

On the Basis of Weight of Raw Material and Finished Products

Depending on the nature or size of the raw material used, industries are classified as heavy industries and light industry.

1. Heavy industry: The industries that use heavy or bulky raw materials as well as produce finished products that are heavy in weight are classified as **heavy industry**. Because of the heavy nature of their inputs as well as output, these industries need an efficient mode of transport that can carry the required load. Examples of such industry are iron and steel, cement, automobiles, ships, refrigerators, etc.

2. Light industry: The industries that use light raw material and produce final goods that are light in weight are classified as **light industry**. For example, fans, garments, electronics, watches, utensils, etc.

On the Basis of Utility

On the basis of utility, i.e., the use to which a particular commodity is put, the industries are classified as follows:

1. Basic goods industries: **Basic industries** are those industries that produce different kinds of fuels, such as high speed diesel and aviation fuel, cement, basic metals, such as sponge iron, copper, and basic chemicals, such as soda and acids, and electricity. These goods are used for further production of new items in manufacturing and agriculture.

2. Intermediate goods industry: **Intermediate goods industries** are those industries that produce incomplete products or inputs that are used in final production of various items. Examples of such industries are the industries producing cotton yarn, plywood, liquefied petroleum gas, aluminium tubes.

3. Capital goods industry: **Capital goods industry** supplies plants, machinery, and other goods used for further investment. The industry manufacturing textile machinery, printing machinery, diesel engines, air and gas compressors, transformers, commercial vehicles, etc., fall under this category.

4. Consumer goods industry: **Consumer goods industry** is the industry that produces final goods, the goods that are used for consumption by the public. For example, bread, biscuits, pen, pencil, eraser, table, chairs, etc. These industries can be further classified as follows:

(i) *Consumer durable goods industry:* The **consumer durable goods industry** produces goods that have a short shelf life and durability. These are final goods which last for a long time, such as cars, scooters, television, refrigerators, sewing machines, vacuum cleaners and watches.

(ii) *Consumer non-durable goods industry:* The *consumer non-durable goods industry* produces goods that have short life span and get consumed quickly such as tea, sugar, bread, bags, milk, biscuits, etc.

On the Basis of Nature of the Manufactured Products

1. Metallurgical industries: The industries involved in extraction, refining, alloying and fabrication of metals are known as **metallurgical industries**. Aluminium industry, iron and steel; industry and non-ferrous metal industry are metallurgical industries.

2. Mechanical engineering industries: The **mechanical engineering industries** deal with designing, manufacturing or maintenance of mechanical structures, engineering equipments and structures. The examples of such industries are: automobile industry, spacecraft industry, textile machinery industry, and the industries manufacturing machineries for printing, paper, wood, leather, rubber, glass and related industries.

3. Chemical and allied industries: The **chemical industries** are involved in the research and development and production of industrial chemicals such as paints, plastic, synthetic fibres and, silicon based chemicals. The main consumers of this industry are consumer good industries, health care, industry, agriculture, paper, textile, transport, defense and construction industries.

4. Textile industries: The **textile industry** is involved in the manufacturing of fibre, yarn and cloth, and textile design and finishing. Apparel industry, garment industry, wool and silk industry, etc., fall under this category.

5. Food processing industries: The **food processing industries** transform raw materials into food and other forms. These industries also deal with processes such as grading, sorting, packaging which enhances the shelf life of food products. In the process these industries provide an important link between the agriculture and allied sector and the manufacturing sector. Beverage industry, bakery and confectionery industry, packaged food industry, milk and dairy product industry, etc., fall under this category.

6. Electricity generation industries: The industries involved in generation of electricity from different sources of energy such as water, wind, coal, nuclear, natural gas, etc. are classified as **electricity generation industries**. Hydroelectric Power Generation and fossil fuel electric power generation fall under this category of industry.

7. Electronics industries: The **electronics industries** manufacturers electronic devices such as radio, television, semiconductors, transistors, computers, and integrated circuits. Electronics Industry is further subdivided as consumer electronics industry, industrial electronic industry, communication and broadcasting equipment industry, strategic electronics industry and electronic component industry.

8. Communication industries: The **communication industries** are involved in communication and distribution of content designed to inform and entertain. Telecommunication industry, cable television industry, publication industry, etc. , fall under this category.

On the Basis of Factor Intensity

On the basis of factor intensity the industries are classified as follows:

1. Capital intensive industries: The **capital intensive industries**, such as textile, iron and ore, cement, oil refineries, etc., require huge investment in plant, building and machinery.

2. Labour intensive industries: The **labour intensive industries** require huge labour force for their operations. Shoes, bidi manufacturing, cracker manufacturing, etc., as require large workforce, are classified as labour intensive industries.

On the Basis of Type of Processing

On the basis of type of processing, industries are classified as follows:

1. Processing industries: The processing industries process raw material and changes its form by altering its physical state, chemical composition, volume or mass so as to make it useful for human beings. For example, food processing industries, fluorocarbon Processing Industries (processors of PTFE and other fluoropolymers), steel processing industries (manufacture power distribution transformer components) are processing industries. Processing industries are further distinguished as initial processing industries and complex processing industries.

(i) *Initial processing industries.* **Initial processing industries** convert a single raw material into a more concentrated or useful form. For example, fruit and vegetable canning, dairy processing, etc.

(ii) *Complex processing industries.* **Complex processing industries** procure several raw materials and subject them to a series of lengthy and complex processes using advanced technology.

2. Fabrication industries: The **fabrication industries** manufacture components that are used in the manufacturing of large machines and structures or buildings. It primarily looks into the assembly of finished and semi-finished products. For example, in building fabrication industries, carpenters, following the design specified by architects, convert milled and dried lumber into buildings and apartments. Similarly, metal fabricating industries manufacture components that are assembled to manufacture various types of automobiles.

11.2.2 Industry Classification System

For uniformity of data collection, policy analysis and administration of policies as well as for various business decisions we need to have grouping of firms/establishments into meaningful categories. Depending on the purpose, the classification can be broad or finer. The classification is kept broad if the objective is to analyze the economy as a whole. But, if the objective is to analyze and understand the economic interactions taking place between different activities then finer/detailed categorization is necessitated. Also, the categorization varies as per the use. Accordingly, various official and private organizations have come up with different **industry classifications** using varied classification criteria (Table 11.3). For example, some classification systems are based on similarity of products, while other systems group industries on the basis of similarity in the production processes. There are also groupings available that are based on the behaviour in the financial markets.

Table 11.3 Some Widely Used Industry Classifications Available in the Literature

Classification category	*Organization*	*Classification criterion*	*Coding structure*	*First/Latest revision*	*Purpose*
International Standard Industrial Classification of Economic Activities (ISIC)	United Nations Statistics Division	Production	4 digits	1948/2008	To collect and report statistics as per the classification. This classification has been adopted by the majority of countries; has become an important tool for comparing data at the international level
North American Industry Classification System (NAICS)	Statistical bureau of US, Canada and Mexico	Production-oriented concept	6 digits	1997/2012	Produce information on inputs and outputs, industrial performance, productivity, unit labour costs, and employment. Used for various administrative, regulatory, contracting, taxation, and other non-statistical purposes
Statistical Classification of Economic Activities in European Community (NACE)	European Community	Principle economic activity	4 digits	1970/2008	Compiling data on production, employment and national accounts

Classification category	*Organization*	*Classification criterion*	*Coding structure*	*First/Latest revision*	*Purpose*
Australian and New Zealand Standard Industrial Classification (ANZSIC)	Australian Bureau of Statistics (ABS) and Statistics New Zealand (Statistics NZ)	Predominant activity	Alphanumeric	1993/2006	Various administrative, regulatory, taxation and research purposes
Global Industry Classification Standard (GICS)	Morgan Stanley Capital International (MSCI) and Standard and Poor's (S&P)	Principle business activity	2-8 digits	1999/2011	To enhance investment research and asset management process for financial professionals
National Industrial Classification (NIC)	India	Economic activities	5 digits alphabetic	1962/2008	Collecting census and sample survey data; using it for policy formulation and analysis
Industry Classification Benchmark (ICB)	FTSE International Limited	Principle business activity	4 digit	2005	Investment research and analysis

Industry classification is used by governments, economic and business analysts, and corporates:

Government

1. For census and sample surveys: Government statistical organizations use industry classification for maintaining standards in data collection, processing and presentation in census and sample surveys.

2. Policy making: Industry classification helps policy makers to ascertain changes in employment and production structure. Tax rates, subsidies, FDI policies and various other policies can be fine tuned to benefit broad or finer categories of industries.

3. Administration: The industry classification is used for various administrative activities as well. For example, tax officials use the classification for computing tax liabilities of different corporate entities.

Corporate Sector

1. Financial sector for determining their exposure to different sectors: Financial sector analyses the growth and the risk and return profiles while providing loans to different industries.

2. Insurance companies fixing insurance premium: Insurance companies collect data on illness and injuries for different industry categories and they decide on the insurance premium as per the estimated risk profile for a particular industry.

3. Filing income tax return: Corporate organizations use the industry classification for estimating their tax liability and accordingly filing the annual income tax returns.

4. Availing subsidies: While availing various subsidies, companies have to indicate their industrial classification number.

5. Eligibility to bid on certain contracts: Often business organizations bidding for government contracts require to quote their industry classification code in the bidding applications.

6. Seeking foreign direct investment: The norms for FDI vary for different industries. Companies can look at the norms that are applicable to the industries in which they fall and decide on the amount of FDI they can invite in their companies.

7. Portfolio management and asset allocation: Industry classification makes it easier for investment analysts and wealth management companies to compare relative valuation and risk-return of companies falling in different industries and use this information for portfolio management and asset allocation.

11.2.3 Industry Structure

Industry structure refers to the number and size distribution of firms in an Industry. The number of firms in an industry may run into one to several hundreds or thousands. A large number of firms (compared to the market size—measured as total sales or total demand) in an industry indicates that each firm in this industry must be small and each may be simply a price taker. A large number may make it difficult for firms to co-ordinate with each other and unite to form a monopoly, and the market may remain fragmented. On the other extreme, a single firm hint that the firm has no rival. Being a monopoly, this firm can exert significant influence on the price of the commodity. In between the two structures there can be just a small number of firms, indicating that each may be commanding a significant proportion of the market share and each may affect the market outcome in terms of price and quantity. The likelihood of fierce competition in such a market, referred to as **oligopoly**, is very high. Also, the small number keeps the possibility of collaboration and consolidation very high. The nature of competition in a consolidated market is very different than that observed in a fragmented market.

Each type of market structure has its advantages. In a fragmented market, co-operation is less likely. The society benefits from such a structure in terms of low price and mass scale production. However, as each firm is too small, the society may be deprived of the benefits arising from the economies of scale that are enjoyed by large size firms. Such firms are also forced to invest in R&D to keep their dominance intact and hence consumers benefit in terms of availability of new, technologically superior products and quality goods.

Given the differences, in the structure of the two types of industries, business firms would need to design different kinds of competition and survival strategies to remain in the market. While formulating public policies, the government analyses the industry structure and tries to alter it so that the desired objectives can be achieved.

11.3 FACTORS AFFECTING LOCATION OF INDUSTRIES

There is a tendency of firms to situate in some specific locations. The location of industries is affected by many factors as depicted in Figure 11.1 and as described hereinafter:

1. Land: An industrial establishment needs flat land to operate. The price of such land is an important consideration while locating an establishment in a particular area.

2. Labour: Highly labour intensive establishments, such as *bidi* manufacturing, prefer to set-up their units in the areas where labour with the required skills is available in plenty.

3. Capital: For capital intensive units, the cheap availability of capital is an important consideration while selecting their locations.

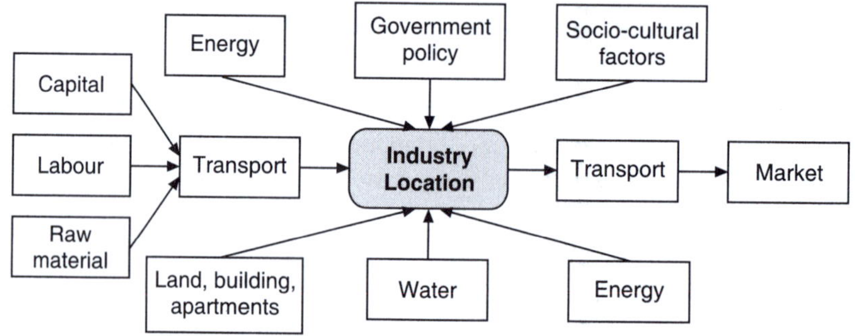

Figure 11.1 Factors Affecting Industry Location.

4. Raw material: Industries that depend on bulky or heavy raw material prefer to locate near the source of raw material. For example, for sugar industries sugarcane is the main input. Sugarcane is almost 8 times bulkier than the output of sugar that it provides. Given the bulky nature of its input, the sugar industries are concentrated in sugarcane growing regions. Similarly, alumina industries use about four tonnes of bauxite to produce two units of alumina. Given the bulky nature of its inputs, alumina industries are located near their source of input. Industries that use perishable raw materials also prefer to locate themselves near their source of input.

5. Energy: Energy intensive units prefer to locate in areas where sources of energy such as water, coal and electricity are available in plenty.

6. Transport and communication: The availability of good transport network—roads, rails, airports, ports—facilitates quick receipt of inputs as well speedy delivery of finished products to the markets. Hence, locations with good transport network are preferred by industrial units.

7. Government policies: Government policies can alter the attractiveness of a particular location for industrial units. Subsidies can make certain locations, such as hilly and remote areas, attractive, whereas regulations can move industrial units away from locations where such regulation are imposed.

11.4 INDUSTRIAL POLICY: WHAT AND WHY?

The **industrial policy** refers to official strategic plans laid down in the form of rules, regulations, principles, policies and procedures for regulating, developing and controlling industrial undertakings. Unlike various macroeconomic policies, such as fiscal and monetary policies, industrial policies are sector specific.

The need for designing and implementing industrial policies emerges primarily because of market failure. **Market failure** can occur in an economy because of the following reasons:

Co-ordination Failure

Each production unit requires support from other production units and supporting infrastructure. For example, construction industry requires easy availability of cement, whereas cement industry, to operate profitably, needs to operate on a large scale, which is possible only if there is a huge demand. In a country with underdeveloped state of construction and other industries, the demand for cement will be very limited, preventing the cement industry from enjoying the benefits of economies of scale and making it unviable. In such countries, cement industry will not grow because there is a lack of demand, while the growth of the construction industry will be limited because, there is no easy availability of the required inputs. Simultaneous investment is required in both of them. But, in the want of proper co-ordination of investment, private initiatives will fail to come up in both cement and construction industry. Another example of **co-ordination failure** is when industrial development, say a food processing industry, in the rural areas fails to take place because of the absence of proper communication and transport network. The government can intervene in such cases by either directly investing in the required industries or by providing appropriate incentives so that there is a better co-ordination of investors in different supporting industries.

Lack of Information or Information Asymmetries

Discovery of lucrative business proposition requires large investment in research and development. At the same time, investors face a risk of failure of their efforts. Once discovered, the new ideas and practices may get copied easily by the competitors, wiping out the excess profits of the investors. The possibility of risk of failure as well the fear of imitations by the competitors often prevent enough investment in knowledge generation. The government can help in the generation of information by protecting ideas and processes, and incentivising the investment in knowledge generation by the private sector.

Information Externalities

Investment in knowledge is subject to large externalities. That is, the benefit accruing to the society of knowledge is much larger than the benefit accruing to the entity investing in the knowledge. Large externalities, thus, discourage enough investment in knowledge generation. For example, a company investing in the training of its staff often fears that the trained staff may join the other industries and the competitors. Such a possibility deters many companies from investing enough in training and development of their staff.

Dynamic Scale Economies

Price signals, emanated from market forces, though lead to the development of the sectors in which the country has a comparative advantage (defined in Section 13.2.1), they often fail to indicate the areas in which the country can achieve comparative advantage over a period of time by learning and doing and by experience. Such areas can be discovered by investing in and experimenting with ideas and processes. The huge amount of investment that is required for such experiments deters private enterprises to venture into and explore such areas. Active intervention by the government in many countries has led to the identification of the areas in which the countries have a dynamic comparative advantage. For example, Brazil, over a period of time discovered its comparative advantage in the aircraft industry. Similar success has been achieved by Korea in the automobile industry.

Environmental Externalities

The environmental externalities arise during the production process; the part of cost/or benefit of production activities gets passed on the entities which are not involved in these activities. The externalities can be negative or positive. The externalities are negative when private cost of economic activities is less than the social cost. That is,

$$\text{Social costs} = \text{Private costs} + \text{External costs}$$

The most often cited example of **negative externalities** is pollution. For example, a factory discharging its chemical waste in a river or lake, affect the life in the water like fish and crabs and threatens the livelihood of people dependent on aqua life. In such cases, as producers bear only part of the cost, they end up overproducing goods. Government policies in the form of taxes on polluting industries help in internalizing the negative externalities and forces the producers to bring down the output to the level that is socially optimal.

On the contrary, positive externalities arise when private benefits are less than the social benefits. That is,

$$\text{Social benefits} = \text{Private benefits} + \text{External benefits}$$

An industry investing heavily in the invention of new technology faces such externalities if the competitors can easily copy their inventions. In such cases, the benefits of the new technology to the inventing firm will be lesser than that of the competitors. This may deter investment in socially beneficial goods and technologies and there will be under production of goods that are socially desirable. Industrial policies in the form of subsidies to the inventors or patent protection help in internalizing the **positive externalities** and help the society to get the optimum level of output.

Though market failure is the traditional justification for the government interventions, at times, government interventions are necessitated for bringing in perfections in the existing markets. Profit maximization objective often forces competitors, especially the ones operating in oligopoly markets, to co-operate and collaborate and form monopolies to strengthen their market position. To promote competition, the governments try to curb such practices by enacting anti-trust or anti-monopoly laws. But, governments, at times, have also been found to be promoting co-operation among firms so as to tap economies of scale.

Public interventions in the form of industrial policies aim at fostering growth by devising interventions that can create markets as well perfect existing markets. These policies do not intend to eliminate markets or replace those by socialist planning. Rather, they improve and promote market forces and channelize resources in the desired directions for achieving sustainable growth.

11.4.1 Objectives of Industrial Policy

Industrial policies try to achieve the following objectives:

Predicting and Facilitating Structural Changes

It is always a challenge to identify the emerging productive sectors that can enhance and sustain the growth. Industrial policy can support the private initiatives by investing in research and development to identify new emerging innovative ideas and technologies, and encouraging the private sector to adopt these technologies in their existing product lines.

Changes in the production structure also bring with it changes in employment opportunities. Often, in the process of structural transformation, labour gets displaced from traditional activities. In the absence of proper skill set, the displaced labour may remain unemployed or may move to the agriculture and/or informal sector. Therefore, while promoting growth via accelerating structural changes one major challenge is to train the displaced worker so that they can be productively deployed in the emerging and highly productive areas. For example, if the service sector is the emerging sector in the economy, the surplus labour in the agricultural sector and displaced labour from the manufacturing sector can be trained by imparting skill set that is required in the services. Such training and investment in human capital can increase the employment in emerging dynamic areas.

Correcting Market Failures

Market failures can occur because of various reasons, such as co-ordination failure and externalities. Market failures restrain entrepreneurs in venturing into emerging activities that can foster growth.

Industrial policies can help in correcting market failures by encouraging private initiatives in generating and disseminating enough information, investing in areas which facilitate better co-ordination of various economic activities. Such policies can also compel the private sector to internalize the harmful impacts of negative externalities and encourage the ones that have a large element of positive externalities.

UBE 11.1 illustrates how industrial policies have been used in correcting market failures in India in the pre-1991 period. At the same time, the case also highlights the type of inefficiencies that crept in the economy during this period. The measures that were taken to overcome the inefficiencies are highlighted in UBE 11.2.

11.4.2 Instruments of Industrial Policy

Though there may be commonalities in the objectives of industrial policies, the blend of policies designed and instruments employed vary widely across countries and over the time. The selection of policies and instruments is largely affected by initial conditions, determined by the potential size of the domestic market, industrial structure, the availability of various factor and non-factor inputs, level of per capita income and its distribution, share of different sectors in the GDP, regional imbalances, socio-cultural factors, the extent of private sector, fiscal position, etc.

The broad instruments used world over are industrial licensing, import licensing, taxes and subsidies, quantitative restrictions and reservation of items for the public sector and the employment intensive small scale sector (UBE 11.1). However, such instruments impose tight control of the working of the industrial sector of the economy. Often such measures limit the capacity expansion, deprive the units the benefits of economies of scale that are enjoyed by the large scale units producing goods in bulk. To overcome the disadvantage arising from the tight control, easing is archived and efficiency is infused by adopting the strategy of liberalization, privatization and globalization (Box 11.2).

Box 11.2 Liberalization, Privatization and Globalization

Controlled or command economy often moves towards market-oriented economies through the process of liberalization, privatization and globalization. These terms are defined as follows:

Liberalization: The term **liberalization** refers to the removal or easing of restrictions by the government on economic activities. The objective of liberalization is to allow the market forces (demand and supply) to play a greater role in all economic activities. Some of the instruments of liberalization are de-licensing and de-reservation. Thus, when the government liberalizes the industrial sector, it implies the removal of licensing restrictions and easing out of many rules and regulations that constrains the production process.

Privatization: **Privatization** refers to the process of transferring ownership or management of an enterprise, agency, establishment, public utility or services and/or public property from the public sector (government) to the private sector. As the private sector tends to lay more emphasis on profit maximization than the government, often the objective behind privatization is to infuse efficiency and enhance productivity of the organizations that are selected for privatization.

Privatization can take various forms; some are listed here:

Complete privatization: **Complete privatization** takes place when there is an outright sale of whole firm or assets by the government to the private sector. Such sale has mostly taken place in transition economies of Central and Eastern Europe. In India, the public sector units that have been completely privatized include Auto Tractors, East Cost Breweries and Distilleries, Goa Telecommunications, Hindustan Allwyn's Refrigeration Division and Rajasthan State Tanneries.

Privatization of operations: In the **privatization of operations**, the responsibility of management and operations is assigned to the private operators though the ownership of the assets remains with the government. In this process, the private entities generate revenue by charging fees to the individuals using the public assets.

Contracting out: In the **contracting out** method, the government outsources production of goods and services to one or more private entities through competitive bidding. The government however, pays for the production of goods and services that are contracted out.

Franchising: Under the **franchising** method, exclusive right of production or providing services, for a period of time, in a specific region, is given to a private bidder offering the most attractive terms. Unlike contracting out, in franchising the consumers pay for the goods and services provided by the franchisee.

Public-private partnership: In **public-private partnership** arrangement, the government and a private entity (or a consortium of private entities) jointly undertake or perform a traditional public activity. The government usually goes for such partnership in large capital intensive infrastructure projects, such as airports, highways and dams. For example, Hyderabad international airport in India is developed under public-private partnership, wherein GMR group holds 63 per cent equity, Malaysia Airports Holdings Berhad owns 11 per cent equity and the Government of Andhra Pradesh and Airport Authority of India each hold 13 per cent equity.

Open competition: At times, government dereserves the sectors erstwhile reserved for the public sector to the private sector and allows the private sector to compete with the public sector units. Such a privatization has taken place in the banking, telephone, electricity and many such sectors in India.

Globalization: The term **globalization** refers to the opening up of an economy to greater trade and capital flows. The process is achieved by easing out of tariff and licensing restrictions on trade flows, liberalizing capital flows and moving towards flexible exchange rate regime. The process of globalization is expected to result in a better integration of the domestic market with the international market. The enhanced competition, larger availability of resources, recourse to better modern technology, as an outcome of better integration, is expected to improve productivity and efficiency in the production process, and enhance the quality of the domestic product.

11.4.3 Parameters for Assessment of Industrial Performance

Industrial policies aim at accelerating growth, improving value addition in different sectors, enhancing the export intensity, boosting net foreign exchange earnings, promoting employment by enhancing the labour intensity and altering the market structure to bring in more competition in the economy. The impact of policies on different aspects of industrial performance can be assessed using various parameters. Some of these parameters are explained here:

Assessing the Contribution to Value Added

One way in which the contribution of an industry to the output can be measured is by finding out the ratio of the output of an industry to the total output. However, total output may be higher due to large use of intermediate inputs in the total value of output. The value added, which ignores the value of intermediate inputs, only reflects the contribution of factor inputs—land, labour, capital and entrepreneurship; hence, it is used for assessing the impact of industrial policies and reform measures on a particular industry.

Assessing the Impact on Exports

1. Export intensity of sales: The performance of the industry on export front is adjudged by the **export intensity of sales**, which is estimated as:

$$\text{Export intensity of sales} = (\text{Exports/Sales}) \times 100$$

2. Import intensity of exports: Though the export intensity of sales gives an idea of the export performance of a unit, it does not indicate whether the unit is contributing to the net foreign exchange earnings (export earnings – export payments). It is possible that the import bill of a highly export intensive unit may be larger than its export earnings. Such units rather than solving the problem of scarcity of foreign exchange will simply be aggravating it. Therefore, to assess the contribution of a unit to net foreign exchange earnings, the parameter **imports intensity of exports** is analyzed. It is estimated as:

$$\text{Import intensity of exports} = (\text{Imports/Exports}) \times 100$$

Assessing the Impact on Industry Structure and the Level of Competition

To make an assessment of the level of competition in the industry, economists, business analysts and the government look at the industry concentration. The two widely used indices for assessing the concentration are:

1. Concentration ratio: The **concentration ratio** (CRn) is defined as the percentage of market share owned by the largest n firms, where n is the specified number of firms. Thus,

$$CRn = \frac{S_1}{TS} + \frac{S_2}{TS} + \cdots + \frac{S_n}{TS} = s_1 + s_2 + \cdots + s_n \sum_{i=1}^{n} s_i$$

where,

S_i = Sales of Industry i

TS = Total sales of the entire industry

$\frac{S_i}{TS} = s_i$ = Share of industry i in Total Sales

The value of *CRn* varies from 0 to 1. It is close to zero even when the concentration ratio for a very large number of firms occupy very small proportion of the total sales in the industry. On the other extreme, *CRn* will be 1 if there is only one firm in the industry, indicating that it is a monopoly. If the *CRn* (say CR_4 or CR_8) is close to 1 it implies that the first few (4 or 8) large firms hold a large share of the total sales in the industry and the market structure is oligopoly.

2. Herfindahl–Hirschman index: Another widely used measurement of the industry concentration is the **Herfindahl–Hirschman Index** (HHI). The HHI, rather than considering the market share, considers the squares of the market share of each firm to place more weight on the share of larger firms, hence, it is considered to be better than the concentration ratio. The HHI is estimated as

$$HHI = s_1^2 + s_2^2 + \cdots + s_n^2 = \sum_{i=1}^{n} s_i^2$$

where,

s_i^2 = Square of the market share of the *i*th firm.

The value of the HHI varies from 0 to 10,000.

Using this ratio, if there is only one firm in the industry, then it implies that it occupies 100 per cent share in the industry and the value of the HHI then will be 10,000. The HHI value of less than 1,000 is considered to be a relatively unconcentrated market, while the value between 1,000 to 1,800 represents a moderately concentrated market. The industry having the HHI value greater than 1,800 is considered to be highly concentrated.

3. Import penetration ratio: The **import penetration ratio** helps in measuring the competition that the domestic units face from imported goods. The ratio is measured as:

$$\text{Import Penetration Ratio} = \frac{\text{Imports}}{\text{Imports} + \text{Output} - \text{Exports}}$$

4. Export intensity of output: **Export intensity of output** or export orientation is defined as the ratio of exports to value of output, i.e.,

$$\text{Export Intensity of Output} = \frac{\text{Exports}}{\text{Value of Output}}$$

5. Capital intensity: **Capital intensity** is defined as the ratio of Capital to Labour. In a competitive scenario, firms try to save on the cost of production by cutting down on the amount of labour. The increased use of capital reduces the employment opportunities in an industry. The capital intensity of an industry can be assessed as:

$$\text{Capital Intensity of Labour} = \frac{\text{Capital}}{\text{Labour}}$$

UNDERSTANDING BUSINESS ENVIRONMENT

UBE 11.1 Overcoming the Problem of Market Imperfection: Industrial Policy In India During the Pre-1991 Period

This UBE illustrates how industrial policies have been used in correcting market failures in India in the pre-1991 period.

During the last two centuries, many present day developed countries achieved rapid growth by adopting the strategy of industrial development. The performance of these developed countries was so impressive that the economic development almost became synonymous with the industrial development.

After independence, in the pre-1991 period, India also adopted the policy of industrialization for achieving mainly the following objectives by addressing the problem of market failure:

- To achieve socialistic pattern of the society by expanding the public sector
- To prevent undue concentration of economic power
- To achieve rapid industrial development through promoting heavy and capital goods industry
- To protect and develop healthy small scale sector
- To reduce regional imbalances
- To create gainful employment opportunities
- To build up co-operative sector
- To modernize industry by upgrading technology
- To alleviate poverty
- To achieve self-sustained growth.

Being a highly underdeveloped country, many markets were either completely missing or under infant state due to co-ordination failure, lack of information and many such reasons. The private sector, in the resource deficit country, of its own could not have expected to overcome these problems and trigger the process of rapid industrialization. Growth, through industrial diversification and development, thus, necessitated government intervention.

To take forward the process of industrialization systematically, the country announced its first Industrial policy in 1948. The policy statement envisioned the Indian economic system as the mixed system with significant role to the government along with the private sector. Accordingly, it kept atomic energy, rail and road industries to be completely in the domain of the public sector. The policy statement also kept exclusive right of initiating projects in six other industries—coal, iron and steel, aircraft, manufacturing and shipbuilding, telephone and telegraph, and minerals though existing units in these areas allowed to continue operating. Besides, the government was empowered to regulate 18 other industries of national importance. Though the first policy statement outlined the broad counters it lacked detail.

The developments on the national front in the subsequent period, such as finalization of the Constitution of India, constitution of the Planning Commission and completion of the first five-year plan in the subsequent period necessitated major changes in the policy. Accordingly, the Industry Policy Resolution, 1956 replaced the Industrial Policy, 1948. The resolution clearly defined and demarcated the role of the government and classified the industries into three categories as follows:

- **Schedule A:** The industries which were the exclusive responsibility of the government fall under this category.
- **Schedule B:** The industries which were expected to be gradually state-owned or the new initiatives to come from the government. The private sector was expected to play just a complementary role in these industries.
- **Schedule C:** All the remaining industries left for the private initiative and developments.

Apart from clearly demarcating the areas for the two sectors, the resolution emphasized the following:

- The private sector should get a fair and non-discriminatory treatment
- The village and small scale enterprises to be encouraged
- The focus should be on reducing regional disparities

The subsequent policy statements addressed some particular facet of industrial development. For example, the Industrial Policy Statement, 1973, to prevent excessive concentration of power with large business houses, emphasized that the preference to be given to small and medium enterprises in enhancing capacity, especially in the industries producing mass consumption goods. The Industrial Policy Statement, 1977, along with assigning a greater role to the cottage, tiny, small and medium enterprises, stressed the need for close integration between industrial and agricultural sectors. This statement accorded highest priority to power generation and transmission. To promote the use of indigenous technology, it issued a list of industries where no collaboration of financial or technical nature was allowed in the areas where such technology was already available. The statement restricted fully-owned foreign companies only in highly export-oriented sectors or highly sophisticated technology areas. For balanced regional development, the statement prohibited the issue of fresh licenses for setting up new industrial units.

Unlike the previous statements, the Industrial Policy Statement, 1980, emphasized improvement in the level of competition in the domestic markets, technological advancements and modernization of industries for enhancing efficiency, productivity and quality of goods.

Mainly, three instruments were used during this period to achieve the various objectives of Industrial policy as follows:

Industrial licensing: Licensing was one of the core instruments of industrial policy in India. As per the Industries Development and Regulatory Act of 1951, even a very small size investors needed to obtain a license before establishing an industrial plant. A license was required not only for starting a unit but also for adding a new product line, changing the output level above the permitted level, and also changing the location of a plant. Such a tight control over the establishments has been cited as a reason for inefficiencies and rigidities in the industrial sector and its poor performance in the past.

Reservation policy: Another widely used instrument to develop the manufacturing sector was the reservation policy for the labour intensive small scale sector. The objective was to enhance the level of employment in the country. The number of products reserved for this sector continued to grow over a period of time. Gradually, the reservation was expanded to all the unskilled labour intensive units and reached to above 800. To avail the various incentives that the government was providing to these units, most of these units preferred to remain small. As an outcome of such protectionist policies, the country lost the advantage that it could have reaped had it allowed large players to expand their capacity.

Import licensing: Trade policy was also formulated to achieve the objectives of industrial policy. In concurrence with the objective of expanding manufacturing base, the trade policy restricted trade flows by imposing large tariff and non-tariff barriers. Import substitution policy was justified by the policy makers using the **infant industry argument**. Similarly, foreign capital flows were also restricted to promote indigenous technology and expertise.

Impact Assessment

The protectionist industrial policies helped the country in brining in the structural transformation of the industrial sector, as is apparent from Table 11.4.

Table 11.4 Share of Traditional Vs Modern Industry in Manufacturing GDP

Year	*Traditional industries*	*Modern industries*
1950–51	73%	27%
1969–70	38%	38%
2007–08	27%	73%

Source: Compiled from Papola (2012), Structural Changes in the Indian Economy: Emerging Patterns and Implications, Working Paper, ISID, (Online) http://58.68.105.147/pdf/WP1202.pdf.

During this period, the share of the registered sector in the total manufacturing sector also witnessed an improvement as is apparent from Table 11.5.

Table 11.5 Performance of the Registered Manufacturing Sector

Year	*Share of registered units in the manufacturing sector GDP*	*Share of registered units in the manufacturing sector growth rate*
1950–51	42%	6.5%
1979–80	52%	4.0%
2007–08	70%	8.0%

Source: Compiled from Papola (2012), Structural Changes in the Indian Economy: Emerging Patterns and Implications, Working Paper, ISID, (Online) http://58.68.105.147/pdf/WP1202.pdf.

The pre-reform period also witnessed a substantial increase in the number of small scale units because people with small savings or capital could start such units. Besides, the government actively supported the setting of such units by providing various tax and non-tax incentives and huge subsidies. These units being labour intensive created huge employment opportunities in the country.

The policies also brought about changes in the use based classification of the industrial sector. During the period 1951–66, the structure changed in favour of intermediate products, such as chemicals, petroleum and machinery. The subsequent two decades, however, show the movement in favour of capital goods such as steel, other basic metals and machinery. Alongwith the improvement in the share of intermediate and capital goods, the country witnessed a decline in the share of consumer goods sector.

Inspite of success in bringing about diversified structure, the overall growth of the manufacturing sector remained low. The share of the manufacturing sector in India's GDP increased from 9 per cent in 1950–51 to 15 per cent in 1979–80; but it remained stagnant thereafter at this level. The main reasons for the stagnation in the industrial growth were as follows:

1. Reservation policy for small scale sector: The objective behind keeping certain products reserved for the small scale industry was to promote employment; but, such a policy deprived the country the benefits that medium and large scale production brings in. The policy also kept the average size of firms small. It was also observed that the policy was responsible for the growth of informal or unregistered sector.

2. Industrial licensing: The policy of industrial licensing prevented reaching the optimum scale of production and was one reason why industrial units could not achieve economies of scale.

3. Import licensing: Import licensing policy prevented the required competition for the industrial units and cited as one of the reasons for inefficiencies in the production.

4. Reservation policy for the public sector: Apart from the import licensing policies, the reservation of number of items for the public sector is also cited as one of the reasons for the lack of competition and lack of efficiency and productivity in the country.

UNDERSTANDING BUSINESS ENVIRONMENT

UBE 11.2 Promoting Competition: Industrial Policy in the Post-1991 Period

This UBE highlights the measures that were adopted in India in the post-1991 period to overcome the inefficiencies that crept in the economy in the pre-1991 period.

To overcome the deficiencies that crept into the industrial segment in the late 1970s and 1980s it was growingly felt that more competition is required to force the existing units to improve the quality of their products. Step in this direction though started in the beginning of 80s with some easing on industrial and import licensing requirements, the serious restructuring of the manufacturing sector began only during the mid-eighties. But, a major blow to the erstwhile highly complex and tightly controlled industrial regime came in the post-1991 period with the complete change in the policy thinking and orientation. The industrial policy in the post-1991 period aims at the following:

- To achieve sustained growth in productivity
- To achieve optimum utilization of human resources and enhance the employment level
- To attain international competitiveness and transform India into a major partner and player in the global arena
- To improve profitability of the public sector units by running them on business principles
- To abolish the monopoly of any sector in any industry except on strategic and security grounds

To achieve the various objectives in the post-1991 period the country adopted the three-prong strategy of liberalization, privatization and globalization (Box 11.2). In the industrial segment, these strategies took the following shape:

Liberalization

Liberalization in the industrial domain has been achieved by delicensing, dereservation and other measures. *Delicensing:* As can be seen from Figure 11.2, by 1997, 94 per cent of the industries were delicensed.

As of now, for health security and strategic consideration only a few industries are kept under licensing regime. These industries are alcohol, cigarettes, hazardous chemicals, electronics, aerospace and defence equipments.

The government also abolished the licensing requirement for location. As of now, no license is required for setting up industrial units in locations other than the cities of more than one million population. In the cities with a population of more than one million, polluting industries are allowed only outside 25 km periphery. But industries of non-polluting nature, such as electronics, computer software, and printing, are permitted even in such cities.

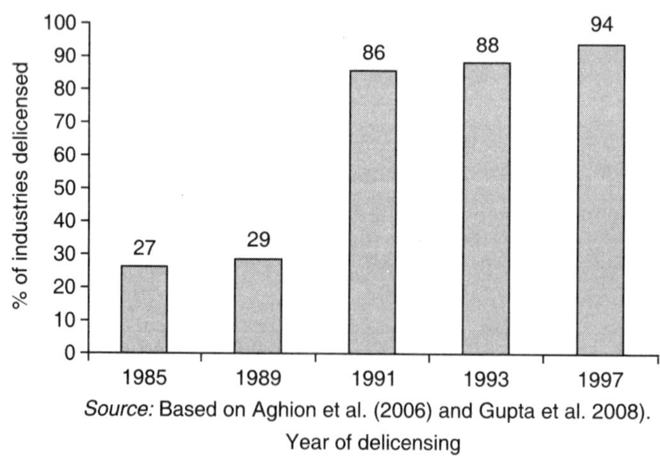

Source: Based on Aghion et al. (2006) and Gupta et al. 2008).

Year of delicensing

(a)

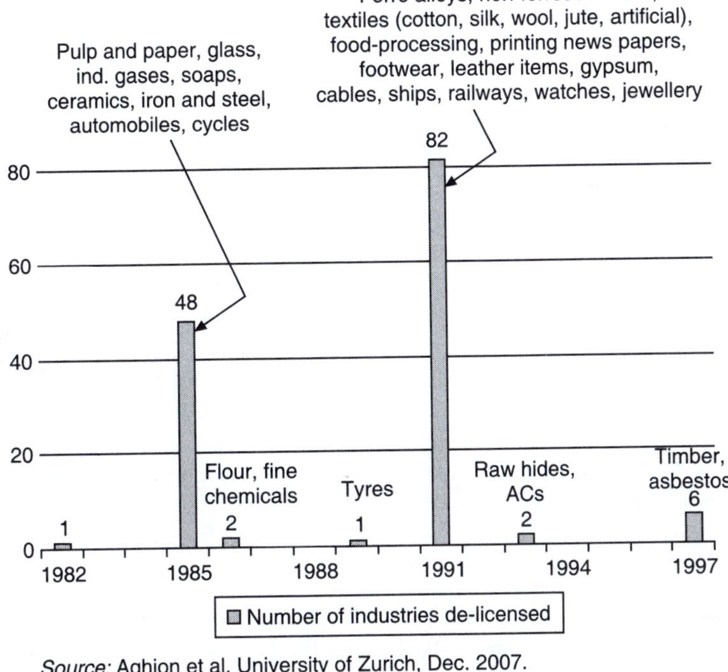

Source: Aghion et al, University of Zurich, Dec. 2007.

(b)

Figure 11.2 Delicensing of Industries.

Dereservation: Dereservation has been implemented for items previously reserved for the public sector and small scale sector.

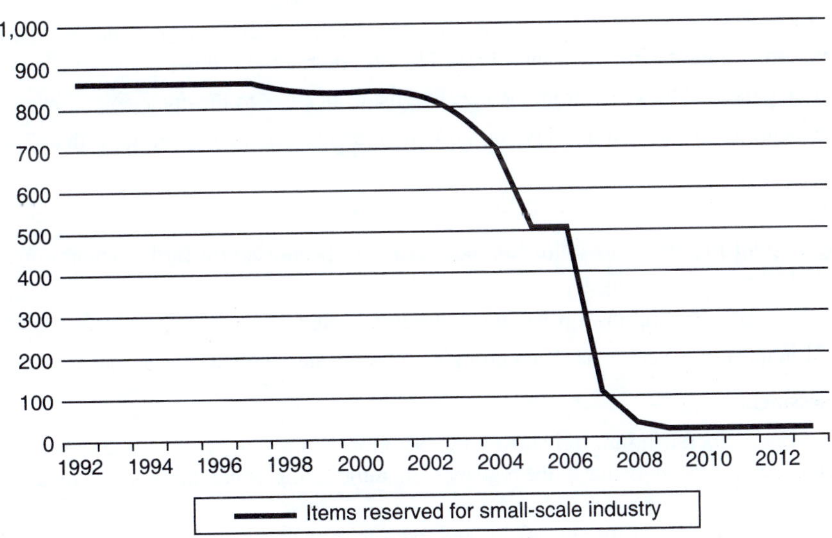

Source: Ministry of MSME, Credit Suisse estimates

Figure 11.3 Dereservation of Items for the Small Scale Industries.

- **Dereservation of items for the public sector:** The process of dereservation of items started in the initial phases of the reform process itself. Gradually, over a period of time, the items reserved for the public sector have been reduced from 17 to 2. These items are: Atomic energy and railway transport
- **Dereservation of items for the small scale industries:** The process of dereservation of items for small scale sector began only in 1997. The total number of products on the list was progressively trimmed from 821 in 1998–99 to 21 items in 2008. As of 31 July 2010 there were only 20 items reserved for the small scale industries (Figure 11.3). These items are: pickles and chutneys, bread, mustard oil, groundnut oil, wooden furniture and fixtures, exercise books and registers, wax candles, laundry soap, safety matches, fireworks, agarbatties, glass bangles, steel almirah, rolling shutters, steel chairs, steel tables, steel furnitures, padlocks, stainless steel utensils and domestic aluminium utensils.

Other measures: Further easing in various processes came with the replacement of Monopoly Restrictive Trade Practices (MRTP) Act, 1969, by the Competition Law, 2002. The MRTP Act aimed at curbing unfair trade practices and preventing the concentration of power in fewer hands. Contrary to the Act, the competition law aims at ensuring freedom of trade and protecting the interest of consumers. Unlike the MRTP Act, the competition law can take suo moto actions and impose punishments to the entities pursuing anti- competitive practices.

Privatization

Privation in India has been achieved by offering part of the government shareholdings in the public sector to the mutual funds, financial institutions, general public and the workers. Other than the outright sale of share of public sector units, privatization has also been achieved by dereserving a large number of sectors for the private sector erstwhile kept reserved for the public sector.

Globalization

Globalization, in the post-1991, has been achieved by switching from fixed exchange rate regime to flexible exchange rate regime and liberalizing trade and capital flows.

Enhancing trade flows: In post-1991 period, the emphasis of the policies is on enhancing exports rather than restricting imports. Trade easing has been achieved by bringing in the following changes:

- Moving most of the items from the negative list of licenses to the open general license category.
- Reducing the peak custom duty on the manufactured products from more than 300 per cent to 10 per cent.
- Easing out the quantitative restrictions on number of items.

Liberalizing Capital Flows: The following measures have been used for further integrating the domestic markets with the rest of the world:

- Most of the areas are now opened up for foreign capital flows
- FDI in most of the cases has been brought under the automatic approval route.

Impact Assessment

Inspite of various liberalization, privatization and globalization measures, the performance of the manufacturing sector, especially that of the registered manufacturing, is not impressive. On many parameters, it is simply dismissal.

The share of industry in the total GDP and even that of the manufacturing sector in the GDP has remained almost stagnant. However, the share of the industrial sector in the total employment has improved as is evident from Table 11.6. But the improvement in the employment share of the industry is due to improvement in the share of the construction industry in total employment rather than that of the manufacturing sector.

Table 11.6 Employment in the Industrial Sector

	Persons employed (million)			*Share in employment (%)*			*Share in GDP (%)*		
	1999–2000	*2004–2005*	*2009–2010*	*1999–2000*	*2004–2005*	*2009–2010*	*1999–2000*	*2004–2005*	*2009–2010*
Mining	2.3	2.6	2.9	0.6	0.6	0.6	3.0	2.9	2.3
Manufacturing	43.8	56.1	52.4	11.0	12.2	11.4	15.1	15.3	16.0
Electricity	1.0	1.2	1.3	0.3	0.3	0.3	2.3	2.1	2.0
Construction	17.5	26.1	44.2	4.4	5.7	9.6	6.5	7.7	7.9
Industry	64.6	85.9	100.7	16.2	18.7	21.9	26.9	27.9	28.1

As can be seen from Table 11.7, there has been an increase in the share of inputs as per cent to total output over a period of time; implying that the share of value added in the organized manufacturing has been on a decline in the post-1991 period. This observation also highlights that there is a low factor productivity in the system. However, the organized manufacturing sector has been able to achieve efficiency in its energy use. Another positive facet of the growth of the organized manufacturing sector is that inspite of a decline in employment in the overall manufacturing sector (organized + unorganized), there is an increase in employment in the manufactured sector. But this increase in employment has been accompanied with a decline in the total emoluments' to output ratio and improvement in the profit to output ratio.

Table 11.7 Some Key Parameters of Organized Manufacturing In India

Characteristics	*1981–1991*	*1991–2001*	*2001–2006*	*2006–2007*	*2007–2008*	*2008–2009*	*2009–2010*
Number of factories	1,01,905	1,27,431	1,32,419	1,44,710	1,46,385	1,55,321	1,58,877
Value of output (₹billion) in per cent	1,450	6,469	13,923	24,085	27,757	32,728	37,228
Input/output	77.20	77.26	81.04	80.89	80.09	81.32	81.54
Fuel/output	8.21	7.01	5.76	4.99	4.67	4.65	4.34
Capital invested/labour (₹ '000)	133	498	872	1,037	1,225	1,355	1,638
Emoluments/output	8.75	6.18	4.35	3.68	3.80	3.96	3.95
Profit/output	3.52	5.58	7.44	10.02	10.72	9.07	8.67
Interest rate of interest	11.90	15.31	11.96	9.64	11.34	12.80	11.06

Source: GOI (2012), Economic Survey, 2011–12.

Reforms have also brought about an improvement in the export intensity of industrial firm as is evident from Table 11.8.

Table 11.8 Export Intensity of Sales of Industrial Firms

Industry	*Exports – Sales Ratio (%)*		
	1997–98	*2003–04*	*2008–09*
Food products	11.8	12.3	16.2
Beverages and tobacco products	9.2	5.0	5.3
Textiles	22.2	22.9	25.4
Chemicals	5.4	9.2	15.9
Non-metallic mineral products	12.8	29.0	26.9
Metal and metal products	10.6	15.4	17.9
Non-electrical machinery	6.9	9.8	13.6
Electrical machinery	9.2	7.9	12.1
Electronics	7.8	8.8	9.8
Transport equipments	6.1	7.3	9.7
Misc manufacturing (paper, leather, etc.)	10.6	11.1	10.5
All manufacturing	8.7	11.4	15.9

Source: Goldar (2010).

Areas that Need Further Reform

Critics have pointed out that there are many regulations in different domains that are restricting the gains of the reforms introduced in the industrial segment. These areas of concern that need further reforms are outlined hereinafter:

Labour Market Regulations

The Indian labour market is governed by different levels of governments – federal as well as state. As per Panagariya (2008) there are 45 different national and state level labour legislations in India. These laws apply only to the **registered sector** or **organized sector**, i.e., the units employing 10 or more workers using power or units employing more than 20 workers without using power. The regulations become more and more stringent as the number of workers employed in this sector increases. With the increasing number of workers in such units, not only the multiplicity of regulations increases but also they are found to be inconsistent. For example, manufacturing units employing more than 10 persons fall under the purview Factories Act, while that employing more than 20 persons are also subject to the Employees Provident Fund and the Miscellaneous Provisions Act of 1950. The units employing 50 or more workers are also mandated to secure health insurance for their employees and are also subject to the Industrial Dispute Act of 1947. Once the size of an industrial unit increases to 100 and above, the unit loses the right to fire workers, or reassign their work. These units are mandated to upgrade the working conditions in the establishment and provide technologically upgraded facilities. Complex and inconsistent laws make hiring and firing of the labourers difficult for an organization in the registered sector and, thereby, limit their expansion plans. By limiting the size of the organizations these laws also deprive the benefits that arise from the economies of scale.

Constraints on Land Acquisition

Along with labour reforms there is also a need for land reforms in the country to speed up the growth of the manufacturing sector. Land laws fall primarily in the domain of the state governments, with very limited role for the Central Government. Given the considerable influence of large landlords in the state politics, land reforms are politically difficult to introduce in India. Apart from landlords there are other political pressures from different constituencies that prevent acquisition of land by the state governments and leasing of the same to industrial units, as was evident from the prolonged protest from farmers on the issue of land lease granted by the West Bengal government to Tata Motors for manufacturing of their budget car **Nano**. The long and violent protest over the inadequate compensation finally compelled Tata Motors to move to Gujarat.

Financial Constraints

Though the financial sector reforms have improved the operational flexibility of banks by substantially bringing down the CRR and moderating the SLR requirement, the SLR requirement is still quite high, which reduces the availability of credit to the private sector and imposes credit constraints on them. In the presence of an ever increasing fiscal deficit, the government borrowings from the market put continuous pressure on the interest rates. Given that the investment in government securities is risk free, there is always a premium that is sought after on lending to the private sector. Thus, the cost of borrowing for the private sector firms remain substantially higher in the presence of ever increasing fiscal deficit.

Infrastructure Bottlenecks

Insufficient and poor state of infrastructure, as is apparent from highly congested roads, overburdened rails and other transport modes, poor and costly electricity supply, the scarcity of water, poor connectivity to the interiors of the country, etc., is one of the important hindrance in the growth of the manufacturing sector, in particular, and overall growth in general. The study by Gupta, et al. (2009) indicated that gain in the manufacturing sector output in the post-delicensing period has remained lower in the states with inferior infrastructure.

Lack of Skilled Labour

India is a labour abundant country. But, in the absence of enough quality education facilities most of the labour remains uneducated or unskilled, constraining their employability in the manufacturing sector. The study by Kochar, Kumar, Rajan, Subramanian and Tokatlidis (2006) indicates that the skill intensity in manufacturing and service sector in India is converging, implying that it is not necessary that the manufacturing sector can absorb more of unskilled labour than the service sector. Like service sector, even the manufacturing sector requires skilled labour. This emerging pattern on the skill intensity of the two sectors emphasizes investment in the education and human capital of the country.

High Level of Corruption

High level of corruption has been found to be a major obstacle in trickling down the impact of various policies at the targeted level. Transparency International (TI) placed India on 94th rank out of 176 countries that it covered in its annual exercise in 2012. The poor ranking of India on these parameters makes it a less attractive destination for foreign investors.

Further Reforms in the Pipeline: The New Manufacturing Policy, 2011

The New Manufacturing Policy (NMP), 2011, aims at enhancing the share of the manufacturing sector in the GDP to 25 per cent. It also aims at creating an additional 100 million jobs over the coming decade by overcoming various obstacles in the industrial growth. To achieve its objectives, the NMP focuses on labour intensive industries, capital goods industries, industries of strategic significance, small and medium enterprises, public sector enterprises and industries in which India has a comparative advantage. For rapid development of the manufacturing sector, it has come up with national investment and manufacturing zones.

References

Aghion, Philippe, Robin Burgess, Stephen Redding, and Fabrizio Zilibotti. 2006. "The Unequal Effects of Liberalization: Evidence from Dismantling the License Raj in India." National Bureau of Economic Research Working Paper 12031. GOI (2012), Economic Survey 2011–12.

GOI (2013), Economic Survey 2012–13.

Goldar, B. (2010), Pro-Market Reforms and Indian Industry: Developments in the Last Two Decades (23 August 2010). Available at SSRN: http://ssrn.com/abstract=1663583 or http://dx.doi.org/10.2139/ssrn.1663583.

Gupta, P. and Kumar, U. (2009), Performance of Indian Manufacturing in the Post-Reform Period Panagariya (2008).

Kochar, K., Kumar, U., Rajan, R., Subramanian, A. and Tokatlidis, I. (2006), **India's Pattern of Development: What Happened, What Follows?, IMF Working Paper,** WP/06/22.

Papola, T.S. (2012) Structural Changes in the Indian Economy: Emerging Patterns and Implications, Working Paper, ISID, (online) http://58.68.105.147/pdf/WP1202.pdf.

SUMMARY

The term industry refers to the people or manufacturers or companies or firms engaged in any type of economic activity producing goods or services that are close substitutes of each other.

Industries are classified using various criteria. On the basis of size, they are broadly classified as small, medium and large scale industries. On the basis of ownership, the classification is as private sector industries, public sector industries, joint sector industries and co-operative sector industries. Using the criterion of source of raw material, industries are classified as agro-based industries, mineral-based industries, forest-based industries, pastoral resource-based industries, Using weight as the criterion, they are classified as heavy and light industries. On the basis of utility, classification is as—basic goods industries, intermediate goods industries, capital goods industries. Using the nature of the product as the classification criterion, the classification is as—metallurgical industries, chemical and allied industries, textile industries, food processing industries, electricity generation, electronic industries, communication industries. Industries are classified as capital and labour intensive industries using factor intensity as the criterion. On the basis of the type of processing, the classification is as—processing industries and fabricating industries. Various official and private organizations have come up with detailed industrial classification systems. Some of these widely known industrial classification systems are: ISIC, NAICS, NACE and GICS. The detailed classification system used in India is known as the NIC.

Industries vary in terms of number and average size of firms, which reflect the industrial structure.

Industrial clusters appear in certain locations. The price and availability of land, labour, capital, raw materials, energy, transport and communication facilities apart from government policies affect the firms' location decisions.

Developing countries often suffer from the problem of market failure which arises because of the co-ordination problem, lack of information, information externalities, dynamic scale economies and environment externalities. Industrial policies, that is, the official strategic plans laid down in the form of rules, regulations, principles, policies and procedures for regulating, developing and controlling industrial undertakings, try to influence the location and industrial structure, with the objective of predicting and facilitating structural changes and correcting the problem of market failure.

The blend of policies and instruments used for achieving the objectives vary across countries depending on their initial conditions.

India in the pre-1991 period, largely inflicted with market failure, adopted industrial licensing, import licensing and reservation policy for the public sector and small scale sector. These policies and instruments though helped the country in broadening its industrial base failed to give a boost to employment in the organized sector. In the post- 1991 period, the thrust of the industrial policies had been to infuse competition so that the productivity of Indian manufactured products enhances and its exports become competitive in the international market. The strategies adopted to achieve these objectives have been liberalization, privatization, and globalization. In spite of two decades of industrial reform the country is not able to achieve very rapid growth of the manufacturing sector. The areas that need further reforms, to achieve the manufacturing sector performance, are land acquisition laws, labour laws, infrastructure, availability of finance and quality of education.

Implications for Managers

Business is the main focus of industrial policies in a country. Unlike fiscal and monetary policies, the industrial policy can directly affect the business environment through various channels.

Industrial policies can directly regulate the price faced by the organizations. By licensing, such policies can limit the capacity of production. Through tax and subsidies, the profit margin is impacted. Even the cost of labour and product gets affected by such policies.

Competition law helps these policies in restricting monopoly practices. Policies on mergers and acquisitions help industrial policies limiting the scale of production and curb monopoly practices. Such policies also alter the market structure.

Industrial policies determine the priority areas for the country. By reserving certain items, these policies can limit or extend the areas in which small, medium or large firms can operate. Industrial policies related to privatization, disinvestment and public-private partnership can create or limit the scope of business opportunities for private organizations.

Industrial policies, with the help of FDI policies, affect the cost of credit and even the technology. Through trade policies, these policies can also expand or narrow the consumer base of the companies. For example, restrictions on exports narrow the consumer base, whereas export subsidies, encouraging sell overseas, widen the consumer base. Similarly, the availability and cost of credit is enhanced by such policies. Ban or restrictions on imported intermediate goods, for example can reduce the availability of intermediate goods and, in turn, increase their cost. Industrial policies by following intellectual property rights can encourage or discourage research and development and innovations.

Industrial policies, through labour laws, organization laws, exit and closure laws can make entry and exit easy or difficult for business units. These policies with the help of licensing and land acquisition policies and environmental regulations can alter the location of business units.

By laying down rules for energy intensity, pollution, forest use, these policies can affect the input composition as well as the locations of companies.

These policies also affect the availability of supporting infrastructure—roads, rail lines, ports, airports, power, etc. and create an enabling environment for the country.

Thus, industrial policies by affecting the price, scale of production, level of competition have a profound impact on the productivity and efficiency of business organizations. Business organizations need to have an in-depth understanding of these policies to survive in cut throat competition or to take advantage of protective environment.

REVIEW QUESTIONS

11.1. What is an industry?
11.2. What are the criteria used for classifying industries?
11.3. What is a small scale industry?
11.4. What is an industrial policy?
11.5. Why do countries formulate industrial policies?
11.6. Why does market failure take place?
11.7. What is the co-ordination problem?
11.8. What is the difference between positive and negative externalities? How do these two types of externalities affect the growth of an economy?
11.9. What is an industrial policy? How does it try to achieve higher sustainable growth?
11.10. What were the objectives of industrial policy in India in the post-reform period?
11.11. What instruments were used to achieve the objectives of industrial policy in India in the pre-1991 period?
11.12. What parameters can be used for evaluating the performance of the Industry?
11.13. What was the impact of industrial policies pursued in the pre-1991 period in India?
11.14. How far the objectives of the industrial policy in the post-1991 differed from that of the pre-1991 period?
11.15. What way the post-1991 industrial policy wants to achieve its objective?
11.16. Differentiate liberalization from globalization.
11.17. What is the difference between liberalization and privatization?
11.18. What are the different forms in which privatization takes place?
11.19. How has the industrial structure changed in the post-1991 period?
11.20. Have the industrial policies in India succeeded in making the growth of the manufacturing sector sustainable?

NUMERICAL PROBLEM

11.1 From the values given in Table 11.9 estimate the import intensity of exports.

Table 11.9 Exports and Imports from India

Year	*Total exports*	*Total imports*
2004–05	3,753.40	5,010.65
2005–06	4,564.18	6,604.09
2006–07	5,717.79	8,405.06
2007–08	6,558.64	10,123.12
2008–09	8,407.55	13,744.36
2009–10	8,455.34	13,637.36
2010–11	11,429.22	16,834.67
2011–12	14,592.81	23,459.73

Source: RBI (2012), *Handbook of Statistics on Indian Economy* 2011–12.

Draw inferences from the values that you obtain for the import intensity of exports.

CASE ANALYSIS EXERCISE

C11.1 Comparative Picture of India and World Manufacturing Production

India is one of the top ten manufacturing countries though its share in total Manufacturing Value Added (MVA) is only about 1.8 per cent. The impact of the post-crisis slowdown on industrial growth has been relatively mild on developing countries including India yet the downward trend in MVA has been significant. The intensity of the slide did vary across countries as shown in Figure in the box. The growth rate of world MVA had declined from 5.4 per cent in Q1 of 2011–12 to 2.2 per cent in Q2 of 2012–13. During the same period China's MVA growth rate declined from 14.3 per cent to 7.3 per cent, but the deceleration rate has been sharper in the case of India as the rate of growth dipped from 7.3 per cent to 0.2 per cent. Analysis of the sub-group level MVAs shows sharp differences between India vis-a-vis other major manufacturing countries. The production of machinery and equipment, one of the key segments of the capital goods sector, has been growing at faster rate in the United States, Canada, China, Malaysia as compared to the deceleration in India's case. A similar pattern is observable in other capital goods segments and high technology sectors. The reason is India's competitive disadvantage owing to low level technology, higher input costs and poor quality infrastructure. A long-term trend analysis from 1995 to 2009 shows that India has lagged behind in increasing its share in MVA of sophisticated products. It has fared better in medium-low technology products in labour-intensive sectors such as textiles, wearing apparel and leather products. Even in these three sectors India's share was low as compared to China, which dominates all three sectors.

A two-digit industry level analysis of world manufacturing shows that in recent years the five fastest- growing sectors were—office accounting and computing; radio, TV and communication equipment; electrical machinery and apparatus, other transport; and basic metal. Other than basic metal all these sectors are medium and high technology activities. India's performance in recent years has been dismal in some of these fast moving sectors. In contrast, China accounted for more than 50 per cent of the developing economies total MVA in 15 out of the 22 industrial sectors—India's share was significant only in a few of these sectors. The latest competitive industrial performance index (CIP) compiled by the United Nations Industrial Development Organization (UNIDO), ranks India 42nd out of 118 countries the same as in 2005. China is ranked fifth.

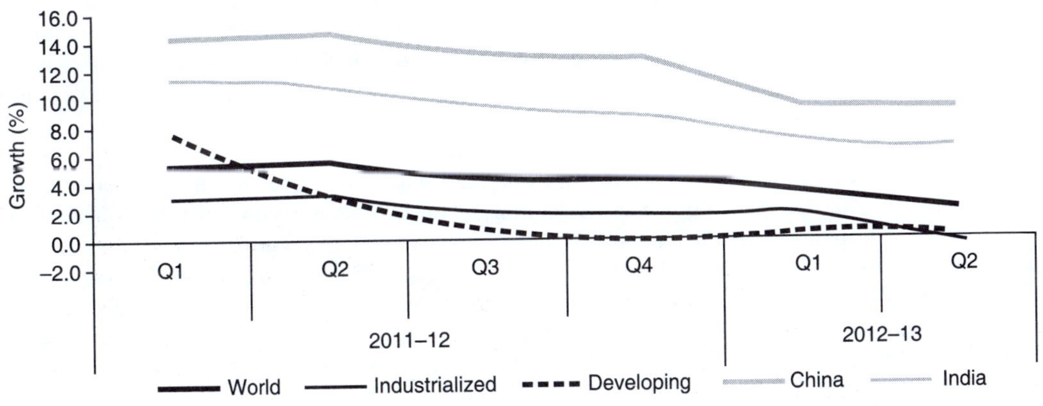

Source: UNIDO-World Manufacturing Production-Quarterly Reports

Figure 11.4 Comparative Manufacturing Value Added Growth.

Source: GOI (2013), Economic Survey, 2012–13.

Questions

1. Why the manufacturing sector growth in the recent past in India and developing countries has decelerated in the recent past?
2. Which segments of industrial sector have contributed to the sharp deceleration in the manufacturing sector growth in India? What is the general characteristics of these segments?
3. In which segments of manufacturing sector India is comparatively better-off?

C11.2 Measuring Industrial Growth through IIP: From Expansion to Slowdown

The **Index of Industrial Production** (IIP) measures the production (gross value added) in the industrial sector for a given period of time as compared to the reference period. It provides a quick estimate of industrial growth till the actual results from the Annual Survey of Industries (ASI) become available in India.

At the aggregate level, the IIP is being compiled by the CSO on a monthly basis. The quick estimate of IIP of any month is released within six weeks from the reference month. This index is subsequently revised twice, namely, in the next month and the following third month. Over a period of time, the index has been revised by shifting the base year to a more recent period, expanding the coverage of items and improving the techniques of construction to appropriately reflect the structure and pattern of industrial growth. The current base year for the series is 2004–05 and the index covers 682 items. Broad sectors, which are covered in the index are manufacturing, mining and electricity. It does not cover gas, water supply and construction sectors. Apart from the sectoral-based classification, the index is also constructed for different use-based classifications, i.e., basic goods, capital goods, intermediate goods and consumer goods consisting of consumer durables and consumer non-durables.

The index is extensively used by the government for policy and planning purpose, and various other organizations including industrial associations, research institutes and academicians. As the IIP data is available at a higher frequency than the GDP data, IIP series is used for assessing the various phases of a business cycle and identifying the turning points in it.

In Figure 11.5(a) the industrial performance using IIP data has been analyzed.

We can ascertain the movements in economic activities in the last two decades from Figure 3.11. We can see that prior to the onset of crisis in 2008–09, during 2003–04 to 2007–08, Indian Industrial sector experienced a very high growth rate. During the high growth phase qualitative and structural changes took place in the industrial sector. Unlike the earlier high growth phase (1993–96), during this phase the capital goods sector recorded double digit growth rate in most of the quarters indicating sound fundamentals of the economy. The growth in this earlier phase of expansion was driven largely by capturing of market share following the opening up of the economy.

Though the signs of moderation in the high growth phase had started surfacing in 2007–08, the year of global financial crisis put a brake to the latest high growth phase and a sharp moderation in industrial activities was registered in 2008–09. Not only the manufacturing sector witnessed a slowdown, but other sectors also registered a steep moderation in their growth rates. The electricity sector witnessed its lowest growth since the introduction of current IIP series (1993–94) on account of deceleration in power generation in all spheres. In terms of use-based classification, basic, capital and consumer goods registered a deceleration, whereas intermediate goods production registered a decline during 2008–09. Though, overall, there was a deceleration in the growth of consumer goods sector, it recovered from a negative growth rate experienced in 2007–08 and recorded a positive growth rate of 4.5 per cent in 2008–09.

Along with the global recovery, the Indian industrial sector recovered and registered a moderate growth rate of 5.3 per cent in 2009–10. There was a further acceleration in the overall growth rate in 2010–11 led by an impressive recovery in the capital goods sector. However, due to moderation in demand, both domestic and external, hardening of interest rates, slowdown in consumption expenditure and subdued business confidence and global economic recovery. Electricity performed better due to the normal South West monsoon, which supported hydro-power generation. The slowdown was registered across all sectors except electricity. The steepest decline was reflected in the mining sector due to low output of natural gas from the Krishna Godvari basin and regulatory and environmental issues, which affected coal mining. Assessing the performance of the industrial sector from the use-based classification (Figure 11.5(b)), we can ascertain that the capital goods and intermediate goods not only registered a decline in the growth rate but the growth rate was also negative. The sharp fall in the growth rate in these two categories was due to dampening of investment climate. The consumer goods also registered a decline in the growth rate in 2011–12 due to hardening of interest rate.

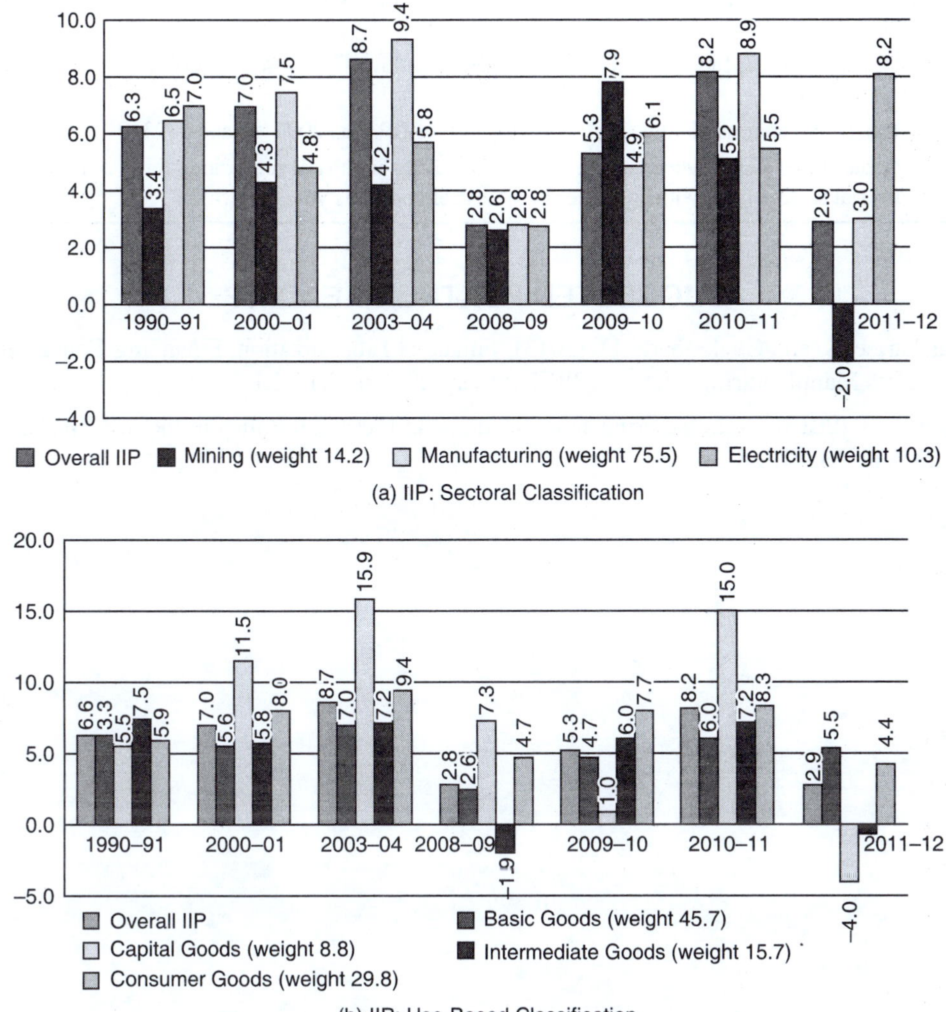

(a) IIP: Sectoral Classification

(b) IIP: Use-Based Classification

Note: The estimates of growth in IIP for years 2009–10, 2010–11 and 2011–12 are based on IIP with base year 2004–05. For other years the growth is based on IIP with base year 1993–94.

Source: The data for the figure is compiled from RBI (2010), Annual Report. Annexure Tables, http://rbi.org.in/scripts/AnnualReportPublications.aspx?Id=991 and CSO (2011), and GOI (2013), Economic Survey 2012–13.

Figure 11.5 Year on Year Growth Rates in the Index of Industrial Production.

Questions

1. What is the IIP? At what frequency is it available in India?
2. What are the different types of classifications for which IIPs are available in India?
3. Why is the IIP often used for identification of turning points in business cycles?
4. Which sector of the Indian economy has the highest weightage in the IIP?
5. Why has there been a sharp deceleration in the growth rate of all major sectors of the economy in 2008–09?
6. Which sector of the Indian economy has witnessed its lowest growth since the introduction of current IIP series? Why?
7. Compare and contrast the two high growth phase of IIP, i.e., 2002–07 and 1993–96.
8. Why has there been a deceleration in the growth of the industrial sector in India in 2011–12? Which industrial sectors have witnessed the sharpest decline in this year and why?

SUGGESTED FURTHER READING

Bhattacharjee, S. and Chakrabarti, D. (2013), Financial Liberalization, Financing Constraint and India's Manufacturing Sector, *EPW*, February 09, Vol. XLVIII, 6.

Chaudhuri, S. (2013), Manufacturing Trade Deficit and Industrial Policy in India, *EPW*, February 23, Vol. XLVIII, 8.

CHAPTER 12

Balance of Payment

Accounting, Adjustments and Imbalances

12.1 INTRODUCTION

In the present world, there is no economy which can be labelled as a completely closed economy. Almost all countries are open to some degree, and allow their residents to purchase imported goods, travel abroad, and sell their factor services to foreigners. Some countries even permit them to purchase shares and debentures issued abroad. Similarly, corporations and traders are also allowed to purchase imported inputs and finished goods and even raise funds from abroad. Likewise, foreigners are allowed to partake in domestic economic activities by supplying their goods and services and investing in domestic companies.

All these transactions, reflecting international transactions in goods and services, movements of factors of production, such as labour, capital and entrepreneurship, and transfer of knowledge and technology, of a country with the rest of the world are recorded in the balance of payment statement following a double entry book keeping system. The statement and its constituents—current account, capital account and official settlement account—provide insights in assessing the extent of integration of domestic economy with the external world, the extent of deficit in different constituents, the amount of adjustment needed to bring about a balance, the pattern of financing deficit and the implications of different forms of financing.

Considering the importance of this statement in an open economy set-up, this chapter has been devoted to understand this statement and analyze the implications of imbalances in any of its constituents.

Section 12.2 describes the general format of the balance of payment statement and the principles on which it is constructed. Section 12.3 deliberates on its constituents, i.e., current account, capital account and official settlement account. The meaning of the terms such as balance of payment deficit and surplus is explained in Section 12.4. Implications of imbalances in the balances of payment are drawn in Section 12.5.

12.2 BALANCE OF PAYMENT: ACCOUNTING OF FOREIGN TRANSACTIONS

All trade and capital inflows to and outflows from a country, get recorded in the **Balance of**

Payment (BOP) statement of that country. Thus, the **BOP statement** is a systematic record of a country's all economic transactions with the rest of the world during a given period of time.

The BOP statement consists of two sides, the credit side and the debit side (Table 12.1).

Table 12.1 Schematic of Balance of Payment Statement

	Credit(+)	*Debit*(–)	*Balance* (+) *Surplus*/(–) *Deficit*
I. *Current account transactions* (*A* + *B*)			(+) Earnings > Payments (–) Earnings < Payments
A. Trade account transactions			
Merchandise transactions	Exports of goods	Imports of goods	(+) Exports > Imports (–) Exports < Imports
B. Invisibles			
Transaction in services	Exports of services	Imports of services	(+) Exports > Imports (–) Exports < Imports
Investment income (Interest/Dividend)	Inflow of investment income	Outflow of investment income	(+) Inflows > Outflows (–) Inflows < Outflows
Private/Government unilateral transfers (remittances, gifts, pensions)	Private transfer receipts	Private transfer payments	(+) Receipts > Payments (–) Receipts < Payments
II. *Capital account transactions* (*A* + *B*)			(+) Inflows > Outflows (–) Inflows < Outflows
A. Long-term capital flows			
Private direct investment	FDI inflows	FDI outflows	(+) Inflows > Outflows (–) Inflows < Outflows
Other private capital flows	Portfolio inflows	Portfolio outflows	(+) Inflows > Outflows (–) Inflows < Outflows
Government capital flows	Borrowing	Lending	(+) Borrowing > Lending (–) Borrowing < Lending
B. Short-term capital flows	Trade debt	Trade credit	(+) Debt > Credit (–) Debt < Credit
III. *Official reserve transactions*			(+) Sale > Purchase (–) Sale < Purchase
Official transactions in reserve assets (Foreign exchange/Gold/SDR)	Sale of reserve assets	Purchase of reserve assets	(+) Sale > Purchase (–) Sale < Purchase
Grand total (I + II + III)			(0) BOP in balance foreign exchange earnings = foreign exchange payments

Receipt of a payment from a foreign country is recorded as a credit transaction, which takes a positive (+) or no sign. Transactions on the **credit side of the BOP** are sources of foreign exchange. These transactions increase the inflow or supply of foreign exchange and, thus, improve the external purchasing power of the recipient country. For example, exports of goods and services, transfer receipts in the form of gifts, borrowings from abroad, investment by foreigners, and sale of foreign exchange reserves by the central bank increases the inflow or supply of foreign currency in a country. On the contrary, a payment to a foreign country is recorded as a debit item with a negative (–) sign. These transactions result in an outflow of foreign exchange and reduce the external purchasing power of a country. The transactions on the **debit side of the BOP** represent the uses of foreign exchange. For example, imports of goods and services, transfer payments such as private remittances and gifts to foreign governments, lending abroad, investment abroad, and purchase of foreign exchange reserves by the central bank result in an outflow of foreign currency from a country.

The BOP statement is constructed on the principles of double entry book keeping, i.e., every transaction is entered twice. Therefore, the BOP statement is always in balance, reflecting that the aggregate of credit side is always equal to the aggregate of debit side. It is an arithmetic equality without any economic significance.

All the transactions recorded in the BOP statement have flow dimension as the statement is prepared for a given period of time.

The BOP statement is widely used in evaluating a country's relative strength in global markets. It is analyzed for the values of its components, their rates of growth, and the interrelationship that exists between them.

12.3 CONSTITUENTS OF THE BALANCE OF PAYMENT STATEMENT

For a meaningful understanding and ascertaining economic significance of the transactions with the rest of the world, the BOP statement is divided into three broad subheads current account, capital account and official settlement account. These subheads of the BOP statement are elaborated hereinafter.

Current Account

All the transactions relating to trade in goods and services, all the receipts and unilateral transfers in a given period of time, that do not result in a creation of an asset or a liability, are recorded in the **current account of the BOP** statement. On the basis of different categories of transactions, this account is further divided into trade account and invisible account.

1. Trade account: The transactions related to merchandise (visible physical goods) imports and exports are recorded in the **trade account of the BOP**. These transactions are recorded at the market value of goods at the point of exit (sea, airport or land border) from the exporting country. The values of exports are shown at free-on-board (f.o.b.), i.e., without any insurance cost (covering the risk of loss or damage to the goods from the point of exit) and the transportation cost from the point of departure from the domestic port to the foreign country. On the contrary, the values of imports are recorded on cost, insurance and freight (c.i.f.) basis.

2. Invisible account: All the transactions not involving any physical transfer of goods are recorded in the **invisible account of the BOP**. Thus, as detailed below, this account consists of all the receipts and payments emerging from exports and imports of services, investment income, and unilateral transfers from private entities and governments.

(i) *Service transaction.* Services, such as banking, insurance, shipping, and consultancy services, etc., are rendered by residents to non-residents. When a country gets such services from other countries it is referred to as the **import of services**. The import of services results in an outflow of foreign currencies. On the other hand, when a country provides these services to other countries, it is referred to as the **exports of services**. The export of services results in an inflow of foreign currencies.

(ii) *Foreign travel.* Spending by foreign tourists results in receipts of foreign currencies to the host country. Similarly, spending by residents of the domestic country in foreign countries, results in an outflow of foreign currencies.

(iii) *Investment income.* The receipt of interest, dividends and profits from abroad, on loans and investment made by domestic participants in foreign countries, result in an inflow of foreign currencies. Similarly, payments of interest, dividends and profits, on loans and investments by foreigners in the domestic markets, result in an outflow of foreign currencies.

(vi) *Transfer payments.* The receipts and payments in cash or kind without quid pro quo (i.e., without any exchange of goods and service) are known as **transfer payments** or **unilateral transfers**. Such transfers can be either private (gifts, remittances) or official (foreign aid, pensions, repatriation benefits).

Capital Account

All the transactions with the rest of the world that result in formation of asset or liability are recorded in the **capital account of the BOP**. Hence, loans and investment in shares and debentures, which either create a liability or an asset, are recorded as capital account transactions.

We should note here that the export of goods results in foreign exchange earnings, whereas the export of capital leads to an outflow of foreign currency from the country. The export of capital, in the form of purchase of foreign shares, bonds, or loans to foreigners, results in an outflow of foreign currency; hence, it is recorded as a debit item. On the contrary, the import of capital, in the form of purchase of shares, bonds by foreigners, and loans from foreign countries, results in an inflow of foreign currency; hence, it is recorded as a credit item.

The capital account transactions are motivated by a desire for economic return. These can take the following form:

1. Short-term capital transactions: Transactions in foreign assets and liabilities of maturity period ranging between three months and less than one year are short-term capital transactions.

2. Long-term capital transactions: Transactions in foreign assets and liabilities with maturity of one year or more are long-term capital transactions. These consist of foreign direct investments, portfolio investment, international loans, and repayment of loans (Section 14.2.2).

All these transactions relating to the financial assets and liabilities are further classified under three sectors, viz., private sector, banking sector and official sector (comprising the government including public sector undertakings and the central bank).

Official Settlement Account

The **official settlement account** or **official reserve assets account** records the changes in official reserve assets held by the monetary authority, i.e., the central bank.

Before proceeding further, we should remember that as the monetary authority and a regulator of money supply and foreign currency in a country, the central bank is exogenous to the system. As the regulator it maintains stock of **reserve assets**, also known as the **foreign exchange reserves** or **forex reserves**, in terms of foreign currency, gold and Special Drawing Rights (SDRs) (Box 15.6) (Figure 12.1). We should know that gold and SDRs have worldwide acceptability. If required, these can be sold or pledged with central banks of other countries and multilateral organizations, like IMF for procuring foreign currency. Hence, a part of forex reserves are kept in these forms. We should also know the special treatment assigned to international gold flows. When gold is used as an ordinary commodity, international transactions in it appear in the trade account. But when the gold is used by the government or the central bank to build up its forex reserves or procure foreign currency to meet the foreign currency requirement, it affects the forex reserves.

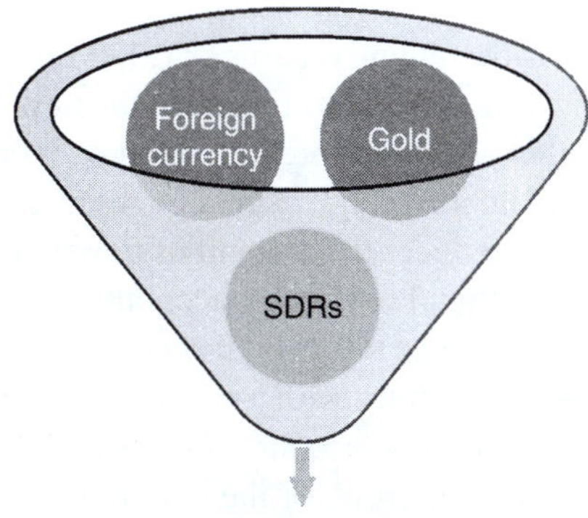

Figure 12.1 Constituents of Official Reserve Assets.

The central bank interventions in the foreign exchange market, in the form of sales and purchases of these assets, lead to variation in its forex reserves. The sale of forex assets results in a decumulation, whereas purchase of these results in an accumulation of forex reserves. Let us now see how these transactions of the central bank are recorded in the official settlement account of the BOP.

A sale of forex reserves reduces the amount of official reserve assets, but increases the availability of foreign currency to domestic participants. Hence, a decumulation of forex reserves is recorded as a credit entry.

On the contrary, a purchase of foreign currency by the central bank from domestic participants increases its forex reserves, but reduces the availability of foreign exchange in the domestic market. Hence, accumulation of official assets is recorded as a debit entry in the BOP statement.

The transactions on the official settlement account are not independent of the size of other items in the balance of payments. These transactions are accommodating in nature and performed to balance the deficit or surplus emerging on account of current and/or capital account of the balance.

Errors and omissions: The discrepancies, arising due to errors in estimation and timing, are recorded as errors and omissions. This is not a separate subhead or account in the BOP statement. However, entry to this effect is made to take care of all the unintended omissions and accounting errors while recording the data.

12.4 BALANCE IN THE BALANCE OF PAYMENT

The BOP statement is prepared on the basis of a **double entry book keeping system** which is a set of rules indicating that every transaction should be reflected in at least two different subsets of an accounting statement, in one as a credit entry and in another as a debit entry. The credit side of an accounting statement accounts all the receipts whereas the debit side accounts for all the payments. Since each item is recorded once as a credit item and once as debit item, the total of credit side is equal to the total of debit side of the statement following double entry system.

Since the BOP statement follows the principles of double entry system, the credit side of this statement accounts for all the sources of foreign exchange for a country, whereas debit side accounts for all the uses of foreign currency. The country's total outgoing of foreign exchange must equal to its total receipts. Therefore, the statement as a whole fully balances without any surplus or deficit.

For illustration, assume that the country earns ₹1,000 crore from exports of wheat and spends ₹800 crore on imports of cloth. It has a current account surplus of ₹200 crore. The country has various alternatives of using this surplus in foreign currency. First, it can be purchased from the market by the central bank to build up its foreign exchange reserves or official reserves. However, this intervention by the central bank reduces the amount of foreign currency in circulation. Hence, it is reflected as a debit entry on the official settlement account. Second, it can be invested in shares and debentures of foreign companies. Since this capital account transaction results in an outflow of foreign currency, it is recorded as a debit entry with a negative (–) sign on the capital account in the BOP statement. Thus, we see that the current account surplus of ₹200 crore balances with a deficit in the official settlement account of ₹200 crore, or the deficit in the capital account of ₹200 crore or as some combination of deficit in the official settlement account and capital account. Adding all these accounts we get a zero, implying that the BOP is in a balance.

If the BOP is always in balance then what does the imbalances in the BOP statement, representing either deficit or surplus, stand for?

The concept of **BOP deficit** or **BOP surplus** basically refers to the deficit or balance in a select sub-group (Figure 12.2). Depending on the group under consideration, one can have different concepts of the BOP deficit and surplus as follows:

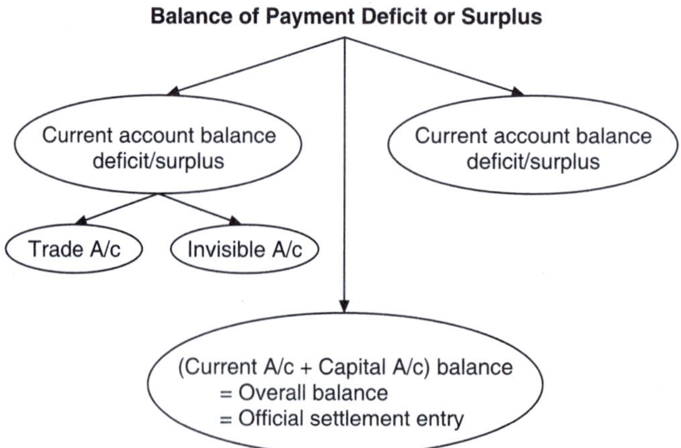

Figure 12.2 Balance of Payment: Deficit or Surplus.

Trade Balance

The difference between merchandize exports and imports depicts the balance on trade account. In the event of insignificant trade of services, the trade balance is an important indicator of income and outgo of foreign currency.

Balance on Account of Invisibles

The difference between total receipts of and total payments in foreign currencies on account of invisibles gives the balance on the invisible account.

Current Account Balance

The current account balance is a sum total of the trade and invisible account balance. It can be in surplus or deficit or in balance.

A surplus on the current account (i.e., current account receipts > current account payments) is often termed as a favourable balance, whereas a deficit (i.e., current account receipts < current account payments) is referred to as an unfavourable balance.

Imbalances in the current account also reflect imbalances in the domestic saving and investment, which we can see from the GDP identity of (Section 3.3.1). We know from the identity that the total income is equal to total expenditure, i.e.,

$$Y = C + I + G + X - M$$

Rearranging this we get

$$(Y - C - G) - I = X - M$$

In this identity, $(Y - C - G)$ indicates the domestic income over and above domestic consumption, i.e., saving. Therefore, the rearranged identity implies that

$$\text{Domestic saving} - \text{Domestic investment} = \text{Current account balance}$$

From the above identity we can also see that a deficit on the current account (i.e., $X < M$) means that the domestic saving is insufficient to fund the domestic investment $[(Y - C - G) < I]$. A country can make up for this deficit by running a capital account surplus (i.e., net inflow of foreign capital) and/or decumulating its official reserves assets. Conversely, a surplus on the current account indicates that there is an excess of domestic saving over domestic investment, which can be used for investing abroad and/or accumulating official reserve assets (Figure 12.3).

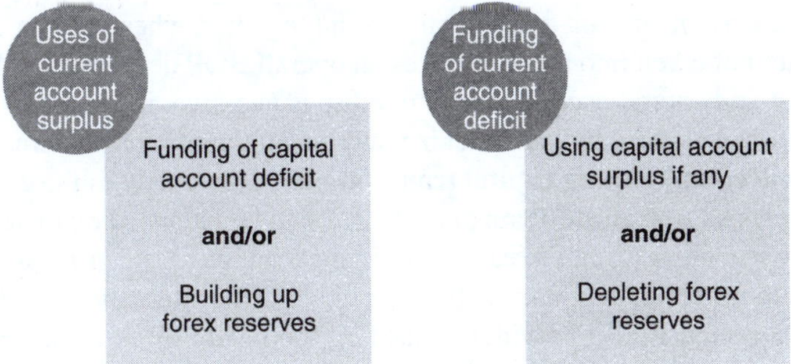

Figure 12.3 Balancing the Current Account of the BOP.

A persistent deficit or surplus in the current account poses serious problems, which are as follows:

Capital Account Balance

Similar to imbalances in the current account, a country can have imbalances in the capital account; implying that over the period for which the balance of payment is prepared, capital receipts need not be equal to capital payments. A country, hence, in any given period, may have either the deficit or the surplus on the capital account.

A surplus on the balance of payment indicates that there is more inflow of capital than the outflow; whereas a deficit indicates that there is more outflow of capital than the inflow. A surplus on the capital account can be used for funding the deficit in current account or building up official reserve assets; whereas a deficit in it is funded from the current account surplus or depleting official reserve assets (Figure 12.4).

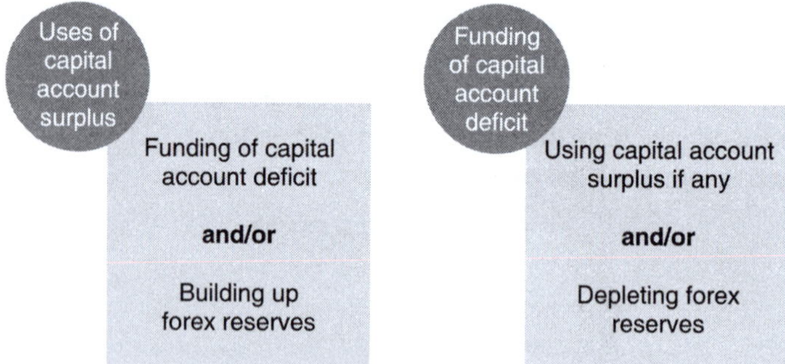

Figure 12.4 Balancing the Capital Account of the BOP.

Not only is the total amount of surplus but also its composition is important. If the surplus is emerging primarily from the short-term capital, such as portfolio flows, short-term deposits and so on, then that poses serious problem for macroeconomic stability; whereas the surplus emerging from long-term capital, such as foreign direct investment and long-term credit, is considered to be stable and hence, not that threatening. Similarly, a distinction between finances obtained on commercial terms, i.e., market determined rates, and on soft terms is important. Larger the former component, the greater the vulnerability of a country to the volatility in interest rates.

Balance of Payment Deficit or Surplus

The balance on the current account and capital account together, when the transactions on official reserve account are not taken into account, gives an overall BOP deficit or surplus. If the balance on current account and capital account taken together is negative, it represents the case of **BOP deficit**. This has to be balanced by the matching surplus on the official settlement account, (these are also known as **accommodating capital transactions**). Conversely, if the combined balance is positive, it represents an overall **BOP surplus**. This has to be balanced by matching deficit in the official settlement account, i.e., an increase in foreign exchange assets or forex reserves.

The BOP statement is an important statement reflecting the integration of a domestic economy with the global economy. It also provides signals on the health of an economy as illustrated in UBE 12.1.

12.5 IMPLICATIONS OF LARGE CURRENT ACCOUNT DEFICIT

As shown in Figure 12.5, continuous capital account surplus, brought about through borrowing, may result in a debt trap or debt crisis; whereas, continuous decumulation of official asset reserves, to finance the persistent current account deficit, causes a balance of payment crisis.

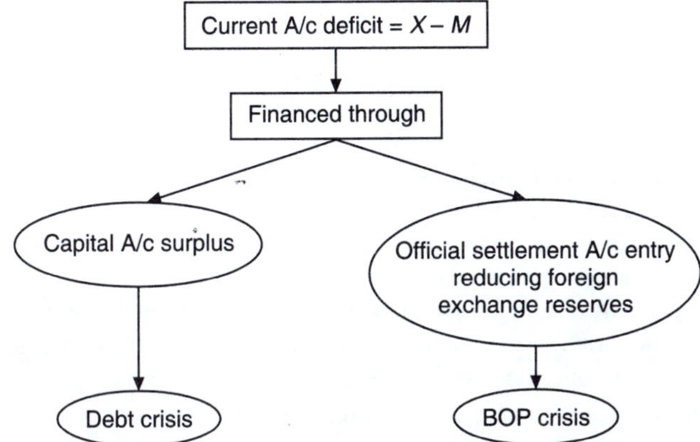

Figure 12.5 Implications of Persistence Large Current Account Deficit.

The problem of persistent current account deficit can be avoided by pursuing the following policies:

1. Control of fiscal deficit: High fiscal deficit puts inflationary pressures and makes exports dearer and uncompetitive in the international market; hence, it may result in persistent current account deficit. Therefore, control of fiscal deficit is essential.

2. Devaluation of the domestic currency: A reduction in the value of the domestic currency in terms of foreign currency makes exports cheaper, and hence, competitive. That helps overcome the problem of current account deficit.

3. Increase in productivity: It is essential to improve the quality of exported goods and reduce their cost of production. An increase in productivity helps improving the quality as well as bringing in reduction in the cost.

4. Reduced dependence on costly external commercial borrowing: A reduction in external commercial borrowing helps in bringing down the interest payment burden and current account deficit. The dependence on external commercial borrowing can be reduced by encouraging and inviting more of foreign direct investment in core and priority industries.

Box 12.1 highlights some of the issues encountered in measuring current account sustainability.

Box 12.1 Current Account Sustainability: Measurement

A continuous current account deficit can lead to continuous depletion of foreign exchange assets of the central bank leading to BOP crisis or a continuous build up of debt leading to a debt crisis. If a persistent current account deficit does not cause such a problem then we can say that the current account deficit is sustainable, i.e., a country can afford to have that amount of deficit on its current account. But, how to measure the sustainability?

Economists widely differ on the definition of sustainable current account deficit and its measurement. It is defined to be sustainable and stable when the current account generates no economic forces of its own to change the growth trajectory of a country. Many economists assess the sustainability by examining the value of a country's external obligations as reflected in the ratio of the country's current account deficit to GDP and the ratio of the country's net international debt to GDP. It has been argued that a current account deficit can be sustained as long as the growth rate of national income exceeds the rate of interest on the nation's liabilities even if the debt to GDP ratio rises over time. A ratio of non-increasing foreign debt to GDP has been identified as a sufficient condition for sustainability. Some argue that the current account deficit is sustainable as long as it does not result in exchange rate or external debt crisis. A set of indicators such as extent of fiscal deficit, credit growth and various reserve adequacy ratios are examined to assess the current account sustainability.

The current account has been identified to be unsustainable when the current account is large relative to the size of GDP, domestic saving rates are low, current account imbalance is caused by a reduction in the domestic saving rate rather than a rise in the investment. Manifestation of unsustainability is in the form of a sharp hike in domestic interest rate, a rapid depreciation of domestic currency, or some other abrupt domestic or global economic disruptions.

UNDERSTANDING BUSINESS ENVIRONMENT

UBE 12.1 India's Balance of Payment

This UBE depicts the development on the BOP front in India since independence which can be used for assessing its openness and soundness.

India started the first five-year plan with a comfortable level of surplus on balance of trade, emerging due to large account of purchases made by Britain to meet its requirements during the Second World War. However, during the subsequent plans, the country faced growing balance of payment deficit due to pursuance of various development strategies, and internal and external shocks.

India adopted "heavy industrialization" as the growth strategy since the second plan period. Implementation of this strategy required imports of heavy machinery and technology which resulted in substantial increase in import bill. Frequent and prolonged drought conditions marked the third plan which made the country to resort to imports of foodgrains on a large scale. To overcome the problem of frequent drought conditions and foodgrain shortage, the country implemented green revolution in the fourth plan, requiring a large scale import of High Yielding Variety seeds and fertilizers, and further worsening the BOP situation. During the fifth plan, on account of the first oil shock, which caused unprecedented rise in oil prices, the country experienced a record deficit of ₹977.2 crore during 1974–75. However, the country adjusted itself to the first oil shock rather quickly and recorded a surplus on the current account in the subsequent two years. The sharp improvement in the BOP was primarily due to an impressive improvement in net invisibles.

The sixth plan period started with the second oil shock, which had a serious negative impact on the Indian economy. During this plan, there was also a gradual decline in the net receipts from invisibles. As the trade deficit was also rising considerably, the contribution of net invisibles in financing deficit declined, resulting in a greater dependence on inflows of foreign capital to balance the current account.

The decade of 1980's also witnessed vigorous pursuit of industrial and import liberalization policies by the government. The import liberalization measures placed an unparalleled pressure on the BOP during the seventh plan. Also, during this period, the private remittances from the Middle East countries declined considerably, adding fuel to the fire.

The period during the 1980s was also marked by a sharp reduction in the flows of concessional assistance. As a result, India had to go for more and more commercial loans, leading to a tripling of its debt service payments on multilateral loans from $ 371 Million in 1984 to $ 1,106 Million in 1989.

Expecting the BOP difficulties in the future, in 1981, India entered into an arrangement with the IMF for a loan of SDR 5 Billion under the extended fund facility. The large current account deficit after 1984-85 was financed by substantial inflows of foreign capital through commercial borrowings and deposits of NRIs.

The final blow came during the year 1990–91 in the form of gulf crisis and political uncertainties in the country, leading to a severe balance of payment crisis. The country, during the crisis year, faced the trade account deficit of 3.0 per cent and current account deficit of 9.1 per cent, and was left with foreign exchange reserves which could have met only two and half months import bills. The situation was rescued temporarily by pledging gold with the central banks of Japan and the UK and procuring foreign exchange to meet the deficit. Also, as an immediate solution, the government implemented various import compression measures which counterbalanced the shortfall in exports.

To restore international confidence, and to achieve an enduring solution, a new BOP strategy was put in place in 1991, emphasizing on exchange rate adjustments, fiscal correction and suitable structural reforms in industrial and trade policy. As a part of the new strategy, a phased series of policy measures were initiated, such as downward adjustments in the exchange rate, trade reforms in the form of substantial rationalization of licensing procedure and lowering of tariffs, liberalization in industrial licensing and foreign investment, phasing of reduction in fiscal deficits, financial sector and tax reforms, and the tight monetary policy.

As a result of the new strategy, there was a considerable improvement, on both domestic and external fronts, in the subsequent decades. During the decade of 1990s, the average trade deficit stood at 2.8 per cent of GDP (Table 12.2). Substantial improvement kept the current account deficit at manageable level of 1.3 per cent of GDP. Generous capital inflows helped India in a steady build up of foreign exchange reserves. On an average, India could maintain reserves that could meet 6.5 months of import bills.

Table 12.2 Balance of Payments: Key Indicators

Item	*Average* 1990–91 to 1999–2000 (10 years)	*Average* 2000–01 to 2009–10 (10 years)	*Average* 2003–04 to 2007–08 (5 years)	2008–09	2009–10	2010-11	2012
I. BOP items (US $ billion)							
(a) Current Account Balance	– 4.4	– 8.3	– 4.7	– 28.7	– 38.2	–45.9	–78.2
(b) Net Invisibles	6.0	44.2	45.8	89.9	80.0	84.6	111.6
Of which							
Services	1.3	21.6	23.4	49.6	36.0	48.8	64.1
Private transfers	7.8	27.9	27.6	44.6	51.8	53.1	63.5
Investment income	– 3.5	– 4.7	– 4.9	– 4.0	– 7.2	–16.4	–16.5
(c) Net Capital Flows (US $ billion)	7.7	31.1	44.4	7.2	51.6	62.0	67.8
Of which							
FDI to India	1.6	16.7	15.3	33.1	31.7	25.9	33.0

FIIs	1.3	7.1	10.6	– 15.0	29.0	29.4	16.8
NRI deposits	1.3	2.5	2.0	4.3	2.9	3.2	11.9
(d) Reserve Changes (BOP basis) (increase(–)/ Decrease (+))	– 3.3	– 22.9	– 40.3	20.1	– 13.4	–13.1	12.8
(e) Reserves Outstanding	22	162	183	252	279	304.8	294.4
II. Indicators (% change)							
(a) Merchandise Exports	8.6	17.7	25.3	13.7	– 3.5	37.3	23.7
(b) Merchandise Imports	9.6	19.5	32.3	20.8	– 2.6	26.7	31.1
III. Indicators (% GDP)							
(a) Trade Balance	– 2.8	– 5.3	– 5.4	– 9.8	– 8.7	–7.8	–10.3
(b) Invisible Balance	1.6	4.8	5.1	7.4	5.9	5.0	6.0
(c) Current Account Balance	– 1.3	– 0.5	– 0.3	– 2.4	– 2.8	–2.7	–4.2
(d) Net Capital Flows	2.2	3.3	4.6	0.6	3.8	3.7	3.7
IV. Openness Indicators (% GDP)							
(a) Exports plus Imports of Goods	18.8	29.5	30.4	41.0	35.5	37.5	43.8
(b) Exports plus Imports of Goods and Services	22.9	39.2	40.8	53.7	47.0	50.4	55.7
(c) Current Receipts plus Current Payments	26.8	45.1	46.6	60.5	53.6	56.0	61.5
(d) Gross Capital Inflows plus Outflows	15.1	33.6	36.8	51.0	47.0	55.6	48.2
(e) Current Receipts and Payments plus Capital Receipts and Payments	41.9	78.8	83.5	111.5	100.6	111.6	109.6

Source: RBI (2012), Annual Report.

In the subsequent decade, inspite of deterioration in the trade balance, there was a substantial improvement in the overall balance of payment situation due to the substantial inflow of invisible receipts and capital inflows. On the one hand, the surplus on invisible account of 4.8 per cent of GDP helped contain the current account deficit at 0.5 per cent in the first decade of this century. On the other hand, the capital account surplus of 3.4 per cent helped in improving the foreign exchange reserves and an import cover of reserves to an average of 12.6 months.

The developments towards the end of the last decade, in the form of global financial crisis of 2008–09, however, increased the current account deficit to almost at the pre-BOP crisis level. But, the BOP of India remained comfortable, because of sufficient surplus on the capital account. However, in the recent period the current account surplus is under severe pressure, with current account deficit widening to 4.2 per cent in 2011–12, due to large increase in imports relative to exports. The capital account though in surplus is not sufficient to offset the widening current account deficit, leading to draw down of foreign exchange reserves. The BOP developments in the post-1991 period also indicate towards growing openness and integration of the Indian economy with the global economy. There was steady improvement in the openness indicators, such as Exports plus Imports of Goods to GDP ratio, Current Receipts plus Current Payments to GDP ratio, Gross Capital Inflows plus Outflows to GDP ratio, and Current Receipts and Payments plus Capital Receipts and Payments to GDP ratio in the post 1991 period up till the onset of global financial crisis.

Reference

GOI (2013), Economic Survey 2012–13.

SUMMARY

Transactions of a country with the rest of the world are accounted in the BOP statement. The statement follows a double accounting book keeping system; with the transactions resulting in an inflow of foreign currency recorded on the credit side and those resulting in an outflow of it recorded on the debit side. It consists of three sub-heads, i.e., current account comprising trade in goods and invisibles, capital account depicting the transaction in financial assets, and the official settlement account balancing the surplus or deficit in the above two accounts.

The BOP statement is always in balance. The deficit or surplus on the BOP refers to imbalances in the current account and/or capital account. The combined deficit or surplus of current and capital account depicts the overall balance in the BOP as the official settlement account is simply a balancing entry.

The deficit in the current account can be financed either through capital inflows or through drawing down of the foreign exchange reserves held with the central bank. Each type of balancing, however, has differing implications. Financing of the persistent current account deficit through continuous borrowings or debt inflows may result in a debt crisis, whereas continuous use of the accumulated reserves to settle such deficit may cause a BOP crisis.

India faced a severe BOP crisis in 1990–91 due to persistent continuous current account deficit and financing of it from the past accumulated reserves of the central bank. Structural reform measures initiated in the post-BOP crisis period helped the country to get better integrated with the rest of the world, to rebuild foreign exchange reserves to a comfortable level, and to restore the confidence in the working of the system in the international market.

Implications for Managers

An understanding of the BOP statement helps business organizations comprehend the developments on trade and capital flows. A careful analysis of the BOP statement helps managers know how far a particular country is integrated with the rest of the world.

An analysis of the trade account of the BOP, especially the destination and product-wise break up, helps managers identify the products that are in demand and destinations that can be explored. The invisible account helps in understanding the evolving services where firms can diversify or expand.

A closer examination of the current account balance, its financing through capital account flows and changes in the official settlement account, indicate whether the imbalances in the current account are sustainable. Or whether there are threats to the macroeconomic stability through debt or foreign currency crisis. Indicators like debt to GDP ratio, short-term debt to total external debt, short-term debt to foreign exchange reserves, short-term debt to current account receipts, help in assessing the sustainability of the current account of the BOP.

Expansion and diversification decisions of business units in external territories can be based on the changes in the BOP and external environment. The business units that do not adopt better technology, better managerial and marketing skills and other practices, do not invent new processes and practices, do not pursue new expansion and diversification strategies and do not evolve as per the changing environment become uncompetitive, obsolete, and get marginalized in the long-run and gradually become extinct.

REVIEW QUESTIONS

12.1 What are the sub-accounts or sub-heads of the balance of payment statement?

12.2 It is said that the balance of payment is always in balance. What do you understand, in such a situation, by the deficit or surplus on the balance of payment account?

12.3 What does official settlement account consists of?

12.4 How is the current account sustainability defined? In what forms the unsustainable current account deficit is manifested?

NUMERICAL PROBLEMS

12.1 Using the information given in Table 12.3 (in ₹ crore), calculate the trade balance and the current account balance of the balance of payment. Is there a deficit or surplus on the current account? How is this deficit financed? Why is the purchase of reserve assets reflected under the official settlement account?

Table 12.3 Current and Capital Account Receipts and Payments

Item	*Receipts*	*Payments*
1. Merchandise	16,000	25,000
2. Invisible		
(a) Travel	9,000	6,000
(b) Transportation	800	1,000
(c) Insurance	100	100
(d) Investment income	600	2,000
(e) Transfer payment	4,000	100
3. Capital account flows		
(a) Private	4,000	2,000
(b) Banking	300	200
(c) Government	12,000	7,000
4. Official settlement account	–	3,400
Total (1 + 2 + 3 + 4)	46,800	46,800

12.2 Using the information in Table 12.4 estimate the trade balance and the capital account balance of the balance of payment. Show that the balance of payment is in balance.

Table 12.4 Balance of Payment Data

Item	*₹ crore*
Exports	18,000
Imports	28,000
Invisible (net)	– 200
External assistance (net)	2,000
Commercial borrowing (net)	2,200
IMF (net) (non-monetary)	1,200
Non-resident deposits (net)	1,600
Rupee debt services	– 1,200
Foreign investment	70
Other flows	2,300
Reserve use	2,030

12.3 Suppose the current surplus for an economy is ₹1,000 in a particular year. During this year its foreign exchange reserves decline by ₹300 and there is a long-term net capital inflow of ₹500. Estimate the amount that this country must be having on its short-term capital account.

CASE ANALYSIS EXERCISE

C12.1 Global Imbalances, Crisis and Adjustments for Stronger Recovery

Global imbalances, in the form of two or more countries having large non-zero current account balances, have preceded many economic crisis in the past. For example, the failure of Bretton Woods System of Fixed Exchange Rate (UBE 15.2) was primarily due to such imbalances. Even the Mexican Crisis of 1994–95 and the Asian Financial Crisis of 1997–98 preceded by a large current account deficit. It has also been argued that a key factor behind the global financial crisis of 2008 was the global imbalances emerging from persistent substantial current account deficit in the USA and some other countries (United Kingdom, Southern Europe, including Greece, Italy, Portugal, and Spain, Central and Eastern Europe) which was financed mainly from corresponding large surplus in China, Japan, other East Asian economies, Germany, and oil exporter countries (Figure 12.6).

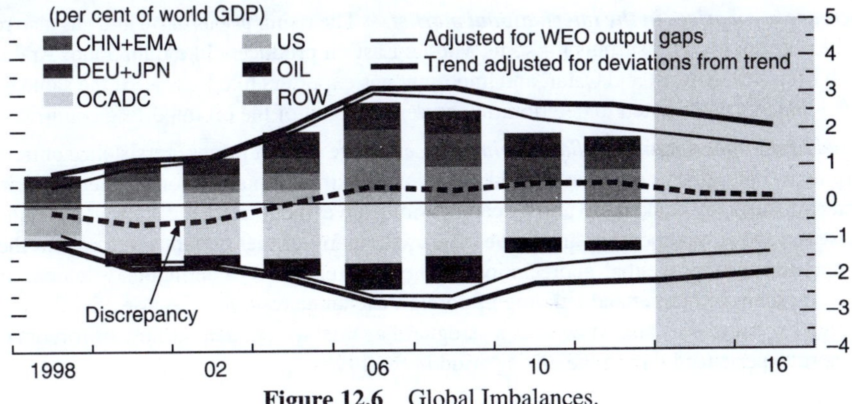

Figure 12.6 Global Imbalances.

Notations

CHN+EMA = China, Hong Kong SAR, Indonesia, Korea, Malaysia, Philippines, Singapore, Taiwan Province of China, Thailand; DEU+JPM = Germany and Japan; OCADC = Bulgaria, Croatia, Czech Republic, Estonia, Greece, Hungary, Ireland, Latvia, Lithuania, Poland, Portugal, Romania, Slovak Republic, Slovenia, Spain, Turkey, United Kingdom; OIL= Oil Exporters; ROW= Rest of the World

Source: IMF (2013), World Economic Outlook, April, (online) http://www.imf.org/external/pubs/ft/weo/2013/01/index.htm

Multiple explanations have been put forward to explain the rise in imbalances (IMF (2009) prior to the sub-prime lending crisis. Some of these are outlined as follows:

- ***Expansionary fiscal and monetary policies in the USA and other advanced countries:*** During the period following the bursting of dot com bubble burst, to give a boost to the domestic economy, the US followed an expansionary fiscal policy which gave impetus to domestic expenditure. This should have resulted in higher interest rates in the economy, but accommodating monetary policy kept them at lower level. Lower interest rates, along with financial innovations, encouraged a housing boom, and increased housing and other prices, resulting in higher wealth. Wealth being an important determinant of expenditure, increase in it provided further impetus to consumption and investment expenditure. Though higher expenditure could stimulate activities in the US, it continuously increased its current account deficit which was financed through cheap imports, especially that from China.
  - Many key industrial economies, including Italy, Spain, Australia, and the UK, also experienced substantial appreciation in housing prices, increase in wealth, expenditure and imports, and growing current account deficit.
- ***Decline in investment opportunities and saving glut in emerging markets:*** Many emerging economies experienced a series of financial crisis in 1990s, including the financial crisis in Russia, Latin America and the East-Asian Crisis. Before these crises, a large openness to capital flows had given an impetus to investment and growth in these economies. However, sudden reversal of capital flows also put them in a crisis and prolonged period of low growth, high unemployment and suffering. In the aftermath of financial crisis in the 1990s many of these economies found themselves with excess capacity, relative decline in profit rate and stagnation in domestic credit, leading to a fall in investment rate in the subsequent period. At the same time, in the last decade, aging population and better fiscal discipline also enhanced saving rate in some of the emerging economies. In the absence of profitable opportunities at home, the excess of saving was invested in already capital rich advanced economies, especially in the US, which financed their current account deficit.
- ***Increase in oil prices in the international market:*** The rising prices of oil and gas also resulted in higher current account surplus for some Middle East oil producers like Iran, Saudi Arabia, United Arab Emirates, Kuwait and Qatar, and important gas exporters like Russia. At the same time, these developments contributed to deteriorating current account of the oil importing countries.
- ***Fixed exchange or managed float regime:*** Left to the market forces, persistence current account surplus in emerging economies should have resulted in an appreciation of their exchange rates, which in turn, by making exports dearer would have moderated the current account surplus. However, viewing exports as an engine of growth, many of these countries, to retain their export competitiveness, prevented appreciation of their currencies by continuously intervening in the foreign exchange market and building up foreign exchange reserves (Section 15.3.2). The build of foreign exchange was also viewed as a safeguard against the sudden outflow of foreign capital, of the sort, experienced during the crisis period in the 1990s.

- ***Financing of current account deficit from capital inflows:*** Alternatively, sustained elevated level of current account deficit in advanced economies could have been moderated had the exchange rate in these countries depreciated. However, the current account deficit in these countries could be sustained at elevated levels for a prolonged period of time because of growing demand for financial assets of the US and that of other advanced countries, owing to their perceived high quality and sophisticated investor protection and lack of investment opportunities in surplus countries, preventing depreciation of their currencies.

Financing of continuous current account deficit through Dollar-denominated liabilities led to speculations that eventually this build up of external claims will turn over through a substantial dollar depreciation. The IMF (2005) had cautioned that an abrupt decline in capital inflows to the US "could engender a rapid dollar depreciation and a sharp increase in US interest rates, with potentially serious adverse consequences for global growth and international financial markets".

The fear did come out to be true in late 2007 and 2008 in the form of global financial crisis and global recession. The dollar depreciation did materialize before the onset of the crisis and during the early stages of the financial crisis, however, a broad-based flight from US assets and a sudden drop in the value of the dollar did not occur because global financial crisis moved the capital to safer avenues, such as US government securities, in flight to safety. The dollar rebounded strongly since September 2008 as the crisis deepened and increasingly engulfed the economies world over (IMF (2009).

The financial crisis, though did not result in a sharp depreciation of the US dollar, accelerated the adjustment of global current account imbalances. The current account of advanced countries declined from – 1.1 per cent in 2008 to – 0.1 per cent in 2009 and remained almost at the same level in the period ahead. On the other hand, the surpluses of emerging and developing economies moderated from 3.5 per cent in 2008 to 1.5 per cent in 2009 and further to 1.4 per cent in 2012. At the country level, the current account deficit of the US, a major deficit country, contracted from – 4.7 in 2008 to – 2.7 in 2009. Though in the period ahead it increased somewhat (at 3 per cent in 2012) it remained much below the pre-crisis level (IMF (2013), whereas the surplus in China, the largest surplus country, moderated from 9.3 per cent in 2008 to 4.9 per cent in 2009 and further to 2.6 per cent in 2012.

IMF (2009) identified three channels of adjustment, which brought down the imbalances in the aftermath of the crisis, as follows:

(i) A reduction in expenditure and an increase in private saving owing to the contraction in housing investment and credit availability in the USA and many other major advanced countries, and the consequent decline in the current account deficit.

(ii) A tightening of global credit conditions, leading to an increase in interest rates and a contraction in consumption expenditure and an improvement in current account balance.

(iii) An improvement in the terms of trade (Box 13.1) for oil importing countries due to a decline in oil prices, reducing the extent of current account deficit. At the same time deterioration in the terms of trade of oil exporting countries, leading to a reduction in their current account surpluses.

IMF (2011 and 2012), however, points out that the adjustment in global imbalances, in the aftermath of the crisis, primarily came from declining demand growth in deficit economies rather than stronger demand growth from surplus economies. There was also significant alignment of real effective exchange rates (Figure 12.7). However, some more alignment is needed from emerging market economies with large surpluses.

Global imbalances though have moderated recently, further consolidation is possible only if the major surplus and deficit countries bring in some major structural reforms. Specifically, the two major surplus countries need to spend more; China on consumption and Germnay on investment. At the same time, the major deficit countries need to enhance their savings. The USA can do so by fiscal consolidation and other deficit economies by improving their export competitiveness by enhancing productivity.

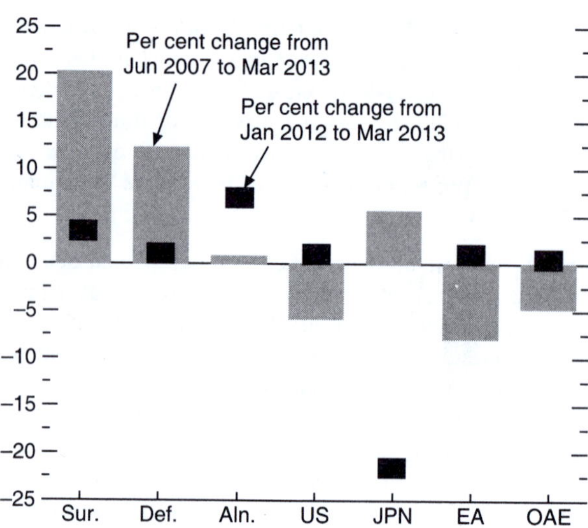

Sur = Surplus Emerging Market and Developing Economies
Def = Deficit Emerging Market and Developing Economies
Aln = Aligne Emerging Market and Developing Economies
US = the United States, JPN=Japan, EA=Euro Area,OAE = Other Advanced Economies

Source: (2013), World Economic Outlook, April, (online) http://www.imf.org/external/pubs/ft/weo/2013/01/index.htm

Figure 12.7 Exchange Rate Movements in Major Regions and Countries.

References

IMF (2005), *World Economic Outlook*, April.

IMF (2009), *World Economic Outlook*, April.

IMF (2011), *World Economic Outlook*, April.

IMF (2012), *World Economic Outlook*, April.

IMF (2013), *World Economic Outlook*, April.

Questions

1. What do you understand by global imbalances?
2. Why did global imbalances rise prior to the sub-prime lending crisis?
3. What factors helped in moderating global imbalances in the aftermath of the sub-prime lending crisis?
4. What is needed for further consolidation of global imbalances?
5. Why global imbalances are considered to be non-zero sum game?

SUGGESTED FURTHER READING

Mohanty, D. (2013), Perspectives on India's Balance of Payment, *RBI Bulletin*, January.

RBI (2013), Developments in India's Balance of Payments during Second Quarter (July–September) of 2012–13, *RBI Bulletin*, February.

CHAPTER 13

Trade Flows, International Linkages and External Environment

13.1 INTRODUCTION

We keep watching variety of products in our markets which are not domestically produced, but are imported from abroad. Some of these imported goods have no substitutes in the domestic markets. However, quite often, we also find that we import goods from abroad despite the availability of similar types of goods in the domestic market. For example, various types of domestically produced cars, such as Tata Indigo, Tata Indica, Tata Nano, Maruti 800, Martui Swift, Maruti Wagan R., etc., are available in India but we do import foreign made cars, such as Toyota Etios, Toyota Fortuner, Toyota Innova, BMW, and so on. Similarly, we do see that domestic producers do not supply all that they produce in the domestic markets, but prefer selling part of it abroad. Why do we export and import commodities? Why do countries participate in international trade?

Countries participate in international trade because it brings in immense benefits to all their constituents.

To producers, it widens the markets for their products and provides them an opportunity to produce at a large scale, enjoy the benefits arising from division of labour, specialization, and thereby, economies of scale. To consumers, it widens their consumption basket and makes available better quality products often at cheaper rates. For a country as a whole, trade widens the market for domestically produced goods, as well as enhances competition in the domestic markets, which helps in enlarging the scale of production and improving the quality of domestically produced goods as well as reducing the cost of production. By opening up its economy, a country can, thus, enhance output and achieve higher growth even when domestic demand is decelerating. Fluctuations in economic activities, emerging from the behaviour of domestic participants, thus, can be moderated with the help of international trade.

However, international trade makes the country dependent on demand from abroad. At the time of crises, such as wars, such sources of growth may become dysfunctional. Also the country, open to trade flows, becomes susceptible to external shocks; severe slowdown or recession can get imported easily in such an economy. Therefore, often countries try to protect their economies by imposing tariff and non-tariff barriers.

Given its importance to business units and a country as a whole, this chapter highlights the need for trade in greater detail in Section 13.2. The arguments for and against protection from free trade are highlighted in Section 13.3. While highlighting the arguments for and against the trade, this section also brings out the reasons for protectionist policies pursued by India in the pre-reform period and the reasons for opening up in the post-1991 period. The arguments in favour of trade have resulted in the constitution of the World Trade Organization. Hence, this section also briefs on its role in promoting and supporting free trade.

13.2 TRADE AND INTEGRATION

13.2.1 Need for Trade

To understand why individuals exchange goods or services among themselves or trade with each other, let us consider a simple economy where there are only three individuals– Rohit, Apporva and Sandeep. To survive they need wheat, clothes and house. Rohit, with sturdy built and a diploma in farming, produces wheat. Apporva can produce all three goods. However, with a creative mind and diploma in fashion designing, she can produce clothes more efficiently than wheat and house. Sandeep, with an engineering degree, can produce all the goods most efficiently, and that too, at the least cost; implying that he has an absolute advantage in the production of all goods. One will agree that Rohit will be required to exchange some of his surplus wheat with others to procure other essential items to survive. Many of us will jump to the conclusion that Apporva need not trade because she can produce all the required goods. However, some of us will be skeptical of this view because though she can produce all the goods, she cannot produce all with efficiency, and argue that she will be better-off by concentrating on the production of clothes and exchanging surplus clothes with other required items. Most of us will view that it is only Sandeep who need not trade with others because he can produce all the goods most efficiently. However, few of us will also not agree with this view. The dissent will argue that if Sandeep tries to produce all the goods, he can produce all those only in small quantities and not at large scale because, like all others he has limited time. Hence, he will be deprived of the benefits arising from a large scale production, i.e., the division of labour, specialization and economies of scale. A large scale production makes possible the division of labour and specialization in the process of production, i.e., different task can be assigned to different individuals. When they repeatedly do the same task, they learn to do it faster and more accurately. In a given time, from given resources, then they can produce larger quantities, and hence, the per unit cost of production declines. Output produced in smaller quantities cannot reap the benefits of division of labour and specialization. In our simple economy all three individuals will benefit if Rohit specializes in the production of wheat because, he can produce it more efficiently than clothes and house. Apporva can focus on clothes as she is more efficient in the production of it than other items. Though Sandeep can produce all the goods at least cost, he should concentrate on building up houses because he is comparatively better off in the production of houses than that of wheat and clothes. Thus, all individuals can produce more by focusing on the production of those goods where they have comparative advantage, and exchanging the surplus of their products over their own consumption with others for those commodities in which others are specializing.

In a nutshell, specialization, in the production of those goods in which the individual is more efficient, increases the total production in an economy or even the global production. Specialization in production lowers the cost of production and prices of commodities. Through exchange of commodities or trade, these benefits are shared among the individuals. The gains from specialization and exchange motivate individuals to trade with each other even when they can produce all the commodities on their own and most efficiently.

The same logic can be extended to international trade, i.e., the trade among the countries. Like individuals, countries differ in many respect from each other. They differ in factor endowment; some countries are labour abundant, whereas others are abundant in capital or natural resources. They differ in factor productivity; in some countries labour is more productive, whereas others have better capital productivity. Differences among countries can even be on account of differences in human skills; some countries have a larger pool of engineers and doctors, whereas others are bestowed more with poets and other creative people. Tastes and preferences also vary across the countries—Asians like more spicy food than Europeans. Product life cycle can also differ across countries; cloud computing may be in the early stages of product life cycle in developing countries, whereas the same may be at the maturity stage or more advanced stage in developed countries. The differences in these factors give comparative advantage to different countries in the production of different commodities and these become the basis for the trade. Let us define the term absolute advantage and comparative advantage before we see in detail how these provide advantage to countries and become the basis for trade.

Absolute advantage in the production of a commodity occurs when an individual or a firm or a country can produce it using least resources or at lower cost than the others. Let us understand this concept by considering the case where two countries, say the US and the UK are producing two commodities, say mobile and laptop. With the use of one unit of resource, say labour, for each of the commodities the two countries can produce the two commodities in quantities as indicated in Table 13.1.

Table 13.1 Absolute Advantage in Production of One Commodity

	Mobiles	*Laptops*	*Pre-trade (domestic) price ratio*
Production per unit of resource used for each commodity			
US	20	10	20:10 = 2:1
UK	10	15	10:15 = 1:1.5
World output	30	25	
Amount of Labour per unit of output			
US	0.05 (=1/20)	0.1 (=1/10)	0.05 < 0.1
UK	0.1 (= 1/10)	0.066 (=1/15)	0.066 < 0.1

From Table 13.1, we can infer that the US has an absolute advantage in the production of mobiles because with the use of one unit of labour it can produce more of mobiles than that can be produced by the UK. Alternatively, we can say that the US requires less units of labour (0.05) to produce one unit of mobile than the UK. Similarly, the UK has an absolute advantage in the production of laptops because it can produce more laptops than the US using one unit of labour. Alternatively stated, the UK requires less units of labour (0.066) to produce one unit of laptop than the US. If these two countries decide not to trade, but remain self reliant, then the US will be exchanging mobiles with laptops in the ratio of 2:1, implying that the cost of one laptop is equal to 2 mobiles.

Similarly, in the UK, mobiles and laptops will be exchanged in the ratio of 1:1.5, implying that the cost of one mobile is equal to 1.5. Mobiles will be less expensive in the USA and more expensive in the UK.

Suppose these countries realize their absolute advantages and each one decides to specialize in the commodity in which it has an absolute advantage. Considering absolute advantage, the US will specialize in mobiles, whereas the UK will concentrate on the production of laptops. The specialization will result in an increase in the world output of mobiles from 30 to 40 (because the US will use both the units of labour for the production of mobiles thus, doubling its production of mobiles) and that of laptops from 25 to 30 (because the UK will use both the units of labour for manufacturing laptops, and thus, doubling its production of laptops). Not only the world output will grow but also each country will benefit from this higher output if they exchange their excess production with the other countries. The USA will benefit if it can procure 1 unit of laptop for less than its pre-trade price of 2 units of mobiles. Similarly, the UK will benefit if it can procure one unit of mobile for less than its pre-trade price of 1.5 units of laptops.

Many of us will wonder whether the trade can take place if a country is more efficient than other countries in the production of all the commodities. As we have seen in the case of Sandeep, the answer to this question lies in comparative advantage.

Even if one country can produce both the commodities more efficiently (has an absolute advantage in the production of both the commodities) the world still benefits from specialization and trade. The argument for trade in such cases is based on the theory of **comparative advantage** proposed by Ricardo. A country is said to have a comparative advantage over another country in the production of one commodity compared to the production of another if the absolute advantage is greater for that commodity than for the other commodities. Alternatively, one can say that the comparative advantage for a country in the production of a particular commodity occurs when the country gives up less of other commodities to produce the given commodity compared to other countries, i.e., the country has lower **opportunity cost** of producing the given commodity than the other countries.

Comparative advantage is worked out from a two country two product comparison, whereas absolute advantage is worked out from a two country one product comparison.

To understand how comparative advantage sets a background for trade, let us assume that two countries, say India and China, are producing two commodities, say wheat and cloth. Table 13.2 shows the production that is possible in the two countries when one unit of resource is used for each commodity.

As can be ascertained from Table 13.2, India has an absolute advantage in the production of both wheat and cloth because it can produce both the commodities in larger quantities with the help of one unit of labour in the production of each commodity. However, it does not have comparative advantage in the production of both the commodities. India has a lower opportunity cost of producing wheat than China because for producing 1 unit of wheat India has to give up just one unit of cloth, whereas China has to give 2 units of cloth. Thus, India has a comparative advantage in wheat production. On the contrary, the opportunity cost of producing cloth is lower in China than India because to produce one unit of cloth India has to give up one unit of wheat, whereas China has to give up just 0.5 units of wheat. Thus, China has a comparative advantage in the production of cloth.

Table 13.2 Production without Specialization

	Wheat	*Cloth*	*Pre-trade (Domestic price ratio)*
Production per unit of resource used for each commodity			
India	50	50	1:1 (50:50)
China	20	40	1:2 (20:40)
World output (Total)	70	90	
Opportunity cost			
India	1 (= 50/50)	1 (= 50/50)	1 < 2
China	2 (= 40/20)	0.5 (= 20/40)	0.5 < 1

The total world output will increase, as can be seen from Table 13.3, if each country uses all its resources (in our example two units of labour) for the specialization in the production of that commodity in which it has a comparative advantage.

Table 13.3 Production from Specialization

	Wheat	*Cloth*
Production per unit of resource used for each commodity		
India	100	0
China	0	80
World output (Total)	100	80

Thus, the concentration in only the production of that commodity in which the country has comparative advantage results in higher world output. The allocation of resources among the nations is most efficient when each nation specializes according to its comparative advantage.

The higher benefits emerging from the specialization can be shared by countries through trading—importing and exporting the commodities. In the process the total output, consumption and welfare improves in the countries involved in trade.

However, for trade to take place among countries it is essential that the appropriate terms or prices exist. In the example above, before specialization and trade, India could get one unit of cloth for one unit of wheat. Thus, if India has to pay one unit of wheat to get one unit of cloth it would not get the benefit. Similarly, before specialization and trade, China could get one unit of wheat for two units of cloth. Thus, if China has to pay two or more units of cloth to get one unit of wheat from India it will not benefit China, and the trade will not take place.

Therefore, for beneficial trade to take place between the two countries, the **Terms of Trade** (TOT), which is the rate at which two goods are traded (Box 13.1), have to be somewhere between the two, i.e.,

1 wheat = 1 cloth (all gains to China) and 1 wheat = 2 cloth (all gains to India).

This implies that if China could get 1 unit of wheat by sacrificing less than 2 units of cloth, and if India could get 1 unit of cloth by giving up less than 1 unit of wheat, each would be willing to trade.

Suppose, China offers to pay India 1.5 units of cloth for each unit of wheat India is willing to sell. This implies the TOT between wheat and cloth to be 1:1.5. The trade will take place at these terms of trade as the countries would be willing to exchange goods. It benefits China as the pre-trade price was 1:2, i.e., one unit of wheat was exchanged for 2 units of cloth. Now, in the post-trade regime, China would be able to get 1 unit of wheat only for 1.5 units of cloth. India also gains from this arrangement as it was able to procure only one unit of cloth by surrendering one unit of wheat in the pre-trade regime. By agreeing to trade with China, it will be able to get 1.5 units of cloth by selling one unit of wheat. In the presence of trade, the international price ratio (i.e., TOT) will be 1:1.5. We can see that free trade also leads to equalization of commodity prices across trading nations.

The more the post-trade price differs from the pre-trade price for a country, for a given volume of trade, the larger the gains from trade for the country. The difference between what the country gains after trade and what it could get by producing it domestically reflects the gains from trade.

We can also see the manner in which specialization and trade can enhance production and consumption possibilities from Figure 13.1. To understand the figure, recollect that when India produces wheat and cloth with the help of one unit of labour each then it can produce 50 units of each commodity (Table 13.2). However, by shifting some of the labour from cloth to wheat it can produce more of wheat (say 60 units) but less of cloth (say 40 units). By specializing, i.e., using all the resources (i.e., 2 units of labour) only in the production of one commodity, it can produce maximum 100 units of wheat or maximum 100 units of cloth (Table 13.3). If we plot all these values we can get India's **Production Possibility Curve (PPC)** (Figure 13.1(a)), the curve which depicts all combinations of amounts of different commodities that an economy can produce with full employment of its resources and maximum feasible productivity. In the absence of trade, the consumption choices of Indian consumers will be limited to the combinations falling on the PPC. However, with the possibility of trade, India can specialize in wheat because, there lays its comparative advantage and can either have 100 units of wheat for domestic consumption or exchange whole of wheat for maximum 150 units of cloth, or it can have any combination of the two commodities (say 75 units of wheat and 50 units of cloth at the TOT of 1:1.5, depicted by the **Consumption Possibility Curve (CPC)**.

Similarly, we can get the PPC of China (Figure 13.1(b)), which depicts the combination of wheat and cloth China can produce given the maximum utilization of resources. China can also improve its consumption possibilities by specializing in cloth (as it has a comparative advantage in it) and can either have 80 units of cloth for domestic consumption or exchange all the units of cloth for maximum 53.3 units of wheat or any combination of the two commodities (say 50 units of cloth and 33.3 units of cloth) at TOT of 1:1.5 as depicted by the trade line in Figure 13.1(b).

Thus, we see that free trade not only enhances the world output but also benefits the countries participating in it by allowing the exchange of surplus and, hence, expanding the CPCs beyond their PPCs as depicted in Figure 13.1.

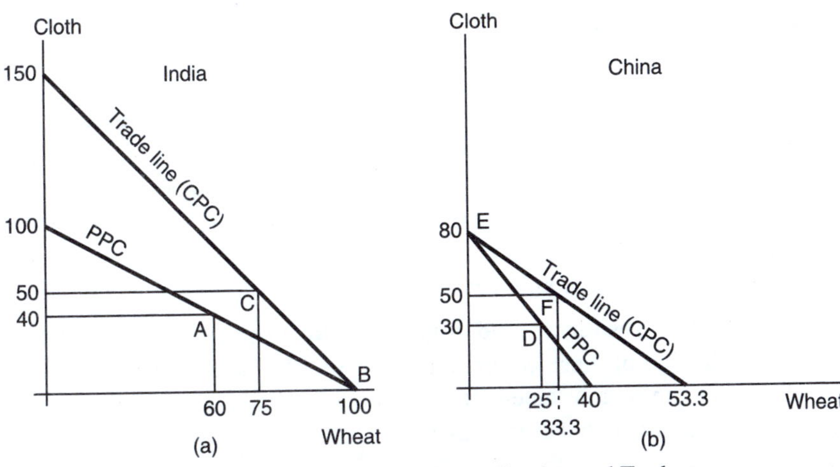

Figure 13.1 Gains from Specialization and Trade.

Box 13.1 Terms of Trade

The **Terms of Trade** (TOT) refers to the ratio of the average price of country's exported commodities to the average price of its imported commodities. Often the TOT is multiplied by 100 and expressed in percentage terms. In a time series analysis of TOT, the base year value is assumed to be 100.

If there are only two countries in the world producing and trading only two commodities, the terms of trade is defined as the ratio of the price a country receives for its exported commodity to the price it pays for its imported commodity. If, for example, a country exports ₹100 worth of a commodity and, at the same time imports ₹200 worth of a commodity for a given volume of commodities, then the country's TOT is 100/200 = 0.5. As export of a country is import of another country, the TOT for the other country is just the reciprocal of the TOT of the first country, i.e., 2 (200/100).

The world consists of a large number of countries and several commodities are traded amongst the nations. Therefore, to represent the overall TOT the ratio of exports price index to that of import price index is estimated. Export and import price indices are often prepared using the Laspeyres' method (Section 4.3). Thus, the export index is the current value of the base period exports divided by the base period value of the base period exports. Similarly, the import index is the current value of the base period imports divided by the base period value of the base period imports. The TOT can be expressed as:

$$\text{TOT} = \left[\left(\frac{\sum_{i=1}^{n} Pxi_1 \cdot Qxi_0}{\sum_{i=1}^{n} Pxi_0 \cdot Qxi_0}\right)\Bigg/\left(\frac{\sum_{i=1}^{n} Pmi_1 \cdot Qmi_0}{\sum_{i=1}^{n} Pmi_0 \cdot Qmi_0}\right)\right]$$

Pxi_1 : Price of exported commodity *i* in the current period
Pxi_0 : Price of exported commodity *i* in the base period
Pmi_1 : Price of imported commodity *i* in the current period
Pmi_0 : Price of imported commodity *i* in the base period
Qxi_0 : Quantity of exported commodity *i* in the base period
Qmi_0 : Quantity of imported commodity *i* in the base period

The TOT fluctuates in concurrence with the changes in export and import prices. A rise in the price of exports or a fall in the price of imports implies an improvement in the TOT, whereas a rise in the price of imports or a fall in the price of exports implies a deterioration in the TOT. The exchange rate and the rate of inflation influence the prices of exports and imports in the international market, and thereby, can influence the TOT.

13.2.2 Advantages of Free Trade Flows

The trade brings in following advantages to countries involved in it:

1. Lower cost of production: Firms catering only to the domestic markets produce only the amount demanded in these markets. Thus, the available domestic demand sometimes limits the optimum utilization of capacity or resources. Trade helps in expanding the level of demand. Under free trade, firms produce not only to meet the demand of domestic consumers, but also that of the foreigners. Thus, trade helps in expanding the level of production and make firms experience economies of scale, i.e., the reduction in per unit cost as the level of production increases.

2. Efficient allocation of resources and higher world output: Trade allows countries to specialize in the production of those commodities where they have comparative advantage or in the areas in which they are more efficient. This improves the allocation of limited resources and increases the total world output and employment.

3. Competitive environment: Trade permits free entry of foreign goods into the domestic market. Imported foreign goods compete with domestically produced commodities and help breaking up the monopoly position of domestic producers, firms and traders. Trade compels domestic producers to respond to higher competition by better work practices, efficient use of resources, better quality of products and adoption of best practices. These changes, in turn, enhance the productivity and bring in cost efficiency in production.

4. Variety to consumers: Through trade, the excess output produced by a country can be exchanged with those commodities produced abroad which either the country is incapable of producing or not as efficient in their production as other countries are. The exchange of commodities provides consumers a variety of products which meet their taste and preferences and increases their welfare.

13.2.3 Disadvantages of Free Trade Flows

The foreign trade has certain disadvantages as follows:

1. Higher dependence on foreign countries: Specialization makes the countries dependent on others even for meeting their basic requirements, such as food, clothing and medicine. The over-dependence creates problems for the countries participating in trade, especially during emergencies like natural calamities and war.

2. Foreign invasion and interference in economic policies: Free trade allows the countries with more efficient production techniques a large degree of control on the production of essential commodities and command over superior technology to invade the not so well-developed countries or interfere in their economic policies or command more favourable TOT for their products. History has numerous such examples. For example, Britishers came to India as traders and eventually took over the complete political and economic governance of the country almost for 200 years. During the last 50 years, the OPEC, a cartel of oil producing countries, has often exploited the situation of lack of close substitutes for oil by raising the price of it. This has imposed a high cost on the oil importing countries and worsened their TOT.

3. Commercial rivalry: Intense commercial rivalry to gain a larger share of world trade may even lead to a war or an invasion.

13.3 TRADE PROTECTION

As seen above, there are several advantages of free trade. However, many countries have been found to be pursuing protectionist policies and imposing restrictions on foreign trade. Protectionist policies aim at protecting the domestic economy by imposing tariffs (Box 13.2) and non-tariff barriers such as quotas (Box 13.3).

Box 13.2 Tariff Barriers

The **tariff** is a tax levied on the price of imports or exports. However, most often it takes the form of a tax on imports only. The tariff affects the price of exported and imported commodities, and thus, influences the demand for these commodities through price mechanism. It can be an *ad valorem* duty or a specific duty. An **ad valorem duty** is levied as a fixed percentage of the value of the good. For example, it can be fixed as 10 per cent of the value of cigarette packet. If the value of cigarette packet is ₹100, then the total tariff will result in revenue of ₹10. If the value of cigarette packet increases from ₹100 to ₹150 the amount of tariff on it will be ₹15. A **specific duty**, on the contrary, is levied as a fixed sum of money per unit of the good. For example, it can be ₹10 irrespective of the value of cigarette packet. If the value of cigarette packet increases from ₹100 to ₹150 the tariff on it will still remain the same.

Tariffs are of two types—revenue tariff and protective tariff.

Revenue tariff: When the tariff is levied with the objective of raising more revenue it is known as the **revenue tariff**.

Protective tariff: When the objective behind imposing the tariff is to protect domestic producers from foreign competition and bring in structural changes in the BOP, by reducing the extent of current account deficit, it is known as the **protective tariff**. The tariff raises the price of imported commodities and makes these dearer for domestic consumers. It is expected that the higher tariff will discourage domestic consumers to demand imported commodities, and thus, will help in correcting imbalances in the current account deficit.

The effectiveness of tariff in protecting the domestic industry depends on the price elasticity of demand for imported commodities. If import demand is highly price inelastic, the tariff will not be efficient in bringing down the demand for imported commodities to the desired extent. In such cases, non-tariff barriers are considered to be more efficient.

The impact of protective tariff is depicted in Figure 13.2. Assume that the world price is P_1. Since free trade equalizes prices across countries, the domestic price is same as the world price, i.e., P_1.

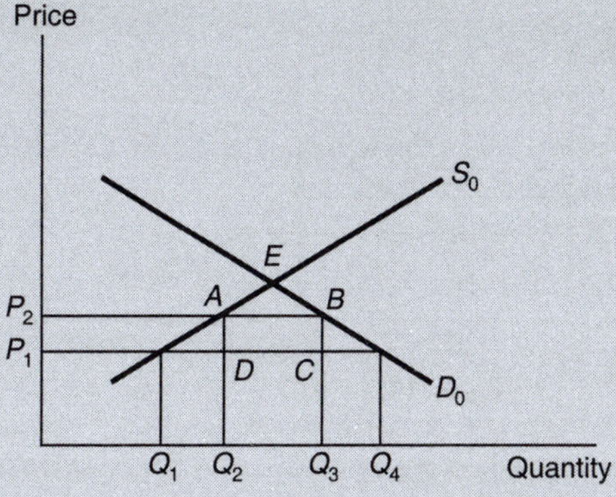

Figure 13.2 Economic Impact of Tariff.

At this price, the domestic demand is Q_4 of which Q_1 amount of demand is met through domestic production and the rest of the demand, i.e., $Q_4 - Q_1$, is met from imports. The imposition of specific tariff raises the price of the imported commodity in the domestic market to P_2, reduces the domestic demand to Q_3, increases the domestic production to Q_2. Hence, it reduces the amount of import from $Q_4 - Q_1$ to $Q_3 - Q_2$. The revenue gain for the government is *ABCD* (import volume $Q_3 - Q_2$ times tariff per unit ${}_1P_2$).

Box 13.3 Non-tariff Barriers

Non-tariff barriers, as detailed below, can take the form of quantitative restrictions, licensing regulation, embargo, export subsidies, and voluntary restrictions.

Quotas: **Quantitative restrictions**, viz., **quotas**, are usually imposed on imports. Quotas are the maximum amount of a commodity that can be imported by traders during a given year. Quotas reduce the quantity imported without affecting their price.

Quotas limit the supply of imported commodities in the domestic market. The supply and demand mismatches, resulting from the imposition of quota, may lead to an increase in the prices of those commodities which are subject to such restrictions. Quotas are found to be more effective than import tariffs in restricting the quantity of imports when the demand for imported commodities is not much sensitive to price changes. Though quotas are more effective in protecting domestic industries, they reduce the revenue of the government. Quotas are also found to be more discriminatory in nature. Tariffs are usually applied equally to all foreign exporters, and hence, non-discriminatory in nature, whereas quotas can be selective and can be imposed on the basis of criteria other than economic efficiency, such as political reasons. Consumers suffer by such discriminations as they have to pay higher prices as well as consume less quantities.

This can be seen from Figure 13.3. Suppose under free trade the price of the commodity is P_1 and the quantity demanded is Q_4. The domestic supply at price P_1 is Q_1. The rest of the demand, i.e., $Q_4 - Q_1$ is met from imports. When the government restricts the imports by imposing quotas by permitting the imports of only $Q_3 - Q_2$ quantities, the total supply in the domestic market reduces to Q_3. This reduction in supply increases the domestic price to P_2.

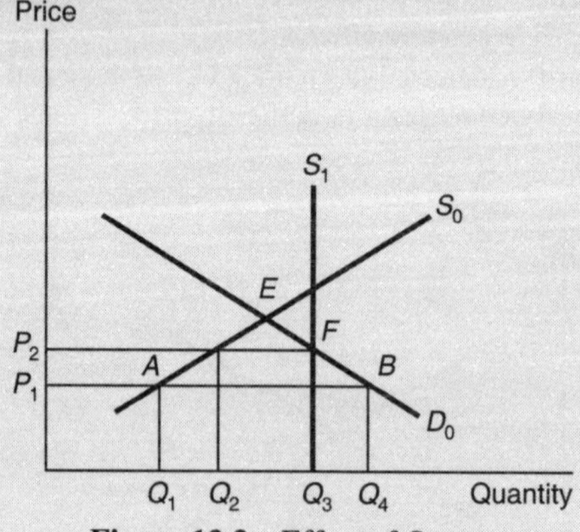

Figure 13.3 Effect of Quota.

Licenses: Traders are not allowed to freely trade in a licensing regime. To import or export commodities they need to procure a **license** from the government. Often quotas and licenses go hand in hand.

Embargo: A complete ban on the imports of certain goods by a country is known as the **embargo**. It is often pursued to prevent the entry of undesired and harmful goods, such as drugs like heroin, arms and ammunition, or punishing a country for political reasons by severing off all the relations with it.

Export subsidies: **Export subsidies** are given by a government to make exported commodities competitive in the international market by reducing their price.

Voluntary restrictions: The government may seek co-operation of foreign governments in the development of domestic industries by requesting them to voluntarily restrict their exports to the country seeking the assistance.

13.3.1 Arguments for Protectionist Policies

The arguments in favour of protection are as follows:

Infant Industry Argument—Development of Domestic Industries and Diversification

New industries usually have a small capacity of production or operate to cater to domestic industries where demand for products is limited. In the initial years of their operations, they cannot compete with well-established foreign firms, which have a superior market and over a period of time have benefitted from the economies of scale. These infant industries may be producing as per the requirement of the domestic country and may have the potential to become efficient if allowed to operate in a protective environment without the fear of damaging competition. Protection allows these countries to expand their production level, learn from experiences, and acquire internal economies of scale, and benefit from various external economies, such as expanding skilled labour force as the country moves on the development path. The **infant industry argument** professes that the infant domestic industries need to be protected from well-established foreign companies until they become efficient enough to compete with them. The development of domestic industries helps the country in achieving the goal of self-sufficiency. Trade barriers can be removed once the domestic industries become cost-effective and competitive. Protection not only allows the domestic infant industries to grow but also the country to diversify in different areas.

Employment Argument

Protection keeps foreign goods out of the country. Domestic consumers need to depend on domestically produced goods to satisfy their demands. Thus, the **employment argument** suggests that the protection enhances demand for domestically produced goods, and thereby, increases domestic output and employment. Higher employment increases the income level which further generates demand and employment in various industries.

Terms of Trade Argument

The **Terms of Trade** (TOT) refers to the rate at which a country's exports can be exchanged for its imports. As per the **terms of trade argument**, the protection in terms of tariff implies exchange of smaller quantities of exports for a given quantity of imports and, thus, an improvement in the TOT.

Anti-dumping Argument

Dumping refers to the practice of selling goods in foreign markets at lower prices than that charged in the home market or below their cost of production. The objective is to capture export or foreign markets, drive out the producers of other countries from their own countries, and then, once in the long-run, the markets have been sufficiently captured, hike the price of exported commodities. Therefore, the **anti-dumping argument** suggests that to safeguard the interest of domestic producers from such practices by foreign countries protectionist policies to be pursued.

Balance of Payment Argument

The **balance of payment argument** professes that protectionist policies, such as tariffs and quotas on selected goods, to be pursued to reduce the demand for imported goods and to overcome persistent deficit in the current account, and thus, restore the BOP equilibrium.

Anti Over-specialization Argument

Trade encourages specialization in those commodities where countries have comparative advantages. However, the **anti-over specialization argument** highlights that over-specialization, quite often, is risky, especially in times of war or natural calamities.

Also, the taste and preferences of consumers keep on changing. The dynamic movements in the taste and preferences of consumers may lead to a drastic fall in the demand for the product in which the country is specializing and the recession may set in the country due to such changes in the world market. The greater the openness and dependence of a country on foreign markets the greater the risks for it due to changing demand conditions in the world market.

Counrties world over use a mix of trade protectionist arguments to protect their markets from foreign produced goods and service. This is illustrated using India as the case in UBE 13.1

UNDERSTANDING BUSINESS ENVIRONMENT

UBE 13.1 Restrictive Trade Practices: Pre-1991 India

The arguments which were used for restrictive and protective policies by India in the pre-1991 period, the shape these policies took, and the outcome of these policies are elaborated in this UBE.

India's trade policies in the pre-1991 period were largely influenced by its colonial experience, which was perceived to be exploitative and growth retarding. Apart from the fears regarding foreign influence on domestic policies and exploitation of domestic resources, there was also exports pessimism which dominated the mindset of policy makers. Considering the low income elasticity for exports for agriculture and other primary products, it was believed that the country cannot achieve export led growth and the growth has to be enhanced through domestic resources by self reliance. Given the fears, export pessimism, and the perceived wisdom of policy makers, with the objective of achieving growth through domestic resources and self reliance, India adopted a closed door policy towards foreign trade and capital flows.

Such policies, were however, not apparent at the very inception of the planning process, because of comfortable level of the Balance Of Payment (BOP) at the time of independence. During the first plan period, food grain production was comfortable and industrialization was not yet a priority for the planners. As the government was not called on to provide for imports of capital goods and machinery on a large scale, it adopted a lenient approach towards imports of these items. However, such import policy soon resulted in a heavy deficit in the balance of trade. In 1956–57 the balance of payment crisis struck the country. To overcome the crises, the government imposed quantitative restrictions on imports since 1957 under the BOP provision of the General Agreement on Tariffs and Trade (GATT) that allowed its signatory governments to set such restrictions on grounds of BOP difficulties.

The second plan contemplated a large scale programme of industrialization for the country, necessitating the imports of machinery and new technology. However, the pressure on the BOP, which surfaced by the end of the first five-year plan, compelled the government to impose restrictions on the imports of all non-essential goods. The axe also fell on the imports of consumer goods to enable the country to go ahead with its ambitious programme of heavy industrialization. Imports were restricted not only through tariff barriers but also through non-tariff restrictions like licensing and quotas (Figure 10.5).

For the purpose of licensing, the commodities were classified into two lists—Open General License and Negative list.

Open General License: The **Open General License** (OGL) list consisted of all those items that could be imported without any quantitative restrictions.

Negative List: The **negative list** carried all those items that required not only license but were also subject to quantitative restrictions. Depending on the severity of the restriction, the items on the negative list fell into one of three categories: restricted, canalized and banned.

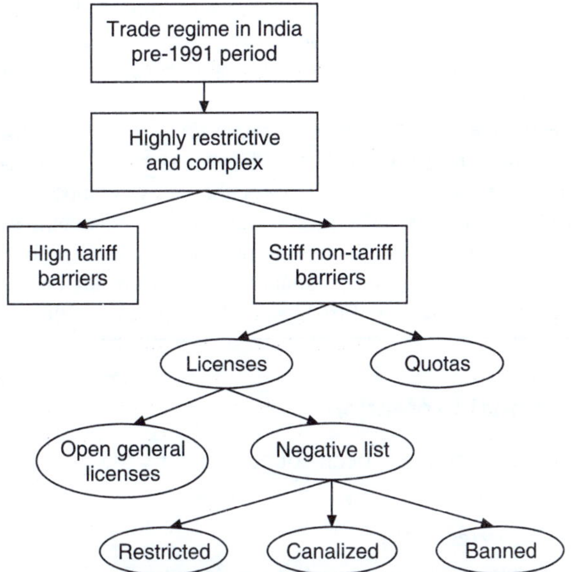

Figure 13.4 Trade Regime in India in the Pre-Reform Period.

Restricted items: The items falling under the **restricted items** category could be imported within the quota limits with government license.

Canalized items: The items which could be imported only by the state monopolies (such as Food Corporation of India, State Trading Corporation) were placed under the category of **canalized items**. Most of the agricultural goods (such as grains, edible oils, oilseeds, and sugar) were placed under this category.

Banned items: Imports of few items was prohibited on the grounds of religious and cultural sensitivity, for example, fat and oils of animal origin. These items formed a part of the **banned items** list.

The Indo-Pak war in the late 1965 led to a withdrawal of foreign aid to the country. At the same time, the drought in 1965–66, necessitated imports of food grains under the PL480 scheme. The high amount of expenditure, arising due to war and supply shocks in the agriculture sector, resulted in severe inflationary pressures in the economy, making Indian exports dearer and imports cheaper in the international market and straining the BOP further.

The severe balance of payment pressures, thus, necessitated the first devaluation of Indian rupee in June 1966. Under the pressure from donor countries and agencies, imports were also somewhat liberalized in 59 priority industries consisting of export industries, capital building industries and industries catering to the needs of common usage, like sugar and cotton textiles. However, these liberalization measures were temporary, the country backed out of its promise of liberalization to the donor countries when sufficient donations did not reach.

Persistence drought and famine conditions led to the advent of **Green Revolution** in 1966, necessitating a large scale import of fertilizers, High Yielding Variety (HYV) seeds, pesticides and insecticides to implement the new strategy. Though the strategy succeeded in improving agriculture production, it stained the import bill.

In the subsequent period, external shocks in the form of 1971 war with Pakistan, international oil price shocks, etc., continued to strain the BOP. In attempts to overcome the unfavourable developments, the country continued to pursue the policy of import restrictions for full two decades right upto the end of the seventies.

Towards the end of the decade of 1970's, the process of import liberalization started taking place which continued in the decade of 1980s as well. Though, the policies, announced annually during this period, were aimed at providing necessary imported inputs for the industrial sector by relaxing the restrictions, they were piecemeal and incoherent.

The restrictive trade regime, though protected domestic industries from foreign competition and provided them the required space to grow, made the Indian industrial sector inefficient. The protective environment in terms of high tariff and non-tariff barriers, the lack of competition from foreign goods and producers, and large demand from the domestic market, though eased the competitive pressures, could not induce the producers to reduce the cost of products and improve their quality. High cost and poor quality of products made Indian products dearer in the international market. As a result, the country faced a severe BOP crisis in 1991, necessitating the restructuring of trade and other segments of the economy.

13.3.2 Arguments against Protection

Each of the arguments for protection has been counteracted by the protagonist of free trade. Their arguments are as follows:

Retaliation by Foreign Countries

When a country tries to protect its domestic markets, by imposing restrictions on imports, it reduces the demand for exports of other countries. Other countries facing reduction in export demand for their products respond by imposing tariff and non-tariff barriers to protect their industries. Thus, the protection by one country invites retaliation by other countries. This adversely affects the demand for exports of those countries which had initiated these measures. Thus, protection results in contraction in global trade and global output.

Loss of Comparative Advantage

Barriers on trade deprive the country the benefits of division of labour, specialization and trade. The total world output declines as a result, and consumption possibility frontier gets restricted to the production possibilities at home.

Inefficiency

Restrictions on free trade, in order to protect domestic industries and market, often breed inefficiencies in production. Supporters of free trade argue that the domestic industrialization can be promoted more efficiently through monetary, fiscal and exchange rate policies rather than trade restrictions.

Protection and restrictions of trade sometimes have been found to be benefitting the country. However, in general, protection for a very prolonged period brings in inefficiencies in the production process, deprives nations from the benefits emerging from specialization and trade, and thus, retards growth. Hence, countries open up their markets for foreign trade as illustrated in UBE 13.2 using Indian experience.

UNDERSTANDING BUSINESS ENVIRONMENT

UBE 13.2 Trade Reforms: Post-1991 Period

Trade reforms in India aim at benefitting from the gains emerging from free trade flows as illustrated in this UBE.

The realization of the unfavourable consequences of restrictive trade practices led the Indian government to initiate the liberalization process during the decade of 1980s itself. However, the attempts towards trade liberation, in the pre-1991 period, were piecemeal and incoherent, and hence, could not solve the severe structural problems that had crept into the system as an outcome of restrictive trade policies. The system finally crumbled under the persistent and continuous BOP pressures and the country ended up with severe balance of payment crisis in the year 1991, necessitating overhauling and restructuring of the entire system.

During the last two decades, as a part of restructuring process, trade policies in India, communicated through **Foreign Trade Policies** (also known as **Export Import (EXIM) Policies**) and the annual Union Budget, have focused at infusing competition, efficiency and productivity in the domestic economy by allowing FDI flows in manufacturing units, eliminating tariff and non-tariff barriers, and enhancing export revenue to restore external payment viability by providing various tax incentives.

Facilitating the market mechanism in the trade segment, the peak custom duty, which stood at 355 per cent on manufactured products in the year of crisis, was gradually brought down to 10 per cent in the budget of 2007–08. Similarly, there has also been a steady decline in the simple average of tariff rates from 113 per cent in 1991 to 5.9 per cent in 2009–10.

To reduce the cost of production and the level of competition, licensing requirements and quantitative restrictions have been substantially eliminated and simplified by shifting most of the items to OGL or freely importable category. Gradually, the list of banned or prohibited items has been cut short to just three, i.e., tallow, fat and oils of animal origin, animal rennet, wild animals including their parts and products and unprocessed ivory. The restricted list though still exist, there has been a substantial abridgment in it as well. Most of the restrictions are on grounds of security, health and environment protection. Some of the items on this list are fire arms, explosives, ammunition, currency paper, freon gases, seeds, plants and animals, insecticides and pesticides, drugs and pharmaceuticals, consumer goods and electronic items. Canalized list has also been pruned and comprises of the imports of petroleum products (by the Indian Oil Corporation), some chemicals and fertilizers (by Minerals and Metals Trading Corporation), Vitamin A drugs (by state trading corporation), oils and seeds (Hindustan Vegetable Oils and State Trading Corporation) and bulk grains (by Food Corporation of India) subject to the cabinet approval regarding the timing and quantity.

There has been a substantial liberalization of exported commodities as well. Only a few items are subjected to export controls to avoid shortage in the domestic market, conserve national resources, and protect the environment. To promote exports, imports are linked with export performance and allowed free of duty for such purpose.

With the implementation of various trade reform measures, India's external sector has emerged with considerable inner strength to meet the challenges of foreign as well as the domestic shocks. However, India is still not a major player in the world trade. There are constraints which continue to hamper export growth. Some of these constraints that need a greater attention are highlighted as follows.

To further enhance export competitiveness in the international market and stabilize the earnings on export front, further tariff reforms are needed. Tariff rates need to be brought down to the levels comparable to those in ASEAN, both for peak rate as well as total duty to improve the competitiveness. Various end use exemptions and tax concessions result in irrational resource allocation and also adversely affect the total revenue collection from custom duties. Hence, further rationalization of tariff reduction is required by eliminating tax concessions and introducing sunset clauses for export promotion schemes.

High transaction cost has been identified as one of the major impediments in the growth of exports from India. The World Bank 'Doing Business' Report indicates that it costs US $945 to export a container from India compared to US $450 and US $500 in Malaysia and China respectively. It takes 17 days to export a container from India compared to 5 days, 12 days and 14 days from Denmark, Brazil and Mexico, respectively. Further reduction in the transaction cost is required to improve India's export competitiveness.

The country also needs to further diversify its export basket as well as markets. As of now, India's presence is significant only in a few items, such as diamonds and jewellery, oil cakes, t-shirts, men/boy's trousers, flat rolled iron products and maize (corn). In other markets such as electronic, electrical, and engineering, its presence is still negligible.

There are other areas as well which need attention and improvement, such as infrastructure constraints, high cost of export finance, complex export and import procedures, reservation of many items with high export potential for the small scale sector, inflexibility in labour laws, quality problems, and ad-hoc export restrictions on agriculture products.

In the best interest of a country and the world as a whole, trade brings in more benefit. However, unilateral moves towards freer trade usually are not very successful in promoting trade as the competing countries may not be very much willing to follow the suite. Therefore, a large number of Regional Trade Agreements (RTAs) (Box 13.4), such as the European Union (EU), Association of South East Asian Nations (ASEAN), Asia Pacific Economic Co-operation (APEC), etc., have evolved over a period of time. Highly organized platforms, such as the World Trade Organization (WTO) (UBE 13.3), have also emerged from the need for greater and freer trade. These platforms try to evolve consensus on various issues through bilateral and multilateral negotiations. There are also organizations that promote trade indirectly. For example, the International Monetary Fund (IMF) provides short-term finance for countries with balance of payments difficulties and enables them to benefit from trade without the BOP problems.

Box 13.4 Regional Trade Agreements

The **Regional Trade Agreements** (RTAs) are broadly of two types—**Free Trading Arrangements** (FTAs) (ex) and customs unions (EX). The FTAs are the agreements, among two or more countries, in which reciprocal preferences are exchanged to cover a large number of goods. The customs unions, on the other hand, not only have exchange of trade preferences but also a common external tariff system.

The RTA has been found to be having two kinds of effects—trade creation and trade diversion. **Trade creation** takes place when a country's domestic production is replaced by lower cost imports from a partner country, whereas **trade diversion** occurs when low cost imports from the rest of the world (outside the RTAs) is replaced by higher cost imports from partner countries because of tariff preferences. Which of these two effects dominate any country at a time depends on a number of factors ranging from the economic structure of the country among the trading partners, diversion of factor endowments, rules governing the RTAs, and products covered under the agreement.

UNDERSTANDING BUSINESS ENVIRONMENT

UBE 13.3 World Trade Organization: Freer and Fair Trade

WTO is an institutional mechanism which has been instituted to promote free trade flows and benefit the participating countries from the gains arising from such flows. Present day trade relations are largely governed by the WTO agreements. This UBE gives insights into the functions and structure of this organization and briefs on the basic principles that govern the agreements on its platform.

In 1944, the United Nations Monetary and Financial Conference was held in the Bretton Woods to look at the issue of restoring peace in war devasted countries, promote growth and development of these countries by restoring trade ties that were disrupted by the 'beggar my neighbour' policies pursued during the inter-war period of 1919–39, and planning the future of the international monetary system. This conference led to the setting up of the **International Monetary Fund** (IMF) and the **International Bank for Reconstruction and Development** (IBRD) popularly known as the **World Bank**. The conference also recommended the setting up of the **International Trade Organization** (ITO).

Formation of General Agreement on Tariffs and Trade (GATT): Since the setting up of the ITO was bound to take some time, the **General Agreement on Tariffs and Trade** (GATT) was signed as an interim measure by the original 23 countries on 30th October 1947. The GATT has sought to dismantle trade barriers through a succession of Multilateral Trade Negotitations (MTN) rounds. The first round was held in Geneva.

The objective of the GATT was to remove barriers to world trade—both tariff barriers and non-tariff barriers. Tariff barriers work through prices, whereas non-tariff barriers work through quantities. The GATT has had limited success in removing NTBs. Its success in reducing tariff barriers has been far more remarkable.

By the time of Dillon Round in 1960–61, the success of GATT was reflected in a reduction of tariffs across the world, particularly for industrialized countries. With the Kennedy round in 1962–67, the focus shifted to the elimination of non-tariff barriers. The reduction of non-tariff barriers received even more serious attention during the Tokyo round in 1973–79. The Tokyo round also led to the fragmentation of the GATT system. A few of the Tokyo round results were incorporated as codes or arrangements for which not all the members of the GATT were signatories. These agreements, known as the **plurilateral arrangements**, formed the 'GATT plus' agreements. Unlike the **multilateral agreements** these did not have universal application.

Tokyo round also led to a realization that there were a host of new areas that impinged on international trade and which might not be part of the original mandate of the GATT. This was natural as international trade flows became more complex and cross-border movements of services, capital and technology increased in importance.

The Uruguay round negotiations covered a wide range of issues and were far more ambitious than earlier rounds. The Uruguay round went beyond trade liberalization (reduction in tariffs and non-tariff barriers and improving market access for partner countries). It talked of rules and disciplines of the trading system (GATT articles, safeguards, agreements and arrangements, subsidies and countervailing measures, dispute settlement and functioning of the GATT system). It also involved discussions in new areas like trade in services, Trade Related Intellectual Property Rights (TRIPS) and Trade Related Investment Measures (TRIMS).

Establishment of the World Trade Organization: After seven years of hard and complicated negotiations, the Uruguay round finally formally concluded at the Ministerial Conference held in Marrakesh in April 1994. Around 110 countries along with India, authenticated the results of the Uruguay round and, 104 countries signed the agreement establishing the **World Trade Organization** (WTO). On 1st January 1995, the WTO came into existence. At present the WTO membership consists of 159 members. The WTO is more global in its membership and the coverage of issues considered by it is much wider than that covered under the

GATT. The GATT was just an agreement, whereas the WTO is a legal entity and a full-fledged international organization. The GATT had restricted itself on agreements on goods, whereas the WTO encompasses besides the trade on goods, the trade on services, and the trade in investment and intellectual property rights. The GATT had a considerable success in bringing down tariff barriers but had only limited success in dismantling non-tariff barriers.

Functions of the WTO: WTO has five specific functions as follows:

(i) Implementation, administration and operation of multilateral agreements in goods, services and intellectual property rights.
(ii) Provides the forum for negotiations among its members concerning their multilateral trade relations.
(iii) Administers the understanding on rules and procedures governing the settlements of disputes.
(iv) Administers the trade policy review mechanism.
(v) Makes the WTO co-operate with the IMF and IBRD and its affiliated agencies with a view to achieve greater coherence in global economic policy.

Structure of the WTO: The organizational structure of the WTO (Figure 13.5) is as follows:

Ministerial Conference: The **Ministerial Conference** is the highest decision-making body. It consists of representative of all the members and meets at least once every two years. The eighth Ministerial Conference of the WTO was held in Geneva, Switzerland in 2011. The ninth ministerial conference is scheduled to be held in Bali, Indonesia from 3–6 December 2013.

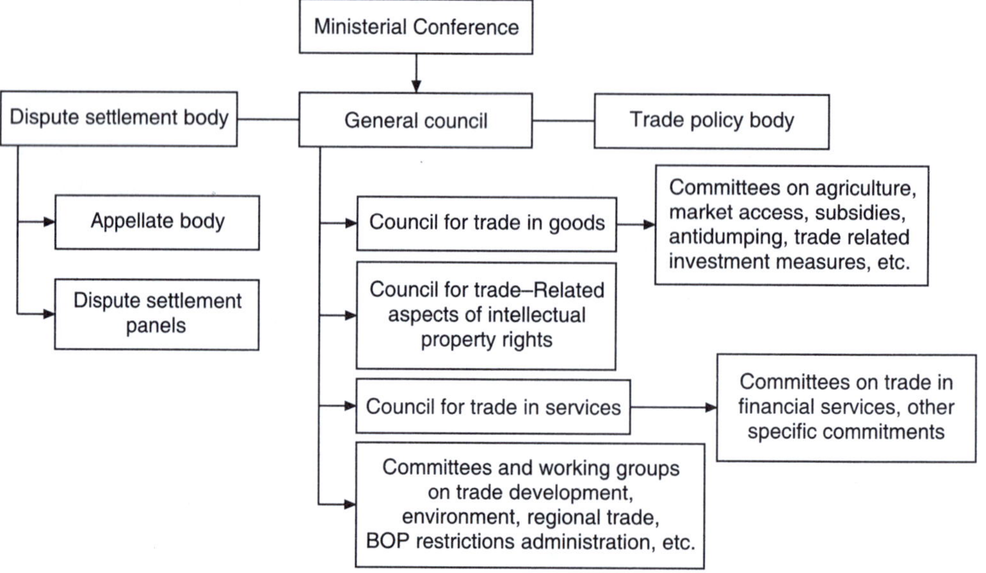

Figure 13.5 Organizational Structure of the WTO.

General Council: **The General Council** consists of representative of all the members. It essentially carries out the functions of the Ministerial Conference in the intervals between the meetings of the Ministerial Conference. It can convene the Dispute Settlement Body (for handling the trade disputes among the member countries) and the Trade Policy Review Body (to monitor the trade policies of member countries).

Dispute Settlement Body handles the trade disputes among the member countries that could not be resolved through bilateral/multilateral talks. The panels of independent experts examine disputes in the light of WTO rules and provide the judgment.

Trade Policy Review Body monitors the trade policies and trade regimes of the member countries. It supervises the implementation of the bindings of tariffs and reduction of non-tariff measures agreed to in the negotiations.

Under the General Council there are three separate councils—**Council for trade in goods, Council for trade in services, Council for trade related aspects of intellectual property rights**. Each council works in a different field. There are six other bodies which report to the General Council on issues such as trade and development, environment, regional trading arrangements and administrative issues.

Decision-making process in the WTO: The WTO continues to practice the procedure of decision-making by consensus followed under the GATT 1947. Wherever the decision cannot be arrived at by consensus, the matter is decided by voting. Each member of the WTO has one vote. However, a waiver from an obligation for a member country is decided by the two-third majority voting. Similarly, an amendment to any of the agreements requires a two-third majority.

Data base of the WTO: The GATT/WTO Secretariat has an **Integrated Data Base** (IDB) into which national schedules of commitments are fed in. Since not all the members of the GATT/WTO are members of the IDB, the figures on tariff reductions that are presently available from the GATT/WTO Secretariat are somewhat biased.

Types of Agreements

The WTO agreements can be classified into multilateral agreements and plurilateral agreements.

Compliance with the **plurilateral agreements** is purely voluntary, and is not binding on all the member countries. Some of the plurilateral agreements had been on agreements on trade in civil aircraft, agreements on government procurement, international dairy agreements and international bovine meat agreements.

On the other hand, the **multilateral agreements** are binding on all the member countries. The Multilateral agreements are based on some general principles as follows:

Protection only through tariffication: The principle of **protection only through tariffication** professes that the interest of domestic producers can be protected only through tariffication. Non-tariff barriers, such as quotas, should be kept to the bare minimum and phased out over a period of time.

Binding of tariffs: Though trade can be protected through tariff barriers the extent of these cannot be very high. The principle of **binding of tariffs** suggest that the member countries need to commit to bring down the tariff levels to the binding limits within the given time framework.

Negation of the most favoured nation: None of the member countries is permitted to grant a favoured status to any particular country **under the negation of the most favoured nation principle** as all the member countries are to be treated as the most favoured, and tariff and other regulations should be applied to imported or exported goods without discrimination among the countries. However, special treatment and preferences to the members of **Regional Trade Block** are permitted.

National treatment rule: The multilateral agreements also follow the principle of national treatment rule. This rule prohibits countries from discriminating between imported products and equivalent domestically produced products once a commodity produced abroad enters the boundaries of a nation crossing the tariff barriers.

In addition, there are rules governing government subsidy, measures to protect the domestic industry from **anti-dumping duties** (i.e., the duties that offset injurious dumping) and **countervailing duties** (i.e., the duties that seek to offset injurious subsidization) and investment measures that are likely to have adverse impact on trade.

The multilateral agreements are broadly classified into four categories, viz, **General Agreements on Trade on Goods** (GATG), **General Agreements on Trade on Services** (GATS), **Trade Related Investment Measures** (TRIMs) and **Trade Related Intellectual Property Rights** (TRIPs).

General Agreements on Trade on Goods (GATG): Unlike the GATT agreements which had focused on trade in goods, the WTO agreements have brought under their purview even the trade on agriculture goods. **Agreements on Agriculture** (AOA) are expected to give better access to the agriculture products originating from the developing nations by making the developed world reduce the level of tariffs and subsidies on these products. These agreements are expected to provide better market access to Indian agricultural commodities by making them more competitive in the international market.

There is also a negation of the **Multi Fibre Arrangement** (MFA). Developed countries were maintaining textile quotas under the MFA. The developed nations had restricted the import of textile products by imposing quotas on each of the textile exporting nations. These have been phased out by 1st January 2005.

Previously, under the quota system, India was routing its textile products via those East-Asian countries that were exporting less than the quota allocated to them. With the eliminations of the quota system, India is expected to increase its exports of textile products.

General Agreements on Trade on Services (GATS): Unlike the GATT, which had considered only the trade on goods, the WTO agreements have even encompassed trade on services. As per these agreements, the member countries need to provide access to service personnel from other member countries into their markets on a non-discriminatory basis.

India is expected to benefit in skilled service exports, such as computer software, consultancy, medical services, films, etc.

Trade Related Investment Measures (TRIMs): The WTO agreements aim at liberalizing global financing services by bringing trade in banking, insurance and securities into multilateral trading agreements.

Trade Related Intellectual Property Rights (TRIPs): The WTO agreements aim at improving the trade in intellectual property, such as discoveries and inventions, books, paintings, software, musical composition, etc., by protecting it by making countries move to product patent from process patent. Under the process patent the same product can be produced using different processes. On the other hand, under the product patent regime the same product cannot be produced using different processes.

The move towards the product patent system was a subject of major controversy in India. It was feared that this move would make medicines very expensive and unaffordable for general public. It was also feared that seeds will become very expensive, which will affect farmers adversely. However, in WTO agreements there are safeguarding mechanism which tries to mitigate these fears. To protect the interest of general public, the WTO has provision which permits the government to take **compulsory licensing** (when the patented product or processes are allowed to be used by someone who is not the owner) for non-commercial public use. Similarly, farmers' and researchers' rights to produce and exchange seeds is protected. Only the commercial sale of branded seeds is affected. Improved intellectual property rights are expected to enhance FDIs to India.

SUMMARY

Trade among countries takes place when they differ in comparative advantage in the production of commodities. A country possesses a comparative advantage when the opportunity cost of producing a good, in terms of foregone output of other goods, is lower than that in other countries. The trade to take place, the TOT, i.e., the ratio of export price to import price needs to be favourable for both the countries, i.e., it needs to lie between the domestic opportunity cost of production in each country.

Inspite of several benefits of trade, many countries try to protect their industries by imposing tariff and non-tariff barriers using arguments, such as infant industry argument, employment argument, terms of trade argument, anti-dumping argument, BOP argument and anti-over-specialization argument. However, protagonist of free trade counteract each of these arguments by pointing out the pitfalls of protection such as retaliation by foreign countries and loss in the world output, loss of comparative advantage and inefficiencies in the production process.

In the post-1991 crisis period, India has moved from restrictive trade practices to a greatly liberalized trade regime. Exports are now looked as an engine for growth and imports are assumed to support exports by making goods cheaper and that of better quality.

To promote free flow of trade among nations a number of bilateral, regional and global platforms have evolved. The WTO is one of the dominant platforms at present that has evolved from the Uruguay round of the GATT. The WTO, a legal entity with 159 member countries and sound organizational structure, addresses the issues related to trade in goods, services and intellectual property rights.

Implications for Managers

With the opening up of the Indian economy since the BOP crisis of 1991–92, a greater integration of the country with the rest of the world through trade flows has been emerging as a principal component of business environment.

A greater integration through trade flows enables greater specialization by business firms in those areas where they have comparative advantage. This reduces wastage of material and cost, and increases output. Exports from domestic producers become more competitive in international markets. An opening up of an economy to trade flows expands the market for indigenously produced goods and services which increases the possibility of higher sales, revenue and profit for domestic business units. The higher integration helps business organizations to safeguard their business interests even when the domestic economy is going through a recessionary phase.

Free trade makes available imported raw material and other inputs at internationally competitive prices and quality for domestic producers. This reduces the cost of production for domestic units. Further, outsourcing and sub-contracting becomes possible which help firms to remain focused on their core areas of competencies and enable them in enhancing the operational efficiency and cutting down the cost of production.

Imported final commodities generate higher competition for domestic firms even when their operations are restricted to only domestic markets. To remain competitive in the domestic and foreign markets they need to cut down cost, enhance the quality and create a brand image for their products by investing in R&D as well as other marketing practices, such as better packaging, higher advertisement, and higher selling commission to the dealers.

REVIEW QUESTIONS

13.1 What is the meaning of absolute advantage in production? How far comparative advantage differs from absolute advantage?

13.2 What is the necessary condition for the trade to take place between countries?

13.3 What is the meaning of terms of trade? What should be the range of TOT so that the trade takes place between the countries?

13.4 What are the advantages and disadvantages of trade?

13.5 What is the infant industry argument in favour of trade protection?

13.6 Are Regional Trade Agreements (RTAs) trade promoting or trade diverting?

13.7 What do you understand by tariff? What is the difference between a revenue tariff and a protective tariff?

13.8 Why export tax is not used widely?

13.9 What are the different types of non-tariff barriers?

13.10 What is the thrust of trade policy in India, since 1990–91?

13.11 What are the different types of agreement on the WTO platform? What are the basic principles behind the multilateral agreements?

NUMERICAL PROBLEM

13.1 Table 13.4 shows the production that is possible in two countries (Bangladesh and Sri Lanka) of two products (Jute and Tea) when one unit of resource is used in the process of production of each product.

Table 13.4 Production Possibilities

	Jute	*Tea*
Bangladesh	4	6
Sri Lanka	2	7

Using this information answer the following questions:

(i) Which country has an absolute advantage in jute production? Which country has an absolute advantage in tea production?

(ii) Which country has a comparative advantage in the production of jute and which country has a comparative advantage in the production of tea?

(iii) In what situation the trade between Bangladesh and Sri Lanka would take place? Answer the question using terms of trade concept.

CASE ANALYSIS EXERCISE

C13.1 Regional Comprehensive Economic Partnership: Will It Make a Difference?

First round of negotiations to establish Regional Comprehensive Economic Partnership (RECP), the world's largest free trade block were held in Bandar Seri Begawan, Brunei Darussalam, between 9 and 13 May 2013. The proposed trade block will consist of all the 10 members of the Association of Southeast Asian Nations (ASEAN), i.e., Indonesia, Malaysia, the Philippines, Singapore and Thailand, Brunei, Burma (Myanmar), Cambodia, Laos and Vietnam, and the six other countries with which the group has free trade agreements (FTAs), i.e., Australia, Public Republic of China, India, Japan, the Republic of Korea, and New Zealand.

The basic objective behind setting up the RECP is to achieve a modern comprehensive economic partnership, which can help in transforming the entire region by enhancing economic growth through cross-border trade and investment. Under its ambit, it will cover trade in goods, trade in services, investment, economic and technological co-operation, intellectual property, competition, and dispute settlement. These agreements will be guided by the following principles:

- To be consistent with the WTO rules
- To result in an improvement in existing ASEAN+1 FTAs
- To take care of the difference in the stages of development of the participating nations and allow differential and special treatment to the least developed nations
- To enable other external economic partners to participte in the RECP at a future date provided that they abide with the groups trade rules and guidelines

Size and Significance of the RECP

The group is expected to exert significant influence on the global trade relationships and economic outcomes as its combined population form 49 per cent of the world population and 30 per cent of the world GDP, which indicates huge size of the market. It also accounts for significant proportion of the world trade in goods and services and FDI inflows and outflows (Table 13.5).

Table 13.5 Size of the Proposed RCEP

	Magnitude (year)	*World share (%)*
Population	3.4 billion (2012)	49
Gross Domestic Product	$ 21.4 trillion (2012)	30
Trade in Goods & Services, Exports and Imports	$ 12.0 trillion (2011)	29
Foreign Direct Investment Inflows	$ 402.8 billion (2011)	26
Foreign Direct Invetsment Outflows	$ 378.9 billion (2011)	22

Source: Compiled from Asian Development Bank (2013), Asian Development Outlook 2013.

Expected Economic Benefits

The RECP is expected to benefit all the member countries through better market access for goods and services, as well as improved technology and skill sets. Larger market will also enable the partner countries to reap the benefits of economies of scale and specialization. The export-oriented economies in South Asia will benefit from greater access to huge domestic markets of China, Japan and India. Besides, the RECP is expected to enhance investment from more developed countries to less developed ones, which will help them integrate better with the other economies in the region.

Referring to the study by Petri, Plummer, and Zhai (2012), ADB (2013) indicates that the RECP will bring insignificant benefits to the member countries (Figure 13.6) and to the world economy in the long-run by increasing the world GDP by 0$644 billion in 2050 (equal to 0.6 per cent of the world GDP).

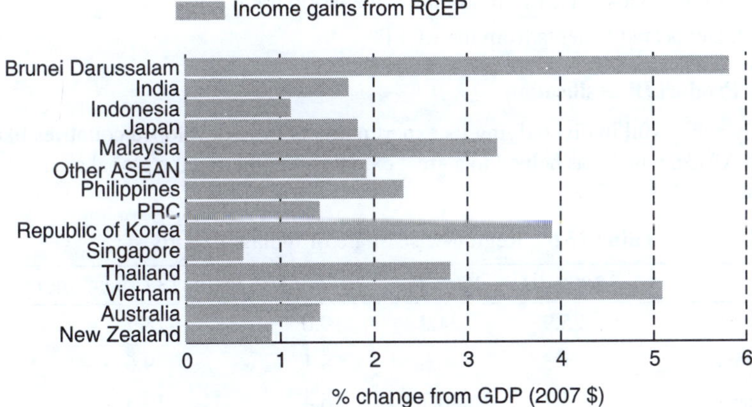

PRC = People's Republic of China, Other ASEAN = Combodia, the Lao People's Democratic Republic, and Myanmar.

Source: Petrl, P.G. Plummer F. Zhal, 2012. Note on Alternative Asial Tract Scenarlos, http://aslapacifictrade.org/wp-content/uploads/2012/11/Asian-track-alternatives.pdf

Source: ADB (2013), Asian Development Outlook 2012

Figure 13.6 Income Gains from RCEP.

Major Challanges Ahead

Though the RCEP is expected to bring in substantial gains to partner countries and the world as a whole. The arrival to agreements on various issues that will be part of the RCEP are not without challenges. ADB (2013) indicates four major challenges as follows:

1. The RCEP is led by the ASEAN. For the successful negotiation it is pertinent that the members of the proposed RCEP respect the leading role of the ASEAN .
2. The countries of the RCEP are at different stages of development. Special treatment and different concessions provided to these countries to take care of their special needs may tantamount to not much trade and investment liberalization, leading to little or no gain from the RCEP.
3. The RCEP aims at covering wide areas of interest including competition poliy and environment. Bringing all the member countries to a consensus on these pertinent issues may be politically very challenging
4. It is quite possible that private organizations, especially small and medium, may not understand the implications of various agreements and may fail to benefit themselves from the possibilities emerging from trade and investment liberalization and other agreements.

For the success of the proposed RCEP, therefore, it is pertinent to build a strong political will, actively involve private sector participation in negotiations, and to outline a clear timetable for concluding negotiations.

References

ADB (2013), Asian Development Outlook 2013, (online) http://www.adb.org/sites/default/files/pub/2013/ado-2013.pdf.

Petri, P., Plummer, G. and Zhai, F. (2012), Note on Alternative Asian Track Scenarios, Asia Pacific Trade.

Questions

1. What is the RCEP? Who are its members? What are its objectives?
2. What makes the proposed RCEP important in the world trade?
3. What are the expected benefits from the RCEP?

C13.2 Market vs Product Diversification

India has been fairly successful in diversifying its export markets from developed countries like the US and Europe to Asia and Africa, which has helped to a great extent in weathering the global crisis of 2008 and the recent global slowdown (Table 13.6).

Table 13.6 Region-wise Share of India's Exports

	2000–01	*2005–06*	*2011–12*	*2012–13 (Apr.-Nov.)*
Europe	25.9	24.2	19.0	18.7
Africa	5.3	6.8	8.1	9.6
America	24.7	20.7	16.4	19.5
Asia	37.4	46.9	50.0	50.4
CIS & Baltics	2.3	1.2	1.0	1.3

Source: Computed from DGCI&S data.

However, in terms of product diversification a lot more needs to be done as can be seen from the following:

- In the top 100 import items of the world at the four-digit HS level in 2011, India has only 6 items in the top 50; it has only 5 items with a share of 5 per cent and above and 18 items with a share of

2 per cent and above (Table 13.7), with 6 new items with high export growth (India) entering the list and 3 going out of the list in 2011 compared to 2010. The new items are medicaments consisting of mixed or unmixed products for therapeutic use; other articles of iron and steel; men's or boys' suits, ensembles; cruise ships, excursion boats, ferry-boats, cargo ships, barges and similar vessels; cane or beet sugar and chemically pure sucrose in solid form; and maize.

Table 13.7 Export Items of India with 2 Per Cent and Above Share in Top 100 World Imports at Four-digit level

Rank# World 2011	*HS4*	*Items*	*India's share in world 2011*	*Growth rate in 2011*	
				India (Export)	*World (Import)*
2	2710	Petroleum oils and oils obtained from bituminous minerals, etc.	6.7	49.0	39.4
7	3004	Medicaments consisting of mixed or unmixed products for therapeutic use	2.1	36.0	5.7
11	2601	Iron ores and concentrates, including roasted iron pyrites	2.3	–32.3	37.8
14	7102	Diamonds, whether or not worked, but not mounted or set	23.8	44.7	14.7
34	7403	Refined copper and copper alloys, unwrought	3.2	–53.7	12.2
39	8803	Parts of goods of heading no. 88.01 or 88.02	3.5	45.4	1.2
3351	6403	Footwear with outer soles of rubber	3.1	23.0	9.2
52	6204	Women's or girls' suits, ensembles, jackets, blazers, dresses	4.9	34.8	9.2
55	7210	Flat-rolled products of iron or non-alloy steel	2.8	0.8	12.2
56	7113	Articles of jewellery and parts thereof, of precious metal	28.5	83.6	13.4
61	2902	Cyclic hydrocarbons	4.4	47.8	27.8
68	7326	Other articles of iron and steel	2.0	97.9	13.9
69	3902	Polymers of propylene or of other olefins, in primary forms	2.8	46.0	17.3
72	6203	Men's or boys' suits, ensembles, jackets, blazers, trousers, etc.	2.3	31.5	16.4
92	6109	T-shirts, singlets & other vests, knitted or crocheted	6.0	22.1	12.1
97	8901	Cruise ships, excursion boats, ferry-boats, cargo ships, barges and similar vessels	2.2	40.0	–25.8
99	1701	Cane or beet sugar and chemically pure sucrose, in solid form	6.0	123.1	20.1
100	1005	Maize	3.4	103.1	34.1

Source: Computed from UN Comtrade data extracted on January 2013.

Note: # Rank is in top 100 world imports.

- India has a very high export share in world imports in the case of only two four-digit HS items, jewellery and diamonds. While India can increase its shares further in the other 16 items given in the table, there are many other simple items in the top 100 world imports with high demand where India has developed its competence. Most of the items come under the three Es, electronic, electrical, and engineering items and some textiles items. Greater focus on these items could lead to a perceptible increase in India's share of exports in world imports.

Source: Internal study, Economic Division, Department of Economic Affairs.
GOI (2013), Economic Survey, 2012–13.

Questions

1. What trade strategy has helped India in weathering the global crisis of 2008 and the recent global slowdown?
2. What is needed for further diversification of India's trade basket?

SUGGESTED FURTHER READING

Bretta, S. and Lenti, R.T. (2012), India and China, Trading with the World and Each Other, *EPW*, November 3, Vol. XLVII, No. 44.

Chaudhuri, S. (2013), Manufacturing Trade Deficit and Industrial Policy in India, *EPW*, Feb. 23, Vol. XLVIII, No. 8.

Hoda, A. and Prakash, S. (2012), Has India's Trade Benefitted from the US's Generalized System of Preferences? *EPW*, Oct. 13, Vol. XLVII, No. 41.

Pailwar, V. and Shah, N. (2009), "Revealed Comparative Advantages for India in Services Trade", *International Journal of Trade and Global Markets*, Vol. 2, No. 2.

Parida, Y, Pratap, D. and Goldar, B. (2012), Impact of Tariff Reduction According to Doha Modalities on India's Trade of Agriculture Products, *EPW*, Jan. 14, Vol. XLVII, No. 2.

CHAPTER 14

Capital Flows, Growth and Macroeconomic Instability

14.1 INTRODUCTION

Benefits emerge not only by opening up an economy to trade flows but also to capital flows. Opening up of an economy to capital inflows eases the resource constraints of firms which they face when they depend only on domestically available resources. It allows domestic firms to access foreign financial markets and funds, and helps them in enhancing their resources. Often they also benefit by low cost of funds prevailing in foreign financial markets. These benefits, along with many other, help domestic firms to enhance their investment and productive capacity, and in turn, scale of production. Foreign capital, at times, also comes in the form of joint ventures and mergers and acquisitions, which enhances the level of competition and compels domestic firms to improve the quality of their production and at the same time reduce the cost of it. Similarly, unconstrained outflow of capital boosts up the level of confidence of foreign investors in the domestic markets by assuring them that they will be able to withdraw their funds easily whenever such a need arises. This assurance of liquidity of funds boosts up the level of capital inflows. Thus, greater financial openness of an economy with the rest of the world helps it boost its overall investment, productive capacity, output and growth.

Not only openness to capital inflows but also outflows benefits the domestic participants. Openness to capital outflows allows domestic households and firms to invest in foreign markets and avail better return than that prevailing in the domestic markets. Therefore, it results in a flow of foreign capital to those markets and economies where returns are higher. Since better returns are an indication of better efficiency, financial openness helps not only a country but also the world as a whole by resulting in more efficient allocation of resources and greater world output.

Global financial openness and integration though can support domestic growth and development, it often brings in a large volatility of output, prices, interest rate, investment and exchange rate, and exposes the domestic economy to global business fluctuations. Therefore, it has a large influence on the macroeconomic policies pursued to stabilize an economy.

This chapter deals with these issues in greater detail. Accordingly, Section 14.2 brings out the importance of foreign capital for an economy. Different types of foreign capital flows have differing impact; hence, this section also describes different types of foreign capital flows and their advantages and disadvantages. Determinants of foreign capital flows are also highlighted in this section. Foreign capital flows though help in enhancing growth they have their own pitfalls. These pitfalls, which are used for arguing against free flow of capital, are indicated in Section 14.3.

14.2 FOREIGN CAPITAL FLOWS

14.2.1 Need for Foreign Capital

Foreign capital brings in both measurable and non-measurable gains along with it as detailed as follows:

We know from previous chapters that capital formation plays an important role in the economic growth. In the initial level of development, in the absence of enough domestic saving coming forward for capital formation, external capital helps by providing the much needed resources for investment. This can also be seen from the GDP identity, discussed in Section 5.3.1. The GDP identity states that the total output is equal to total demand or expenditure in an economy, i.e.,

$$Y = C + I + G + X - M$$

This identity can be rearranged as follows:

$$(Y - C - G) + (M - X) = I$$

where $(Y - C - G)$ represents the excess of domestic output over domestic private and government consumption, i.e., domestic saving. M represents foreign saving because imports are that part of foreign production that is not consumed abroad. Similarly, X represents that part of domestic output that is not consumed in the domestic market and made available to foreign consumers. Exports, hence, can be viewed as domestic saving used by the foreigners. Thus, $M - X$ represents **net foreign saving** used by domestic participants. Thus,

$$\text{Domestic saving} + \text{Net foreign saving} = \text{Domestic investment}$$

By further rearranging, one gets the extent of resource gap as follows:

$$\text{Resource gap} = \text{Domestic investment} - \text{Domestic saving} = \text{Net foreign saving}$$

Thus, foreign saving or capital helps in bridging the domestic **resource gap**.

Foreign capital plays a significant role even when a country has sufficient domestic saving to meet the requirements of domestic capital formation. The process of production needs not only capital formation but also some imported raw materials. Sometimes, the advanced technical know-how, which determines the productivity of capital, is also missing from the country. Imported raw materials, new improved machinery and advanced technology in the country can only be brought, in most of the cases, through paying foreign exchange. In the initial stages of development, even exports are not sufficient to meet the foreign exchange requirements of the country. This **foreign exchange gap** (exports earnings being less than import payment requirements) can also be filled by the foreign capital.

Foreign capital also brings in with it certain non-measurable gains. It opens up the new marketing channels for domestically produced commodities as the multinational units operating in the domestic economy have better knowledge of and access to foreign markets. These units also bring in new managerial skills. An opening up of the economy to foreign capital inflows and outflows increases the access of the domestic participants to foreign financial markets. The presence of more market players enhances competitiveness, which helps in bringing down the cost of domestically produced commodities. Higher integration, through capital flows, also results in movement of capital from those countries where interest rates are lower to those countries where interest rates are higher, implying the movement of capital from less productive uses to more efficient ones. However, an outflow of capital reduces the amount of capital in low return countries, and given the demand for funds, increases the return in these countries, whereas in the recipient countries higher supply of capital depresses interest rates. The process continues until the returns equalize across the countries. Thus, free flow of capital results in an efficient allocation of resources and equalizes interest rates across the countries.

Relaxing the domestic saving and foreign exchange constraints, the flow of foreign capital, thus, provides access to superior technology, managerial skills, marketing channels and foreign financial markets, and creates a competitive environment. In the process, it increases efficiency by better allocation of capital and other resources.

14.2.2 Types of Foreign Capital

Foreign capital can be from different private and government sources (Figure 14.1).

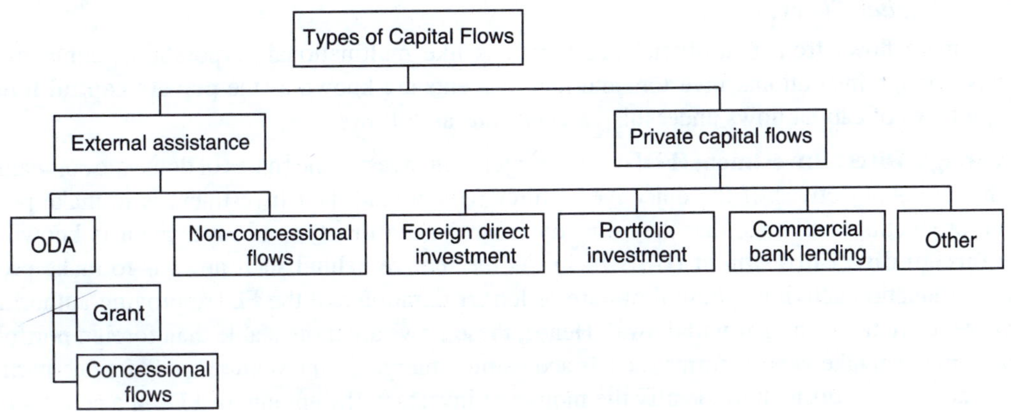

Figure 14.1 Types of Foreign Capital.

The characteristics of different types of capital flows are outlined as follows:

External Assistance

Concessional and non-concessional flows from official sources are known as the **external assistance**. These are administered with the objective of promoting economic development and welfare in developing countries.

1. Official Development Assistance: Capital flows to developing countries from bilateral (country to country basis) as well as from multilateral organizations (such as the IMF, World Bank, Asian Development Bank, etc.) are known as the **Official Development Assistance (ODA)**. These flows can be further distinguished as:

(i) *Grants.* When the recipient country is neither required to pay principal nor interest on foreign capital than it is known as the **grant**.

(ii) *Concessional loan flows.* Any loan with more than 25 per cent of grant element is known as the **concessional flow**. It implies that the borrower is required to return only less than 75 per cent of the amount of principal and interest. For example, suppose a multilateral organization gives a loan of ₹90 crore to a country. Suppose the amount of interest on it, at the market determined rate, is ₹10 crore. If there is no concessionality involved then the borrower would be required to pay in total ₹100 crore at the time of maturity to the lenders. Now suppose, the lender gives a concession of ₹30 crore to the borrower then the borrower will be required to repay only ₹70 crore to the lender. Since the amount of concessionality involved is more than 25 per cent it is a concessional ODA.

2. Non-concessional Flows: Any loan that is provided through official channels without any concession or at less than 25 per cent grant element is considered as **non-concessional flow**. For illustration, in the above example, if the amount of concessionality is just ₹20 crore and the borrower is required to return in total ₹80 crore to the lender then this loan will be classified as a non-concessional flow. Such capital flows include credit from official export credit agencies and commercial borrowings from the private sector window of multilateral financial institutions, such as International Financial Corporation (IFC), Asian Development Bank (ADB), Canadian Development Corporation (CDC), etc.

Private Capital Flows

The capital flows from non-official organizations like multinational corporations, commercial banks, foreign institutional investors and non-residents are known as the **private capital flows**. Major types of capital flows under this category are as follows:

1. Foreign Direct Investment (FDI): Foreigners can invest in the shares of domestic companies with various objectives. If the objective of foreigners behind their investment is to make profit from production activities, that they directly control, then this type of investment is known as the **foreign direct investment** (UBE 14.1). As the motive behind such flows is to make profit from production activities, these flows are of longer duration and the FDI approving authorities impose restrictions on their withdrawal. Hence, these flows are more stable than foreign portfolio flows. FDI can take various forms such as acquisition, merger, joint venture, production sharing, etc. Though, it is difficult to identify the motive of investors, the amount of FDI in a country can be ascertained from the data available with the authorities granting permission for the FDI in a country (UBE 14.2).

2. Foreign Portfolio Investment (FPI): When the objective of foreigners behind investment in shares of a domestic company is to make profit from share market fluctuations rather than controlling the production activities then this type of investment is known as the **foreign portfolio investment**. These flows are motivated by short-term profit opportunities, and therefore, are highly volatile in nature. Compared to FDI flows, these flows are subject to lesser restrictions on withdrawls.

3. External Commercial Borrowing (ECB): The loans from commercial banks and other financial institutions at market determined rates are known as **External Commercial Borrowing**. (The term commercial borrowing, which is often found in the literature, includes non-concessional loans not only from private sources but also from official sources.)

4. Other Credit: The credit from foreign private sector can also be in the form of buyers credit, suppliers credit, securitized instruments, such as floating rate and fixed rate bonds, etc.

UNDERSTANDING BUSINESS ENVIRONMENT

UBE 14.1 Components of Foreign Direct Investment

Considerable difference may exist across countries in the types of assets included in the FDI as indicated in this UBE. Therefore, a cautious approach needs to be adopted while comparing the FDI data of different countries.

The main difference between the FDI and FPI, conceptually, lies in the lasting interest expressed by a non-resident direct investor in a resident enterprise of the domestic economy. The FDI emphasizes the non-resident investor's desire to be associated with the long-term business activities of resident enterprises by exerting significant influence on their management.

Given the underlying principle, the definition of FDI adopted by the International Monetary Fund (IMF) includes twelve different elements—equity capital, reinvested earnings of foreign companies, inter-company debt transactions, short-term and long-term loans, financial leasing, trade credits, grants, bonds, non-cash acquisition of equity, investment made by foreign venture capital investors, earnings data of indirectly held FDI enterprises, control premium and non-competition fee.

The data available on FDI in India, before 2000–01, included only equity capital reported on the basis of issue or transfer of equity or preference shares to foreign direct investors in the FDI definition. However, in the subsequent period, in order to bring India's FDI data reporting system in alignment with international best practices, a new definition of FDI has been adopted by the RBI that includes three categories of capital flows, viz., equity capital (equity in branches, shares in subsidiaries, and other capital contributions), reinvested earnings (retained earnings of the FDI companies), and other direct capital (inter-corporate debt transactions between associated corporate entities). As a result of the adoption of new definition, the estimates of amount of FDI inflows into India during 2000–01 and 2001–02 were revised upwards by US $1.7 billion and US $2.2 billion, respectively.

There are, however, considerable differences among countries as far as the reporting system of FDI is concerned. For example, China's definition of FDI is much broader. Apart from the 12 components identified by the IMF, it also includes project imports as the FDI. In India these are recorded as imports. Also the private transfers in the form of remittances inflows from non-resident and capital inflows in the form of NRI deposits are recorded in China largely as the FDI, whereas in India these are shown as separate categories under invisibles under the current account and NRI deposits inflow under the capital account, respectively.

Part of the difference between the FDI in China and India, can be attributed to "round tripping". Special treatment extended by the Chinese authorities towards foreign investors vis-a-vis domestic investors results in a substantial amount of FDI (reported to be 30 per cent of the reported FDI by the UNCTAD, 2003) made by the resident Chinese from foreign locations. The extent of **round tripping** (in the context of foreign capital round tripping means the act or practice of two or more companies located in different countries trading assets or securities back and forth at approximately the same price to avail various tax benefits) is much smaller in India and takes place mainly through Mauritius under **double taxation treaty** (double taxation means imposing tax on the same amount of income or gain twice. It occurs when income is earned in one country and paid to entities of another country, which is often the case with multinational organizations. Double taxation, thus, discourages capital flows. Countries trying to promote capital flows mutually agree to avoid double taxations. These agreements, hence, are known as double taxation treaty).

UNDERSTANDING BUSINESS ENVIRONMENT

UBE 14.2 Channels of Foreign Investment

There is a multiplicity of organizations granting permission for FPI and FDI as indicated in this UBE which at times creates confusion among investors.

Foreign investment in India is permitted in the form of Foreign Portfolio Investment (FPI) as well as Foreign Direct Investment (FDI). The process of getting approval for these investment categories is handled by different organizations as depicted in Figure 14.2.

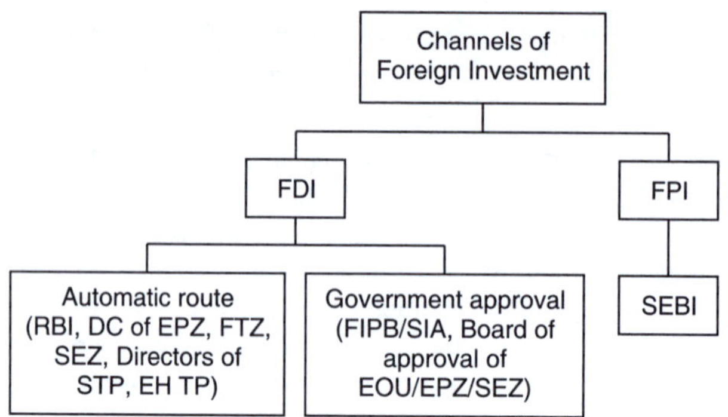

Figure 14.2 Channels of Foreign Investment.

The Foreign Portfolio Investment (FPI) in Indian companies is through acquisition of shares in the primary and secondary market as well as in unlisted, dated government securities, TBs and units of domestic mutual funds without any lock in period. It includes the FPI investment by foreign institutional investors (FIIs), issue of global depository receipts (ADRs) and offshore funds. The FPI by the FIIs, such as pension funds, investment trusts, asset management companies, etc., requires the registration with the Security and Exchange Board of India (SEBI). The FIIs are permitted to open a foreign currency account and/or a non-resident rupee account in India with a designated branch of an authorized dealer. The purchase and sale of permitted securities are routed through this account only. NRIs do not need any approval for the FPI.

The Foreign Direct Investment (FDI), including Global Depository Receipts (GDR)/American Depository Receipts (ADR)/Foreign Currency Convertible Bonds (FCCB), has been permitted in almost all the areas except a small list of strategic importance without an approval either by the government or the RBI through the **automatic route**. The foreign investors have to simply notify the regional office of the RBI within 30 days of the receipt of inward remittances, and file the required documents within 30 days of the issue of shares to foreign investors. The automatic route is only for fresh issues by an Indian company.

The FDI not covered under the automatic route requires a prior approval from the government. Such applications by foreign investors are considered by the **Foreign Investment Promotion Board (FIPB)** in the Department of Economic Affairs, Ministry of Finance, Government of India. Application by Non-Resident Indians (NRIs) are considered by the Secretariat of Industrial Assistance (SIA), Department of Industrial Policy and Promotions, Ministry of Commerce and Industry, which expeditiously process the application. No approval is needed from the RBI once the approval of the government is obtained. The **Foreign Investment Implementation Authority (FIIA)** in the Ministry of Industry and Commerce facilitates speedy implementation of approved FDIs.

For setting up industrial parks/industrial model towns/ Special Economic Zones (SEZs) in the country 100 per cent FDI is permitted under the automatic route. The DC of Export Processing Zones (EPZs), Free Trade Zones (FTZs) and SEZs accord the automatic approval for such projects. All proposals which do not meet any or all of the parameters of automatic approval are considered and approved by the Board of Approval of EOU/EPZ/SEZ.

The directors of Software Technology Parks (STPs) and the designated officers in respect of Electronic Hardware Technology Park (EHTP) accord the automatic approval in these areas. All other proposals in these parks are covered by the FIPB.

14.2.3 Determinants of Capital Flows

Though the ODA flows are determined by the development needs of the recipient countries, the other kinds of flows are determined by various types of pull and push factors (Figure 14.3).

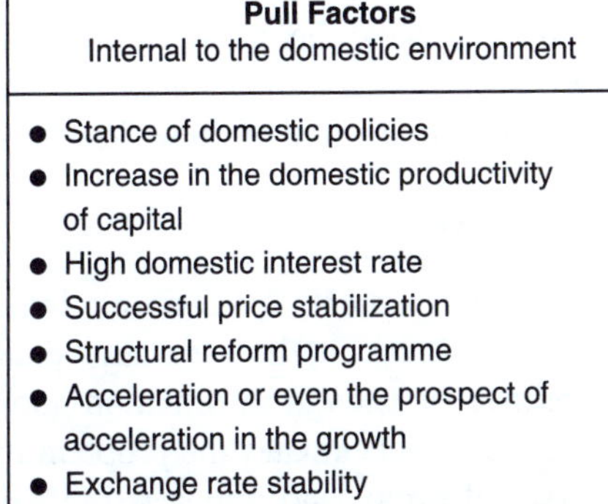

Pull Factors
Internal to the domestic environment

- Stance of domestic policies
- Increase in the domestic productivity of capital
- High domestic interest rate
- Successful price stabilization
- Structural reform programme
- Acceleration or even the prospect of acceleration in the growth
- Exchange rate stability

Push Factors
External to the domestic environment

- Decline in available profit opportunities abroad
- Falling interest rate abroad
- Existence of recessionary conditions abroad
- Band wagon effect

Figure 14.3 Pull Factors vs Push Factors.

The pull factors are country-specific and related to the policies followed by recipient countries and the prevailing domestic business and economic conditions. Successful price stabilization measures affecting the aggregate efficiency of resource allocation, structural reform programmes, measures that increase openness of the domestic financial markets to foreign investors, sustainable debt and debt service reduction and timely repayments, acceleration or even the prospect of acceleration in growth, exchange rate stability, improved ability of the country to absorb shocks, high domestic productivity of capital, high domestic interest rate attract/pull the foreign capital to the domestic markets.

The push factors, on the contrary, are unrelated to the policies pursued by recipient countries. A fall in external interest rates, decline in profit opportunities abroad, existence of recessionary conditions in foreign countries, herd mentality in international capital markets push the capital from external markets to domestic markets.

14.3 ARGUMENT AGAINST FREE FLOW OF CAPITAL

There is no denying the fact that the foreign capital is essential for the development of an economy. However, it also poses certain risk and problems which are highlighted as follows:

14.3.1 Macroeconomic Instability

The East Asian Currency crisis of 1997 (UBE 14.3) highlighted that though high growth can be registered with the help of foreign capital flows, a cautious approach needs to be adopted while opening up the doors of an economy to such flows. An economy, in the presence of large foreign capital is more prone to instability and external shocks, especially when a higher proportion of capital flows is of short-term duration. As we will see in Section 15.4, free entry and exit of capital can result in exchange rate volatility, sharp fluctuations in money supply and inflation rate, and thus, by creating uncertainty in the environment can jeopardize the macroeconomic stability. Thus, large flow of foreign capital places additional responsibility of protecting the economy from the adverse impact of these flows on the monetary authority.

Not only the amount, but the composition of private capital flows also needs to be monitored.

To reap the benefits from capital flows as well as overcome the associated problems, policies need to be moulded in such a way that they promote stable and long-term capital flows. Short-term deposits and portfolio flows tend to be more volatile and make the country more prone to instability. Appropriate taxation policies, taxing the short-term capital gain at a high rate, may be formulated and pursued to bring in favourable changes in the composition of these flows.

14.3.2 Adverse Selection and Moral Hazard Problems

Global financial integration enhances the choice of financial instruments for domestic investors. Thus, by providing avenues for risk sharing and portfolio diversification, the integration enhances the efficiency of financial services. However, in the absence of enough information about the working of companies located in the far-off destinations, it also accentuates the problem related to the asymmetric information (moral hazard and adverse selection) and imposes limits on the efficiency of resource allocation.

Therefore, strengthening of the financial sector is desirable before opening up an economy on a large scale to the foreign capital flows. Imposition of prudential norms such as stricter capital adequacy and income recognition norms, can limit the danger related to the moral hazard and adverse selection problems to a certain extent. These norms compel domestic financial institutions to invest their resources in viable projects and help them compete with foreign financial institutions.

14.3.3 Drain of Capital

It has also been observed in some countries that the drain of capital, in the form of repatriation of profits and dividends, in the long-run turns out to be much more than the initial inflow of foreign capital. Thus, rather than benefitting, unrestricted capital flows can drain out the resources from the country and retard its growth.

To prevent drain of capital in the form of dividend and interest, the companies can be incentivized to reinvest such payments in the domestic market itself.

14.3.4 Unbalanced Regional Growth

Often capital flows to already developed regions, with well-developed infrastructure, of a country and the undeveloped regions get deprived of such flows due to lack of enabling facilities. Thus, foreign capital often perpetuates unbalanced growth and already existing regional inequalities.

Some of the regions in their endeavour to attract large capital flows give large tax incentives to foreign investors. This wipes out the net gains from these projects and, thus, defeats the very purpose of inviting the FDI.

Common policies, thus, need to be framed that can restrict these undue concessions and benefits to foreign investors, but at the same time lead higher foreign investment to already neglected states.

14.3.5 Replacement of Domestic Saving

A large increase in capital inflows surges share prices in stock markets, and thus, increases the wealth of domestic households. Wealth being one of the important determinants of household consumption, an increase in it reduces saving. Thus, there is a possibility of foreign saving reducing and replacing domestic saving.

Continuous financial innovations, which increase the choices of financial instruments and their liquidity for investors can, to a certain extent, help in mitigating the impact of foreign capital flows on domestic saving.

UNDERSTANDING BUSINESS ENVIRONMENT

UBE 14.3 Was High Growth in East Asian Economies Driven by Foreign Capital?

Rapid growth can be achieved by opening up an economy to capital flows. However, as indicated in this UBE, cautious approach is needed towards such an opening to prevent crises.

In the aftermath of the Second World War, between 1950s and 1970s, many developing and underdeveloped countries, which had just got independence from colonial rule, feared opening up their economies to trade and capital flows primarily for the following reasons:

First, these countries feared that if they open up their economies to trade and capital flows, foreigners may capture their governance as they had done in the past.

Second, many of these countries were dependent on agriculture and allied activities for their livelihood. As we all know that these activities produce food grains, vegetables and other essential products for which income elasticity is very low. Low income elasticity implies that as the income increases the demand increases, but proportionately less than the increase in the income. Hence, these countries were very export pessimist. They feared that even if they open up their economies there will not be much demand for their indigenously produced goods from developed countries that have already achieved a very high level of development and have low income elasticity for agricultural and other related products. At the same time, they perceived that the opening up will flood their markets with cheap foreign products and prevent development of their domestic industries. Low demand for exports and high demand for imports, they felt that, will simply put pressures on the balance of payment.

Third, the fear that imports will hinder the development of their domestic industries compelled many countries to pursue import compressing measures. Such measures kept their foreign exchange requirements to the minimum. Whatever foreign exchange requirement and other resource requirements they had, they could meet those from ODA and other debt flows that were easily available from donor countries and multinational organizations

However, the oil price hikes in 1973 and 1979, and the series of major external shocks which persisted till the opening years of the 1990s increased their requirements for foreign exchange tremendously. At the same time, during this period dismemberment of the former USSR, German unification, war and political uncertainities in Arab countries, and the large fiscal and balance of payment deficit of the USA, led to drying up of traditional sources of ODA funds to developing countries. The ODA was used for the development of the east European countries and highly underdeveloped African countries. Thus, though net flow of foreign capital to developing countries increased over the period 1985–1995, a marked change was noticed after the year 1991 in the composition of these flows. The net ODA flows registered a declining trend during the first half of the 1990s, whereas non-concessional debt flows increased substantially, putting many of the developing countries into debt difficulties.

At the same time, during the 1980s and 1990s, many East Asian countries registered high growth rates. These countries adopted outward oriented strategy and invited large scale private capital flows leading to a sharp increase in their net private flows to GDP ratio (Table 14.1). These flows were used for investment purpose which improved their investment to GDP ratio (Table 14.2). The consequent expansion in productive capacity helped them register rapid economic growth as is evident from Table 14.3.

The sustained economic growth rate in these countries lasted until the currency crisis of 1997. It was surprising why these countries which were witnessing rapid growth rate faced the severe economic crisis which led them into prolonged period of large scle unemployment and human suffering. A closer examination of Table 14.1, provides a possible explanation for such a crisis. These countries registered a heavy inflow of foreign capital, however, they did not bother to keep a check on its composition. Most severely affected East Asian countries like Thailand, Indonesia, Malaysia and Phillipines had a very large proportion of their private capital flows in the form of short-term flows such as portfolio flows and short-term liabilities. Short-term flows, since can be easily withdrawn, leave countries with smallest decline in the confidence in their economies. Thus, when signs of weaknesses in the working of these economies started surfacing, a large proportion of private capital left these countries overnight, leaving them in a highly uncertain situation.

Table 14.1 Net Private Capital Flows to GDP Ratio: Selected Asian Countries

(Average: Per cent of GDP)

Country	1975–82	1980–91	1992–96
China			
Net private capital flows	0.3	1.1	3.5
Net direct investment	0.1	0.6	4.2
Net portfolio investment	–	0.1	0.3
Short-term liabilities	0.2	– 0.2	– 0.2
Indonesia			
Net private capital flows	1.1	2.6	4.8
Net direct investment	0.5	0.6	1.8
Net portfolio investment	0.1	0.1	0.7
Short-term liabilities	– 0.8	1.4	2.4
Malaysia			
Net private capital flows	5.1	4.1	10.5
Net direct investment	3.7	3.6	6.5
Net portfolio investment	–		–
Short-term liability	0.8	0.5	3.5
Philippines			
Net private capital flows	5.5	– 0.8	4.8
Net direct investment	0.5	1.0	1.7
Net portfolio investment	0.1	0.1	0.1
Short-term liabilities	2.9	– 2.0	2.3
Thailand			
Net private capital flows	4.0	5.7	8.8
Net direct investment	0.4	1.3	1.0
Net portfolio investment	–	0.8	2.2
Short-term liabilities	1.7	2.8	4.7

Country	1975–82	1980–91	1992–96
India			
Net private capital flows	– 0.2	1.4	1.5
Net direct investment	–	0.1	0.4
Net portfolio investment	–	–	0.8
Short-term liabilities	0.1	0.7	– 0.1

Source: Data is Compiled from IMF, *World Economic Outlook*, October 1998.

Table 14.2 Investment to GDP Ratio: Selected Asian Countries

(Average: Per cent of GDP)

Country	1960–69	1970–79	1980–89	1990–96
Hong Kong	—	24	28	30
Republic of Korea	18	28	30	37
Taiwan Province of China	25	29	24	24
China	35	35	34	39
Indonesia	18	19	27	32
Malaysia	15	23	30	38
Philippines	19	25	23	23
Thailand	22	25	28	41
India	16	18	22	24

Source: Compiled from IMF, *World Economic Outlook*, October 1998.

Table 14.3 Annual Growth Rate in Real GDP: Selected Asian Countries

(US$ Million)

Country	*Average* 1983–92	1993	1994	1995	1996	1997	1998	1999	2000
China	10.2	13.5	12.6	10.5	9.6	8.8	7.8	7.1	8.0
Indonesia	6.3	7.3	7.5	8.2	8.0	4.5	–13.1	0.8	4.8
Malaysia	6.6	9.9	9.2	9.8	10.0	7.3	–7.4	6.1	8.3
Philippines	1.0	2.1	4.4	4.7	5.8	5.2	–0.6	3.4	4.0
Thailand	8.4	8.4	9.0	9.3	5.9	–1.4	–10.8	4.2	4.4
India	5.4	5.0	6.9	7.7	7.3	4.9	5.8	6.8	6.0
Pakistan	5.8	2.7	4.4	4.9	2.9	1.8	3.1	4.1	3.9
Sri Lanka	4.1	6.9	5.6	5.5	3.8	6.4	4.7	4.3	6.0
Total (Asian countries)	7.3	9.4	9.7	9.0	8.3	6.5	4.0	6.1	6.8

Source: Compiled from IMF, *World Economic Outlook*, October, 2001.

On the contrary, the countries like China, though open to private capital flows, but limited exposure to short-term flows, were not affected by the crisis because of high proportion of stable flows, such as FDI in the total flows.

The growth experience of the East Asian countries brought in a sea change in the ideology of the developing countries in the late 1980s. Rather than viewing the flow of foreign capital, especially the private foreign capital, as a danger to the national economy, they started viewing it as a vehicle of economic growth. However, the crisis of 1997 also made them realize that unhindered entry of capital is never desireable. A cautious approach needs to be adopted while opening up an economy to such capital flows. Also, the financial sector should be strengthened by imposing prudential norms before opening up an economy to such flows. Not only the total amount of capital is important but also its composition matters a lot. For the stability of a country, more of FDI and other long-term flows to be encouraged and exposure to the short-term flows should be minimized.

UNDERSTANDING BUSINESS ENVIRONMENT

UBE 11.4 Has the Opening Up Improved Foreign Investment Flows to India?

This UBE highlights how far the opening up of the Indian economy to foreign capital flows, in the aftermath of BOP crisis of 1991, has succeeded in bringing in desirable changes.

The balance of payment (BOP) crisis of 1991, in India, necessitated structural reforms and a move towards opening up of the economy in a big way. The experiences of the East Asian countries with foreign capital flows also made it clear that trade and capital flows can be an engine of economic growth and prosperity. The country realized that a sustained inflow of foreign capital cannot be achieved through the Overseas Development Assistance (ODA) flows. The ODA flows were drying up and over the years had become thinner and thinner. Even the prospects of increasing the ODA flows to India in the future were not very bright because of the drying down of its traditional sources. It was increasingly realized that the ODA flows are more likely to flow to the neediest countries, particularly in Africa, and for specific purposes, such as famine relief, poverty alleviation, infrastructural development (both physical and human), and structural adjustment programmes. As far as the flow of commercial bank lending was concerned, these move to countries with superior growth performance and declining debt service ratio. Therefore, it was realized that primary reliance for external finance had to be placed on private funds, both the Foreign Direct Investment (FDI) and the Foreign Portfolio Investment (FPI). This realization changed the orientation of policies in favour of private capital flows.

In an effort to encourage foreign capital flows to the country, a number of structural reform measures were initiated since 1991. These consisted of changes in regulatory framework and exchange rate liberalization. India signed multilateral investors protocol for protection of investors on 13 April 1992, and set up the Foreign Investment Promotion Board (FIPB) in 1992–93, for those cases of FDI that do not fall under the category of direct approval under the RBI. To facilitate foreign exchange transactions, the Foreign Exchange Management Act (FEMA) replaced the Foreign Exchange Regulation Act (FERA) (UBE 15.6). To correct the distortions emerging on account of the fixed exchange rate regime (Section 15.3.2), the rupee was made convertible on the current account in August 1994, The country has gradually started moving towards full capital account convertibility (Section 15.4) since then.

Apart from introducing various structural reform measures, the inflow of FDI, FPI and other capital flows is encouraged through various incentives and promotional schemes. The country has gradually brought all the FDI, except a small negative list, under the automatic approval route. The FIIs are allowed to invest in the Indian capital market upto 24 per cent in a paid-up equity capital issued by a particular company subject to registration with the SEBI. They are allowed to invest in the dated government securities and T-bills and units of mutual funds both through primary and secondary markets. Interest rate swaps, currency swaps and forward agreement for the authorized dealers have been permitted. To promote the inflow of the NRI deposits, the NRI rupee account schemes are exempted from income and wealth tax and are fully repatriable. The Foreign Currency Non-Resident (Banks) (FCNR(B)) Account Schemes are available in the US Dollar, Pound

Sterling, Yen and Deutsche Mark with repatriability. The External Commercial Borrowings (ECBs) have been permitted for expansion of the existing capacity as well as for fresh investment. For such borrowings, high priority is given for the projects in infrastructure and core sectors. Even the Indian corporate sector has been permitted to access capital market abroad through the American Depository Receipts (ADRs) and the Global Depository Receipts (GDRs) without any end use restrictions except the restrictions on investment in real estate and share market.

The efforts of the Government of India in attracting the flow of foreign capital, especially the foreign direct investment, have yielded positive results. Apart from the changes in domestic policies and economic structure, the favourable external factors till 2007–08 also helped the country to attract a large amount of capital flows especially private flows comprising the Foreign Direct Investment (FDI) and Foreign Portfolio Investment (FPI). Though in 2008–09, the period of a crisis, there was a sharp decline in portfolio flows these have resumed with vigour in the subsequent period (Table 14.5).

India accounted for minuscal share of 0.19 per cent of total FDI flowing to developing countries in 1991 (Table 14.4). As a result of various promotional strategies and liberalization policies, within two years, it doubled its share of FDI flows to all developing countries. Notwithstanding year-to-year fluctuations, since then there has been a substantial rise in this share, reflecting the improvement in perception about India as a long-term investment destination. The fact that India has been able to receive significant amount of foreign capital even during the period of global crisis and recession, highlights India's resilience to adverse conditions.

Table 14.4 Share of India in Total FDI Inflows

	1991	2001	2005	2006	2007	2008	2009	2010	2011
World	154072.7	827617.3	980727.1	1463351	1975537	1790706	1197824	1309001	1524422
Developing economies	39833.89	216865.1	327247.8	427163.4	574311.5	650016.8	519225	616660.7	684399.3
India	75	5477.638	7621.769	20327.76	25505.59	43406.3	35595.9	24159.2	31554.03
Share of India in developing countries (%)	0.19	2.53	2.33	4.76	4.44	6.68	6.86	3.92	4.61
Share of India in the World (%)	0.05	0.66	0.78	1.39	1.29	2.42	2.97	1.85	2.07

Source: Computed on the basis of data available from UNCTAD STAT; (online) http://unctadstat.unctad org/, as on 13/5/2013.

SUMMARY

The foreign capital consists of external assistance (the ODA concessional and non-concessional flows and loans) and private capital flows (FDI, FPI, ECB and other private flows).

The foreign capital flows from one country to another because of various pull and push factors. The pull factors are country specific, such as the changes in domestic productivity, interest rate, and stabilization and reform measures initiated by the country. The push factors, on the contrary, are related to the changes in external environment that push the capital from other markets to domestic markets.

Foreign capital flows help in bridging resource gap and foreign exchange gap and also brings in non-measurable gains, such as better access to markets, new technology and new management skills.

Learning from the growth experiencess of many East-Asian countries and realizing the problems of closed door policy, India has been pursuing an open door policy towards these flows since 1991. The reform measures and various incentives provided to give a boost to private capital flows have made India as one of the attractive destinations for FDI flows. By pursuing these policies, India has been able to improve the share of non-debt creating flows in its total capital inflows.

However, since these flows, especially the portfolio flows and other short-term flows, have the potential to jeopardize the macroeconomic stability, India is pursuing a very cautious approach as far as their composition is concerned. Efforts are to promote more of stable rather than short-term volatile flows.

Implications for Managers

With the opening up of the Indian economy since the BOP crisis of 1991–92, greater integration of the country with the rest of the world through trade and foreign capital flows has been emerging as a principal component of business environment.

Higher integration, through capital flows, leads to a higher access to foreign capital markets for domestic firms. In the process, domestic financial markets and domestic interest rates get aligned with the international markets and interest rates. Higher volume gets traded in the domestic financial markets, which deepens them. The liquidity in the domestic financial markets improves which helps in the further development of these markets. The greater integration of the domestic financial markets with the financial markets located abroad and the global sourcing of funds by domestic units reduces their cost of capital. It facilitates domestic firms to raise financial resources at internally competitive interest rates.

Higher capital flows enhance investment, which leads to an improvement in the infrastructure and the productive capacity of an economy. MNCs bringing in foreign direct investment also bring with them new technology, new marketing skills and new business practices. Domestic producers benefit by observing and adopting these practices. They also benefit from higher competition resulting from more and more units setting up their units in the domestic economy.

Higher capital flows enhance the availability of foreign currency which helps a country in stabilizing the exchange rate and building up its foreign exchange reserves. This builds up the confidence of foreign investors and traders. A higher reputation of the country and better credit rating for the economy create a conducive environment for business organizations.

Globalization of the country brings in immense benefits to domestic business firms. However, the greater integration also makes a country and business organizations vulnerable to external shocks. Trade and capital flows become highly unstable with even small changes in the world environment. To safeguard their interest, business units need to continuously watch the trade performance, development on the capital account, and the build-up of foreign currency reserves, and take actions accordingly.

REVIEW QUESTIONS

14.1 What types of benefits are expected from foreign capital flows?

14.2 Foreign capital flows bring in immense benefits for the host country. Why do most countries, then, usually follow a very cautious approach towards opening up their economies for these flows?

14.3 What are the different types of foreign capital flows?

14.4 Differentiate among the different types of foreign capital flows. Which of these are more desirable from the point of view of the macroeconomic stability of a country?

14.5 What are the determinants of foreign capital flows?

14.6 What are the constituents of FDI in India? How far are these different for China?

CASE ANALYSIS EXERCISE

C14.1 Is India's Debt Unsustainable?

India's external debt has increased over a period of time in absolute terms. It stood at US $305.9 billion at the end of March 2011, and rose to $345.4 billion at the end of March 2012 and further to $365.3 billion at the end of September 2012 (Table 14.5). The rise in external debt stock in the first half of 2012 is mainly on account of a rise in NRI deposits, short-term debt and external commercial borrowings.

Over the years, due to various internal and external reasons, there has been structural shift in the composition of India's external debt. First, external concessional flows, known as ODA, since early 1990s has been increasingly flowing to highly underdeveloped countries. Consequently, the share of concessional flows to India is declining. At the same time, large scale liberalization has enable the country to raise resources from private entities. These developments have reduced the share of concessional debt to total external debt. Second, large scale liberalization of norms has increased the share of short-term external debt in the total external debt, reflecting deteriorating quality of the external debt.

These adverse compositional changes have been raising doubts about the external debt sustainability of the country.

However, there are other features of India's external debt which indicate that as of now India is capable of withstanding these unfavourable compositional changes. Inspite of an increase in the value of external debt in absolute terms and deterioration in the quality of the debt, India's debt sustainability indicators—solvency and liquidity indicators—have remained fairly stable and its external debt has remained within manageable limits. India's has an external debt to GDP ratio of 19.7 per cent, which is much lower than the countries which have much lesser indebted (Table 14.7) and debt service ratio of 6 per cent in 2011–12. India's foreign exchange reserves can still finance more than 80 per cent of its total external debt and more than 70 per cent of short-term debt.

The cautious external debt policy, which focused on raising funds from less expensive sources with longer maturities, prepaying high cost loans, restricting end use, enforcing limits on ECBs, encouraging non-debt creating capital flows, and constant monitoring of short-term debt, helped in containing the accumulation of external debt and maintaining external debt within manageable limits. These policies improved the position of India among developing debtor countries. In 1991 India was the third largest among the developing debtor countries. Its position improved to eighth in 2004. However, since then there has been again a deterioration in India's position. It stood at the fourth position among the top ten developing debtor countries in 2011 (Table 14.6).

Table 14.5 India's Key External Debt Indicators

(Per cent)

Year	*External debt (US $ billion)*	*Ratio of total external debt to GDP*	*Debt service ratio*	*Ratio of foreign exchange reserves to total external debt*	*Ratio of concessional debt to total external debt*	*Ratio of short-term debt* to foreign exchange reserves*	*Ratio of short-term debt* to total debt*
1990–91	83.8	28.7	35.3	7.0	45.9	146.5	10.2
1995–96	93.7	27.0	26.2	23.1	44.7	23.2	5.4
2000-01	101.3	22.5	16.6	41.7	35.4	8.6	3.6
2005-06	139.1	16.8	10.1	109.0	28.4	12.9	14.0
2006-07	172.4	17.5	4.7	115.6	23.0	14.1	16.3
2007-08	224.4	18.0	4.8	138.0	19.7	14.8	20.4
2008-09	224.5	20.3	4.4	112.1	18.7	17.2	19.3
2009-10	260.9	18.2	5.8	106.8	16.8	18.8	20.1
2010-11	305.9	17.5	4.3	99.6	15.5	21.3	21.2
2011-12	345.4	19.7	6.0	85.2	13.9	26.6	22.6
End Sep 2012 QE	365.3	–		80.7	13.2	28.7	23.1

Notations: QE: Quick Estimates

Note: *Short-term debt is based on original maturity Debt-service ratio is the proportion of gross debt service payments to External Current Receipts (net of official transfers)

Source: GOI (2013), Economic Survey 2012–13, (online) http://indiabudget.nic.in/survey.asp

Table 14.6 International Comparison of Top Ten Developing Debtor Countries, 2011

	External debt (US$ million)	*External debt (% of GNI)*	*Short-term debt (% of total external debt)*	*Short-term debt (% of total reserves)*	*Concessional debt (% of total external debt)*
China	6,85,420	9.3	69.5	14.6	5.6
Russian federation	5,42,980	31.1	12.8	14.1	0.4
Brazil	4,04,320	16.6	10.4	11.9	2.8
India	3,34,330	18.2	23.3	26.1	15.6
Turkey	3,07,010	40.1	27.2	95.2	3.4
Mexico	2,87,040	25.1	17.8	34.4	1.1
Indonesia	2,13,540	25.9	17.8	34.6	21.3
Ukraine	1,34,480	83.2	24.3	102.9	0.9
Romania	1,29,820	72.3	22.9	61.9	6.7
Kazakhstan	1,24,440	77.9	7.1	30.5	0.9

Note: Countries are arranged based on the magnitude of total external debt stock.

Source: World bank database 2013, World development indicators online as on 13/5/13 http://data.worldbank.org/data-catalog/world-development-indicator

Questions

1. Is there a cause for concern as far as the composition of India's external debt is concerned?
2. What indicators reflect on debt solvency and what factors can be used for assessing debt liquidity?
3. Is India's external debt sustainable?
4. As a manager, does debt sustainability of a country matters to you? What are the likely implications of India's debt reaching unsustainable level?

SUGGESTED FURTHER READING

Dhar, B. (2012), India's Bilateral Investment Agreements: Time to Review, *EPW*, December 29, Vol. XLVII, No. 52.

Jadhav, A.M. (2013). Does FDI Contribute to Growth? Evidence from the Capital Goods Sector in India, March 23, XLVII, 12.

Khan, H.R. (2012), Outward Indian FDI—Recent Trends and Emerging Issues, *RBI Bulletin*, April.

Mohanty, D. (2012), Global Managing Capital Flows, *RBI Bulletin*, December.

Obstfeld, M. (2012), Gross Financial Flows, Global Imbalances and Crisis, *RBI Bulletin*, January.

RBI (2009), Report of the Committee on the Global Financial System on Capital Flows and Emerging Market Economies.

Subbarao, D. (2013), *Rethinking Macropolicy II: Capital Account Management*, *RBI Bulletin*, May.

CHAPTER 15

Exchange Rate Regimes and Currency Convertibility

15.1 INTRODUCTION

In the modern era, transactions of goods, services and even financial assets require currency. Different currencies are used by different countries as a means of payment, representing their sovereignty. Transactions, whether of commodities or financial assets, among the countries, thus, necessitates transactions of currencies as well. Hence, when we travel abroad we get exchanged our domestic currency into foreign currencies. Similarly, when producers import raw material and other inputs, and final goods they exchange their domestic currency with foreign currencies to make the payment to foreign producers. Many other such transactions in our daily life as well as in our working sphere require trading of domestic currency with foreign currencies. The trading, however, is always at some rate. The rate at which currencies are traded in the international market is known as the **exchange rate**. The value of the exchange rate is determined by the prevailing exchange rate regime in the country.

The prices of foreign goods faced by the domestic households and producers are determined not only by the prices prevailing in foreign countries but also by the rate at which domestic currency is exchanged with foreign currencies. An increase in the price of domestic currency in terms of a foreign currency, i.e., an increase in the value of domestic currency, reduces the prices of foreign goods faced by the domestic participants. The converse holds true when there is a depreciation of the domestic currency. Therefore, changes in the exchange rate, by exerting influence on the prices faced by domestic participants, affect their consumption and production decisions and play a significant role in international trading decisions and financial management of international business.

The changes in exchange rate not only affect households and firms but also the country as a whole. By affecting the prices of imported and exported commodities, exchange rate fluctuations bring in substantial changes in the current account and, through it, in the overall Balance of Payment (BOP). The central bank, to maintain the BOP in a balance often intervenes in the foreign exchange market by purchasing or selling foreign currency. Purchase or sell of a foreign currency by the central bank impacts the foreign exchange assets on its balance sheet, and influences money supply, domestic price level, inflation rate and other macroeconomic variables. To control trade and capital flows sometimes restrictions are imposed on the convertibility of the domestic currency in foreign currencies, which in turn, have bearing on the macroeconomy.

This chapter examines various issues related to the exchange rate that are of relevance for domestic firms and for the macroeconomic stability of a country. Section 15.2 defines the exchange rate. The process of determination of exchange rates in different exchange rate regimes is elaborated in Section 15.3. Issues in currency convertibility and their implications are dealt in Section 15.4.

15.2 FOREIGN EXCHANGE MARKET AND EXCHANGE RATE

Foreign exchange or foreign currency, including paper currency and bank deposits denominated in foreign currency, is traded in the foreign exchange market. Trading of foreign exchange requires expressing the value of one currency in terms of another currency. The price of one currency in terms of another currency is known as the **exchange rate**. Or alternatively, the exchange rate is a rate at which two currencies can be bought or sold in the foreign exchange market.

The exchange rate helps in converting the price of a commodity that is quoted in terms of foreign currency into domestic currency. The price in terms of domestic currency can be calculated by multiplying the foreign currency price by the given exchange rate, i.e.,

Price of a commodity in terms of domestic currency
= Price of the commodity in foreign currency × Exchange rate

15.2.1 Direct and Indirect Quotation of Exchange Rate

In the commodity market, the price is quoted as per unit of a commodity. For example, when we buy a television, the shopkeeper quotes the price per television. The similar pattern of quotation is followed in the exchange rate market. Since the exchange rate is a price of one currency in terms of another currency, one of the currencies is treated as the price currency and the other one as the quantity currency. Depending on whether the home (or domestic) currency is treated as the price currency or the quantity currency, the exchange rate is quoted in two different ways, known as the direct quotation and indirect quotation. As explained below, each of these ways of quoting the exchange rate has certain advantages, and hence, both are in use.

The **direct quotation** expresses the exchange rate by treating the home currency as the price currency and the foreign currency as the quantity currency. To understand this method of quotation let us suppose that Indian rupee is the price currency and the US $ is the quantity currency. Then the quotation of ₹45 = $1 or ₹45/$1 implies that one unit of the US $ costs ₹45 in the foreign exchange market. From the perspective of India, this is the direct quotation.

The **indirect quotation**, on the other hand, treats the home currency as the quantity currency and foreign currency as the price currency. If the Indian rupee is the quantity currency and the US $ is the price currency and the quotation is US $0.02 = ₹1 or $0.02/₹1, then it implies that the price of one unit of Indian rupee is $0.02. From the perspective of India, this is the indirect quotation.

The value of domestic currency varies inversely with the value of direct quotation. A fall in the direct quotation indicates the rise in the value of domestic currency and a rise indicates the fall in the value of the domestic currency. For example, if the quotation changes from ₹45 = $1 to ₹40 = $1, it indicates the decline in the direct quotation and implies that to procure one unit of the US $ economic agents have to pay now less of Indian rupee. Alternatively, ₹45 can now procure more than one unit of the US $. On the contrary, if the rate changes from ₹45 = $1 to ₹50 = $1, it implies that to procure one unit of the US $ economic agents have to pay now more of Indian rupee. Alternatively, ₹45 can now procure only less than one unit of the US $.

Unlike direct quotation, the value of the domestic currency varies directly with the value of the indirect quotation. An increase in the indirect quotation implies an appreciation in the value of the quantity currency or the home currency whereas converse holds true in case of a reduction in the value of this quotation. For example, a change in the quotation from US $0.020 = ₹1 to US $0.022 = ₹1 implies that one unit of rupee can procure more of the US. Alternatively, we can say that US $0.02 can now buy only less than one unit of the Indian rupees.

The direct quotation facilitates easy computation of requirement of the domestic currency to procure one unit of a foreign currency, whereas the indirect quotation is much more convenient for economic analysis as the value of the domestic currency varies directly with it. Therefore, in this chapter for all analytical purposes the indirect quotation has been used.

15.2.2 Buying Rate vs Selling Rate

Dealers in the foreign exchange usually quote different rates at any particular time for selling and purchasing—a selling rate and a buying rate. The difference between the buying rate and the selling rate is referred to as the **spread**. Apart from the spread, the foreign exchange dealers also charge a separate fee or commission for their services.

15.2.3 Spot Exchange Rate vs Forward Exchange Rate

Foreign exchange is traded in a foreign exchange market where the market can be a spot (current) market or a forward market. The exchange rate resulting from the foreign exchange transactions in the current market, i.e., the market where foreign exchange is quoted and traded for immediate delivery and payment, is known as the **current exchange rate** or the **spot rate**. On the contrary, the **forward exchange rate** refers to an exchange rate that is quoted and traded today, but for delivery and payment on a specific future date. For example, if the three-month forward exchange (buying) rate for the US $ is quoted on 1 June as $1 = ₹46, then it implies that an Indian importer can ensure paying a rate of ₹46 per Dollar for a fixed amount of Dollars on 1st September by buying the Dollars forward on 1st June. The forward price (which is determined by the spot price and the interest rate differential between the two countries) can be higher than (at a premium to) or lower than (at a discount to) the spot price. Forward exchange transactions provide importers and exporters with an opportunity to cover themselves against the risk of future changes in the spot exchange rate.

15.2.4 Appreciation and Depreciation vs Revaluation and Devaluation

Changes in the exchange rate can occur in two ways. First, the changes can be an outcome of fluctuations in demand for and supply of the foreign currency. Second, the changes can be due to government decisions. The changes in the exchange rate due to market forces, i.e., demand and supply forces, are termed as **appreciation** or **depreciation**, whereas the deliberate resetting of the exchange rate by the government or monetary authority is known as **revaluation** or **devaluation**.

We will see in the coming sections that the flexible exchange rate regime allows market forces to play a role in the determination of exchange rate. Hence, an appreciation or a depreciation of the exchange rate takes place in this regime. On the contrary, in the fixed exchange rate regime, the value of the exchange rate is set by the monetary authorities, it is not allowed to float freely. Hence, a revaluation or a devaluation of the exchange rate takes place in the fixed exchange rate regime.

Expressed as the indirect quotation, the appreciation or revaluation increases the value of the domestic currency vis-à-vis a foreign currency; whereas depreciation or devaluation reduces the value of the domestic currency vis-à-vis a foreign currency.

The depreciation/devaluation implies that the domestic traders have to pay more units of the domestic currency to procure one unit of a foreign currency. Alternatively, for one unit of the domestic currency they receive fewer units of a foreign currency. The appreciation/revaluation of the domestic currency, on the contrary, implies that the traders can procure more units of a foreign currency for one unit of the domestic currency while they have to surrender fewer units of the domestic currency to procure one unit of a foreign currency. The depreciation or devaluation of domestic currency makes imported commodities dearer, and exports cheaper and more competitive. Conversely, the appreciation or revaluation makes imports cheaper and reduces the competitiveness of exports by making them dearer.

For example, the impact of movements in the exchange rate on the rupee price of foreign goods is illustrated in Table 15.1. Suppose initially the exchange rate is ₹1 = $0.020. At this rate, the rupee price of US car worth $10,000 is ₹5,00,000. Suppose an appreciation in the value of Rupee makes the exchange rate as ₹1 = $0.0208. The appreciation in the exchange rate makes the imported US car cheaper with the car costing ₹4,80,000. Conversely, had there been a depreciation with exchange rate being ₹1 = $0.0193, the imported US car would have been dearer with the car costing ₹5,20,000.

Table 15.1 Impact of Movements in Exchange Rate on the Rupee Price of Foreign Goods

Dollar price of US car	*Exchange rate*	*Rupee price of US car*	*Appreciation/Depreciation of rupee*
$10,000	₹1 = $0.0208	4,80,000	Appreciation
$10,000	₹1 = $0.0200	5,00,000	
$10,000	₹1 = $0.0193	5,20,000	Depreciation

15.2.5 Nominal Exchange Rate vs Real Exchange Rate

The **nominal exchange rate** is a rate at which one organization can trade one currency with another currency. The exchange rate quoted at any particular time (in money terms) in the foreign exchange market is the nominal exchange rate.

Nominal exchange rate adjusted for the price level is known as the **real exchange rate**, i.e.,

Real exchange rate = (Domestic price level/Foreign price level) × Nominal exchange rate

From the above formula we can see that, given the nominal exchange rate, the value of the real exchange rate varies directly with the changes in the domestic price level and inversely with the foreign price level. For example, a 10 per cent increase in the domestic price level, with no change in the foreign price level and nominal exchange rate, would result in a 10 per cent increase or appreciation of the real exchange rate or real value of the domestic currency. The increase in the domestic price level, for a given nominal exchange rate, increases the price of exported commodities in the international market. Thus, an appreciation in the real exchange rate reduces export competitiveness. On the contrary, a depreciation in the real exchange rate reduces the price of domestically produced commodities and enhances the export competitiveness.

Both nominal and real exchange rates fluctuate. However, the variations in the value of real exchange rate are more frequent than the variations in the value of nominal exchange rate as changes in both price level and nominal exchange rate can have an impact on its value. For example, the nominal exchange rate remains constant in the fixed exchange rate regime. However, the real exchange rate can vary even in this regime due to changes in the price level in the domestic market vis-a-vis the markets in the trading partner countries.

Though while buying and selling we just consider the nominal value of exchange rate, the real exchange rate is more important than nominal exchange rate while assessing the effect of exchange rate changes on exports, imports and the balance of payment as it takes into account the changes in many more factors than simply the nominal change in the value of the domestic currency.

15.2.6 Bilateral vs Effective Exchange Rates

All quoted exchange rates in the foreign exchange market are **bilateral exchange rates** as these involve the currencies of only two countries. For example, we see quotations like ₹45 = $1 or ₹80 = £1.

Every country in a particular period, however, trades or transacts with a number of other countries with different bilateral exchange rates applicable in transactions with different countries. Bilateral rates, in a particular period, vary by different degree and in different directions. One bilateral exchange rate (say, Rupee vs Dollar), may be increasing, whereas another one (say, Rupee vs Euro) may be decreasing in a particular period of time. Bilateral exchange rates, in such a situation, are inefficient in expressing the average or effective exchange rate faced by the domestic country.

An overall measure of the movement in the domestic currency vis-a-vis major currencies can be obtained by calculating the **effective exchange rate** (also referred to as the **multilateral exchange rate**). To know the effective exchange rate a composite index is needed. This composite index is a weighted average of different bilateral exchange rates faced by a country. The weights in this index are either the shares of different countries in the total trade or the shares of exports to different countries in the total exports of the country in consideration). The composite index based on trade weights is referred to as the **trade-weighted exchange rate**, whereas that based on export weights is referred to as the **export-weighted exchange rate**.

The effective exchange rates are expressed in both nominal and real terms (Box 15.1). The **Nominal Effective Exchange Rate** (NEER) is obtained by calculating the weighted average of the bilateral nominal exchange rates, while the **Real Effective Exchange Rate** (REER) is obtained by estimating the weighted average of the bilateral real effective exchange rate (i.e., the bilateral nominal exchange rates adjusted for the relative price differentials between the domestic and foreign countries).

An increase in the NEER indicates an overall or effective appreciation in the value of the domestic currency, whereas a fall in it indicates a depreciation in the overall value of the domestic currency. An appreciation of the NEER reduces the export competitiveness, whereas a depreciation in it boosts up the export competitiveness.

Changes in the value of the REER are outcomes of changes not only in the nominal bilateral exchange rates but also the ratio of price level in the domestic market to that of price level of trading partners. An increase in the price level of the domestic currency appreciates the value of the REER and, thus, reduces the export competitiveness of a country. A fall in the domestic price level, on the contrary, boosts up the export competitiveness.

The movements in effective exchange rate and its impact are illustrated in UBE 15.1 using Indian context.

Box 15.1 Computation of the Effective Exchange Rate Indices

The **effective exchange rate** is the weighted average of bilateral exchange rate. Often it is estimated in an index form. While constructing the index, all the bilateral exchange rates are first expressed in some common numeraire which is either some commonly accepted currency, such as the US $ or a basket of currency such as the **Special Drawing Rights** (SDRs, Box 15.6). After expressing all the bilateral exchange rates using some numeriare, all the bilateral rates of given period are compared with their values in the base period. A weighted average of these ratios provides an estimate of the effective exchange rate.

The effective exchange rate can be **Nominal Effective Exchange Rate** (NEER) or **Real Effective Exchange Rate** (REER). These are estimated in the indexed form as follows:

The NEER is a weighted average of bilateral nominal exchange rates of the home currency in terms of foreign currencies. It can be calculated using the arithmetic average as follows:

$$\text{NEER} = 100\sum_{i=1}^{n} wi\left[\frac{(e_t/e_o)}{(e_{it}/e_{io})}\right]$$

where

e_t = Current period exchange rate of the home currency (₹) against a numeraire (SDR)

e_o = Base period exchange rate of the home currency (₹) against the numeraire (SDR)

e_{it} = Current period exchange rate of currency i against the numeraire (SDR)

e_{io} = Base period exchange rate of currency *i* against the numeraire (SDR)

w_i = Weight attached to currency/country *i* in the index

n = Number of countries/currencies in the index other than the home or domestic country

(it can be noted that as the indirect quotation method is used for expressing these rates, the numeraire, say SDR appears in the numerator and the other currencies appear in the denominator. Therefore, et, for example, is expressed as the number of units of SDR for one unit of domestic currency. Similarly, values of other exchange rates are expressed.)

The REER is a price deflated NEER. While estimating the REER, the NEER is adjusted by the ratio of domestic price level (P_t) to foreign price level (P_{it}). The REER is expressed as:

$$\text{REER} = 100\sum_{i=1}^{n}\left[\frac{(e_t/e_0)}{(e_{it}/e_{io})}\left(\frac{P_t}{P_{it}}\right)\right]$$

These indices can also be estimated using geometric averages as follows:

$$\text{NEER} = 100\prod_{i=1}^{n}\left[\frac{(e_t/e_0)}{(e_{it}/e_{io})}\right]^{wi}$$

$$\text{REER} = 100\prod_{i=1}^{n}\left[\frac{(e_t/e_0)}{(e_{it}/e_{io})}\left(\frac{P_t}{P_{it}}\right)\right]^{wi}$$

UNDERSTANDING BUSINESS ENVIRONMENT

UBE 15.1 Do Movements in Exchange Rates Affect the Indian Economy?

For assessing the effective exchange rate, India estimates NEER and REER indices. This UBE compares the direction of trend in these indices and assesses whether REER matters for the working of the Indian economy.

The NEER and REER are used as indicators of effective changes in the exchange rate and external competiveness of a country over a period of time. The NEER captures the average movements in cross-currency exchange rates, whereas the REER captures not only the movements in cross-currency exchange rates but also inflation differential between the domestic country and its major trading partners. In India, the Reserve Bank of India (RBI) has been constructing monthly estimates of 6 currency and 36 currency indices of the NEER and the REER using the SDR as the numeraire. The 6 currency index includes the US, Euro zone, the UK, Japan, China and Hong Kong, whereas the 36 currency index includes the currencies of Argentina, Australia, Bangladesh, Brazil, Canada, China, Egypt, Euro, Hong Kong, Indonesia, Iran, Israel, Japan, Kenya, Korea, Kuwait, Malaysia, Mexico, Nigeria, Pakistan, the Philippines, Qatar, Russia, Saudi Arabia, Singapore, South Africa, Sri Lanka, Sweden, Switzerland, Taiwan, Thailand, Turkey, the UAE, the UK, the USA and Vietnam. To reflect the dynamically changing pattern of India's foreign trade, these indices use a 3 year moving average trade weights. In the estimation of REER, the Wholesale Price Index (WPI) is used as a proxy for Indian prices and the Consumer Price Index (CPI) is used as a proxy for trading partner countries. The 6 currency index updates the WPI data every week, whereas it is updated monthly for the 36 currency index. The 6 currency index is estimated for two base years, the fixed base which remain fixed until further revision and the moving base which gets revised every year. At present, the fixed base year is 2004–05 while the moving base year is 2010–11.

The year on year percentage changes in the NEER and REER presented in Figure 15.1 exhibits that in 2012–13 there was a deppreciation of 6 currency and 36 currency trade based NEER as well as REER. However, the depreciation in REER was lesser than that in NEER, implying that the overall price level in India was higher than that in its major trading partner countries. From the figure, we can also ascertain that there was lower depreciation in the 6 currency REER than that in the 36 currencies REER, reflecting that the six major trading partners had higher inflation than the other countries included in the 36 country index.

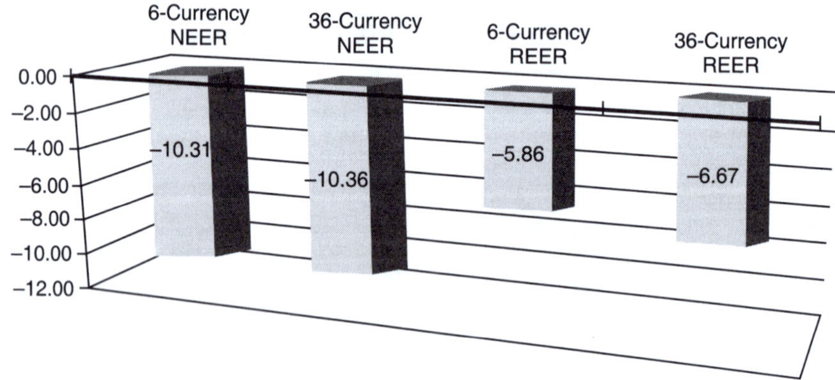

Source: Based on the data available from RBI (2013), *RBI Bulletin*, May.

Figure 15.1 Appreciation (+)/ Depreciation (–) of Indian Rupee.

It is important to analyze the movements in effective exchange rates because these movements can affect the economy through various channels:

- First, the exchange rate appreciation can lower the cost of imports expressed in domestic currency, and hence, moderate inflation.
- Second, the exchange rate appreciation can weaken the comparative advantage in exports and hence, can adversely affect exports.
- Third, the exchange rate appreciation by promoting exports and retarding exports can weaken the current account and the BOP of a country.

To assess whether these channels operate in India, the RBI (2010) made an empirical assessment of movements in exchange rate on the Indian Economy. While making such an assessment it refers to three studies, viz., RBI (2004), Khundrakpam (2007) and its own recent assessment.

The RBI (2004) and Khundrakpam (2007) make an assessment of exchange rate movements on the price level. RBI (2004) estimates indicate that a 10 per cent depreciation of exchange rate increases wholesale price based inflation by 0.4 per cent during the period 1970 to 2004. While Khundrakpam (2007) estimates for the post-reform period (August 1991 to March 2005) indicates that a 10 per cent change in the exchange rate leads to change in the final prices by about 0.6 per cent in the short run and 0.9 per cent in the long run. Thus, RBI (2010) concludes that exchange rate movements can be used for stabilizing inflation in India.

For making an assessment of exchange rate movements on trade balance, RBI (2010) carried out a simple regression of trade balance (ratio of exports to imports, i.e., LXM) on exchange rate (6 currency trade weighted REER, i.e., LREER), seasonally adjusted domestic real GDP (LINGDP) and World GDP (seasonally adjusted OECD GDP, i.e., LOECDGDP) using the data for the period 1996 Q_2 to 2009 Q_4. The estimates of the study, as presented in the following equation, indicate that the currency appreciation worsens the trade balance significantly by invoking around 0.7 per cent deterioration in it.

$$\text{LXMt} = 4.28 - 0.73\text{LREERt} - 0.99\text{LINGDPt} + 2.56\text{LOECDGDPt}$$

t-stat (3.53)* (– 2.34)* (– 5.88)* (5.15)*

$R^2 = 0.48$ DW = 1.83

*Significant at 5 per cent level

All variables are in log form.

Given the negative relationship between the exchange rate movements and the price level and inflation, in 2009–10 when the country was reeling under high inflationary pressure and required strong recovery, it was viewed in some quarters that the RBI should aim at appreciating exchange rate by intervening in the forex market so as to moderate the inflation rate. However, the RBI has restrained using exchange rate policy to control inflation because, an appreciation of the exchange rate, by dampening exports, also undermines the growth objective. It rather prefers managing the inflation-growth objectives through monetary policy.

References

Khundrakpam, J.K. (2007), Economic reforms and exchange rate pass-through to domestic prices in India," BIS Working Papers 225.

Reserve Bank of India (2004), Report on Currency and Finance 2002–04.

Reserve Bank of India (2010), Annual Report 2009–10.

15.3 EXCHANGE RATE REGIMES AND DETERMINATION OF EXCHANGE RATE

The body of rules that govern the buying and selling in the foreign exchange market is referred to as the **exchange rate regimes**.

All over the world three different types of exchange rate regimes are pursued (Figure 15.2). The fixed exchange rate regime and flexible exchange rate regimes are the two extremes of the foreign exchange rate regimes, whereas the managed flexibility regime is a combination of fixed and flexible exchange rate system described as follows:

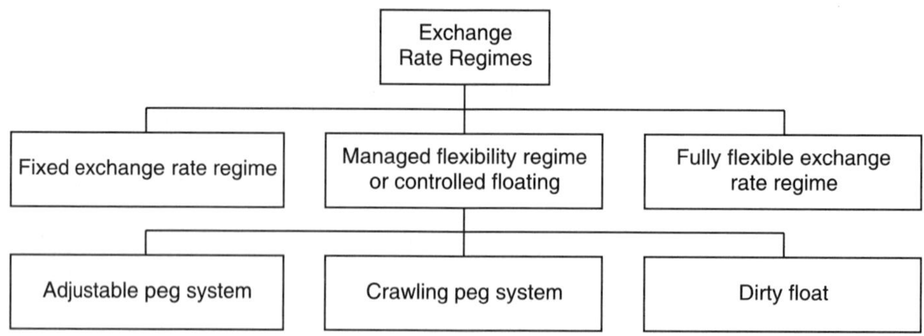

Figure 15.2 Types of Exchange Rate Regimes.

15.3.1 Fully Flexible Exchange Rate Regime

In a fully flexible exchange rate system, the exchange rate is determined by the movements in demand for and supply of domestic currency in the foreign exchange market (or alternatively demand for and supply of foreign exchange in the domestic market). The movements in the demand and supply in turn are dependent on the factors that affect international transactions in goods, services and financial assets as explained as follows:

The demand for domestic currency, say rupee, emerges in the foreign exchange market when foreigners purchase or demand domestically produced goods, services or financial assets. Foreigners surrender their own currency to procure the domestic currency to make payments to the domestic suppliers. The demand for domestically produced goods by foreigners (or the demand for exports of the domestic country) is inversely related with the price that they are required to pay. As the exchange rate appreciates, domestically produced goods become more expensive, and thus, foreigners are required to pay more of foreign currency to procure one unit of domestic currency. Demand for domestically produced goods, hence, declines. As the demand for domestic currency is linked to the demand for domestically produced goods, an appreciation in the exchange rate not only reduces the demand for goods and services but also reduces the demand for domestic currency. Thus, there is a negative relationship between the exchange rate and the demand for the domestic currency, which is shown by a downward sloping demand curve for domestic currency in Figure 15.3.

A shift in the demand curve for domestic currency takes place when variables other than the exchange rate change. For example, an increase in foreign income increases the demand for domestic exports for each given exchange rate, and hence, shifts the demand curve towards right and vice-versa. Similarly, changes in the preference of foreigners in favour of domestically produced goods, reduction in tariff barriers, etc., increase the demand for domestically produced goods, and hence, shift the demand curve for domestic currency towards right. Not only changes in foreign environment affect the demand for domestic currency but also changes in the domestic market can influence the demand for it. For example, an improvement in domestic productivity makes domestically produced goods cheaper, and hence, enhances demand for them, which in turn, shifts the demand curve for domestic currency towards the right. An increase in the export subsidies and a reduction in domestic price level also have a similar impact.

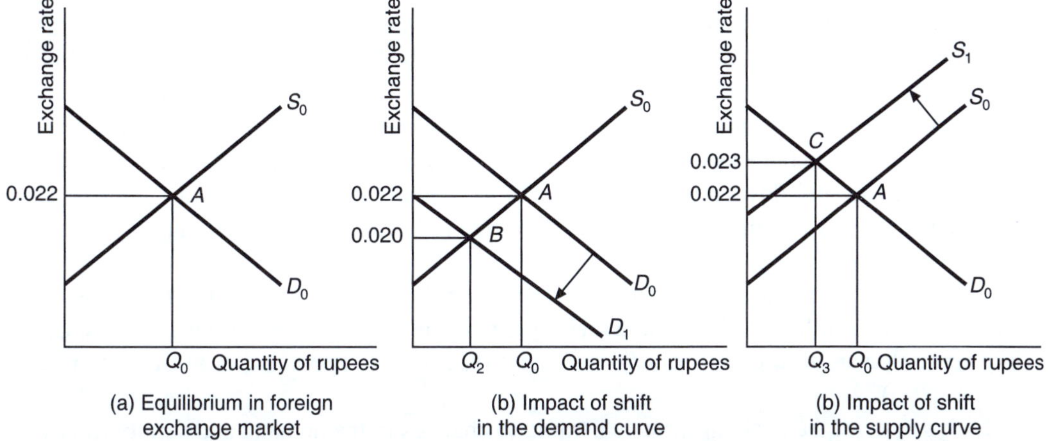

(a) Equilibrium in foreign exchange market (b) Impact of shift in the demand curve (b) Impact of shift in the supply curve

Figure 15.3 Determination of Exchange Rate in Fully Flexible Exchange Rate Regime.

Unlike the demand, the supply of domestic currency in the international market emanates from the demand (or imports) for foreign goods and services and assets by domestic participants (say, Indians). For making payments for imports, the domestic participants surrender domestic currency and purchase foreign currency. As the exchange rate increases, imports become cheaper and demand for imports increases which, in turn, increases the demand for foreign currency or the supply of domestic currency. Thus, there is a positive relationship between exchange rate and imports. This also implies a positive relationship between the exchange rate and the supply of domestic currency, which is shown by an upward sloping supply curve in Figure 15.3.

A shift in the supply curve of the domestic currency takes place when there are changes in the domestic or world economy other than the exchange rate. Changes in the domestic income levels, taste and preferences, tariff and non-tariff barriers are some of the domestic factors that can change the demand for imported commodities, and thereby, shift the supply curve. Similarly, changes in productivity abroad, price level in foreign countries and export subsidy by foreign countries are also some of the factors that can shift the supply curve.

The factors that affect the flow of goods and services, such as productivity, consumer taste and preference, etc., take several years to change. Hence, these affect the exchange rate in the long-run. In the short-run, exchange rate is affected by the flow of financial assets. Financial assets move from one country to another in response to changes in interest rates and also due to expected movements in exchange rates over the maturity period of financial assets.

We can also ascertain the factors affecting the demand for and supply of domestic currency in the international market from the Balance of Payment (BOP) statement. The credit side of the BOP statement indicates the amount of foreign exchange earnings of the domestic country. When a foreign currency arrives in the domestic market, it is exchanged for domestic currency by the domestic participants. Hence, credit side also reflects the demand for domestic currency. On the contrary, the debit side of the BOP statement reflects the amount of foreign exchange payments by the domestic participants. Since to purchase foreign currency domestic agents surrender domestic currency, the debit side also reflects the total supply of domestic currency in the international market.

Given this understanding of the factors affecting the demand for and supply of domestic currency in the international market, we can understand the determination of exchange rate in a fully flexible exchange rate regime diagrammatically. In Figure 15.3, the initial equilibrium exchange rate between the Indian rupee and the US Dollar is ₹1 = $0.022 as indicated by point A (the point where the supply curve of rupee intersects the demand curve for rupee). If some autonomous changes in the economy lead to a decline in the demand for Indian exports the demand curve for rupee will shift down towards left from D_0 to D_1 in Figure 15.3(b). The new demand curve for rupees intersects the supply curve at point B which indicates that the rupee has depreciated in terms of the US Dollar.

On the other hand, an autonomous increase in the demand for imports by the Indians leads to higher demand for the US Dollar, and thereby, more supply of the Indian rupee. This shifts the supply curve upward to the left from S_0 to S_1, and results in an appreciation of the Indian rupee (Figure 15.3(c)).

In this system, the exchange rate is flexible to changes in the demand and supply forces and floats along with them. This market determined system of exchange rate takes into consideration both commodity trade and capital transactions. Hence, it is also known as the **balance of payment theory** of exchange rate determination.

Advantages

1. Self-correcting mechanism: A market determined exchange rate changes along with the demand and supply forces. Therefore, any disequilibrium (deficit or surplus) in the BOP gets corrected automatically without any intervention by the government or the monetary authority, i.e., the central bank. Deficit in the BOP, for example, indicates that the aggregate of debit side entry is higher than the aggregate of credit side entry. It implies that the foreign exchange payments are more than foreign exchange earnings. Alternatively, we can say that the demand for domestic currency is less than its supply. The demand being less than the supply, the exchange rate will decline. The depreciation of the domestic currency, on the one hand, will make exports cheaper, boost the demand for it and improve foreign exchange earnings. On the other hand, it will make imports dearer, will shrink the demand for it, and reduce foreign exchange payments. The appreciation of the domestic currency will continue until foreign exchange earnings are equal to foreign exchange payments and the BOP is brought back to equilibrium. On the contrary, surplus in the BOP results in an appreciation of the exchange rate, which makes the exports expensive and reduces demand for them. At the same time, it makes imports cheaper for the country in surplus and reduces import bill. In the process the surplus declines. The appreciation continues until the surplus is completely wiped out and the BOP is brought back to an equilibrium. Thus, we see that the variations in the exchange rate automatically correct the imbalances in the BOP and keep it in a balance.

2. No speculation: In a flexible exchange rate regime the adjustments in the exchange rate are gradual and reflect the market realities. Hence, any disequilibrium get corrected instantaneously, leaving no scope for speculation about its value.

3. Independence in monetary policy: We will see in Section 15.3.2 that in a fixed exchange rate regime the central bank maintains the exchange rate at a given parity by continuously intervening in forex market either by purchasing or selling foreign currency. When central bank purchases foreign currency from the market it pays in terms of the domestic currency and, hence, money supply in the economy increases. Conversely, when it sells foreign currency, the buyers of foreign currency surrender domestic currency to the central bank leading to a contraction in the money supply. Thus, in the fixed exchange rate system money supply gets affected by exchange rate considerations. Hence, the central bank loses control over money supply and its independence in setting money supply and pursuing monetary policy. In contrast, in a fully flexible exchange rate system, since the exchange rate is determined by the market forces, the central bank does not have to intervene in the foreign exchange market. Hence, money supply does not get influenced by the exchange rate considerations and can be decided independent of exchange rate policy. Thus, the central bank can pursue independent monetary policy. Even the government can pursue independent fiscal policy to formulate it solely in response to domestic issues.

4. Minimization of foreign exchange reserves: As we will see in the next section, to maintain fixed exchange rate, the central bank needs to continuously intervene in the foreign exchange market by either buying or selling foreign currency. The central bank interventions require sufficient reserves of foreign exchange which, however, involve cost. These reserves are like idle cash and do not provide any return to the central bank. The central bank can get higher return if these reserves are invested in earning assets.

In a fully flexible exchange rate regime, no such interventions by the central bank are required. Therefore, there is no need for the central bank to keep large foreign currency reserves. The flexible exchange rate, thus, helps in minimizing foreign exchange reserves. The excess reserves can be invested in assets that are more productive and yield a high return which increase the profitability of the Central Bank.

Disadvantages

1. Volatility in the exchange rate market: In a fully flexible exchange rate system, the exchange rate keeps changing along with the changes in demand and supply reflecting market realities. However, too frequent changes create an uncertainty for traders. A highly volatile exchange rate market, on the one hand, discourages traders from exporting or importing or investing in financial assets, and, on the other hand, encourages speculative activities in the foreign exchange market which may further accentuate fluctuations in it.

2. Lack of discipline: As we will see in Section 15.3.2, in the fixed exchange rate regime continuous interventions by the central government affect money supply and inflation. For example, continuous purchase of foreign currency by the central bank increases money supply and puts inflationary pressures. To contain inflationary pressures, the central bank tries to maintain strict discipline on the monetary policy by ensuring that money supply does not increase from other channels, such as central bank credit to the government or financial institutions. Similarly, the government follows fiscal prudence to check inflation. Thus, fixed exchange rate brings in a greater degree of discipline on monetary and fiscal policies. However, flexible exchange rate does not affect the money supply. Hence, often the government and the monetary authority become lax on fiscal and monetary policy front. The lenient approach, reflected in the form of easy fiscal and monetary policy, often lands up a country in a highly inflationary situation in a flexible exchange rate regime. At times, the situation gets ignored until it turns into a full-blown crisis.

3. Impact of domestic policy on the exchange rate: Though movements in exchange rates do not cause changes in monetary or fiscal policy, the exchange rate is affected by the changes in these policies. For example, easy monetary policy increases the overall price level, makes export dearer, and thus, reduces foreign exchange earnings on the trade account. Easy monetary policy also reduces interest rates, which adversely affect the inflow of foreign capital to the country. Thus, the balance of payment gets affected adversely by the easy monetary policy, which may cause depreciation in the exchange rate. Converse holds true when a tight monetary policy is pursued. Thus, the attempts to pursue independent monetary policy may lead to substantial volatility in the exchange rate market.

15.3.2 Fixed Exchange Rate Regime

Under a **fixed exchange rate regime** the exchange rate is fixed by the central bank, at a pre-announced 'par' value that is changed only occasionally when the existing rate can no longer be defended. Sometimes fixed exchange rate regime takes up a very rigid form such as the Currency Board Arrangement (CBA) (Box 15.2) or dollarization (Box 15.3).

Box 15.2 Currency Board

A **Currency Board Arrangement** (CBA) is the strongest form (next to a full currency union) of fixed exchange rate regime in which the central bank, qua currency board, fixes the exchange rate in terms of some commonly accepted currency (say US $ or Euro). The board is committed to supply or redeem, without limit, its monetary liabilities, which consists of currency in circulation and bank reserves (Section 6.6.1), at the fixed exchange rate. Such a commitment necessitates the currency board to maintain foreign exchange reserves of at least equal to the value of its monetary liabilities, i.e., a one to one ratio between the domestic currency and foreign exchange reserves. Unlike other systems where the foreign exchange reserves simply back up only a fraction of total monetary liability or monetary base of the central bank, in the CBA there is full backing of the monetary liability with the foreign currency reserves. Therefore, an inflow of foreign currency automatically increases the money supply, whereas the outflow of it automatically contracts the money supply. Also, as there is one to one relationship between the monetary base and the foreign exchange reserves, the system never encounters either excess or shortage of demand or supply of domestic currency in the foreign exchange market. Therefore, the official interventions to bring back the value of the domestic currency to the parity level are not required.

The functions of currency board are confined to fixing the exchange rate at a particular level and defending it at that level. The currency board cannot perform other functions of a central bank, such as a lender to the government or lender of the last resort to the financial institutions. Hence, the only channel or source of money supply (Sections 6.6.1 and 6.6.5) in this system is the purchase of foreign currency by the central bank. The other channels such as the central bank credit to the government or central bank credit to financial institutions become dysfunctional because currency board is not permitted to lend to the government or financial institutions. This restricts the power of currency board to influence money supply and via it short-term interest rates. In such a system, the interest rates in the domestic market get aligned with the interest rates of the country to which the domestic currency is anchored to.

The CBA gives credibility to the fixed exchange rate regime. It helps in stabilizing the price level in the economy as money supply is tightly linked with the availability of the anchor currency and does not get influenced by the other factors such as fiscal deficit and health of financial institutions. The exchange rate and price stability boost the confidence of investors in the market, and hence, is expected to promote the growth and development.

For the CBA to be successful, a considerable amount of fiscal discipline is necessitated because the currency board cannot lend to the government. Therefore, funding for the government expenses from this source is not possible. Similarly, soundness of the financial system is equally important as the currency board cannot act as a lender of the last resort unless it has more foreign exchange (FOREX) reserves than required. Financial sector weakness, in the absence of a lender of the last resort, can cause a severe damage to the system by triggering crises. Similarly, structural weaknesses in labour and product markets may cause a problem especially when the system also has the wage and price rigidities. For example, price changes bring an equilibrium between the demand for goods and services and their supply; but if the price is fixed, and there is an excess of demand, the imbalance between the demand and supply will persist which may result in unsatisfied demand and unsatisfied customers. Similarly, in the presence of wage rigidities, excess supply of labour results in persistent unemployment problem and unrest in the system. The CBA may not be able to solve such problems by reducing money supply (thus reducing the demand for goods and services) or increasing money supply (thus, enhancing credit availability and production and creating employment opportunities). Therefore, structural rigidities and weaknesses in the system may prevent self-correcting mechanism to operate. The inability of the CBA to address such problems may lead to a collapse of the system and even the abandoning of it in favour of more flexible exchange rate regime. However, the cost of such switching to other exchange rate systems turns out to be more expensive because when the government is not able to defend the CBA it loses its credibility which leads to a conversion of financial assets denominated in domestic currency into assets denominated in foreign currency and a massive capital out-flight. A large scale withdrawal of capital from domestic financial institutions and other organizations results in a severe shortage of funds which reduces funds for working capital and investment purpose and results in severe contraction in economic activities and a prolonged recession.

The CBA has been experienced by countries like Argentina, Hong Kong, China and many others.

Box 15.3 Dollarization

The fixed exchange rate can even take the form of **unified exchange rate system** widely known as **Dollarization** or now even as **Euroization**. Under this arrangement the country abandons its independent domestic currency in favour of some foreign currency. The price of the domestic currency is permanently set against the foreign currency, say Dollar, or some other strong foreign currency say Euro.

Dollarization eliminates the risk of devaluation, reduces the risk premium and the cost of servicing the public debt. Possibility of speculative attacks and contagion, though not completely eliminated, gets reduced from dollarization. Dollarization also helps in promoting financial integration as well as trade integration, and thus, helps in boosting growth.

However dollarization has its own pitfalls as indicated below:

First, for enacting dollarization, the government is necessitated to withdraw domestic currency from circulation and replace it with another currency. As there is no necessity of printing new notes or currency in the coming period the country going for dollarization loses the income from seigniorage, which can be significant. Under the CBA, the country does not forego income from seigniorage as the domestic currency printed by the domestic government remains the legal tender.

Second, under dollarization the Central Bank cannot act as a lender of the last resort and address and avert banking or financial crises. The CBA, though faces a similar constraint, has more flexibility in this regard if the countries maintain more foreign exchange reserves than required for meeting their monetary liability. However, under dollarization large foreign banks play an important role in the financial system, and therefore, the chances of bank run are minimized.

Third, an exit option is almost absent in dollarization. It is much more difficult to reverse dollarization than to modify or abandon the CBA. It is very difficult to make public accept a new currency and displace the existing strong and convertible foreign currency.

Fourth, in dollarization the cost of overvaluation is also very high. The real devaluation in such economies is possible only through a fall in nominal prices and wages which most often are rigid. Adjustments in wages are often resisted by the workers, and a price fall adversely affects the profitability of business firms, which often sets in recessionary situation in an economy.

In the fixed exchange rate regime, the central bank defends the parity (fixed exchange rate) through interventions in the foreign exchange market.

Often the objective of fixing the exchange rate is to provide stability to it and avoid volatility and uncertainty experienced in the flexible exchange rate regime. Ideally the exchange rate should be fixed at the rate which reflects the market reality such as shown in Figure 15.4(a). However, often the other objectives are also pursued by fixing the exchange rate. For example, a country may aim at boosting its exports or minimizing its imports and improve its balance of payment position. Hence, it may deliberately fix the exchange rate either above the equilibrium level [Figure 15.4(b)] or below the equilibrium level [Figure 15.4(c)].

An overvalued (or appreciated) exchange rate [as indicated in Figure 15.4(b)] keeps the export price higher and import price lower for the domestic participants. By keeping the exchange rate at overvalued level it is expected that the import will be lower and export earnings will be higher. This expectation, however, is based on the assumption that the imports and exports are inelastic in nature (Box 15.4).

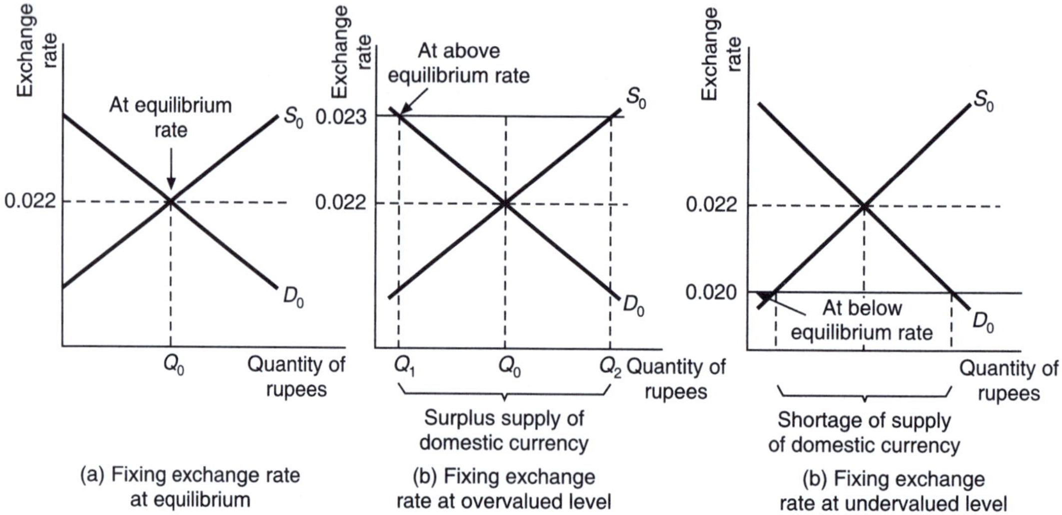

Figure 15.4 Pegging of Exchange Rate in a Fixed Exchange Rate Regime.

Similarly, the country fixing the exchange rate at undervalued level assumes that the demand for imports and exports is elastic. An undervalued exchange rate makes imports dearer for the domestic participants and the exports of domestic commodities cheaper for foreigners. Given the elastic demand for imports, the higher prices of imports are expected to reduce the demand for imported commodities and, thus, help the country in controlling its import bill. At the same time, the elastic demand for exports is expected to boost up the exports earnings by lowering their prices for the foreigners.

The value of the domestic currency can be fixed in terms of gold or some foreign currency or a basket of currency as elaborated hereinafter.

Box 15.4 Exchange Rate Elasticity and the BOP

The impact of fluctuations in the nominal or real value of exchange rate on exports, imports and the BOP depends on the exchange rate elasticity.

Elasticity is a measurement of sensitivity of variable X when there is a variation in variable Y. It shows by what percentage X changes when there is a given percentage change in Y.

This concept is widely used for measuring price elasticity of demand for a commodity, which indicates by what percentage the demand for a commodity changes when there is a given percentage change in the price of the commodity, i.e.,

$$Edz = \frac{\%\Delta Qdz}{\%\Delta Pz} = \frac{\Delta Qdz}{\Delta Pz} \cdot \frac{Pz}{Qdz}$$

where,

Edz = Price elasticity of demand for commodity Z

Qdz = Quantity demanded of commodity Z

Pz = Price of commodity Z

The value of price elasticity of demand is always negative because, price of a commodity and the demand for it are negatively related, i.e., an increase in the price reduces the quantity demanded and vice versa. The demand is considered to be elastic when in absolute terms (i.e., without considering the sign) $Ed > 1$, i.e., when $\%\Delta Qd > \%\Delta Pz$, and inelastic when $Ed < 1$, i.e., when $\%\Delta Qd < \%\Delta Pz$. The concept is useful for managers when they want to assess the impact of price change on the quantity demanded of their products, and hence, on their revenue. Since price and quantity demanded are negatively related, the revenue increases when the price elasticity is greater than one, implying that a one percentage change in the prices results in more than one percentage change in the quantity demanded.

The exchange rate being a price, the exchange rate elasticity is similar to the price elasticity. We can estimate the impact of exchange rate changes on the quantity demanded of exports (and, hence, on the total value of exports) and imports (and, hence, on total value of imports) by estimating the exchange rate elasticity of exports (*Edx*) and imports (*Edm*) respectively as follows:

$$Edx = \frac{\%\Delta Qdx}{\%\Delta Px} = \frac{\Delta Qdx}{\Delta Px} \cdot \frac{Px}{Qdx}$$

$$Edm = \frac{\%\Delta Qdm}{\%\Delta Pm} = \frac{\Delta Qdm}{\Delta Pm} \cdot \frac{Pm}{Qdm}$$

where

Edx = Price elasticity of exports

Edm = Price elasticity of imports

Qdx = Quantity demanded of exports

Qdm = Quantity demanded of imports
Px = Price of exports
Pm = Price of imports

Exports and imports are considered to be elastic when $Edx > 1$ and $Edm > 1$, respectively. On the contrary, exports and imports are inelastic when the values of these elasticities are less than one.

The value of export elasticity helps us in ascertaining the impact of changes in exchange rate on our export earnings, whereas the value of import elasticity helps us in ascertaining the impact on our import bill. To understand the impact of exchange rate elasticity on exports, assume that there is an overvaluation or appreciation of the exchange rate, implying that there is an increase in the price of exported commodities. The increase in the price of exports will reduce the demand for our exported commodities. If the $Edx > 1$, then it will imply that the overvaluation has reduced the demand for our exports more than proportionately, Hence, revenue generated by our country through exports will decline. The converse will hold true if $Ed < 1$. In this case also an overvaluation will reduce the demand for exports but less than proportionately. Hence, the exports earning will increase.

Similarly, from import elasticity we can ascertain the impact of changes in exchange rate on our import bill. To understand the impact of exchange rate elasticity on import bill, again assume that there is an overvaluation of the exchange rate. The appreciation implies that we have to pay less of domestic currency to procure one unit of foreign currency. Hence, in terms of domestic currency, imported commodities become cheaper and demand for them increases. The impact on import bill, however, depends on whether export elasticity of imports is elastic or inelastic; $Edm > 1$ will increase our import bill, whereas $Edm < 1$ will result in decline in it.

Thus, a country can succeed in improving its balance of payment by the overvaluation of exchange rate only if exports and imports are inelastic, i.e., they are highly insensitive to exchange rate changes. Similarly, it will be able to improve its BOP by the undervaluation or depreciation of exchange rate only if exports and imports are elastic, i.e., they are highly sensitive to exchange rate changes.

Fixed Exchange Rate vis-à-vis Gold (Gold Standard)

Under the gold standard, the price of the domestic currency is fixed in terms of gold (e.g., 1 Pound = 2 Gram of gold). The rate of exchange under the gold standard is known as the **mint par** of exchange or the gold par of exchange. To defend this parity, the central bank intervenes in the market by purchasing gold or selling gold. Purchases of gold result in an increase in the amount of domestic currency in circulation, whereas sale of gold reduces it.

Unlike currencies, the availability or supply of gold is limited in the world. The supply of gold cannot be increased as easily as the supply of currencies by printing notes. The limited supply of gold makes it a valuable anchor with which the value of currency can be pegged. Given the limited supply of gold, the amount of currency pegged with gold cannot be increased unless the country discovers more gold or able to import it from the other countries. Difficulties in increasing the supply of gold, helps controlling the money supply and price level. Thus, gold standard provides stability to the value of the currency and helps the country in maintaining confidence in its currency. However, given the limited stock of gold, the system also prevents expansionary monetary policies even when these may be required.

Fixing the value of two different currencies in terms of gold implies fixing the value of these two currencies in terms of each other. Thus, all countries on the gold standard also maintain stable exchange rate with each other's currencies.

Under the gold standard, the imbalances in the balance of payment gets corrected by an inflow (import) and outflow (export) of gold. For example, a deficit in the BOP on the trade account reflects that the country is importing more than it is exporting. This imbalance in the BOP results in a net outflow of gold from the country. As the country begins to loose gold, money supply in the country contracts, and the prices of goods and services start declining. Exports become cheaper. On the contrary, the countries that had been the net recipient of gold face higher money supply and higher inflation rate. This makes imports dearer for the country which was initially in deficit. Thus, changes in the domestic price level due to a net inflow and outflow of gold from trading countries bring in corrections in the BOP imbalances and re-stabilize the equilibrium in the balance of trade with no more net gold flow.

The gold standard was widely in practice in most countries before the First World War. However, the war necessitated a large scale expenditure on arms and ammunitions which required more funds with the government. For the war financing, the hostile nations raised the funds primarily by increasing the money supply. Given the limited stocks of gold with each of these nations, the increase in money supply was not possible under the gold standard. Hence, these countries abandoned it to meet their war financing requirements. Even the Bretton Woods System of Fixed Exchange Rate, discussed in UBE 12.2 was based on the gold standard.

Fixed Exchange Rate vis-à-vis One Currency

The exchange rate can be fixed against a single currency of international repute, known as the **official parity**. To defend the parity, the central bank intervenes by buying and selling the anchor currency whenever the exchange rate deviates from a stated percentage from the fixed (constant) rate.

This system was widely used by most countries even under the Bretton Woods System (UBE 15.2), which expected the countries to fix the value of their currencies in terms of gold.

Fixed Exchange Rate vis-à-vis a Basket

Rather than fixing the value of the domestic currency in terms of a single foreign currency, the rate can even be fixed with reference to the basket of currencies.

A target parity for a basket of currencies was adopted by some countries after 1972. Some countries chose the Special Drawing Rights (SDRs) (Box 15.5), some Euro Currency Units (ECU), while others like India chose a basket of their choice.

UNDERSTANDING BUSINESS ENVIRONMENT

UBE 15.2 The Bretton Woods System of Fixed Exchange Rate

The Bretton Woods System of Fixed Exchange Rate, which ruled the world for almost three decades, is described in this UBE.

The delegates of 44 allied nations gathered in Bretton Woods, Hempshire, for the United Nations Monetary and Financial Conference in July 1944, to draw a plan for rebuilding the II World War devastated nations and to restore trade and financial linkages. The system of exchange rate which emerged from these meetings, is known as the **Bretton Woods system** of fixed exchange rate (Figure 15.5). This system required each member country of the IMF to adopt a monetary policy that maintained the exchange rate of its currency, within a fixed value (parity)—plus or minus one per cent (band), in terms of gold by intervening in foreign exchange markets. Thus, the system provided the advantage of both freely floating and tightly pegged exchange rate regimes.

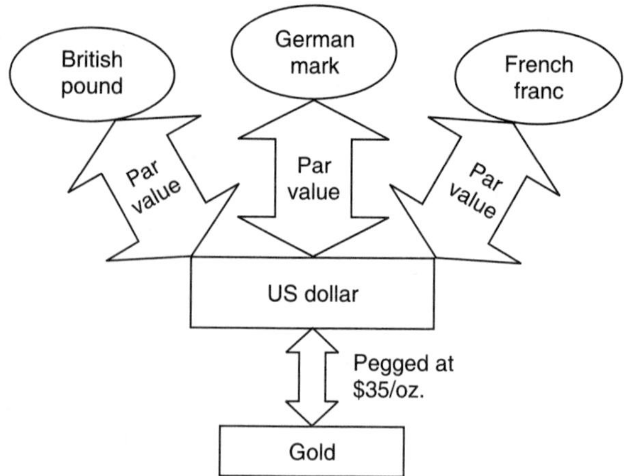

Figure 15.5 Bretton Woods System, 1945 to 1972.

Under this system, the US agreed to link the dollar to gold at the rate of $35 per ounce of gold. Gradually, the US dollar, with highest purchasing power, emerged as the strongest currency. All the European nations that were involved in the World War II were highly in debt. They transferred large amounts of gold into the US, which further contributed to the supremacy of the US and US dollar.

Given the supremacy of the US dollar, the member countries maintained the parity and the reserves in the form of US dollar rather than gold. However, since the US $ was linked with gold, all the currencies linked with the US dollar automatically became convertible into gold (Figure 15.4). The member countries intervened in the foreign exchange market by buying and selling the US dollar whenever the exchange rate deviated from plus or minus 1 per cent band. Under this system, the member countries facing fundamental disequilibrium in the balance of payment could only change their par value with the IMF approval.

However, during the period 1958–1971, the US experienced a persistent deficit in its balance of payment, putting pressure on the value of dollar to depreciate. To prevent the depreciation and to maintain fixed parity with gold, the US financed its BOP deficit by continuous depletion of its gold reserves. By 1963, the US gold reserves declined to such a low level that the stock was merely sufficient to cover the liabilities of foreign central banks. The depletion continued further in the coming period. The crucial turning point came between 1970 and 1971, when gold reserves depleted from 55 per cent to barely 22 per cent of the liabilities of foreign central banks weakening the confidence in the US dollar. The lack of confidence resulted in a massive flight from the dollar which persuaded the US to halt gold convertibility on 15 August 1971, and the system collapsed.

The Group of Ten, in a meeting at the Smithsonian Institute in Washington DC in December 1971, decided to go for a temporary arrangement via which the member countries were allowed to vary their exchange rate within margins of +/– 9/4 per cent after currency realignment with devaluation of dollar to $38/Ounce

However, the Smithsonian agreement could not succeed in bringing in instability in the system. In February 1973, the Bretton Woods currency exchange market closed with the devaluation of the dollar to $ 44/Ounce and reopened in March, in a floating currency regime.

Impact of Fixed Exchange Rate Regime on Domestic Economy

Under the fixed exchange rate regime, imbalances in the BOP rather than getting self-corrected are adjusted through variations in the reserve assets or foreign currency reserves that the central bank of a country maintains in terms of some foreign currency of importance and international reputation, gold and/or the SDRs (Box 15.5 and Box 15.6). The variations in reserve assets, in turn, affect the money supply, price level, inflation rate and other macroeconomic variables.

Box 15.5 Reserve Adequacy

Foreign exchange reserves, as defined by the IMF, are "external assets that are readily available to and controlled by monetary authorities for direct financing of external payment imbalances, for indirectly regulating the magnitudes of such imbalances through intervention in exchange markets to affect the currency exchange rate, and/or for other purposes" (IMF Balance of Payments Manual, 5th edition).

Central banks maintain reserves for the following reasons:

- First, reserves are maintained to stabilize the value of the domestic currency in the international market. Central banks sell foreign currency, from its reserves, to prevent depreciation of the domestic currency, whereas they purchase foreign currency to prevent sharp appreciation in it.
- Second, at the time of crisis often a massive out flight of capital takes place, leaving financial institutions and other organizations with lack of funds and shortage of liquidity. If enough liquidity is not provided in such a situation on time, then sharp contraction in production and other economic activities becomes unavoidable. To prevent their countries slipping into a sharp slowdown or recession, central banks ensure liquidity by depleting their foreign exchange reserves. Thus, sufficient reserves ensure liquidity at the time of crisis.
- Third, sufficient level of reserves indicates that the country is capable enough of meeting its external obligations like principal and interest payment on borrowed amount and ensures confidence of the outside world and credit rating agencies in its functioning. Thus, an adequate level of foreign exchange reserves helps in getting a better credit rating for the country, which promotes foreign capital inflows.

However, these reserves also have associated costs for central banks as follows:

Opportunity cost: Reserves assets are non-earning assets as they do not provide any return to central banks. Central banks can earn certain return if they invest their reserve funds in earning assets. Thus, by maintaining reserve assets, central banks forego some return. Hence, these assets have an opportunity cost.

Sterilization cost: Central bank interventions in the foreign exchange market impact the money supply; the purchase of foreign currency increases money supply, whereas the sell reduces it. To mitigate the impact of foreign exchange purchases and sales on money supply, inflation and other economic variables, sterilization measures, often in the form of open market operations, are pursued. The cost of such sterilizations turns out to be substantial if the interest rate on domestic borrowing exceeds the interest rate on reserves. For example, if the central bank decides to absorb excess liquidity from the market, arising from the purchase of foreign currency, by selling government securities, then more of government securities can be sold in the market only by increasing interest rate on them. Since reserves mostly are non-earning assets, and the government securities carry interest, the cost of sterilization measures turns out to be positive.

In addition, the conduct of sterilization measures is associated with some carrying cost. To pursue open market operations to sterilize the impact of foreign exchange reserves, central banks need to maintain enough of government and other approved securities. Thus, central bank funds get locked up in such securities resulting in carrying cost.

Sterilization is also associated with some indirect costs. By affecting the money supply and inflation rate, it affects the real exchange rate and, thus, the balance of payment.

Balance sheet risk: Changes in the value of domestic currency affect the central bank balance sheet by affecting the value of reserves in domestic currency. Appreciation, for example, leads to a decline in the value of reserves in terms of domestic currency.

Other costs: There are some other costs as well. For example, the build-up of reserves through external debt (rather than non-debt creating flows) results in interest payment on these debts, and thus, imposes additional costs on central banks.

The build-up of foreign exchange reserves as entails benefits as well as costs, the determination of an adequate level of foreign exchange reserve is an issue of debate among policy makers and economists. Since there is no consensus on the amount of adequate reserves, variety of measures are suggested to central banks for identifying an adequate level of foreign exchange reserves. These measures are outlined as follows:

Traditional Measures of Reserve Adequacy

Certain traditional indicators used for determining the adequate level of reserves for an economy are:

Import adequacy: Foreign currency is required for making payments of import bills. The **import adequacy** measure addresses this aspect of foreign transactions and indicates that the reserves should be sufficient enough to meet the import bill requirement of certain months to be considered to be adequate. The broad rule-of-thumb for reserve adequacy followed by the IMF is that the reserves should be sufficient enough to pay for about three to four months of imports.

This traditional measure of reserve adequacy focuses on the current account. For economies with little or no access to financial and private capital markets, this measure remains on focus. However, for economies with large capital flows this criterion is not sufficient.

Monetary adequacy: Capital can be withdrawn from a country not only by the foreigners but also by the domestic participants. Domestic participants, when they loose confidence in domestic monetary and fiscal policies, convert their domestic currency assets into foreign currency denominated assets. Thus, the aggregate money stock reflects the extent of resident-based capital flight that can take place in a time of crisis. The monetary adequacy indicators of reserves, i.e., the ratio of reserves to broad money or the ratio of reserves to monetary base, provide a useful indicator of crisis in those economies that have a fixed exchange rate regime, unstable demand for money and a weak banking system.

These measures of reserve adequacy have been in use for many decades in countries with fixed exchange rate regime, especially under the gold standard, and had gained acceptance well before the import-based measure came into the common use. In a very strict form of fixed exchange rate regime such as the CBA, this ratio is 100 per cent (i.e., there is one to one ratio between domestic money supply and foreign exchange reserves). Countries with more flexible exchange rate regimes require to maintain reserves equals roughly 5 to 20 per cent of M_2 for boosting the confidence in the value of domestic currency and reduce the risk of capital flight by domestic participants.

However, for countries where money demand is stable and confidence in the domestic currency is high, the reserve over money ratio tends to be lower and it is not a good predictor of capital flight. These measures also do not capture comprehensively the potential for domestic capital flight as they simply consider the possibility of conversion of domestic currency into foreign currency and assets and neglect the possibility of resident shifting out of other domestic assets, such as short-term debt of public sector, into foreign assets. The capital flight in such a situation will be much larger, and higher reserves would be required to maintain than that indicated by monetary adequacy.

Debt adequacy: The reserves should be sufficient enough to meet the obligations of external debt payment, particularly short-term debt liabilities by remaining maturities. **Debt adequacy**, thus, is measured by the ratios of reserves to total external debt and short-term debt.

Short-term debt is the main source of capital outflow. As the short-term capital flows are highly volatile, the economies open to capital flows need to constantly keep a watch on the reserves to short-term debt. In the absence of external current account deficit (implying that no reserves are required to meet import bill or other current account transactions) or overvalued exchange rate (which often causes current account deficit), for countries with sizable, but uncertain private capital flows the reserves to short-term external debt by remaining maturity of 1 is considered to be sufficient for crisis prevention. However, presence of significant external current account deficit (or significant overvalued exchange rate) and short-term liabilities requires significantly higher reserves than that indicated by debt adequacy indicators.

New (Post Asia Crisis) Measures of Reserve Adequacy

Tremendous increase in cross-border capital flows, with lagging trade volume under managed float in post Asia crisis, also created a possibility of their large scale withdrawal. To prevent the possibility of a crisis occurring from such an event, it became pertinent to build up **confidence reserve**, i.e., the build up of reserves to maintain the confidence in the domestic economy. However, there is a disagreement on the adequate amount of confidence. Hence, again some new measures of reserve adequacy have surfaced as outlined as follows:

Debt servicing adequacy: The **debt servicing adequacy** suggests that to prevent crises, countries should manage their external assets and liabilities in such a way that they become capable of living without the foreign borrowing for upto one year, i.e., the foreign exchange reserves should exceed schedule amortization. Alternatively, countries should maintain sufficient reserves for debt servicing (interest + repayments) for one year without any new net borrowing. This measure is known as the **Guidotti Rule**.

Liquidity at risk measures: We operate under uncertain environment. Therefore, we cannot ascertain very accurately the extent of capital flight which can take place in an upcoming period. Since there are different possibilities of capital out flight, and hence, of liquidity shortage, the **liquidity at risk** measure suggests that to assess the liquidity at risk, a country's external liquidity position should be calculated taking into account the full set of external liabilities and assets over a wide range of possible outcomes for relevant financial variables such as exchange rate, commodity prices, and credit spreads. An appropriate level of reserve is the one that provides sufficient external liquidity for one year without new borrowing with high probability (say 95 per cent of the time). This is known as the **Greenspan Rule**.

Box 15.6 Special Drawing Rights

The Special Drawing Rights (SDR), created by the IMF in 1969 to support the Bretton Woods fixed exchange rate system (UBE 15.2) as supplement to two reserve assets—gold and the US Dollar, are now primarily used as a unit of account of the IMF and some other international organizations. It is neither a currency nor a claim on the IMF, but represents a potential claim on the currencies of the IMF members.

The value of the SDR was initially defined in terms of gold. However, after the collapse of the Bretton Woods system in 1973, the value of the SDR is defined in terms of basket of currencies. The composition of basket is reviewed every five years in the light of evolving trade and financial system. At present, as per the revision in January 2011, this basket consists of the Euro, Pound Sterling, Japanese Yen and United States Dollar. The weights to each of the currencies in the basket are determined on the basis of the value of the exports of goods and services and the amount of reserves denominated in the respective currencies which were held by the member countries of the IMF. The value of the SDR in terms of the US dollar, posted on the IMF's website, is determined daily on the basis of the exchange rates of the currencies making up the basket in terms of US $, as quoted at noon at the London market (As on 31/5/2013, US $1 = SDR 0.667215 and SDR1 = US $1.498767).

The SDRs are allocated to members by the IMF in proportion to their IMF quotas. These are costless assets as these do not earn any interest. However, the excess holding of SDR earns interest and the members are also required to pay interest if their holding of the SDRs fall short of their allocated quotas. The SDR interest rate is determined weekly as a weighted average of representative interest rates on short-term debt in money markets of the SDR basket currencies.

The process through which the parity is defended in the fixed exchange rate regime is explained hereinafter.

In Figure 15.6, the initial demand curve for and supply curve of domestic currency, say rupees, in the foreign exchange market are D_0 and S_0, respectively. The exchange rate is fixed at 0.022, which is also an equilibrium rate that matches the demand for domestic currency with the supply of domestic currency in the international market. An autonomous increase in the demand for domestically produced commodities shifts the demand curve for rupee to D_1 [Figure 15.6(a)]. At the fixed exchange rate there is more demand for rupees than the supply. Left to the market forces, this shortage of rupees would have been self-corrected by the variations (appreciation in this case) in the exchange rate. However, the exchange rate is fixed. To defend this parity, the central bank intervenes in the market by artificially creating demand for foreign currency; it purchases foreign currency, builds up foreign exchange reserves and supplies more of the domestic currency until the supply curve of rupee shifts to S_1. The supply of more currency though is able to defend the fixed parity, affects the domestic economy and the BOP through two routes.

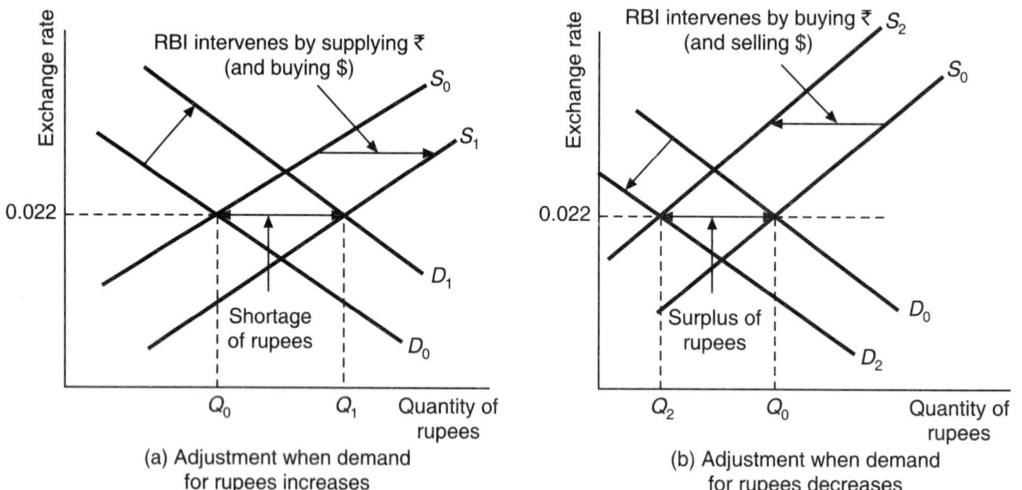

Figure 15.6 Adjustments in Fixed Exchange Rate Regime.

First, the increase in the supply of domestic currency increases the monetary base and, through money multiplier, affects the total money supply. Without the matching supply of goods and services, the increase in the money supply increases the overall price level and inflation rate.

Higher prices of domestically produced goods make exports uncompetitive in the international market which worsens the trade balance and the current account of the BOP. The demand for rupee declines and the pressure on the rupee to appreciate comes down. The higher money supply also increases the growth of output, and thus, enhances the demand for imports, which further eases the pressure on rupee to appreciate.

Second, changes in the money supply affect not only the price and the output, but also the interest rate. An increase in the money supply increases the credit availability, and thus, reduces the interest rates. A lowering of the domestic interest rates discourages the inflow of foreign capital. As a result, the supply of foreign currency and the demand for domestic currency go down.

Thus, the central bank interventions, through the purchase of foreign exchange and the sale of domestic currency in the foreign exchange market, restore the BOP through the current account as well as the capital account balance.

On the other hand, an autonomous decline in the foreign demand for Indian commodities shifts the demand curve for rupee downward towards the left to D_2 [Figure 15.6(b)], which results in a surplus of rupee. To defend the exchange rate parity, the central bank decumulates its foreign exchange reserves, increases the supply of foreign currency, and absorbs the excess domestic currency from the foreign exchange market by artificially creating demand for it until the supply curve of rupee shifts upward to S_2.

A reduction in the supply of domestic currency, as a result of the central bank intervention, reduces the price level, which, on the one hand, improves the export competitiveness and, on the other, reduces the demand for imported goods. As a result, there is an improvement in the balance of trade and the current account.

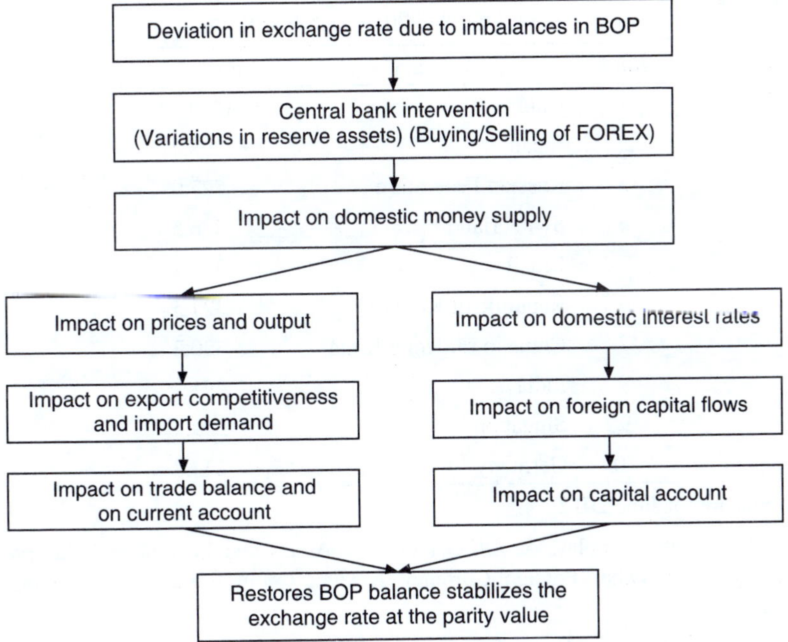

Figure 15.7 Macroeconomic Adjustments and Exchange Rate Stabilization in a Fixed Exchange Rate Regime.

A reduction in the money supply also increases the overall interest rate, which attracts more capital inflow in the country. The capital account of the BOP improves and the supply of foreign exchange or demand for domestic currency increases. The pressure on the depreciation of the domestic currency, as a consequence, eases.

Thus, in the fixed exchange rate regime, the interventions in the foreign exchange market by the central bank affect not only its reserves of foreign currency but also have economy-wide implications, which help in restoring the BOP imbalances (Figure 15.7) and mitigates the pressures on the exchange rate to deviate from its fixed parity.

UNDERSTANDING BUSINESS ENVIRONEMNT

UBE 15.3 Are there Excess Reserves in Developing and Newly Industrialized Asia?

To maintain the fixed exchange rate regime, or to moderate large fluctuations in the exchange rate, central banks often maintain large reserves. However, such reserves have associated costs. This UBE reveals that many Asian countries are holding reserves far in excess and would be better off by actively investing them in earning assets.

Central banks, to ensure against the currency crises and support the value of their domestic currency, often maintain large reserves of foreign exchange.

The Asian financial crisis of 1997–98 made it believe that larger the amount of the foreign exchange reserves, the better it is. This belief is reflected in the fact that six out of the top ten reserve holders in 2013 were the developing and newly industrialized Asian countries (Table 15.2).

Table 15.2 Top Ten Reserve Holders (As on February 2013) (US $ million)

Rank	*Country*	*Reserves*
1	China	3240.0*
2	Japan	1298.4
3	Russian Federation	527.0
4	Switzerland	526.5
5	Brazil	373.7
6	Republic of Korea	327.5
7	China, p.r. : Hong Kong	320.3
8	India	291.7
9	Singapore	259.1
10	Germany	244.8

*Figures for China are for June 2012.

Source: IMF (2013), Data Template on Official Reserve Assets and International Reserves and Foreign Currency Liquidity (item: Other Foreign Currency Assets), (online) www.imf.org/external/np/sta/ir/IR Process Web/topic.aspx.

For China: State Administration of Foreign Exchange (2013), Monthly Foreign Exchange Reserves, (Online) www.safe.gov.cn.

It has been argued that reserve levels in many Asian countries are far in excess of most of the benchmarks of reserve adequacy (Table 15.3).

Considering the informal tests, based on widely used rules of thumb (as indicated in Table 15.3), and the formal analysis, based on econometric techniques carried out by Park and Estrada (2009), it can be concluded that the developing and newly industrialized Asian countries have substantial excess reserves.

Green and Tongerson (2007) estimated costs of holding excess reserves and argued that the opportunity cost (foregone return) associated with the excess reserves are large and the net marginal return to additional reserves is low.

Park and Estrada (2009), supporting Green and Tongerson (2007), also suggest that the developing Asia would be better off investing those reserves more actively to maximize risk-adjusted returns (only after they have acquired sufficient institutional capacity to do so). However, citing the example of attack on Korean currency and stock market in 2008, inspite of comfortable level of reserve as per the conventional tests, they indicate that the conventional measures of reserve adequacy are not sufficient to guide the policy makers, and hence, there is a need to develop a more sophisticated approach (such as contingency based approach) for measuring reserve adequacy (as discussed in Box 15.5).

Table 15.3 Developing and Newly Industrialized Asia: Reserve Adequacy Ratios (As on 31 December 2011)

Rank	*Country*	*Reserves (exc gold) (billion US$)*	*Reserves/months of imports*	*Reserves/short-term debt (%)*	*Reserves/M (%)2*
1	China	3,212.6	22.1	6.7	23.8
2	Taiwan	390.6	16.7	na	36.5
3	India	297.9	8.0	3.8	21.6
4	South Korea	306.4	7.0	2.3	20.1
5	Hong Kong	285.4	7.1	0.4	27.5
6	Singapore	237.8	12.0	na	69.8
7	Thailand	175.1	12.0	3.9	40.9
8	Malaysia	133.6	7.6	3.1	35.0
9	Indonesia	110.1	7.4	2.9	34.7
10	Philippines	75.3	10.8	10.8	72.1
	Benchmark		3.00	1.00	5.20

Source: Computed on the basis of data available from ADB (2013), Statistical Data Base System (SDBS), (Online) https://sdbs.adb.org/sdbs/index.jsp, as on 20/5/13 and World Bank (2013), Data, (online) http://data.worldbank.org/indicator/DT.DOD.DSTC.CD, as on 20/5/2013.

References

Green, R. and Torgerson, T. (2007), Are High Foreign Exchange Reserves in Emerging Markets a Blessing or a Burden? Department of the Treasury, Occasional Paper No. 6, March, Office of International Affairs, US.

Park, D. and Estrada, G.B. (2009), Are Developing Asia's Foreign Exchange Reserves Excessive? An Empirical Examination, ADB Working Paper, No. 170, August.

Advantages

Fixed exchange rate system has the following advantages:

1. Stability in exchange rate: The fixed exchange rate system creates certainty about the exchange rate. Traders know exactly how much of the domestic currency they would receive when they export a commodity or would be required to pay when they import it. They are also sure of the value of their assets denominated in foreign currency. This boosts the confidence of traders and investors in carrying out the transactions that require a foreign currency, and thus, promotes international linkages through trade and capital flows.

The fixed exchange rate regime stabilizes the value of the exchange rate to a given parity which helps in curbing speculative activities in the foreign exchange market to a large extent.

2. Large degree of discipline in policies: The fixed exchange rate system requires prudential fiscal and monetary policies so that these do not become the cause of imbalances in the balance of payment of the country. Profligacy in monetary and fiscal front causes severe imbalances in the BOP, imposes a heavy cost on the economy, and has a potential to destabilize the economy. For example, high government expenditure financed from central bank borrowing results in higher inflation and real appreciation of the domestic currency, which reduces export competitiveness and increases current account and the overall BOP deficit. The persistence deficit financed from foreign exchange reserves results in the depletion of foreign exchange reserves and lowers the credibility of the country in the international market. The threat of losing credibility imposes discipline on domestic economic policies. The government is restrained from excessive borrowing from the central bank to prevent inflationary pressures in the economy or imbalances in the BOP. The central bank is also restrained from boosting up or controlling the economy through very easy or tight monetary policy.

Disadvantages

Fixed exchange rate system also has certain disadvantages as follows:

1. Persistent imbalances in the BOP and destabilizing forces: The fixed exchange rate regime, in which the exchange rate is set without considering market realities, can cause serious problems. It can persistently result in imbalances in the balance of payment, causing continuous accumulation or decumulation in the foreign exchange reserves of the central bank and continuous inflation or deflation in the domestic market. Thus, an incorrectly set exchange rate has a potential to destabilize the macroeconomy.

2. No independence in monetary policy: The central bank loses its autonomy in the conduct of monetary policy in the fixed exchange rate regime. Monetary (as well as fiscal) policies in such a regime are often guided by the exchange rate considerations. The central bank cannot regulate the money supply in concurrence with the domestic growth and stabilization requirements. For example, the growth rate improvements demand easing of interest rates in a developing economy or in an economy trying to recover from a recession. However, the central bank cannot go for an expansion of money supply because that would have an adverse impact on the capital inflows, the BOP and the value of the exchange rate. Similarly, in a highly inflationary situation, the need is to control inflation by pursuing tight monetary policy, which contracts money supply. However, this increases interest rate and enhances the inflow of foreign capital. The consequent appreciation in the exchange rate necessitates central bank interventions to maintain the parity.

3. Speculations: Serious imbalances in the BOP and large deviations of the fixed exchange rate from the rate supported by the market forces may even encourage speculative activities in the foreign exchange market and further jeopardize the macroeconomic stability of the country.

Persistent current account deficit, for example, reflects that the exchange rate is fixed at an overvalued level. This, undermining the central bank's ability to support the rate, either from its reserve balances or through borrowing, generates an expectation of devaluation of the domestic currency. Speculators, anticipating such a move, may postpone their exports and prepone imports, thus, further worsening the current account. Speculators may even convert their domestic currency into foreign currencies or invest in foreign assets with the expectation of benefitting later when the domestic currency gets devalued or the fixed exchange rate regime is abandoned. This adversely affects the BOP through accentuated imbalances in the capital account. The central bank, under severe speculative pressures may run out of its foreign exchange reserves and ultimately devalue the currency or even abandon the fixed exchange rate system.

Persistent current account surpluses in the BOP, reflecting undervalued domestic currency, on the contrary, lead to continuous build-up of foreign exchange reserves which are potentially inflationary. Such a situation generates expectation of revaluation of the domestic currency in the coming period. Speculators, anticipating such a move, may postpone their imports and prepone exports, further increasing the current account surpluses. At the same time, there would be a higher capital inflows leading to surpluses in the capital account as well. Continuous inflationary pressures and continuous surplus on the current and capital account may necessitate a revaluation of the domestic currency.

4. Large amount of foreign exchange reserves: The central bank requires to maintain sufficient forex reserves to maintain the fixed parity in the fixed exchange rate regime. But, these reserves have associated cost as detailed in Box 15.5.

Continuous accumulation or decumulation of foreign exchange reserves to stabilize the exchange rate value may expose the country to continuous inflation or deflation. In the event of insufficient foreign exchange reserves it also poses threat to the macroeconomic stability or currency crisis.

To overcome the above problems associated with the fixed exchange rate and, at the same time, to enjoy the benefits of the fixed exchange rate regime, central banks often address the problem either by re-fixing the value of the domestic currency or by sterilizing the impact of changes in the foreign exchange reserves on the money supply through sterilized interventions described as follows:

Revaluation–Devaluation of the Domestic Currency

Persistent current account deficit or surplus reflects that the value of the domestic currency is set at a level which is deviating far from the level that reflects the market reality. In such situations, one way to stabilize the value of the domestic currency, in terms of foreign currency, is by refixing it.

An overvalued exchange rate results in a persistent current account deficit. Therefore, supporting this overvalued exchange rate strains the foreign exchange reserves of the central bank. In such a situation, to prevent further decumulation of foreign exchange reserves, the central bank can devalue the domestic currency. A devaluation of the domestic currency is expected to correct the current account deficit by encouraging an inflow of foreign exchange (as exports and investment in domestic assets become cheaper for foreigners) and discouraging an outflow of foreign currency (as imports and investment in foreign assets become dearer for the domestic participants) under the assumption that the demand for the two is elastic enough to bring about the desirable changes in the BOP.

On the other hand, the undervalued exchange rate can cause persistent current account surplus. To defend the undervalued exchange rate, the central bank continuously purchases foreign currency from the market which results in continuous accumulation of foreign exchange reserves. However, a continuous build-up of foreign exchange reserves exposes the country to severe inflationary pressures. To stabilize the economy, the central bank can revalue the domestic currency which corrects the imbalances in the BOP by making exports and purchases of the domestic assets dearer for the foreigners (which discourages an inflow of foreign currency), and imports and purchases of foreign assets cheaper for the domestic participants (which increases an outflow of foreign currency).

The revaluation/devaluation reduces the need for central bank interventions in the currency market. However, for the revaluation and devaluation to have the desired impact on the economy and the BOP it is essential that certain conditions are met. These conditions are as follows:

First, the revaluation or devaluation needs to be real rather than nominal. The real competitiveness comes not from nominal changes in the currency value but requires real changes. Given the nominal revaluation/devaluation the real changes depends on the price level. Hence, price stability is important when the country is trying to fix the problem of surplus or deficit on the BOP by nominal revaluation or devaluation.

Second, the export and import need to be elastic enough to the changes in the exchange rate resulting from the devaluation and revaluation to bring about the desirable changes in the BOP and the economy. In the presence of inelastic demand for exports and imports the devaluation or revaluation, rather than correcting the imbalances in the BOP, would further accentuate the problem and destabilize the economy.

Third, the impact of refixing of the exchange rate on the BOP and the economy may not be immediate and may take longer time than required. Refixing of the exchange rate though changes the prices of exports and imports instantaneously, the impact on the volume is with a lag.

Fourth, it is also essential that the country going for a revaluation or devaluation of the domestic currency prevents speculative attacks. In the case of serious imbalances in the BOP, the currency becomes subject to speculative attacks. The devaluation, particularly, triggers a speculation of further devaluation and creates uncertainty in the currency market which may result in a collapse of the system. The problem of revaluation may not be that serious, but it may lead to other types of problems. For example, for a country experiencing high growth rate through exports in response to an undervalued currency, the revaluation slows down the economic growth. Therefore, countries like China, pursuing export led growth, resist revaluation of their currencies inspite of persistent surpluses on their BOP.

Sterilized Interventions

An attempt to stabilize the value of the domestic currency by the central bank, under the fixed exchange rate regime, results in a sale or purchase of foreign currency. However, whenever the central bank purchases foreign currency it has to make payment in terms of domestic currency. The converse holds true whenever the central bank sells foreign currency. Therefore, such interventions affect the monetary base and, through money multiplier, the total money supply in the economy which leads to changes in the overall price level, inflation rate and other economic variables. To counteract the impact of its interventions in the foreign exchange market on the money supply, inflation and other economic variables, the central bank pursues **sterilized interventions** as follows:

1. Sterilizing the impact of heavy inflows: In the case of heavy inflow of foreign currency, resulting in a build-up of foreign exchange reserves and the increase in money supply, the central bank sterilizes the impact by pursuing tight monetary policies. These can take the form of (i) open market sale of government securities, (ii) increase in the policy rate, i.e., bank rate, repo/reverse repo rate, and (iii) impounding of bank reserves through an increase in the CRR.

2. Sterilizing the impact of heavy outflows: On the contrary, the impact of a heavy outflow of foreign currency, resulting in a sharp depletion in foreign exchange reserves, and consequently, a sharp reduction in the money supply, is sterilized through pursuing an easy monetary policy. This can take the form of (i) open market purchase of government securities, (ii) reduction in the policy rate, i.e., bank rate, repo/reverse repo rate, and (iii) releasing of bank reserves through a reduction in the CRR.

Limitations of sterilization

However, sterilization also has its limit. Any of the methods adopted as **sterilization measure** has the associated **sterilization cost**. For example, to carry out sterilization through open market operations, the central bank has to maintain large stock of government securities in its own account. Thus, its funds get locked up in such securities. Similarly, when sterilization is carried out through raising the CRR, the funds of commercial banks get locked up in non–earning assets and they end up paying the cost of sterilization.

15.3.3 Managed Flexibility or Controlled Floating Regime

Both fixed and flexible regimes have their own advantages and disadvantages. The fixed exchange rate though creates conducive environment by generating certainty regarding the exchange rate, it is at the cost of loosing autonomy in pursuing macroeconomic policies. Thus, it makes the country susceptible to macroeconomic crises. On the contrary, the flexible exchange rate though reflects the market reality, it may also result in large volatility and uncertainty in the environment. Therefore, to have the benefits of both the regimes, and at the same time to avoid the adverse consequences of them, many countries, rather than pursuing purely the fully flexible exchange rate regime or the tightly fixed exchange rate regime, are pursuing a mix of these two types of regimes, known as managed flexibility regime.

The **managed flexibility regime** comprises characteristics of both the fixed exchange rate regime and the flexible exchange rate regime. Under this regime, the exchange rate is declared either as fixed or flexible. When it is kept as fixed, the monetary authority reserves the right of changing it periodically depending on the emerging economic scenario and evolving market realities. Alternatively, when the exchange rate is kept flexible, the monetary authority intervenes in the market whenever a large deviation from the desired level of exchange rate occurs.

Classification of Systems under the Managed Flexibility Regime

Depending on what mix of flexible and fixed exchange rate regimes is pursued, broadly, three different systems of managed flexibility regime are distinguished as adjustable peg system, crawling peg system and dirty float. These systems are described as follows:

1. Adjustable peg system: The country sticks to the fixed exchange rate until its foreign exchange reserve position permits under the **adjustable peg system**. Once the foreign exchange reserves are exhausted or get accumulated to a very high level, the country moves to another equilibrium exchange rate by resorting to a devaluation or revaluation of the domestic currency. Sometimes, such a system leads to a large adjustments in the exchange rate value.

2. Crawling peg system: The adjustments are made in the rate of exchange in the light of changing demand and supply conditions under the **crawling peg system**. The system assumes that the large devaluations at long intervals should be avoided. Therefore, the adjustments in the exchange rate are made at regular intervals according to the set of indicators or the judgment of the monetary authority. Some of the important parameters that are considered are the differences in inflation rate in the domestic country vis-a-vis foreign countries, level of reserve assets or foreign exchange reserves, growth of money supply, the current actual market exchange rate relative to the central par value of the pegged rate. Like the adjustable peg system, the crawling peg system is also closer to the fixed exchange rate regime.

Some Latin American countries have adopted this type of system whereby the official parity is revised frequently. Often, inflation and balance of payments data are built into the formula used for revising the rate.

3. Dirty float: The exchange rate is declared to be market determined in the dirty float system. However, the central bank pursues some unofficial target for the exchange rate and seeks to have some stabilizing influence on it without clearly announcing it to the public. As the central bank officially does not make it public that it has some desirable level of exchange rate for the domestic currency and still tries to regulate it by frequent interventions, this system of flexible exchange rate regime is known as the **dirty float**.

4. Clean float: Under the **clean float** system the exchange rate is market determined, but contrary to the dirty float system, the central bank does not have any desirable exchange rate though it may intervene in the market to avoid large destabilizing fluctuations in the exchange rate threatening the macroeconomic stability of the country. Unlike the adjustable peg and crawling peg systems, dirty float and clean float systems are closer to the flexible exchange rate regime.

Advantages and Disadvantages of Managed Flexibility Regime

Under the managed flexibility regime though the uncertainty regarding the exchange rate is not completely eliminated it gets reduced substantially. At the same time, it avoids large changes in the exchange rate which reduces the possibility of severe speculative attacks on the currency. Thus, it creates conducive environment for the traders and the business firms. However, the implications for the economy of the central bank interventions to stabilize the exchange rate remain.

Different regimes have their own advantages and disadvantages. The regime which is most suitable for a country depends on its economic structure and objectives. Changes in the objectives and the structure necessitate changes in the exchange rate. However, a move from one regime to another requires adjustments in legal and policy framework (UBE 15.6), price stabilization, strengthening of the financial sector, improvement in productivity and overall enabling environment for the new regime to be successful. UBE 15.4 describes the experiences of three countries that switched to flexible exchange rate regime.

UNDERSTANDING BUSINESS ENVIRONMENT

UBE 15.4 How did Chile, India, and Brazil Learn to Float?

Though flexible exchange rate regime causes volatility, the countries planning to adopt such a regime can safely do so by improving their monetary and financial policy framework as described in this UBE.

Several emerging market countries moved to greater exchange rate flexibility over the past decade, despite the potential costs of exchange rate fluctuations in terms of output and inflation volatility, and unfavourable balance sheet and debt-service effects (see, for example, Calvo and Reinhart, 2002; Hausmann, Panizza, and Stein, 2001). Recent work has emphasized that countries can "learn to float" by improving monetary and financial policy frameworks, which directly addresses the key vulnerabilities (Rogoff and others, 2004). For example, an independent Central Bank committed to price stability may be able to stabilize inflation expectations, and thus reduce the pass-through of exchange rate changes to prices. Similarly, strong prudential regulations can moderate the balance sheet mismatches in the financial and corporate sectors. This segment illustrates these points by examining the experiences of three countries—Chile, India, and Brazil, that moved to greater exchange rate flexibility during the 1990s. These three case studies were selected because they offer a range of experiences across regions, types of transitions, and evolution of policy frameworks.

Chile

Chile made a transition from a crawling band to a free float in September 1999, having significantly enhanced its monetary and financial policy frameworks over the previous decade (see Kalter and others, 2004; Duttagupta, Fernández, and Karacadag, 2004; Morandé, 2001; and Ariyoshi and others, 2000). After gaining full independence in 1989, the central bank started anchoring inflation expectations by publishing short-term inflation targets and over the time built a reputation for an anti-inflationary bias. In 1998, the central bank further shifted its policy framework towards influencing expectations by setting the rate of crawl for the Peso at expected inflation. When the crawling band was abolished in 1999, the central bank adopted a full-fledged inflation targeting framework, making price stability its only monetary policy objective.

During the 1990s, the crawling band for the Peso was widened several times and the central parity adjusted in response to strong capital inflows. To dampen pressures for exchange rate appreciation, Chile maintained restrictions on the capital account, mainly in the form of unremunerated reserve requirements on certain financial inflows (1991–98). Fluctuations of the exchange rate within the crawling band increased incentives for the deepening of forward and futures markets in foreign exchange, which helped to limit the impact of currency fluctuations on the real sector.

Chile had substantially strengthened its banking supervision before the transition to free floating. The banking law of 1986, and the subsequent amendments in 1989 and 1997, gave the regulators the essential tools to control risk taking by banks. The measures strengthened balance sheets by tightening capital requirements, imposing strong liquidity management rules, limiting bank's exposure to foreign exchange risk, and increasing banks' capital requirements in line with the recommendations of the Basel Committee.

India

India announced the transition from the peg of the Rupee to the US Dollar to a managed float in March 1993, though the IMF de facto classification system dates the transition to August 1995. While India shifted to greater exchange rate flexibility when reforms to policy frameworks were still in progress, the managed float has been maintained without major distress, even during times of international market turbulence.

In 1991, India embarked on a wide-ranging liberalization programme. Financial sector reforms were an important component of this reform programme and were implemented gradually, beginning with interest rate liberalization, the introduction of greater competition in the banking system, measures to develop domestic securities markets, and steps to strengthen financial sector supervision (see Acharya, 2002; Ariyoshi and others, 2000; Chopra and others, 1995). Liquidity in financial markets benefitted from fiscal reforms: the government shifted to borrowing at market interest rates (1992–93) and the automatic monetization of fiscal deficits by the Central Bank was phased out (1994–97). In the period after the floating of the Rupee, many of the reforms launched in the early 1990s, continued to be implemented and enhanced. Moreover, foreign exchange dealers were allowed to use derivatives to hedge their positions (1996–97) and the prudential requirements regarding the risks of foreign exchange exposures were tightened.

External financial liberalization was also gradual, and focused on the long-term foreign direct investment and equity portfolio inflows. Extensive controls on short-term borrowing were retained throughout the 1990s, which together with the existing prudential norms limited foreign exchange vulnerabilities in the banking and corporate sectors and increased India's resilience during international financial crises. The policy of maintaining limited external public debt (and on concessional terms) also diminished the exposure of the economy to exchange rate volatility.

Monetary policy in India has traditionally focused on the twin objectives of maintaining price stability and supporting growth. In the first half of the 1990s, a surge in capital inflows pushed inflation higher, but in the second half of the decade, the Reserve Bank of India succeeded in keeping inflation low. After abolishing the peg of the Rupee, the central bank actively intervened in the foreign exchange market to reduce volatility. The exchange rate against the US Dollar remained quite stable until the end of the 1990s, with occasional shifts at the times of large unfavourable shocks. In the past several years, the Reserve Bank of India has allowed even greater exchange rate flexibility, but still maintains many controls on residents' capital account transactions.

Brazil

Brazil abandoned the crawling peg of the Real to the US Dollar in January 1999. However, the rapid adoption of inflation targeting has helped to contain inflation expectations after the initial depreciation and moderate the adverse impact of a more volatile currency (see IMF, 2003; Bogdanski, Tombini, and Werlang, 2000). To influence expectations, the bank increased the transparency of its decision making, communicated extensively with the public, and explained its performance relative to the inflation targets.

The financial sector weathered the sharp depreciation of the Brazilian Real as a result of wide-ranging structural reforms launched in 1994, that reduced systemic foreign exchange and credit risks. In addition, both financial and corporate sectors had a little exposure to foreign exchange risk because of extensive hedging through Dollar-indexed government securities, derivatives, or foreign receivables. The prudential measures against the foreign exchange risk were further tightened after the crisis.

Restrictions aimed at discouraging short-term capital inflows (1993–97) were ineffective given the sophistication of the Brazilian financial market. This stands in contrast with India, where capital controls were more effective, reflecting in part the relatively less developed financial market.

Concluding Remarks

The three case studies provide us with some interesting insights. First, all three transitions were associated with an improvement in the monetary and financial policy frameworks, which helped to diminish the potential costs of exchange rate flexibility in terms of inflationary and balance sheet effects. Second, the timing of improvement in policy frameworks varied across the three cases. Chile made significant enhancements to its policy framework before the transition; India started off with partial reforms that continued after the transition; and Brazil quickly adopted a new nominal anchor following a crisis. Finally, the experience of India suggests that even with an imperfect policy framework, the potential costs of exchange rate volatility can be kept in check by capital controls, though looking forward gradual liberalization supported by strengthened policy frameworks would likely help to boost the growth (see Chapter IV of the October 2001 *World Economic Outlook*).

Note: The main author of this segment is Martin Sommer.

Source: IMF (2004): *World Economic Outlook*, September.

15.4 CURRENCY CONVERTIBILITY

All our transactions with foreign countries require conversion of the domestic currency into foreign currencies. For example, for enabling our travel abroad we need to convert the domestic currency into the currency of the country where we intend to travel. Similarly, for enabling our investing in shares and debentures issued by foreigners in foreign currencies we need to convert the domestic currency into foreign currencies. Even donations to foreigners require such conversion.

However, often when we approach foreign exchange dealers, such as Thomas Cook, American Express and commercial banks, we encounter two types of restrictions as follows:

First, the dealer sometimes is unwilling to give us all the amount of foreign currency that we want and restricts it to the government permitted limit. For example, whenever an Indian travelling abroad converts rupees into a foreign currency he is informed by the dealers that he cannot procure more than US $10,000, i.e., the permitted limit set by the Indian government for such transactions. Similarly, whenever an Indian company tries to raise resources in the form of external commercial borrowing (ECB) it is informed that it cannot borrow more than US $500 million in a year, i.e., the permitted limit set by the RBI for ECB.

Second, the dealer may restrict the price, i.e., exchange rate, at which one currency can be converted into another currency.

The absence of first restriction implies that the country is open to all kinds of trade and capital flows; there are no quantitative restrictions on such flows. The absence of second restriction implies that the country is pursuing the flexible exchange rate regime and permitting the conversion at the market determined rate. The absence of both the restrictions, at the same time, implies that the country is allowing currency convertibility.

Thus, the **currency convertibility** may be defined as the freedom to convert one currency into other internationally accepted currencies without any quantitative restrictions at market determined exchange rate (Figure 15.8).

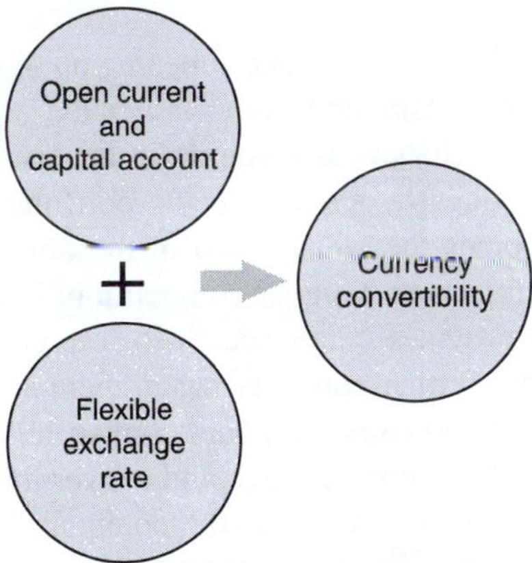

Figure 15.8 Currency Convertibility.

As the currency convertibility necessitates opening up of the economy to trade and capital flows, it is expected to enhance such flows. Since currency convertibility also implies flexible exchange rate, it assures traders and investors that they will receive the amount that is determined by the market forces. Such an assurance further promotes trade and capital flows. It has been argued that the viability of balance of payment is achieved by flexibility and realism in the exchange rate and macroeconomic policies, and therefore, currency should be fully convertible.

The currency convertibility can be on current account and/or capital account.

15.4.1 Current Account Convertibility

The **current account convertibility** exists when currency conversion is permitted for transactions (purchase or sell) related to goods and services, factor payments and all other transactions recorded under the current account of the balance of payment without any quantitative restrictions at the market determined rate. The current account convertibility does not preclude restrictions in the form of taxes and tariffs on the current account transactions.

The Article VII of the Articles of the Agreement of the IMF enjoins the member countries from imposing restrictions on the making of payments and transfers for current international transactions or from engaging in discriminatory currency arrangements or multiple currency practices unless the measure is approved by the IMF on grounds of the balance of payment difficulties.

The current account convertibility is in place in most countries as this ensures market determined earnings and payments for the traders and encourages the trade flows.

15.4.2 Capital Account Convertibility

The **capital account convertibility** exists when currency conversion is permitted for transactions (purchase or sell) recorded under the capital account of the balance of payment without any quantitative restrictions at market determined rate. The transactions on the capital account consist of inflow and outflow of Foreign Direct Investment, foreign portfolio flows, debt flows and other capital flows. Thus, the capital account convertibility implies freedom to convert domestic financial assets into foreign assets and vice-versa at the market determined rate. However, the capital account convertibility does not preclude restriction in the form of **Tobin tax**, i.e., the tax on currency transactions.

The capital account convertibility necessitates opening up of the capital account, and hence, brings in the measurable and non-measureable gains associated with an open capital account (as highlighted in Section 14.2.1). It enhances investment in the country through greater access to capital; it enhances domestic savings by expanding the portfolio choice of domestic savers to include foreign assets; it overcomes the weaknesses in the domestic financial system through access to international capital markets and higher competition; it improves the return on capital; it reduces the cost of funds; it provides better access to foreign markets and it brings in new managerial skills. These gains are further enhanced when there are no exchange rate restrictions on capital flows, i.e., when there is full capital account convertibility.

Despite these expected benefits, the capital account convertibility is resisted because an open capital account, which is accompanied with it, has the potential to jeopardize the functioning of an economy. The capital flows, especially the short-term flows, are much more volatile than the trade flows. Small changes in the macroeconomic environment can bring about large changes in the capital account, and hence, threaten the macroeconomic stability of a country as elaborated below.

To understand the threat from an open capital account, consider a situation where there is a sudden surge in portfolio flows. A large inflow of foreign capital in a flexible exchange rate regime results in an appreciation of the exchange rate, which in turn, deteriorates the export competitiveness. To retain export competitiveness, often, the central bank prevents the appreciation by purchasing foreign exchange from the market and paying for it in terms of domestic currency. However, such an intervention increases the foreign exchange assets and the high powered money in the economy. An increase in the high powered money, given the money multiplier, enhances money supply, and hence, domestic inflation rate. To combat inflationary pressures, sterilization measures are implemented, which require pursuance of tight monetary policy. Tight monetary policy can take the shape of an open market sale of government securities or an increase in the CRR or increase in the policy rates. In either case, the real interest rate in the economy increases, which further attracts capital inflows (Figure 15.9), and the country finds itself in the same situation with which it had started with.

Now assume that there is some exogenous shock to the economy, which results in a sudden reversal of capital flows. A large outflow of capital causes a sharp depreciation of the exchange rate, and a large current account deficit. To prevent unfavourable impact on the balance of payment, the central bank intervenes by selling foreign currency; but this contracts money supply and reduces price level. To stabilize price level, the central bank pursues expansionary monetary policy but that reduces interest rate and accentuates further withdrawal of capital from the country.

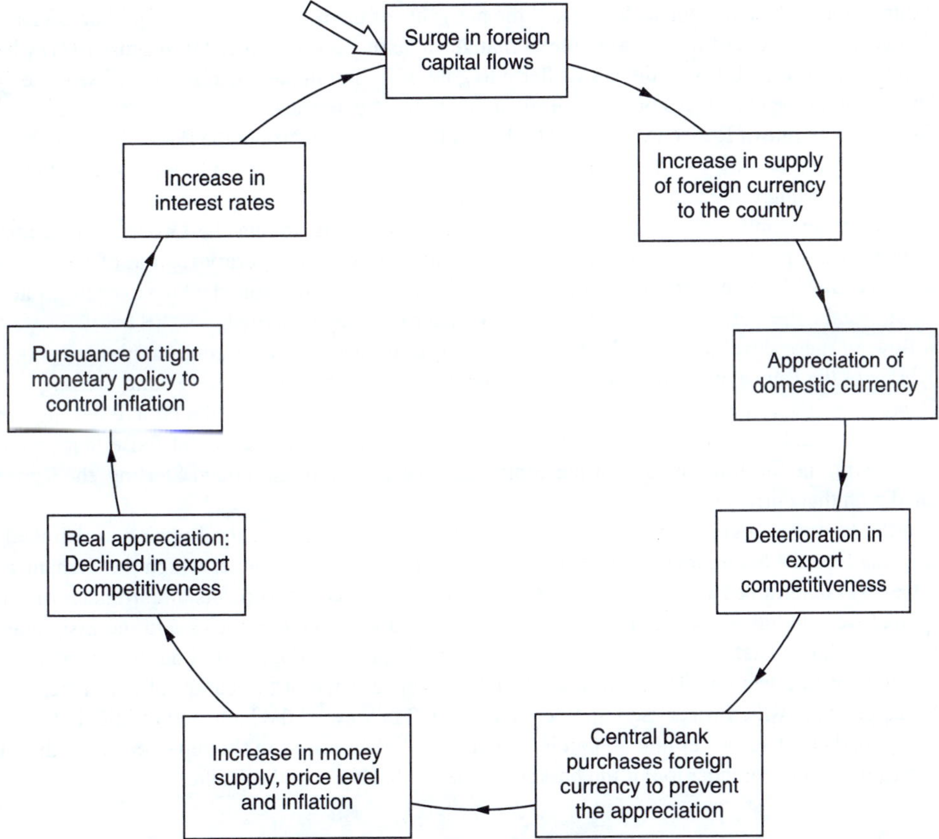

Figure 15.9 Foreign Capital Flows and Macroeconomic Stability.

Thus, we see that in the presence of an open capital account, the country one day finds itself with very high inflation rate and interest rate; but the very next day, if there is a reversal of capital, it also experiences sharp decline in inflation rate and interest rate. Therefore, an open capital account and capital account convertibility has the potential to jeopardize the macroeconomic stability of a country.

To safeguard from potential destabilizing forces, countries follow a very cautious approach in opening up their economies for capital account flows and making their domestic currency fully convertible on the capital account. They try to prepare for such changes by strengthening their real, financial and fiscal sectors, and also by bringing in regulatory changes. India has been the case in place as described in UBE 15.5, UBE 15.6 and UBE 15.7.

UNDERSTANDING BUSINESS ENVIRONMENT

UBE 15.5 Exchange Rate Regimes in India

This UBE describes the gradual transition of India from the fixed exchange rate regime to the flexible exchange rate arrangement and India's attempt towards currency convertibility.

Pre-liberalization Period: Controlled Exchange Regime

Historically, the Rupee was linked with the Pound Sterling for financing external transactions. India's membership of the IMF entailed a declaration of the par value of the Rupee in terms of gold or US Dollar. A major change in the system of maintaining the exchange value of Rupee occurred in August 1971, when the US suspended the convertibility of the US Dollar into gold, resulting in the collapse of the fixed rate system and the floatation of the currencies of many of the industrialized countries.

The exchange rate of Rupee was pegged to the US Dollar until 1971, but the Pound Sterling continued to be the intervention currency in the exchange markets, i.e., the RBI continued to intervene in the foreign exchange market through sale and purchase of Pound Sterling.

Following the Smithsonian Agreement in 1971 (arrangements among the Group of 10 countries), a realignment of the parities of major currencies came into being. A temporary regime of wider margins (2.25 per cent against 1.25 per cent permitted by the IMF) and central rate around which exchange rate could fluctuate was established. However, the situation remained extremely unsettled.

Following these developments, the Government of India decided to discontinue the pegging of the exchange rate of the Rupee, with the US Dollar and repegged its currency with the Pound Sterling in 1971.

The result of the re-pegging of the external value of the Rupee in terms of the Pound Sterling was that the Rupee also floated in relation to the SDR and all other world currencies except those that maintained fixed parities with the Sterling. In view of the continued depreciation of the Pound Sterling, the Rupee also depreciated with that currency.

In order to impart a greater measure of stability to the exchange rate, the Rupee was delinked from Pound Sterling from 24 September 1975. A new arrangement was adopted under which the exchange value of the Rupee was determined with reference to the daily exchange rate movements of currencies of selected countries that were India's major trading partners. The selection of the currencies and the assignments of the weights to them was left to the discretion of the central bank. The Pound Sterling, however, continued as the currency of intervention. The bank maintained the Rupee value of the basket of currencies within a band of 2.25 per cent, which was raised to 5 per cent in 1979 in view of the large and erratic fluctuations in the currency markets. The basket link helped in moderating the variations in the rupee rates. To discourage speculations, the actual composition of the basket was never disclosed to the public.

Changes Since 1991

Liberalized Exchange Rate Management System, 1992

As a part of the reform measures initiated in the year 1991–92, the Government of India also exercised changes in the exchange management and the control by the RBI in the foreign exchange market. The measures in this direction were initiated with the introduction of the Liberalized Exchange Rate Management System (LERMS), i.e., partial floatation of the Rupee in February 1992.

With the introduction of the LERMS, the RBI became obliged to supply foreign exchange to the Authorized Dealers (ADs) only for the import of specific items to the extent authorized by the Ministry of Finance. These items included Government departmental needs, crude oil, diesel, kerosene, fertilizers and other specified items.

The ADs were required to ensure that they surrender 40 per cent of the entire invoice value of exports to the RBI at the official rate of exchange.

For exporters and others who were in receipts of foreign exchange earnings, the LERMS meant more earnings in terms of Rupees. Such persons could, under the new system, exchange 60 per cent of their foreign exchange earnings at the market rate and the balance 40 per cent at the official rate. This entitled them for more proceeds than they could get under the old system when 100 per cent of foreign exchange earned could be converted only at the official rate of exchange. However, for importers and those who required foreign exchange to be sent outside the country, the new arrangement meant that they had to acquire their foreign exchange 100 per cent at the free market rate. This meant more outgo in terms of Rupee.

The LERMS was criticized for its discriminatory treatment towards exporters. The government was talking of boosting exports on one hand, and on the other hand, imposing a tax on exporters in the form of compulsory conversion of part of their export proceeds at the official exchange rate.

As far as capital account transactions were concerned, the LERMS continued to subject them to control. The transactions permitted by the government, however, could be executed at free market exchange rate.

In another move the RBI replaced the Pound Sterling by the Dollar as the intervention currency.

Replacement of the LERMS by the Unified Exchange Rate System, 1 March 1993

In 1993, the LERMS was replaced by the Unified Exchange Rate System. The new arrangements did away with the dual exchange rate system; the rupee was made fully convertible on the trade account. The dual rate system was abandoned and the exporters were permitted to sell their foreign exchange earnings to the authorized dealers at the market rate of exchange. However, the RBI continued to hold the right to intervene, namely buying and selling foreign exchange as and when it deemed fit in the market and continued to fix its official rate on the basis of prevailing market rate.

With the modification of the LERMS, the Rupee came to float freely. Receipts and payments under the trade account of the balance of payments could be converted by the ADs at the market determined rate of exchange. This did not make the Rupee fully convertible, however, as all the transactions in foreign exchange were subject to exchange control regulations. Indian residents who were in receipt of foreign exchange were required to surrender their foreign exchange holdings to the Authorized Dealers unless they had been generally or specifically permitted by the RBI to retain the same with banks in India or abroad.

The RBI, under the new arrangements, suspended the purchases and sales of the Pound Sterling, Deutsche Mark and Japanese Yen. This was done because under the new arrangements the ADs were no longer obliged to sell any portion of their foreign currency receipts to the RBI. Now the ADs could sell their receipts to other ADs for permissible transactions. Since the RBI purchases only the US Dollars, the ADs who want to sell their foreign currency holdings to the RBI should first convert those to the US Dollars and then sell to the RBI.

Rupee Convertible on the Current Account, 19 August 1994

With the introduction of the current account convertibility in 1994, the authorized dealers (ADs) are allowed to provide foreign exchange for effecting current payments upto specified indicative limits, beyond which foreign exchange could be obtained for bonafide current payments after making a reference to the Reserve Bank. Further relaxations are made by permitting the ADs to provide exchange facilities to their customers without prior approval of the Reserve Bank, beyond the specified indicative limits for purposes such as travel, studies and medical treatment.

Since then India has been moving gradually towards the capital account convertibility.

UNDERSTANDING BUSINESS ENVIRONMENT

UBE 15.6 Acts Relating to Foreign Exchange Controls

The opening up of the Indian economy, currency convertibility at current account and move towards capital account convertibility necessitated a change in the regulatory framework. Hence, as described in this UBE, in 2000 the FERA, a very restrictive regulatory framework, was replaced by the FEMA, a facilitative approach.

Inadequacy of foreign exchange resources in India, had led the GOI to employ the technique of exchange control for using the limited foreign exchange resources according to the scheme of priorities.

In India, exchange controls were imposed in 1939, under the Defence of India Rules. Under the Foreign Exchange Control Act, 1947, provision was made for restrictions on dealings in foreign exchange, on import and export of currency and bullion and regulation of payment for goods and exports. Under the 1957 Act, powers were vested in the Government to impose exchange control between India and the rest of the world and a Directorate of Enforcement was set up to enforce the provisions of the Act. The Act was revised to control the entry of foreign capital in the form of branches and activities of resident foreigners and concerns, due and prompt realization of export proceeds and plugging the leakage of foreign exchange through invoices manipulation. The new Act, the **Foreign Exchange Regulation Act** (FERA), dealing with these issues, came into existence in January 1974. The FERA was too restrictive in its approach. It aimed at regulating the foreign exchange transactions. It was a criminal law as contravention of the FERA implied even imprisonment.

The opening up of the economy, currency convertibility at current account and move towards capital account convertibility necessitated more facilitating approach towards foreign exchange transactions. Accordingly, the FERA, which was known as the law to "Control", has been replaced by the **Foreign Exchange Management Act** (FEMA), the law to "Manage" foreign exchange transactions, with effect from 1/6/2000. The FEMA is a civil law unlike the FERA which was a criminal law. Contravention under the FEMA results only in an imposition of a monetary penalty and not an arrest. There are 49 sections in all in the FEMA. Of these, only seven sections, namely, Sections 3 to 9, deal with certain acts to be done or not to be done in connection with transactions involving foreign exchange, foreign security, etc. Sections 16 to 35 relate only to adjudication and appeal. Thus, the NRIs and residents have much easier time under the FEMA.

UNDERSTANDING BUSINESS ENVIRONMENT

UBE 15.7 Capital Account Convertibility: Certain Issues and Challenges

Fiscal, monetary and financial consolidation and strengthening of productivity and production efficiency is essential before opting for full currency convertibility. This UBE discusses these issues in the Indian context.

The group supporting the full convertibility of the Rupee argues that the full currency convertibility would provide a signal to the international community that the country intends to manage its affairs without exchange restrictions which would enhance international confidence in the country's policies. The elimination of exchange restrictions is also expected to lead a turnaround in capital inflows.

The Committee on Capital Account Convertibility (CAC) set up by the RBI under the Chairmanship of Dr. S.S. Tarapore, indicated that "CAC refers to the freedom to convert local financial assets into foreign financial assets and vice versa at market determined rates of exchange. It is associated with changes of ownership in foreign/domestic financial assets and liabilities and embodies the creation and liquidation of claims on, or by, the rest of the world. The CAC can be, and is, coexistent with restrictions other than on external payments. It also does not preclude the imposition of monetary/fiscal measures relating to foreign exchange transactions which are of a prudential nature".

The committee has recommended in June 1997 a phased road map for making the capital account convertibility and suggested that the country should achieve fiscal, monetary and financial consolidation prior to achieving the full capital account convertibility by targeting at low fiscal deficit (3.5 per cent of GDP), low inflation (3 to 5 per cent), efficient financial system, healthy foreign exchange position ($26 billion).

The committee recommendations were criticized on the grounds that it failed to recognize that convertibility depends not only on the financial preconditions, but also on the real factors such as technology, infrastructure, management practices, productivity, labour quality, which influence the competitive strength of an economy. The committee on CAC has not recognized that the poor, the industry and exports in India would be exposed to the vagaries of exchange rate movements originating in capital movements in a regime of full convertibility. No amount of exchange reserves would be adequate to protect the economy unless the competitiveness of the economy is strengthened.

It was also argued that the full convertibility should be the last stage of the reforms. An economy, which is internationally competitive, can initiate the process of full convertibility. It is not simply fiscal deficit or its relationship to GDP that is a matter of concern but the more important indicator of fiscal prudence is the revenue deficit. Deficit financing for capital formation or asset creation, which augments supply, is accepted.

The East-Asian crisis of 1997, which set in after the recommendation of the committee, also subdued the demand for capital account convertibility.

However, in the first half of the first decade of this century, the country enjoyed robust external sector performance with relative macroeconomic stability in terms of price stability, comfortable foreign exchange reserves, stability on fiscal and financial front and high growth rate. Therefore, some quarters that argued that a conducive environment for the capital account convertibility has already been created and the country should go for full-fledged currency convertibility to promote capital flows. Considering the demand, the second committee on fuller capital account convertibility was set up, which submitted its report in July 2006.

The committee considering the risk associated with the capital account liberalization, as experienced by many countries with liberal capital account, had argued for a strong macroeconomic framework, sound financial system and markets, and prudential regulatory and supervisory architecture. As an indicator of stable and sound system, the committee has recommended meeting of certain indicators/targets which include meeting the Fiscal Responsibility Budget Management (FRBM) targets, shifting from the present measure of fiscal deficit to a measure of the Public Sector Borrowing Requirement (PSBR), imparting greater autonomy and transparency to the RBI in the conduct of monetary policy, segregating the government debt management and monetary policy operations through the setting up of the office of public debt independent of the RBI, further strengthening of the financial system by a range of reforms in the banking sector, such as a reduction in the share of government/RBI in the capital of public sector banks, maintaining the current account deficit to GDP ratio under 3 per cent and maintaining adequate reserves that cover not only import requirements, but also liquidity risk associated with present types of capital flows.

The committee detailed a broad five-year timeframe for movement towards fuller convertibility in three phases: Phase I (2006–07), Phase II (2007–08 to 2008–09), and Phase III (2009–10 to 2010–11). Some of the measures that needed to be implemented in gradual manner over these three phases were: gradual removal of overall ceiling on external commercial borrowing (ECB) and removal of end use restrictions; raising the limits for outflows on account of corporate investment abroad in phases from 200 per cent of net worth to 400 per cent of net worth; providing Exchange Earners Foreign Currency Account Holders access to foreign currency current/saving accounts with cheque facility and interest bearing term deposits; prohibiting the FII from investing fresh money through participatory notes; allowing non-resident corporate (and non-residents) to invest in the Indian stock markets, through the SEBI—registered entities; allowing institutions/corporates other than multilateral ones to raise Rupee bonds subject to an overall ceiling; linking the limits for borrowing overseas to paid-up capital and free reserves and raising it gradually over the phases; abolishing the various stipulations on individual fund limits and the proportion in relation to net asset value; raising the annual limit of remittances abroad by individuals; allowing non-residents (other than NRIs) access to Foreign Currency Non-Resident (Bank) (FCNR(B)) and Non-Resident (External) Rupee Account (NR(E)RA) Schemes.

SUMMARY

The exchange rate is a rate at which two currencies are traded in the foreign exchange market. Exchange rates that are quoted in the market are bilateral nominal rates. The weighted average of bilateral rates gives the effective exchange rate. These can be the Nominal Effective Exchange Rate (NEER) or Real Effective Exchange Rate (REER).

The value of exchange rate is determined by the exchange rate regimes. These are classified as fully flexible exchange rate regime, fixed exchange rate regime and managed floating regime. In the flexible exchange rate regime, the exchange rate is determined by the market forces, whereas it is fixed by the monetary authority in the fixed exchange rate regime. In the managed floating regime, the exchange rate is either fixed (as in adjustable peg and crawling peg) or flexible (as in dirty float), but the monetary authority intervenes in the market to stabilize the rate.

The value of exchange rate can change in all the regimes. In the fixed exchange rate regime the changes are deliberate, and are known as revaluation and devaluation, whereas in the flexible exchange rate regime changes are determined by the market forces and are known as appreciation and depreciation.

The flexible exchange rate regime provides independence in the pursuance of domestic macroeconomic policy, whereas the fixed exchange rate regime provides greater stability to the exchange rate. In the flexible exchange rate regime there is high volatility, whereas in the fixed exchange rate regime the macroeconomic policies are subservient to exchange rate policy. The managed floating regime tries to provide greater stability to the exchange rate regime and, at the same time, brings in more flexibility to the exchange rate.

The fixed exchange rate and managed float regimes require maintenance of adequate foreign exchange reserves to provide macroeconomic stability. Empirical studies indicate that the emerging market economies are maintaining reserves that are much more in excess of the required reserves in terms of import adequacy, monetary adequacy and debt adequacy.

To promote trade and capital flows it has been argued that there should be currency convertibility, i.e., the freedom to convert one currency into another currency. Currency convertibility can be on the current account or capital account. Though, IMF member countries have adopted current account convertibility, many of them are following a much more cautious approach towards the capital account convertibility as it also necessitates opening up of the country for capital flows, which are more volatile in nature and subject the economy to macroeconomic instability.

India has moved from the fixed exchange rate regime to the flexible exchange rate regime in the aftermath of the balance of payment crisis of 1991. A dual exchange rate regime in the form of LERMS was introduced in 1992. The rates were unified; the rupee became convertible on the trade account in 1993, and on the current account in 1994. Since then there is also a move towards the full currency convertibility. To facilitate the move towards the capital account convertibility, a more facilitating approach towards foreign currency transactions has been adopted in the form of enactment of the FEMA, 2000 which replaced the restrictive FERA, 1974. The Tarapore Committee Report has suggested Five Year Programme (2006–2011) and has emphasized the strengthening of the financial and fiscal sectors and macroeconomic stability before the country adopts the full capital account convertibility.

Implications for Managers

Variations in exchange rates affect foreign exchange earnings as well as foreign exchange payments of business firms, which, in turn, have bearing on their profitability.

Decisions related to foreign exchange transactions are greatly affected by the level of exchange rate or the expected value of the exchange rate. The exchange rate, which traders or business firms are likely to face, gets determined by the prevailing exchange rate regime. In the fixed exchange rate regime, traders know for certainty the rate at which they would be able to transact with the rest of the world. However, in the flexible exchange rate regime the exchange rate keeps on fluctating along with the market forces. Therefore, traders need to be prepared for a certain amount of volatility in the exchange rate and fluctuations in their earnings emerging from such volatility. To a certain extent, they can protect their earnings by hedging their positions in the forward foreign exchange markets. In the managed flexible exchange rate regime though the uncertainty regarding the exchange rate is reduced, it is not completely eliminated.

The central bank interventions in the foreign exchange markets to stabilize the value of the domestic currency though help in reducing the fluctuations in exchange rate, these have economy-wide implications from which business firms are not immune. Not only the firms trading in the international markets but also the firms confining their operations to the domestic territory need to understand the implications and dynamics of such interventions on the economy and their business operations.

The changes in the foreign exchange market affect the firms trading in the international market, as well as the domestic firms which do not have such exposures. The central bank interventions in the foreign exchange markets affect even the money market, and through economy-wide linkages, the other markets in the economy. These affect the overall price and interest rates. The output and employment also get affected in the process. No business organization can remain immune to such changes as business decisions, though the territory of such organization may be just restricted to the domestic domain, are affected by the changes in price level, interest rate and also other economic variables.

Thus, it is pertinent for the firms and managers to understand the exchange rate regimes, the process of determination of exchange rate, and the impact of the central bank interventions in the foreign exchange market on the economy and their business organizations.

REVIEW QUESTIONS

15.1 What is foreign exchange? Where is foreign exchange traded? What is the exchange rate?

15.2 Differentiate between the spot rate and the forward rate.

15.3 What is the effective exchange rate? What is the difference between the Nominal Effective Exchange Rate (NEER) and Real Effective Exchange Rate (REER)?

15.4 What is the difference between depreciation and devaluation? What impact the devaluation of a domestic currency has on the balance of trade? What conditions are required to be met for the devaluation to have a favourable impact on the balance of payment?

15.5 What do you understand by the term exchange rate regime? Differentiate between the fixed exchange rate regime and the fully flexible exchange rate regime. How far the managed floating or controlled floating regime differs from the above two regimes?

15.6 At times countries maintain exchange rate above the rate that can be supported by the market forces. What is the underlying assumption for such a peg?

15.7 What is the Currency Board Arrangement (CBA)? How far the CBA differs from dollarization?

15.8 Fixed exchange rate regime is criticized for the absence of self-correcting mechanism. How do the deviations in exchange rate due to imbalances in the BOP get corrected in such a regime?

15.9 What is the impact of central bank interventions in the FOREX market on an economy?

15.10 What is import adequacy? Is this measure of reserve adequacy sufficient for countries with large capital flows? What measures have been suggested for countries with substantial access to capital markets? What are the new measures of reserve adequacy?

15.11 In what type of economic environment monetary adequacy is an acceptable measure of reserve adequacy? What are its limitations?

15.12 What is the adjustable peg system? How far does this differ from the crawling peg system?

15.13 What is the difference between dirty float and clean float?

15.14 Which exchange rate regime gives independence to the monetary authority in pursuing monetary policy?

15.15 It is often pointed out that in the fixed exchange rate regime the monetary policy cannot be pursued independent of exchange rate considerations. Why do countries then pursue fixed exchange rate regime?

15.16 What are the advantages of the flexible exchange rate regime?

15.17 Why is the managed floating regime pursued in many emerging countries world over?

15.18 What do you understand by the currency convertibility? Differentiate between the currency convertibility on current account and capital account. What is the difference between open capital account and currency convertibility on the capital account?

15.19 Why do countries follow very cautious approach towards the currency convertibility on capital account?

15.20 As per the revised estimates, how many currency REER and NEER indices are estimated in India? Do movements in REER matter for the Indian economy? Substantiate your answer.

15.21 Empirical assessments indicate that there is a negative relationship between effective exchange rate and inflation. Inspite of this in 2009–10 when country was reeling under high inflationary pressures, the RBI did not use exchange rate policy for controlling inflation. Explain the reasons for the RBI's decisions.

15.22 Are emerging market economies maintaining excess reserves? If yes, to what extent? What are the lessons from the Korean experience as far as the level of reserve adequacy is concerned?

15.23 Differentiate the pre-liberalized exchange rate regime from the post-liberalized exchange rate regime in India?

15.24 What are the issues involved in the capital account convertibility in India? What are the recommendations of the Tarapore Committee Report II in this context?

15.25 Compare and contrast the experience of Chile, India and Brazil in the context of a move towards flexible exchange rate regime.

NUMERICAL PROBLEMS

15.1 Suppose that at the exchange rate of $1 = ₹45, an Indian product is sold for $50 in the USA. What will be the price in dollar in the USA if exchange rate changes to $1 = ₹50. Has the Rupee appreciated or depreciated in this case?

15.2 You have been given the bilateral exchange rate (indirect quotation using numeraire as SDR) between Indian Rupee and the currencies of its two major trading partners in Table 15.4. Along with the bilateral rates, the trade shares and the inflation rates in India and in the trading partner countries are specified.

Table 15.4 Bilateral Exchange Rates (in terms of SDRs)

Date	*Indian rupee (INR)*	*UK pound sterling (GBP)*	*US dollar (USD)*
14 Mar 2001	0.0166	1.1303	0.7778
14 Mar 2011	0.014	1.0212	0.6341
Inflation (%)	6	8	5
Weightage	–	0.4	0.6

(i) Using these bilateral rates and assuming 2001 as the base year, compute trade weighted nominal and real effective exchange rates for the year 2011.

(ii) Which of these indices is higher and why?

15.3 In Table 15.5 the trends in nominal and effective exchange rate are presented.

Table 15.5 Trends in Nominal and Real Effective Exchange Rate of Rupee in 2010–11 (Trade Based Weights; Base 2004–05 = 100)

Month	*Nominal effective exchange rate*		*Real effective exchange rate*	
	6 currency	*36 currency*	*6 currency*	*36 country*
April	94.70	96.35	116.00	103.78
May	94.24	95.55	116.19	102.95
June	93.51	94.66	115.23	102.30
July	90.96	92.03	112.64	99.98
August	90.91	92.02	112.71	99.57
September	91.38	92.87	113.96	100.75
October	92.32	94.51	115.20	102.66

Month	Nominal effective exchange rate		Real effective exchange rate	
	6 currency	36 currency	6 currency	36 country
November	91.52	93.34	115.08	101.67
December	92.47	93.82	117.94	103.52
January	91.46	92.72	117.31	102.65
February	90.37	92.32	115.54	101.78
March	90.43	92.54	115.56	102.88

Answer the following questions using the information given in Table 15.5.

(i) Is there more appreciation or depreciation in the NEER than the REER between April 2010 and March 2011? What must have been the reason for it?

(ii) Which of the indices is more stable? What must have been the reason for it?

CASE ANALYSIS EXERCISE

C15.1 The Influence of Commodity Prices and Capital Markets on Developing Country Exchange Rates

The experience during two earlier periods of sustained increase in international commodity prices and private capital flows is illustrative. Between 2003 and mid-2008 prior to the Lehman crisis, prices of industrial commodities rose more than 164 per cent in real terms and crude oil prices rose to 230 per cent, implying annual increases of 21 per cent and 26 per cent. A second price rally occurred following the financial crisis with prices recovering close to the pre-crisis peaks in just over two years, helped by fiscal stimulus measures and sustained monetary easing in high income countries, and a quick rebound in developing countries' growth compared to a much weaker growth in high income countries. The period of near-zero interest rates and quantitative easing in the US, UK, Japan and other high income countries caused capital flows to developing countries to surge again. The influx of commodity-seeking inflows as well as private capital flow (attracted by faster productivity growth), together resulted in a significant appreciation of developing countries' currencies.

The extent of appreciation of developing countries currencies, however, varied along two dimensions—the importance of primary and industrial commodities in overall imports, and the extent of financial market openness. We measure the latter as the share of foreign portfolio equity inflows as a share domestic product (GDP), which signals the extent of integration into global financial markets. As box figure ExR 1.1 shows, developing countries that are in the top third along both dimensions (e.g., Brazil, South Africa) experienced the steepest appreciation, especially compared to other developing countries that are relatively well-integrated into financial markets, but not significant commodity exporters (e.g. India, Turkey, Thailand). By contrast, the real exchange rates of other commodity exporters that are in the bottom third in terms of our measure of financial market integration (e.g. Gabon, Cameroon, Iran) were on average flat during the first period and lost value in the second period.

This suggests that commodity prices and capital flows can interact in complex ways to influence currencies of developing countries. A commodity price boom can attract not only foreign direct investment into resource intensive sectors raising overall levels of FDI (box figure ExR 1.2), but in countries with relatively higher levels of financial openness, it can also cause short-term speculative inflows into non-tradable sectors, for example, real estate, that benefit from the increased demand caused by commodity revenues, in the process further appreciating the currency. Eventually, when international prices retreat or investor risk aversion rises, the process is reversed, as sudden capital outflows depreciate the exchange rate, in the process raising the local currency burden of foreign currency-denominated liabilities (Ostry et al. 2010). Such a commodity price boom-fueled real exchange rate appreciation, especially in countries with relatively higher levels of financial market integration, can exacerbate risks to firm and sovereign balance sheets (Korinek 2011). Although some financially-integrated commodity exporters have made efforts to mitigate these risks through controls on cross-border flows, such as Chile's—Encaje || in the 1990s and Brazil's more recent IOF tax on inflows, such controls may come at the cost of reduced allocations of portfolio capital that is often redirected towards countries with more open exchange rate regimes (Forbes et al. 2012), and over time, lower investment rates, productive capacity and welfare. When there is significant cross-border spillovers of a country's capital control policies that can exacerbate existing distortions in others, multilateral co-ordination of such unilateral policies may be beneficial (Ostry, Ghosh, and Korinek 2012).

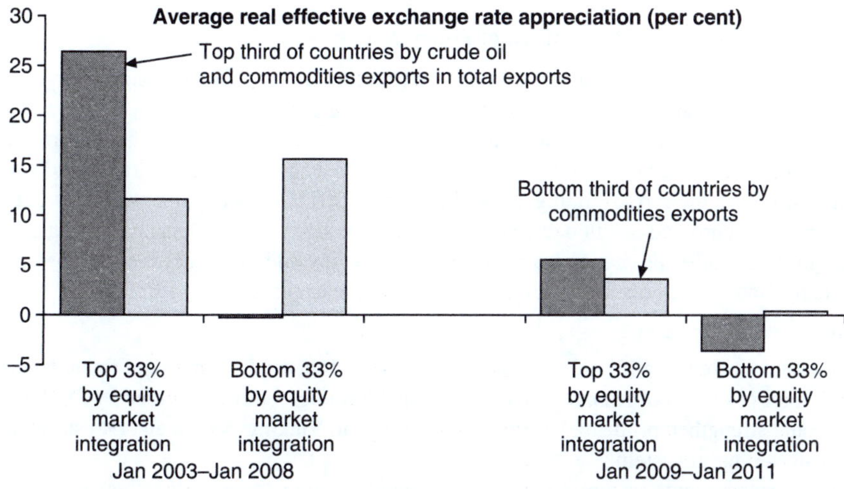

Source: IMF International Financial Statistics, J.P. Morgan and World Bank.

Figure 15.10 Currencies of Commodities Exporters that are also Financially-Integrated Experienced the Largest Gains During Periods of Commodity Price Increases and Capital Flows.

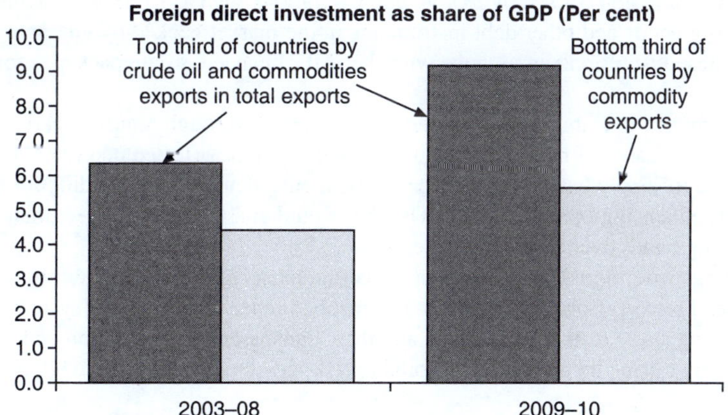

Source: IMF International Financial Statistics, J.P. Morgan and World Bank.

Figure 15.11 FDI is Stronger in Commodity Exporting Countries.

Source: The World Bank (2013), Global Economic Prospects, Volume 6, January 2013. Washington, DC: World Bank.

DOI: 10.1596/ 978-0-8213-9882-1 License: Creative Commons Attribution CC BY 3.0

Questions

1. Why was there a surge in capital flows to developing countries following the global financial crisis?
2. What was the impact of surge in capital flows on the value of developing countries currencies?
3. The extent of appreciation of exchange rate due to surge in capital flows varied across countries? What factors can account for the differences in the impact?
4. How is the financial market integration measured?
5. What risks a commodity price boom fueled exchange rate appreciation posed to firms and sovereign balance sheet?

C15.2 Euro Area Crisis – An Assessment of Policy Action

The euro area is caught in a deep, structural and multifaceted crisis characterised by large fiscal deficit, enormous public debt, banking problems and consistently eroding competitive position manifested in a gradually deteriorating current account balance. Beginning with the peripheral euro area in 2009, the sovereign debt crisis has of late cascaded to engulf core euro area economies, like France and Austria, which were downgraded from their AAA rating status in January 2012. It has also brought Greece closer to a possible exit from the euro and resulted in a spillover to a banking crisis in Spain and Portugal. As countries in a currency union, the affected economies are faced with a policy dilemma since they do not have the liberty of using exchange rate and monetary policy as stabilisation measures.

Policy Measures

The policy measures taken to alleviate the crisis were mainly four-fold: (i) regional financial arrangements and euro-IMF joint provision of resources, (ii) exceptional liquidity facility provided by ECB, (iii) measures to recapitalise and strengthen prudential norms in the European banking system and (iv) structural measures to correct a distorted fiscal system.

Financial arrangements in the region were effected through the establishment of new institutions, such as the European Financial Stabilisation Mechanism (EFSM) in May 2010, the European Financial Stability Facility (EFSF) in August 2010 and the European Stabilisation Mechanism (ESM) that is being operationalised but has not found favour for a banking license as yet. While EFSM involves funds raised by the European Commission backed by EU budget, institutions such as EFSF were authorised to mobilise resources by issuing bonds and other debt instruments in the market backed by guarantees of 17 euro area member states. These institutions, in alliance with the IMF, financed rescue packages for Greece, Ireland, Portugal and Italy.

The ECB arranged to stabilise the sovereign debt markets through security market programmes that involved sterilised purchases of both public and private debt of the affected countries. In December 2011, the ECB committed to supply banks in the euro area with euro-denominated funding for three years in two special long-term refinancing operations (LTROs) that would enable banks to meet their potential funding needs from maturing bonds over the next few years.

Since the large sovereign debt holdings of European banks raised the probability of a spillover of the crisis to the financial sector, efforts were made to inspire confidence in the banking system. Popular measures included encouraging stress tests for the banks and their transparent dissemination and the recapitalisation of 65 major banks by raising their core tier I capital to risk-weighted assets ratio to 9.0 per cent by end June 2012.

In terms of medium-term policy measures, European leaders often reiterated their commitment to implementing fiscal austerity measures. At the Brussels Summit in December 2011, EU members agreed that general government budgets should either be balanced or in surplus. Besides, institutions outside the euro area have extended their support through measures, such as central banks' provision of contingent swap lines in 2010 and again in late 2011, and also announced easy and unconventional monetary policy measures.

Besides, various structural measures are currently being undertaken including the recent (June 2012) European Council decision on "Compact for Growth and Jobs" which aims to mobilise 120 billion euros for immediate investment by unlocking domestic potential for growth, including through opening up competition in network industries, promoting the digital economy, exploiting the potential of a green economy, removing unjustified restrictions on service providers and making it easier to start a business.

There is also a line of thought that though not very likely, exit of troubled nations like Greece from the union may allow more policy flexibility to the affected countries in the medium-term.

Assessment

The policy measures taken by the euro area, viz., bailing out affected economies and liquidity provision have not proved to be effective in debt crisis resolution. Concerns over fiscal sustainability and solvency of these economies still remain. For example, in June 2012, Spain's economic condition worsened necessitating bail-out packages for its banks. These appear to be aimed at staving off the crisis rather than addressing its structural issues.

Since the economies in a currency union do not have the option to adjust the exchange rate, the necessary adjustment has to come through fiscal consolidation. However, the ongoing fiscal austerity measures are likely to impact near-term recovery. The clear inter-temporal choice between fiscal consolidation and near-term growth then necessitates concrete collective effort to establish a fiscal union. Besides, efforts should be made to encourage domestic savings and develop indigenous government bond markets to reduce the reliance on foreign capital to finance public debt.

Second, regional arrangements have limited firepower, and may require multilateral financial assistance to supplement resources. But this would have direct implications for IMF resource mobilisation, and since the ratification of the 2010 quota reforms is a protracted process, the IMF may have to rely on borrowed resources that may deviate from the equilibrium ratio between quota and borrowed resources, with potential governance implications. This not only pre-empts resources from low-income countries that have become more vulnerable to global economic uncertainties but also puts pressure on crisis by-standers that may be facing an uncertain macroeconomic situation.

Third, increased liquidity provision in the region may add to global liquidity, which, in turn, may feed into global inflation and raise monetary policy challenges for EDEs. If increased global liquidity is channelled into commodity markets, rising commodity prices, particularly oil, will stretch current account deficits in oil importing economies, like India. Tightening the prudential norms in the European banking systems may lead to deleveraging, which may increase exchange rate volatility in EDEs.

Against this backdrop, there has been a debate about whether the crisis response in the euro area has been appropriate. One argument is that the "troika" of the EU, the ECB and the IMF has delayed in responding to the crisis. Douglas J. Elliott, Fellow at Brookings Institution in his testimony argued that the euro crisis could plunge Europe into a deep recession and put the US into at least a mild recession. There are those who argue that the economics of austerity may fail in the euro area. Others argue that the currency union is inherently unsustainable and taxpayer money is being drained through unworkable bailouts. The problem is whether others in the periphery can be ring-fenced and how to thwart a likely strong contagion. Broin (2012) warns that if loss-sharing cannot be agreed on, a messy default is likely to end in a forced exit with far-reaching implications for the rest of the world.

Brutti and Saure (2011) find that exposure to Greek sovereign debt and the debt of Greek banks constitute an important transmission channel in the case of the euro area and, overall, financial linkages explain up to two-third of the transmission of sovereign debt in the euro crisis. Further, if Greece leaves the Union, the apprehension about probable exit of other countries from the euro area is likely to increase considerably as their situation is equally fragile. Portugal and Ireland may have to restructure their public debt regardless of whether Greece defaults. Illiquid but solvent countries like Italy and Spain will have to be rescued through lender of last resort support to avoid default. It would have a cascading impact on German and French bank balance sheets as they hold majority of the Greek loans. Subbarao (2012) has pointed to the trilemma being faced by the central banks, including the ECB, in managing price stability, financial stability and sovereign debt sustainability at the same time. This new trilemma has emerged after the global crisis.

References

Broin, Peader O. (2012), "The Euro Crisis: Orderly Default or Euro Exit", The Institute of International and European Affairs, Report No.8.

Brutti, Filippo and Phillip Saure (2011), "Transmission of Sovereign Risk in a Euro Crisis", December, Swiss National Bank Study Centre, Gerzensee Working Paper No.12.01.

Subbarao, Duvvuri (forthcoming), "Price Stability, Financial Stability, and Sovereign Debt Sustainability Policy Challenges from the New Trilemma", Macroeconomics and Finance in Emerging Market Economies.

US Congress (2011), "What the euro crisis means for Taxpayers and US economy", Testimony of Douglas Elliott before House sub-committee on Troubled Asset Reconstruction Programme (TARP), Financial Services and Bailouts of Public and Private Programs, December 15, 2011.

Source: Reserve Bank of India (2012), Annual Report 2011–12.

Questions

1. What is the euro crisis? Is it a soverign debt crisis or fiscal crisis or currency crisis?
2. Where did the euro crisis trigger? Which countries did it engulf subsequently? Which countries of the e are though illiquidity are solvent? Which countries of the European Union are fundamentally sound?
3. What policy measures have been taken to alleviate the euro crisis?
4. Why the countries in the zone do not have the option to adjust the exchange rate?
5. What are the likely implications of increased liquidity provision in the euro zone for global liquidity?
6. What structural measures have been taken to promote growth and enhance job opportunities in the euro zone?
7. What justifies establishment of a fiscal union in the euro zone?
8. What is the troika of the European Union?
9. What new trilemma has emerged after the global crisis?

SUGGESTED FURTHER READING

Chandra, N.K. (2008), India's Foreign Exchange Reserves: A Shield of Comfort or An Albatross, *EPW*, Vol. 43, No. 14, April 05–11.

Mallick, S. and Marques, H. (2013), Exchange Rate Pass-through by Indian and Chinese Exporters, *Live Mint* and the *Wall Street Journal*, May 30.

Rangarajan, C. and Patra, M.D. (2012), Can the SDR become a Global Reserve Currency? *EPW*, March 17, Vol. XLVII, No. 11, RBI (2013), Report on Foreign Exchange Reserves.

Subbarao, (2011), India and the Global Financial Crisis What Have We Learnt, *RBI*, Speech, June.

CHAPTER 16

Legal Environment of Business

16.1 INTRODUCTION

An active and aggressive preserver of its intellectual property, American multinational Apple was recently in the news headlines for dragging South Korean consumer electronics giant Samsung into a legal battle. The recent feud between Apple and Samsung started in April 2011 when Apple Inc. filed a patent infringement case against Samsung in a US District Court in Northern California for violating its intellectual property rights. Apple claimed that Samsung was copying Apple's iPhone and iPad designs. In August 2012, Apple won a huge victory in this case and was awarded $1 million. This ruling is under appeal as of now. If Apple wins this case in the court, Samsung will be subject to heavy fines with a possibility of some of its products being banned for sale in the US market. Competing for market share, these two giants in the electronic industry are in patent disputes in many other countries as well.

Several other companies are also in disputes with their competitors over infringement of their intellectual property rights. For example, Amazon filed lawsuit against Barnes and Noble in 1999 for copying its patented one click option for making payment for online shopping. The lawsuit took three to four years to settle. Similarly in 2009, Google was accused of selling the trademarked name "Rescuecom" as a keyword to Rescuecom's competitors.

Not only the competing companies are involved in several legal disputes but also workers and consumers have dragged many companies to the courts as is evident from the cases cited hereinafter.

In February 2009, Abercrombie & Fitch, an American retailer, which focuses on casual wear for consumers aged 18 to 22, was in feud with California state labour regulators. The regulators alleged that its "Appearance/Look Policy" forced its employees to buy and wear its clothes while on the job. The company, though confirmed that it offered discounts to its associates to encourage them to purchase the company's clothes, denied that wearing the goods was a requirement. The company lost the case. To settlement agreement required the company not to force workers to buy its clothes and reimburse former employees for Abercrombie-brand clothes purchased for working in California stores during that period. The settlement required the company to pay a fine of $2.2 million and not to force workers to buy its clothes.

In India, in 2009, a consumer won a case against Concorde Motors. Vinay Sreenivas, an IT consultant in Bangalore, purchased a red colour diesel Fiat Palio from Concorde Motors for ₹5,47,810. The very next day of the delivery of the car, he noticed dents and paint defects in the car. The engineer at the service centre confirmed that the car had been repainted. On receiving complaints from Vinay, the management of Concorde Motors, offered either to paint the car once again or replace damaged parts with parts from a brand new car. Rejecting the offer, Vinay demanded a brand new car. Receiving no reply to this request, Vinay filed a case against the company in a consumer court which gave the ruling in favour of the consumer.

Governments, world over, control business activities both directly and indirectly. Various government policies, such as fiscal policy, monetary policy and trade policies, have more indirect influence, whereas various legislations have more direct influence on business activities. The incidents highlighted in the previous paragraphs stress the fact that the infringement of laws and indifferent attitude towards legal issues and regulatory policies not only results in heavy monetary losses for a firm but can also tarnish its brand value.

Given the importance of legal environment for business, this chapter in Section 16.2 defines legal environment and details on types of laws in Section 16.3.

16.2 WHAT IS LEGAL ENVIRONMENT?

The functioning or behaviour of a company always impacts its stakeholders (Figure 16.1). **Stakeholders** in a company are the people or groups of people who supply their resources and, thereby, have an interest in the working of the company. The stakeholders can be broadly classified into two categories, viz., internal stakeholders and external stakeholders. **Internal stakeholders** consist of groups within a business, such as shareholders or owners, managers and workers; whereas **external stakeholders** are groups outside a business, such as suppliers, consumers and communities.

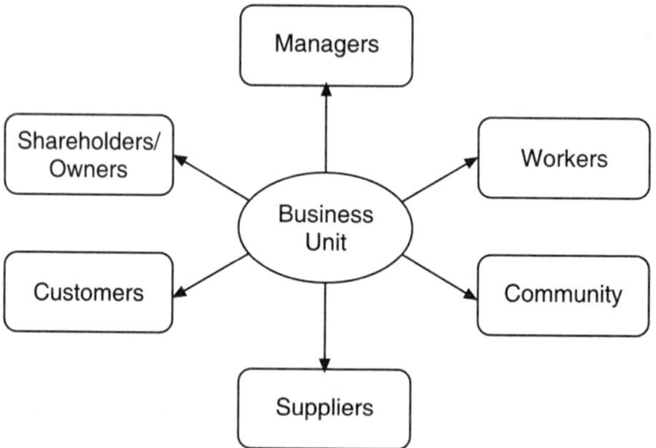

Figure 16.1 Types of Stakeholders in a Company.

The different stakeholders have dissimilar interest in the working of an organization. For example, shareholders are the owners of the company; they are most interested in the profit made by the company. The managers and workers are primarily interested in their salaries and retaining their jobs. Input suppliers want the business to continue as it is a customer for their products, while lenders and other creditors want the business to do well so that they get timely payment of their dues. Consumers are interested in quality and price of the products to satisfy their needs. Community is interested in business so that more people get employed. They are also affected by the activities of business organizations as these affect the natural environment of the community.

At times, the interest of the company and that of its stakeholders may conflict and the working of the company can have a negative or harmful impact on its stakeholders. For example, a factory may want to operate even during night so as to meet the growing demand for its products. But in the process, the noise at nights may be very disturbing the local community. Similarly, air and water pollution may be very harmful to the local residents. The government intervention may be required to restrain the damaging effects of such unsafe business practices. Hence, the government often enacts laws to protect the interest of stakeholders or to minimize the harmful impact of the functions of companies.

16.3 TYPES OF LAWS

Broadly, the laws affecting business activities can be classified as laws protecting consumers, society and public interest, and laws affecting business organization (Figure 16.2). An overview of these laws is presented hereinafter.

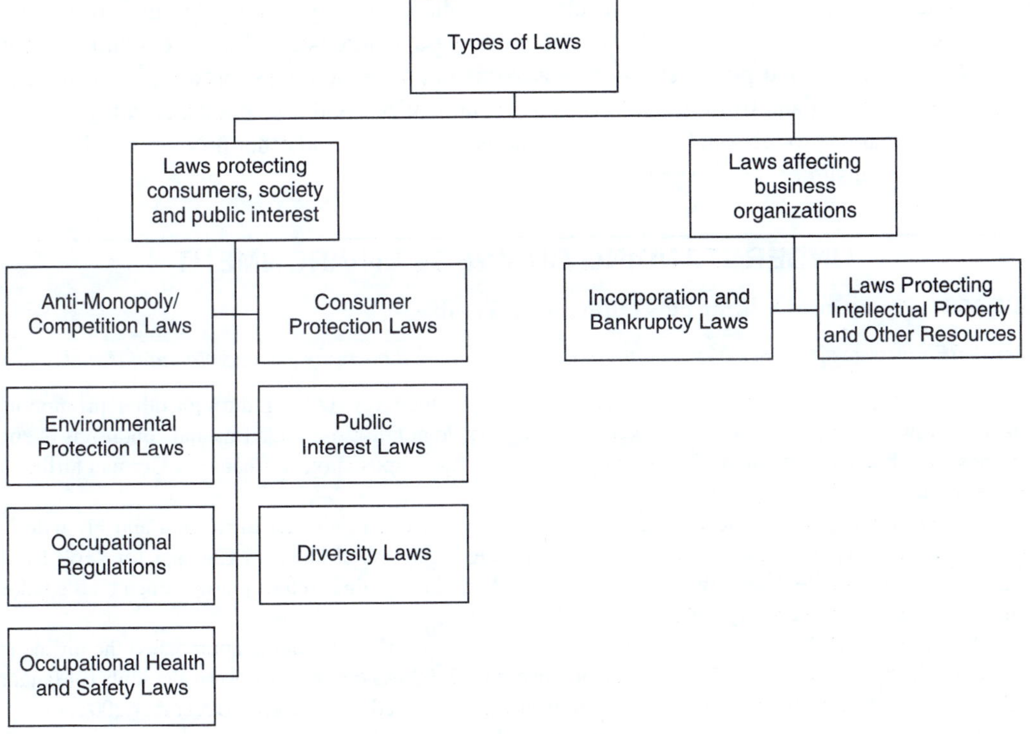

Figure 16.2 Types of Laws Affecting Business.

16.3.1 Laws Protecting Consumers, Society and Public Interest

The laws protecting consumers, society and public interest are as follows:

Anti-monopoly or Competition Laws

Competitive environment promotes efficiency and encourages innovations in an economy. It creates pressure on companies to invent and innovate, differentiate products and improve the quality of their goods and services. However, such improvements come with a cost. To enhance their profits or their relative market position, companies often collude with each other and pursue anti-competitive practices. Anti-competitive practices can take a variety of forms; ranging predatory pricing to collusive practices, such as fixing the price, market sharing to type of goods produced, inputs as well as final products tying, and sharing of the market. However, such practices hurt consumers by the resultant higher prices of the commodities and the reduced choices. Therefore, many countries have formulated **anti-monopoly laws** to protect the interest of the public. These laws are known by various names. For example, in the USA these are referred to as **anti-trust laws**, whereas in the UK, Europe and India these are known as **competition law**. The type of business practices that are considered to be anti-competitive also vary from country to country.

Consumer Protection Laws

A consumer is defined as someone who acquires goods or services for direct use rather than for resale or use in production and manufacturing. **Consumer protection laws** (UBE 16.1) are designed to ensure the rights of consumers by enhancing transparency through information disclosure and fair trade practices. These laws encompass a large body of laws regulating various business transactions and practices, such as advertising, sales practices; product branding; mail fraud; sound banking and truth in lending—credit applications and collections, credit ratings and credit repair issues; product quality and safety; housing material and other product standards; and other types of consumer transactions.

UNDERSTANDING BUSINESS ENVIRONMENT

UBE 16.1 Promotional Scheme Puts Lufthansa in Trouble

This UBE illustrates how lack of transparent practices can put a business organization in a trouble.

Companies often lure customers by offering discounts on their products or through other promotional schemes. However, they can end up in deep trouble if they do not disclose the terms and conditions of such schemes, which amounts to an anti-consumer practice. A fine imposed on Lufthansa, a German airline, in the past highlights this.

Lured by low price air ticket offered by Lufthansa, a German airline, Bhaskaran and his wife, an elderly couple, purchased return journey ticket from the airline travel agent in Chennai for ₹160,160 in August 2002. The couple flew to the US on 8 August 2002, but kept their return journey open on the tickets which were valid up to February 2003 (Deccan Herald, 2012).

While in the USA, Bhaskaran fell ill. Deciding to return early, the couple approached the airline for their return journey sometime in the last week of November 2002. As the seats were not available till January 2003, the couple bought fresh tickets on another airline and returned to India on 1 December 2002.

On their return, the couple was taken aback when Lufthansa refused to return the unused amount on the grounds that they had already charged the couple way below the cost price under an excursion fare scheme.

However, the National Consumer Disputes Redressal Commission pulled up Lufthansa for a non-transparent promotional scheme; for neither specifying on the tickets nor revealing by means of any leaflet that the tickets were issued to the couple under an excursion fare scheme or that no refund was permitted for partially unused tickets.

Imposing a fine of ₹80, 080, the commission stated that the code word that were used for identifying the tickets were concessional were totally for internal consumption; consumers cannot be expected to understand the implications of such codes.

Reference

Deccan Herald (2012), Consumer court pulls up Lufthansa, orders fine, August 22.

Environmental Protection Laws

Environmental laws are complex body of national environmental laws and international treaties on environment protection. These laws broadly fall into two categories, viz., laws aiming to control pollution and laws aiming at resource conservation and management. Laws pertaining to pollution control focus on controlling emissions into different environmental mediums, such as air, water and soil (UBE 16.2). These laws also specify liability for exceeding permitted emissions and responsibility for cleaning up on the defaulting parties. The basic objective of these laws is to preserve the natural environment as well as human health. Laws pertaining to resource conservation and management focus on conservation of natural resources, such as forests, animal species and wildlife, and mineral deposits and natural gas. These laws aim at balancing the benefits of commercial exploitation of resources at present with the benefits arising from the preservation of these resources in the future.

UNDERSTANDING BUSINESS ENVIRONMENT

UBE 16.2 Coca-Cola Blamed for Environmental Damage

Non-compliance with the environmental laws can tarnish the image of a company as highlighted in this UBE.

Coca-Cola had been blamed for environmental damage and many other problems in several countries including India. In March 2010, the company was asked to pay $47 million for the environmental damage at a bottling plant in the southern Indian state of Kerala.

Coca-Cola, one of the best known product names in the world, has long been the leader of the soft drink industry in the international market. The company has weathered several ups and downs and litigations in its journey and had struggled hard to retain its leadership position.

It had been part of several controversies in India. After returning from a two decade absence stemming from a dispute with the government over its domestic ownership, it again landed up into several disputes. Initially, a report issued by a group in New Delhi indicated that the products sold by major carbonated beverage giants Coca-Cola and PepsiCo contained high levels of pesticide residue. Subsequently, later in that year, the company was accused for depleting the ground water in Plachimada village in Kerala. An Indian court ordered it to stop using its Plachimada bottling plant Hindustan Coca-Cola Beverages Private Ltd. (HCBPL). However, the protest continued. The opponents of the company could gather worldwide support and succeeded in getting Plachimada plant closed since 2005. A front page article in the Wall Street Journal (Stecklow, 2005) indicated that the company lost millions of dollars due to reduced sales and legal fees in India as well as growing damage to its reputation elsewhere.

Though the report published by an Indian research group TERI, which found the allegation about pesticide contamination baseless, gave some respite to the company; the report had not given a clean chit to it. The report questioned the setting up of the bottling plants in already water stressed areas.

In 2010, a committee in Kerala that examined the allegations against Coca-Cola found that the factory located in Plachimada had caused excessive depletion of the groundwater resources (Frontline, 2010). The committee also indicated that the company caused severe damage to farms and the local environment by dumping wastewater sludge on area crops from 1999 through 2004. The report by the committee indicated that the villagers experienced severe unemployment since 2000, resulting in 72 per cent of the migration of the worker to the neighbouring villages in search of jobs. The Kerala government accepted the panel's findings and recommended the fine of $48 million to compensate for agriculture loss, health damages, water provision, wage and opportunity loss, and pollution of water resources.

Arguing the report findings baseless, the company challenged the ruling. However, the Kerala government accepted the findings and passed the legislation *Plachimada Coca-Cola Victims' Relief and Compensation Claims Special Tribunal-2011* to provide compensation to individuals for harm and losses caused by the environmental damage done by the Coca-Cola bottling plant.

References

R. Krishnakumar (2010), *Plachimada's Claims*, Vol. 27, No. 15, Jul. 17-30.

Steve Stecklow (2005), How a Global Web of Activists Gives Coke Problems in India, *The Wall Street Journal*, June 7.

Public Interest Laws

The term public interest refers to the common well-being or general welfare. **Public interest laws** try to protect individual rights and enhance general well-being. The agencies that look into general welfare are government agencies, non-profit organizations, international organizations and prosecutor and public defender offices.

Occupational Regulations

Some occupations and professions, such as doctors, lawyers, chartered accountant, architects, teachers, insurance agents and electricians, in public as well as private sectors require professional qualifications. **Occupational regulations** often require procurement of a licence, certificate or registration or membership before a person can begin working in a regulated occupation. A regulatory body sets standards for the occupation and after assessing the qualifications and certificates determines whether the person is qualified to pursue the intended job. Ensuring the required skill sets among professionals, these regulations help serving the public interest. Preventing unethical hiring practices, such regulations also ensure that only those who have the required skill set get hired rather than the person known to the employer.

Diversity Laws

Companies need employees with varied skills, personality traits life experiences to succeed in business. Diversity in workplace, in terms of race, gender, age, disabilities, religion, job title, physical appearance, nationality, ethnicity, competency, training, experience, and personal habits, thus, helps in achieving better relationship with the customers and meeting their needs, and in turn, enhancing customer base as well as opening up new markets. However, diversity also poses tremendous challenges, dealing with which requires fair understanding of the national laws governing diversity. Like occupational laws, the laws governing diversity also intend to prevent unethical practices in hiring process and promote equality in the society by laying down the rules for hiring, promotion, demotion, and firing abuses in workplaces. Most often, these laws emphasize equal pay for equal work. These laws also protect the employees who have filed a discrimination charge or participating in discrimination proceedings or opposing discriminations.

Under these laws, companies can be sued by people who feel they have been discriminated. Proved of discrimination, companies can be fined for such practices (UBE 16.3).

UNDERSTANDING BUSINESS ENVIRONMENT

UBE 16.3 An American Organization Fined for Discrimination in Hiring Practices

Discrimination at work places is prohibited in the USA and in many other countries. This UBA illustrates a case when an American organization was fined for following discrimination in hiring practices.

In the USA, Immigration and Nationality Act (INA) protects work authorized immigrants by prohibiting recruiters discriminating on the basis of citizenship status. Companies violating the provision of this act can be fined as is evident from the ruling given by the Justice Department, which went against the hiring policies of the American Academy of Paediatrics.

Based in Elk Grove Village I11, the American Academy of Paediatrics (AAP) is an American organization of 60,000 paediatricians. It was alleged that AAP impermissibly allowed postings on its website that restricted application for postings as doctors, nurses and other professionals to US citizens and certain visa holders. Finding the allegations to be true, the Justice Department held the view that other work authorized immigrants should have been allowed to apply as well and imposed a penalty of $22,000 (The US Department of Justice, 2011). Apart from the penalty, the settlement agreement required AAP to monitor its job postings to ensure that the work authorized individuals are treated equally. As a part of the settlement, it also agreed to train its PedJobs personnel about its non-discrimination responsibilities under the INA, and to submit periodic reports to the department for three years.

Reference

The United States Department of Justice (2011), Justice Department Settles Allegations of Immigration-Related Employment Discrimination Against American Academy of Paediatrics, Press Release, May 31, (online) http://www.justice.gov/opa/pr/2011/May/11-crt-705.html

Occupational Health and Safety Laws

Safe work environment is not only crucial for the success of the business but also one of the ways to retain staff. Such measures not only help in reducing employee injury and illness-related costs, including medical care, sick leave and disability benefit costs but also help in minimizing the punitive actions taken by the court or compensations paid to the victims in case there is a mishap. By reducing the incidents of mishaps these measures also enhance productivity. In spite of knowing the importance of safety measures in the workplace, companies at times ignore these or follow shortcuts as health and safety equipments can be very expensive. To make companies abide by proper health and safety measures, occupational health and safety laws are introduced. **Safety laws** set out the rights and duties of employers as well as workers to ensure that sufficient measures are in place at the workplace.

16.3.2 Laws Affecting Business Incorporation and Constitution

Although companies are free to organize their employees as they see suitable, to enhance the survival of business organizations, many countries have enacted laws concerning their incorporations and bankruptcy.

Incorporation and Bankruptcy Laws

Most legal jurisdictions specify the forms of ownership that a business can take. Though the forms of business organization vary across jurisdictions, there are some common forms, such as sole proprietorship, partnership, privately and publicly held corporations, and co-operative. **Incorporation laws** vary as per the type of organization. These laws dictate the type of information and the format in which the relevant information need to be made public by a particular type of organization. For example, companies raising capital from the stock markets need to provide detailed information about their financial conditions periodically.

Bankruptcy laws also vary as per the type of organization. For example, in the USA there are three types of bankruptcy—Chapter 7 (Liquidation), Chapter 11 (Restructuring) and Chapter 13 (Personal bankruptcy applicable for sole proprietorship form of organization). In India also bankruptcy laws vary as per the type of organization. For example, if a private limited company becomes insolvent then only the assets of the company are used to clear the debts. The managers of the company have no personal liabilities in such forms of organizations and their assets remain untouched. Managers of such companies can incorporate another company if they wish to do so. On the contrary, if a sole proprietorship or a partnership firm becomes insolvent then the creditors can claim not only the assets of the company but also the property of the person who is the sole proprietor or partners in the company.

Laws Protecting Company's Intellectual Property and Other Resources

Companies spend enormous time, efforts and money to invent new products, and manufacture and market them. The years of efforts and lakhs of money can go waste if the competitors can easily copy these products. In societies where such process is easy, the investment in R&D will be very limited, which will restrict the growth of the country. Hence, laws protecting intellectual property and other valuable resources, such as patent, copyrights and trademarks, which give exclusive right to the company (Box 16.1) to own and control their productive resources and profit from them over a period of time. Such laws, thus, protecting the rights of the inventors, boost technological advancements and create processes more efficiently.

Box 16.1 Intellectual Property Laws

Intellectual property laws deal with protecting the rights of those who create original work of arts or science. These can be divided into two broad categories: (i) The laws protecting industrial property and (ii) the laws protecting literary and artistic work.

Laws Protecting Industrial Property

Industrial property is protected by granting the following by the national government:

Patent: A **patent** gives the inventor an exclusive right to use, sell or manufacture the invented product or process for a certain period of time. Patents protect against the unauthorized use of patented products. For example, patent granted to Suven Life Sciences (Suven) by New Zealand and Australian Patent office for their New Chemical Entities (NCEs) for the treatment of disorders associated with neurodegenerative diseases are valid until 2024 and 2025, respectively; during these years these patents provide Suven exclusive right over the patented product.

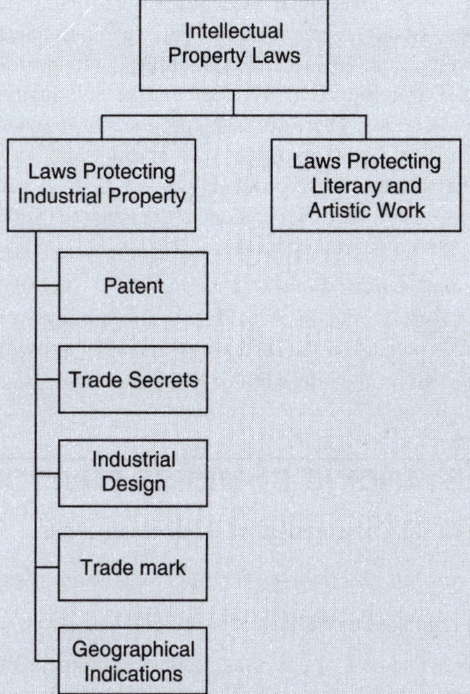

Figure 16.3 Types of Intellectual Property Laws.

Trade Secret: A **trade secret** is a formula, process, device, design or other business information that is kept confidential to maintain an advantage over competitors. It is essentially an internal instrument, the responsibility of protecting a trade secret lies with the owner. For example, the formulation of the drink coca-cola is a trade secret, which is guarded by keeping it locked in a bank vault in Atlanta. The vault can be opened only by a resolution of the company's board and is known to only two employees only at the same time. Unknown to the public, these two employees are not allowed to travel together. Similarly, Google's proprietary search algorithm is a trade secret. Stealing trade secrets is a punishable offence.

Industrial Design: Designs are used in various industries and for various products, such as medical, electrical appliances, computers, jewellery, footwear, apparels, etc. An **industrial design right** protects the outward appearance of a product or a part of it, resulting from the lines, contours, colours, shape, texture, materials, etc. and offers protection for owners of the design and helps in safeguarding the ornamental and aesthetic elements of the object. To be eligible for registration the design has to be unique. For example, Apple has patents over its iPhone and iPad designs.

Trademark: Distinctive single words, numbers, symbols, two or three-dimensional forms, sounds or colours and short phrases cannot be patented. However, **trademark law** protects these identifying marks of products and companies and prevents others using these words/phrases and signs for selling similar products. Trademarks help consumers easily distinguish competing brands from each other. For example, trademark "Coca-Cola" distinguishes the brown colour soda water of a particular manufacturer from its competitors like Pepsi. Similarly, the trademark "Just Do It" is associated with the sport apparel and accessories manufacturer Nike Inc., an American multinational corporation. Trademark protection can be maintained indefinitely.

Geographical Indications: A **geographical indication** is the name or sign used on products to reflect the specific attributes—quality, reputation or some specific characteristics—of their original geographical location of production. In India, for example, Kolhapuri Chappals, Bikaneri Bhujia, Agra Petha, Basmati Rice, Darjeeling Tea, Malabar Coffee and many such products have been granted their geographical indications. There are many products from other countries as well that have received geographical indications. The examples of such products are Scotch Whisky, Irish Whiskey, Florida Oranges and Idaho Potatoes. These products possess distinct peculiar features and quality. Geographical indication laws ensure that the consumers get genuine products of specific quality, and are not deceived by dishonest commercial operators.

Laws Protecting Literary and Artistic Work: Literary works such as novels, poems and plays, films, musical works and artistic works, such as drawings, paintings, photographs and sculptures, and architectural designs are protected by national governments by providing copyrights. Copyrights, represented by symbol ©, do not protect ideas but only the way these ideas are expressed.

UNDERSTANDING BUSINESS ENVIRONMENT

UBE 16.4 Acts Influencing Legal Environment of Business in India

This UBE highlights some of the acts and policies that affect the business environment in India.

In India business activities are regulated by various acts and policies. Some of these acts are detailed here:

The Sale of Goods Act, 1930: The sale of goods act defines and amends the laws relating to the sale of goods. It also governs the contracts relating to the sale of goods, which includes transfer of ownership of goods, delivery of goods rights, duties of buyers and sellers, remedies for breach of contract, conditions and warranties implied under a contract for sale of goods.

Indian Companies Act, 1956: The Companies Act, 1956 regulates the formation, functioning, financing and winding up of companies. The objectives of the act are:

- To help the development of companies in a healthy way
- To protect the interest of shareholders as there is separation between ownership and management of companies
- To safeguard the interest of creditors
- To achieve the ultimate ends of social and economic policy of the government
- To empower the government to intervene in the affairs of a company so that the interest of all its stakeholders is protected

The act has been amended from time to time in the light of changing economic environment. The latest amendment was in 2006.

Income Tax Act, 1961: Income tax is levied with two-fold objectives. First, it aims at an equitable distribution of the tax burden. Second, it aims at raising resources for the government. With these two objectives, the Government of India enacted the Income Tax Act, 1961. Over a period of time, because of various amendments and policy changes, this law became very cumbersome and uncomprehensible for a common man. Considering the deficiencies of the existing income tax laws, the Direct Tax Code, 2012, will replace the five decade old income tax, which is expected to be economically efficient, effective and equitable and likely to improve voluntary compliance, increase the tax to GDP ratio, and reduce the scope for disputes and minimize litigations.

The Consumer Protection Act, 1986: The Consumer Protection Act is meant to be for an ordinary consumer, i.e., the person who buys goods for his personal use and not for resale or for any commercial purpose. The objectives of the act are:

- To protect the consumers from marketing of goods which are hazardous to life and property
- To safeguard the consumers from unfair trade practices
- To provide consumers an access to a variety of goods and services at competitive prices
- To ensure availability of sufficient information to consumers regarding quality, quantity, potency, purity, standard and price of the goods that they aim at purchasing.

The latest amendment to the bill was made in 2011 for speedy execution of court rulings to provide quick justice to aggrieved consumers.

The Weights & Measures Act, 1976: To provide better protection to consumers by ensuring accuracy in the weights and measurement, the Standard of Weights and Measurement Act, 1976 replaced the large number of weights and measures used in the trade and commerce. As, its enforcement lies with the state governments, a new act, known as the Standards of Weights and Measures (Enforcement) Act, 1985 was enacted.

Environment Protection Act, 1986: With the objective of providing protection and improvement of environment, which includes water, air, land, human being, other living creatures, plants, micro-organism and properties, and matter connected with the environment, the Environment Protection Act was enacted in 1986. The act has provision for fine of upto ₹ 1 lakh and imprisonment of up to 5 years or both for non-compliance with the various sections of the act.

Patent Act, 1970 and Patent (Amendment) Bill 2005: A patent confers legal rights to the owner for the exploitation of an invention and prevents others from copying the invention. However, such a protection also creates patent monopolies and leaves scope for large difference between marginal cost of production and the price charged to the consumers. Therefore, patent policies try to balance between protecting the rights of innovators and ensuring access to resources at reasonable prices. In India the Patent Act of 1970 emphasized the public interest (availability of goods to the public at cheaper rates) over monopoly rights; hence, patents were only issued for methods of producing products and not for the products themselves. However, compliance requirement under the World Trade Organization (WTO) agreement on Trade Related Aspects of Intellectual Property Rights (TRIPS) and the growing recognition that a low cost-driven strategy is not conducive for research and development and innovations compelled the government to amend the existing act. Accordingly, the Patent (Amendment) Bill, 2005, replaced the process patent with the product patent.

Labour and Employment Laws: Laws relating to labour and employment fall broadly under the category of Industrial Laws which try to take care of the complex relationship between the workers and business. There is a plethora of such laws in India. Some such laws are:

- *The Factories Act, 1948:* The Factories Act enacted in 1948 aims at promoting the growth of factories in a systematic manner. It also aims at improving the working conditions in the factories by regulating working hours, leaves, holidays, overtime, employment of children, women and young persons and ensuring adequate safety measures by setting minimum requirements for safety, health and welfare of workers.
- *The Minimum Wage Act, 1948:* The Minimum Wage Act binds the employer to pay the minimum wages fixed under the Act from time to time. Thus, it tries to ensure the interest of the workers primarily in the unorganized sector. The fixation of minimum wages depends on factors such as level of income and paying capacity, prices of essential commodities, productivity, local conditions, etc. As these factors vary from State to State there is wide variation in the minimum wages across

the states. Hence, to bring in more uniformity, initially, the Central Government introduced a 'national floor level minimum wage' at ₹ 35 per day. As per the latest revision, which took place in 2011, the floor is at ₹ 115 per day.

- *Industrial Disputes Act, 1947:* The Industrial Disputes Act, aims at settlement of industrial disputes by mediation, conciliation, adjudication and arbitration. This act has a provision for payment of compensation in case of lay-off and retrenchment.
- *Employees' State Insurance Act, 1948:* Sickness benefit, maternity benefits, disablement benefit and medical benefit are addressed by the Employees' State Insurance Act.
- *Employment (Standing Orders) Act, 1948:* This act enforces industrial organizations to clearly specify the conditions of employment under them and make them known to their workmen.
- *Employees' Provident Fund Act, 1952:* This act seeks to make a provision for industrial workers after their retirement or retrenchment or for their dependents after their premature death.

Some other laws addressing the labour and employment issues are Maternity Benefit Act, 1961, Payment of Gratuity Act, 1972, Equal Remuneration Act, 1976, etc.

MRTP Act and Competition Act: To prevent the concentration of wealth and the means of production in a few hands, and to promote competitive forces for better product and reasonable prices, the Monopolies and Restrictive Trade Practices (MRTP) Act came into force in 1969. The MRTP act was replaced by the Competition Law in 2002. The object of the new law is to promote and sustain competition in markets as well as to ensure the freedom of trade and to protect the interest of consumers.

FERA, 1973 and FEMA, 1999: With the objective of preventing the outflow of Indian currency the Foreign Exchange Regulation Act (FERA) was enacted in 1973. However, in the post-reform era, the stance of the government towards foreign exchange transaction has shifted from regulation to facilitation of transactions. To have more facilitating environment towards external trade and payments and foreign exchange market, the FERA was replaced by the Foreign Exchange Management Act (FEMA) in 1999.

SUMMARY

At times, the interest of a business organization may be in conflict with the interest of its various stakeholders, such as shareholders, employees, consumers, and society in general.

Various laws and government policies, which constitute the legal environment of business, try to protect various stakeholders of a business organization, by influencing business activities.

Broadly, the laws affecting business activities can be classified as the laws protecting consumers, society and public interest and the laws affecting business organizations. Anti-monopoly or competition laws, consumer protection laws, environmental protection laws, public interest laws, occupational laws, diversity laws, occupational health and safety laws focus at protecting consumers, society and public interest, whereas incorporation and bankruptcy laws and intellectual property laws affect business incorporation and constitution.

Promoting and infusing competition in the market, competition laws help consumers by lowering prices and improving quality. Such laws necessitate information disclosure and compel companies to follow fair trade policies. Environmental protection laws help the society by limiting pollution and promoting resource conservation and management. Preventing unethical hiring practices and maintaining quality of services, occupational regulations try to ensure right jobs for right persons. Diversity in terms of race, gender, age, religion, etc., is ensured by diversity laws. Safety at the workplace is maintained by occupational health and safety laws.

The forms, working process and bankruptcy procedures for companies are dealt by incorporation and bankruptcy laws. Intellectual property and other resources of business organizations are protected by intellectual property laws, such as patent, trade secrets, industrial design, trademark, geographical indications, and copyright.

India also has several laws affecting business activities and practices. Some of these laws are: Sale of Goods Act, Weights and Measurement Act, Indian Companies Act, Consumer Protection Act, Income Tax Act, Patent Act, Labour and Employment Laws, Factories Act, Minimum Wage Act, Industrial Disputes Act, Employment Act, Employees Provident Fund Act, MRTP Act and Competition Act, and FERA and FEMA.

Implications for Business

Various business activities and practices, such as establishing a new organization, hiring and firing practices, marketing strategies, dividend policy, resource acquisition methods, are significantly influenced not only by the existing domestic framework but also by the global legal framework in an open economic environment. With rapid changes in technology and integration of economies, the legal environment is becoming dynamic and complex. Survival in a growing complex environment and achieving a competitive edge over the competitors require good understanding of the existing legal framework.

There are manifold benefits of keeping abreast of legal environment of business. On the one hand, the knowledge of laws relating to business organizations help a company remaining ahead of competition without getting victimized by the malpractices pursued by the competitors, keeping intellectual property rights intact, and accessing resources at the right price. On the other hand, the knowledge of laws protecting consumers, society and public interest helps companies maintaining their brand image and retaining the goodwill of their stakeholders.

Though legal experts can be hired by a company to comply with legal issues while making business decisions, it is expensive as well as risky as the legal experts may not be well-versed with business objectives, its operations, and current market and economic realities. Better results can be obtained when managers, with some broad understanding of the legal environment, work jointly with legal advisors.

Ignorance of legal issues can cost the company not only in monetary terms but also in non-monetary terms like loosing goodwill of consumers and other stakeholders.

REVIEW QUESTIONS

16.1 What do you understand by legal environment?

16.2 Whom do various laws and government policies try to protect?

16.3 What types of laws are applicable for business organizations?

16.4 What are anti-monopoly or competition laws? Whose interest these laws serve?

16.5 What are the different types of laws that protect the interest of consumers, society and public?

16.6 What is the objective of diversity laws?

16.7 What laws affect business organizations?

16.8 What are the different types of laws that protect intellectual property?

16.9 What are the differences between trademark and copyright?

6.10 What are the differences between trademark and geographical indications?

6.11 Which type of protection is granted to business organizations forever?

6.12 What are the different types of laws that are applicable to business organizations in India?

6.13 Which law at present in India tries to promote competition in India?

6.14 Which law is applicable to foreign exchange transactions in India?

6.15 Which laws in India try to protect the interest of employees?

6.16 Whose interest the Weights and Measures Act in India tries to protect?

CASE ANALYSIS EXERCISE

C16.1 Google in Controversy

Google Inc., an American multinational, in the recent period is once again in a controversy. Founded in 1996 and incorporated in 1998, Google provides various internet related products, such as internet search, cloud computing, software and advertising technologies. Of these services, Google Search dominate the internet search market not only in the USA but many other countries including the European Union.

Recently, the company is in news headlines of many leading newspapers in the USA. It is likely to be hit with an anti-trust case in the USA. The New York Times, a leading newspaper, in its edition of 12 October 2012, reported that the Federal Trade Commission (FTC) is preparing a case that looks at the question of whether Google manipulates its search results to favour its products, and whether it makes it more difficult for rivals' products to appear prominently in those results.

The probe by the FTC was initiated on receiving complaints from many of Google rivals regarding its anti-competitive practices in ad pricing, shopping search and the ranking of Websites in search results and ad listings. Facing a sharp decline in online traffic from Google Search, NexTag, a competitor in comparison shopping service, in its complain to FTC, has argued that Google is manipulating its search results to harm commerce competitors. The opponents have cited that a simple Google search for "Miami flights" displays a large Google results box underneath the top sponsored links featuring airfare quotes from Google's partners. On the whole, the internet search giant has been accused by rivals that Google is using its dominant position to foreclose competitors from the search marketplace, especially in high traffic segments like travel, jobs, health, real estate, media and local search. In an attempt to curtail competition, Google is unfairly demoting rival products and favouring its own commercial services, such as Google Shopping for buying goods and Google Places for advertising local restaurants and businesses over rival specialized search engines and search advertisers.

Critics of the probe, however, are arguing that having a monopoly in a given market is not, in itself, illegal. Though it is illegal to retain a monopoly power through anti-competitive practices, Google has not built a dominant position through anti-competitive methods but through the merits of its superior products. Consumers are using Google services because of their superior quality. In a rapidly changing technology sector, various players can create their own space. Dominance of Facebook and Twitter in the social networking sites and Google's failure to make inroads into such sites proves the point. Google has been arguing that the US anti-trust law is aimed at protecting consumers; but most of the complaints directed against it are from its rivals rather than consumers. Google has monopoly power only in search services; in no ways this power has been used for exploiting consumers. It is neither charging exploitative price (as such services are free) nor preventing consumers from switching to a rival search engine. In other internet product markets it does not command monopoly. For example, Google advertising competes closely with other online advertising, such as display ads and mobile ads, and even traditional forms of advertising, such as print, TV, radio, etc. Google, the owner of its search page has the prerogative to display its own services.

Supporting the Google stand, it has been argued that heavy regulation will simply hamper technological innovations, and it will constrain not only the growth of fast moving industry—internet search, online commerce and smart phone field but also the economies depended heavily on this industry. Critics of the Google practices, on the contrary, have been emphasizing that Google, being a monopoly in the search engine, has less competitive pressure to improve; hence, it is more likely to lose sight of consumer/customer interests.

The charges of anti-competitive practices on Google are not new. Also in the past, Google has been charged for following anti-competitive practices. Previously, to resolve the charge that it bypassed Apple Safari browser privacy settings that blocked cookies for their users, Google reached a record $ 22.5 million settlement with the FTC in July 2012. Similarly, in April 2012, after finding that Google deliberately delayed an investigation into how it collected data for Google Street View, a technology used in Google Maps and Google Earth, the FTC fined the company $25,000.

Google has faced an anti-trust investigation not only in the USA but also in Europe. The European Commission launched an investigation into the company's search practices on receiving complaints from other search engines, such as Foundem, eJustice. Fr and Microsoft's Ciao, that the company favoured its own Web services in search results on Google.com over theirs. The rivals argued that such practices by Google put them at a significant competitive disadvantage in the market. The coalition opposing Google includes the FairSearch.org consortium, which is composed of several of Google's competitors including Microsoft.

Speculating over the outcome, the anti-trust experts in the USA indicate that most likely the regulators would push for a commitment from Google for not using it's dominate position in the internet search market to discriminate small competitors to get an unfair advantage in its own other businesses. If the FTC and Google fail to agree on a settlement, the lawsuit against Google is the likelihood, which will be the major action taken against any technology company since a similar action taken against Microsoft in the 1990s by the government.

Reference

The New York Times (2012), Drafting Antitrust Case, F.T.C. Raises Pressure on Google, October 12.

Questions

1. Why Google is in controversy?
2. In your view, is Google pursuing anti-competitive practices? Why?
3. What will be the outcome if the internet market is heavily regulated? Show the impact diagrammatically.
4. What are the possible outcomes if anti-competitive practices are not curbed?

FURTHER SUGGESTED READING

Centre for Trade and Development (2010), Competition Law and Indian Pharmaceutical Industry, Competition Commission of India, (online) http://www.cci.gov.in/images/media/completed/PharmInd230611.pdf.

Institute for Social and Economic Change (2012), **Competitive Assessment of Onion Markets in India** Competition Commission of India, (online) http://www.cci.gov.in/images/media/completed/AO.pdf.

CHAPTER 17

Demographic Environment of Business

17.1 INTRODUCTION

Kenneth Gronbach, internationally recognized demographer and expert in generational marketing in his book *The Age Curve* shares an experience of sales cycles faced by American Honda Motorcycle, a client of his marketing company for advertising. In 1979, the client company was selling 4,00,000 motorcycles that were targeted to motorcycle buying men 16 to 24 years old per year and had a 40 per cent share of the market. The success continued till the mid-1980s until a jolt came in 1986 in the form of screeching halt in sales.

To push up the sales figure, Honda tried various strategies from moulding the design, increasing marketing budget, reducing prices and advertising through various media like billboards, print, radio and TV, albeit without any success. Between 1986 and 1992 sales dropped by almost 80 per cent, leading to the closure of 130 dealerships. Not only Honda but other motorcycle manufacturers—Suzuki, Kawasaki and Yamaha—also saw dwindling in their sales figure without any inkling of what was going wrong.

Suspecting a change in the behaviour of generation X, which was at that time in the target age group of 16 to 24 years, for this fall in the demand, Gronbach made his research department study the behaviour of this generation. The research indicated that the behaviour of Generation X was not much different from Baby Boomers, but it was a small group. This finding gave the clue to Gronbach that it was the total number of men in the target age group that was much lesser in Generation X than the Boomers, causing a sharp decline in the sales figure. Had the motorcycle manufacturers looked at the size of this age group, a very crucial demographic aspect, while estimating the potential demand rather than focusing only on other factors that affect demand (such as disposable income, employment, other alternative mode of transports, etc.), they would have been able to better manage their production plans.

The above incident highlights the importance of demographic changes for demand forecasting and production planning. However, demographic changes pose challenges not only from demand but also from the supply side. With baby boomers preparing to retire, countries with higher proportion of aging population, such as the USA, Germany, Japan, Singapore, Australia, China, South Korea, are facing severe labour shortage apart from other challenges associated with such a demographic change. The governments of some of these countries like the USA and

Singapore have already initiated the process to deal with the shortage by raising the retirement age and/or bringing in social security reforms while the government of some other countries like China and South Korea are intending to bring in some such reforms. Another supply side challenge that is predominantly emerging from the demographic challenge is for countries like India where the population of children is increasing rapidly and putting the burden on education system. Educational shortage may turn into skill shortage in these countries.

Demographic changes are of concern for everyone—individuals, families, business organizations and governments. Such changes can alter individual priorities, family structure, business marketing, production and hiring decisions, and influence government policies. Given the significant influence of changes in demographic environment on strategic decisions this chapter looks into various aspects of demography. Section 17.2 highlights the meaning of demography and details on the different components of demography. Section 17.3 describes the determinants of demography, whereas Section 17.4 details on the uses of Demography for Business Managers.

17.2 DEMOGRAPHY AND ITS CHARACTERISTICS

Demography is the study of the three basic characteristics of human population, i.e., size, composition and distribution. The basic determinants of these characteristics are fertility, mortality and migration.

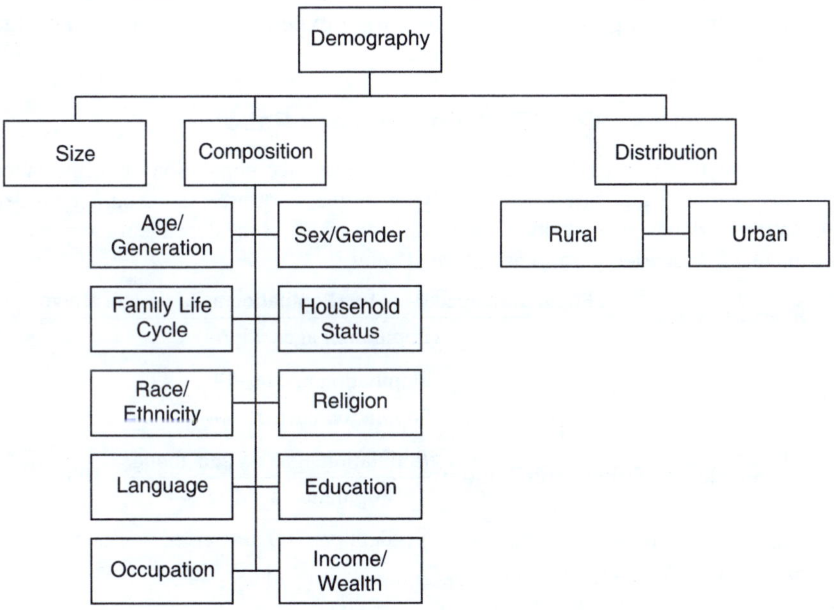

Figure 17.1 Characteristics of Demography.

The characteristics of Demography as depicted in Figure 17.1 are described hereinafter.

1. Size: We can estimate the size of a country by counting the number of people in that country. The size of the population and its growth rate has both demand and supply side effects. There is an old saying that with every mouth God sends a pair of hands. Going by the saying and drawing an analogy, an expansion in the size increases the consumption needs (representing the number of mouths), and hence, demand for different goods and services. But, at the same time, it also enhances the amount of labour (representing the pair of hands), which is a factor of production enhancing the production capacity.

2. Composition: The composition of population can be assessed by classifying it by using different criteria described as follows:

3. Age Composition/Generations: Classification of total population into different age groups provides the **age composition** of the population. Broadly the population is divided into three groups as follows:

(i) Child Population: Population aged 0–14 years

(ii) Working Population/Labour Force: Population aged 15–64 years

(iii) Aged Population/Retired: Population aged 65 and above

Such a classification is widely used by different economic agents.

Governments, the world over, use such a classification to estimate the dependency ratio (Box 17.1) and plan their regional socio-economic policies. Regions dominated by the child population require allocating larger government expenditure on school education, whereas that dominated by teenage or young adult population necessitate larger diversion of funds for higher education or vocational training programmes. Similarly, dominance of the middle-aged population necessitates focus of policies toward the creation of employment opportunities, whereas greater proportion of aged or retired population requires larger expenses on medical health facilities and pensions.

Box 17.1 Dependency Ratio

The population aged 15 to 64 is considered to be working age population or in the labour force. The population below 15 and above 65 is usually out of the workforce; hence, it is considered to be dependent on the working age population. Depending on which of the dependent group is considered, we can estimate the **dependency ratio** as indicated here:

$$\text{Total Dependency Ratio} = \frac{(\text{Population aged 0–14}) + (\text{Population aged 65 and above})}{(\text{Population aged 15–64})} \times 100$$

$$\text{Child Dependency Ratio} = \frac{\text{Population aged 0–14}}{\text{Population aged 15–64}} \times 100$$

$$\text{Old Age Dependency Ratio} = \frac{\text{Population aged 65 and above}}{\text{Population aged 15–64}} \times 100$$

All these ratios are presented as the number of dependent per 100 persons of working age population.

The dependency ratio is important for various reasons as outlined here:

- First, the ratio reflects the burden of supporting children and aged on the working population. The burden is not only in the form of direct expenses on education, healthcare, etc. but also in the form of higher taxes that the government imposes when the dependency ratio increases to cover up its expenses.
- Second, the dependent population is a bigger recipient of government spending in the form of scholarships, education, pensions, healthcare, etc.; hence, the burden on fiscal exchequer increases with the increase in the dependency ratio. For countries like Italy high dependency ratio has been identified as one of the reasons for high public debt ratio.

- Third, the dependency ratio has a significant influence on government policies. The increasing dependency ratio has made some governments to raise the retirement age to take care of the shrinking labour force. Some governments have tackled the problem by encouraging immigration of young working age people, whereas some others have tackled pension burden on the fiscal exchequer by reducing the amount of state pensions and encouraging private pension schemes.

Consumer needs vary as per their age, and hence, the age distribution is equally important for business organizations for segmenting the markets and designing and targeting products for specific age groups. Business organizations also divide the population into generations, which is one way of classifying the population using the age criteria, to design and target products and effectively communicate with different generations as indicated in UBE 17.1. The world population is aging, though that is expected to bring in new challenges, but also new opportunities for business organizations as highlighted in UBE 17.2.

UNDERSTANDING BUSINESS ENVIRONMENT

UBE 17.1 Communicating Effectively with Different Generations in the USA

For effective communication with different types of clients, often business organizations divide the population into different generations as illustrated in this UBE.

Business organizations have to interact with different age groups and generations simultaneously. For effective communication with different generations, they usually differentiate their characteristics and devise and adopt methods which work well with them.

In the USA, for example, the generations are classified as Veterans or Seniors (born before 1945); Baby Boomers (born during 1946 to 1964); Gen X (born during 1965–1979) and Gen Y (born after 1980). The specific characteristics of each of these of generations and their communication needs are as follows:

Veterans or Seniors: The **generation of seniors**, which is already retired from the workforce, had seen very hard time during the Great Depression and the Second World War, is characterized by high moral values and dedication to the work. However, many of this generation are uninitiated to the new technology like the internet, and hence, sceptical of its use. This generation can be better dealt with direct communication through traditional methods, such as landline telephone, postal mail, handwritten or typed circulars.

Baby Boomers: Born in the post World War Second period of food rationing and massive social restructuring, the generation of **baby boomers** was forced to imagine and invent new methods to enhance productivity and fulfil its needs. More liberated, better educated and better travelled, this generation not only experienced personal success but also drastic change in family structure and relationships. The generation that was known for its rebellious nature in teens and twenties, over the period of time has become quite possessive of whatever it has created – family, business, property and does not want to lose its control over its own creations. Though many of this generation have already embraced the internet and mobile phones in their lifestyle, the preferred mode of communication for them is still direct contact or mail rather than the virtual interaction.

Generation X: The **generation X** is often referred to as "baby busters" as they are attributed to a rapid decline in birth rates caused by delaying marriages and parenthood. This generation is more resourceful and educated than the previous generation "Baby Boomers". Sceptical of the authority commanded by the baby boomers, the generation X focusses on outcomes and skills. Their loyalty is to the return they receive rather than the organization for which they work. Well-educated and well-versed with the recent technological developments, the generation X prefers internet, though selective, for communication and gathering information.

Generation Y: The **generation Y**, known as the Millennials, the Google generation or the iPod generation, brought up with fewer siblings and in a comparatively stable economic environment, is highly individualistic, overly ambitious and impatient, and highly demanding. This generation values quality and authenticity. At work place, they look for "inclusion and collaborative" rather than the "command and control" approach.

Living with a blurred vision of work and social life, the generation Y prefers multi-tasking communicates with the peers in a complex but integrated structure with a rapid speed. Not hesitant to make public their personal life, it is all open to see on Facebook, which is bewildering and hard to digest for their previous generations. This generation can be best approached or contacted through a variety of technological mediums.

UNDERSTANDING BUSINESS ENVIRONMENT

UBE 17.2 The Aging World Population: Challenge or Opportunity?

Changing composition of world population is bringing in new challenges for business organizations, but also many opportunities as highlighted in this UBE.

The world population has been exploding—some decades ago this used to be cited as one of the main problems of many developing countries. However, exploding population had been leveraged as one of the main assets of growth by some of the countries like China, and is not considered to be a major problem now-a-days. Presently, what the world, especially the developed world, fearing is the changing composition of this population. The population world over is growing older, year after year, and is projected to be older further with the declining share of child population. As per the World Population Prospects (the 2010 revision) in 1950, 34 per cent of the world population was child population. The share of this group has declined to 26 per cent in 2010, and is projected to be around 18 per cent by the end of this century. On the contrary, the share of aged is increasing year after year, increasing from 8 per cent in 1950 to 10 per cent in 2010 and projected to increase further to 22 per cent by the end of the century (Figure 17.2).

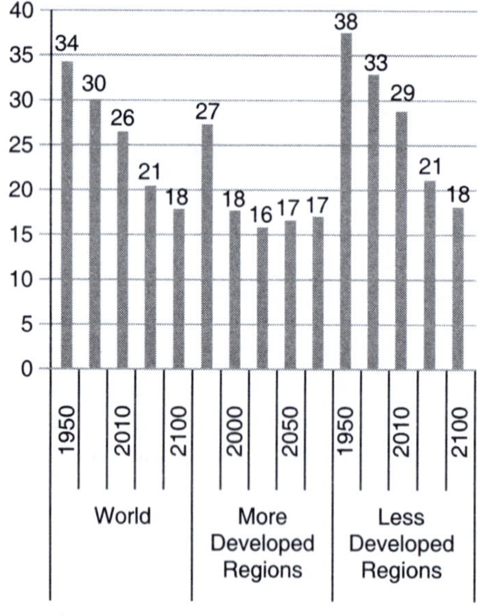

(a) Percentage population age 0–14 years

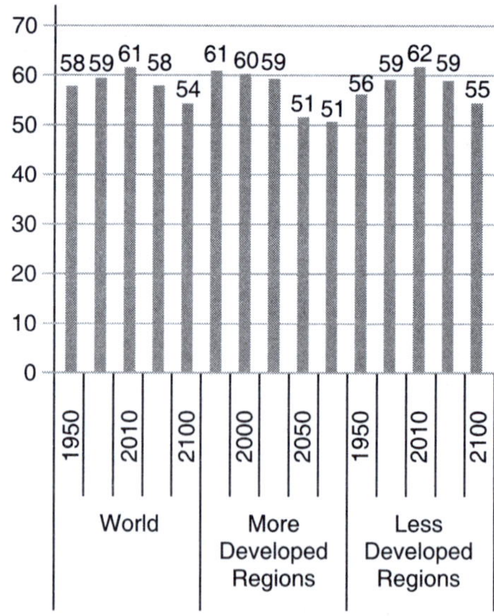

(b) Percentage population age 15–59 years

Figure 17.2 *Contd...*

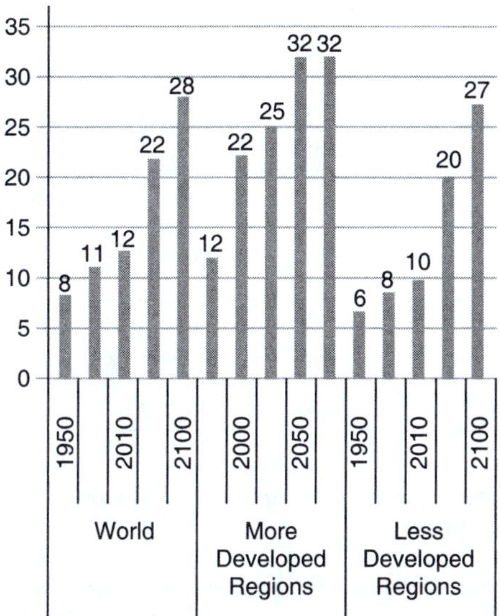

(c) Percentage population age 60 and above

Source: Figures are plotted on the basis of data available from the United Nations' Department of Economic and Social Affairs/Population Division (2012), World Population Prospects: The 2010 Revision.

Figure 17.2 Percentage Distribution by Age Group.

Major affected are the already rich countries like Japan, South Korea, Taiwan in Asia, Germany, Italy and Spain in Europe and Russia in Eastern Europe. The less affected amongst the advanced countries are the USA, the UK, France and many Nordic countries which have a comparatively good share of the child population to keep the countries young.

Problem of aging population is not yet so alarming for the developing countries as of now, but would be engulfing even them by the end of this century when the share of the child population in these countries would be almost equal to that in the advanced countries. The fear is that when these countries will be entrapped into old age problem, the enormity of the problem will be far more severe for them, because these countries are so populous that they might find it difficult to manage the number of aged. Though overall these countries are yet young, with children under age 15 accounting 29 per cent of the population and young persons aged 15 to 24 accounting for further 18 per cent, some countries are aging fast. For example, China's "one child policy" though managed to curb the population growth in the last 30 years, has also been responsible for its rapidly aging population.

What is causing aging worldwide?

There are two long-term trends that are blamed for the alarmingly growing population of aged as outlined here:

- First, families world over are having far less children now than that in the last century, resulting in a decline in the crude birth rate as well as fertility rate (Table 17.1). Work pressures, by increasing the opportunity cost of raising children, restricting the size of the family, on the one hand, and government policies restricting the number of children a couple can have on the other, have contributed to the declining trend. The declining trend in birth rate and fertility rate has been steadily reducing the share of children in the total population (Figure 17.2 a.).

  This trend was first noticed in developed nations, but gradually also gripped the developing world.

Table 17.1 Crude Birth Rate and Total Fertility Rate by Major Regions

Major Regions	*1950-55*	*2005-10**	*2050-55**	*2095-100**
Crude Birth Rate (births per 1,000 population)				
World	36.9	20.0	13.8	12.1
More Developed Regions	22.4	11.4	11.1	11.4
Less Developed Regions	43.5	21.9	14.3	12.2
Total Fertility Rate (children per women)				
World	4.95	2.52	2.15	2.03
More Developed Regions	2.81	1.66	1.99	2.07
Less Developed Regions	6.07	2.67	2.16	2.02

* Projected Values

Source: Compiled from UN Department of Economic and Social Affairs/Population Division (2011), World Population Prospects: The 2010 Revision.

- Second, better healthcare services and awareness have resulted in lowering of crude death rate and improved the life expectancy at birth initially in more developed regions and then gradually in less developed regions as well. During 1950–55, the life expectancy at birth for the world was just around 47 years. By now it has almost doubled and stands around 68 years. Substantial improvement are expected to enhance it further to 81 years by the end of this century (Table 17.2).

Table 17.2 Crude Death Rate and Life Expectancy at Birth by Major Regions

Major Regions	*1950–55*	*2005–10*	*2050–55**	*2095–100**
Crude Death Rate (deaths per 1,000 population)				
World	18.7	8.4	10.2	11.5
More Developed Regions	10.3	10.0	12.4	10.6
Less Developed Regions	22.6	8.0	9.9	11.6
Life Expectancy at Birth (years)				
World	47.7	67.9	76.3	81.1
More Developed Regions	65.9	76.9	83.3	88.2
Less Developed Regions	42.3	65.9	75.1	80.1

* Projected Values

Source: Compiled from United Nations' Department of Economic and Social Affairs / Population Division (2011), World Population Prospects: The 2010 Revision.

Why aging a cause of concern?

Concerns are manifolds:

- First, countries of the aging population will face not only a sharp reduction in working force but also in productivity; hence these countries are threatened by the prospects of declining output growth in the coming decades.
- Second, the aging population will increase the age old dependency ratio. Health expenses of the aged are much more than that of children. This is expected to increase the total expenditure of families, especially on healthcare and medicines.

- Third, in countries where pensions are the main source of income for the elderly and the retired, the burden on fiscal exchequer will increase enormously unless the governments' of these countries reform their pension system, which might be politically a sensitive issue. Some countries even have generous public healthcare system. As the population becomes old and frail the expenses on healthcare will also grow, putting further pressure on fiscal exchequer.
- Fourth, to support the aged, working population may be subjected to higher taxes, which may be disincentive for work and investment. Therefore, there may be further fall in productivity.
- Fifth, contraction in growth is feared not only because of shrinkage in labour force and productivity but also because of decline in overall saving and investment. The basis of such fears is the Life Cycle Hypothesis formulated by Modigliani and Brumberg which points out that individuals plan their consumption and saving behaviour over their expected life duration. They build up assets in the initial stages of their working life and make use of these assets to meet their expenses post-retirement to maintain the lifestyle that they are used to. Going by this hypothesis, larger share of aged population will reduce the overall saving, and hence, the overall investment in the economy, reducing the productive capacity of the economy.

Are there only problems or even opportunities for businesses?

Changing age structure possess not only challenges but also creates new opportunities for businesses. In the economies with rising share of aged, business will faces challenges not only on supply (work force) front but also on demand front. The aging population though will shrink the overall demand, it will create new opportunities for business. The structural changes in the demand will give a boost to inventions and innovations of new technology that can help aged to maintain their health, independence and quality of life. There will be huge demand for healthcare, telemedicine, nutrition, home remodeling, tourism, sports, home security and other products catering to the needs of aged. Customization will be the mantra of success in such a market. Many companies, from diverse fields, have already initiated customizing their products. For example, mobile companies have come up with customizable font size and sound speed. Automobile companies like Ford Motors have designed a hands free parallel parking system. Confectionary manufacturers have come up with baked potato chips or mutli-grain biscuits targeting specifically the aged. Catering the needs of old, insurance companies like Allianz have developed holistic pension solutions that offer asset management as well as insurance, providing guaranteed returns and protection against market volatility and inflation. More or more such initiatives and strategies are surfacing on business front.

---

4. Race/Ethnicity: Classification of population on the basis of race or ethnicity is subjective as individuals usually identify their own race or ethnicity in the population census conducted by their countries. For example, in the USA Census there are six race/ethnic categories: American Indian, Asian, Black, White, Hispanic and Others.

Such a classification is used by different economic agents for variety of reasons.

Government officials formulate development policies that can tackle the problem of ethnic groups. Political parties often design political campaign that can lure the dominant racial group or ethnic group of their area. NGOs and Social activities use such data to defend their request for grants for activities and schemes targeted towards specific ethnic or racial groups from donor organizations. Business organizations also use such a data for a variety of business strategies. They often use such a data to design advertisement that can attract the dominant category. Similarly, investment decisions are often based on such information. For example, in a predominantly Hispanic area investment in start up Spanish Radio is considered to be a lucrative business proposition but not in an area dominated by the Asian community.

5. Religion: Religion categories in demographic classification also vary across countries. For example, in India major religions are Muslim and Hindu.

Business organisations take care of the religious sentiments while designing their products. For example, McDonalds sells burgers through its outlets worldwide. However, the ones sold in India are made from lamb rather than beef because of religious sentiments.

6. Language: Depending on the major language spoken in a particular country, the classification of population according to language also varies across countries.

Businesses use such information for a variety of reasons. For example, regional radio stations develop their programmes in a language or a dialect that is commonly spoken in a specific region. A regional station situated in Agra district of Uttar Pradesh in India prefers preparing and offering programmes in Braj Bhasha, the regional language of that area. Similarly, Konkani is the preferred language for regional radio stations located in Dabhol in Maharashtra in India. Likewise, businesses use population classification on the basis of language to select the language of advertisement for their products. Multinationals entering a new market often use such information for deeper penetration of their products. For such purposes, often they hire specialist conversant in widely spoken local languages.

7. Education: Education profile is assessed by enumerating the number of people of 18 years and above attaining a specified level of education.

The education profile communicates a variety of aspects of the population of a country. First of all it hints at the skill set available in the country. Governments use such information for designing employment generating schemes. For example, in areas where education level is very low or the majority of the population is just middle class or higher school classifications, the jobs that require unskilled or semi-skilled labour need to be created to increase the level of employment in that region.

Such information is also used by businesses. For example, IT companies in India prefer setting their units in places like Bangalore or Pune where skilled labour force (people with a degree in information technology or some professional qualifications in this area) is easily available. Similarly, California is one of the preferred destinations in the USA for IT companies.

Education level also often influences income, product choices and standard of living. Businesses, hence, often use such information for market research and product targeting.

8. Occupation: Different countries have been using different occupation classification. The classification has been varying not only inter-spatially but also inter-temporally. In early classification systems, the emphasis was on the industry in which one worked, whereas in the most recent classification systems the emphasis has shifted to the characteristics of the work done by the person.

Occupational data is used by businesses for targeting and pricing their products. For example, insurance companies use the occupational classification to estimate accident risk while pricing their insurance policies covering the risk of car driving. They give discounts on premium to the purchases of such policies from preferred occupational categories. Usually teachers, engineers, doctors are considered to be low risk and benefit from such discounts. On the other hand, professions requiring significant night time driving are considered risky. Similarly, banks often give loans at a slightly cheaper rate to teachers as they are considered to be a less risky occupational category.

9. Income: Income, being a primary measure of well-being of a person, influences his/her purchasing power and choices. Income can be aggregate income of a person or per capita income. It can be nominal or real.

Governments as well as business organizations use this attribute of the population to make decisions. Governments constantly monitor the changes in aggregate and per-capita income to assess the overall health and progress of their economies and changes in the standard and cost of living in the country. They manoeuvre their polices to give a boost to the economy in a slowdown or continuously expand the growth rate.

Businesses use this attribute of the population to assess overall demand for their products as well as to design their product mix. Brands are specifically developed and positioned within particular income segments to maximize turnover and profit. Some business units target affluent income categories of consumers whereas some target that of lower and middle income consumers. For example, Rolls Royace cars are designed for the affluent class whereas the Tata Nano is targeted at lower and middle income classes.

10. Gender composition: One of the basic characteristics of demography, the gender composition largely reflects the underlying social, economic and cultural patterns of a society.

The gender composition, also known as the sex composition, is estimated as the number of females per 1,000 males in the total population. It measures the extent of equality between males and females in a society prevailing at a given point of time. The ratio is affected by various factors, including sex differential in mortality, sex selective migration and skewed sex ratio at birth.

Gender classification of population is often analyzed by businesses as men and women have different psychological and physiological needs and they shop differently. Such a segmentation is widely used within cosmetics, clothing and magazine industry. For example, fair and handsome fairness crème is promoted as the fairness crème for men, whereas fair and lovely is promoted as the crème for women. Similarly, Femina is viewed as a magazine for women.

11. Family life cycle: The stages of life through which families go through is known as family life cycle. The life cycle begins with young unmarried single persons and ends with old persons left single with the death of a spouse. It is, hence, often expressed as bachelor, married with no children (DINKS: Double Income, No Kids), full-nest (married couple with the children staying with the couple), empty-nest (married couple with children living separately), or solitary survivor.

Need of the families varies over the cycle. For example, families with no children will not be demanding paediatric services, and would show no interest to such professionals. On the other hand, families with young children would not only be targeted by paediatric service providers but also by baby care product manufacturers, educational institutions, entertainment service providers, etc. Similarly, families with older couples whose children have left home (empty nest) would be targeted by companies manufacturing elderly care products.

Governments also make use of such segmentation for designing family welfare policies. For example, to encourage families with one child some governments give scholarships or free education to children of such families.

12. Distribution: Distribution of population depicts the density in a particular area. **Population density** is estimated per square mile of land area and measured by the following formula:

$$\text{Population Density} = \frac{\text{Total population of the area}}{\text{Size of the area}}$$

Population density is used for identifying geographical locations as urban or rural (UBE 17.3). However, there is no unique internationally accepted definition applicable to all countries. Different countries have their own definition of urban and rural areas. For example, in the USA, the agglomerations of 2,500 or more inhabitants having a population density of 1,000 persons per square or more are considered to be urban, whereas in Canada the same is defined as places of 1,000 or more inhabitants having a population density of 400 or more per square kilometer. Similarly, India has its own definition with places having 5,000 or more inhabitants, a density of less than 1,000 persons per square mile or 400 per square kilometer being considered as urban.

Population density is an important indicator of quality of life. With the changes in density, structural changes in land use occur. For example, as the density rises, agriculture land is often acquired for more profitable residential or industrial purposes. Though such structural changes boost the overall economic activities in that area, they also have their associated costs. Structural changes in favour of industrial activities often increase air and water pollution. At the same time, overall increase in economic activities increases the number of vehicles plying on roads, causing traffic slowdown and aggravating air pollution. Increasing density also increases the property prices to skyrocketing levels, making a decent living unaffordable and turning habitations into slums and causing various physical and mental health problems.

Population density also influences government planning and policies. For example, many infrastructural enhancement decisions, like construction of roads, over bridges, etc. do get influenced by the population density.

Even safety regulations by governments are often influenced by the density of the population. For example, the speed limit is kept low in dense areas. Helmet wearing made compulsory in cities.

Population density has bearing even for business decisions like setting up of retail outlets.

UNDERSTANDING BUSINESS ENVIRONMENT

UBE 17.3 Urbanization in India and China: What is in Store for Business Organizations?

Urbanization creates huge business opportunities but brings in within many problems as highlighted in this UBE.

The world urban population, as per the projections made by UN (2012), is expected to grow by 72 per cent by 2050, from 3.6 billion in 2011 to 6.3 billion in 2050. Most of this growth will be concentrated in urban areas of the less developed regions, whose population is projected to increase from 2.7 billion in 2011 to 5.1 billion in 2050. Even in the less developed world, urban population is concentrated in a few countries, with China and India projected to account for about a third of the increase in the urban population in the coming decades (Tables 17.3 and 17.4). Part of this increase will be due to migration from rural areas, leading to fall in the rural population and continued urbanization in less developed regions.

Unlike the past trend, the future urban population is expected to be concentrated in large cities of one million or more inhabitants. By 1970, the world had only two megacities: Tokyo in Japan and New York in the USA. Over the four decades, their number has increased noticeably to 23 accounting for 9.9 per cent of the world population. Most of these megacities are located in developing countries.

Table 17.3 Percentage of Population Residing in Urban Areas

	1950	*2010*	*2050*
World	29.4	51.6	67.2
India	17.0	30.9	51.7
China	11.8	49.2	77.3

Source: Compiled from UN (2012), World Urbanization Prospects: The 2011 Revision

Table 17.4 Population of Urban and Rural Areas and Percentage Urban, 2011

	Urban	*Rural*	*Total*	*Percentage Urban*
World	36,32,457	33,41,579	69,74,036	52.1
More Developed Regions	9,64,240	2,76,140	12,40,380	77.7
Less Developed Regions	26,68,217	30,65,439	57,33,657	46.5
India	3,88,286	8,53,206	12,41,492	31.3
China	6,81,508	6,66,058	13,47,565	50.6

Source: Compiled from UN (2012), World Urbanization Prospects: The 2011 Revision

Rapid urbanization in China and India will bring fundamental shifts in these countries, which will bring significant changes not only in these two countries but also affect the global economy as a whole. Rapid urbanization will accompany with a rapid increase in per capita income, providing new opportunities for business organizations by expanding consumer base.

Detailing urbanization in China and India, Dobbs and Sankhe (2010) that by 2025, indicate that the largest expansion will be in the markets for transportation and communication, food and healthcare, personal products, housing and utilities, and recreation. Besides, both countries will also experience a massive increase in demand for urban infrastructure. For example, India will need at least additional 350 to 400 kilometres of metropolitan railways and subways annually while the requirement in China for such infrastructure will be approximately 1,000 km. Both the countries are already open to the public private partnership mode in infrastructure development. Business can reap such opportunities by infusing not only capital but also knowledge in major public projects.

In both the countries many cities are already facing severe traffic congestion and air and water pollution has reached to critical proportions. To make these cities livable, a major cleaning drive is required. Thus, business organizations also have the scope for innovations in areas such as energy conservation, water recycling and clean technology.

No doubt rapid urbanization will bring massive opportunities for business organizations, but there will be major infrastructural constraints faced by them, especially in India, hampering their productivity. The Mckinsey report points out that China has much better infrastructure than India, which is an outcome of systematic and internally consistent planning, policies, funding, implementation and governance. China has invested heavily and ahead of demand. The better infrastructure at the grass root level is also an outcome of the autonomy and flexibility provided at the local level. City mayors play an important role in the development of their cities: they raise resources and can retain 25 per cent of the revenue coming from the value added tax. China's urbanization planning is consistent with its planning for land use, housing and transportation.

India, on the contrary, so far has hardly paid attention to systematic urbanization and failed to incorporate the competing demand for space, housing and transportation in its planning. Even the capital city Delhi lags behind the tier 2 cities of China in terms of basic facilities, Mumbai, which is projected to be the second largest city in the world by 2020 is known as the world's slum capital. As a result, its urban areas are under severe pressure to provide basic civic amenities to a rapidly growing population.

References

Dobbs, R. and Sankhe, S. (2010), Comparing Urbanization in China and India, Insights and Publications, MaKinsey and Company, July.

UN (2012) : World Urbanization Prospects: The 2011 Revision.

17.3 DETERMINANTS OF DEMOGRAPHY

Fertility, mortality and migration are the three basic factors that affect the different characteristics of demography. The meaning, measurement and the impact of these three factors is detailed here.

Fertility

The term **fertility** refers to the number of children that an average woman bears during her productive years. The fertility rate can be ascertained from **crude birth rate**, i.e., the number of live births for every thousand people in the population. Thus,

$$\text{Crude Birth Rate} = \frac{\text{Number of live births in the year}}{\text{Total population}} \times 1{,}000$$

Decline in the fertility rate, given the mortality rate and migration, reduces the overall population size and the proportion of children in total population, on the one hand, and increases that of the adult and older person, on the other. Such a structural change often reduces the child dependency ratio or increases old age dependency ratio.

Mortality and life expectancy

The number of deaths in a year in a country represents the mortality. **Mortality rate** can be ascertained by estimating the **crude death rate** as follows:

$$\text{Crude Death Rate} = \frac{\text{Number of deaths in the year}}{\text{Total population}} \times 1{,}000$$

To assess average life expectancy of the population, often infant mortality rate is estimated. An assessment of **life expectancy** is made through the following formula:

$$\text{Infant Mortality Rate} = \frac{\text{Number of deaths of infants of less than one year old}}{\text{Total population}} \times 1{,}000$$

Impact of mortality rate on the overall size of the population is opposite of that of fertility rate. However, it affects the dependency ratio in a much more complex manner than the fertility rate. The impact depends on the age group that benefits from the decline in the mortality rate. In the initial stages of mortality decline, it is the infant group (age group 0–5) that benefits proportionately more. A decline in the infant mortality rate has a similar influence as an increase in the fertility rate. It makes the population much younger and increases the child dependency ratio. Subsequently, as the life expectancy improves and crosses 70 years of age, the proportion of older persons in the population expands, which in turn increases the old age dependency ratio.

Migration

The movement of people from one place to another is referred to as **migration**. Migration into an area is known as **immigration**, whereas the migration out of an area is known as **emigration**. Immigration and emigration are estimated through immigration and emigration rate as follows:

$$\text{Immigration Rate} = \frac{\text{Number of people entering a region}}{\text{Total population}} \times 1{,}000$$

$$\text{Emigration Rate} = \frac{\text{Number of people leaving a region}}{\text{Total population}} \times 1{,}000$$

Migration from other countries can also alter the overall size, age structure and the distribution of the population. Usually the migration is that of the working age group, and hence, it is expected to reduce the dependency ratio. Also, the migration is from rural areas to urban areas; hence, it is one of the important determinants of urbanization.

17.4 USES OF DEMOGRAPHIC PROFILE BY BUSINESS ORGANIZATIONS

1. Production analysis: The knowledge of changing composition (classification of population using age, gender, income, etc. parameters) is used for identifying purchase behaviour, the changing demand pattern, and designing and developing new products accordingly.

2. Establishing selling outlets: Information on the distribution of population is used for identifying the locations for establishing selling outlets.

3. Determining advertising and communication strategies: At any point of time population of a country consists of several generations. Not a single way of communicating and advertising is effective in such a setup. The differences in the attitude, psychology, patterns of living, etc. is often used for designing an effective advertising campaign and communicating with different generations.

4. Strategic planning: Long-term or strategic planning, which consists of identifying new markets, designing and launching new products, etc., is based on thorough analysis of projected changes in various components of demography.

SUMMARY

Demography is the study of size, composition and distribution of population in a country. Size refers to the total number of people in the country, whereas composition refers to the classification of population on the basis of age, gender, family life cycle, household status, race, religion, language, education, occupation, and income and wealth. Classification of population into rural and urban areas depicts its distribution, which depicts the density of these areas.

Various demographic characteristics—size, composition and distribution—are determined by fertility rate, mortality rate and life expectancy, and migration. The fertility rate is ascertained from the crude birth rate, which is the number of live births for every thousand people while the mortality rate is estimated from the crude death rate, which is the number of deaths for every thousand people. Migration refers to the movement of people from one place to another. Migration into an area is known as the immigration while migration out of an area is known as emigration.

One of the important emerging demographic characteristics is that the world is rapidly aging; especially the advanced countries are expected to severely affected from both the demand and supply side. Rapidly aging population expected to shrink the overall demand and change its composition, on the one hand, and shrink the overall supply of labour force and its productivity, on the other.

Though, overall the world is aging, some of the developing countries, like India, are expected to experience larger workforce and lower dependency ratio in the coming decades. It is expected that this will provide a demographic dividend to the country.

Rapid urbanization is another noteworthy emerging demographic characteristic. Most of the growth of urban areas is projected to be in the less developed regions, especially that in China and India.

Implications for Managers

Business managers can use different aspects or components of demography for varied managerial decisions, such as designing, developing and marketing the products of their companies as well as as pursuing various HR practices.

The size of the population can be used by the managers to assess the overall market size of a country. Even developing countries like India with relatively lower per capita income, but huge population size create large opportunities for business organizations and attract multinationals.

It is not only the overall size but also the other aspects of demography that affect business decisions and profits. For example, the changing age structure changes the composition of demand; hence it influences the production and industrial structure in a country.

REVIEW QUESTIONS

17.1 What is demography?
17.2 What are the different characteristics of demography?
17.3 What way we can assess the composition of the population?
17.4 What do you understand by the age structure or age composition of the population?
17.5 What is the dependency ratio? Why is it known as the dependency ratio?
17.6 What use governments and business organizations can make of the concept of dependency ratio?
17.7 How are generations classified in the USA? What use managers can make of such a classification?
17.8 How does the family life cycle affect the behaviour of individuals?
17.9 What do you understand by the distribution of population?
17.10 How is the population density measured?
17.11 What are the basic determinants of different demographic characteristics?
17.12 Differentiate fertility rate from mortality rate? How do these factors affect the demographic characteristics?
17.13 What do you understand by life expectancy? How does life expectancy affect the demographic characteristics?
17.14 What is migration? How can we measure immigration and emigration?

NUMERICAL PROBLEMS

17.1 From the information given in Table 17.5 estimate the total dependency ratio, child dependency ratio and the old age dependency ratio. Is this country going to experience demographic dividend? Give reasons for your answer.

Table 17.5 Age Distribution of Population

Age slabs	*Total population*
0–14 years old	250
15–64 years old	1,000
65 years and above	750

17.2 From the information given in Table 17.6 estimate the population density for China, India, Japan, the UK, the USA.

Table 17.6 Population and Land Area per Square Kilometer in 2010 for some selected countries

Country	*Population*	*Land area sq km*	*Density*
China	1,33,83,00,000	93,27,480	143.48
India	1,22,46,15,000	29,73,190	411.89
Japan	12,74,51,000	3,64,500	349.66
UK	6,22,32,000	2,41,930	257.23
USA	30,93,49,000	91,47,420	33.82

Source: World Bank Database (Online), as on 25 May 2012.

Calculate birth, death rate, total immigration, emigration rates.

CASE ANALYSIS EXERCISE

C17.1 Changing Age Composition: Demographic Dividend or Nightmare for India?

India is the second largest populated country, next to its neighbour China. In 2010, India had a population of 1.21 billion, and the dependency ratio was 55, which was much higher than that of China. In 2030, when the figure is expected to hit 1.48 billion, India will overtake China in numbers. By then, its dependency ratio will lower to 48 (Table 7.17).

Table 17.7 Dependency Ratio

	India			*China*		
Year	*Total*	*Child*	*Old Age*	*Total*	*Child*	*Old Age*
1950	68	63	5	63	56	7
2000	64	57	7	48	38	10
2010	55	47	8	38	27	11
2030	47	35	12	45	21	24
2050	48	28	20	64	22	42

Source: Population Division of the Department of Economic and Social Affairs of the United Nations Secretariat, World Population Prospects: The 2010 Revision, http://esa.un.org/unpd/wpp/index.htm Sunday, May 13, 2012.

Favourable demographic changes in India are leading to contemplation the world over whether India will be able to leverage its demographic dividend and achieve rapid growth in the coming three decades or so.

Demographic dividend is the term used by demographers to depict a situation of rapid growth rate achieved by a country because of young labour force growing faster than the dependent population of the retired force and children. The term was first applied to describe the favourable circumstances and rapid growth achieved by the tiger countries—Singapore, Taiwan, Hongkong and South Korea—for more than 20 years in the second half of the last century. Apart from these countries, some other noticeable examples of demographic dividend are Japan in the 1950's, China in 1980's, and Ireland in 1990s.

The economists who are expecting a demographic dividend for India are basing their arguments on the following reasons:

- First, the direct increase in the number of bread winner will increase output. Of this working group population, the majority will be of young age group. Implying higher productivity and higher growth of output.
- Second, the decline in the dependency ratio will also be accompanied by a reduction in the child dependency ratio occurring due to a decline in fertility rate. With fewer children being worn, it is likely that more women will join the workforce, which will increase the number of bread winners and the growth of output in the economy.
- Third, people save most during their working years for meeting the expenses during their post retirement years. An increasing working force, hence, will also imply increasing savings. Besides, a decline in the dependency ratio is also expected to contribute to the overall saving. Higher saving, which is expected to be above 30%, will boost investment and productivity in the economy.

On the flip side, however, it has been argued that the payoffs may not be as large as those of China for the structural weaknesses in the Indian economy as outlined here:

- First, as noted in UBE 3.1, service sector contribute most to the GDP, whereas the contribution of the agriculture is the least. On the contrary, agriculture employs more than 50 per cent of India's labour force which is extremely inefficient because of small and fragmented land holdings, poor land management, dependence on the vagaries of monsoon for water supply, and poor storage and other infrastructure and supply chain management. Though service sector is the second largest employer, the majority of employment in this sector is in low value added and thereby, low paying services. The high value added services like information technology and software services employ relatively much lower numbers.

  Given the present employment structure, it is unlikely that the additional young population entering the labour force will find any gainful employment. India needs to create millions of productive employment opportunities to absorb the growing workforce and achieve rapid growth through favourable demographic trend.
- Second, for garnering the demographic dividend, the quality of the workforce is very important. Education standards largely affect the human capital and the quality of the labour force. Looking at the Indian education system, one can clearly see that it is in a miserable state from bottom to top. India's literacy rate is around 63 per cent, much lower than that of China's 93 per cent. Of the 63 per cent population, which is literate, most have come from poor quality schools with inadequate infrastructure and poorly paid de-motivated and frequently absent teachers. Not only school education but higher education also lacks quality and is well below global standards, requiring the hiring companies to invest heavily in training the engineering and other graduates to prepare them for their work requirement. Though, the country also has centres for higher education that can meet global standards, such as IITs and IIMs, the graduates passing from these centres prefer leaving the country for greener pastures. The number of such centres is much lower than the growing demand for quality education, and the deficit is likely to continue in the future, leaving the country with a possibility of unemployable poor quality massive work force.

- Third, higher growth requires not only qualified workforce but also good quality infrastructure. But, India rate poorly on infrastructure (Table 17.8).

Table 17.8 Some Growth Enabling Parameters (for the latest available year)

	India	*China*
I. Key Infrastructure Endowment		
Percentage of population with access to electricity	66.3 (2009)	99.4 (2009)
Paved roads (per cent of total roads)	49.3 (2008)	53.5 (2008)
Number of cellular phone	61.42 (2010)	64.04 (2010)
Percentage of population with access to electricity		
II. Education		
Adult literacy (15+) literacy rate total (%)	62.8 (2006)	94.3 (2010)
Average years of total schooling	7.1 (2010)	10.9 (2010)
Pupil teacher ratio	40 (2004)	18 (2008)
Employment		
Employment rate (aged 15 years and above)	57.7 (2005)	...

Source: Compiled from ADB (2011), Framework of Inclusive Growth Indicators: Key Indicators for Asia and the Pacific 2011, Special Supplement.

Thus, on balance, we can say that demographic changes though erecting a window of opportunity for Indians, there is no guarantee that this demographic change will turn the country into an economic miracle. A whole lot will depend on the policy environment and the preparedness of the country to exploit the opportunities by investing heavily in manufacturing, infrastructure and education. Otherwise, supporting the large young unemployed will simply be a nightmare.

Questions

1. What is the meaning of demographic dividend?
2. For which countries the term demographic dividend was first applied to?
3. Why India is expected to reap the demographic dividend in the coming decades?
4. Why is it feared that India may not be able to reap its demographic dividend?

SUGGESTED FURTHER READING

McKinsey and Company (2010), Urban World, Cities and the Rise of the Consuming Class, June,
GOI (2013), Seizing the Demographic Dividend, Economic Survey, 2012-13, Chapter 2.

CHAPTER 18

Technological Environment

18.1 INTRODUCTION

In the past decade, Ford motors revolutionized the way cars were manufactured at that time. Unable to satiate the demand for its car, Henry Ford installed a moving industrial line in his factory, which enabled his employees to build cars one piece at a time instead of one car at a time. The new process also enabled him to implement the principle of division of labour, which improved the productivity tremendously. The new system produced cars not only quickly and efficiently but also lowered the cost of assembling cars and prices to the end consumers. As the competitors, in turn, were forced to deploy the same process to decrease their costs; it was a significant leap in the production process followed by the car manufacturers.

Similarly, American Airlines in the USA took a lead in the airline reservation system in 1950 by adopting automated airline booking system. Initially, the automation was limited to the intrinsic application in the airline system. American Airlines worked closely with IBM and launched the Semi-Automatic Business Research Environment (SABRE) in 1964. The impact of computerized airline reservation system on the growth of the aviation industry, in terms of accurate record keeping, speed in response to ticketing/ticket reservation, efficiency in information handling and reliability and cost effectiveness, has been of great economic value.

Adoption of Radio Frequency Identification (RFID) technology in 2005 gave Walmart a competitive advantage over other retail giants. The implementation of the new technology was done throughout the supply chain, which ensured easy checking in and out of products, and continuous reordering of out of stock products. The study carried out by researchers at the University of Arkansas in 2005 on Walmart's use of RFID technology showed that the RFID controlled stores were 63 per cent more effective in replenishing out-of-stocks than those without. The success of Walmart was so impressive that other competitors also started deploying the same technology.

We can see that the technological advancements, for centuries, have been widely adopted by business organizations to improve production, volumes and profits. Technological changes, time and again, have revolutionized the ways in which business is conducted and has provided competitive advantage to its adopters. However, technology also poses several threats, which need to be managed for efficient utilization of the technology.

Given that the technological changes are the driving force behind the global development, in this chapter we look at the meaning of technology in Section 18.2. We identify the types of technology in Section 18.3 and briefs on classification of technology in Section 18.4. In Section 18.5 we ascertain the relationship between technological development and overall happiness. Section 18.6 details on the impact of technology. Section 18.7 discusses the threats of technology and management of such threats.

18.2 TECHNOLOGY: A DEFINITION

Technology is the application of science, art and other fields of knowledge used in designing tools and equipments that aid in acquisition, manipulation and communication of information and performance and enhancement of productivity of factors of production, such as labour and capital.

18.2.1 Science, Technology and Industry: A Difference

The words science and technology are often used together or interchangeably. However, there are significant differences between the two terms. **Science** is the system of acquiring knowledge based on scientific methods and the organized body of knowledge, whereas **technology** refers to the items of use, emerging from the practical application of science. For example, in the energy as a science study, solar panels is a scientific discovery, while technology is the use of the scientific knowledge of solar panels in solar powered lights, calculators and cookers. However, technology is not always a subset of science. There are several other important differences between the two terms as evident from Table 18.1, which gives technology a distinct identity.

Table 18.1 Differences between Science and Technology

Parameter	*Science*	*Technology*
Motto	Reductionism, involving the isolation and definition of distinct concepts	Holism, involving the integration of many competing demands, theories, data and ideas
Mission	The search for and theorizing about cause.	The search for and theorizing about new processes
Focus	Focuses on understanding natural phenomena	focuses on understanding the man made environment
Goal	Pursuit of knowledge and understanding for its own sake (New knowledge)	The creation of artifacts and systems to meet people's needs (new products)
Result Relevance	Making virtually value-free statements	Activities always value-laden
Evaluation Methods	Analysis, generalization and creation of theories	Analysis and synthesis of design
Goals Achieved Through	Corresponding Scientific Processes	Key Technological Processes

Contd...

Parameter	*Science*	*Technology*
Development Methods	Discovery (controlled by experimentation)	Design, invention, production
Most Observed Quality	Drawing correct conclusions based on good theories and accurate data	Taking good decisions based on incomplete data and approximate models
Skills Needed to Excel	Experimental and logical skills needed	Design, construction, testing, planning, quality assurance, problem solving, decision making, interpersonal and communication skills

Source: Compiled from Science vs Technology, (online) http://www.diffen.com/difference/Science_vs_Technology as on 11/9/12.

Though first scientific revolution played a very limited role in the first technological and industrial revolution, often scientific breakthroughs have led technological advancements and industrial revolutions (Table 18.2). For example, during the second technological and industrial revolution many new technologies and industries emerged from new scientific knowledge. Similarly, fifth technological revolution is expected to be emerging from the scientific breakthrough in the field of biotechnology and the sixth revolution is expected to be based on new physics revolution.

Table 18.2 Scientific, Technological and Industrial Revolution

Time	*Scientific revolution*	*Technological revolution*	*Industrial revolution*
Sixteenth and Seventieth Century	First Revolution: Birth of modern astronomy, physics and development of modern science		
1763–1870		First Technological Revolution: Steam engine and mechanical revolution	First Industrial Revolution: Mechanization
1870–1945		Second Technological Revolution: Electric power, internal combustion engine, chemistry, telecommunication, and transport	Second Industrial (Transport) Revolution: Electrification
1946–1970	Second Scientific Revolution: Relativity and quantum theories, astronomy, genetics, geography, etc.	Third Technological Revolution: Electronics, computers, microcomputers and automation	Third Industrial (Science) Revolution: Automation
1970–2020		Fourth Technological Revolution: Information revolution and internet	Fourth Industrial (Knowledge) Revolution: Informatization

Contd...

Table 18.2 *Contd...*

Time	*Scientific revolution*	*Technological revolution*	*Industrial revolution*
2020–2050	Third Scientific Revolution: New biology revolution	Fifth Technological Revolution: Fusion of biology and technology, information conversion, bionics, creation and regeneration of life	Fifth Industrial (Biological/ Regeneration) Revolution: Life engineering
2050–2100	Fourth Scientific Revolution: New Physics Revolution	Sixth Technological Revolution: New energy, new space time and new transportation	Sixth Industrial (Physics/Space Time) Revolution: Transport engineering

18.3 TYPES OF TECHNOLOGY

Technology is of two types as depicted in Figure 18.1 and as detailed in the following paragraphs.

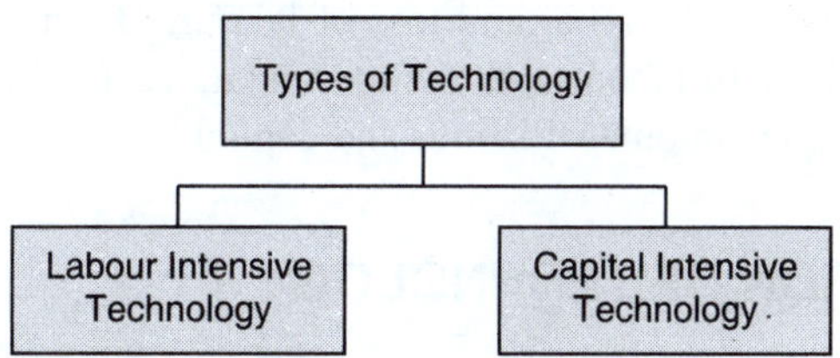

Figure 18.1 Types of Technology.

Labour Intensive Technology

The technology which requires a high level of manpower compared to the level of capital, for a given level of output, is known as **labour intensive technology**. The labour intensive technology is suitable for the production of customized products or production on a small scale. Rising labour intensity increases capital productivity. It is widely preferred in industries, such as small scale enterprises, agriculture, mining, hospitality, apparel and footwear.

The amount of labour used in the process of production usually varies with the level of output. Therefore, the cost associated with it is usually considered variable. Given that the amount of labour is a variable input, it can be scaled up or down more easily than other factors of production. For example, in a downturn scarcity of demand necessitates scaling down the level of production and reduction in cost to maintain profitability. In the labour intensive technology it is much easier to achieve downsizing by retrenching labour. However, a major disadvantage of the labour intensive technology is that it cannot be used for mass production and does not bring much economies of scale in the process of production.

Capital Intensive Technology

The technology that requires a high level of capital investment compared to labour cost is referred to as **capital intensive technology**. Rising capital intensity increases labour productivity. Examples of industries using capital intensive technology are: automobile industry, steel industry, aviation industry, oil industry, etc.

Capital intensive technology is often used in mass scale production and in the processes that can be automated. However, capital intensive technology requires huge investment in financing capital, maintaining it, and making provision for its depreciation.

We can understand the difference between labour and capital intensive technology more clearly with the help of a hypothetical example presented in Table 18.3.

Table 18.3 Labour Intensive vs Capital Intensive Technology: A Numerical Example

Type of technology	*Amount of labour*	*Amount of capital*
A (Capital Intensive)	100	400
B (Equal Amount)	200	200
C (Labour Intensive)	400	100
Total amount of output	1 unit	1 unit

As can be seen from Table 18.3, one unit of output can be produced with different combinations of labour and capital, representing three different technology—A, B and C. Technology A is capital intensive as it uses more of capital and less of labour. On the contrary, technology C is labour intensive as it uses more of labour and less of capital. Technology B is neither labour nor capital intensive as it uses equal amount of labour and capital.

18.4 CLASSIFICATION OF TECHNOLOGY

Technology is classified on the basis of various categories explained as follows:

1. Information technology: The **information technology** (IT) refers to the technology that uses computers, networking, software programming, and other equipment to store, process, retrieve, transmit and protect information. In some companies it is referred to as the Management Information Services (MIS) or simply as the Information Services (IS)

2. Medical technology: The **medical technology** is an application of medical science that consists of wide range of healthcare products used for early diagnosis and less expensive monitoring and treatment of diseases with the help of medical devices, information technology, bio-technology and healthcare services. The objective of medical technology is to extend the life of patients, relieve pain and reduce the risk of diseases.

3. Education technology: The **educational technology** consists of communication skills and approaches to teaching and learning through diverse and most efficient technological developments, such as slides, films, case studies, computers, simulation games, etc.

4. Space technology: The systematic application of engineering and scientific discipline to the exploration and utilization of outer space is referred to as the **space technology**. The space technology enables entry and survival of human beings and spacecrafts for a prolonged period of time. It also enables the return of objects and human beings into the earth's surface from outer space.

5. Mobile technology: The technology based on cellular communication is known as **mobile technology**. As devices based on such a technology can be used while on the move, this technology is also known as mobile technology. Examples of devices using mobile technology are smartphones, Global Position System (GPS) devices, wireless debit/credit card payment terminals, laptop and palmtop computers. These devices use mobile technology such as wireless fidelity (Wi-Fi), Bluetooth, third generation (3G), Global System for Mobile communication (GSM) and General Packet Radio Services (GPRS) data services, dial up services and virtual private networks.

6. Transportation technology: The transportation technology refers to the system used for or assisting in moving people and objects from one place to another through land, water, air and space. Scooter, car, bus, train, airplane, boat are some examples of **transportation technology**.

As transportation is crucial to all business and economic activities, there has been an enormous amount of invention and innovation addressing the problems impeding transportation such as traffic congestion, traffic safety, fuel cost, air pollution, global warming and even regulatory policies. The technological advancements that have addressed some such problems in the recent period are special purpose system (GPS) as a travel aid, providing information on routes and travel time, intelligent transport system or transport telematics, such as ramp metering, adaptive signal control, GPS navigation, collusion avoidance, automatic fare or toll collection, alternative fuels, such as Liquefied Petroleum Gas (LPG), Compressed Natural Gas (CNG) or Liquefied Natural Gas (LNG), methanol, ethanol, electricity, and hydrogen, new mode of transport, such as New Large Aircraft (NLA), high speed rail and megaships.

7. Assistive technology: The **assistive technology**, also known as the *adaptive technology*, consists of assistive adaptive and rehabilitative devices used by individuals with disabilities to perform day-to-day activities, which otherwise may be difficult or impossible. It includes devices, such as wheelchairs and walkers, specially designed hardware, software and other accessories to enable people with disabilities to access computers and other information technology devices, and many more such devices.

18.5 ROLE OF TECHNOLOGY IN DEVELOPMENT

Technology plays a fundamental role in wealth creation. It is the primary engine of economic growth. Technology is instrumental in transforming a society and improving the quality of life and overall well-being of humans.

The countries that viewed technology not as a consumable item but an asset to be created and produced invested heavily in its creation. They could enhance the income of their people and bring in overall prosperity and progress (UBE 18.1) by improving productivity and efficiency and cutting costs. For example, technological innovations in cotton spinning, steam engine, iron smelting enabled industrial revolution first in the United Kingdom and subsequently in the Western European countries in the 19th century. The revolution changed almost every aspect of these economies. In the 20th century, the industrial revolution transformed the United States from an agrarian economy to an industrial superpower. Technological innovations in robotics, automobiles, and consumer electronics also transformed Japan, dependent on rice field, to an industrial force, a threat to then industrial giants USA, UK and other major industrial European countries. In the last century, exploiting technological advancements in the form of silicon microelectronics many other south-east Asian economies like Korea and Taiwan became industrialized countries. In the recent period, China and India have registered sustained growth with the help of advancements in manufacturing and information technology respectively.

On the contrary, sub-Saharan African countries, such as Tanzania, Sudan and Mozambique, and other countries, such as Pakistan, Nepal and Nicaragua that viewed technology simply as a consumable item ignored investment in it and still largely remain low in skill levels and lagging much behind the technologically superior countries.

UNDERSTANDING BUSINESS ENVIRONMENT

UBE 18.1 Technology, Development and Happiness

It is widely claimed that technological advancements and economic development and happiness go hand in hand. This UBE explores this relationship.

It is widely recognized that science and technology helps in stimulating and sustaining development by addressing the problem of food and energy scarcity, environmental degradation, diseases, communication inadequacy as well as building and developing markets in goods and services and bringing in overall prosperity and progress.

Technology, unlike land, labour and capital, is an intangible factor of production. For centuries, it has been a key driving force behind economic prosperity. In the past century, technological advancements in manufacturing systems and processes led to the growth of many of the present day developed countries. In the 21st century it is the software, robotics and biotechnology that are determining the lead in efficiency and productivity.

To assess the level of development of intangible factors like technology in a country, the Martin Prosperity Institute (2011) has prepared The Global Creativity Index (GCI). The index is based on three intangible factors—technology, talent and tolerance (3T). Technology in this index is estimated as a composite of the following three factors:

1. The financial resources devoted to research and development as a share of total economic output
2. The share of human resources devoted to R&D measured as the share of the total labour force made up of researchers
3. Patents granted per capita

As per the estimation in 2011, Sweden ranked highest on GCI followed by the United States and Finland (Table 18.4).

Table 18.4 Overall Global Creativity Index Rankings

Total rank	*Country*	*Technology*	*Talent*	*Tolerance*	*Global creativity index*
1	Sweden	5	2	7	0.923
2	United States	3	8	8	0.902
3	Finland	1	1	19	0.894
4	Denmark	7	4	14	0.878
5	Australia	15	7	5	0.870
6	New Zealand	19	5	4	0.866
7	Canada	11	17	1	0.862
8	Norway	12	6	11	0.862
9	Singapore	10	3	17	0.858
10	Netherlands	17	11	3	0.854
50	India	42	75	30	0.382
58	China	30	76	-	0.327

Source: Compiled from Martin Prosperity Institute (2011), Creativity and Prosperity: The Global Creativity Index

However, it is Finland that tops the list of technology index (Table 18.5). Home to Nokia and many innovative small firms, Finland ranks first in researchers, third in R&D investment and fourth in innovation. Next to Japan, which ranks fourth in R&D investment, third in researchers and second in innovation, is the United States. Home to many high-tech startups such as Microsoft, Apple, Google and Yahoo, the United States is first in innovation and sixth in R&D investment and seventh in researchers and ranks overall third in technology index list.

Of the total 75 countries considered in the study, India ranks 42 on technology index. It is 27th on innovation, 36th on researchers and 38th on R&D investment.

Table 18.5 Global Technology Rankings

Country	*R&D Investment*	*Researchers*	*Innovation*	*Technology Index*
Finland	3	1	4	1
Japan	4	3	2	2
United States	6	7	1	3
Israel	1	-	5	4
Sweden	2	2	6	5
Switzerland	5	11	3	6
Denmark	9	5	9	7
Republic of Korea	7	16	–	8
Germany	8	13	7	9
Singapore	11	4	11	10
China	26	39	–	30
India	38	36	46	42

Source: Compiled from Martin Prosperity Institute (2011), Creativity and Prosperity: The Global Creativity Index.

The study indicates that these measures of global creativity are closely associated with various indices of economic and social progress (Table 18.6), with nations having a high score on the GCI also have higher levels of economic output, entrepreneurship and overall economic competitiveness, human development, life satisfaction, and happiness and equality.

Table 18.6 Correlation of GCI and Indices of Economic and Social Progress

Measure of economic and social progress	*Overall GCI*	*Technology*	*Talent*	*Tolerance*
1. Economic Output (GDP per capita)	0.84	0.72	0.78	0.63
2. Economic Competitiveness (Global Competitiveness Index developed by M. Porter)	0.79	0.82	0.66	0.59
3. Entrepreneurship (Global Entrepreneurship Index developed by Z. Acs and L. Szerb)	0.81	0.55	0.74	0.71
4. Inequality (Gini Index- World Bank's World Development Indicators) 0.82	–0.43	–0.47	–0.52	–0.06
5. Human Development (Human Development Index prepared by UN)	0.82	0.63	0.83	0.57
6. Happiness (Gallup Organization's 2009 Gallup World Poll)	0.74	0.65	0.65	0.66

Source: Compiled from Martin Prosperity Institute (2011), Creativity and Prosperity: The Global Creativity Index.

18.6 IMPACT OF TECHNOLOGY

Technology affects a country through various dimensions as detailed here.

18.6.1 Social Impact

Technological advancements bring in immense social changes. These change the societal structure, social relations and social communication. For example, industrial revolution displaced many people from their homeland to find work in crowded cities. In the process, strong family ties, self-sufficiency and land ownership were replaced with weak family units, dependency on others and tenancy of land. In this decade, information technology has further brought in several changes in social relations, social communication, and living pattern. In the new era, because of easy availability of internet many off-line activities, such as shopping, learning, fund transfers and other banking activities, have become online, which have reduced the need for human interface. Internet tools are also increasingly used for community-oriented communications, voicing opinions, sharing photographs, greeting on birthdays, receiving communication on school events, weather conditions and even traffic congestions. The new technology has also created more job opportunities for women which otherwise were confined to men. However, increased job opportunities are also responsible for the absence of women from home for longer duration, reduced time for rearing children, lowering the fertility rate and reducing the family size. At times, such a changing system is also blamed for increasing divorce rate world over and growing number of single parent families.

18.6.2 Economic Impact

Technological changes have had tremendous impact on the way goods and services are produced, exchanged and distributed to final users. For example, before the widespread use of internet, until the end of the last century, business decisions were constrained by the limited and lagging knowledge of customers' needs, location of inventories and flow of material in the supply chain. The lack of sufficient knowledge necessitated large inventories of material as well as staff as a backup to deal with uncertainties in the environment and mis-assessment on the part of organizations. Widespread use of IT has enabled easy accessibility of relevant information; hence there is now lesser inventories and lesser uncertainty in the environment. The speed with which the knowledge is generated and used for production, has enhanced productivity and efficiency. The impact of higher productivity is on wages as well as on the standard of living.

18.6.3 Business Impact

Businesses have been extensive users of new technology. They always look for new technology that can reduce time, increase productivity and reduce costs, and provide them with an edge in a competitive market. However, adoption of a new technology requires several changes in the manner in businesses operate. Some of these are described here:

1. Investment in technology: To reap the benefits of new technology, business units are required to invest heavily in enabling infrastructure. As most businesses nowadays are conducted over personal computers and other communication devices, companies are required to invest in computers and information technology. For example, according to Ovum (a research and consultancy organization) study, annual spending on IT among global retail banks is expected to increase by $3.6 bn in 2012 and by 2015 it will hit $135 bn. Most of this increase is expected to be in delivery channels, especially online services. Technologies that improve selling and services, such as customer analytics and customer data management are expected to be a hot area of investment in the coming period.

2. Hiring and outsourcing policies: Advancements in technology have enhanced the speed with which information travels across the world. Such advancements have made the world boundary less and distances meaningless, and enabled outsourcing overseas possible. Companies with the help of new technology outsource part of their process, such as computer programming and customer care services to the destinations where manpower is available at a cheaper rate.

3. Inventory management and quality control: Technology like Radio Frequency Identification (RFID) is used for management of inventory. An RFID tag, which consists of a tiny microchip and a small aerial, can store range of digital information (like the number equivalent of a barcode) about a particular product, the places where the chip has travelled, etc. The information, thus recorded on the tag, can be read and modified remotely. Thus, the information recorded can be used for:

- Identifying individual products and components and tracking them through the supply chain from production to point of sale.
- Preventing over stocking and stocking of products
- Increasing stock security, by positioning tag-readers at points of high risk, such as exits, and causing them to trigger alarms
- Improving quality control, particularly of stock items with a limited shelf life

The technology is particularly helpful for retailers, wholesalers or distributors who stock a wide range of items, and to manufacturers who produce a variety of products for different customers.

4. Improved security and confidentiality: Technology like RFID tags are also used to tighten the security of business premises by implanting tags in employees. Signals emitted by such tags can be read by access control readers; hence these are used for restricting the entry to the office premises only to the authorized persons.

5. Reduction in time/improvement in speed: Computer modeling has dramatically reduced the time and cost required to design items not only on factory floors and in distribution channels but also in services. For example, in health services, medical diagnoses have become more comprehensive, accurate and faster and have enabled speedier treatment of patients. At the same time, advancements in biotechnology have also enhanced the potential for discovering more effective treatments. The speed has also improved drastically in financial services and transactions because of technological advancements. Further improvements in technology used in electronic market that solicit bids from suppliers have the potential for further reducing search and transaction costs for firms and improving productivity.

6. Improving the speed of communication: Technological advancements have changed the ways in which people and organizations communicate. Cellular technology as well as satellite communication has made the communication easier and faster. Through the internet it is now possible to carry out several transactions within minutes which otherwise would have taken several days or months. Improved speed of communication, hence, has been facilitating volume of transactions and improving productivity.

7. Widening customer reach: Even small business units can reach the remotest households through the use of IT. Cloud computing has enabled use of IT in the business practices of small and medium enterprises.

8. Reduction in travel cost/reduction in distances: As communication has become faster, barriers to distance are disappearing. Technological advancements have made outsourcing of jobs, such as computer programming and telephone customer services, overseas easier where the cost of production of a particular goods or services is cheaper. Not only outsourcing of jobs has become easier, but even various business meetings can be conducted through videoconferencing, eliminating the gap of space and time. The saving in travelling costs, when it is possible to cut on travel to perform business activities, is substantial.

9. Efficiency in recruitment process: Selection options for employees in the job market have increased remarkably due to advancement in technology. While filling their vacancies, firms need not restrict themselves now only to the local market. They can easily advertise about their requirements and vacancies over the net which has global access. Candidates from abroad also can easily access information about such vacancies. The shortlisted candidates now need not visit the factory or office premises of the recruiting firm, but can face the interview panel via the webcam on Skype. Companies are able to save on travelling cost by conducting interviews on Skype.

18.7 MANAGEMENT OF TECHNOLOGY

As we have seen in previous sections, technology provides immense advantages to the firms and countries investing in its creation and generation. However, it poses many problems and risks not only to the firms entering with new technology but also to incumbents, as discussed hereinafter.

1. High cost: Technological advancements require large investment in R&D and in training scientists and engineers; hence, these are costly. For example, inspite of sharp and continuous reduction in the cost of computers and softwares, the cost of each of these runs in several thousand rupees. On top of it, it is not a one time expense. Continuous inventions and innovations make the existing machineries outdated quickly. Companies, aiming to remaining competitive in the fast changing scenario, end up incurring expenses in updating instruments and softwares and training the professional operating these machineries year after year.

2. High risk: At the same time, it is also highly risky; the large investment made by a firm may not result in the desirable outcome and the fund investment may simply go waste. Besides, the competitors may come up with more advanced technology, which may make the inventions and innovations of firms soon outdated.

3. Displacement of labour: Technological advancement though creates jobs in those areas where the new technology is adopted, it also displaces labour from traditional sectors dependent on old technology. Often, the displaced worker is not competent for jobs in the emerging sectors, which require new skills and knowledge and/or end up accepting low salary jobs. For example, in the USA advancements in the internet technology have enabled many companies to outsource many of their manufacturing activities. Many former manufacturing workers have ended up accepting comparatively lower paying service jobs.

Technological changes are often the reason for structural unemployment in many countries—a situation where there is high unemployment, but at the same time large vacancies in some sectors. India faces such a problem. There is large scale unemployment among the unskilled workers. But many educational institutions, for example, are constantly looking for trained and qualified teachers, but are unable to get enough.

4. Destruction of the existing industries: Companies which do not upgrade their technology become uncompetitive and compelled to exit the market ultimately. Kodak faced this situation in the recent past (UBE 18.2).

UNDERSTANDING BUSINESS ENVIRONMENT

UBE 18.2 Is Technology Destroying Kodak?

Technological advancements are very rapid. The companies not adopting the changes quickly are driven out of the market as reflected in this UBE.

Kodak, the company that invented film photography for the masses and also the technology for mobile phone photography is struggling hard to survive its photography business. It has already shut down its digital camera business, and is in the process of selling its photographic paper and still camera business. It is also planning to be out of the business of inkjet printer manufacturing. In January 2012, the company ended up filing for Chapter 11 protection in the US Bankruptcy? What has led a more than 130 old icon on the verge of bankruptcy?

George Eastman, founder of the Eastman Kodak company, in 1988 invented a machine that captured images on large plates of glass. Subsequently, he developed roll film and the Brownie Camera. His inventions helped his company to become a household name in America. In 1975, Steve Sasson, an engineer at Kodak invented the digital camera. But the company failed to recognize its mass market potential and remained focused on its camera in niche markets. The company failed to see that the new technology will kill its film camera market and remained focused on its camera in niche markets. A setback to the company came when Sony launched its own digital camera in 1981. Inspite of the realization of the mistake, Kodak introduced its first every day use digital product, in the form of photo CD, in the market only after a decade in 1991. After 5 years, in 1996, it also launched its pocket size digital camera. It's biggest push, Easy Share brand came in 2001; but by then the market was already flooded with similar products from Canon and other Asian manufacturers. The bigger competition, however, came not from similar cameras, but from Smartphones.

The digital camera technology that Kodak invented has been used by mobile companies to incorporate photography features in mobile devices, such as Smartphones and tablet computers. It is not now uncommon to find smartphones featuring digital cameras and 10, 12 or 14 mega pixel resolutions. Cheap image editing applications in these devises enable users to transform, stylize and perfect their photos on the devise itself, and internet facility allow them to share these photos more easily and quickly with family and friends on social networking sites. These devices are all the time with the people, and thus, driving out the cameras with standalone features. Companies like Kodak that lagged behind taking advantage of the new technology and diversify their business are either on the verge of bankruptcy or are already out of the market.

What is Technology Management?

Excessive caution and haste both are undesirable in the use of new technology.

Technological competitiveness is necessary for corporate survival. A corporation with inferior technology cannot compete with a corporation with superior technology. However, it is not a sufficient condition. There are various domains of business, which are equally crucial for the success of a business organization. The success of business organizations depends on the strategic adoption of technology in all domains of business—finance, marketing and sales, operations, etc. While successfully integrating technology in the various business domains, a company has to have a clear answer to the following questions:

- What markets the company wants to explore and how? Which products and services will help the company in exploring and capturing the intended markets?
- What technology supports the company's expansion plans in the intended markets and the products? Will the new technology benefit the company in terms of lower cost or value addition?
- Should the company acquire the required technology through licensing or go for in-house development by spending on research and development (R&D)?
- Does the R&D staff have access to development in various functional areas of the company? Do they have access to the company's key customers? Are they aware of their requirements and preferences?

The integration of technology with business units and business strategies is referred to as the technology management. It is a part of the total management system. Managing technology involves the following four concepts:

1. New ventures: While radically new products and new ventures may seize the public's imagination and provide an entrant a leading edge they involve risks related to developing new products and creating new markets. Making incremental technological improvements in existing product lines is less risky and often more profitable.

2. Innovations: Innovation is a process that involves several activities ranging from creating a new technological knowledge to implementing it in new or existing business units.

3. Research: New technology generates new knowledge of production and marketing process, which often requires substantial investment and research by corporates. Investment in research requires assessment of the present technological structure of the company as well as assessment of the emerging trends in technology and the technologies adopted by its competitors. Effective research management for technological development requires organization of research, project management, management of research personnel and the pursuance of corporate research strategy.

However, short-term profit goals often seem to conflict with the research and development programmes that brings in the long-run sustainability and valuation of a firm

4. Research infrastructure: Corporate research activities may get constrained by the available supporting infrastructure in the country. Better infrastructure in the country creates a conducive research environment and facilitates technological innovations. Technology management, thus, also necessitates large investment by the government of a country in setting up supporting infrastructure. To facilitate setting up of such an infrastructure, many countries like India pursue consistent science and technology policy (UBE 18.3).

UNDERSTANDING BUSINESS ENVIRONMENT

UBE 18.3 Science and Technology Policy in India

To promote research environment which can create a conducive technological environment many countries pursue research and technology policy. This UBE deliberate on the science and technology policy pursued in India.

India realized the importance of production and creation of technology in the growth and development of the country very soon after its independence. To foster scientific and technological developments, the country moved the Scientific Policy Resolution, in 1958. The resolution aimed at ensuring an adequate supply of research scientists and technical personnel of high quality. Further, to give a clear direction for the growth of indigenous technology and acquisition of technology from outside. The Technology Policy Statement was introduced in 1983. Subsequently, as an offshoot of the Seventh Plan, in 1985, the Technology Mission was launched to bring in improvements in the fields of literacy, immunization, oilseeds, drinking water, dairy products and telecommunication. The technology policy adopted in 1993 was designed to further strengthen the Indian economy and assist it in fulfilling its role in the global economic environment. This policy emphasized the role of market forces and industries in promoting scientific and technological developments and responding to the needs of the users and markets. The Science and Technology Policy adopted in 2003 emphasized the issues related to technology governance, utilization of existing resources, development of innovative technology for management of natural hazard, management of intellectual property and creating awareness about the benefits of science and technology.

The latest policy statement in India is the New Science and Technology Policy, 2013. The Science, Technology and Innovation (STI) policy aims at accelerating the pace of discovery and delivery of science led solutions for faster and inclusive growth. The thrust areas of the policy are as follows:

- Higher investment in R&D: Raising gross expenditure on R&D from current 1 per cent to 2 per cent in this decade.
- Excellence and relevance in R&D
  - Fostering excellence against global benchmarks
  - Nourishing the roots: Promoting grassroot innovations through mechanisms such as "Risky Idea Fund" and "Small Idea Small Money" schemes
  - Assigning greater role to NGOs in delivering and diffusing rural technologies
  - Higher Gender Parity
  - Establishing inter university centre for research
  - Linking performance with rewards and incentives in public funded institutions including universities
- Directed and focused STI interventions
  - Identification of 10 sectors of high impact potential for focused attention
  - Integration of agriculture R&D policy with the national R&D policy and the STI policy
- Greater private sector investment in R&D
  - Emphasis on public private partnership mode: Establishing a new National Science, Technology and Innovation Fund in a Public Private Partnership mode
  - Treating private sector research on par with the public institution in accessing public funds in research and development
- Diffusion of scientific outputs and technology intervention
  - Increasing full time research and development personnel by two thirds within five years

- Increasing India's share in Global publications from the current 3.5 per cent to around 7 per cent by 2020.
- Increasing the publication record in the world's top 1 per cent of journals by four folds

• Fostering academia research—Industry Partnership

• Gaining global competitiveness through collaborations
  - Establishing a new regulatory framework for data access and sharing of Intellectual Property Rights

• Public awareness of Indian STI sector
  - Promoting scientific temperament across all sections of the society
  - Creating a national knowledge network

SUMMARY

Technology is application of various field of knowledge used for designing tools and equipment that adds to the productivity of various factors of production. There are two types of technology, viz., labour intensive technology and capital intensive technology. Labour intensive technology requires higher level of manpower compared to capital. It enhances capital productivity, and is suitable for the customized products production at a small scale. Capital intensive technology, on the contrary, requires higher level of capital investment compared to labour cost. It enhances labour productivity, and is useful in mass scale production. Depending on the field in which technology is applied, the technology is classified as information technology, medical technology, education technology, space technology, mobile technology, transportation technology and assistive technology.

Technology plays an important role in wealth creation. It is fundamental in transforming a society and bringing in overall improvement in the quality of life. The Global Creativity Index (GCI) prepared by the Martin Prosperity Institute reaffirms this relationship: Nations having high score on the GCI also have higher levels of economic output, entrepreneurship and overall economic competitiveness, human development, life satisfaction, and happiness and equality. Technological changes, along with them bring in changes in the society, economy as well as in business practices.

Adoption of new technology affects business as it brings in improvement in outsourcing and outsourcing practices, inventory management and quality control practices, improves security and confidentiality, reduces time in designing items, improves the speed of communication and widens customer reach.

Though new technology brings in immense benefits to firms adopting these, it also entails several challenges such as high investment in research and development, high risk of failure of new ventures, displacement of labour from traditional sectors dependent on old technology, and also destructions of existing industries.

To minimize the possible threats and maximize gains, new technology needs to be managed efficiently. Technology management, i.e., integration of technology with business units and business strategies, entails a cautious approach towards new ventures, imaginations, research on assessment of emerging trends in technology. The government also needs to support business units in their efforts to manage technology by creating supporting infrastructure.

REVIEW QUESTIONS

18.1 Define technology.

18.2 What are the different types of technology?

18.3 Differentiate labour intensive technology from capital intensive technology. Give examples of industries that use labour intensive technology.

18.4 What are the advantages of labour intensive technology?

18.5 When will you use capital intensive technology?

18.6 What are the different classifications of technology?

18.7 What is assistive technology? How far it is different from medical technology?

18.8 What are the differences between information technology and mobile technology?

18.9 In what form technology is used in education?

18.10 How does space technology benefits human beings?

18.11 What role technology plays in the development process?

18.12 What is the Global Creativity Index? What does it highlight?

NUMERICAL PROBLEM

18.1 Using the information available from Table 18.7, identify which of the technologies C, D and E is labour intensive and which is capital intensive.

Table 18.7 Types of Technology and Factor Inputs

Type of technology	*Amount of labour*	*Amount of capital*
C	400	400
D	600	200
E	200	800
Total amount of output	1 unit	1 unit

CASE ANALYSIS EXERCISE

C18.1 The "Energy Revolution", Innovation, and the Nature of Substitution

Large and sustained price changes alter relative input prices and induce innovation (Hicks 1932). The post-2004 crude oil price increases did just that in both natural gas and oil exploration and extraction through new technologies, such as horizontal drilling and hydraulic fracturing. Because of these technologies, the US increased it natural gas production by almost 30 per cent during 2005-12. Similarly, US crude oil production increased by 1.3 mb/d during the past 4 years. To put this additional oil supply into perspective, consider that global biofuel production in terms of crude oil energy equivalent was 1.2 mb/d in 2011.

The sharp increase in natural gas supplies, not only put downward pressure on prices but also induced substitution of coal by natural gas in various energy intensive industries, notably in electricity generation and petrochemicals. Natural gas, which traded just 7 per cent below oil in 2000–04 in energy-equivalent terms, averaged 82 per cent lower in 2011–12, and it has been traded close to parity with coal (figure Box Comm 1.1). On the other hand, growing US oil supplies, coupled with weak demand, caused WTI to be traded at 20 per cent below Brent, the international marker (figure Box Comm 1.2). The discount is expected to persist until 2015 when new pipelines and reversal of existing pipelines will move oil supplies from the mid-continent US to the US Gulf.

Yet, the shift from crude oil to other types of energy, notably electricity and natural gas, with potential use by the transportation industry (which globally accounts for more than half of crude oil consumption) has been very slow. Such slow response reflects the different physical properties these types of energy, namely density (the amount of energy stored in a unit of mass) and scalability (how easily the energy conversion process can be scaled up). The energy densities of the fuels relevant to the transportation industry are 37 MJ/liter for crude oil, 1 MJ/kg for electicity, and 0.036 MJ/liter for natural gas (in its natural state); Compressed Natural Gas (CNG), used by bus fleets in large cities, is about 10 MJ/liter, while the density of Liquefied Natural Gas (LNG) is 24 MJ/liter. Energy density is measured in megajoules (MJ) per kilogram or liter. For comparison note that one MJ of energy can light one 100-Watt bulb for about 3 hours.

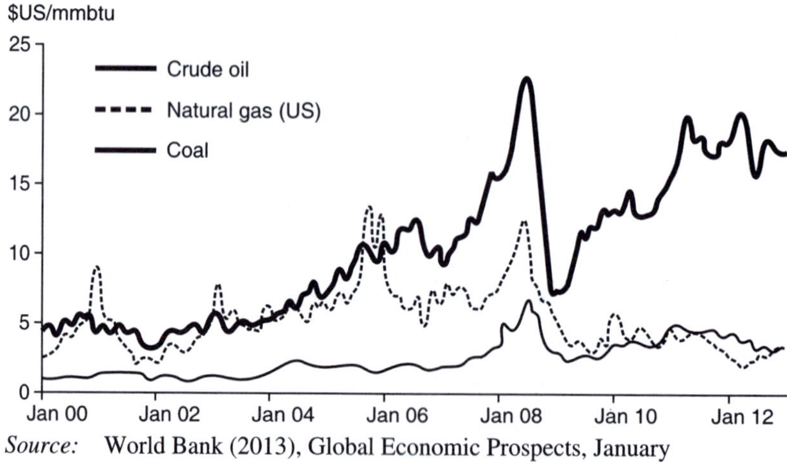

Source: World Bank (2013), Global Economic Prospects, January

Figure 18.2 Energy Prices.

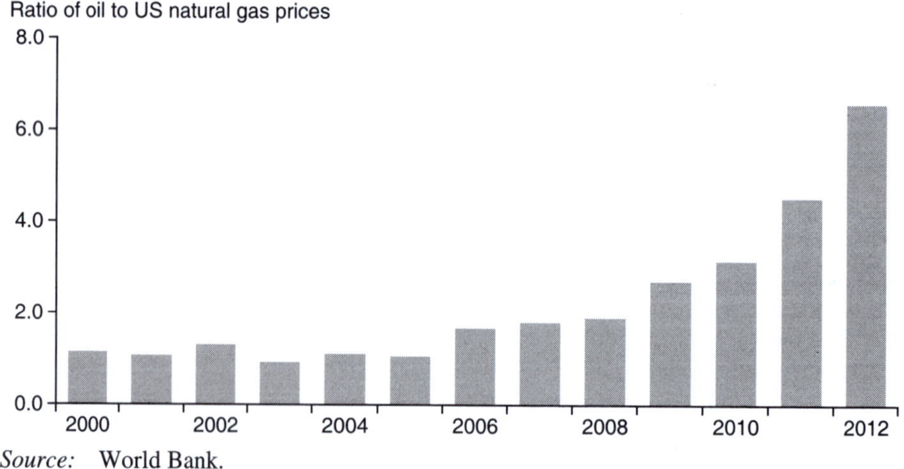

Source: World Bank.

Figure 18.3 Oil to Natural Gas Price Ratio.

Source: World Bank (2013), Global Economic Prospects, January

To gauge the importance of energy density associated with various fuels and technologies consider the following illustrative example. If a truck with a net weight capacity of 40,000 lbs were to be powered by lithium-sulphur batteries (currently used by electric-powered vehicles) for a 500-mile range, the batteries would occupy almost 85 per cent of the truck's net capacity leaving only 6,000 lbs of commercial space. That is, an energy conversion process that works at a small scale (a passenger car) does not work at larger scales (a truck, an airplane, or an oceanliner). Similarly, to increase the energy density of natural gas, it must be liquefied, which involves cooling it to about –62°C at a LNG terminal, transporting it in specially designed ships under near atmospheric pressure but under cooling, and then off-loading at destination, gasified and reinjected into the natural gas pipe network. This is a technically demanding process adding considerable costs at delivery. Contrary to natural gas, crude oil products have convenient distribution networks and refueling stations that can be reached by cars virtually everywhere in the world. Thus, in order for the transport industry to substitute crude oil by natural gas at a scale large enough to reduce oil prices, innovations must take place such that the distribution and refueling costs of natural gas become comparable to those of crude oil, which explains why the transport industry is slow to utilize natural gas.

Questions

1. What new technological innovations have taken place in natural gas and oil exploration field?
2. What factors compelled discovery of new exploration technology?
3. What advantage the new technology has provided to the USA?
4. What is the impact of new technology?
5. What factors are responsible for switch from crude oil to other types of energy sources?
6. What further innovations are needed to enable transport industry to switch to natural gas at a rapid pace?

SUGGESTED FURTHER READING

Government of India (2013), Science, Technology and Innovation Policy 2013. (online) http://www.dst.gov.in/sti-policy-eng.pdf.

Coad, A. and Reid, A (2012), The role of Technology and Technology-based Firms in Economic Development:Rethinking Innovation and Enterprise Policy in Scotland, Technopolis |group|, August (online) http://www.scottish-enterprise.com/~/media/SE/Resources/Documents/PQR/Technology%20and%20Technology-based%20Firms%20in%20Economic%20Development.pdf.

CHAPTER 19

Natural Environment and Business Sustainability

19.1 INTRODUCTION

Cadbury New Zealand, in early 2009, as a cost saving strategy, substituted palm oil and other vegetable fat for coca buffer. However, country wide protest by environmental groups who blamed palm oil production for destruction of rainforests across Indonesia and Malaysia, a key habitat for orangutans and other endangered species, forced the candy maker to phase-out palm oil out of Cadbury milk chocolate products.

In the subsequent periods, similar protests forced Nestle, Unilиver and Kraft to severe their ties with Sinal Mas—one of the largest supplier of palm oil—and switch to certified sustainable palm oil or other environmentally sustainable substitutes.

Some confectionery manufacturers, as indicated in the previous paragraphs switched to environmental inputs due to protest from environmental groups, while some others like Seventh Generation have set goals to switch to such inputs voluntarily.

Not only confectionery manufacturers but business organizations, in general, now-a-days are trying to use more environmentally sustainable inputs and processes. Delta Airlines, for example, in 2011, as a part of its recycling programme of non-hazardous waste, recycled 495 tons of papers which is expected to save 8,257 trees, 3.4 million gallons of waste, 2,23,411 gallons of oil and 12 kWh of electricity.

As a part of their environment sustainability approach, some companies like Land Securities, Deloitte, Marks and Spencer, are aiming to use cloud computing to reduce their energy and water usages.

Why companies are bothered about environmental sustainability? What forces them to adopt environmentally sustainable inputs and processes? Why environment protection is necessary? Why many companies are reluctant to move to more environmental friendly solutions? This chapter looks at some issues related to natural environment and its sustainability to get an answer for many such questions. Accordingly, Section 19.1 defines natural environment. Section 19.2 outlines the forms of environmental degradation takes, whereas Section 19.3 discusses its causes. Policy instruments to prevent environmental degradation are outlined in Section 19.4. Interdependence of natural environment and business activities is indicated in Section 19.5. Section 19.6 outlines the environment costs, their accounting and the types of business decisions that are affected by environmental costs.

19.2 FORMS OF ENVIRONMENTAL DEGRADATION: THREAT TO BUSINESS PROSPERITY

Environmental degradation is a process of erosion of the natural environment through depletion of natural resources, destruction of ecosystem and loss of biodiversity. The process can be either natural in origin or caused by human activities or a combination of both. The process of degradation has increased significantly since the industrial revolution and accelerating with the increasing globalization of economic activities. It is one of the major areas of concern for the planet as life health and sustainability is dependent on the quality of the environment it is surrounded by.

Environmental degradation can take various forms. Some of these are described here:

Soil Degradation

Degradation of soil is primarily in the form of soil erosion and soil salinization. **Soil erosion** refers to the gradual process of wearing away of soil layers from fields by water and wind flow. Soil erosion is a common phenomenon in areas with steep slopes, barren lands and over populated areas. It is a natural phenomenon, which is commonly found in areas with steep slopes and barren lands. Though some amount of soil erosion is necessary for the soil formation itself, accelerated amount of erosion results in the loss of valuable soil and its nutrients that are essential for crops to grow, which increases the risk of malnutrition of farmers as well as availability of foodgrains to human being and availability of raw material for manufacturing activities.

Soil salinisation occurs due to increasing salt content in the soil. The salinisation is common in naturally dry areas that are continuously used for multiple cropping with irrigation from river or other sources of ground water without allowing any fallow periods for the land to recover. All the groundwater irrigation contains salt, which remains behind in the soil after the water evaporates. The salt, making it more difficult for plants to absorb soil moisture, affects the root growth, which in turn suppresses plant growth. The soil affected by salinisation is very difficult and expensive to rehabilitate and often remains unused and abandoned.

Water Pollution

Clean water is an important resource for life on earth as it transports nutrients and chemicals within the biosphere to all forms of life—whether plants or animals or human beings. At the same time it also holds the surface of the earth. However, only around 2.5 per cent of all the water on Earth is fresh water, of which 70 per cent is frozen in ice caps located in Antarctica and Greenland and the rest 30 per cent is available for consumption.

Water gets contaminated from the discharge of industrial waste, chemical waste and heavy metal in the river. Not only the surface water but also the underground water gets contaminated by such discharge. Such a contamination not only harms human life but also aquatic life.

Air Pollution

Industrial production, vehicles and energy generation increase the sulphur dioxide concentration and make air polluted. Respiratory disorders and lung cancer are commonly noticed problems in polluted areas which are a major factor affecting productivity. Besides, acid rain, as an outcome of water pollution, creates problems for vegetation, forests and water bodies.

Deforestation

Forests protect the environment by preventing soil erosion and regulating the ecological balance of the nature. Excess deforestation destroys tropical rain forests and plants and animals natives to such forests. Growing industrialization and urbanzination has been causing rapid loss in the forest cover, which in turn is contributing to soil erosion and ecological imbalance.

Desertification

Permanent degradation of land due to loss of soil nutrients, moisture and vegetation, and salinisation is known as **desertification**. Such degradation occurs because of unsustainable land use and global warming, and converts productive lands into non-productive deserts. Desertification is more common in semi-arid areas, such as Kenya, Sudan and Namibia, because water scarcity in these regions make them sensitive to the effects of climate change, and human development.

Biodiversity Loss

Biodiversity represents the diversity of living creatures genetically, individually and ecosystem wide. The diversity in the species is important, because all have a unique role to play in the cycle of earth. However, due to varied human activities, like deforestation and hunting, the natural habitats as well as the survival of several species are being threatened. Excessive deforestation, desertification, overexploitation of natural resources, water and air pollution, and climate change reduces this variability and contributes to biodiversity loss. The loss will affect the number of pollinators, which will hamper crop yield and food production. The extinction of plant and animal species also has the potential of endangering genetic resources required for the development of new drugs. The reduced biodiversity will aggravate the emergence and spread of infectious diseases and will question mark life survival on earth.

Atmospheric Changes

Earth is surrounded by a thin layer of gases consisting nitrogen (78 per cent), oxygen (21 per cent), argon (0.9 per cent), carbon dioxide (0.03 per cent) and trace amount of other gases that is retained by Earth's gravity. These gases, which form the atmosphere, insulate the earth from extreme temperatures and make it livable. The atmosphere protects the life on earth by trapping heat and oxygen and blocking some of the ultraviolet rays reaching Earth.

Excessive release of greenhouse gases and other pollutants in the air by indiscriminate industrialization, urbanization and deforestation, however, are causing imbalances of gases and damaging the Earth's atmosphere, the manifestation of which are in the form of global warming, ozone holes and acid rain.

Global Warming (Greenhouse effect)

The term **global warming** signifies an increase in the atmospheric temperature near the Earth's surface. An increase in atmospheric temperature occurs due to imbalance in the greenhouse gases; hence global warming is also known as the **greenhouse effect**.

Box 19.1 Greenhouse Gases

Greenhouse gases in the Earth's atmosphere comprise water vapour (H_2O), carbon dioxide (CO_2), methane (CH_4), nitrous oxide (N_2O), and ozone (O_3). These gases act like the glass panes in the greenhouse. They can absorb and emit infrared radiation emerging from sunlight. They let in light but keep heat from escaping, maintain the right temperature required for life on Earth. Imbalances in the proportion of greenhouse gases would make the Earth warmer than usual. Over time, the energy absorbed from the sun must be balanced by outgoing radiation from the Earth's atmosphere, leaving the temperature of the Earth's surface roughly constant.

Over a period of time, especially since large scale industrialization that began around 150 years ago, the level of several greenhouse gases have increased by about 25 per cent, increasing the average temperature on earth and causing global warming. Global warming is blamed for drier soils in mid continental areas, substantial rise in sea levels worldwide and severity of tropical storms such as hurricanes and cyclones. Global warming is causing food supply shortage by massive crop failure and is responsible for widespread extinction of species, which is a threatening news for humans and other life forms on earth.

Ozone Depletion

Earth's atmosphere consists of many layers. Ozone gas, which is a form of elemental oxygen, is found in two such layers—troposphere and stratosphere. Troposphere is closest to Earth, i.e., at the ground level. Ozone in this layer is an air pollutant that damages crops, trees and other vegetation and also causes breathing problems in human beings. It is a main ingredient of urban smog. Ozone in the stratosphere, on the contrary, is considered to be good; it protects life on Earth from Sun's harmful ultraviolet (UV) rays. Ozone is produced naturally in the stratosphere, but is destroyed by man-made chemicals, such as chlorofluorocarbons (CFCs), hydrochlorofluorocarbons (HCFCs), halons, methylbromide, carbon tetrachloride, and methyl chloroform used in and released by air conditioners, refrigerators, fire extinguishers, pesticides, aerosol sprays, etc. and air conditioners, are considered to be the main cause of ozone depletion. Depletion of ozone in stratosphere enables entry of larger amount of UV rays to Earth. Overexposure to UV rays causes problems like skin cancer, cataracts and affects the immune system. It also damages sensitive crops such as soybeans and reduces crop yields and affects marine phytoplankton—which are the base of ocean food chain.

Acid Rain

Acid rain is a broad term used for describing deposition of acid from atmosphere. The deposition can be in wet form such as acidic rain, snow, dew, fog and frost or in dry form such as acidic hail and dust.

Rain water always contains some impurities in the form of dust particles and other gas absorbed from air. These pollutants make water acidic. Normally, the acidity or alkalinity of water, measured by its pH level is 5.6. But, rain water that is highly polluted and acidic will usually have a pH of below 5. Acid rain (or even as acid snow, dew, fog, frost, hail, dust) can harm crops and plants that depend on rain water for their survival. Not only life gets affected but even buildings and monuments can get damaged by such chemicals. Discolouration of Taj Mahal is one such example.

Acidity in rain water can occur from lightening, volcanoes and forest fires, and rotting organic matter, which are the natural phenomena, or can be due to human activities, such as burning of coal and other fossil fuels in the process of electricity generation and other industrial and day-to-day activities.

UNDERSTANDING BUSINESS ENVIRONMENT

UBE 19.1 World GHG Emissions and Historical Responsibilities

This UBE highlights the countries that are responsible for the high level of GHG emission.

The largest share of historical and current global emissions of GHGs has originated in developed countries. While the worldwide emissions of GHGs have increased since 1945, with the largest increases taking place in CO_2 emissions, scientists attribute the global problem of climate change not to the current GHG emissions but to the stock of historical GHG emissions (Figure 19.1).

Most of the countries, particularly the industrialized countries, having large current emissions are also the largest historic emitters and the principal contributors to climate change. Industrialized countries with the largest total emissions also rank among those with the highest per capita emissions.

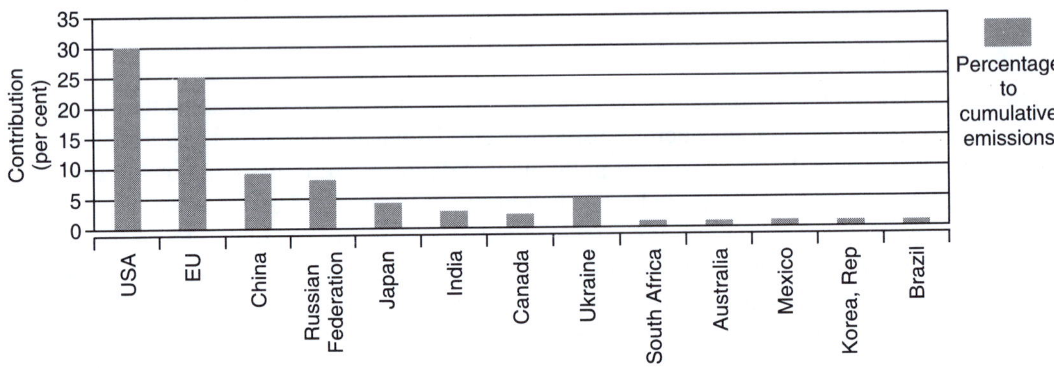

Source: Earth Trends (http://earthtrends.wri.org) Searchable Database Results Provided by the World Resources Institute (http://www.wri.org).

Figure 19.1 Percentage Contribution to Cumulative Emissions1900–2005.

Source: Government of India (2012), Economic Survey.

19.3 CAUSES OF ENVIRONMENTAL DEGRADATION

Environmental degradation is an upshot of the dynamic interplay of a range of factors as outlined here:

19.3.1 Demographic Factors

Social factors, such as population size, poverty and urbanization can cause rapid environmental degradation as outlined here.

Increase in population beyond certain threshold limits increases the demand for natural resources tremendously. For example, demand for housing increases which in turn results in higher demand for wood and other natural resources. A sharp increase in the demand causes rapid decline in natural resources. At the same time, with increasing population there is a substantial amount of waste generated through daily activities and discharged into water bodies, air and soil which cause pollution and add to environmental degradation. Poverty and environmental degradation have bidirectional relationship, i.e. one accentuates the other and makes the relationship complex. In the absence of alternative resources poor are more dependent on natural resources; and hence they deplete natural resources faster than the rich. However, depletion of natural resources accelerates poverty and impoverishment as they experience contraction in their natural assets such as forests, wildlife, water, fish, etc. and depletion in their sources of earnings.

Large scale migration by people seeking for employment opportunities in urban areas puts stress on the limited infrastructure—energy, housing, transport, communication, water supply and sewerages and recreational amenities—of cities. Unplanned expansion results in proliferation of slums and rapid degradation of urban environment.

19.3.2 Economic Factors

Major economic factors that cause environmental degradation are as follows:

1. Market failure: **Market failure** occurs when markets for environmental products do not exist or even when they exist they malfunction. In the presence of market failure, prices cannot be properly determined or even when they are determined they under price the underlying products. Consequently, we end up producing and consuming environmental products too much. The environment bears the cost of our excess production and consumption. Market failure can occur due to externalities, under-pricing, lack of markets and information, and policy failure as outlined here:

Externalities: Production and consumption of goods and services often carry with them externalities. The term **externalities** refers to unintended effects of the actions of certain producers and consumers of the society. Externalities can be positive or negative. **Positive externalities** confer unintended benefits to others. For example, if usherance of a mega housing complex increases sales of local shops, even when they are not bearing the cost of the complex, then we can say that the local shop owners are enjoying externalities. **Negative externalities**, on the contrary, result in unintended harmful effects for others. For example, waste discharged by factories into water-bodies causes water pollution, damages marine life and make many depended on marine life unemployed. Thus, the cost of pollution, which ideally should have been on the polluters, gets passed on to the society in general. The cleanup cost of such damage is often borne by the community and/or the government.

Both, positive and negative externalities, cause market failure. As there is a separation between the perpetrator and the affected parties and the effects are unintended and often non-quantifiable, it is difficult to get the perpetrator to incorporate the cost of the harmful effects and the beneficiaries to pay for benefits. Therefore, divergence between private cost and social cost or private benefits and social benefits can occur. The social cost and social benefits are defined as follows:

$$\text{Social Cost} = \text{Private Cost} + \text{External Cost}$$

$$\text{Social Benefits} = \text{Private Benefits} + \text{External Benefits}$$

The divergence between private and social costs and benefits causes market failure. To understand this more clearly let us consider the case of positive externality.

In the case of **positive externalities**, as indicated in Figure 19.2, the social cost is equal to the private cost, because the society does not have to pay anything extra for the benefits that it derives from the positive externality. However, the amount of social benefits exceeds the amount of private benefits, i.e., Social Benefits > Private Benefits because benefits are not simply confined to the party that has incurred the cost to get such benefits. The producer aiming at maximizing profit will equate Private Marginal Cost (PMC) with Private Marginal Benefits (PMB) to identify the profit maximizing level of output. In the diagram the profit maximizing output occurs at quantity Q_p;

hence, without any government or external intervention, left to the market forces, the optimum production or consumption will be equal to Q_p. However, this is socially inefficient because at given Social Marginal Cost (SMC) and Social Marginal Benefits (SMB), the society would like to produce or consume Q_s amount which is higher than Q_p.

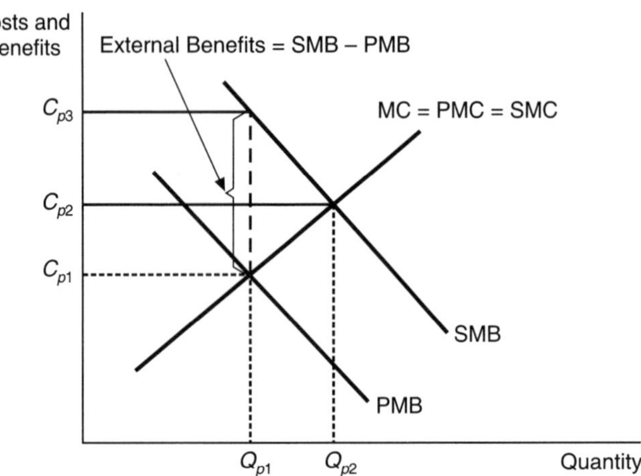

Figure 19.2 Positive Externalities.

Similarly, negative externalities result in an outcome which is not economically efficient or socially optimum. In the case of **negative externalities**, social benefits are equal to private benefits; however, there is a divergence between the social cost and private cost as indicated in Figure 19.3. The profit maximizing producer, in such a case, will produce Q_{n1} quantity. However, at this level of output marginal cost to the society (C_{n3}) is higher than that to the private sector (C_{n1}). For the society, the optimum output occurs when SMC is equal to PMC. This occurs at the output of Q_{n1} which is lower than what will be produced in the free market. The activities such as cigarette smoking, pollution from automobile driving, garbage disposal on streets, etc., involving negative externalities, are carried out in greater quantities than what will be socially optimal.

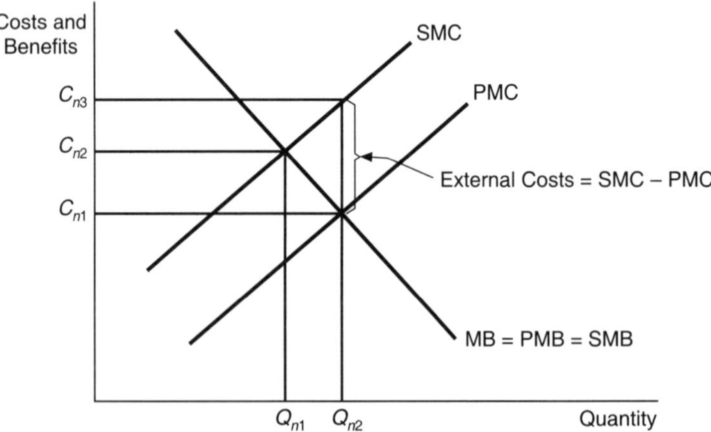

Figure 19.3 Negative Externalities.

Under pricing: Markets in general usually account for pecuniary cost and unable to make provision for the environmental cost of production. Environmental resources, such as clean air and water in water bodies like river and lake, are in most countries in the public domain, i.e. no specific group of a society own these. Such resources are open access resources or public goods. Hence, users of these resources consider them free and end up imputing zero cost for them. This results in under costing and under pricing, overexploitation of natural resources and environmental degradation.

Policy failure: At times, government polices also result in market failure. For example, government subsidies on urea and other chemical fertilizers to farmers, result in under pricing and excess use of fertilizers by the farmers, often causing loss in soil fertility and contamination of groundwater in the long run.

Lack of information: Lack of sufficient information often gives a distorted picture of the availability of resources to the users. If the impression is that of scarcity, the resources get overpriced and underutilized. On the contrary, the impression is that of abundance, the under pricing, and overexploitation and environmental degradation take place.

Macroeconomic factors: It has been argued that the models of developments pursued by developing countries are unsustainable. In most countries, the population is depended on primary activities, such as agricultural, forestry, fishing and mining. For development they import machinery, manufactured and technological products. The foreign exchange required for the payment of these items is earned by exporting primary products. In the development process, overexploitation of natural resources causes severe loss in the bio-diversity in the country and the development process becomes environmentally unsustainable. For example, Myanmar had excessive deforestation resulting in a downward trend in animals like tigers and elephants. Currently the country is trying to balance its economic growth with environmental biodiversity and sustainability.

2. International trade related factors: Growing globalization and international trade agreements are also identified to be one of the reasons for environmental degradation. Some of the agreements arrived at multilateral platforms, such as the TRIPS agreement on WTO, supersede national laws and prompts companies to get patent on natural resources—seeds, plants and other organism, which otherwise belong to the society as a whole. Such patented resources, it has been argued, accelerate the monoculture cropping and destroy bio-diversity.

3. Technological factors: Even scientific and technological advancements that contribute to the rapid economic growth can cause environmental degradation. For example, technological advancements in the form of steam and internal combustion engines though helped UK to achieve industrial revolution, but the same advancements also polluted many of its cities, leading to thousands of deaths every year from respiratory illness. Similarly, India achieved green revolution with the help of hybrid variety seeds and fertilizers which demand large quantities of water. Over exposure to such technology has depleted water levels sharply in the regions like Punjab which were the main beneficiaries of the revolution. Not only the depletion of the ground water, but also the salinity in the water making the soil infertile.

4. Institutional factors: Institutional factors are related to structure and mechanism that govern the behaviour of individuals and help the society in establishing co-operation. Most environmental problems emerge from conflict between collective and individual rationality in a society. These conflicts can take varied forms. For example, prevention of deforestation require co-operation from individuals. One of the co-operation required in this direction is the recycling of waste papers and using the recycled papers. In the absence of a robust institutional mechanism, such as proper affordable recycling facilities, it becomes difficult to make individuals co-operate on this front. Similarly, use of public transport can greatly help in controlling pollution. However, poor transport facilities often deter people to use them and prompt them to switch to private transport, which in turn increases pollution. In some countries it is the absence of properly defined property rights that have been leading to overexploitation of natural resources and environmental degradation. Property rights confer privileges as well as responsibilities in the use of natural resources, which help in better use of resources as well as the conservation of environment.

As setting up institutional mechanism is a costly activity, institutional set-up varies across countries depending on their level of income, preferences of society and pressure from the environmentalist groups within and outside the country.

19.4 POLICY INSTRUMENTS TO PREVENT ENVIRONMENTAL DEGRADATION

It has been argued that to prevent the problem of environmental degradation in the form of air pollution, water contamination, soil erosion, resource depletion etc., the public in general and businesses in particular to be encouraged to adopt environmentally friendly and sustainable processes and uses. However, such a change in the behaviour does not occur automatically. Hence, governments, the world over, are following environmental policies that aim at influencing the behaviour to prevent environmental degradation and achieve business and economic sustainability (UBE 19.3 and UBE 19.4). Policies are enacted broadly, as indicated in Figure 19.4, through four types of instruments. These instruments are outlined hereinafter:

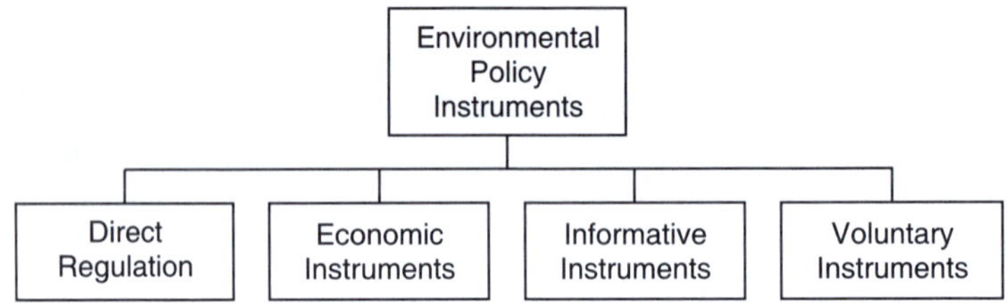

Figure 19.4 Instruments to Control Environmental Degradation.

19.4.1 Direct Regulation

Tax and subsidy and market-based regulations work through the market mechanism. Such instruments may or may not be effective in bringing in the required changes. In case the other instruments are not able to bring in the desirable changes, regulation-based instruments are resorted to. The regulation-based instruments regulate the behaviour and performance of polluters directly to achieve a desired, prescribed environmental quality targets. These can take various forms such as—licenses, permits, registrations, land and water extraction restrictions, bans and prohibitions, planning and building controls, quantitative limits on emissions, guidelines setting technical standards, like engineering standards, performance standards, emission or effluent standards, environmental quality standards, process and equipment standards, etc.

The important advantage associated with the regulatory instruments is that they have direct and certain impact on the target; hence these are considered to be more effective than the other instruments. However, they are also subject to criticism as follows:

- They are difficult and costly to implement and enforce
- They leave scope for corruption
- The fines and penalties imposed are usually set so low that these instruments are unable to deter the violators

19.4.2 Economic Instruments

Unlike the regulation-based instruments which consists of enforcements and restrictions, economic instruments are designed to provide financial incentives that promote environmentally-friendly forms of production and consumption. Economic instruments affect the costs and benefits of alternative processes available to individuals and firms and leave polluters to respond to certain stimuli/incentives (for example subsidies) and deterrents (for example taxes). As they operate through market forces, i.e., demand and supply forces, they are also known as the market-based instruments. These instruments include:

1. Charges and levies: Effluent/emission charges, user charges, product charges and administrative charges, congestion charges, resource taxes, etc.

2. Subsidies: Subsidies act as incentive to polluters to modify their behaviour. This instrument takes the shape of grants, concessional loans and tax incentives (such as tax credits and accelerated depreciation on equipments used for controlling pollution) and exemptions.

3. Financial enforcement incentives: To encourage compliance with environmental standards and regulations financial enforcement incentive are used. These take the form of non-compliance fees and fines and performance bonds. At times, these also take the form of denial of public subsidies and financing, termination of licence or suspension of plant operations.

4. Deposit refund: The consumers of durable or reusable, but potentially polluting products are made to pay a deposit in the form of a surcharge. When these products (such as cold drink bottles, automobile batteries, pesticide containers) are returned to the approved centre for recycling or proper disposal, the deposits are refunded.

5. Market instruments: These instruments give the rights to economic agents for potential pollution. The buyers, however, can sell these rights to others at a premium, which is market determined. Examples of such instruments are pollution credits, emissions trading (UBE 19.1), price intervention and liability insurance.

UNDERSTANDING BUSINESS ENVIRONMENT

UBE 19.2 New Zealand Adopts Emissions Trading Scheme

The market mechanism for controlling pollution is gaining popularity in the recent period. New Zealand is one country which has adopted this mechanism in the form of the Emission Trading Scheme as illustrated in this UBE.

Emission trading is a cost-effective instrument that is used by governments to regulate emission of pollutants through the market mechanism. While using this instrument, the government first sets a limit for total acceptable emission level and then divides this into tradable units, often referred to as credits or permits. These units are then sold in the market for such units. The pollutants, who cross the amount of permissible level of emissions, as reflected in the permitted credits, can buy units from those units that have reduced their emissions and have surplus units to sell.

A signatory to the Kyoto Protocol (UBE 19.2), New Zealand is committed to reduce its greenhouse gas emissions back to 1990 levels by 2012; otherwise it will be required to pay for the extra emission. As an instrument to meet its commitment, since 2008 New Zealand has chosen **Emission Trading Scheme** (ETS) as mandatory scheme for the following reasons:

- ETS moves the cost of emission only to those who contribute to it.
- ETS works through the market mechanism; hence it provides more flexibility than simply a tax on pollution.

Through this instrument, New Zealand expects that there will be

- Lower emissions
- Higher investment in clean technology and renewal power generation
- Larger tree plantation
- Strengthening of the country's green brand, which will help the country in trading in international markets where consumers are increasingly demanding environmentally friendly products.

The ETS works as follows in New Zealand:

In New Zealand, tradable units authorizing the right to generate pollution are termed as New Zealand Units (NZUs). One NZU provides the right to emit one ton of carbon dioxide, or the equivalent amount of certain other greenhouse gases. Different organizations are made to participate in the scheme in different ways as follows:

- Organizations emitting greenhouse gases, such as companies that mine natural gases, surrender NZUs to the government
- Organizations absorbing greenhouse gases, such as owners of forests, earn NZUs from the government
- Organizations that might face a significant increase in energy costs, but are unable to pass the same to customers, are given NZUs by the government.
- The above groups are permitted to trade NZUs with each other; those with spare NZUs can sell them to those who have to surrender NZUs.

A schematic of the ETS is presented in Figure 19.5.

The ETS adopted by New Zealand since 2008, is mandatory and currently covers emissions from forestry, stationary energy, industrial processes and liquid fossil fuels, which are collectively responsible for roughly 50 per cent of New Zealand's emissions. There will be further expansion of the coverage of the scheme by including waste and synthetic gases in 2013, and agriculture in 2015.

Apart from New Zealand, twenty eight other countries have adopted or in the process of adopting ETS. The scheme is also adopted by some states of Australia and the USA. For example, the European Union was the first one to adopt the scheme; it is in practice since 2005 there and is mandatory. Japan is also operating the scheme since 2005, but it is voluntary there. China is scheduled to launch pilot emissions trading schemes in six provinces and cities in 2013 with a view to develop a nationwide trading scheme by 2015.

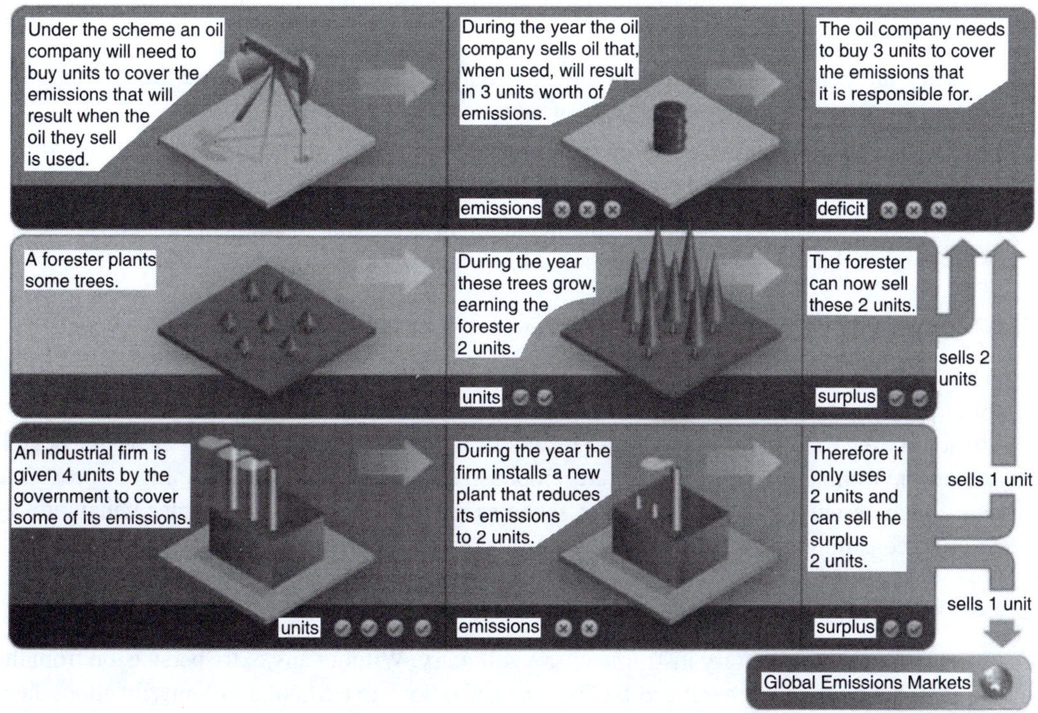

Source: New Zealand, Ministry for the Environment, (online) http://www.climatechange.govt.nz/emissions-trading-scheme/about/ets-diagram.html, as on 20/6/2012.

Figure 19.5 Mechanism of ETS in New Zealand.

Economic instruments have several advantages as follows:

- These instruments are considered to be economically efficient.
- They allow the polluter to incorporate pollution prevention and control charges in his costs thus, they help in incorporating the appropriate pricing of environmental resources, such as water and air, which otherwise treated as free. Appropriate pricing of the resources helps, in the long run, in better allocation and use of resources.
- Such instruments encourage innovations in the area of pollution control technology and non-polluting products that can help not only in environmental degradation but also reduce the costs of the adopters.
- They provide flexibility to the polluter of selecting the technology that is both effective in reducing pollution and his costs.
- Some of these instruments generate revenue for the government, which can be used for controlling pollution.

Notwithstanding these advantages, the economic instruments have following critics:

- The effectiveness of these instruments is subject to market uncertainty. For example, taxes on polluters though might increase their cost of production may not encourage them to adopt the pollution controlling techniques if the cost of these technologies is substantially higher.

- They are perceived as giving polluters a right or permission to pollute the environment after making payments in the form of taxes.
- These may not be effective in achieving the objective of controlling pollution if the polluters are able to pass on the higher costs to the consumers.
- The costs associated with the implementation of economic instruments are considered to be higher than that of regulation-based instruments.

19.4.3 Informative Instruments

When it is difficult to clearly identify the root causes of environmental problems, authorities usually use softer policy instruments to improve public awareness of the consequences of environmental degradation. Often extensive research and results of monitoring work are published. In a school curriculum environment related issues are emphasized and even special training is provided. Measures such as environmental labelling schemes aim at controlling consumer behaviour by encouraging consumption of goods and services that are environmentally friendly.

19.4.4 Voluntary Instruments

As the name suggests, voluntary instruments are voluntary. Without any extra persuasion from the government, the public in general and business organizations in particular voluntarily adopt these instruments and process and innovate and adopt technologies that are not only environmentally friendly but also reduce their cost of production.

Some forms that these instruments can take are as follows:

1. Environment or eco labelling: The **eco label** is a warded by an impartial third party, which certifies that the product meets certain eco-label standards. The prominent logo that appears on such certified products help consumers about the environmental impact of the labelled products. The label makes the products stands out on store shelves distinctly, and expected to motivate the competitors to redesign their products in a way that they too become environmentally friendly and get the required eco label certification to attract/retain customers.

2. Eco audits: **Eco audits** are voluntary arrangements adopted by firms that provide consumers the information about environmental management practices pursued by them. These measures not only foster better relationship with customers, suppliers and other stakeholders but also help firms discover processes that are more efficient through self-evaluation.

3. Voluntary agreements: The **voluntary agreements** are agreements between government and society and firms that aim at achieving desirable social outcomes. For example, firms may agree to certain emission targets. Such agreements may be legally binding or maybe simply an informal declaration of intent of the firm towards its commitment to the desirable target.

Governments often give a boost to such initiatives by various mechanisms, such as persuasion, providing information and bringing in changes in the law. For example, it can give the citizens ‘environmental rights’ to sue individuals or companies that break particular environmental laws or transfer rights of land ownership to a set of local individuals who assign more priority to the environmental friendly use of the land.

Voluntary instruments since are voluntary, require least administrative cost. However, critics of these instruments argue that since these are based on political bargains rather than price signals, they may not produce economically efficient outcomes and may not be effective in controlling environmental degradation.

Environmental degradation is a global problem, hence, the problem has been discussed at the global level to bring about appropriate solutions (UBE 19.3). At the country level also a mix of measures is adopted for environmental sustainability (UBE 19.4).

UNDERSTANDING BUSINESS ENVIRONMENT

UBE 19.3 Climate Change: A Global Concern

Environmental degradation is a global problem. Hence, joint efforts to combat the problem are going on as illustrated in this UBE.

Climate change is not a localized phenomenon as the countries pursuing environmentally friendly policies and practices also get affected by the climate change in other countries. Recognition of the fact that the whole world is a stakeholder, joint efforts to combat climate change started as early as June1992 when the "United Nations Framework Convention on Climate Change" (UNFCCC) in Rio de Janeiro was set up to take coordinated and effective action to limit average global temperature increase and the resulting climate change. The convention came into force in 1994. As on date there are 195 countries that are parties to the convention.

The convention recognizes that already developed countries (labelled as Annex I countries; belongs to OECD countries) are the source of most past and current greenhouse gas emissions they do most to cut emissions on home grounds. Annex I countries were expected by the year 2000 to reduce emissions to 1990 levels. Many of them have taken strong action to do so, and some have already succeeded.

The convention though has realized that the share of greenhouse gas (GHG) emissions emitted by developing nations will grow in the coming years, it has not yet imposed stricter norms on these countries as that may hinder their economic progress. However, to enable them to take voluntary mitigation and adaptation measures, industrialized nations have agreed to provide financial and technical assistance to developing countries to support their efforts in climate protection.

The conventions keep a check on the climate change activities pursued by Annex I countries. They are required to report regularly on their climate change policies and measures and need to submit an annual inventory of their greenhouse gas emissions, including data for their base year (1990). Even developed countries (non –Annex I countries) are subject to such disclosures but in more general terms and less regularly than Annex I countries.

The legally binding quantitative time bound targets for developed countries came into force in the convention held in 1997 in Kyoto, Japan. The Kyoto protocol sets limits of 5% below 1990 levels on six greenhouse gas emissions by 37 industrialized countries, individually or jointly, in the first commitment period 2008–12.

Realizing the difficulty in meeting the targets by domestic measures alone, the protocol provides considerable flexibility in meeting the targets through three measure as follows:

Clean Development Mechanism (CDM)*:* Clean Development Mechanism allows a industrialized country to finance mitigation projects in developing countries. Such projects earn saleable certified emission reduction (CER) credits, which can be used to meet Kyoto targets.

Joint Implementation (JI)*:* Mechanism of Joint Implementation allows an industrialized country to earn credits from an emission-reduction or emission removal project in another industrialized country, which can be counted towards meeting its Kyoto target.

Emission Trading (ET): Emissions trading allows countries that have emission units to spare—emissions permitted them but not used—to sell this excess capacity to countries that are over their targets.

The main shortfalls of the Kyoto protocol is that it did not set very ambitious targets. Two developed countries, Australia and the United States, did not sign ratified protocol, further limiting its reach. Another constraint which limited its impact was that the quantitative ceilings were not applied. The achievement of the Kyoto Protocol in the first five year commitment period is far from satisfactory as many parties not only miss the modest targets set in the Protocol but also record higher emission than the base year 1990 (Figure 19.6).

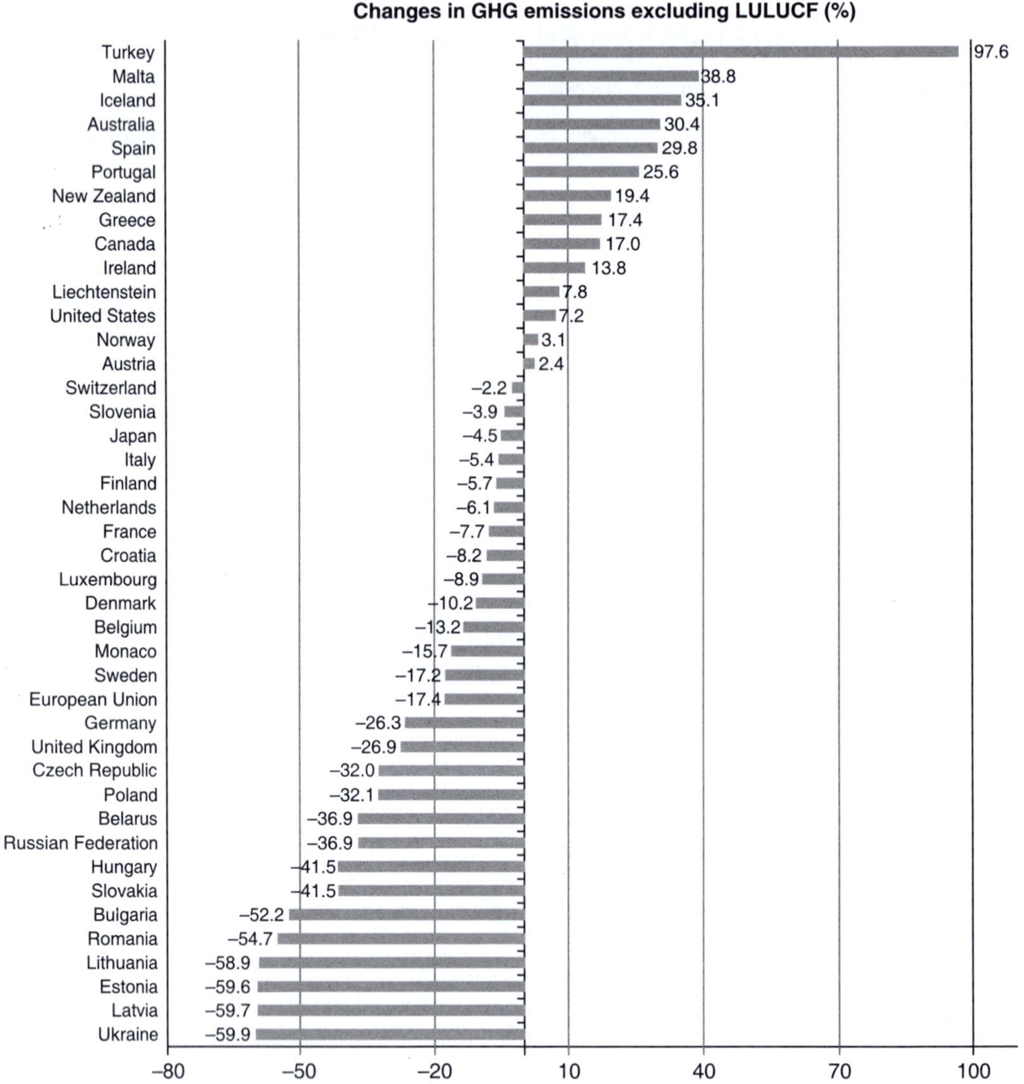

Source: United Nations Framework Convention on Climate Change (online), http://unfccc.int/ghg_data/ghg_data_unfccc/items/4146.php

Figure 19.6 Total Aggregate Greenhouse Gas Emissions of Individual Annex I Parties, 1990–2009, excluding Land Use, Land Use Change and Forestry (LULUCF) (%).

The Conference of Parties (COP) is the supreme body of the Convention. It meets annually and reviews the implementation of the Convention. Its recently held meeting in Durban from 28 November to 10 December 2011 (COP 17) marks an important step forward in the climate change negotiations. The Durban outcomes, outlined hereinafter, made significant contribution towards Climate Change by setting the second commitment period of the Kyoto Protocol and operationalized some of the key agreements of previous COP.

Key Durban Outcomes

- The Durban conference established a second commitment period of the Kyoto Protocol, which will begin on January 1, 2013 and end on December 2017 or December 2020.
- It operationalized some of the key Cancun agreements related to Green Climate Fund (GCF) and Technology Mechanism (TM).
- To enhance transparency, its sets more elaborated reporting guidelines for developed countries (Biennial Reports) and developing countries (Biennial Update Reports).
- It launched a Durban Platform for discussion on the post 2020 arrangements for the global climate regime.
- Progress was made on issues relating to Reducing Emissions from Deforestation and Degradation and Sustainable Management of Forests in Durban Conference.

UNDERSTANDING BUSINESS ENVIRONMENT

UBE 19.4 Environmental Protection and Management in India

Some of the laws enacted for environmental protections in India and their main thrust is highlighted in this UBE.

In India, good environment is a constitutional right. As per this right it is the duty of the State to protect the environment and to safeguard the forests and wildlife of the country. The Ministry of Environment and Forests (MoEF) is the apex administrative body that formulates environmental policy and oversees the implementation of environmental and forestry programmes. Environmental policies and regulations are formulated by the centre, but the implementation and enforcement of these policies is by state governments.

Systematic approach in dealing with environmental protection started in India after the United Nations' conference on Human Environment in 1972 and many policies and laws and their enactment took place in the subsequent period. As of now, India has a comprehensive environmental management system, which consists of environmental laws, regulatory institutions and institutional framework. Some of the laws enacted for environmental protections by the central government and their main thrust is highlighted here:

The Environment (Protection Act), 1986: It is one of the most encompassing legislation to protect the environment. This umbrella legislation authorizes the central government to protect the environment from pollutant from all sources and to take steps to improve the quality of the environment. Accordingly, the central government can prohibit or restrict the setting up and operations of any industrial activity on environmental grounds.

In addition to this all encompassing act, India also has different legislation for different constituents of environment as follows:

Water Pollution: Acts relating to water pollution, such as the Water (Prevention and Control of Pollution) Act, 1973 (amended 1988), the Water (Prevention and Control of Pollution) Cess Act, 1977 (amended 1992) and the Water ((Prevention and Control of Pollution) Cess (Amendment) Act, 2003, aim at preventing pollution of streams, inland water, subterranean waters as well as sea or tidal water by prohibiting disposal of polluting matters in the water.

Air Pollution: The Air (Prevention and Control of Pollution) Act, 1986 (amended 1987) and the Motor Vehicles Act, 1988 are specifically formulated to prevent, control and abate pollution from emission from industrial sources, motor vehicles and other sources.

Noise Pollution: Noise levels in public places from various sources like industrial activity, construction activity, loud speakers, music systems, electricity generators, vehicles and other mechanical devices are controlled by the Noise Pollution (Regulation and Control) Rules, 2000 and its amendment in 2010.

Hazardous Waste: Hazardous Wastes (Management and Handling) Rules, 1989 and its amendments in 2000 and 2009, the Ozone Depleting Substances (Regulation and Control) Rules, 2000, Batteries (Management and Handling) Rules, 2001, the Recycled Plastics Manufacture and Usage (Amendment) Rules, 2003, Bio-Medical Waste (Management and Handling) (Amendment) Rules, 2003 and E-waste Management and Handling Rules, 2011 regulates the generation, collection, treatment, import, storage, and handling of hazardous substances such as flammables, explosives, heavy metals, nuclear and petroleum fuel by-product, dangerous microorganism and synthetic chemical compounds like DDT and dioxins, electrical and electronic equipments and components.

Ozone Depleting Substances: Ozone Depleting Substances (Regulation) Rules, 2000 prevents the production of ozone depleting substances.

Forest Conservation: The Forest (Conservation) Act 1980, (amended 1988) enacted to conserve the country's forests by restricting and regulating the de-reservation of forests for non-forest purposes, while the Schedule Tribes and Other Traditional Forest Dwellers (Recognition of Forests Rights) Act, 2006, recognizes the rights of traditional forest dwellers in the forest areas.

Wildlife Protection: To preserve the natural habitats as well as the population of the wildlife across the country, India enacted The Indian Wildlife (Protection) Act. The act was amended in 1993 and further in 2003, making the punishment and penalty for offences under the Act more stringent.

Biological Diversity: The Biological Diversity Act, 2002 covers conservation, use of biological resources and associated knowledge occurring in India for commercial or research purposes or for the purposes of bio-survey and bio-utilization.

Public Liability Insurance: To provide for damages to persons affected by accidents occurring while handling any hazardous substances, India has enacted Public Liability Insurance Act, 1991.

Apart from enacting various acts, rules and regulations, India is also active on various international platforms addressing the issue of environmental protection. It is signatory to many international agreements including The Convention on International Trade in Endangered Species of flora and fauna (CITES), 1975, The Convention on Wetlands of International Importance, 1991, The Framework Convention on Climate Change, 1992, The Convention for Conservation of Biological Resources, 1992, The Vienna Convention/ Montreal Protocol on substances that deplete the ozone layer, 1985 and The Rio Declaration on Environmental and Development and the Agenda 21.

Inspite of plethora of policies, rules and regulations, India is one of the largest polluter in the world. It was placed 125 out of 132 countries by on the Environmental Performance Index (EPI) 2012 prepared by Yale University (Table 19.1). Air and water pollution seems to be a major area of concern for the country.

Increasing population pressure, rapid depletion of resources to achieve rapid economic growth and poor implementation of rules and regulations have been pointed out to be the main reasons for India's poor performance on environmental protection front.

Table 19.1 India's Ranking on Various Environmental Parameters

Level of Aggregation	*Performance*	
	Score	*Rank*
Environmental Performance Index	36.2	125
Environmental Health	25.7	119
Air (Effects on Human Health)	3.7	132
Environmental Burden of Disease	37.1	110
Water (Effects on Human Health)	24.7	104
Ecosystem Vitality	40.8	94
Agriculture	11.7	126
Air (Ecosystem Effects)	38.9	73
Biodiversity and Habitat	41.8	97
Climate Change	51.9	55
Fisheries	29.2	39
Forests	98.1	21
Water Resources	6.9	122

Source: Yale University (Online) Environmental Performance Index http://epi.yale.edu/epi2012/countryprofiles, as on 19/6/2012.

19.5 NATURAL ENVIRONMENT AND BUSINESS: AN INTERACTION

Natural environment consists of all natural resources such as raw material and energy sources such as water, air and climate. Some of the resources/energy sources are renewal whereas are others are non-renewal. Renewal resources, such as wind, solar or geothermal power, are replenished by natural processes, and thus can be used repeatedly; while non-renewal resources, such as nuclear power, coal, crude oil and natural gas, exist in a fixed quantity and will eventually run out, if used continuously.

There is no business activity which is not dependent on natural resources and/or energy sources either directly or indirectly in its supply chain. Agricultural activities are heavily dependent on water availability, soil fertility and so on. Allied activities, such as fishing is dependent on fish population. Not only agricultural but manufacturing activities draw their inputs from the nature.

Abundance of natural resources and energy sources, thus, enhances business prosperity.

However, business activities also influence the natural environment (Figure 19.7). Excessive use of non-renewal natural resources, such as oil and coal, leads to their sharp depletion. Some renewal resources also may become non-renewal by excess human use. For example, excessive deforestation and animal hunting can affect regeneration of both the plants and animals as many animals help in pollinate flowers and disperse seeds and plants that provide shelter and food to many animals. Similarly, hazardous residuals emanated from manufacturing and other business activities can pollute the natural energy sources and make them unusable. The polluted natural resources not only become unusable for business activities but also for the bio-diversity that is dependent on these resources. For example, water pollution gets into marine animal lungs and kills them. Such an incident took place in 2010 when the Zijin Mining Group, a top mining company, allowed a toxic waste water to spill into the Ting River, killing nearly 1900 tons of fish and threatening the fishing industry in the area. Thus, such an environmental degradation reduces the availability of natural resources, constrains business activities and limits future economic opportunities and economic growth.

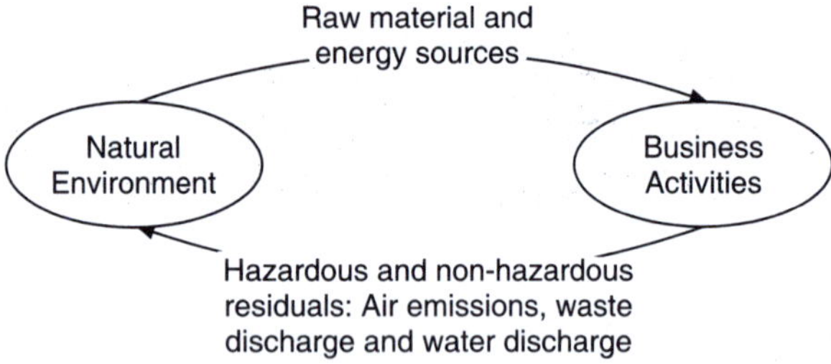

Figure 19.7 Interaction between Natural Environment and Business Activities.

19.6 ENVIRONMENTAL ACCOUNTING AND BUSINESS DECISIONS

With global warming and energy prices prominently in the news, consumers demanding green products, shareholders preferring for corporations that rein in environmental liabilities and government regulations mandating firms to account for environmental costs and benefits, environmental aspects are increasingly getting considered by companies in their decision makings. As a consequence, some of them, rather than simply confining themselves to traditional or conventional costing have also started accounting for environmental costs (UBE 19.5). The **environmental costs** (Figure 19.8) are those costs that the company incurs to prevent the environmental damage that is likely to occur while pursuing certain activities or to clean up or make up for the environmental damage that has been caused by its activities.

The literature on **environmental cost accounting** indicates that the full environmental cost consists of internal as well as external costs (Figure 19.8). The **internal environmental costs** are those environmental costs that are borne by the company, whereas the **external environmental costs** are those that are passed on to the society in the form of environmental and health cost. For example, driving entails road congestion, accidents and air pollution. All of these have some element of internal as well-external costs. The cost of congestion is internalized by paying the parking fees. However, congestion causes delay for the other commuters; hence the cost of delays to others, which does not get covered in the parking fees, is an external cost of driving activity. Similarly, accident will cause harm to the driver as well as the other parties involved in the accident. To the extent, the driver is made to compensate the injured party for all medical and treatment expenses incurred by the injured than to that extent the cost is internalized. However, to the extent the pain born by the injured remain uncompensated the cost is external. Pollution, as we all know, causes respiratory problems for the public, and hence, driving results in a health problem. Pollution tax imposed on a driver internalizes the cost but to the extent the health problem and the costs incurred by others for treatment is not paid by drivers the cost remains external. We can also understand the difference between internal and external environmental costs by another example.

A nuclear energy plant consists of several external costs, which include health and environmental impacts of radioactive releases in routine operations, radioactive waste disposal and the effects of severe accidents and future financial liabilities arising from dismantling of nuclear facilities. While some of these costs are internalized voluntarily by the industry, government regulations in the form of stringent limits to atmospheric emissions and liquid effluents from nuclear facilities mandate many other costs to be internalized.

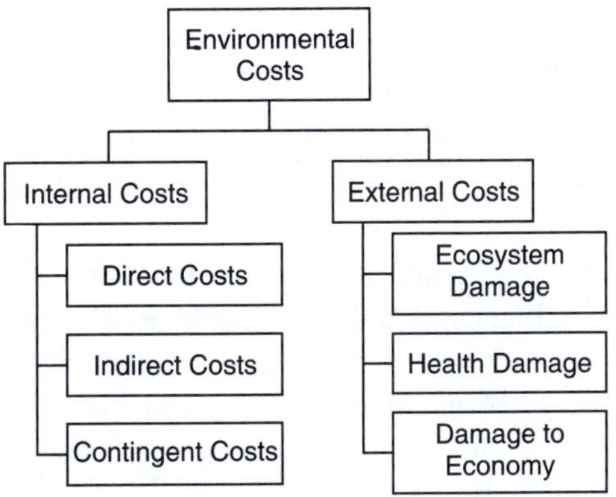

Figure 19.8 Types of Environmental Costs.

19.6.1 Internal Environmental Costs

The **internal environmental costs** of a firm consist of the following broad categories:

1. Direct costs: The **direct environmental costs** can be attributed to a particular product, site and pollution prevention programme, such as waste collection, treatment and disposal costs.

2. Indirect environmental costs: **Indirect environmental costs** are those costs that are incurred for common or joint activities and cannot be attributed readily to a particular project and activity. For example, cost incurred by a company on environmental training, record-keeping and reporting, research and development, activities such as tree plantation carried out to create a positive image, etc., benefit in general the company in minimizing the cost of damage.

3. Contingent environmental costs: The **contingent environmental costs** are subject to the occurrence of an event that may impact the operations of the firm. For example, the compensation made by a company to the victims of gas leakages from a nuclear plant is an actual cost, but the insurance premium paid for covering the third party damage occurring due to unexpected gas leakage from a nuclear plant is a contingent cost. Or accident insurance of mining workers is a contingent cost. Unexpected regulatory changes changing the material input costs, methods of production or allowable emission are also contingent costs.

19.6.2 External Environmental Costs

The costs for which firms are not legally liable or the cost that cannot be enforced through the existing legal system are known as the **external environmental costs**. They can be in the form of damage to the natural environment and damage to human health and their property.

1. Environmental damage: Damage to the environment due to business activities is in the form of climate damage, bio-diversity loss, water scarcity, and overall ecosystem degradation. Waste released by industries and excessive use of natural resources often cause damage to the environment. For example, high emission of greenhouse gases from fossil fuel based power production plants cause drastic change in climate. Global warming is such a case. Similarly, excessive use of wood by paper industry results in rapid deforestation and, consequently, loss of bio-diversity.

2. Health damage: The toxicants released into air, water and soil from industrial and agricultural activities enter into the human body through inhalation, ingestion and absorption, which result in many health problems, such as skin disorders, respiratory abnormalities, abdominal and intestinal problems, ear and eye infections, blood disorder and lung cancer, malaria and many other diseases. To the extent, human beings are not compensated for these sufferings by the pollutants, the cost remains external to the industry.

3. Economic damage: Environmental degradation has been attributed as a cause of global warming, recurrent floods and landslides. These factors are not only resulting in health damage to human beings but also to their property and overall productivity, which cost the economy. For example, landslides damage buildings, roads, railways, pipelines, communication networks and agricultural land. Similarly, global warming affecting weather conditions, rainfall and regional changes in agricultural productivity.

19.6.3 Impact of Environmental Costs on Business Decisions

Environmental costs affect business decisions in several ways, some of these decisions are listed here:

- Capital budgeting
- Investment decisions
- Product mix decisions
- Choosing manufacturing inputs
- Product costing or pricing
- Evaluating waste management decisions
- Identifying the location for manufacturing unit
- Research and development decisions
- Identifying and adopting pollution preventing technologies
- Outsourcing decisions

UNDERSTANDING BUSINESS ENVIRONMENT

UBE 19.5 Sport Lifestyle Company Declares to the World Its Environmental Costs

The corporate world is increasingly becoming conscious of environmental costs, and has started accounting for them. Puma has pioneered in this area as highlighted in this UBE.

Puma, a sport and lifestyle company, outsources most of its products across the globe. The overall winner of the Guardian Sustainable Business awards, Puma has pioneered in the area of environmental accounting by placing a cost on the impact of its business has on the environment, across its entire supply chain (Figure 19.9). It is the first one to reveal, by publishing its first ever full Environmental Profit and Loss (EP&L) Account in November 2011, a true picture of the cost of producing its goods in terms of the natural resources used and the environmental impacts of its operations—from the stage of raw materials purchases to the stage of retail transactions.

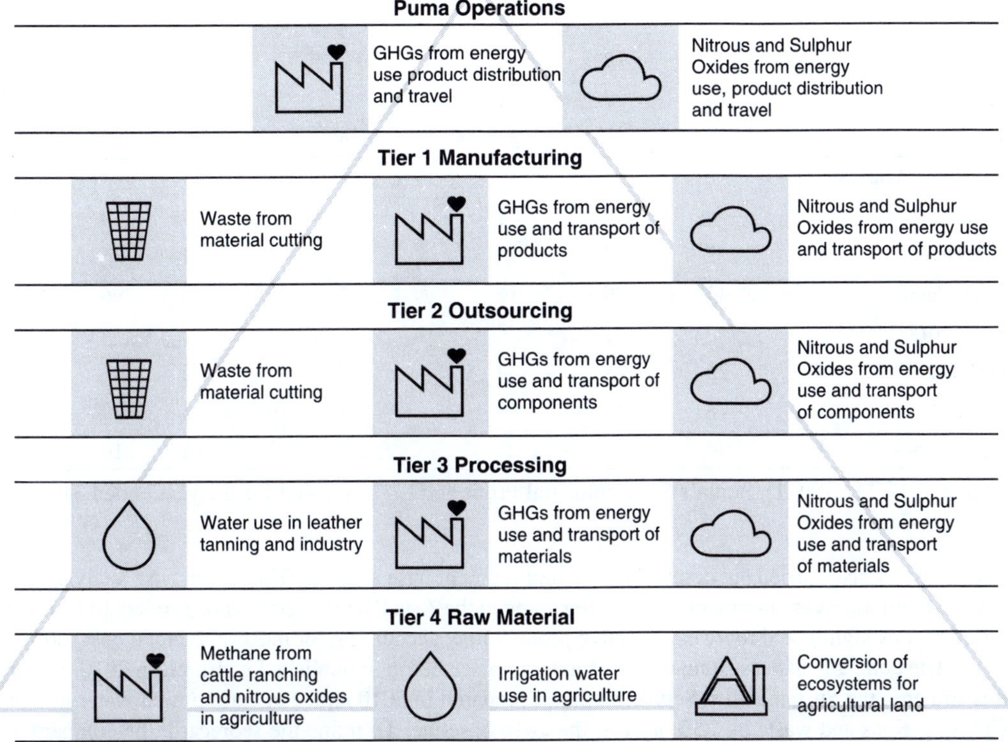

Source: Puma (2011), Annual and Sustainability Report.

Figure 19.9 Puma's Supply Chain and Related Environmental Impacts.

The estimated costs are enormous (Euro 137 million) which forces the executive chairman, Jochen Zeitz, to state that the current economic model, which originated in the industrial revolution some 100 years ago, must be radically changed and a new business paradigm which works with nature, rather than against it, to be adopted.

The company carried out the cost estimation exercise with the objective of identifying the magnitude of environmental cost to managers and stakeholders and to locate where in the supply chain they were being incurred so that appropriate action can be taken to address them and achieve business sustainability. Initially, it started with assessing the cost of greenhouse gas (GHGs) emissions and water usages and subsequently also estimated the cost of land use, air pollution and packaging throughout its operations and supply chain.

The analysis of the estimated cost reveals that only 6% of the costs lay with the company's own direct operations, such as offices (Table 19.2). Most of the costs (83%) were accounted by its Tier 4 suppliers, covering the actual sourcing of raw materials, such as leather, cotton and rubber, over which the company has the least control.

Table 19.2 PUMA's 2010 EP&L Results (in EUR Million)

	Water Use	*GHGs*	*Land Use*	*Other Air Pollution*	*Waste*	*Total*	*% of Total*
	33%	33%	25%	7%	2%	100%	
Total (EUR million)	**47**	**47**	**37**	**11**	**3**	**145**	**100%**
PUMA operations	<1	7	<1	1	<1	8	6%
Tier 1	1	9	<1	1	2	13	9%
Tier 2	4	7	<1	2	1	14	9%
Tier 3	17	7	<1	3	<1	27	19%
Tier 4	25	17	37	4	<1	83	57%
Regional Analysis							
EMEA	4	8	1	1	<1	14	10%
Americas	2	10	20	3	<1	35	24%
Asia/ Pacific	41	29	16	7	3	96	66%
Segments							
Footwear	25	28	34	7	2	96	66%
Apparel	18	14	3	3	1	39	27%
Accessories	4	5	<1	1	<1	10	7%

Source: PUMA (2011), Puma's Environmental Profit and Loss Account for the year ended 31 December 2010.

The company also carried out detailed region and segment wise analysis. The region wise analysis indicated that most of Puma's environmental cost is generated in the Asia Pacific region while product line or segment-wise analysis highlighted footwear, its main product line, accounting for most of the total cost (66%).

The company had a sustainability strategy in place before it published its EP&L in 2010. As a part of this strategy, the Sustainability Scorecard that it prepared in 2010 aimed at cutting total water use, energy, CO_2 emissions and waste by 25% against the 2010 baseline. To refine the scorecard, the company is now feeding its analysis based on EP&L into its strategy.

As a step towards implementation of its sustainability strategy, Puma in close collaboration with its Tier 1 suppliers, has introduced fully automated cutting machines and new sewing technologies that cut down on discarded material. It has also developed Puma Re-Suede made of 100% recycled polyester fibres, recovered from manufacturing scrap waste. This move is expected to cut energy use and emissions by 80%.

SUMMARY

Environmental degradation is a process of erosion of the natural environment through depletion of natural resources, destruction of ecosystem and loss of bio-diversity. Some forms that it can take are: soil degradation, water pollution, air pollution, deforestation, desertification, bio-diversity loss, and atmospheric changes. Environmental degradation is an upshot of an interplay of a range of factors including demographic factors, economic factors (market failure and economic factors), international trade related factors, technological factors and institutional factors.

To prevent the problem of environmental degradation, a range of policy instruments is used the world over. These instruments include direct regulation, economic instruments, informative instruments and voluntary instruments.

Natural environment and business activities are affected by each other. Business organizations are dependent on the natural resources for various raw material, whereas natural environment is affected, often adversely, by various economic activities, which can constraint business sustainability. Nowadays, increasingly business units have started accounting for environmental cost so that they do not overuse natural resources and help in preventing rapid depletion of natural resources. Environmental costs consist of internal as well as external costs. Internal environmental costs are the costs that are borne by the company, whereas external environmental costs are the costs that are passed on to the society in the form of environmental and health costs. Internal environmental costs consists of direct costs, indirect costs and contingent costs, whereas external environmental costs consists of ecosystem damage, health damage and economic damage.

Implications for Business

Business units are an integral part of ecosystem and depend on it in many ways. The ecosystem helps businesses by providing basic raw materials, fuel, energy, water, timber, etc. The nature also supports businesses by contributing to soil formulation, nutrient recycling and maintains balance in the climate. Without such basic support services, business units cannot think of sustaining themselves in the long run. Business units can also affect environment positively as well as negatively. The impact is usually negative, especially when the cost of using environmental resources and energy forces is not accounted for by business activities. Such a neglect of environmental costs often results in excessive use of resources, pollution of natural energy forces such air, water, and soil, and damage to bio-diversity by the release of industrial waste to rivers, seas, soil and atmosphere. The impact on the environment is positive when proper accounting of environmental forces help business units to identify the activities, processes and stages in the supply chain that are degrading the environment and may be a cause of concern. In the process, it highlights the areas where the environmental-friendly processes need to be adopted by companies to reduce their environmental costs as well as their total cost of production. Such strategies help them in identifying more sustainable materials, designing eco-friendly products and packaging that can also help the units to survive in the market for a longer period. Such a move also helps companies in generating goodwill among the employees, building a green image and gaining customers, which are becoming more and more environmentally conscious and growingly demanding environment friendly products, in the long run.

REVIEW QUESTIONS

19.1 What is the natural environment?

19.2 Differentiate renewal resources from non-renewal resources.

19.3 How are business activities and natural environment related?

19.4 What are the different environmental policy instruments?

19.5 What are the regulation based instruments? Why are they used? What are their major disadvantages?

19.6 What are the economic instruments? How do they work? What are their major advantages?

19.7 What is the environmental cost? What are its components? Is the environment not considered at all in the traditional accounting process?

19.8 How internal environmental cost is different from external environmental costs?

19.9 Why are companies trying to incorporate environment cost in their accounting methods?

19.10 What types of decisions are affected by environmental cost?

CASE ANALYSIS EXERCISE

C19.1 Who is Responsible for a Slow Death of Noyyal?

The Noyyal, a once—pristine river originating from Vellingiri in the Western Ghats bordering Tamil Nadu and Kerala in India, of late has been facing a slow death, to rapid industrialization and urbanization in the surrounding area.

Covering an area of 160 km, the Noyyal passes through the districts of Tirupur, Coimbatore and Erode, and ends in the river Cauvery, near Karur and is a life source for tens of thousands of villagers living in the neighbouring areas. The two districts Tirupur and Coimbatore in Tamil Nadu, in the last two decades, beginning from the early 1990s, have achieved astonishing success in cotton manufacturing and exports. It brought prosperity to the region by employing 5 lakh people and contributing almost 75% of India's knitwear exports.

But, this huge success was not without a price. In textile processing, bleaching and dyeing are the two major activities. These activities require a large amount of water which gets discharged as affluent after processing. Even the textile units located in Tirupur and Coimbatore region, all these years dumped the polluted water into the river unabated, affecting tens and thousands of villagers living in the vicinity of the river. Because of the continuous disposal of the waste water, Total Dissolved Solids (TDS) in the water were estimated to be on an average above 9,000 parts per million (ppm), much higher than the stipulated norm of 2,100 ppm. The level of TDS increases in summer when water evaporation is higher. The water waste affecting the physical environment as well as the economy of the region. Jayanth, Karthik, Logesh, Srinivas and Vijayanand (2011) indicates that, due to activities of textile industry, the area is facing following adverse impacts:

- Water levels in the borewells are lowering due to the large scale exploitation of groundwater and the water has become unsuitable for drinking as well as the textile industry.
- The non-perennial river Noyyal now flows throughout the year because of the effluent discharge from the industries. The water quality is poor because of the level of dissolved solids, chlorides, sulphate, oil and grease are higher than the permissible limits.
- Salinity in the water has increased which has made it unfit for agriculture. Due to high salinity yield has declined sharply. As a consequence, many farmers have switched to selling clean water at a premium price rather than tilling the land for their livelihood.
- Fish mortality has increased substantially, which has compelled the Fisheries Department to stop fish culture.

The Noyyal river sports a dam in Orathupalayam village. It has been observed, the world over, that usually, the people living upstream prefer keeping the shutters of the dam closed to have better access to water and those living downstream eagerly wait for the release of the water. However, the situation reversed here in 1990s with people living upstream demanded a release of the water and those living downstream vehemently opposed its release. The reason was simple; the waste dumped into the river had made it toxic, unusable and hazardous; the stench foul emanating from it spread panic among the people, both upstream and downstream, feared damage to their crops and livestock.

Fearing loss of their livelihood, farmers joined hands and have taken the matter to the courts. In response to the litigation filed in 2003, the Madras High Court ordered in 2011 closure of all common effluent treatment plants (ETPs) and some 750-odd dyeing and bleaching units in Tirupur.

Reference

Jayanth, S.N., Karthik, R., Logesh, S., Srinivas, Rao K. and Vijayanand, K. (2011), Environmental Issues and Its Impact Associated with the Textile Processing Units in Tirupur, Tamil Nadu, a paper presented in 2nd International Conference on Environmental Science and Development, IPCBEE Vol. 4, IACSIT Press, Singapore.

Questions

1. Explain the role of Noyyal in the development of the districts Tirupur and Coimbatore?
2. What are the causes of the slow death of Noyyal?
3. What are the likely consequences of the damage to Noyyal?

SUGGESTED FURTHER READING

UNEP (2012), Global Environment Outlook 5 for Local Governments: Solving Global Problems Locally.

UNEP (2013), UNEP Yearbook 2013: Emerging Issues in Our Global Environment.

Index